ROBERTSON
SUMNER
WILSON
RUTHERFORD
WARREN
BEDFORD
LINCOLN
FRANKLIN
MARION

Correspondence of James K. Polk

VOLUME II, 1833–1834

James Knox Polk and Sarah Childress Polk. These paintings were done by Ralph E. W. Earl during the 1830s. They are in possession of the Polk Memorial Association and hang in the Polk home in Columbia, Tennessee.

Correspondence of
JAMES K. POLK

Volume II
1833-1834

HERBERT WEAVER
Editor

PAUL H. BERGERON
Associate Editor

1972
Vanderbilt University Press
Nashville

Library of Congress Cataloguing-in-Publication Data

Polk, James Knox, Pres. U.S., 1795–1849.
Correspondence of James K. Polk.

CONTENTS: v. 1. 1817–1832.—v. 2. 1833–1834.
I. Weaver, Herbert, ed. II. Title.
E337.8.P63 973.6′1 75–84005
ISBN 0–8265–1146–5 (v. I)
ISBN 0–8265–1176–7 (v. II)

Printed in the United States of America
by Kingsport Press, Inc., Kingsport, Tennessee

Sponsored by

Vanderbilt University
The National Historical Publications Commission
The Tennessee Historical Commission
The Polk Memorial Association

To
Harvie Branscomb
and to the memory of
Daniel M. Robison and Philip M. Hamer

PREFACE

The two years spanned in this volume were important to the political career of James K. Polk both at the state level and on the national scene. Before the second session of the Twenty-second Congress adjourned on March 2, 1833, Polk had become a member of the influential Ways and Means Committee and was generally recognized as Jackson's floor leader in the House. Yet when he returned to Tennessee in the spring to campaign for re-election, he faced a serious challenge. His district had been reduced from four to two counties, Maury and Bedford, and in the latter there was strong opposition. Businessmen who were alarmed by the attacks on the Bank of the United States were determined to punish Polk for his part in that controversy. On the other hand, voters who disliked the Bank were stirred to even greater efforts in Polk's behalf because of his unyielding hostility to that institution.

In the 1833 campaign Polk again was opposed by Theodorick F. Bradford of Bedford County and also by the lesser-known Thomas J. Porter of Maury County. It became clear in the early stages of the canvass that Bradford was receiving powerful support from outside the district. Anti-Polk materials that flooded the region were traced to Nashville, to Washington, and even to the Bank itself. Polk may have gained some satisfaction to learn that he was such an important target, but he had many uneasy moments. By fighting off the initial attacks and by exposing their sources, he gained confidence and carried the fight to his chief opponent, Bradford. Polk once more demonstrated his prowess as a stump speaker and campaigner; finding Bradford vulnerable at many points, he pushed his unrelenting attacks with vigor. One effective stratagem was the exposure of excerpts from letters of recommendation written in support of Bradford for a federal appointment during the John Quincy Adams administration. These letters from prominent men in Tennessee described Bradford as a strong anti-Jackson man. Perhaps more important to Polk's success, however, was the service he had done for Bedford County by obtaining a tri-weekly mail delivery on a new stage line from Nashville to Huntsville, Alabama. The battle for political survival was a complete victory: Polk's vote more than doubled the combined vote of his two competitors.

After his impressive triumph in Tennessee, Polk returned to Washington, and early in the new session he was elevated to the chairmanship of the Ways and Means Committee. This represented not only a reward for his previous work against the Bank but also an acknowledgment that he was expected to lead the fight to remove federal deposits from the Bank, an action upon which Jackson had already determined. Polk's speech of December 30, 1833, seems to have turned the tide against Nicholas Biddle and his allies. Following a hard fight, the removal of deposits was accomplished and efforts to recharter the Bank were defeated. Requests for copies of his December 30 speech came from all parts of the country; Polk had become a figure of national importance almost overnight.

In June 1834, near the end of the first session of the Twenty-third Congress the House witnessed a development that was to have serious consequences for both Polk and his party. Andrew Stevenson, Speaker of the House, had been expected to resign from the House for some time, and various members, including Polk, had begun maneuvering to succeed him as Speaker. By the time the vacancy appeared, Polk had the support of a majority of his party, but he did not have enough votes to win. A contest developed between Polk and John Bell, also of Tennessee and nominally of the same party. Eventually Bell attracted significant support from the opposition and won the post. The defeat angered many loyal Jacksonians, and Polk determined to prove Bell's apostasy and to drive him out of the Jackson ranks. Matters were further complicated because both Bell and Polk were being mentioned as possible gubernatorial candidates in Tennessee.

During the congressional session many of Polk's friends had urged him to return home and serve as a delegate to the forthcoming Tennessee Constitutional Convention. The convention met more than a month before Congress adjourned, however, and Polk could not leave his strategic post in Washington. Back in Middle Tennessee late in the summer of 1834, he discovered that dissatisfaction with Martin Van Buren as a presidential candidate was developing into an incipient revolt within the Jackson party in Tennessee. Political figures who had previously followed the President without question now openly expressed their strong disapproval of Jackson's choice for his successor. Still intact after the divisive effects of nullification and of the Bank fight, the legions of Old Hickory in Tennessee were torn by internal dissension that could imperil the whole party organization in the state. Senator Hugh Lawson White, whom Polk liked and respected, was being put forward by Bell and his friends as a presidential candidate more acceptable than Van Buren.

Soon after the Tennessee congressional delegation returned to Washington in December 1834, the plans for White's candidacy began to take shape. Late in the month in a series of meetings, Tennessee congressmen considered strategy for promoting White and sought to enlist support for him. Polk and Grundy refused to attend, and several other members decided that they would not support White unless he received the nomination at the Democratic national convention. By the end of 1834 it was apparent that should White agree to become a candidate, a party split was inevitable. The latter months of 1834 generated further anxiety among Polk and his friends because Tennessee newspapers, especially those in Nashville, were almost completely under the control of Bell-White forces. As the year ended it was evident that Polk would have to exhibit remarkable political agility to maintain the ascendancy he had achieved.

Polk's deep absorption with politics left too little time for private affairs. The estates of his father, father-in-law, and the three brothers who had died in 1831 had been settled except for a few minor details, but his law practice languished. In search of additional income, he looked to his plantation in Fayette County. To his new overseer, Ephraim Beanland, he sent additional family slaves. Beanland's handling of the slaves was unsatisfactory but Polk dealt with him patiently. When crops were short in 1834, Polk decided to sell the plantation and establish another in Mississippi. He asked Beanland to move to the new plantation and further showed his confidence in his overseer by placing much of the settlement of the affairs in Fayette County in his hands.

In Columbia, Polk's mother, Jane Knox Polk, less than sixty years of age, presided over the family in staunch matriarchal fashion. The loneliness of widowhood was relieved considerably by the presence of daughters, sons, sons-in-law, and an increasing number of grandchildren. All four daughters lived nearby; this was a mixed blessing, especially in the case of Ophelia, whose instability and marital troubles became sources of worry. The two youngest children, William H. and Samuel W., were away at school. Samuel first entered Manual Labor Academy (later, Jackson College), located a few miles away at Spring Hill, but in the fall of 1834 he, his nephews James Hays Walker and Joseph Knox Walker, and his friend William F. Cooper went to New Haven and enrolled at Yale College. In late 1832, William H. Polk went to Bingham School in Hillsborough, North Carolina, to prepare himself for admission to the university at Chapel Hill. He began attending classes at the university early in 1833 and continued to do so in 1834 although a deficiency in Greek prevented his admission as a regular student. William's spendthrift ways continued to worry Polk. In the summer of 1834, William returned to Tennessee and later entered the University of Nashville.

Polk continued to be dependent upon his brothers-in-law for assistance with business and political matters. Among the husbands of his sisters, James Walker was the most active correspondent as well as the one most involved in politics. Adlai O. Harris and Silas M. Caldwell supplied information and advice, principally about the plantation and other business affairs. Dr. John B. Hays was the most silent of the group, there being no letters to or from him in 1833 and 1834; perhaps personal concerns and his tempestuous wife, Ophelia, kept him from being of much assistance to Polk at this time. Sarah Polk's brother John W. Childress and brother-in-law Dr. William R. Rucker, both of Murfreesboro, frequently provided political news and counsel. In view of Polk's political activities and various family concerns, it is probable that his stamina was severely taxed.

This Volume

The amount of correspondence in 1833 and 1834 made selectivity mandatory for this volume. After scrutiny of almost 850 letters, 664 were chosen for publication: 512 in full, and 152 in summarized form. The remaining pieces were too routine and inconsequential to merit publication. Approximately a hundred of those selected are family letters, principally exchanges with brothers-in-law. There is only one to Polk's wife, Sarah, which is not surprising since she was with him in Washington as well as in Columbia. More than a hundred other letters are almost entirely political in nature, including about sixty communications with more than twenty-five members of the House of Representatives. Faithful Archibald Yell contributes seventeen letters to his interesting, but one-sided, correspondence. The twenty-one letters from Ephraim Beanland afford the rare privilege of seeing through the eyes of an overseer the problems of operating a cotton plantation for an absentee owner. Many letters concern jobs, recommendations, pensions, land claims, mail routes, and other matters of importance to Polk's constituents.

Continuing under the assumption that their primary responsibility is to assemble and make available the significant correspondence of James K. Polk, the editors have made no important changes in the editorial procedures adopted for Volume I. Selectivity has been necessary, but otherwise the editors have continued in their efforts to reproduce the correspondence in a form as faithful to the original text of each letter as possible; original spelling, punctuation, capitalization, and grammar have been preserved except when slight alterations were required for the sake of clarity. Lower-case letters at the beginning of sentences have been converted to capitals. When it has been impossible at other places to determine whether the writer intended upper- or lower-case, current style has been followed. Commas and semicolons have been inserted sparingly in sentences that lack clarity or are deficient in punctuation. Superfluous dashes have generally been deleted, and those that appeared at the ends of sentences have been converted to appropriate punctuation marks. Words unintentionally repeated by the writers have been deleted. These minor changes have been done silently, without editorial indications of where they occur. Letters that were particularly difficult to decipher or those written by semiliterate persons have been given special attention, and that fact is indicated in the footnotes.

The appearance of three ellipses marks within brackets indicates that a word (or words) is illegible, usually because a part of the manuscript is torn or blotted. Where several words are missing because of a damaged manuscript, this fact is explained in a footnote. To conserve space, complimentary closings have been deleted; the ellipses marks at the end of the last sentence of a letter means that the complimentary closing began as a part of that sentence. These editorial procedures, of course, do not apply to summarized letters.

As all letters published herein are either to or from James K. Polk, his name is not included in the headings except in cases of multiple authors or recipients. Regardless of their position in the original manuscript, the salutation, provenance, and date appear on a line just below the heading. An unnumbered note at the end of each letter gives the place to which the letter is addressed, place and date of previous publications, if any, and information as to such markings as "confidential" or "private." The repository possessing the letter is also indicated unless it is from the Polk Papers, Division of Manuscripts, Library of Congress. All items are autograph letters signed, unless noted otherwise.

Numbered footnotes immediately follow the unnumbered one. A brief explanation or identification is given upon the first mention of a person, place, or special subject. Subsequent appearances of such persons, places, or subjects usually receive no additional annotation. Identifications that are in the first volume are generally briefer in this volume. To identify everything has been neither possible nor desirable. The editors believe, however, that in some cases when only meager information is available, it should be provided in a note. Some persons have been left unidentified either because efforts to establish identity were abortive or because there was uncertainty as to which of two or more persons by the same or similar name was intended. Where appropriate, the editors have provided cross references to other letters in this or in the first volume. The index will help in locating identifications.

The annotations often have been taken from several sources. Frequently the sources are so obvious as to need no citation. Because of these and other considerations, the editors have decided to forego the citation of sources in footnotes.

Acknowledgments

Although the number of persons to whom we are indebted for help in preparation of this volume is too large for us to mention each of them individually, we acknowledge our gratitude to them all. For their steadfast support and unfailing encouragement we are especially grateful to Dr. Oliver W. Holmes, executive director of the National Historical Publications Commission, and to Messrs. Robert A. McGaw and Stephen S. Lawrence, chairman and executive director, respectively, of the Tennessee Historical Commission. The staffs of the Tennessee State Library and Archives, Joint University Libraries, the National Archives, and the Division of Manuscripts in the Library of Congress have put us deeply in their debt by their unselfish assistance. The fruits of the intelligent labor of Maury County researchers Jill McKnight Garrett, Evelyn B. Shackelford, Marise P. Lightfoot, Rose Harris Priest, and Virginia Wood Alexander continue to save us many tedious hours. We are also appreciative of the kindnesses of Mrs. Alex Pirtle Jr. and Mrs. Harriet Quin of the Polk Memorial Association.

The accuracy and dispatch with which Mrs. Jean Voegeli has typed the manuscript for this volume and the yeoman service done by Mrs. Anita Tidwell Fruzzetti in four years of faithful transcription from original manuscripts are gratefully acknowledged. We are obligated to Miss Henrietta Medlock and Gary G. Gore of the Vanderbilt University Press for their editorial and production work. To Blanche Henry Weaver, to whom the first volume is dedicated, we owe more than we can say for accomplishing the many things that have made the work of the editors less burdensome.

Again we express our indebtedness to the three institutions that have financed this undertaking: Vanderbilt University, the Tennessee Historical Commission, and the National Historical Publications Commission. To the men who guided these institutions in their initial commitment to our support, we humbly dedicate this volume.

H. W.
P. H. B.

CONTENTS

1834

ILLUSTRATIONS

Chronology of James K. Polk

1795	November 2	Born in Mecklenburg County, North Carolina
1806	Fall	Moved to Maury County, Tennessee
1812	Fall	Underwent major surgery by Dr. Ephraim McDowell in Danville, Kentucky
1813	July	Began study under Robert Henderson at Zion Church Academy
1814	July	Began study under Samuel P. Black at Bradley Academy, Murfreesboro, Tennessee
1816	January	Entered University of North Carolina as a sophomore
1818	June	Graduated from University of North Carolina
	Fall	Began reading law in office of Felix Grundy
1819	September	Elected clerk of the senate of Tennessee General Assembly
1820	June	Admitted to the bar
1823	August	Elected to lower house of Tennessee General Assembly
1824	January 1	Married to Sarah Childress of Murfreesboro
1825	August	Elected to United States House of Representatives
1827	August	Re-elected to House of Representatives
	November 5	Death of his father, Samuel Polk
1829	August	Re-elected to House of Representatives
1831	January 21	Death of his brother Franklin, aged 28
	April 12	Death of his brother Marshall, aged 26
	August	Re-elected to House of Representatives
	September 28	Death of his brother John, aged 24
1833	August	Re-elected to House of Representatives
	December	Became chairman, Ways and Means Committee

1834	June	Defeated by John Bell for Speaker of the House
1835	August	Re-elected to House of Representatives
	December 7	Elected Speaker of the House over John Bell
1837	August	Re-elected to House of Representatives
	September 4	Re-elected Speaker of the House
1839	August	Elected Governor of Tennessee over Newton Cannon
1841	August	Defeated in gubernatorial election by James C. Jones
1843	August	Defeated in gubernatorial election by James C. Jones
1844	May	Nominated for the presidency at Democratic National Convention
	November	Elected President of the United States over Henry Clay
1845	March 4	Inaugurated as President of the United States
1849	March 4	Yielded office to his successor, Zachary Taylor
	June 15	Died in Nashville

Correspondence of James K. Polk

1833

FROM [REUBEN M. WHITNEY][1]

Dear Sir [Washington?] [1833?]

Mr Adams in his Report page 404 of Doc. 1831–2 says *"the price current of bank Stock, the Thermometer of public confidence."* Now on referring to the accompanying papers you will [see] how the thermometer bore relatively between the Bank of the U.S. and the Banks selected in New York & Philadelphia prior to their having been employed by the Treasury as its agents. Those in New York are the Manhattan, Mechanics, & America. In Phila. The Girard.

On the 31st August	U.S.B. Stock	112⅞—	Manhattan Bk Stock	128—
4th September—	ditto—	110¼	Mechanics—do—	117½
			America—do—	110¾
6th September—	ditto—	110	Mechanics—do—	119
9th Sept In Philadelphia—			Girard Bank—	122½

These are the Banks in the two largest Commercial Cities. You may say that the Stock of *nearly all* if not of every Bank, employed by the Treasury was above that of the Bk of the U. States in the market at the time they were employed by the Treasury.

W.[2]

Directed to Polk without address or date and presumably delivered by hand.

1. A Philadelphia businessman and former director of the Bank of the United States who became a trusted adviser to Jackson and to the Treasury Department. During 1833 he assisted Polk in an investigation of the Bank.

Since this seems to be a part of that collaboration, the 1833 date is suggested.

2. Someone has written the name of Richard Henry Wilde just below the signature, and the Library of Congress has erroneously identified this congressman from Georgia as the author of this letter.

FROM McKAY W. CAMPBELL[1]

Col. Polk Columbia Jany 3d 1833

I send Mr. [Nathaniel] Simmons application[2] for a pension which be so good as to hand to the proper office. Any communications on the subject send to me.

I wish you would have the Globe sent to me. If you pay it in advance I will hand it to you on your return.

I wish You would let me hear from the applications for pensions which I mentioned to you in a former letter.

Your friends &c are all well. You will see the announcement of *Mrs. Joseph Porter* (Jef's mother).[3]

M. W. CAMPBELL

Addressed to Washington.

1. At this time Campbell was practicing law in Columbia.

2. This application seems to have been unsuccessful, since the name of the applicant does not appear on the list of pensioners reported by the Secretary of War in 1835. Simmons is unidentified, but he was probably a resident of Maury County.

3. Mrs. Porter, mother of Thomas Jefferson Porter, had died recently.

FROM CHARLES C. MAYSON[1]

My Dear Sir Columbia Janry 3 1833

I recd a few weeks since a letter from my friend Ch. J. Colcock[2] of So C in which he stated to me that he would procure & transmit to you certain documents proving my fathers revolutionary services. If he should do so I will thank [you] to keep them & suggest what it will be necessary for me to do—whether to present a petition or not.

Since I wrote to you, I have become your Tenant. I am now in your house & expect to remain here until the first of March when I expect to go to Mississi.[3] Will you urge upon my brother-in-Law Major Glynn[4] to pay me the sum I want, the $200. I never expect to be so much in want of that amount again. Let me beg you to write me what Mr. Glynn says in this respect. If he dont pay me I must put the claim in suit but I hope he will let me have the money. I am sorry to trouble you with this *dunning* business but I hope you can do it without much trouble & will excuse me. *My poverty* not *my will* forces me to trouble you.

Your friends are all well here & so are the people generally.

CHS C MAYSON

Addressed to Washington.

1. A lawyer in Columbia.

2. A leading nullifier in South Carolina who presided for some years over the court of appeals in that state.

3. It is not known when Mayson left for Mississippi, but by the summer of 1833 he had become editor of the Jackson *State Rights Banner.*

4. Anthony G. Glynn was a clerk in the office of the Secretary of War. Mayson's persistence in trying to collect from Glynn may be seen in three previous letters that he had written to Polk, May 19, December 3, and December 18, 1832.

FROM WILLIAM S. MOORE[1]

Dear Sir Columbia 3d Jany 1833

I understand their is to be a Surveyor general appointed for the Chickasaw Nation Shortly and a Mr William Dickson[2] of Madison County Alabama who is a friend of mine is an applicant for the office. Mr Dickson is a verry responcible man and Evry way qualifiyed to fill the office with Cridit to himself and to the Sattisfaction of the Govermnt. And any thing that you may doo for him Shall be most Cordially remunerated by you humble Servant.

WM. S. MOORE

NB. Mr Dickson is an acquaintance of Judge [Hugh Lawson] Whites and Clemt C Clays[3] and to them I would refer you for his Standing.

WM S M.

Addressed to Washington.

1. A Columbia merchant.

2. Although there were in that region several William Dicksons of such age as to suggest them as possible appointees, this is probably the one who was one of the first justices of peace in Madison County.

3. At this time Clay was representing Alabama in the United States House of Representatives, and White was in the Senate.

FROM ROGER B. TANEY[1]

My Dear Sir [Washington] Jany 3, 1833

I send you a letter I received some days ago from Philadelphia in relation to the conduct of the Bank of the U. States.[2] If an examination should take place it may be worthy of attention.

R. B. TANEY

Marked "Private," this letter was directed to Polk without any address.

1. At this time he was United States Attorney General, but within a few months he became Secretary of the Treasury.

2. The enclosure was a letter from John Yatman of Philadelphia, citing an example of what appeared to be sharp practice by the Bank of the United States.

FROM EBENEZER J. SHIELDS

Pulaski. January 4, 1833

A Pulaski lawyer serving in the state legislature (later Polk's colleague in the House of Representatives) inquires about the status of the pension application of William Wells, who had served in the Virginia line during the Revolution.

Addressed to Washington.

FROM FREDERICK E. BECTON JR.[1]

Dear Sir, Murfreesboro Tenn. Jany 5, 1833

I beg to draw your notice to some efforts making in some parts of this County having for their object, the removal of Mr. Wendel[2] our Post Master.

I assume that the people who transact business at Mr W's office and all the inhabitants of this place with but few exceptions are decidedly opposed to his removal. Those who aspire to his office are the only discontents, and they disagree upon his successor.

As Mr. Wendel and I, have not spoken to each other for more than two years except in his office and as we are politically unfriendly, I hope my testimony in his favor may be of some use in keeping him his position. He is a good, faithful officer and though a little dissatisfied with some of Genl. Jacksons plans, is a temperate, upright calm oppositionist, who meddles not with business that does not concern him.

Please say to the P. Master Genl that the people who have business at the P. Office here are pleased that Genl Jackson is President and that Mr. Wendel is our P Master. We wish him retained.

FRED. E. BECTON JR

Addressed to Washington.

1. A Murfreesboro physician who had moved to Rutherford County shortly after his graduation from the University of Maryland.

2. David Wendel was an early settler and former mayor of Murfreesboro. It must have been refreshing to Polk to receive a letter supporting a man "politically unfriendly" because he had been a good public servant. A letter from John W. Childress, January 9, 1833, attests to the general satisfaction of the community with the services that Wendel had rendered. He was not removed at this time.

FROM SAMUEL BIGHAM[1]

Rock Creek Bedford Co. Te.

My dear sir Jany 5th 1832[1833][2]

I advertised and sold the Thompson place at auction shortly after you left Tennessee. It went off at the sume of $396, to be paid in three equal annual payments, the first of which is to be next Christmas, and I think the money well secured. The post office department has I understand ordered Mr. Woods[3] not to come this way with the mail on his passage from Macon to Cornersville, but Dr. Haywood[4] has addressed you on that subject, therupon I will only say to you that I have seen his communication and know it to be a correct statement of the case. If the late Chickasaw purchase should be made a new surveyors district, I wish you to write me immediately who is appointed surveyor. If should be a Tennessean I want to make early application for part of the surveying. We have recd the presidents proclamation. The people unanimously as far as I can learn say that of all the acts of his useful life, this is the greatest. It will no doubt be esteemed a valuable state paper after we are all dead and gone, and will I have no doubt in a good degree have the effect of restoring tranquility in the south.

S. Bigham

Addressed to Washington.

1. At this time he was postmaster at Rock Creek, Bedford County. See his letter to Polk, November 2, 1832.

2. Although the letter was dated 1832, it is evident from the contents that the correct date is 1833.

3. Not otherwise identified.

4. George W. Haywood, son of the famous Judge John Haywood, was a prominent physician in the western part of Bedford County.

FROM BENJAMIN CLEMENTS[1]

D Sir Fayetteville Jany 5th 1833

In my letter Some time Since to you I informd. you of my application to the president of the U. States for the office of Surveyor for the district of Country about to be obtaind. from the Chickasaw Indians.

I then mentioned to you that I likely would be at the City the latter part of this month but find it will not be convenent for me to be there so soon if at all as I am compeld to be at Tallahassee, Florida the latter part of this Instant & Expect to leave home the 8th Instant for that point.

Sir I askd. you to give me your aid to the president in my application. You will please Excuse me for trobling of you but Sir I hope you will do me the faviour to give me your aid in the

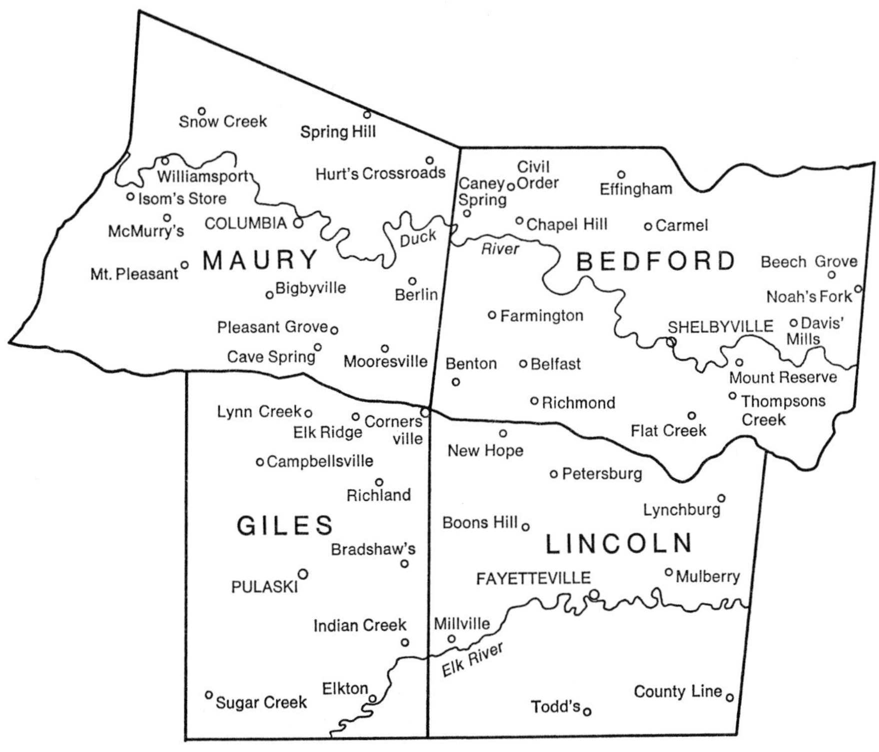

POLK'S CONGRESSIONAL DISTRICT

The district from which Polk was first elected in 1825 was composed of Maury, Bedford, Lincoln, and Giles counties. After the redistricting in 1833, Polk's district included only Maury and Bedford counties.

above matter and in the event I fail in the above application I hope you will faviour me by mentioning to the president my name as an applicant for Some other office in his gift of which I likely can discharge the duty of.

Sir will you please let me hear from you at Tallahassee, Florida on the recpt. of this & you will also inform me if necessary for me to come to the City. I likely will remain at Tallahassee till Some time in February.

Sir I hope you will give the above mentioned matter a little attention as your humble Servant is so needy.

BENJA. CLEMENTS

Addressed to Washington.

1. An early settler in Lincoln County. See his letters to Polk, January 11, February 2, and November 22, 1833.

FROM GIDEON J. PILLOW[1]

Dear Colo. Columbia Jany 6th 1833

Enclosed you will find recommendations from the Columbia, Pulaski and Franklin Bars, in behalf of Judge [William E.] Kennedy as an applicant for the office of District Judge of the United States for West Tennessee.[2] Judge Kennedy directs me Say to you that any Services of yours in forwarding his views with the President will be *kindly remembered* by him and you have a positive assurance from me Col. that his *friends* throughout the State, will gladly seek an opportunity of evincing their sense of the personal obligations the exercise of your influence with the President will place them under to you. Col. Bell and Col. Johnston[Johnson] will co-operate with you in such measures as your judgement may suggest as proper.[3] The Judge was in the army with the president. If the circumstance shall have escaped his memory would it not be well to remind him of the fact? Our Friends are all well. There are unusual embarrasments in our County. There have been a number of failures, but none of much consequence since you left us.

GIDEON J. PILLOW

P.S. Be pleased to lay these documents before the President immediately Col. McNairy[4] has actually resigned his office, and I presume his successor will be appointed at an early period. If you get from the President any *intimation* of his intentions do us the favour of writting us immediately. You Know the anxiety a man [and] his friends have under such Circumstances. This I hope will be sufficient apology for the haste manifested in the manner of the communication.

G. J. P.

Addressed to Washington.

1. A Columbia lawyer and one of Polk's close friends.

2. A circuit court judge who had formerly lived in Fayetteville, Kennedy did not receive the appointment, which went instead to a Nashville lawyer, Morgan W. Brown.

3. This is a reference to John Bell and Cave Johnson, Polk's colleagues in the House of Representatives.

4. John McNairy of Nashville, who had been a United States district judge for more than thirty years.

FROM SAMUEL H. LAUGHLIN[1]

My dear Sir, Nashville, Tenn. January 8, 1833

I have no news to communicate, Nashville being this winter truly a dull place. Trade languishes, there being no cotton in market worth naming, and in truth none in the country to bring to market.

I want a Washington newspaper. Duff[2] I have long given up as being damned and unworthy of all trust & patronage. The Globe I take with a next door neighbor, and it is not upon the whole a much better paper than it should be. I care not for hot decoctions & concoctions of politics. I want *news* and I want a fair report of your Debates. I must therefore beg of you to have forwarded to me (including all the papers if possible from the 1st day of this month) the *National Intelligencer*. It is the country paper—triweekly I think or twice a week—which I want. I have not time to deal in Dailies.

The Presidents Proclamation meets universal approbation in this country. Even Hoover, Trott[3] &c. of Rutherford give the President unlimitted praise on account of it. It is certainly the next most important State paper ever issued in this country since the Declaration of Independence. It is far more important than Washington's Proclamation of neutrality, and parts of it will be hereafter remembered as partaking of the deep patriotism and fatherly solicitude for the welfare and preservation of the integrity of the United States which are found in the best parts of Washington's farewell address. What is to become of South Carolina?

How much are you willing to give me for my interest in our little Maury place & all rents &c. due & to become due?[4] I am, owing to purchase of property here and removal, and the scarcity of cash in these parts, very much pressed in money matters. I owe Maj. A. J. Donelson,[5] of Washington City several hundred dollars. Now I hereby empower you for yourself and as my attorney in fact to fix just such price as you please. Such that you cant loose and must gain by upon my interest in the concern. Then obtain from Donelson his receipt to me for so much of his debt left in the hands of John McGrigor[6] against me as you may fix that price at and send it to me, and I will instantly make a deed to you and either forward it to you or to James Walker[7] as you may direct. I am sued for the money. I will have to pay it by first of Summer. I must get out of debt; and I must sell my interest in this affair of ours. I am unwilling to sell to any person but you. I want the proceeds for Donelson. He will give you time til end of session or until next session of Congress. Therefore my dear friend fix a price you can afford to give and take it & settle so much with him. Any price you fix I assure you will meet my entire approbation.

For want of usual freights in cotton & tobacco, our steamers belonging to this port and engaged in our trade are carrying thousands and thousands of barrels of corn in sacks of cotton bagging, in the ear, to Mississippi and Louisiana. It is expected they will find a good account in the business.

Send me Joe's paper,[8] bad as his politics are, and let me hear from you.

SAML. H. LAUGHLIN

Addressed to Washington.

1. Editor of the Nashville *Union*.

2. Duff Green, editor of the Washington *United States Telegraph,* had by this time turned against Jackson.

3. Andrew J. Hoover and Henry Trott. Hoover later served briefly in the state legislature and was a Whig elector in 1836. Trott was for a long time a resident of Murfreesboro but later moved to Cannon County, where he was elected to the state legislature, serving 1843–47.

4. In 1831 Polk and Laughlin had bought from John Royall for $431 a 36–acre farm on the Little Bigby.

5. Andrew Jackson Donelson, Jackson's private secretary and a nephew of Jackson's wife Rachel.

6. Not positively identified. It is possible that he was the same man who helped Sam Houston financially when Houston was leaving the state after having resigned as governor.

7. Columbia businessman who was Polk's brother-in-law and loyal political supporter.

8. The Washington *National Intelligencer,* edited by Joseph Gales.

FROM JOHN W. CHILDRESS[1]

Dear Sir Murfreesboro Jany 9th 1833

I have been solicited by a friend of ours, (Mr James C Moore)[2] of this place, to ask your aid in behalf of a Mr [William] Dickson of Alabama who is a near relation of Mr Moore, and is now offering his services to the Executive, for the appointment of Surveyor in the Chickasaw Country. I Know nothing of Mr Dickson except what I learn from Moore. He speaks very highly of him. Should you be willing and have it in your power to do him any service you will greatly oblige Mr Moore who is a very good friend of yours. Our peaceable little town has been somewhat excited for a day or two past, on account of some exertions that are making to have our Post Master removed from office. Martin Clark[3] of the firm of Ledbetter & Co. has a paper out for signatures, petitioning for the removal of Mr [David] Wendel and the appointment of himself. A very large majority of the people would be opposed to the change. The only signatures he can procure will be among his Methodist bretheren, and some warm partisans of a political party. Surely Mr [Felix] Grundy will do his best to prevent the appointment of *Clark* (should Mr Wendel be removed) who is constantly reading [Nicholas] Biddles pamphlet, and urging upon the people that Grundy is a nullifier. Such is his course with every person he meets. Mr Bell cannot urge Mr Wendels removal, who has been his devoted friend and should it be determined that Mr Wendel is to be removed, it is expected by your friends here that you will give some other person your aid rather than Clark. I once addressed [you] upon this subject with reference to my own pretensions. I have come to the conclusion that my chance is bad for making a living in any way than by the sweat of the brow, and have given over any idea of sharing in the *loaves and fishes;* tho my means are extremely limited, yet I can live and that is as much as a reasonable man should wish. Tis at least as much as I expect. It is expected that Coln. Cannon[4] will be announced in a few days, a candidate for Congress in this district. Should he be a candidate it is thought Bradys[5] prospects will be much better. Cannon, Dickinson and Murray[6] will divide the votes of Williamson, and leave Brady, Rutherford, pretty much undivided, and a tolerable share in Williamson. There is no news here of interest. We are all well and Mah seems to be better contented in town. Give our love to Sarah and tell her to write to us frequently. I should be glad to hear from you soon.

JNO W CHILDRESS

Addressed to Washington.

1. A younger brother of Polk's wife and a Murfreesboro lawyer.

2. Not positively identified but probably a relative of William S. Moore. See the latter's letter to Polk, January 3, 1833.

3. A charter member of the first Methodist church established in Murfreesboro, Clark later became a Methodist minister. In 1834 he bought out his partners in the firm R. Ledbetter and Company. He was also connected briefly with a local newspaper.

4. Newton Cannon of Williamson County. Cannon did not seek the congressional seat and instead ran unsuccessfully for a place in the General Assembly.

5. William Brady had served for ten years in the lower house of the General Assembly.

6. Probably Abram P. Maury of Williamson County. After sitting in both houses of the state legislature, he was in Congress for two terms, 1835–39. David W. Dickinson, John Bell's brother-in-law, was successful in the 1833 congressional race.

FROM EZEKIEL P. McNEAL[1]

Bolivar. January 9, 1833

At James Walker's request, McNeal, Polk's first cousin and agent, sends a duplicate which he has signed of a lease on a tract of land belonging to the heirs of the late Marshall T. Polk.

Addressed to Washington.

1. See McNeal to Polk, March 7, 1828.

FROM JOHN RAYBURN

Waynesboro. January 9, 1833

Rayburn, a former sheriff of Wayne County, requests information on pension applications of William Barnett and William Rutledge, old and needy citizens of that county.

Addressed to Washington.

FROM BENJAMIN CLEMENTS

Fayetteville. January 11, 1833

Clements reminds Polk of earlier correspondence concerning his desire to be appointed surveyor in the lands acquired from the Chickasaws. He asks Polk to discuss the matter with the president and notes that he will soon leave for Tallahassee, Florida.

Addressed to Washington.

FROM JAMES W. WYLY[1] TO JAMES K. POLK AND JAMES STANDIFER[2]

Dear Gentlemen, Greeneville January 11th 1833

I take leave to address you a line without having any important information to communicate. There is in this section a perfect dearth of domestic news. The political movements of South Carolina and the Presidents proclamation, produced for a while much excitement. It is thought however nothing serious will result except the public disgrace which will always attaint the characters of the nullifiers. The leaders of that doctrine in South Carolina I think ought to pull hemp. There is no doubt that their sole object was a seperation of the union—but they cant effect that object. Mr Calhoun will have to live under the administration of Genl Jackson and after him, some other good republican, or leave the United States. If he should choose the latter I dont believe their would be any killing grief for his departure. He is as politically defunct as Aron Burr than whom in principle he is not superior. And Gove[r]nor Hamilton[3] recommended the Legislature to pass a law to authorize the Gove[r]nor to organize two thousand militia at Charleston and throughout the State. Ten thousand to be called the State guard. What for? to resist the union. How ridiculous—and the Gove[r]nor requested the passing a resolution desiring the President to remove the United States troops from the Citidal at Charleston, so as to give them a chance. The old chief could rally force enough if necessary, upon two weeks notice from other States to Stand on the Saluda Mountain[4] and piss enough, (I ask your pardon for the language but I know no other word so appropriate to connect with nullification) to float the whole nullifying crew of South Carolina into the Atlantic Ocean. The proclamation of the President electrified the Legislature of that State. Mr Preston[5] flew into a paroxism of rage—others, whilst that part of the proclamation was reading which addressed the citizens of that State in the affectionate language of a father to his children, were convulsed with a *holy laugh.* I presume Gov[r]nor Hamilton has his militia in proper training. It will be a complete army of Gentlemen each furnished with a servant to help his master, the soldier, on and off his warlike steed; this would be an indispensable requisite for at least one half of the South Carolinians are unable to get on their horses, with one foot in the Stirrup, under three fair trials.

Did Coln. Standifer procure Coln. Jacobs & Doct. Cock[6] to write the piece against his opponent James I Greene[7] which lately appeared in the Knoxville Register? If so he has commenced the Campaign early and is rallying his forces for a hard fight. I am told T. F Bradford[8] is exciting the good people of

Bedford on account of the organization of the congressional districts by the Legislature by which he expects to sail into Congress. He accuses certain members of East Tennessee of combining to prevent Bedford from having a representative in Congress. This is untrue—but they did defeat Mr Theodorick in his manouvering to attach Bedford to some small county (thereby disorganizing the nature & fitness of things) for the purpose of working the wires to suit his own ambitious views. Coln Polk must not let such a federal hypocrite in politicks defeat him.

Judge McNairy is about to resign his office of Judge of the Federal Court. It would afford me the greatest pleasure to have that appointment conferred on my friend Judge Wm E Kennedy of Columbia. I hope your greatest exertions will be used to that effect. He possesses every requisite of a Judge—impartial, industrious & profound in his profession. I wrote to White & Blair[9] on his behalf. Write to me on reception.

JAS. W. WYLY

Give my respects to Genl Hall, Cave Johnson & Fitzgerald[10] & tell them write me without fail.

Addressed to Washington. Letter has been published in Paul H. Bergeron, editor, "A Tennessean Blasts Calhoun and Nullification," *Tennessee Historical Quarterly,* XXVI (1967), 383–386.

1. A lawyer in Greene County and, at the time of this letter, a member of the upper house of the state legislature, in which he served two terms, 1831–35. He moved to Missouri in 1835.

2. From the Sequatchie valley, Standifer was in the House of Representatives at this time. He served in the House 1823–25 and 1829–37. He was a leader in the effort to have Tennessee's congressional delegation endorse Hugh Lawson White for the presidency in 1836.

3. By the time this letter was penned James Hamilton had been succeeded as governor of South Carolina by Robert Y. Hayne.

4. An eminence at the extreme northwest corner of South Carolina that theoretically overlooked the whole state.

5. A strong nullifier, William C. Preston was a lawyer in Columbia, South Carolina, and a member of the state legislature. Later in 1833 he was elected to the United States Senate, where he served with John C. Calhoun until 1842. He was president of South Carolina College, 1845–51.

6. Probably Solomon D. Jacobs, an influential businessman in Knoxville, and John Cocke, a former congressman from East Tennessee.

7. A state senator from East Tennessee, 1827–33.

8. Theodorick F. Bradford of Bedford County, who ran unsuccessfully against Polk in 1833. He had represented his county in the General Assembly for four terms.

9. A resident of Jonesboro, John Blair was a member of the United States House of Representatives, 1823–35.

10. William Hall, Cave Johnson, and William T. Fitzgerald were members of the Tennessee delegation in the House of Representatives.

FROM WILLIAM P. BRADBURN

Nashville. January 13, 1833

A former printer's apprentice who had been appointed midshipman in the navy some months before asks Polk to ascertain why he had not been ordered to active duty.[1]

Addressed to Washington.

1. See Polk to Levi Woodbury, May 6, 1832, and Woodbury to Polk, May 8, 1832.

FROM MARSHALL P. PINKARD

Williamsport. January 13, 1833

A merchant and deputy postmaster at Williamsport, Pinkard calls attention to the inadequacies of the mail service to his community and suggests means of improving it.

Addressed to Washington.

FROM WILLIAM H. POLK[1]

Dear Brother Hillsborough N.C. January 13th 1833

The session will commence on tomorrow. I received A letter from Brother Samuel[2] on yesterday saying that they were all well and that the Cholera was said to be in Nashville and in the western district. I want you to send me some newspaper so as I can see what is said and done about nullification and what is doing in Congress. I received A letter from sister Laura[3] saying that Ma[r]shall[4] could walk and had got perfictly well. Tell sister Sarah I have been looking for A letter from her and am in hopes that she will not disapoint me. You must answer this when you receive this. Nothing more at presant.

W H Polk

P.S. You must not forget to sen[d] me that paper so I can read it when I have got my lesson.

W H Polk

Addressed to Washington.

1. Polk's oldest living brother, who was almost eighteen years old at this time.

2. Samuel Washington Polk, fifteen years old.

3. Laura Wilson Polk, widow of Polk's brother Marshall T. Polk.

4. Born in Charlotte, North Carolina, in May 1831, one month after his father's death.

FROM JOSEPH BROWN[1]

Dear Col Cave Spring Maurey Cty Te January 14th 1833

I have Taken my pen to acknowlege the recept of yours of December last in which you inform me that you are not of Opinion that Mr Plummer[2] nor my self Could be of aney Service in giting My Claim Allowed Which Coresponds with my own Exsept this. As the preasident had been long aquintid with me and Knew that My own privet Intrest had neaver hindred me from dowing a publick good, I had Concluded that me being thare might be the Means of the Oald Gentelman a Saying something to Aney of the Members that was Known to be Inimmical to My Claim that might remove their prejudice, and I also Concluded that if the law passed I would have to gow thare, and if so I would rather be thare at the time Congress would be in Session. But if the law passes as I have had all the Troubel with it and some of the hairs lives in the State of Mississippi (to wit Wm & George Brown)[3] and William is Cripled by a wound he Received from the Indians when I was a prisnor by them. On that ground the law had better be passed in My Name as hair of James Brown Deceased that when I went to git My own I might git the whole as I think I have hounesty enough to do what is right. I have but on[e] sister a living and my two Brothers above named and I have two sisters that are dead that have left hairs.

One of them is by the name of Margaret Hamilton, and the other by the name of Jane Collinsworth. My Sister that is living is by the Name of Ann Anderson,[4] and I feell Vearey thankfull to you for writing to me as you did for I should now have been on the rode, but I asure you it was a trip that I dreaded at this season of the year and I feell vearey glad to git leave to stay at home. My family is in Common health.

Jos. Brown

Addressed to Washington.

1. An early settler in Maury County and one of its most respected residents. See Brown to Polk, December 6, 1832.

2. Probably James R. Plummer, a leading merchant in Columbia who at one time served as its mayor.

3. In May 1788 James Brown, a Revolutionary War veteran and father of the writer of this letter, led an expedition down the Tennessee River expecting to ascend the Cumberland and settle in the Duck River region. The party was intercepted by Indians, and several of them, including James Brown, were killed. The others were held captive, and members of the Brown family were widely separated during this captivity. Joseph was about fifteen years of age in 1788; George was some six years younger. William Brown, an older brother, was already in Middle Tennessee and was preparing for the arrival of the rest of his family. Eventually the Browns were freed, and the family reunited.

4. Not otherwise identified.

FROM WILLIAM R. RUCKER[1]

Dear Colonel Murfreesborough 15th Jany 1833

I employ a leisure hour to write you a short letter to redeem my pledge. There is very little transpiring here that will interest you and Sarah. Time passes very much as it has done for the last year or two. It has hitherto been a much milder winter than the last, though there has been a great deal of rain. But Cholera the many headed monster has not yet made its appearance in Murfreesborough and it is very much doubted whether it has really been in Nashville, the report of the Board of Health to the Contrary notwithstanding.

Mrs. McIver will be married next Thursday to a Lawyer Fentress[2] of the Western District. The parties have all arrived. Your relation Miss Polk[3] is at this time at Mr Wendell's but will accompany Mrs Fentress when she goes home. I am told the Groom is rather an elderly looking gentleman.

It is rumoured here that there is a probability that Mr Wendell would be removed from his appointment of Postmaster and that Martin Clark of this place would be appointed in his place. Now I do not believe that we could get a better Post Master in Murfreesborough or one who would give more general satisfaction than Mr Wendell, And (however he was opposed to the Election of Genl Jackson) less obnoxious to the Presidents friends. If he should be removed I would have no objection [to] the appointment of Mr Clark. He is honest and capable.

I will be much obliged to you if you will send me the Intelligencer and pay the Subscription of one year & I will pay when you return.

We hear & read a great deal on the subjects of South Carolina Nullification and the Presidents Proclamation. These are eventful times and may God grant us a safe deliverance from our threatened evils. The Proclamation will be long read in our country as our *constitutional* Text Book and its author will stand in fame next to our beloved Washington.

We are all well. Susan would write to Sarah but says she has nothing to write about.

W. R. RUCKER

Addressed to Washington.

1. A Murfreesboro doctor who was married to Susan Childress, a sister of Polk's wife.

2. On January 17, 1833, a marriage license was issued in Murfreesboro to David Fentress and Matilda C. McIver. She was a member of the Wendel family and the widow of Evander McIver. Fentress was a prominent lawyer of Hardeman County and later represented that county in the lower house of the General Assembly.

3. Apparently one of James K. Polk's first cousins and probably a resident of Hardeman County.

FROM JONATHAN WEBSTER[1]

Dear Sir Noah's Fork Bedford Cty. Ten Jany 15th 1833

About the 6th of Decm last, I wrote you relative to my new invented water wheel, asking the favour of you to exammon the pattent Office, and see if there has been any such before. I have not yet recieved your answer. Therefore I beg permission to trouble you again on the subject. I expect to start on a jorney in the course of two or three weeks, but should like to hear from you on my return home but still hope to get a line from you before I start.

I stated that my invention was water buckets on the top of the inclined wheel with water gaps in the edge to discharge the water at the lowest point, while the water would be coming in at or over the uper part, as an over shot. Doors are to be fited in those gaps to open very quick when they come to the place for the discharge of the water, and shut again themselves. Above this wheel there is to be a Horse floor, so that Horse and water can operate together or separate from each other. I had heard that a gentleman in Huntsville was studying on my plan, and asked you to exammon and assist me in securing the right. I am told that I should have a circular from the Secretary of State.

I have just heard that a man by the name of ——— Wheelor[2] has obtained a pattent for a similar invention. They say he calls it the inclined race wheel. If convenient please send me the exact description of his wheel. He lived in the Western District, Shelby Cty. Should I not hear from you I shall mail a small modle directed to you, as I am told that I have the right and that it is the practis.

You take the Shelbyville papers. We have no other news here to send you. Cannon[3] I believe, will walk over the turff alone. I shal not (as I now think) oppose him. I should have met [Theodorick F.] Bradford, had he not gone back. And appear when he may (My friends aside) I shall be with him.

If Maury puts up two for Congress, I shall then look out for Bradford, but he will not, I think attack you alone.

Jacksons & Whites success has made me so fat that I allmost "lard the ground as I walk."

J. WEBSTER

Addressed to Washington.

1. A Bedford County resident of considerable political influence who served in both houses of the General Assembly. Since the extant portion of Webster's letter of December 6, 1832, does not mention the water wheel, it appears that more of that letter is missing than was at first thought.

2. Not otherwise identified.
3. Robert Cannon, a prominent Bedford County political figure who ran successfully for the state senate.

FROM A. W. BILLS[1]

Dear Sir, Millersburgh [Kentucky] Jany 16th 1833

It is perhaps to you of little importance especially at this time to receive this trifling memento from an old friend with so few claims to be remembered unless for his Youthful follies. Of these you was a personal witness. Yet I believe and will venture to hope that time and experience have not altogether wasted their influence in correcting and maturing the mind for appropriate usefulness.

Yours has been an uninterrupted course of publick turmoil and I would say success, perhaps to the intent of your wishes.

My own has been one of varied success marked thruout with the relentless hand of affliction from disease; at one time upon the verge of the grave and again permitted to hope for health and ability to accomplish the arduous duties which pressed of necessity upon me.

In this manner I have lived, hoped, aspired and despaired then taken courage when health would permit and sometimes succeeded in my wishes. In health I have improved materially for these last two years. Have now a family of five likely and promising children if you will take my word in the matter. These are sometimes a source of concern and again of solace, such as should be expected by all reasonable men. But without too much circumlocution I had as well come to the point which at present has called for this letter.

It is thought another nomination to Columbia[Colombia] will be made since Mr. Moore[2] has been permitted to return. Now do not be startled. I do not ask to go as Minister. But might I not be allowed to calculate upon the confidence of the Government as Charge des Affairs or Secretary of legation as the case may be? We have already lost two prominent men from our State on missions to those countries and more than possible from the want of efficient medical skill. This might if urged in connection with official ability in the applicant have a material weight in determining the selection. To the Minister himself it must be an important consideration. I therefore place myself before the cabinet with the aid of your kindness to see the Secretary of State and President in person upon the subject. And if nominated our Friend the Hon Felix Grundy will upon your request vindicate my claims in the Senate. I have other friends viz—A Kendall and Majr. Barry[3] to whom you might if thought necessary make mention of the matter with a request that they might advance my pretentions. Our present representative Mr. Marshall[4] being politically opposed I feel unwilling to commit any thing confidential to his keeping. He knows full well that I was no advantage to his election and I have nothing to hope at his hands.

I anticipate the want of celebrity in a public capacity and other minor difficulties which alone can be obviated by your zeal to serve and old and now ardent friend. I have read minutely the history and achievements of our Southern Republicks and have constantly entertained a strong desire to visit and witness their exertions for the establishment of independence and equal rights.

I am the more inclined to hope for it with the strongest conviction that my health and constitution would be greatly benefitted.

But I may be consuming time and wearying your patience to no purpose for these things may have all been settled before this time. But should they not and any chances seem to present themselves your friendly assistance is respectfully solicited.

I will not further trespass upon your patience unless to request an early reply.

I could if room and time permitted take a passing notice of the intersting posture of our national affairs as presented in this country. But of these things you are well advised. It is only necessary to state that in all probability the apportionment will be so arranged that we shall loose most if not all our representatives hereafter in Congress—as by similar management we are so much in the minority in the Legislature, but when we come to even balloting for Govr. we out count them. Consequently Jackson Men enjoy nothing of state patronage.

A. W. Bills

Addressed to Washington.

1. A physician who had helped organize in 1831 and 1832 a Christian church in Millersburg. The organizers were Baptist dissenters who later united with Presbyterian dissidents under Barton Stone. Bills had lived in Middle Tennessee and was possibly a kinsman of John H. Bills, at this time a resident of Bolivar, Tennessee.

2. Thomas P. Moore had served in the United States House of Representatives, 1823–29, and had received the Colombia appointment from Jackson in 1829. When Moore returned from South America in 1833, he failed in an effort to be re-elected to Congress.

3. Amos Kendall had been a prominent newspaperman in Kentucky before he moved to Washington in 1829, where he became an influential member of Jackson's Kitchen Cabinet. William T. Barry, also of Kentucky, served as Postmaster General, 1829–35.

4. Thomas A. Marshall served two terms in the United States House of Representatives, 1831–35. Afterward he had a long judicial career in Kentucky and became chief justice of the state supreme court.

FROM THOMAS COLLIN[1]

Sir Tennessee State, Bedford County. January 16 1833

I take pleasure in informing you that I receved your polite faver in forwarding to me the presidents Message acompanied with additional statements relative to the comerce and navigation of the United States which communications is gratefuly acknoledged by me and will be on all ocatisons[occasions]. Much excitement is stiring up with your peopel on the nulfing [nullifying] questen or tariff. We all cry out save the union. We grone and complain under the presure of the times, and if sides has to be choosed hear I doubt we will see wors times than you or me has ever seen, for it would [take] a wiser head than me to devine or tell what the peopel will do hear. You have no sarten oponent yet to my knoledge. Bradford and his friends apears to be feeling but I think he will not stand the pull.

Col. R. Canon is out for Sineter in State Legislator. Col. [Jonathan] Webster is talked of as his oponent but not sarten. For the Comons, Kincaid, Col. An[d]erson, and S. Philips.[2] Pleas give my kind complyments to judg Felix Grundy. Let him know Springer[3] and myself has setteled our seuts in Murfreesbourow. But our seut has returned from Sparta Supreme Cou[r]t to Winchester, Franklin Co. Circuit Cou[r]t for new tryel and set on the first Monday of July for tryel. This I wish him to set down as one of the peticler memorandum note for on that day I hope to see him thear in good health. Another matter I wish to cumunicate to you and think I once stated sumthing of the case to you, that is this. Shortly after the defeat of Nickejack towen in the Cherocee nation, at that time I was living in Sumner County, sum of the lying out Indens after the treaty was made came near to Bletchers Lick and stole several horses. They took mine and James Carothers[4] at that time. It was the articals of the treaty that if the Cherocees stole any horses from the whites that the[y] should be paid sixty dollars per head out of the Cherocees anuel selery. James Carothers and myself as I consider maid pointed proof by an evidence wos[whose] caracter could not be disputed. That was Robert White[5] of Sumner C. and Archey Coody[6] the Inden Linkester who seen our horses in the nation in posesion of sarten Indens which the[y] name in thear depositions. I purched Carothers clame and laid it with my owen before Col. Henly[7] and then before [. . .] who was agents for the Cherocee nation. The[y] allways made sum excuse that the[y] had no mony or had to write to the war office and so on that I coud get no mony out of them and I did not know how to compel them. About the decleration of the last war I sent on the peapers to judg Grunday who was a mimber to Congress at time. Buisness was so presing he dun nothing as know of.

Pleas to have the goodnis to name the caus to judg Grunday and if you can do any thing for me in that case it will gratefulled acknoleges by me. . . .

THOMAS COLLIN

N B One hundred and twenty dollers will do me more good now than one thousand would have don ten years ago.

THO COLLIN

Addressed to Washington.

1. The handwriting in this letter is almost impossible to read. The signature could not be deciphered with assurance, and the writer has not been identified. Since he was trying to get payment for a horse allegedly stolen about thirty-eight years earlier, he was probably well advanced in years.

2. Joseph A. Kincaid, a physician, had represented Bedford County for

two terms in the lower house of the General Assembly. Kenneth L. Anderson was active in political affairs and had served as county sheriff. Samuel Phillips, also politically active, was a brother of Archibald Yell's first wife.

3. Unidentified.

4. Possibly James Caruthers of Lincoln County, a War of 1812 veteran and a Tennessee legislator for one term.

5. An officer in the Sumner County militia.

6. A halfbreed Cherokee who spoke and wrote English and who served as an interpreter and as a messenger between the settlers and the Indians.

7. Unidentified.

FROM ARCHIBALD YELL[1]

My Dear Sir. Fayett[e]ville Jany the 16th 1833

I am so much of a partizan that I am always for *Jackson Right or Wrong.* At the same time I must confess to you that I am now and ever have been, since I have had any Politicks at all, so much of a *Desorganizer* if you will allow me to give it no worse a name, that I have held more to the Virginia docterine than the docterines laid down in the Proclamation. I am not a Nulifyer if I know realy what I am, and I am much further from being in faver of *Consoladation.* I imbrace the Virginia Resolutions that the Genl Government was framed by the States in their soveregn Capasity, that all Powers they had under the old Confederation and not expressly parted with, they still retain, but whether under any view of their powers, they have a right to secede. If they have, then our Goverment is held together by a very weak cord. If they have not, then there is in my view grate danger from the Genl Govnmt. Is it posable that I have all my life bin mistaken and that this *Umpire* is the Federal Judiciary that in my view is worse than either result? But it must rest some where but where it is I am for further *argument.* One thing is now certain there has been a verry sudden converssion. The *Enimy* has come over. Or we have gone to them (how is it)? We are waiting with trembling anxiety to see what Congress will do with the Tariff. You can preserve the *Union* or permit the fire brands to go forth. That may result in a disolution of this Republic. Our prayrs are all here that the "Cup may pass" and that order may be restored. But I greately fear the time is not far ahead (4 years) when this fabric will tumble to pieces, and perhaps sooner. One thing may prevent it. The Eastern states would be the loosers. That may teach them what they should do. These are subjects perhaps about which we should not allow ourselvs to speculate.

I see my successor is old Maj Chambers of Ky.[2] quite a clever fellow. Here permit me to tender you my warmest thanks for your attention to my letter of Resignation. Your influence and exertion and the kindness of the President will not be easily forgotten. You can more easily imagine my feelings of Gratitude than I can express them.

Judge McNary will shortly resign and you I presume know the applicants. I am for *Lea,*[3] tho. I live amidst [William E.] Ken[n]edys relations. I have so written to Judge Hu L. White. You I presume will be "hands off." I think it probible I have not consulted my own interest as his friends may entertain some unkind feelings because I refused to sign his letter of Recommendation. Be it so, I have always been in the habit of giving way to my feelings and they were for *Lea,* not because I know him personally for I do not. But for his sterling Integrity, and perhaps because he was defeated by that *Rascal* Arnold[4] and because he is the friend and relative of Judge White.

State Politics

1st, as to yourself. Your mail Rout I am informed by some of our Bedford frnds who was here a few days since (Col Sam Mitchell & Doct McKisick)[5] has been a *quietus* upon *Theo.*[6] It has done you more service in Bedford than all your *Big* speeches in Congress and they are clearly of the oppinion that *Cousin Theo* will not run. They say his frinds have seased to talk about his being a candidate. (I though[t] he was too smart for that.) So is quite probible you will be reelected without opposition. (So mote it be.) Bob Cannon is out for the senate. [Jonathan] Webster will oppose him and also [Joseph] Kincaid as some think. If all run the result doubtful. Chances in favr of Cannon, perhaps. As yet no body out for the H. R.

Here I am almost afraid to say any thing for fear you conjecture that I am opposed to Inge.[7] That is not true. Yet the Result I conceive as doubtful. Majr Field[8] is out for the Senate. On yesterday some of the strongest men in this county, such as Bright, Fulton, McKinny and others wrote Col Moore[9] a letter requesting him to be a Candidate for the Senate. Moors answr has not been recievd, but I fear there is but little doubt he will oppose Field for the H. R. Col. James Smith, John R. Greer, and F. G. McConnel[10] are out. There will be some more started, who will probably beat them all. Doct. Smith[11] is strongly patriotic but as yet he objects. I think it not improbible that John H Morgan[12] will run. It seems dificult to select some man on whom the People will unite that would run.

Be so good as to present me to Col *Sevier* and say to him that I had prepared a letter for the President for Judge Johnson,[13] but by the same mail had the pleasure to see his reappointmt. I receved a few days since a letter from Judge Johnson. All was well.

I have settled down contentedly in the little vilage of Fayettville. My prospects here are as flatering as I could have anticipated. Write me when you find leasure, and present me to your good Lady, whose friendship I hope I yet retain and accept for yourself my best wishes for your health and happiness &c.

YELL

Addressed to Washington.

1. One of Polk's close political and personal friends for many years. After a political career in Bedford and Lincoln counties, Yell moved to Arkansas, where he achieved even greater political success.

2. Benjamin S. Chambers replaced Yell as receiver of public money at Little Rock, Arkansas. He died in October 1833.

3. Pryor Lea had been a congressman from East Tennessee but had been defeated when he ran for re-election. He left the state in 1836, moving first to Mississippi and thence to Texas.

4. Thomas D. Arnold, a strong anti-Jackson man, had defeated Pryor Lea in the congressional race in 1831. He served one term and ten years later was elected to another term.

5. Samuel Mitchell, a colonel in the militia, had represented Bedford County in the General Assembly, 1829–31. Spivey McKissick was an early settler in Spring Hill and was its first mayor. He was absent from the state at this time. See McKissick to Polk, January 18, 1833.

6. Theodorick F. Bradford.

7. William M. Inge was a Fayetteville lawyer. He had recently represented Lincoln County in the General Assembly.

8. William H. Feild was a Pulaski lawyer and a member of the state senate, 1831–33. This is the correct spelling of the name although it was probably more often spelled Field.

9. James Bright, an early settler in Lincoln County, was for many years clerk of the circuit court and was one of the commissioners appointed in 1831 to settle the boundary dispute with Kentucky. James Fulton was a highly regarded lawyer in Fayetteville. McKinny is probably Ira McKinney, who later was elected from Lincoln County to the lower house of the General Assembly, serving 1839–41. William Moore, Yell's brother-in-law, was successful in his bid for the state senate seat for Lincoln and Giles counties, serving two terms, 1833–37.

10. James Smith was the son of William Smith, Revolutionary War veteran, and was also a brother-in-law of Isaac Southworth. John R. Greer was probably a relative of Vance Greer, but he has not been fully identified. Felix Grundy McConnell served as postmaster at Fayetteville, 1830–33. In 1834 he moved to Talladega County, Alabama, where he engaged in a successful political career.

11. Probably William F. Smith, a Fayetteville physician.

12. Yell's law partner in Fayetteville for a short time. Later he moved to Memphis and became its mayor in 1838.

13. Ambrose H. Sevier, kinsman of John Sevier and a native of Tennessee, was the delegate to Congress from Arkansas Territory, 1828–36, and later served as United States senator from the newly admitted state of Arkansas, 1836–48. Benjamin Johnson, brother of Richard Mentor Johnson of Kentucky, had served as a federal judge in Arkansas under Monroe and Adams and was twice reappointed by Jackson.

FROM HERBERT BILES[1]

Stat of Tennessee, Fayett Co, Summerville

Dear Sir January the 17th 1833

I take my pen in hand to Let you [k]now how we are dowing. My helth is very good except my Back and that is much better then when you war hear. Thar has bean a grat Deal of Sickness Among the niggars senc you war hear. Severl of them is Complaining at this time. Seasor has got well. Lizabeth is on the mend; she got married in the Crismas times to a boy in the neighborhood and I am in hopes that he will [. . .].[2] I am dun my Cotton and am sorry to say it has turned out so sorry I onley maid twenty eight thousand. I have geathered my Corn and am afraid that I will not hav anuff. I hav Commenced Claring and intend to start my plows in a day or too. We hav had a very wett fall and winter but now[no] snow yet. I received your letter of the 17th of December and wold hav written sooner but I was wating for the boyes to come with the hoggs. But Doctor Colwell[3] has gon to Kentuckey to buy niggars and thay will not bea down for too weeks yet which will keepp me out off their work six week by his smartness. Lucys Little girl Silvey Died on the 9th of December. Wally has behaved himself very well and I think will make me A first rate hand. Mr Warrick has got down with Mr Rutlidge[4] hands and Mr Rutlidge will be down the first of Febuary. Georg Moore[5] sais that his Cotton has turned out very sorry. He sais that off of 80 Akers that he wont make Eight thousand and Mr [James] Walker sais that Kibble[6] has don wors then either of us. Kibble has left Mr Walker and gon to himself. The first five bailes of Cotton that I Sent off weyed 2491 lb. The second Lode was Delivered on Sunday and was not wayed. Thar is another Lode reddy and it will Start as soon as the rod[e] gets so that we can travel. Nothing more. . . .

H Biles

Addressed to Washington.

1. Overseer on Polk's Fayette County plantation.
2. Two words illegible.
3. Silas M. Caldwell, husband of Polk's sister Lydia Eliza.
4. William Rutledge of Rutherford County had apparently bought land in the region and was moving to it. In a letter of August 11, 1832, he had asked Polk about a tract of about 300 acres that Polk owned. It appears that Warrick was Rutledge's overseer, but this has not been firmly established. It also seems likely that Biles's wife was related to Rutledge.
5. A highly regarded overseer on one of James Walker's plantations in Fayette County.
6. Unidentified other than that he had been an unsuccessful overseer for James Walker.

FROM DANIEL LEATHERMAN

Bradshaw's Creek, Giles County.
January 18, 1833

A Giles County resident, who claims to be Polk's old and true friend, wants to build a mill in the Chickasaw lands and seeks Polk's political support.

Addressed to Washington.

FROM SPIVEY McKISSICK

Dear Sir Roxb[o]ro N C 18th Jany 1833

Living at this time remote from my home and friends in the western country and in bad health and hearing much of nulification and anxious to know what will be the final result of all this excitement I have thought none could give me more light or information upon the subject than my representative in the national councils and have addressed this letter to you under an impression that you will devote a few moments of your time in giving me your views upon the South Carolina doctrines. We have but very little difference of opinion in North Carolina in Person County. I understand we have only one nulifier and he is trying to work out of former opinions. We believe in this part of the state that the president in his proclamation has given us the true doctrines of the constitution and have no doubt at this time but what General Jackson is more popular with the people in this part of the state of North Carolina than previous to the presidential election.

Mr Smith[1] of Roxbro wrote on to Mr Blair[2] to send him his paper. Mr Smith is a solvent and respectable man. Please know his reasons for not forwarding the paper.

S McKissick

Addressed to Washington. This letter has been published in Elizabeth Gregory McPherson, editor, "Unpublished Letters from North Carolinians to Polk," *North Carolina Historical Review,* XVI (1939), 76–77.

1. Unidentified.
2. Francis P. Blair was editor of the Washington *Globe.*

FROM SAMUEL BIGHAM

Dear Sir Livingston,[1] Bedford County Te. Jany 19th 1833

I am requested by Willis M. Hopwood[2] to say to you that he wishes his Globe discontinued at the end of the year and that he will pay you the money as soon as you return home. He wants to take a Nashville paper. Major Davis[3] would take the Globe but complains of being in debt and money is very scarce. From the present aspect of public affairs it seems as if you will have a very responsible session this term but we all know here that you will use every exertion in your power to restore harmony, and save our happy and flourishing country and invaluable government from dissolution. I see Duff Green has got a well merited castigation for using his slanderous epithets so liberally. If you have time let us know what is likely to be done respecting the tariff law or any other matter of importance to your constituents, that may come before you.

S. BIGHAM

Addressed to Washington.

1. For a short time there were two post offices in Tennessee with this name, one in Bedford County and another in Overton County. The one in Bedford was discontinued.

2. A merchant who lived in that part of Bedford that later was incorporated into Marshall County. At Lewisburg, the county seat of Marshall, he served as constable, deputy sheriff, and sheriff.

3. Probably the Thomas Davis who was postmaster at Shelbyville.

FROM DANIEL STEPHENS[1]

Very dear sir Columbia, Tenn. Jan. 19, 1833

The purport of this short letter is to trouble you (if it will not be too great an intrusion on your time) to attend to the application of my son William H. Stephens,[2] for a situation as Cadett at West Point. You will recollect that you handed in his application and recommendations last spring, to the Secty. of War.

We only wish you to attend to whatever etiquette may be necessary on the subject, and to apprize us, in due time, of the result.

Your friends here are all well.

DANIEL STEPHENS

Addressed to Washington.

1. Rector of St. Peter's Episcopal Church, Columbia. In 1834 he moved to Bolivar, Tennessee, where he established an Episcopal church and served as its rector until 1846.

2. Polk had written to Secretary of War Lewis Cass in support of his application, but Stephens never attended the Military Academy. See Polk to Cass, June 11, 1832.

FROM AARON V. BROWN[1]

Dear Sir Aspen Hill [Giles County] Jany 20th 1833

Some time since I wrote you enclosing some valuable papers (perhaps) & requesting a reply from you—touching all the S. Carolina events—but I have received no answer. Has my letter miscarried? or is Giles no longer a part of your disctrict? Oh now I can account for it. You are so *intensely engaged* in public concerns, that you have no time to devote to private friendship! Atlas never supported half such a burden as now rests on one poor pair of stooping shoulders! Nullification shaking her "snaky crest" on the one hand & the "Gorgon head" of consolidation on the other. Wont this do as well as "Sylla & Caribdis"? Send me one of Duffs pamphlets containing the *quintessence* on both sides. What does Mr. *Adams* mean by his call?[2] Does he mean to seek distinction *in the fray* or is he only collecting materials for another epic?

Well I vow I do not very well know which side to take in some respects. S. Carolina is determined to destroy herself by her folly & pricipitance & the proclamation in some parts leaves the "old Virginia" doctrines of state rights far on the left. *Subrosa* what will you state rights sticklers do now? "What will Mrs Grundy say"?[3] Now *nullification* I always believed to be nonse[n]se but what about *secession?* If made by a state in time of peace & with as little injury as the nature of the act will admit of is it then a *causa belli* on the part of the other States? If so must not *Congress* declare it? Can the Executive? Do not all the laws now in force contemplate an unauthorised resistance by a mob or other association of private individuals in cases where the *President* can interfere? These are vital questions, which the crisis will decide & decide against the Virginia doctrines. *The sword* cuts all Gordian Knots like these Whilst the politician is dreaming over his abstractions.

Tell the President that my remedy for nullification is—if we loose S. Car. let us get Texas in its stead—though I had rather have both. Why dont you send Carroll[4] there; he would I think come as near getting that country as any one else whatever. Now to another topic. Cant you all at Washington prevent any contest next fall between E. & G.[5] for Senator which can be gotten through the Senate? If E. cant perhaps G. could for something worthy his acceptance. Look to this & *if practicable* prevent an issue which I should regret, let it fall either way.

It is understood here, that [William E.] Kennedy shoves against [John] McNairy & [William H.] Feild & Bramblett,[6] Kennedy—all wanting to be successor. How will the first come out at the City? When you answer *that* I will say who will come out here.

A. V. Brown

Addressed to Washington.

1. Polk's former law partner and one of his strongest supporters in Giles County.

2. This is probably a reference to a resolution submitted to the House of Representatives by Adams on December 18, 1832, in which he sought to have Jackson submit to the House the correspondence with the Republic of Buenos Ayres that had resulted in a threatened diplomatic break. The trouble concerned seal fishing rights in the Falkland Islands.

3. Mrs. Grundy, a character in Thomas Morton's play *Speed the Plough,* first produced in 1798, became the symbol of conventional propriety in nineteenth-century England.

4. Governor William Carroll had been prominently mentioned as a possible diplomatic representative in Mexico.

5. John H. Eaton and Felix Grundy. A called session of the General Assembly in the fall of 1832 had been unable to reach a decision in a contest for a seat in the United States Senate, Eaton and Grundy being the chief contenders.

6. Lunsford M. Bramlett, a Giles County lawyer who later held state judicial positions.

FROM ISAAC SOUTHWORTH[1]

Hon. James K Polk Fayetteville (Tenn) 21st Jany. 1833
Monday Night

Your polite acknowledgement of the reception of mine of Nov 27th '32, which bears the date of the 29th Ulto. came to me this morning.

I thank you most cordially for so readily and so courteously complying with my wishes. You have also the heartfelt thanks—I am authorised to say—of the worthy old soldiers in whose behalf I was primarily induced to break through the severe forms of refined etiquette and address you upon no better authority than the broad basis of being your fellow citizen. Pray permit me to avail myself of the latitude which I am, in consequence of your kind attention, emboldened to exercise, to lay before you the following facts, and to bespeak for them your patriotic regard.

By the last mail which left this place, there was transmitted to the Hon. Mr. Grundy a M.S. intitled 'Frank Confessions of an Experienced Manufacturer.' The production is from my pen and is my maiden effort of a political nature.

It is purposely written in such a manner as to lead the public to lay the authorship of it at the door of some Northern devotee of the Union, who is willing and anxious to sacrifice upon the altar of patriotism. And goes to show; 1st. That particular circumstances now, as heretofore, afford protection to the artisan independent of the aid of government. 2dly That it is the belief of the writer, that it is partially owing to ignorance among artificers, that they do not give ground—and not to want of patriotism solely—that they so strenously adhere to the 'American System.' It further proceeds to prove, as I conceive, that the inhabitants of the agricultural states are indeed an oppressed people and furnishes detailed calculations demonstrating the Tariff Laws to be unreasonable, unjust and unneeded. Now the object I have in thus troubling you is, to say, that the gentleman, who transmitted the paper, has suggested to me, since its departure, that the Hon. gentleman to whom the 'Confessions' are addressed *may* avail himself of the arguments therein contained and withhold the publication. I shall dislike to lose my labour, or to see anything of mine in a mutilated or garbled form. And, therefore, beg you to add to your condenscension by noticing whether aught answering to the above described M.S. appears shortly in either of the Washington papers, or in the Richmond Enquirer; and to give me such information as the tenour of these remarks may seem to require.

An an[x]ious, sleepless desire that the Union may be perpetual induced me to come out upon this subject; and had it not been for my great obscurity I would have given the 'Confessions' the sanction of my name. But *poverty* forbade. I may, with propriety, add that the facts divulged are well known to me—aye & to thousands of others, but their selfish views will not permit them to disclose the secret—from practical experience. I was born & raised in that part of our country where spinning by machinery was first introduced. I can clearly remember the period; and my subsequent opportunities have been such as to give me a thorough knowledge of the subject of which I have treated.

The Union! would to God my feeble powers might be employed for its preservation. I have nothing to leave my children but Freedom, the sacred and sole patrimony I inherited; and *that shall* be their portion if my blood can preserve it for them.

With renewed thanks for your kindness, (I recd. the Treasurer's Report) hopes of its continuance, and prayers for the perpetuity of the union, the happiness of the patriot at its head, & for your welfare, dear sir.

Isaac Southworth

P.S. Not till after finishing the foregoing did it occur to me that your stay in Washington will not probably continue until I can get an answer, & you receive my reply. I therefore propose to myself to transmit you a copy of the above mentioned article so soon as I can find leisure from my daily associations to prepare it. I.S.

Addressed to Washington.

1. A Fayetteville lawyer. See Southworth to Polk, November 27, 1832.

FROM ISAAC J. THOMAS[1]

Dear Sir Maury Cont, Ten Janry 22d 1833

I Received yours of the 2nd Inst & am truly gratifyed at the prospect (which you express to be good) of Receving an appointment to visit West Point. I will hold myself in Readiness to accept if you succeed which I hope you will. With Respect to the Chickasaw Business, on mature Reflection I most cordialy concur in the opinion that you have so readily & clearly expressed & I take the present opportunity to express to you my gratitude for that opinion.

The Idea was addressed you on first thought Just as I would have done If the subject had come in mind & I had met you on the square in Columbia & I am happy to see by your letter that so you understood it. I very clearly see that neither of the places would be an advantage to me. The other appointment I am very desirous to obtain & have no doubt of your success in geting it if attention will procure it for me.

The local matters of our countery are various. On the 26th Inst the stockholders of the bank of our state meet in Nashville to Elect the Directory. I expect to attend. A number of our citizens have sent a part of their hand[s] to Mississippi state to make cotton farms. Mr Littlefield & Rob. Webster & Co., Messrs Booker & Smizer[2] is preparing to send & some others; Mr. Booker & Mr Mason[Charles C. Mayson] being the principal advocates for Nullification about Columbia their stand is not desireable. The[y] are commonly in a fret. I do most sincerely wish all such deranged & fanatical polititions or statesmen could be brought back to a sence of their error & a right view of the principals of our happy union. My most ardent prayer is for the success of those principal set forth in president proclamation. That document strikes my mind with more force & clearness than any thing I have ever seen on the principals of our glorious connstitution.

The ingathering of our cotton crops is very short & the pressure in money matters very great. But we are looking forward to the opperations of the Bank when it start for some Relief. We have general good health. The winter has been mild & the weather at present very pleasant.

Isaac J Thomas

Addressed to Washington.

1. A Maury County physician who had formerly served in the General Assembly. He was the father of James H. Thomas, who later became Polk's law partner, and of John A. Thomas, a cadet at West Point. Polk had been trying for many months to secure for Thomas the appointment as visitor to the United States Military Academy. See Thomas to Polk, December 18 and December 24, 1832.

2. Edward B. Littlefield, Robert Webster, Peter R. Booker, and James Smizer were Columbia businessmen. Smizer was also a lawyer and, with

Webster, promoted Duck River navigation companies. Littlefield became a leader of the anti-Polk faction in Maury County.

FROM JOHN A. THOMAS[1]

Dear Sir U S. M[ilitary] Academy January 22d 1833

Contrary to my most sanguin expectations when I arrived at this Institution I have attained within one examination of graduating. And notwithstanding the disadvantages that every Western man must labour under who comes here, I do not regret coming, but will ever look back to it with pleasure and satisfaction, and will owe a debt of Gratitude to the one whose influence placed me in the situation.

We Tennesseans have not succeeded well, out of four who came on last June, only two remain. McCrabb[2] of East T. & myself will according to the common course of things graduate in June, when there will be but four Tennesseans left. I would be glad to know who is to take my place from our district.

J. A THOMAS

Addressed to Washington.

1. A son of Isaac J. Thomas. He was graduated from the academy in 1833; nine years later he became its commandant.

2. John W. McCrabb was graduated with Thomas, served in the Seminole War, 1837–39, and died at St. Augustine in 1839.

FROM SAMUEL P. BLACK[1]

[Abbottsville] Rutherford County, Tennessee

Dear Sir, 23rd Jany. 1833

I have lately been told that an attempt has been made, or is now making to remove our Post Master at Murfreesboro, Mr. David Wendel, for the purpose of giving the Office to another. I imagine I need say nothing to you about Mr. Wendel, for if I mistake not you are well acquainted with his character, and know that he is often named as a *pattern of punctuality* and *correctness*. What charges are laid or about to be laid against him I know not; but I am persuaded no man will perform the duties of the post office better than he has done, or more acceptably to the people. Whatever has been done in this business has been done very insidiously, and perhaps the project is abandoned, but should it be otherwise, I hope that you will oppose it, and thereby confer a favour on a worthy man, as well as gratify almost every man who has any thing to do with the office.

Before I close this letter, permit me to enquire whether you have settled the claims against the estate of Joel Childress Decd. agreed on at the time we made the compromise, & if you have, whether there is any surplus in your hands of what you received from the estate?[2] I wished to enquire into the situation of this business when you were last in Tennessee, but had no convenient opportunity, and was the less concerned on this account as I have always had the fullest confidence that you would give me the information wanted as early as you conveniently could.

SAML. P. BLACK

Addressed to Washington.

1. A Murfreesboro businessman who had taught Polk at Bradley Academy. He had once represented Sumner County in the General Assembly.

2. Black was one of the several men who signed as securors of Anderson Childress in the administration of the estate of Joel Childress, Polk's father-in-law.

FROM SAMUEL W. POLK

Dear Brother Columbia Ten Jan 23 1833

I have deferd writing so long that I am almost ashamed. I have no apology to offer but the want of some thing that would be interesting to you. I dislike to write to a Congressman and have nothing to say but tell him all the little things that happen about town, but I have to come to it at last or have no letter.

Your two boys Ben and James arrived here the Saturday before Christmas in health and good spirits but unfortunately for you Dr [Silas] Caldwell heard of some cheap Negroes in Kentucky and started off three or four days before the boys got here. No one in town knew that he was agoing untill he was gone and he staid three weeks and returned without any.[1] The hogs were delivered according to agreement and there remained untill a fiew days since. Mother fretted no little I assure you; she said they were there on expence and the boys loosing time but he has at length started. Joe went with him the first day and they went very well.

Mr [James] Walker has returned from the district; he says that your and his crops fell short of your expectations but upon the whole they were doing tolerably well business. Knox[2] went with his father and I staid in the post office while he was gone. The time is now nigh at hand when I shall return to school again. When you went away it was doubtfull whether Mr Laberee[3] would stay or not, but he has consented to remain as teacher in that Acadmey and has took charge of the Columbia church entire. The people are very much pleased with him.

We have received several letters from William.[4] Mother is very much cheerd with the manner in which he write and says she hopes he will yet do well.

Ther is nothing talked of among the Gentleman here but the new bank and Nullification. There is but three Nullifiers in town and they are Booker, Mayson and Ketchum[5] and they are carried high. I do ashure you Booker gets so mad that he raves.

Dr Hays[6] has bought new servants from Mr McDowel[7] and has moved home and is doing well so far. Mother says tell Sister Sarah she must be sure and write to her. She is so uneasy for fear you are sick. The Cholera is actually in Nasvhille; there has been Twenty cases and six deaths. Give my love to Sister Sarah. No more.

S W Polk

Addressed to Washington.

1. The writer here echoes the disapproval of Caldwell's actions that was expressed by Herbert Biles and James Walker letters to Polk, January 17 and January 24, 1833.

2. Joseph Knox Walker, Polk's nephew, was the son of James Walker. At this time he was fifteen years old. Later he became Polk's private secretary.

3. Benjamin Labaree moved to Tennessee from Massachusetts and settled at Spring Hill, where he became the first head of the Manual Labor Academy.

4. William H. Polk was at this time in school in North Carolina.

5. Probably Levi Ketcham, a Columbia businessman. Again, Polk's young brother echoes the views of his elders. See, for example, the refer-

ences to Columbia nullifiers made by Isaac J. Thomas in his letter to Polk on January 22, 1833.

6. John B. Hays, a Columbia physician, was the husband of Polk's sister Ophelia Clarissa.

7. Probably Samuel McDowell, who was one of the directors of the Columbia Bank when it was established in 1819.

FROM JOHN C. WORMELEY[1]

Dear Sir Beechwood [Maury County] Jany 23rd 1833

I thank you most sincerely for the kind reception given my former letter.[2] In it I thought I had informed you of my intention of removing to some part of the Chickasaw Country as soon as Settlers would be permitted and that I did not want the office I was asking from the President on account of any great salary attached to it, as I did to make it auxiliary to other business. I find that it will not do for me to remain longer in Maury as making of cotton here is out of the question and I have too large a family to stay where I can not make enough for their maintaince. In asking the office of Register (which is my first choice) I thought if I succeed, it would assist me whilst I was preparing a plantation.

We have nothing new worth relating in this part of the world. The South Carolina Heresy is all the talk, at first I confess I was a good deal concerned for fear our Blessed Union might be dissolved, but the more I reflect on the absurd position taken by that State the more I am disposed to consider it a mere Braggadocia. But Virginia, Good Old Virginia, Oh! How I have been disappointed. Instead of a firm and manly disavowal of the miserable doctrine of Nullification She comes out with a laboured commentary on the Presidents Proclamation and at the same time advocates the right of a State to secede from the Union. This is a refinement in Politicks that Old Folks like myself can't understand. I had thought that our present happy Constitution was formed and adopted for the purpose of making a more perfect Union. More perfect than What? The answer I should think would be the Old Articles of Confederation. Under that I think a State might have seceded, but not now unless consentively.

I have just finished reading with feelings of the most profound contempt a peice Signed [by] a member of the convention. I had not gone far before I was convinced it proceed from the pen of a Gentleman, of Cummin memory, and before I finished I could not help laughing at the idea of what Champions of Liberty these Silk Coat Heroes think themselves. I must quit Politicks or I sh'an't know when to stop. Present our best respects to Mrs Polk and tell her we had another fine Son added to our family on the 7th of this month.

JOHN C. WORMELEY

Addressed to Washington.

1. An early settler in Maury County.

2. This probably refers to one of two letters from Wormeley to Polk: December 12, 1832, or December 26, 1832.

FROM LINCOLN COUNTY CITIZENS

Fayetteville. January 24, 1833

The ten signers of this letter express pleasure with a proposed stage route from Murfreesboro to Huntsville, Alabama, via Fayetteville. They dissent from a recommendation of some citizens that the route go by way of Lynchburg, arguing that the route is longer and the roads poorer. To settle the matter of distances, they refer Polk to a map of Tennessee done by Matthew Rhea of Columbia in 1832.

Addressed to Washington.

FROM ELISHA S. CAMPBELL

Hinds County, Mississippi.
January 24, 1833

A former resident of Tennessee, having established himself in Mississippi, asks Polk to help him obtain a government appointment in that region.

Addressed to Washington.

FROM JOSEPH COTTON

Memphis. January 24, 1833

Not being acquainted with William T. Fitzgerald, the representative from his district, the writer asks for help in getting appointments to West Point for his two sons. He asks Polk, should no vacancies exist, to send information regarding Georgetown College.

Addressed to Washington.

FROM JAMES WALKER

Dear Sir, Columbia, January 24th 1833

I have just returned from the district, and am at some loss what to say to you in relation to your affairs there. [Herbert] Biles is in better health than when you was there, and I think it likely his health will be sufficient to enable him to pay proper attention to your business. He has gathered your Corn & Cotton both of which turns out to be a light crop. It is probable you had about 200 barrels of Corn the 1st of the year and about 28000 of Cotton or say 14 heavy bales, 10 of which has been shipped & probably sold. He is still clearing the same ground he was at when you were down—thinks he will be able to finish that and clear 40 acres more. He thinks he can next year plant & cultivate 125 acres in Cotton and the same in Corn, and if he does this well, I think you will have no right to complain. Your Horses & cattle look well. Little Ben & Jim arrived here the day before Christmas, agreeable to your orders. Dr. Caldwell went off to Kentucky to purchase some negroes, and delayed starting down until yesterday morning.[1] Of course your pork will be late in killing & Jim & Ben have lost a months work. Upon the whole your Pork arrangement has turned out a very expensive business. Biles has not bought stock Hogs, on account of the price in the district. He wrote to me just before I went down to purchase. I had no opportunity to do so and left the order to buy with Mr. Harris[2] & Dr. Caldwell. They did not purchase, and it is perhaps as well so, as you will most likely have to purchase Corn anyhow.

I examined your a/c with Biles; the expenditure since you was there is about $135—the largest items for beef. I thought every thing right about it. I paid your $40 note, gave Biles $75 to pay blacksmith & Doctor's Bills (I had not time to get these a/cs myself) and gave him an order on Levin Coe[3] for the ballance he owes you. I went to see Coe, but he was gone off some distance to a sale. If Biles gets this money it will answer in what you owe him.

The worst feature I see in your concern, is the great complaint of sickness among your negroes. 5 of them were sick when I was at your plantation, and Biles says there is frequently 10 or 11 sick at a time, generally with colds, which he thinks he could cure directly if he had permission to steam them. He says Salts are pernicious in colds, that red pepper & steaming is the remedy—is utterly opposed & refuses to give Calomel under any circumstances. I advised him to use no more red pepper or steam medicines, and when the negroes had bad colds to give them salts and if that did not do, to send for a Physician.

Upon the whole I think it will be well for you to look out for another overseer, as Mr. Biles will hardly suit you. Tho you might be worsted he seems dissatisfied that he cannot have his own way and I think it very probably you can get a better manager.

My new ground Cotton turns out very little. I shall not make more than 60 bales at both plantations. I think Biles & Kibbles management about the same. I have a new overseer at the Kibble place, that I hope will do better, but I am determined not to be sanguine.

Nothing new here. We are all well, but somewhat uneasy in consequence of the Cholera being at Nashville.

James Walker

Addressed to Washington.

1. The various people who wrote to Polk about conditions on his plantation mentioned without much comment the somewhat eccentric actions of Dr. Silas M. Caldwell at this time.

2. Adlai O. Harris was a Columbia businessman and husband of Polk's sister Naomi Leetch.

3. Levin H. Coe was a lawyer and a prominent political figure in Fayette County.

FROM RUSSELL M. WILLIAMSON[1]

Dear Coln. Vernon [Mississippi] January 24th 1833

With much pleasure I assume the responsibility of addressing you, though unsolicited, I hope not unwelcomely.

The affairs of our common country have arrived at a crisis, which must carry in its train, consequences, greatly to be deprecated. However much we may deplore the causes which led to it, whether from "vaulting ambition," or a settled design to mar and destroy this beautiful fabric, or to bring our instituttions back to their democratic purity, is a question well worth the attention of the statesman, altho it cannot facilitate him in its proper adjustment. The proclamation of the president is bitterly denounced by all the nullifiers in the state while many of the Clay party are highly pleased with the doctrines it contains. Nullification is in some degree gaining ground, but I do not believe that it will ever become formidable in this State. The party have been indefatigable in their exertions to make proselytes, and by this great *"boogaboo"* the tariff to alienate the friends of President, the pressure of which we feel. But every thing has been made to hang on this loop of his constitutional principles, with a perversion of his acts and advices. If the subject of nullification were addressed to the people, unconnected, with the tariff, few there are who would not look upon, and denounce it as a political heresy. And this, in the South, is the only channel through which the popularity of the President has been assailed and then only with miniature success. Our Legislature has been in session some weeks. Senator Poindexter[2] will not be invited to resign his seat as I once thought he would, nor is it possible that any resolutions can be passed approbatory of the course of South Carolina. The adaptation of the statutary laws of the State to the new constitution engrosses the attention of the Legislature.

I have written to our representative Mr. Plummer[3] upon the subject of an individual claim against the government, for property taken in '94 by the Cherokee Indians at which time the father of the petitioners was Killed by them at or near the Muscle Shoals. Your co-operation and assistance will doubtless serve the true interests of your Country, and reduce a large and extensive family in this State under grateful obligations. Any political documents you may think proper to send me, or any leisure moments you will devote to my information, will be gratefully hailed. . . .

R. M. WILLIAMSON

Addressed to Washington.

1. A man of some prominence in Madison County, Mississippi. He represented his county in the constitutional convention of 1832, and in the state

legislature, 1840–41. In 1834 he was appointed surveyor general of lands south of Tennessee.

2. George Poindexter was a former governor of Mississippi and was in the United States Senate, 1830–35.

3. Franklin E. Plummer was one of Polk's colleagues in the House of Representatives, 1831–35.

FROM JOHN H. ANDERSON[1]

D. Sir Shelbyville 25th January 1833

Enclosed you will receive the declaration of Joseph Rogers,[2] who you will see is very old and blind, and I do assure you he is very poor. He has no family except himself and wife who is also very old and helpless, and one son who is subject to fits and almost an idiot. I wish you in behalf of the old man and for the sake of that noble principle called charity to the aged and afflicted, and particularly to one who States upon his oath, that he raised his feeble arm in Support of liberty in the days that tried mens Souls, to press his case, (in an Honorable way tho) for a pension and should he get one to enclose his certificate to me without delay. I wish you also, at the request of your old friend Esqr. Dial who says he made a declaration in order to obtain the benefit of the act of the 7th June 1832 which was drawn out by Thos. G. Whit[e]side Esqr.[3] and transmitted to the propper department in August last. He says he has heard nothing of it since. Pleas to inquire what situation it is in, and inform me when you write. I have Enclosed Some amended declarations to the principle clerk of the Pension office, directed to the Honr. J. L. Edwards,[4] and not having heard of them, perhaps they were impropperly directed. Should that be the case please to present my appology—(Ignorance). You will confer a favour on me and others of your friends to inquire into the situation of a number that have been sent to the department. I have wrote 20 or 30 and the old men are generally very poor and unable to work, and although the amount claimed is generally Small yet to them, it will be of vast importance in procuring something to Subsist upon the few days that remain for them here.

I am happy to inform you that the great *Bugaboo,* about the mail three times a week, upon which the friends of the Black

Hawk up here, you know who I mean, were making so much noise has disappeared, Since the publication of your corrispondence with the postmaster general on that Subject.

My old friend I want you to stand up for Old Hickory through thick and thin; dont give up the Ship. Recollect, we are somthing like the Virginians Horse, Should it be necessary (*We are Here*). I myself would be willing again to feed on parched corn, raw hide, Beech & Hickory nuts before the *Union* Should be disolved by the d——d tadpole Eating crew of S. C. Write to me and send me every publick document you can and Col be sure and do what you can for the old vetrons and believe me to be your friend in reality.

JNO. H. ANDERSON

Addressed to Washington.

1. One of the early settlers in Bedford County. In the first elections held in Shelbyville, in 1819, Anderson was chosen as an alderman.

2. Rogers served in the South Carolina militia during the Revolution and was placed on the pension list within a month of the date of this letter.

3. A Bedford County lawyer, Whiteside was to serve as state attorney general for the Fifth District, 1836–42. His client, Jeremiah Dial, was already on the pension list but had not received notification.

4. Commissioner of the Pension Office.

FROM HIRAM HOLT

Bedford County. January 25, 1833

A farmer and storekeeper of Flat Creek, Holt desires the establishment of a post office at his store about midway between Shelbyville and Lynchburg and asks Polk to deliver a petition to the proper authorities.

Addressed to Washington.

FROM COLLIN S. TARPLEY

Florence, Alabama. January 25, 1833

Tarpley, who studied law with Polk and Aaron V. Brown and practiced in Pulaski before moving to Alabama, supports the application of his friend Robert Tinnin for appointment to a post in a land office in Mississippi.[1] He refers Polk to Clement C. Clay for further information on Tinnin.

Addressed to Washington.

1. Tinnin was appointed register at the Pontotoc land office in March 1833 and served for several years.

FROM LINCOLN COUNTY CITIZENS

[Lincoln County]. January 26, 1833

Some citizens of Lincoln County send a petition asking Polk to help establish a post office in their county, the office to be called Elk River.

Addressed to Washington.

FROM BARKLY MARTIN,[1]

Sir Hamilton [Georgia] 26th Jan 1833

I was acquainted with you when I lived with my Father in Bedford Cty, W. T. at the time when you were first a candidate for the honorable station which you now occupy. I was then a boy and perhaps you may have forgotten me, and may not feel for me on application at this time. I reside in a little village a majority of whose citizens (not of the County) are of that detestible class of politicians called nullifyers, and loud on opposition to the Proclamation of the old "Tennessee War Horse," among whom are applicants for the office of P. Master to fill the vacancy occasioned by the removal of the present P. Master. Permit therefore to say to you that a Mr. Biddle has made application who is to all intense and purposes a nullifyer, and consequently opposed to the administration. A friend of mine a Mr. Lee[2] has applyed for the office but has given way to me, and will be satisfyed if I should receive the office. I ask you to use your influence and secure me the appointment. My frind Judge Wayne[3] I have written to and with him I would be glad you would consult. For the sake of the common cause of the union and in the name of all that makes our country dear to us use your influence to prevent the appointment from falling into the hands of those disunionist who are opposed to evry thing like government and order. I again ask you to consult with my friend Jas. Wayne. He is personally acquainted with me and will coopperate with you if you should favor my application in presenting me before the P office department for the office.

BARKLY MARTIN

PS. Tell the President, In Harris County we are a majority of "union men" and will rally to his Banner when he is in the field marching to Carolina. B. M.

Addressed to Washington.

1. His father (Barkly or Barclay) was one of the early settlers in Bedford County. The father had moved with his family to Georgia some years before and had died there. The son was active in the affairs of Harris County, Georgia, and represented it at an antitariff convention held in Georgia in November 1832.

2. Biddle and Lee are unidentified.

3. James M. Wayne of Savannah, Georgia, was in the House of Representatives. Later he was appointed to the Supreme Court and participated in the *Dred Scott* case.

FROM JOHN ELIOT[1]

[. . .]Swamp Wayne County [North Carolina]

Dear Sir Jany 27th 1833

Permit me to renew our college acquaintance longe since suspended with regret by introducing to you my friend Mr Benjamin I Borden[2] who wishes to become a pupil Student of Georgetown College. He has been raised in my neighbourhood, has at different times been my pupil for about five years at different times the last eighteen months of which he has lived with me in the same house. He has been apt to learn, assiduous in his application and correct in morals. His good qualities have endeared him to his friends and some of them I fear will expose him to imposition from the artful and designing. Naturally of an ingenuous and ardent feeling none but honourable motives in his own bosom and consequently suspecting none in others he will be a fit object for the designs of Knaves & villains. He will be almost an entire stranger in the District having no acquaintance there but a cousin in the College & Mr Wm R. King[3] who has not seen him so long that perhaps he may hardly know him. A friendly adviser you readily perceive will be of great service to him and I could recommend him to apply to none sooner than yourself. Though his education (owing to limited means) has been very defective he knows more of man from what he has read than from what he has seen. He has little knowledge of the world & has not the tact to acquire it.

As his friend as well as Guardian I shall (as well as himself) be much obliged by any kindness and attention you may show him.

JOHN "GHOST" ELIOT

P.S. I saw in Wilmington a few weeks ago several of our college friends who were all well and doing well, Owen Holmes, William M. Green and Thos H. Wright and William J. Harriss.[4] Had I time I would write a long letter. But Borden will be here to start shortly. I should be happy to hear from you occasionally if you have leisure and inclination. I am still unmarried, a pedagogue and forever living with my parents who have now no child but myself. I have however two nephews and a niece to educate.

GHOST

Addressed to Washington but delivered by hand.

1. One of Polk's schoolmates at Chapel Hill.

2. Unidentified.

3. A native of North Carolina, King moved to Alabama in 1818. At this time he was in the United States Senate, where he served from 1819 until he resigned in 1844. In 1852 he was elected Vice-President of the United States.

4. Holmes, Green, and Wright were students at the University of North Carolina while Polk was enrolled there. Holmes, a lawyer, served in the state senate of North Carolina. Green became a prominent Episcopal clergyman. Wright was a physician who also served as president of a bank at Cape Fear. The last name seems to be a reference to William J. Harrison, also a former student at Chapel Hill, who later practiced medicine.

FROM HENRY ROBERTSON[1]

Dear Sir Fayetteville Tennessee January 27th 1833

During the last session of Congress I never Receved a single scrap of a pen[?] from you. A few days since I Recd the presidents Message Franked by you which had been forwarded long since. I have thought in all probability I may have done you injustice in my owne mind and that the any communication that you may have sind has been Neglectd to of handed to me or Miscarried. I should be glad to Know if you Ever did write to me during the last of Congress or not. Your compliance will afford me much satisfaction to Know whether I have been forgoten by the post office or yourself.

I have never been very troublesome to any public gentlemen. I believe all the information I asked of you was that if any appropriation was made to the west for labour to let me Know and who had the letting out the contract.

H. ROBERTSON

Addressed to Washington.

1. A Lincoln County farmer who took a great interest in politics.

FROM SAMUEL G. SMITH[1]

Dr Sir Nashville Jny 27th 1833

I am informed by Jesse Blackford Esqr that Grants No 1755 for 640 acres and Grants No 1728 for 640 acres to James Robertson and Grant No 3202 for 640 acres to Robert McConnell all from North Carolina were conveyed to James O'Harra[2] of Pittsburg[h] and that part of them are taken by superior titles. In that event a warrant can issue for so much as may be taken. He also informs me that a Mr Dana[3] now a member of Congress married the heir of O'Harra & Mr Blackford proposes to undertake an investigation of the claims and procure the warrants at his own expense for one half. He will also in making the agreement undertake to sell the warrant and account to him for his half. I have no knowledge of these claims but by his request I ask the favour of you to See Mr Dana and inform him of the proposition.

It is but a small matter but he is here and would attend to it. If he is disposed to employ him some authority can be forwarded for that purpose. I will be responsible for a faithful attention and account of the whole matter. Warrants are not valuable and in a short time will not justify attention.

The election of Directors to the Union Bank commencd yesterday but has not yet closed. There seems to be much solicitude by some on this subject for what purpose I am unable to say.

You will notice the appointments made by the Executives. For the Presidency Genl. Gibbs & Col Hynes[4] are candidates. It is said the Executive influence & Messrs Yeatman & Woods[5] are for the Genl as you would suspect. Consequently he is looked upon as prominent. For my own part I have not permited myself to be involved in this matter on either side, either in feeling or action.

If the institution should assume the character of monopoly privvileges &c. it will give strength to the mammoth institution that has caused the republican party so much difficulty. If it is understood here that our Executive is the organ of the President and such may be wished down upon us, those Such as Judge White, yourself & the others who have fought faithfully for eight years will have to struggle in a desperate contest when the old chief will be out of the way.

I may imagine things without cause but I do not believe anyone can observe the present aspect of affairs without any concern. While the Genl Government is involved in difficulties Tennessee is approching a period of the highest importance to her as a state. You are aware that public sentiment is ripe for a convention to revise our State Constitution and her future political complection will very much depend upon those who have the ascendancy. The necessity of the President to silence the discontent in the South has offered a pretext for many to come in who were looking to such a movement but they will never divide upon the most trifling matter.

Should such a power exist either avowededly or secretly it will not only modle our State government to suit them but make great strides to controle public sentiment in the next canvass for the Presidency as far as Tennessee is concerned.

I should be gratified to hear from you at any time. Your fast friendship will always be cherished in my recollections and I shall proudly embrace any opportunity to testify my obligations. This careless scrall is for your own eyes alone.

SAM G SMITH

Addressed to Washington.

1. Tennessee's secretary of state.

2. Blackford and McConnell are unidentified. O'Harra, long deceased, had been a merchant in Pittsburgh. See McKay W. Campbell to Polk, November 23, 1833.

3. This should have been spelled Denny. Harmar Denny was a Pittsburgh lawyer who served in Congress from 1829 until 1837.

4. George W. Gibbs was an influential lawyer and politician in Nashville for many years. He represented Davidson County in the state legislature for one term, 1825–27, and later moved to West Tennessee. Colonel Hynes was probably Andrew Hynes who had a copper and tin manufacturing firm in Nashville.

5. Thomas Yeatman, Joseph Woods, and Robert Woods were partners in a banking business in Nashville. Earlier they had been commission merchants. The development of an iron works in Stewart County was one of their enterprises. Yeatman died in June 1833, but the firm continued under the old name for several more years. Yeatman's widow married John Bell in 1835.

FROM REUBEN M. WHITNEY

Strether Hotel [Washington]
Sunday Evg 27th Jany [1833][1]

My Dear Sir

It is of the utmost importance that some person should be sent to the Secretary of the Treasury to examine certain accounts upon the books of the Bank of the U States as well as to call for and obtain certain correspondence, all of which form most important links in the chain of examination about to take place in relation to some of the transactions of that institution, and which cannot now be obtained excepting under the authority delegated to the Secretary in the charter. There is no time to spare now in sending this agent. I know of no person so well qualified as Mr Kendall or who could without any body in Phila. to pilot him, get at the important facts which it is necessary to possess the Committee of Ws & Ms of. I therefore would recommend you seeing the Secretary in the morning and urge him to make the appointment, delegating to him all the powers which he possesses under the charter as broadly and as distinctly as possible. It is very desireable that he should have time on Tuesday so as to take the Boat at Baltimore on Wednesday for Philadelphia.

It is of the utmost importance that while the investigation is undertaken, it should be as thorough as possible, and the exposures as complete, particularly to those who take a conspicuous part in the Committee, and I assure you that I feel no small degree of Intrest myself. I beg of you to see the Secy. and the President both, *tomorrow morning* upon the subject.

R M WHITNEY

Delivered by hand, presumably in Washington.

1. Whitney omitted the year. The Library of Congress has placed the date as 1839, but internal evidence strongly suggests 1833. See Whitney to Polk February 9 and February 11, 1833.

FROM CHARLES C. MAYSON

Columbia. January 28, 1833

Mayson requests Polk to find out what has happened to pension applications of Jacob Gillam, Edward McFadden, and Caleb Farris, all of whom served in the Revolution and were from South Carolina. He also repeats his request that Polk ask Anthony Glynn about a debt that Glynn owed Mayson.

Addressed to Washington.

FROM WILLIAM H. POLK

Dear Brother Chapel Hill N. C January 29th 1833

I received your letter of the 24th enclosing the half hundred dollar bill this morning and have entered college. I received a letter from sister Laura a fiew days since and all was well. I do not know wether I can enter college on Greek or not. I know I canot if the faculty mak me stand but I made a proposition to them a fiew days ago that if they would let me join on Greek and if I did not stand amongst the best in the class by the end of this session I would quit the class on Greek. They have not given me an answer as yet but as soon as they do I will let you know if they do let me in. I will try to reap the same honours that you and Brother Marshall did when you were here however vain the atempt may be. Give my love to sister Sarah.

WILL. H. POLK

Addressed to Washington.

FROM SHADRACK PENN JR.

Louisville, Kentucky. February 1833

Penn, editor of the Louisville *Public Advertiser* and subsequently editor of the St. Louis *Reporter,* informs Polk of the mail-carrying activities of the Ohio and Mississippi Mail Line Company. Special action by Congress is needed, however, to permit the company to have a contract with the Post Office Department. Penn entreats Polk's attention to this matter.

Addressed to Washington.

FROM ISAAC SOUTHWORTH

Fayetteville. February 1, 1833

Southworth encloses a rough copy of his article "Frank Confessions of an Experienced Manufacturer," which he had described in his letter to Polk, January 21, 1833.

Addressed to Washington.

FROM A. M. M. UPSHAW

Pulaski. February 1, 1833

A prominent Giles County resident asks whether or not Polk has received from William D. Sims the papers of William A. Thompson concerning a land claim. He also requests Polk to ascertain whether or not Upshaw's father is eligible for a pension.

Addressed to Washington.

FROM JOHN K. YERGER

Pulaski. February 1, 1833

Pulaski Postmaster Yerger asks Polk whether or not he had received John Donly's[1] draft on the Post Office Department, which was due January 1, in favor of Jacob Shaw. Yerger desires that Polk make available to him a check for the amount of the draft, the check to be on the branch bank at Nashville.

Addressed to Washington.

1. John Donly of Nashville was a stage operator and mail contractor who competed with James Walker for contracts to carry mail between Natchez and Nashville. Donly's daughter was the wife of Greenwood Leflore, a Choctaw chieftain who later was prominent in Mississippi politics. At one time Donly was in partnership with Joseph H. Hough of Nashville.

FROM JOHN W. CHILDRESS

Dear Sir Murfreesboro Feby 2nd 1833

I recieved a letter yesterday from Will H Whitsitt[1] of Demopolis Alabama, proposing to buy all the Land we have in Marengo Co. and pay the cash. I have examined the list of Land you obtained from the Commissioners office in Washington, and cannot find any of the Land he describes as belonging to us in Marengo. The list you got purports to be, a List of Lands purchased in the St Stephens District in the year 1819. Is it not possible Lands may have been purchased at other sales and at other times of which you have not obtained a list? On one quarter there has been paid $110. and opposite is written—"further credited in first class"—which leads me to think there were other lands purchased than those of which you obtained a List. There were Land sales at Tuscaloosa and Catawba. Would it not be well to examine the Commrs. office again? I have written to ascertain what Patents we have, and all the information the agent Mjr. Childress[2] of Tuscaloosa can give. You will please let me know what further information in rey you can get in Washington as soon as possible.

JNO W CHILDRESS

Addressed to Washington.

1. He was a kinsman of Sarah Childress Polk; the exact relationship has not been established. Sarah's mother was Elizabeth Whitsitt before her marriage. The Joel Childress estate included large landholdings in Alabama.

2. James Childress was an early settler in Tuscaloosa; his original home was built on the site that afterwards was selected for the state capitol. He was a brother of Joel Childress. His son James L. Childress was later Tuscaloosa's mayor.

FROM BENJAMIN CLEMENTS

Tallahassee [Florida]. February 2, 1833

Clements reiterates his plea for Polk's assistance in securing an appointment for him as surveyor in new Chickasaw lands.[1] He wants to know who will get the position if he does not.

Addressed to Washington

1. See Clements to Polk, January 5 and January 11, 1833.

FROM LOUIS McLANE[1]

Washington. February 3, 1833

McLane urges Polk to support a requested raise in the salary of Asbury Dickens, a War Department clerk, and hopes that the salary will be made $3,000.

Marked "Private" and delivered by hand to Polk's boardinghouse.

1. McLane had been Secretary of the Treasury since August 8, 1831. He resigned from that post on May 29, 1833, and was immediately appointed Secretary of State.

FROM ANDREW MATTHEWS

Columbia. February 3, 1833

Writing at the instance of Daniel McKie, who claimed to have served in the Virginia line during the Revolution, Matthews asks what action has been taken on McKie's papers that were forwarded to the War Department.

Addressed to Washington.

FROM JOSEPH KNOX WALKER

Dear Uncle: Columbia Feb 3d 1833

I ought to have written to you before this but have not had either time or subject to write upon. There is a very great excitement here for a week or two back, about the Union Bank. There has been a mighty split or rather cross split in this county upon that subject. Mr. [Edward B.] Littlefield has been utterly defeated in his attempt to be president of the principal bank, or even any office of the bank either here or Nashville. Papa influenced all the western district votes against him which blasted all his hopes. Littlefield threatens vengeance & has been going night & day to defeat Mr. [Adlai O.] Harris's election. He is in favor of P. W. Porter.[1] It is thought Mr. Harris will be elected but is not certain. Littlefield is opposed to E. W. Dale & Jas. S. Walker[2] being directors in the branch here. The Looneys[3] & Littlefield have joined in their conspiracy & Nicholson's[4] friends have supported Harris & our party. Papa is *at a stand what to do in the next election.* He says without some of his friends offers he wont vote at all.

I am very much pleased with my trip to the district. So much so that I have picked me out a place for a plantation on the five thousand acre tract between Poplar & Bear creeks in Haywood County which is as good a spot of ground perhaps as is in the district or as good as most any in Maury. We were at your plantation in our rout which turned out equally as well as the Greezy plantation but not so good as the Haywood plantation. The cotton crops at all of the plantation[s] did not turn out as well as was expected on account of the weather princaply. Papa has got a new overseer at the upper plantation by the name of Shelton.[5] It is thought that he will do pretty well if it could be told in so short a time.

The Manual Labor Academy commences on next Monday which is tomorrow. There is no mail[male] school here of importance at presence. Ma says tell aunt Sarah that news reached town to day that Lucius Polk[6] had a daughter & that he is much mortified because he cant name it Andrew Jackson. Aunt Naomi and Ophelia are very much rejoiced.[7] But should it be a mistake there will be great woe. Give my best to Aunt Sarah. Answer this letter, if it deserves it.

J. Knox Walker

Addressed to Washington.

1. Parry Washington Porter, a brother of Thomas Jefferson Porter, was cashier of the Union Bank in Columbia.

2. Columbia businessmen. Walker was a cousin of James Walker, Polk's brother-in-law.

3. Abram Looney was a wealthy merchant in Columbia and the head of a large family.

4. Alfred O. P. Nicholson was editor of the Columbia *Western Mercury* at this time. Later he edited influential newspapers in Nashville and Washington.

5. Unidentified.

6. Son of Colonel William Polk of Raleigh, North Carolina, he was Maury County's representative in the state senate at this time.

7. These sisters, Naomi Polk Harris and Ophelia Polk Hays, had daughters only and had been the subject of jests by Lucius Polk.

FROM LOUIS McLANE

My dear Sir [Washington] Feb. 4. 1833

I hope you will let me see you, before the examination of witnesses in the case of the Bank is finally closed. Should Mr. Biddle's[?] report[1] not appear in the Phila. papers to-day can't you procure me a sight of it without disclosing to your chairman[2] the fact?

LOUIS McLANE

Addressed to Washington. It is marked "Private."

1. This may be the report of the Bank's exchange committee to which Reuben M. Whitney refers in his letter to Polk dated February 11, 1833.

2. Gulian C. Verplanck of New York, chairman of the Ways and Means Committee.

FROM LEWIS CASS[1]

Sir, Department of War Feby 6 1833

I received your letter suggesting Dr [Isaac J.] Thomas as a proper person to be selected as a Visiter to the Military Academy from Tennessee and should have answered it sooner,[2] but that all the applications not being before me, I could not determine what course would be ultimately determined upon, nor can I yet answer definitively your letter of the 2d Inst on the same subject. I understand that East Tennessee has never had a Visitor, and I therefore considered it just, upon the recommendations of Judge [Hugh Lawson] White to select Dr Coffin[3] for this trust more particularly as West Tennessee had two Visitors at the Military Academy last year. I will when the period for selection arrives, examine the subject and do all I can to gratify you, consistently with the pressure there may then be upon the Department from the different sections of the Union.

L. CASS

Addressed to Washington. This is a clerk's letter-book copy in Records of the United States Military Academy (RG 94), National Archives.

1. Secretary of War.

2. See Cass to Polk, December 29, 1832, and Thomas to Polk, January 22, 1833.

3. Charles Coffin, a Presbyterian minister, had served for several years as president of Greeneville College and as pastor of a Presbyterian church in Greeneville. In 1827 he became president of East Tennessee College in Knoxville, a position that he held until his resignation in 1833.

FROM JONATHAN WEBSTER AND MOSES HART[1]

Dear Sir Noah's Fork, Bedford Cty, Ten, Feby, 6th 1833

I hope you will not consider us very troublesome though we often tax your patience. The object of this address is to inform you that two days ago we learnt here, for the first time on Noah's Fork, that a scheme has been formed to break up this post rout on Noahs Fork and of course to move the office.

The facts, so far as we can learn, are these. There has been a petition, at Caldwell's Store, in Shelbyville, for some weeks, praying for a *Stage Rout* from McMinnville to Shelbyville by the way of Davis Mills, and today we learn that some of our citizens on this creek saw it there and Signed it, believing as they did, that it was intended for the present *Mail rout*, but they are now awake. They see perhaps too late their error, for William S. Wat[t]erson,[2] we understand, has latly been boasting that it is to pass the Beech Grove, and that they have got as many petitioners as they want and will have the stage running by his House, in a short time.

If fairness had have been the object why keep the petition at Shelbyville, beyond the reach of the people on this creek and this present Mail rout? Why not let the people here know it? Why keep it secret, even in the neighbourhood of the Beech

Grove for even there, but few were made acquainted with the project? The truth is, Wat[t]erson has for a long time been trying to turne this Road by the Beech Grove, but publick opinion was against him. Of this fact you were made acquainted some years ago, and you got a law passed, making it the duty of the contractor, to carry the Mail by Websters House, Since which untill latly he has been silent. We view this attempt as a piece of management by him and his friends, to cheat us out of the Road, for his aggrandisment.

You will doubtless recollect, the petition we Sent you to have this Mail rout established. By a reference to that paper you will find that it Declares this to be the nearest and best way, and that William S. Watter[son], Subscribed to it. We now Say the same, and more, that the rout proposed by him is yet to be cut out except a small bridge way, and we protest against having that work to do, when we have a good road now open. We are no enemy to the Grove, but contend for our Rights, which we donot wish taken from us in this underhanded manor. We are not opposed to a Stage rout. We pray that one may be established, but let it be on the most direct rout from McMinnville, by the way of Noahs Fork, or Websters and Davis's Mills to Shelbyville. We know not to whom the petition is addressed, whether to the Post Office Department, or to Congress. Be that as it may, we pray you to attend to the matter, and see that your old enemies, donot [. . .] your friends, before they are heard.

You may look out for a petition from this quarter, for a stage rout. It will be sent to you either to lay before Congress, or the Department. We shall act above board, and not get our Distant friends to manage others out of their rights.

We write from hear say, and shall be sorry to find that we have done injustice to any one but we believe what we have wrote.

Your attention will much oblige your true friends.

J. Webster   Moses Hart

[Robert] Cannon is the only candidate for the Senate, as yet. I am about to start a Jerney, and donot wish to leave my name as a target. I cannot say as yet whether I will offer or not.

Jacob Greer, is out for the lower House, Isarel Fonveal

[Fonville], and Col. Arnold are spoken of. I am looking for Col. Abram Martin[3] for the last named place. [Theodorick F.] Bradford is silent, at least I hear nothing from him. He is blown in the uper end of Bedford. If Maury does not Start an opponent, you will "walk over the turf alone" (as I think).

Please write to me on the receipt of this scrawl.

J. WEBSTER

Feby. 7th

Please write us immediately relative to the Stage rout and let us know how that matter stands, and what we had better do.

J. WEBSTER MOSES HART

Addressed to Washington. Although signed by both men, this letter was in Webster's handwriting and was probably composed by him.

1. A former postmaster at Noah's Fork.

2. A wealthy resident of Bedford County and postmaster at Beech Grove.

3. These men were of some prominence locally. Greer was probably related to the Greers of Lincoln County, the best known of whom was Joseph Greer. Israel Fonville, of a large family, lived in Shelbyville, as did James Arnold. Abram Martin was a Shelbyville lawyer.

FROM WILLIAM DEARING[1]

Dear Sir Giles Cty Lynn Creek Feby. 7th 1833

After my best Compliments to you I have taken the Liberty of writing a few lines to you requesting the favour of you to have my name entered at the Globe office as a Subscriber to the Globe for his weekly paper. You'l please pay Mr Blair the Subscription in advance for me and I'll Certainly pay you on sight. I am pleased with his paper. Direct it to Lynn Creek Post office. I thank you kindly for your favour to me. I recd. your pamphlet showing the state of Income and Expenditures of the Gover'-ment. We are here as Usual Like the handle of a Jug all for the administration which I Know is Gratifying to you. Your old friend Laird[2] Says if he was not so old he would move over to be in your District. He is Doubtful he'l never have such another representative from his District & I feel Concious he is rigt. I am of the same oppinion. The Nullifyers of South Carolina ought to be put down & I believe its the General opinion of your Constituents.

Our old friends & acquaintances here are all in good health. Old Father Reynolds[3] Sends his respects to you & requests the favour of you to let him Know about his chance with regard to his pension. He is getting Very old & Cant Enjoy it long should he get it. He requests the favour of you to give his best respects to Col Richd. M. Johnson,[4] his old friend & Neighbour. I add no more but wish you all the success in the world & remains your friend.

WILLIAM DEARING

Addressed to Washington.

1. One of the early settlers of the region, having moved into the Lynn Creek vicinity in 1807.

2. Unidentified.

3. Aaron Reynolds of Giles County had served in the Virginia line during the Revolution. He was placed on a pension roll on April 6, 1833, and died ten days later.

4. A congressman and political leader from Kentucky, Johnson served as Vice-President under Martin Van Buren.

FROM JONATHAN S. HUNT[1]

Dear Sir Pleasant Grove T. Feby 7th 1833

I discover an Extract from P[. . .] Advertiser stating it as a fact not generally known that Every incorporated Library company in the United States is entitled as a Donation from Congress to a Copy of the Diplomatic Correspondence of the American Revolution in twelve volumes valued fifty Dollars.[2] I wish you to search into the Subject & let me know if it is a fact, & if so let me know how to obtain the said work. You are perhaps aware that we have a Library incorporated by the Legislature of this State by the name of the Fountain Library Company, passed 3rd Dec 1826. If there is an act of Congress to this effect we are entitled to the benefits of it, & should you need any proof you will let me know how to prove it. Probably you have seen it in the acts of the Legislature that year. No other news in this County worthy your attention. The Cholera is at last in Nashville.

JONATHAN S HUNT

Addressed to Washington.

1. Postmaster at Pleasant Grove in Maury County and trustee of the Pleasant Grove Male Academy.

2. Edited by Jared Sparks, this set was published, 1829–30.

FROM A. O. P. NICHOLSON

Dear Sir Columbia, Feby 7th [1833][1]

The inquiries, made by those persons who have forwarded their Declarations for pensions from this county, are so frequent, that I have thought it best to request you to give me such information touching the fate of the several applications as may be in your reach. I cannot expect you to give special information of each individual application, but such general inteligence as will be of service to me in satisfying the inquiries. Perhaps it might be well for you to write an answer which being made public would give much satisfaction. It has always been desired by us, that you would communicate more freely and frequently on all the subjects of interest. We are much obliged to you for the public documents you have forwarded to us, and would be glad to receive any that you may send.

I know of nothing here of sufficient moment to interest you, but as I have a strong aversion to *blank paper,* I'll not stop here. The only subject of conversation and excitement here is the arrangement of the Union Bank of Tennessee. We are in great danger of falling into considerable party excitement, unless the Nashville Directory make a speedy appointment of Directors for Columbia. A O Harris, Parry W Porter, and Sam. Craig[2] are applicants for the Cashier's place here. It is entirely uncertain who will succeed.[3]

We have three Candidates for the Senate, declared, and one in reserve. Dr Greenfield,[4] who goes for Jackson, Van Buren, *Eaton,* and the Union—Cahal,[5] who is uncommitted as to U. S. Senator. Littlefield, who is also uncommitted, and I think Dr. Thomas will also run. For the lower House, there is as yet but one candidate, your humble Sert. You have no opposition nor is it supposed by any body that you will have any. I believe I have troubled you, with enough of the *news,* so I bid you good by.

A O P NICHOLSON

Addressed to Washington.

1. Nicholson omitted the year. The letter was assigned an 1832 date and filed under that date in the Library of Congress, but his comments about the bank controversy show that it was written in 1833.

2. A Columbia businessman who was at one time a collector of United States revenue in Maury County.

3. In his letter of February 3, 1833, J. Knox Walker had said that Nicholson's friends were supporting Harris. In this letter Nicholson is noncommittal on the matter.

4. A native of Maryland, Gerrard T. Greenfield had moved to Maury County as a young man. He was a successful physician and farmer and was active in the affairs of St. Peter's Episcopal Church.

5. Terry H. Cahal, a young lawyer in Columbia, was just beginning a political career that gave him prominence in state affairs for some years.

FROM MATTHEW RHEA

Dear Sir Columbia Feby 7th 1833

I take the liberty of sending herewith a draft on Messrs Thompson & Homan booksellers of the City for a small amt of $50.00 or upwards, due me on the sale of Maps of Tennessee. I have herewith advised them of the draft being forwarded to you. Will you be so good as to present it, and if paid, to bring the amt on your return.[1]

Your favour of Jany 12th came duly to hand. I tender you my thanks for your Kindness in presenting my application to the President. A few letters on the subject of my competency as a Clerk &c will soon be presented also from proper persons. I have determined at present to make the office of Register of the Chickasaw lands when Created, my object of application. Any act of Kindness which you may find consistent to make, further, in this respect, shall be duly acknowledged.

M. RHEA

Addressed to Washington.

1. Appended was a note to Thompson and Homan instructing them to pay Polk any money that was due from sale of maps.

FROM LOUIS McLANE

Washington. February 8, [1833][1]

McLane encloses a draft of a bill that would authorize the Secretary of the Treasury to sell government-owned shares in the Bank of the United States and asks that the bill be presented in Polk's handwriting. The letter asks also that Polk arrange for McLane to see William W. Ellsworth and Nathan Appleton[2] during the morning.

Delivered by hand to the House of Representatives.

1. McLane provided only the month and day. The year 1833 is suggested on the basis of the material in the letter and the fact that McLane resigned as Secretary of the Treasury in May 1833.

2. Members of the House of Representatives from Connecticut and Massachusetts, respectively.

FROM LOUIS McLANE

Washington. February 9, [1833][1]

In reply to a note from Polk, McLane says that he would be happy to receive at his office at seven o'clock that evening Polk and such others as Polk chose to invite.

Delivered by hand to the House of Representatives.

1. McLane failed to include the year in the date on his letter; thus the 1833 date is conjecture.

FROM REUBEN M. WHITNEY

Dear Sir Baltimore Feby. 9 1833

Since I saw you yesterday I have been considering how much you yet have to do in the examination of the Bk Directors and Exchange Committee,[1] and the short time you have to do it in. I would reccommend most particularly that your Committee sit during the Session of Congress next week, for you ought to finish the examination by this day week, to give time to prepare your report, the great importance of which will require much time and labour. You will see that there will be but a short time after it is made to have it printed and circulated. I am under the impression that the Bank and its friends are perfectly willing to spin out the time & so to prevent the Report being made in season to be printed and circulated before the close of Congress. This should be thought of. This I consider the most important moment for the Bank which there has yet been. It is the *crisis* of the contest, between the Govt & the Bk. and the question is now at a point which cannot be blinked, which shall triumph? The Govt or the Bank?

We shall have all the materials which we shall want, to determine it to our satisfaction and that of our friends, in case you take care not to let your antagonists undermine you. I again repeat, the *absolute necessity* of placing the testimony as fast as taken in such a place that *no friend* of the Bank can get it to show to other friends or witnesses. I doubt not that you would feel as distrustful as I do if you had seen as much of the power of the Bk to enlist recruits in its service as I have. I am well satisfied from my observations of yesterday, that J. Q. Adams and John Sergeant[2] both aid and assist, and consult with some members of your Committee, and some of the Bank Directors—say Eyre & Bevan.[3] I mention this to place you upon your guard, that you may know the force we have to contend with & that you may pursue all advantages. If you get *Honest* copies of all letters from Cadwalader[4] to the Bank, they will I think be of vast importance. I have no doubt but his letter of the 22d August inclosed a copy of the contract with Barings, and that letter must have been receved on the 20th Sept. If so it will damn the Report of the Exchange Committee. I have written Mr [Amos] Kendall today and given him the data for a few very important interrogatories for to be put to Eyre & Bevan. Sullivan[5] informed me that there was an objection yesterday to the inquiries as to loans to Editors while under protest, and while reported overdrawers. These are very important facts, which ought to be officially laid before the people, for, so far as they relate to the Intelligencer and the Pennsylvania Inquirer, which they do to each, they are cases of Bribery and Corruption of the worst Kind.

I am detained here on a/c of the stoppage of the Steam Boat & the Ice, but shall leave at 2 oclock in the Mail for Phila.

where I shall arrive about 10 O clock tomorrow, and intend to be with you again on Thursday next.

W

Addressed to Washington.

1. This was an internal committee of the Bank of the United States that had been established to deal with foreign and domestic exchange. The House Ways and Means Committee was obtaining testimony from members of that committee as well as from some of the Bank directors.

2. An intimate friend of Nicholas Biddle, Sergeant was serving as an attorney for the Bank. In 1832 he had sought the vice-presidency on the ticket with Henry Clay, and prior to that he had served several terms in Congress.

3. Manuel Eyre and Matthew L. Bevan were Pennsylvanians and long-time directors of the Bank.

4. Thomas Cadwalader of Philadelphia, a director of the Bank, was one of Biddle's close advisers. In 1832 he went to Europe to persuade foreign holders not to submit the Bank bonds for redemption. He finally arranged for the English firm, Baring Brothers, to buy the bonds.

5. John T. Sullivan was a government director of the Bank and an anti-Bank lobbyist.

FROM NOAH'S FORK CITIZENS

Noah's Fork, Bedford County
February 11, 1833

Disturbed by news that a new stage route from McMinnville to Shelbyville will bypass Noah's Fork to go through Beech Grove, twenty-two citizens protest and ask Polk's support.

Addressed to Washington. Although he did not sign it, the letter is in the handwriting of Jonathan Webster.

FROM REUBEN M. WHITNEY

Dear Sir Philadelphia Feby. 11th 1833

I find since I arrivd here, that the Bank party place great reliance upon the ability of [Gulian C.] Verplan[c]k to outgeneral his antagonists of the committee. They also think that Gilmore[1] will ultimately go with Verplan[c]k in favour of the Bank, and they believe that the Session is now so far advanced that there will not be time to complete the examination and make a Report. I communicate to you these facts to show you the importance of hastening the examination, and of your taking care that Gilmore is not tamperd with. No effort will be left uninvestigated[?] to save the Bk and its President. I beg of you to guard against the secret machinations of your adversaries of the Committee, and particularly of the Chairman. I would not permit him to have access to the testimony which has been taken, unless one of our frinds accompanies him. By that being shown to the Bank party serious injury will be done. I hope that you will be able to complete the whole investigation this week.

The Report of the Exchge Committee has been printed here by the Bk. I will obtain two or three copies and take with me on my return to Washington.

R. M. Whitney

Addressed to Washington and marked "Confidential."

1. John Gilmore, a Pennsylvanian, was a member of the Ways and Means Committee and did, indeed, go along with the pro-Bank faction of the committee.

FROM ADLAI O. HARRIS

Dear Sir Columbia 13th Feby 1833

I know that I owe you a long apology for my silence, and I really feel so ashamd. of my negligence that to attempt to paliate the matter would make it worse and I must plead a little guilty in the management of the business you left for me to do. Mr Mathews[1] in settling of the cost of the Royal place gave me a good deal of trouble, and finally refused to pay for more than 25 acres of ground—saying that there was not more than that quantity in cultivation. I recd. 60 Barrels corn, and we are to have the place measured and he is to account for the ballance. I have contracted with a Stone Mason to do the work in front of your House & shall probably have the wall altogether of stone, as there is no brick to be had, and the brick work would increase the expense very much, without adding much I think to its beauty. You will probably be at home in time to have brick, or the stone work if you prefer it. The weather has been too bad to do any thing of consequence at it yet.

I have not heard from [Silas M.] Caldwell since he took

your hogs down in January. We have recd acct sales of 10 Bales your Cotton @ 9¢.

I hand you herwith Duff Greens rect. to Mr Willis[2] for $20. which Mr. W. says is considerably more than he owed. He said that he had handed you some money at two different times perhaps on acct of the "Telegraph" and promised me he would write to you on the subject explaining the matter. I return the rect. thinking that there may be some mistake in Greens acct.

The Election for Directors of the Union Bank came on 26th ulto. You have no doubt seen a list of the Directors long since. Our County man Mr Littlefield left no stone unturned to get into the Directory and then be made President. And he at one time had a very fair prospect of success—but the Western District votes in the hands of Mr Armour, Dr. Butler &c &c came to our assistance and decided his fate.[3] He was left out by a large majority. He took care to inlist Mr Craighead[4] against me before he left Nashville and through his influence, and great exertions he may get me left out of the Cashiership of our Branch. The Directors at Nashville will appoint our Directors & Cashr. next week. The Bank will go into operation in about four to six weeks and never was the assistance of a Bank more needed than just at this time. The U. S. Bank gives the screw a turn every week. They call almost every note as it falls due—but are compeld in self defence to renew a part of almost all of the notes that they can.

The Cotton Crop in our Country will not average I think more than 250 lb pr acre and the quality of this little is very inferior. The Winter, though very wet has been very mild and our Farmers predict a fine Cotton season for the next crops—may it prove so.

Naomi says do make some apology to Sarah. She says that she never wanted to see her so bad in her life, but—the fact is I can offer no excuse that would be a plausible one.

L J Polk has a *daughter* three weeks old tomorrow. No cholera here yet. The premonitions[?] are very general in Nashville and there has been some deaths. But it has been very mild. There is no alarm felt here of any consequence.

All Well.

A. O. Harris

Addressed to Washington.

1. He had rented the Royal place that had been owned jointly by Polk and Samuel H. Laughlin. See Harris to Polk, December 19, 1832.

2. Unidentified.

3. William Armour and Dr. William E. Butler of Madison County were among the financial leaders of the Western District. Armour was a civic and political leader and was among the first trustees of the educational institution that was the forerunner of Union University. In his letter to Polk on February 3, J. Knox Walker gave his father credit for having persuaded the men of the Western District to oppose Littlefield.

4. Probably David Craighead, a Nashville lawyer who represented Davidson County in the state senate for one term, 1835–37.

FROM HERBERT BILES

Stat of Tennessee Fayett County

Dear Sir Febuary the 15th 1833

Ben and Jim got home on the 3rd of this month with the hoggs. We have had some very warm weather senc I killed them but I have taken A great Deal of pains with the meat and am in hopes that it will not spile. Thar has not bean Any snow hear untel yesterday thar fell A snow About four inches Deep. My health is Agetting much better then it has bean. The niggars is tolarable helthy. Elizabeth has got much better but has not got the youse of her arm yet. I hav broke up thirty Akers of my new ground and Am getting Along very well with my claring and think that I will get as much land as we can cultivat this year. The people are helthy hear. I hav comenced geting the gin timbers. I Received your letter to Day of the 25th of January complaining of my not writing oftener. I wrot to you sum time past which I expect you hav Received before now. I will writ to you Again About the time you get to Columbia. Nothing more. . . .

H. Biles

Addressed to Washington and postmarked Somerville. This letter is in the Manuscripts Section, Tennessee State Library and Archives. At the end of the letter Biles wrote February 16, a day later than the date he had given above.

FROM BENJAMIN CARTER

Pulaski. February 15, 1833

A Giles County physician and businessman who formerly lived in Maury County asks Polk's help in getting a Revolutionary War pension for his father, Daniel Carter, who still lives in Maury County.

Addressed to Washington.

FROM WILLIAM H. POLK

Dear Brother Hillsborough N.C. February 17th 1833

I enclose to you a catalogue of studies preparitory to enter college. I would have sent it sooner but I could not get one till I sent to Chapel Hill for it. Sister Sarah said in her letter that you wanted to know whether I had entered my class or not. I have not entered it yet nor I dont know whether I can or not but I will still continue to study hard and if I can not enter college when the the rest of the class does I will study under some of the professors all vacation and I think that I can enter when the session commences. I think that Mr Bingham[1] treated me rite bad. He said that he would hear me private lessions in the vacation but when I returned from Raleigh he said that he could not hear me lessions. I did not stay in Raleigh but 4 days. But I think that I can enter college by stud[y]ing next vacation. It is generally thought that Mr Bingham will not live long if he still continues to keep school and his eyes are very bad. Nothing more at presant.

W H Polk

Addressed to Washington.

1. William J. Bingham was a classmate of Marshall Tate Polk at the University of North Carolina, from which they were graduated in 1825. He headed the Bingham School in Hillsborough for many years.

FROM SAMUEL G. SMITH

Dear Sir Nashville Febry 18th 1833

I very much fear you are ready to conclude I am officious but the friendship I profess towards you and greatful feelings for your past kindness are offered as an excuse. You are aware that it is now understood a hostility exists between this administration and United States Bank, of the fact however I am entirely ignorant. It has been aleged that the Branch at this place is cited to prove that the Bank has caused the country to be overtraded and that here unparalleld losses have been sustained by the institution. Such is said to be the charges made against the Bank implicating the managers of it here and causing excitement not only against the administration but against some of the warm supporters.

If I am not mistaken for the last day or two it has been stated in the street that it should have come from Judge White. I have no doubt the mother Bank will call for information here as to the losses and solvency of the debts to prove (what they say has been charged to her) misrepresentation. I can see no other object but to fix down that such charges originated with Judge White and then prove the safe condition of the institution. I do not profess to know any thing of these matters nor have I any facts to produce but in the course of my observation have been induced to make this intimation to you. I intertain the highest respect for the gentlemen who manage this institution here and from their great caution have no doubt it is as safe as any other Branch. I cannot however, remain indiferent when I see any one for whom I intertain such exaulted opinion as for Judge W and see things taking a course with a view to prejudice a single individual against him. If you or any other person were to intimate to me how far to go in opposition or defense of such attempts to create prejudice then I should most cheerfully do so.

Any thing said would be confidential and so considered on my part. It is not with a view to any profit or advancement on my part nor any unkind feeling for persons here as I intertain the highest respect & friendship for them. Genl Jackson is now out of the way of political ambition but I am not satisfied that the persecutions of Judge W & yourself with many others who have stood by him in all his difficulties will yet cease. If such a move is aimed at Judge W it is not of Tennessee origin as he is too well secured in the affection and confidence of the people of Tennessee to affect him at home.

I have said this much in a hasty and careless manner knowing I was communicating to a friend.

SAM G SMITH

Addressed to Washington. This letter is marked "Confidential."

FROM ELIJAH HAYWARD

Washington. February 19, 1833

The Commissioner of the General Land Office states that examination of land sales in Alabama prior to 1820 shows no purchases by Joel Childress except those in the St. Stephens District, and he returns to Polk the letter that John W. Childress had written to Polk, February 2, 1833.

Addressed to Washington. Clerk's copy in Miscellaneous Letters Sent, General Land Office (RG 49), National Archives.

FROM JAMES ROBERT DONALDSON[1]

Dear Sir New York 26 Feby 1833

I avail myself of the priviledge of an old college acquaintance to request the aid of your influence in procuring a Midshipman's warrant for a young man in whose welfare I feel much interested. His name is John James Kelly,[2] is a native of North Carolina, but lately a resident of this city, and is now on a voyage of preparation to Canton. He is an orphan, has been educated by my Brother, and for a few years acted in the capacity of clerk in my Compting room; but his passion for the sea was so uncontrollable, that we thought it might be happier for himself, and more advantageous to his country, to allow him to follow the bent of his inclination.

An application was made last year to the Hon. C. C. Cambreleng,[3] but the appointments of that year were made previously. It is probable the claims of North Carolina to her quota of appointments, may afford this young man an additional chance of success. I shall consider any interest you may take in this affair as a personal favor.

I assure you it will give me great pleasure to be of any service to you here. Can you furnish me with the address of Mr. Lucius Polk of Tennessee?

JAMES DONALDSON

Addressed to Washington.

1. One of Polk's classmates at Chapel Hill. Donaldson had moved to New York, where he was a lawyer and businessman. Although he signed his name James, he generally had been known as Robert.

2. Unidentified.

3. A New York businessman who went into politics and served in the lower house of Congress, 1821–39. When Polk became chairman of the Ways and Means Committee in December 1833, Cambreleng became a member. Later he became chairman of the committee.

FROM LOUIS McLANE

Washington. March 2, 1833

This explains an amendment (about which Polk had some reservations) favoring Customs House officers and expresses the hope that Polk will support it.

Marked "Private" and presumably delivered by hand.

TO JAMES L. EDWARDS

Dr. Sir Washington City March 4th 1833

I herewith return the pension papers of William Alexander,[1] accompanied by a grant for land which he swears was the reward for his revolutionary services. You requested me to state in writing the rate per hundred acres at which the lands were granted to the soldiers of N. Carolina, which I now do. By the laws of N. Carolina the lands were granted at the rate of ten pounds N. C. currency per hundred acres. The pound, N. C. currency, was reckoned at 8 shillings to the dollar; and of course the land granted was estimated in dollars at $25. per hundred acres. In this case 500 acres having been granted, the amount due the applicant for his service would be $125.00 from which you can estimate amount of pension which may be due to him.

You will confer a favour if you will have the case immediately acted on and send the certificate to my lodgings before 11. O.Clock tomorrow, as at that hour I shall leave the City. Return also the grant for the land, as it constitutes the only evidence of title.

If you cannot get it ready before I leave tomorrow send the certificate to my residence by mail, and retain the grant for the land with the other papers, as I do not wish to risk so valuable a paper by the mail.

JAMES K. POLK

Addressed to Washington. This letter is in the Historical Society of Pennsylvania.

1. A resident of Maury County, who was placed on the pension roll less than a week after this letter was written.

FROM WILLIAM DAVIDSON[1]

Dr Sir Charlotte No. C March 9th 1833

I have Transferred to my friend Mr John Irwin[2] of this place your receipt from debts due me in Tennessee Contained In the last of notes placed in your hands for Collection. The amount received by me of Collections made and remitted By Drafts and otherwise has been duly entered on the receipt. The Balance as soon as Collected which you will please have Done as soon as possible Consistent with my interest. You will please remit to Mr Irwin or pay over to his order.

Circumstances has rendered it necessary For me to make this Transfer. You will however please to pursue the Same Course in the Collection of the debts and the Settlement of the business in relation to all matters Conected with the land in Such way as you Shall Consider Just and equitable and in the same manner as you would have done had no Transfer Been made, Save only that when the money is Collected you will remit to Mr Irwin or pay to his order, and advise me thereof.

Mr Irwin has no wish other than that which will be Consistent with my Interest of which he will advise you.

WM DAVIDSON

No address is available, but presumably, the letter was addressed to Columbia.

1. A wealthy North Carolinian who had retained Polk to attend to his landholdings in Middle Tennessee.

2. Unidentified.

TO CLEMENT C. CLAY

My Dear Sir Columbia March 25th 1833

After we seperated from you at the mouth of the Cumberland we had a long voyage to Nashville. We reached home however on the 21st—but not without having quite an adventure on our way from Nashville to this place. We left Nashville in the stage about 2. O.Clock in the morning and about sunrise and before we knew it, the driver had driven into a swift stream that was swimming. The Stage filled with water up to the seats and it was with some difficulty that we escaped. Mrs. P. and most of the passengers were taken out from the stage on a horse. We all however escaped unharmed, except that we got a genteel wetting. Since it is all over Mrs. P. seems to consider it the greatest adventure of her life, but would not I judge be willing to try the experiment again. I apprehend from what the Capt. of the Memphis told me, that you were detained at the mouth of the Tennessee several days. Write to me how you got home and the state of your health. Make our kind respects to Mrs. Clay. . . .

James K. Polk

Addressed to Huntsville, Alabama. This letter is in the Duke University Library.

FROM ISAAC S. LYON

Boonton Falls, New Jersey. March 25, 1833

Lyon, a publisher and bookseller, requests a copy of Polk's speech on the Bank of the United States for inclusion in a collection of notable congressional speeches that he is preparing for publication.

Addressed to Knoxville and delivered to Polk in Columbia, presumably by hand.

TO CAVE JOHNSON

Dear Sir: Columbia, Tennessee April 24, 1833[1]

I am surprised to learn from your letter of the 17th Inst. that your fidelity to the administration is doubted. In answer to your inquiry I have to state, that I have always regarded you as a friend of the administration, and am well satisfied that you are so regarded by the members of the House generally. Your general course has certainly sustained the measures of the administration and I have never for one moment doubted the sincerity of your support. Your general conduct, when examined, cannot, I should think, but be satisfactory to all on that point.

James K. Polk

Presumably addressed to Clarksville.

1. This is the first of a series of letters from Polk to Cave Johnson published in St. George L. Sioussat, editor, "Letters of James K. Polk to Cave Johnson, 1833–1848," *Tennessee Historical Magazine,* I (1915), 209–256. These letters have since disappeared, probably destroyed by a Clarksville fire many years ago. The editors, therefore, have been forced to rely upon the scholarship of Professor Sioussat and have made only minor editorial modifications for the sake of uniformity, but they have supplied their own annotations. Hereafter, letters in this collection will be cited as Sioussat, editor, "Polk-Johnson Letters."

TO JAMES L. EDWARDS

Sir Columbia Tenn. May 8th 1833

Enclosed I return the Declaration of John Culver[1] for a Pension, with the best additional testimony of service, which it is in his power to produce. He is very poor, is a man of excellent character and is universally reputed to have served as he has declared. It is impossible for him to procure direct testimony of his services. I flatter myself that the proof now forwarded may be satisfactory.

James K. Polk

Addressed to Washington. This letter is in Pension File R2573 (RG 15), National Archives.

1. A resident of Bedford County, Culver was granted a pension in June 1833 for his services in the Revolutionary War.

TO LEVI WOODBURY[1]

Sir Columbia Ten. May 16th 1833

Mr George W. Meek[2] a young gentleman of good character and respectable standing in society, expresses a desire to obtain the appointment of midshipman in the Navy. He is a good English scholar and is about twenty years of age. I desire to be informed whether there be now any vacancies, and what the prospect of his appointment during the present year may be. My impression is, that there are but few midshipmen from Tennessee in the service, and if there be any new appointments shortly to be made, that may possibly be a circumstance that would have some influence upon the Department in their selection. Will you do me the favour of giving me an answer, as soon as your convenience may permit?

James K. Polk

Addressed to Washington. In Miscellaneous Letters Received by Secretary of the Navy (RG 45), National Archives.

1. At this time he was Secretary of the Navy; in 1834 he became Secretary of the Treasury.

2. Not positively identified. It is possible that he was a relative of William Meek of Chapel Hill, Bedford County.

FROM ANDREW JACKSON DONELSON

Dr. Sir, [Washington] May 30th 1833

For your own information I send you extracts from the recommendations in favor of [Theodorick F.] Bradford in 1827 as an applicant for the office of Marshal.[1] But I do not wish you to use my name in connection with them, not feeling myself at liberty to take official copies and believing as a general rule that the Government should regard such communications as not intended for the public eye.

I cannot suppose that Mr. Bradford or any friend of his would undertake to deny that at the period of writing those communications he was politically opposed to the election of Genl Jackson.

Your friends here take a deep interest in your election and are well apprised of the instruments which are employed to defeat you. We have great confidence that the people of your district are too much enlightened not to see that the support and approbation of the measures of the administration which they have so cordially manifested will be unavailing, if an advocate of the Bank or any one not identified with the leading views of the President and his friends, should be selected to represent them.

It is obvious from all the demonstrations recently made by the opposition that the exertions to bring into discredit the character of the administration are to be renewed with increased violence. We shall have occasion therefore in Congress for the service of men able to vindicate both the character & the measures of the President.

We shall set out in a few days on the tour to the south in the course of which probably I shall write you.

The President is in only tolerable health. He unites with Mrs. D & myself in tending you and Mrs. Polk the kindest regards.

AND J DONELSON

P.S. You may rely upon the extracts as correct. With the knowledge which they convey of Mr. Bradfords political views you may perhaps address yourself more effectually to the people.

A J D

I rely upon your discretion not to use the extracts or connect me in any manner with any allusion to the facts which they prove.[2]

The Secretary of State has no knowledge of my having read the letters.[3]

Presumably directed to Columbia although no envelope has been found. Donelson wrote across the top of the letter: *"Private and for your own eye alone."*

1. These extracts, in Donelson's handwriting, are available. They consist of statements by Thomas H. Fletcher, Thomas Yeatman, John P. Erwin,

John Williams, and Thomas Washington, written in 1827 when Bradford was still pretending to be a Jackson man. Fletcher said: "He is a devoted friend to the [Adams] Administration and is perhaps with the exception of Col. Williams more obnoxious to the Jackson party than [any] other man in Tennessee." This, and similar statements by the other men, were most useful to Polk in his campaign against Bradford.

2. This sentence and the one following it were written along the margins of the letter.

3. When Polk attempted to obtain true copies of the letters, he was told that such copies could not be released without the consent of the writers. See Polk to Louis McLane, June 24, 1833, and McLane's annotation thereon.

TO JAMES L. EDWARDS

Sir Columbia Tenn June 11th 1833

Enclosed is the amended Declaration of William Newsum[1] for a Pension. Be pleased to decide the case as early as convenient & advise me of the result.

JAMES K. POLK

Addressed to Washington. The letter is in Pension File, S4612 (RG 15), National Archives.

1. A resident of Mt. Pleasant, Newsum was placed on the pension rolls in July 1833.

FROM EBENEZER RICE[1]

Dear Sir Maury County June 12th 1833

I was raised from my childhood a democratic republican and was taught to believe that our government was of that Carracture and that the powers of our General Government Emenated from the several States as seperate Independant Communities, Each State Conceeding to the General Government such powers as was thought necessary for the general good of the whole which powers were Expressly dellegated in the Constitution of the United States and all powers not there Expressly dellegated were retained to the States. And in the Exersise of those powers so retained to the States they are as Independent as though the general government never had have been formed and I have ever thought that one great object of thus expressing the powers that were to be exercised by the general government was for the purpose of restraining the majority from opressing the manority. Taking this view of the subject it dose appear to me that the general government ought not to exercise any power from Construction but that the Constitution should be its own Expositer and that Congress should not attempt to exercise any power that is not expresly dellegated in that Compact. Let Congress pursue that Course and there is no danger of nulification Cecession or any other remidy that a state may adopt to stop the encrochment of the general government on their reserved rights, but the states will all moove on like brethren of the same general stock and peace and harmony will prevade our happy and beloved Country.

Having in a brief manner laid before you my views of the formation and nature of our government I will now proceede to lay before you some of the difficulties that are presented to my mind from the recent Course of our republican pollititions. It dose appear to me that they have abandoned the posision they have heretofore ocupied and have assumed the same ground with the federal Consolodationists. If I understand their arguments right they certainly take the same position which is that the powers of the general Government Emenated from the WHOLE people of the States Consolodated into one great mass which to my mind distroyes the verry Idiea of state rights. But still when I listen to their speaches they Strongley Contend for state rights from which I infer that they honestly do believe that the states have reserved rights. And now Comes the greate difficulty with me. If the states have those rights there sertainly is some way for them to assert them because a right without the liberty of exerciseing that right is no right at all. Therefore to my mind we must either give up state rights altogether or point out some way for the states to exercise them should the general government Encroch upon them.

And now sir my object in addressing you on this subject is that you may releive my mind from those difficulties and point out the remidy by which the states are to maintain their reservd rights, for I acknowledge to you that I am but a weak minded man at best and possessed of but little lerning and therefore would be glad to be instructed. I hope you will not view me as a flaterer when I tell you that I have ever had a high opinion of you as a pollitition and as a man of strict Integraty and political honesty. Therefore with the more confidence I make this communication to you hopeing you will try to relieve my mind from those difficulties. I will Just here name some of the remidies that I have heard spoken of among some of our pollititions which I think are hardly as good as a school boy might have brought. One of them is that the remidy is at the pols. (Say they) if your public servants do not do their duty turn them out and put in them that will. Now sir the manority may have representitives of the verry best Carracture that is possable to have and yet be as though they were not represented at all, the majorrity always bearing them down and they canot be heard. Another sais the Fedral Court is the place for a state to redress her grievences in case of encrochments upon her rights by the general government. But the fedral Court being a creture of the general government the Judges holding theire office at her will, it is Equally futile and delusive.

Dear sir believe me when I say to you that I love my Country and highly appreciate the blesings of our government, believeing it to be the verry best ever enjoyed by man. And I must say to you that the greatest danger of the downfall of our republic is from the greate popularity of men. Let us therefore be carefull lest the great popularity of some particular friend should exercise so greate an influence over our minds. This letter is not intended for the public. I hope therefore to receive a private answer. You will please excuse bad writing & spelling.

E. Rice

Addressed to Columbia with the inscription "To be opened by Col. Polk alone." It was delivered by hand.

1. A skilled and highly respected blacksmith in Maury County.

FROM THOMAS B. COLEMAN

Williamson County. June [16], 1833

Coleman encloses affidavits certifying that his father, John Coleman, had died in 1814 while in military service.

Addressed to Washington.

TO CAVE JOHNSON

Dear Sir: Shelbyville, Tennessee, June 20, 1833

I think I am entirely safe in my election, the probability being that I will receive many hundred more votes than both my competitors together; have notwithstanding an angry and most violent contest. I am assailed from all quarters, first upon the Bank question as you have seen, next upon the Military Academy at West Point, thirdly upon the vote upon the proposition to enquire into the expediency of repealing or modifying the 25th section of the Judiciary act of 1789, fourthly upon the vote for the outfit and salary of Mr. Randolph[1] to Russia. All these, together with some minor matters have been met and in succession put down. Lastly I am charged with being *"systematically opposed* to bettering the condition of the soldiers of [the] Revolution." I do not know that it will be necessary but lest it may be, I desire that in reply to this you will state whether in conversation upon the subject of the various pension bills which have been before Congress since you have been a member, I have not by my course, and in conversation uniformly expressed the opinion that it was unjust to confine the pension granted by the Government, to the soldiers of the continental line alone; whether I have not uniformly announ[ce]d my opinion that the pension should be extended to the soldiers of the militia, state troops and volunteers, who were poor and needy, as well as to the continentals; providing for all alike who had performed services equally meritorious, without regard to the line or corps in the army to which they belonged. I voted against the *House bill* of 1832, after having failed by my votes to have it amended in such manner as to make it equitable and just. For the *Senate bill* of 1843,[2] which passed and is now the law, upon the question of voting it to be ordered to a third reading I voted as the Journal shows in the affirmative; upon the final passage the yeas and nays were not taken. I think I have conversed with you and communicated my opinions, but I have no distinct recollection that I ever did. If I did I wish you to state upon receipt of this your recollection of my opinions as expressed to you. For such men as *Wade Hampton,*[3] my kinsman *Col. Polk*[4] of N. C. and others who were wealthy; who did not need and had never asked a pension, I did not think it necessary to provide, and would have preferred that the law which did pass should have been confined to those who were in moderately reasonable circumstances, and to [whom] the pension would be a comfort.

[I w]ish you to give me an answer immediately on receipt of this, but in the mean time I do not care that it should be publicly known that I have written to you on the subject, my object being to be prepared to meet any false representations which my political enemies may possibly attempt to make upon the eve of the election. I am anxious to hear what your prospects in your election are. Write me upon that subject also.

Direct your letter to Columbia.

James K. Polk

Addressed to Clarksville. This letter is in Sioussat, editor, "Polk-Johnson Letters," *Tennessee Historical Magazine,* I, 211–212.

1. John Randolph of Roanoke had been appointed by Jackson as minister to Russia. In 1830, after only a month on duty there, he resigned because of ill health. He died a month before this letter was written.

2. The date 1843 appears in Sioussat's edited version of this letter; obviously it should have been 1832.

3. A South Carolina plantation owner who, at the time of his death in 1835, was reputed to be the wealthiest planter in the country. Hampton served in the Revolutionary War and in the War of 1812.

4. William Polk of Raleigh, a first cousin of Polk's father, was a highly successful businessman who engaged in many business ventures in Tennessee.

FROM EDWIN A. KEEBLE

Murfreesboro. June 24, 1833

At the request of William Brady, Keeble, a Murfreesboro lawyer and editor, informs Polk that the papers of Daniel McKie have been received and returned to Washington.

Addressed to Columbia.

TO LOUIS McLANE

Dear Sir Columbia Tenn. June 24th 1833

If it be not contrary to the regulations of your Department to permit it, I desire to obtain copies of certain letters now on file in your office written in November and December 1827—recommending *Theoderick F. Bradford* for the appointment for Marshall of West Tennessee. The letters, copies of which I wish to obtain, were written by *Thomas H. Fletcher, Thomas Yeatman, John P. Erwin, John Williams* & *Thomas Washington.*[1] If copies are permitted to be taken by the rules of your office I desire that they may be forwarded to me immediately.[2] If you prefer it the copies need not be certified officially. If I am sure that they are true copies it will answer my purpose. It may be important to me to have them, and if I should find it necessary to use them, I will of course do it prudently, and in a way to prevent any injury to the administration for furnishing them.

I congratulate you upon your accession to the Department of State. The labours of your new situation will I trust be less severe than those of the Treasury, which pressed so heavily upon you during the last winter.

James K. Polk

Addressed to Washington. In Miscellaneous Letters, Department of State (RG 59), National Archives.

1. Andrew Jackson Donelson had already provided Polk with extracts from these letters (Donelson to Polk, May 30, 1833). Fletcher was president of the Nashville branch of the Bank of the United States, and Washington, a lawyer, was a member of the board of directors of that bank. Fletcher had also served as United States Attorney for West Tennessee and as Tennessee's secretary of state. Erwin was a Nashville lawyer who had served as the city's postmaster, 1826–29; he became mayor in 1834. Williams was probably the United States senator from Tennessee who had been defeated for re-election by Jackson in 1823.

2. McLane noted at the bottom of the letter that on July 6, 1833, he replied that the rules of the department would not permit copies of such letters to be furnished without the consent of the writers.

FROM CAVE JOHNSON

Dear Sir, Clarksville 25th June 1833

I recd your letter of the 20th of June to day.[1] I recollect to have conversed with you frequently during the time I have been in Congress with you in relation to the pension system, & its inequality & injustice as regulated by the act of 1818. I think it was expectedly the subject of conversation between us whenever the subject was under the consideration of the House. You always avowed your opinion to be, that the act of 1818 was unjust in its operation being limited as it was to the Regular soldiers of the Revolutionary War and that it ought to be extended to the Militia, volunteers & State troops upon the same terms that it was to the Regular Troops, and if I am not much mistaken you were the first individual that pointed out to me the great inequality produced by the act of 1818 in the disbursments of the public monies. The Eastern States having generally furnished Regular troops & the Southern States militia, volunteers or State troops and of course the disbursements under the act of 1818 would be verry unequal giving to the Eastern States a verry decided advantage over the Southern States & also over the Southwestern States which had been principally settled from Virginia, the Carolinas & Georgia.

In our conversations as to the Bill which finally became a law in 1832, I recollect that both of us objected to it because it was not limited to that class of the Revolutionary soldiers who needed the aid & bounty of the Government, believing it to be unjust to extend it to those who were wealthy & independent and I recollect your speaking in strong language as to the impropriety and injustice of placing on the pension roll men of such fortunes as Genl Wade Hampton & some others. But notwithstanding this exception to the Bill, you seemed inclined to vote for the Bill upon the ground that the Bill would be less unfair, less unequal and less unjust, than the previous pension laws, limited as they were to the regular soldiers. I recollect urging the impropriety of voting for any such law without some such limitations as we both thought just, & the impression is strongly fixed upon my mind, that when we last conversed upon the subject, that you would vote for the Bill & that I should vote against it—& if I am not mistaken I verry shortly after was taken sick & did not vote upon the Bill.

I have given you my recollection of the opinions expressed by you to me at various times & I do not recollect any difference of opinion between us on those subjects except as above stated. I regret that I have not my Journals at hand that I might examine them. They might recall to my recollection, by an examination of the various stages of the Bill, other conversations which would more clearly shew your views & opinions upon the subject. I do not think I ever heard the opinion expressed by you shewing that you was disinclined to render comfortable & independent those venerable men who served during the Revolutionary War. I am well satisfied that your object & wish was to have all who performed similar services to the country placed upon a footing of equality, without any regard to the kind of troops to which they were attached, whether regulars, militias, volunteers or State troops.

I am much gratified I assure you to learn that your prospects are so favorable. I was fearful that the Bankmen, with their *cunning* & *money* & their double handed game against you might trouble if not beat you. As to myself I am bedevilled enough in the same way. Cheatham, Marable & Hewling & Frey[2] all on my back aided by Mjr [. . .] the author of J[. . .] & the Republican but I believe I get stronger the more I am attacked & I think at present the only doubt is whether I shall beat both or not. I am satisfied that I shall beat either much farther than I beat Marable before. Fitz [3] writes me, that it is a verry hard case that has to be beaten for his vote for the Force Bill & I for my vote agt. it. I think we shall beat Mr. Hewling this time, if so Mr G.[4] gets the vote. Powells[5] prospects in Robertson is said to be the best & he will vote for G. In Humphreys, Perry & Stewart both the candidates for the lower House are for G & it is said Andrews[6] if elected will vote for G. Bullock[7] his opponent is decidedly & openly for G. Batson & Gordons[8] election is considered verry doubtful. B– will vote for G– if elected. I have not been lately to Hickman & know but little of that. I go next week. If my opinion is not as full as you desire or you can recall to my recollection any thing write me to Centreville.

C. JOHNSON

Be pleased to remember me to Madam & tell her I recd today by mail *Miss Mary Brooms*[9] *card* & of course I must return it in the winter. I shall say so to my constituents.

I expect my letter to Majr. B. G.[10] in behalf of Grundy last fall has rendered him luke warm if not agt. me & I shall hold you accountable for it.

C. J.

No address is available. Since this is in reply to a letter in which Polk asked Johnson to direct his reply to Columbia it is presumed to have been sent there.

1. It is not known how much Polk used this letter in his campaign. He was confident of his election at this time, but he must have taken some comfort in the prompt reply to his request. Johnson's statement accurately describes Polk's attitude toward pension legislation.

2. Richard Cheatham of Robertson County served in the state legislature, 1827–33, was a member of the state's constitutional convention in 1834, and concluded his political career with one term in Congress, 1837–39. John H. Marable was a Montgomery County physician who had served two terms in the United States House of Representatives, 1825–29. In 1829 Cave Johnson had beaten Marable in his effort to be re-elected. Frederick W. Huling of Montgomery County served in the General Assembly five successive terms, 1825–35. Henry Frey, a Robertson County farmer and politician, was sheriff of that county, 1818–23, and then served nine nonconsecutive terms in the state senate, 1823–35 and 1837–43.

3. William T. Fitzgerald.

4. Felix Grundy, who was hoping to be elected to the United States Senate by the Tennessee General Assembly in 1833.

5. Richard P. Powell was successful, and he served one term in the General Assembly, 1833–35. Earlier he had been sheriff of Robertson County.

6. Cullen Andrews was at this time in the state senate, serving 1831–35.

7. Micajah Bullock, a lawyer, represented Henderson County twice in the lower house of the state legislature, 1835–37 and 1841–43. He moved to Madison County and served in the same body from that county, 1845–47.

8. A resident of Dickson County, Richard Batson had served one term in the legislature, 1825–27. Boling Gordon of Hickman County served in the lower house of the legislature, 1829–35, and then was elected to the state senate.

9. Unidentified.

10. Boling Gordon.

FROM JOHN BLAIR

Dear friend: Jonesborough [Tennessee] June 26th 1833

I received yours of the 13th inst. in reference to the votes of the majority of the Tennee. Delegation in the several pension bills before congress since 1828. To make my answer as explicit as possible I can say that at all times that portion of the Delegation from the state who supported the present Administration, have harmonized on most of the questions of import. On the pension bills I know that there was a great coincidence in opinion, and I will give you what I understood to be their course in that subject. In 1828 a bill was before the House which in our estimation done unequal justice to all classes & it f[o]und the support of the Delegation, see page 331 of the 2d Session of the 20th Congress. *This bill failed in the Senate.* Both the bills to which you refer were unequal in their provisions & moreover grossly unjust & ought not to have receved the sanction of a disinterested man—being pretty much the same in principle. I give you the objection to the last, I mean the bill of the HR. of 1831–2. That bill proposed to give an annuity to the Revolutionary soldier, without reference to his circumstances, the rich as well as the poor on the ground that the Govt had promised pay & failed to give it & that was to make up the defect. The bill tho, gave to the soldier who served 9 mo the same amount as was allowed to him who served seven years. This certainly could not be justified by any one, seeing that a pension never should be given to a man of wealth, but this was to make good his pay. Then justice required that he who served longest & lost most should have in return the highest annuity. Again, it would have taken from six to seven millions out of the treasury & if you recollect the President told us that he would not be prevented paying the public debt, & spoke expressly in reference to that very bill. Again we had at the same time before the senate the bill which has passed & is now the law of the land with which all are satisfied within my acquaintence. It proposed to do justice and promote equality amongst the soldiers. Why vote for the oposite when we had choice of the two, (if desire only to vote for a pension bill) surely take that makeing the nearest approach to your opinions of justice. I know that the Tennessee Delegation (in general) have expressed equal solicitude with the members of any other state, to provide for the soldiers of the revolution including militia & volunteers, but because a bill happened to be entitled *Pension bill* they did not choose to vote for it without seeing that it was just & right. If you look to the amendments proposed to the House bill of 1831–2 & rejected, you will see something of the feeling of the north on the subject of Pensioning our fellow citizens. 1st the Kingsmountain men who turned the ball of the Revolution. Who are they who opposed the amendment? See yeas & nays. 2d These who fought at Guilford, see same. 3d Indian fighters proposed by Wickliffe[1] & rejected by yeas & noes, see names. This is indicative of the feeling which pervaded the north, & for myself I wish my folk to have a fair participation at least when such immense benefits are to be conferred. I write in haste & you must excuse omissions as I have not time to review. I am in the midst of the Supreme Court & its affairs.

J Blair

P.S. I can only be affected by a union of the friends of Carter[?][2] and [Thomas D.] Arnold, which I think would not take place if either should draw back.

J. B

Addressed to Columbia.

1. Charles A. Wickliffe, a Kentucky congressman who became Postmaster General in 1841.

2. Probably William B. Carter of Elizabethton who had been a colonel in the War of 1812 and had served in both houses of the General Assembly. In 1834 he was the presiding officer of the Tennessee Constitutional Convention.

FROM JOHN ROBB[1]

Washington. June 29, 1833

This acknowledges a letter concerning the desire of Dr. Jonathan Bostick of Chapel Hill, Bedford County, to obtain an appointment as surgeon or assistant surgeon, and regrets that there are no vacancies.

Addressed to Columbia. Clerk's letter-book copy in Letters Sent Relating to Military Affairs (RG 107), National Archives.

1. Chief clerk in the War Department. Robb occasionally served as Acting Secretary of War.

FROM CLEMENT C. CLAY

My dear Sir, Huntsville [Alabama] July 2d 1833

Your favor was not recd. till it was too late to answer by the last mail, in consequence of my absence, during the last week, in the country.

I regret to learn that you are charged with being "systematically opposed to bettering the condition of the soldiers of the Revolution &c."[1] Having boarded in the same house with you, during the two first sessions of my service, and having been intimately associated with you, throughout the last four years, I should have been as little astonished to find you assailed on any other ground, as that of hostility to those who fought for Independence. I have no hesitation in declaring that I always found you ready to make ample provision for those survivors of the Revolutionary army, who *might be presumed to stand in need of their country's assistance.* Your votes & conduct in the House and *your conversation out of it,* always favored the justice and policy of such provisions. The only difficulty with you as well as myself, was to limit measures, having this object in view, to *those who were needy*—whether they belonged to the *continental line, state troops, militia, or volunteers.* For those who were *wealthy,* who *did not stand in need,* and *who had never asked a pension,* I did not deem it necessary or proper, to increase the public burthens, by making any provision—and, in this opinion, I am satisfied, you fully concurred. To tax the widows, and the orphans of those who had fallen, fighting our Revolutionary battles, or who had not been so fortunate as to live as long as others, who are still amongst us, to *provide pensions for some of the wealthiest men in the Union,* did not seem to me consistent with justice, or sound policy; and, on such grounds, I always understood you to speak & act, while you evinced a desire to make *comfortable provision for the poor & needy.* If my testimony upon this or any other subject can be of any service to you, I shall most cheerfully record it, as an act of justice.

C. C. CLAY

Addressed to Columbia.

1. Polk's letter to Clay has not been found. It is obvious, however, that Clay—like Cave Johnson, John Blair, William T. Fitzgerald, and perhaps others of the Tennessee delegation in the House of Representatives—was being requested to clear Polk of the charge being circulated by the opposition in his district that he was unfriendly to proposals for Revolutionary War pensions. The statement here given seems to be a direct quotation from Polk's letter to Clay.

FROM WILLIAM T. FITZGERALD

Dr Sir Dresden July 3rd 1833

Your favor of the 24th ult I have just received. I do not at this time ever remember to have had but one conversation with you on the subject of the pension Bill & that was on the House Bill of 1832. I have not time to examine the Journals but if I remember right I voted for the Bill in every shape it assumed. Tho. I voted for the amendments which confined its benefits to the poor I think I was alone from the state on this Bill on several occasions with the exception of [Thomas D.] Arnold (not very good company for a Jackson man). The conversation to which I allude took place on the floor of the House of Representatives and related wholly to the propriety of limiting its provisions to those who were needy. I remember you told me that it was not right that such men as Wade Hampton & Colo. Wm. Polk should be pensioned on the Government &c &c. I well remember your giving me them as instances of the injustice of the provisions of the Bill as it then stood. I never understood you as having any other objection to the Bill. I understood you and all the other members from the state as in favor of the principle of pensioning the needy. I gave myself more latitude than any of you for I would have gone it in almost any shape it had ever assumed. In the midst of all the misrepresentation & abuse that is heaped on me here I enjoy most infinite amusement at the various expedients resorted to in the different districts in Tennessee to displace the late incumbents. (If this be rotation in office I am clearly opposed to it *at present*). One is assailed in one district because he voted for some measure & another is assailed in another because he did not. [Cave] Johnson is abused because he voted against the Force Bill and I am assailed because I voted for it. (I wish there was some law to hang demagogues.) I think I shall be elected. If not I intend to have fun enough during the canvass to compensate me for the loss of my election,[1] for no misfortune troubles me long. One sound nights sleep & all is settled. Make my respects to Mrs Polk and do just what you please with this letter.

W Fitzgerald

Addressed to Columbia.

1. Fitzgerald's attitude probably stood him in good stead; he was defeated for re-election by David Crockett, the man whose seat he had won two years before.

FROM ARCHIBALD YELL

My Dear Sir Mulberry [Lincoln County] July the 10th 1833

I have made this my place of retreat for the last 2 weeks. The Cholera has pretty much subsided in our vilage for the last few days. I hope we will be authorised in a few days more to get back to Town. Shelbyville now presents a view of woe and trouble. I have lost some good friends & so have you. I hope you have been prudent & will continue so in avoiding the exciteing causes &c.

I have not heard from your District for the last 10 days. Can you give me any news? I am told The. F. [Bradford] has made a publication & designs another before the Election. I wish you would drop me a line for I feel much more interest in your success than I do for *Monsur Combs*.[1] You will be interested when you learn that I am for that *Yanky* but its because he is the only chance to beat [William M.] *Inge* who I wish defeated about as much as I do *Bradford*.[2] He is a right clevr sort of a fellow but he has made War on my frnds & are seeking their defeat which he may effect by the accidental union of the frinds of [Aaron V.] Brown in Giles. They with Brown at the head are supporting Inge because they personally dislike Combs & they are voting for Kincannon[3] because he is in favor of Fields[4] for Judge. Those circumstances combined operate grately against Moore[5] & may cause his defeat tho. he & his frinds are very sanguine. But under a diferent state of things I am well assured that Brown & his imediate frinds would not go against Moore. I am & always have been attached & devoted to Brown & to him. Our folks here have been looking too at the candidate at the next election to represent the District. But who may be elected? But some of the knowing one begin to say that *Brown* & Inge will not oppose each other. If *Brown* declines & Inge runs there will be a man from Giles who has more strength & sounder politicks than poor Combs. The opposition here to Inge will run him. If Inge backs out & Brown runs, a Gentlemn from Lincoln will be on the tract. Nothing would give him more pain than to be placed in that situation; & I am certain he has no desire to engage in a political Contest. But that arrangemt will bring it about. But if Brown acts as I think & believe he will, he will receive from 1000 to 1500 vots over against Inge.

I have written once or twice to Brown, but I have had no intimation from him what he will do at our other election. He is no[t] for Inge, of necesity not from choice, for to Inge & his frinds here is Brown indebted for the loss of many of his old frinds in this County upon the subject of the Congressional Districts.

Inge is a Jackson man, but while a member of the Legislature in 1829 he was a Bank man & voted for all those subjects of Internal Improvemt. But he has been taught better by public oppinion & he has voted praise & Honor to the old Chief for all his *Vetoes*. He has a circular now under advisemt. I will send it to you with a *Review* that will follow it. Combs choice at present is pretty good & if he continues to gain as he has done for the last month he will be elected. In the three lower Countis Combs will get a majorty of from 600 to 1000. His chance is now good for a majorty in Giles. In this County he will receive from 500 to 800 vots. *Inge* can not [get] ov[e]r 2000 vots here but many of those also who will not vote for Inge will not vote at all. If a *Rally* can be effected here for Combs to the No. of 800 he will be Elected. So you have my oppinion of his strength, but I would take Inges chance much the soonest but he is on the decline & if his Circular does not Reinstate him he may be defeated. If the latter part is not better than the first it will do him but little service, as I think & a part [. . .].

On this subject I have written as I always do without disguise & Reserve. I know you will regret my whim in the choice I have made in Candidates. Indeed I regret it myself but it's forced upon me. Thats my appology & sufficnt too as I conceve &c.

Write me if you can find liesure.

A. YELL

Addressed to Columbia but not sent through the mails.

1. James W. Combs, a Pulaski lawyer.

2. Yell had shifted gradually from nominal support of Inge to outright opposition. It seems likely that he had never liked Inge and that his opposition increased because Inge had damaged the political fortunes of Aaron V. Brown, Yell's friend.

3. Andrew A. Kincannon, a Fayetteville lawyer who had served as county sheriff. He represented Lincoln County at the state constitutional convention in 1834. In the 1840s he moved to Mississippi, where he had a successful career in politics and education.

4. William H. Feild, whose name Yell consistently misspelled.

5. William Moore was Yell's brother-in-law. Although Yell does not say so, he was probably visiting in Moore's home at Mulberry when this letter was written.

TO FRANCIS P. BLAIR

Dear Sir, Columbia Ten. Augt 8th 1833

I have been forcibly struck with your article in the Globe of the 27th July, expressing the relations which subsist between the Intelligencer & the Bank of the U. States. The Bank it seems is the real owner of the establishment and the Editors are its mere servants and journeymen. The Bank of course is the real *printer* to the next Ho. Repts. Under the circumstances, it cannot longer be pretended by any, even the warmest partizan and zealous advocate of the Bank, that the Intelligencer can longer be regarded as a free press, so far at least, as the Bank's interests are concerned. The influence of the Bank upon the freedom of the press, is visible in every quarter of the Union, though its power is perhaps not so absolute over any other single press, as it is over the Intelligencer. Even in Tennessee it has its instruments, of which the "*National Banner*"[1] at Nashville is most prominent. In the late canvass for Congress, the (result of which you have seen) the whole power of the Bank, through its organ here, (*The "Banner"*) was brought to bear on my Congressional District. Throughout the whole contest too, I had to contend with the secret influence of the Bank, which was made to operate whenever it was supposed it could produce effect. Early in the canvass I was assailed through the *"Banner"* upon my *Minority Report* from the Committee of Ways & Means upon the Bank question. This I met satisfactorily to my constituents by my speech delivered in April, and which was afterwards republished in the Globe.[2] Passing over various other efforts secretly to affect me before my constituents, on the eve of the election, (and to this I wish specially to call your attention) several extra sheets were printed, at the *"National Banner"* office at Nashville, Entitled *"National Intelligencer Extra"* and purporting to have been published at Washington, filled with Bank matter, and eulogies on the Bank, and special reference is had to me in terms of censure, for my course on the Bank question at the late Session of Congress. The *forgery* and the object to be effected were too palpable, and in a publication addressed to my constituents (a copy of which I send you) I met and exposed the *fraud.* Is the *"National Banner"* at Nashville authorized to use the title & speak in the name of the *Intelligencer* in sustaining the Bank? The fact now disclosed that the Bank owns & controls the *"Intelligencer,"* may contribute to unveil the mystery. These *sheets* were extensively circulated in my Congressional District on the eve of the election, and I doubt not, though I have no positive evidence of the fact, that the expense of publication was paid by the Bank itself. I have forwarded to Mr. Kendall the only copies of these *Extra Sheets* which I preserved. Would it not be well [. . .] you to examine them, and expose in the Globe this trick, this insidious attempt on the part of the Bank to interfere in the elections in this quarter? I do not doubt, but that it is the settled purpose of the Bank to organize a Bank party in Tennessee, and in my judgment the means employed to effect it cannot be too soon met and exposed. These suggestions I make for your own consideration, for my letter is not designed for publication. If necessary hereafter, however I can and will sustain the statements which I make under the responsibility of my name.

JAMES K. POLK

Addressed to Washington. This letter was marked "Private." It is in the Princeton University Library.

1. In nearly every case Polk put the names of newspapers in quotation marks and then underlined for emphasis.

2. Polk's speech to his constituents was made on April 15, 1833, and was widely circulated in his district. Polk's minority report of March 1, 1833, had been a vigorous attack upon the Bank.

FROM LEWIS CASS

Washington. August 10, 1833

This acknowledges Polk's letter recommending William Hunter as an agent to superintend the emigration of the Chickasaws and assures him that the recommendation will be given full consideration.

Addressed to Columbia. In Letters Sent, Bureau of Indian Affairs (RG 75), National Archives.

TO WILLIAM B. LEWIS[1]

Dear Sir Columbia Tenn. Augt. 13th 1833

Our elections as you have seen have terminated, and though in my District, we have had a warm and even an angry contest, having had to grapple, as I did, with the whole power of the Bank and its advocates and organs in this quarter, openly as well as secretly brought to bear upon my constituents, yet as the result of the election shews, my triumph has been complete. My majority over both my competitors was more than three to one.

When I saw you at Nashville in the Spring, you thought it still probable, (and indeed I take it for granted that it is so) that our friend S.[2] would go to England. In that event it will be important that a successor of the true political faith should be selected. Before the adjournment of the late Session of Congress, in anticipation of such an event, some of our political friends of the Ho. Repts. conversed with me on the subject and suggested that I would probably be as acceptable to the party as any other. Since that time and during the recess, I have received letters from others making similar suggestions. Now I have only to say that should I be voluntarily selected by our friends, it is a station which no man would decline, but on the contrary I would regard it as a mark of high confidence on the part of those political friends with whom I have so long acted. Still I would not wish to thwart the wishes of friends, or be instrumental in disturbing the harmony of the party. I make these suggestions in *strict confidence* and for yourself alone. Can you inform me whether Mr. S. will certainly go abroad, and if so whether before or after the meeting of Congress; and if his seat in the House should be thus vacated, are our friends at Washington looking to any other person as his probable successor. I think I may with truth affirm that I possess the confidence of all our true friends of the House, in as unqualified a degree and to as great an extent as any other. I have long acted with them, (having now been a representative for eight years, & under two administrations) and have been uniformly, sincerely, and consistently, fou[n]d sustaining all the great measures of public policy which have marked the course of the existing administration. I was among the earliest of Genl. J.s friends & supporters for the Presidency; voted for him as a member of the Legislature, for the Senate of the U.S.—upon principle opposed the administration of Mr. Adams; warmly and at all times and under all circumstances have supported the election of Genl J., and since his election, have constantly and zealously stood by him and sustained his administration, as I intend to do. In a word, amidist all the political summersets and revolutions which we have witnessed since I have been in the public service, my fidelity has never been doubted or questioned by a human being. I have never asked office of any human power but my constituents and now if the political friends with whom I have acted (and some of them have intimated to me their desire to do so) should think proper to place me in the station to which I have alluded, I will not disguise the fact that I should regard it as a most distinguished honour.

But little is said here as yet in regard to the next Presidential election. V. B. I doubt not will be able to carry the vote of this state, by a large majority, should he be the candidate of the Republican party as I doubt not he will be. The coincidence of his views and opinions with those of the existing administration, and especially upon the Bank question, and the absurd doctrines of nullification must make him strong in Tennessee. Is it contemplated to have a convention at Baltimore to make the nomination? If such convention should be convoked, I think it pretty certain that the nominations there made will succeed. Can you inform me what the views of our friends at Washington are on this subject? Is it deemed most prudent to wait for the assembling of a convention, or that the Legislatures of the States should make the nominations? We had some conversation on this subject when you were at Nashville and I should be pleased to have your present views.

JAMES K. POLK

This letter is marked "Confidential" and presumably was sent to Washington. It is in the Ford Collection, New York Public Library.

1. A close friend and adviser to Jackson, Lewis was at this time Second Auditor of the Treasury. There was a marked coolness between Lewis and Polk at this time although both were trusted by Jackson. Polk seems here to have been taking some political risk in revealing his hopes and plans.

2. Andrew Stevenson, Speaker of the House, who was expected to receive a foreign post.

FROM CLEMENT C. CLAY

My dear Sir, Huntsville [Alabama] August 19th 1833

Your favors of the 5th and 14th inst. were not recd. till night before last, in consequence of my absence on a visit to the southern part of the state, for the last three weeks—hence the delay of my answer. I was highly gratified, and offer you my congratulations on your triumphant reelection—notwithstanding the violent opposition you encountered from the U.S. Bank, and other quarters. I never doubted your election and always answered others who did, that you had served your constituents assiduously, faithfully, ably and that *no man could rise earlier, or lie down later.*

The elections in Tennessee have generally gone very much to my satisfaction with the exception you mention (the notorious Davy Crockett) and the defeat of poor little Isacks.[1] He ought not to have been a candidate it is true, but as he was, I regret that he is beaten.

In this state, as you will have seen, the elections for Congress have resulted in our favor, except as to Dick Lewis,[2] who had no opposition. McKinley[3] is elected, after a close contest—accounts vary his majority from 270 to 350—and it is further rumoured that his election will be contested. Mardis[4] had two competitors, each of whom he beat in his own county, and his majority over their united vote will be considerable. Murphy has beaten Dillitt[5] in the 5th (Mobile) District more than a thousand. My own election, you have seen, was without opposition.

As regards the subject to which you allude in your last, confidentially, I should be much pleased if it could be managed successfully. Should the vacancy of which you speak occur, I know no other member whose election to fill it would be more agreeable to my own feelings than yours.

Mrs. C. will accompany me to Washington. In what mode we shall travel is yet undetermined probably, however, in a private conveyance. We must communicate hereafter, and endeavour to meet on the way.

Mrs. C. tenders her best regards to Mrs. P. & yourself. Please present me, also, most respectfully, to Mrs. P.. . . .

C. C. Clay

Addressed to Columbia.

1. Crockett defeated William T. Fitzgerald. John B. Forester, a lawyer from McMinnville, defeated Jacob C. Isacks of Winchester, who had served for ten years in the United States House of Representatives. Forester served two terms, 1833–37.

2. Dixon H. Lewis of Montgomery was a member of Congress from 1823 until his death in 1848; he served in the Senate after 1844.

3. A Florence lawyer, John McKinley served in the United States Senate, 1826–31. He served one term in the House of Representatives, 1833–35.

4. Samuel W. Mardis, a native of Tennessee, was at this time a resident of Montevallo. He served in the United States House of Representatives for two terms, 1831–35. He moved to Talladega County and died shortly thereafter.

5. John Murphy of Monroe County was a former governor of Alabama. James Dellett, a long-time state legislator, was also from Monroe County. In 1839 he defeated Murphy and served in Congress 1839–41 and 1843–45.

FROM HUMPHREY H. LEAVITT[1]

My dear Sir, Steubenville (O) August 26, 1833

I have had the pleasure to receive, through the medium of the newspapers, the gratifying intelligence of your re-election to

Congress, by a very flattering & triumphant majority. To be thus sustained by your constituents, must under existing circumstances be peculiarly grateful to your feelings, and is an event that will not fail to give pleasure to your numerous personal and political friends both in Tennessee and elsewhere. But, without further notice of the auspicious result of the late canvass in your District, I will proceed at once to state the object I have in view in obtruding this letter upon your notice.

I am not in possession of any *state secrets,* and can not therefore say whether our late speaker, Mr. Stevenson is to be sent abroad or not. But it seems to be generally taken for granted that he is to be thus disposed of, and it has occurred to me that the subject of selecting his successor, in the next Congress, is worthy of the early and serious consideration of the friends of the administration. In anticipation of the happening of the event to which I have alluded, I have heard the names of several gentlemen mentioned for the speakers chair and among them, you have not been the least prominent. I know not whether this matter has been presented for your consideration by your friends, but supposing it would be important to the harmonious and successful movements of our party in Congress, in regard to the election of a Speaker, that there should be some previous concert and understanding among the members composing it, I have taken the liberty to address you on this subject. Without any design to be unnecessarily complimentary, permit me to say that insofar as my knowledge extends, I know of no one in our ranks who could become a candidate with a better prospect of success than yourself. Let me therefore inquire of you what your views are in relation to this matter, and let me assure you how sincerely desirous I am that you will permit your friends to consider you as a candidate for the Speakership, in the event of Mr. Stevenson being sent to England.

The West, as you are well aware, will be strong in the next Congress and I think that insofar as the democratic portion of its representation is concerned, they will be nearly, if not altogether unanimous, in your favor.

Be good enough to let me hear from you on this subject, as soon as your convenience will permit. It will probably be in my power to do something towards effecting union & concert among the democratic members from Ohio in the election of Speaker, and I need not assure you with what pleasure I shall exert my limited influence for the promotion of your Success, should you give your consent to be a candidate.

H H Leavitt

Addressed to Columbia.

1. A resident of Steubenville since 1819, Leavitt had served several terms in the state legislature. He was in Congress from December 1830 until he resigned to accept an appointment as a United States district judge in July 1834.

FROM WILLIAM M. INGE[1]

Dear Sir, Fayetteville August 28th 1833

I received yours of the 13th Inst which gave me much pleasure. I should have answered it before, but when it reached Fayetteville I was confined at Pulaski with the bilious fever. Since I have received it, I have felt unable to answer it from indisposition. I am now convalesing from an attack of what I should call the cholera judging from the way it wrenched my internals. But for these things I would have answered you earlier.

You estimate me rightly when you suppose me to be your friend, and there is nothing which I could do to forward your views or prospects but I would most cheerfully perform. Your letter I consider confidential and shall not be shown to any one. If the Republican party should fix upon you for speaker, which I would prefer, I would give you my hearty and cordial support.

It is a station which you ought not to decline, and it is one which I think you can filll with ability, and with satisfaction to all concerned. More when I see you. Nothing would give me more pleasure than to travel with you to Washington. I hope we can so arrange it. How will you go, & when will you start? Will you go through N Carolina? This I would prefer. I want to revisit my native land once more, to retrace the scenes of my youth—the land where my ancestors lie buried for several generations! I would be glad to see you here at the circuit Court. All your old friends would. If you come over I will try & arrange my business so as to go on with you to Nashville. I intend visiting Nashville during the session of the Legislature. If the convention has carried I would think the legislature would not sit more than 3 or 4 weeks.[2] I shall expect you over during our court. If you would come on Monday the second week of court I could certainly go on with you to Nashville. I may be detained at Court professionally the first week.

Permit me in conclusion to congratulate you upon your distinguished success, for I do consider it so under all the circumstances. Bad health admonishes me to quit. More when I see you at Court. Until then may you enjoy all the good things of this life that I desire you to have. If you should you will be happy.

WM. M. INGE

Write me on receipt of this.

Addressed to Columbia.

1. Inge had just been elected to the House of Representatives from Lincoln County, which had been in Polk's district.

2. This apparently is a reference to the proposal for a constitutional convention in 1834.

FROM CAVE JOHNSON

Dear Sir, Clarksville Augt. 29th 1833

I recd the enclosed from C. C. Clay on yesterday.[1] I shall again write him in a day or two suggesting to him the propriety of writing to some of his intimates, making the suggestion to them & thus have as far as practicable a concerted movement. I shall make the suggestion also to Burns & Bynum.[2] I have written Leavitt.[3] We should be there at least two weeks before hand. I shall leave home about the 20th Oct. & travel on Horseback. I also wrote [James] Standifier and [John] Blair but have recd no reply.

C. JOHNSON

Addressed to Columbia.

1. The enclosed letter from Clay was retained by Polk. Clay acknowl-

edged receiving a letter from Johnson proposing Polk for Speaker of the House and expressed his approval of Polk's candidacy for the post.

2. Robert Burns, a physician from Grafton County, New Hampshire, and Jesse A. Bynum, a lawyer from Halifax County, North Carolina, were in the House of Representatives for the first time.

3. See Leavitt's letter to Polk, August 26, 1833. Although Leavitt does not mention the letter from Johnson, it is possible that he had received it before he wrote to Polk.

FROM ANDREW JACKSON

My Dr. Sir Washington August 31st 1833

You will find from the inclosed,[1] that I have at last thro the Government Directors got a *small peep* into their expence account, and the corruption practised by that institution on the morales of the people. In two years $80 odd thousand expended to corrupt the people & buy a Recharter of that mamoth of corruption. I think when these scenes of corruption are made known to the people, and that by an order of the board of directors, the whole funds of the Bank are placed at the disposal of Mr. Biddle to appropriate as he pleases without [. . .][2] voucher, to [. . .] of the Bank by the most bold specious[species] of corruption ever practised by any body of people in the most corrupt governments & in the most corrupt times. Can any one really say, from this expose that the U.S. Bank is a safe deposit for the peoples mony?

I send it to you that you may use the facts without stating from whence you got them. I would not that you would let it be known that it came from me as we have not yet taken an order on the deposits. We will act as soon as Mr. Kendall makes his report & can find that the State Banks will be a safe deposit. He has just returned.

I write in haste. Present me to Mrs. Poke, & all the family & to Lucius & Mary[3] & the old Genl & his family as with you.

[ANDREW JACKSON]

Addressed to Columbia and marked "Confidential." The signature is missing, but the letter is in Jackson's handwriting. It has been published in John Spencer Bassett, editor, *Correspondence of Andrew Jackson,* 7 vols. (Washington, D.C.: Carnegie Institution, 1926–35), V, 173–174.

1. The enclosure, which Polk retained, was a letter from government directors H. D. Gilpin, John T. Sullivan, and Peter Wager dated August 19, 1833. It, also, has been published in Bassett, *Correspondence of Andrew Jackson,* V, 160–165.

2. At this point a corner of the letter is torn away. The two gaps indicated here represent about a half line each.

3. Lucius J. Polk and his wife, Mary Eastin Polk.

TO JAMES L. EDWARDS

J. L. Edwards Esqr Columbia Tenn. Sept 1st 1833

Enclosed I return the Declaration of Edward McFaddin [McFadden][1] accompanied by my certificate as to the official character of the Judge and Clerk before whom the same was originally taken. I enclose also an amended Declaration made by Mr McFaddin before a Justice—the applicant being so old and infirm as to be unable to appear personally at Court. From the character of the applicant I have full confidence in the truth of his statement as to his services. If a Pension be granted enclose the certificate to me & I will carry it to the applicant.

James K. Polk

Addressed to Washington. This letter is in Pension File S2790 (RG 15), National Archives.

1. Identified earlier. He was placed on the pension rolls on September 13, 1833.

TO JAMES L. EDWARDS

Sir Columbia Tenn. Sept. 4th 1833

Enclosed I return the original Declaration of John Jones[1] for a pension, accompanyed by his amended declaration, and also the testimony of service which he has been enabled to procure.

I hope the case may now be satisfactorily made out, so as to entitle him to a pension. The applicant is old and very poor & I believe has procured all the testimony in his power. If a pension be granted, forward his certificate to James H. Thomas[2] or myself, to be handed to the applicant.

James K. Polk

Addressed to Washington. This letter is in Pension File S1678 (RG 15), National Archives.

1. A private in the Virginia militia during the Revolution, Jones was placed on the pension rolls within a few days after this letter was written.

2. A Columbia lawyer who was later Polk's law partner.

FROM JOSEPH W. CHINN[1]

Dear Sir Oakley. Lan.[Lancaster] Cty. Va. [Sept. 7, 1833][2]

I have to thank you for a copy of yr. address to the citizens of yr district and to congratulate you that they have appreciated it, as I did, by triumphantly returning you to yr. former seat. Mrs. Chinn & myself shall be extremely happy in meeting again you & Mrs. Polk. Our family will consist of the same number, and if yrs. is larger in number, it will only enhance the pleasure of our meeting. We shall be in by the commencement of the Session, and shall be pleased if we are again thrown together in the caste of messes.

I like *close racing* (to borrow a figure from the turf) but in my last, as you saw from the returns, I was not more than a neck ahead. But I am perfectly satisfied, altho I was confoundedly jockeyed, and so were my friends. Mrs. C. unites in kind regard to Mrs. Polk & yourself.

J. W. Chinn

Addressed to Columbia.

1. A Lancaster County, Virginia, lawyer who had been Polk's colleague in the past Congress and who had been re-elected. After serving two terms in the House of Representatives, he moved to Richmond and resumed the practice of law.

2. No date was placed at the beginning of the letter. The writer put on

the envelope merely the month and day. Polk's notation that he answered the letter on September 26, 1833, provides the correct date.

TO CAVE JOHNSON

Dear Sir: Columbia, Tennessee, September 7, 1833

It may be a matter of some importance that a proper man be selected as speaker of the Senate of the next Legislature, especially in the event the present incumbent in the Gubernatorial office should rceive [*sic*] his long-looked-for preferment.[1] Some of our friends here are solicitous that Col. [James W.] *Wyley,* the Senator from Green[e], should be elected. Wyley is a clean fellow, and has I believe been always right in his politics. I am aware that this is a matter that it does not become you and me to in[ter]fere in much, but at the request of friends I suggest it to you, that if you concur with me in opinion you might suggest it to *Mr. McMeans, Rayburn*[2] and perhaps to some other friends. I know not who the *"little knot of politicians"* at Nashville who undertake to control the politics of the State, and who have recently given you as well as myself so much trouble, will run, but doubtless they will have their man, and there is as little doubt that that man will not be Col. W., for he would not suit their purposes.

You must not fail to meet me at Nashville on Thursday of the first week of the Session of the Legislature. I am obliged to be at the Fayetteville Circuit Court on Monday and will come from there to Nashville.

James K. Polk

Addressed to Clarksville. This letter is in Sioussat, editor, "Polk-Johnson Letters," *Tennessee Historical Magazine,* I, 212.

1. Governor William Carroll had been mentioned as a possible representative of the United States in Mexico. Had he resigned as governor, he would have been succeeded by the speaker of the state senate.

2. James R. McMeans, a Henry County lawyer, and John Rayburn of Wayne County had been elected to the state senate to succeed Robert Murray and William Davis.

FROM JOHN TURNEY

Galena, Illinois. September 18, 1833

Referring to himself as an old friend, Turney commends to Polk one Addison Philleo, former mail contractor in Illinois, as a reliable person and a friend of the administration.

Addressed to Washington and delivered by Philleo.

TO CAVE JOHNSON

Dear Sir: Columbia, Tennessee, September 26, 1833

Since I wrote you last I have received letters from some of our friends in Congress, on the subject upon which we have heretofore corresponded; and among others one from our friend *Jesse Speight* of N. Carolina.[1] I think from his letter that he has some views of his own. I learn too that Judge [James M.] Wayne of Georgia is now in New York, and is looking to the station. I think it important for me if you have not already done so, that you should write to *Jarvis* of Maine and *Hubbard* of New Hampshire,[2] and to any others with whom you are intimate, but especially to those two gentlemen. I fear I am imposing too much on your kindness, but hope I may have it in my power in some way to reciprocate the favour.

I understand you are to be at Nashville next week. If you should meet with *Mr. Ferrister* [Forester] or *Peyton*[3] (Genl. Hall's successor) mention the matter confidentially to them.

I regret that I did not see you at Nashville last week. My impression was when I left that our friend G's election was tolerable secure.[4] His friends counted for him 27 votes on the first balloting. You will probably be there at the election, and as I start to the Western District in the morning, I must ask the favour of you if you are at Nashville when the election takes place to drop me a line to *Somerville* apprising me of the result.

I expect to be able to leave Murfreesborough for Washington about the 1st Nov. Inge spoke of going on horse-back and travelling with us. I will write you again more definitely as to the time we will start immediately on my return from the District.

JAMES K. POLK

Addressed to Clarksville. This letter is in Sioussat, editor, "Polk-Johnson Letters," *Tennessee Historical Magazine,* I, 212–213.

1. Speight had served in both houses of the North Carolina legislature before being elected to Congress. After serving from 1829 to 1837, he moved to Mississippi and subsequently was elected to the United States Senate from that state.

2. Leonard Jarvis served in the House from 1829–37. Henry Hubbard was in the House from 1829 through 1835 and then served in the Senate, 1835–41. He was governor of the state, 1841–43.

3. John B. Forester and Balie Peyton had been elected to the United States House of Representatives. Peyton, a Sumner County lawyer, succeeded William Hall.

4. On October 8, 1833, the General Assembly elected Felix Grundy to the United States Senate.

TO WILLIAM B. LEWIS

My Dear Sir Columbia, Tenn. Sept. 26th 1833

In consequence of my absence from home your letter of the 7th Inst. was not received until yesterday, and I have to thank you for the information which it communicated. I am induced to think that the sentiment cannot be general among the friends of the administration, of the Ho. Repts. that Tennessee should be excluded from the Speakership (in the event Mr. S.[1] goes abroad) on the ground that at the late Session Judge White happened to be President Pro. tem. of the Senate. I know at least that it is not universal. It is a matter about which I had not thought until it was voluntarily suggested to me by some of the *true friends* of the administration, members of the House, from several of whom I have received letters during the summer, expressing a desire on their part, that I might be selected by the party in the event of a vacancy, and desiring to know what my views were upon the subject. I think it a matter of great importance that the Speaker should be a man not only *true* in his politics, but one who has *always* been so, *never suspected,* and one who would give to the administration an honorable and hearty support. I will not permit myself under any circumstances to be the means of disturbing the harmony of the party, or preventing the success of our cause; but if our friends elect to the next Congress should be disposed to unite upon me (and I know some of them are so disposed) I do not see that the objection to Tennessee is at all a substantial one, and more especially as at the next Session of Congress the Vice President will preside in the Senate in person. When we meet at Washington however the friends of the administration can *confer* together and be enabled to have some understanding upon the subject, whereby they will be enabled to act together. Should Mr. S. retain his seat in the House, of course he will be the Speaker.

In regard to your little son, it would afford us pleasure to bring him on with us, and we will do so if we possibly can. We have not yet positively determined on our mode of travelling. Should we take the Stage it would put us to no inconvenience; and should we take a private carriage I will still endeavour to arrange it so as to bring him.

We expect to leave early in November, so as to reach Washington a few days before the meeting of Congress. If you have any further information on the subject of the Speakership, I should be happy again to hear from you on receipt of this. In the mean time I desire our correspondence on the subject (for the reasons given in my last) to be considered as confidential and resting between ourselves alone.

JAMES K. POLK

Addressed to Washington. This letter is in the Bancroft Library, University of California. It is marked "Confidential" at the beginning and "Private and Confidential" on the envelope.

1. Andrew Stevenson.

FROM HENRY HORN[1]

My Dear Sir Philada. Octor 5 1833

It is the fate of those engaged in trade to be obliged sometimes to resort to the Law for the recovery of their Just rights. I enclose you therefore a note drawn in favour of our house by Mess. Dale & Duncan[2] of your place for One Hundred and

Twenty nine Dollars 90/100 which you will perceive has been long since due.

The mode of collecting it must be left entirely to your discretion. If it can be done in a Reasonable time without coersive measures you may take that course. Otherwise you will proceede by the most Speedy and effectual means to secure and recover the amount in which case the suit should be brought in the names of Henry Horn & Christian Kneass.[3] Please advise of the Rect of this by return mail.

The success which we have recently obtained at our ward elections over our political opponents gives us the strongest assurances of a compleat triumph on Tuesday next. The Bank of the United States is losing its power over the people by the loss of the Public deposites. Thus the President God bless him has disarmed the tyrant of its most destructive weapon. Divested of the Peoples money the monster will be almost powerless and our triumph over it will be easy and certain.

Henry Horn

(You will add interest to the note from its maturity.)[4]

Addressed to Columbia.

1. Recently one of Polk's colleagues in the House of Representatives.

2. A general store in Columbia. Edward W. Dale and Lemuel H. Duncan were partners in this business.

3. Christian Kneass and Henry Horn were partners in a business that specialized in silver plating.

4. Polk noted on the envelope that he had collected from Dale and Duncan $142.24, which included $12.34 interest.

FROM TERRY H. CAHAL

Dear Sir Nashville Oct. 8, 1833

I am here yet. It is near 5 p.m. The thing is just over. All is well. Grundy is elected, having after a hard fight all day, got 33 votes on the 13th ballotting. I have never seen such a scene of confusion. When 31 votes came out the lobby, crowded to overflowing, raised a shout and rushed out like a tumultuous mob. Eaton in a letter to the Speaker of the Senate[1] withdrew this morning after the first balloting, but a few of his friends instantly announced publicly their determination still to support him. Bell was then nominated by [Boling] Gordon and got 23 votes. I send you the various ballotings. I can write no more I am too well pleased.

TERRY H. CAHAL

Addressed to Somerville, Tennessee.

1. David Burford, representing Smith and Sumner counties.

FROM JAMES L. EDWARDS

Washington. October 8, 1833

Edwards reveals that the claim of Samuel Hillis, alias Hillhouse, was returned to Charles C. Mayson in March and that the papers of Alexander McKay have not been received from William Brady.

Addressed to Columbia.

FROM EPHRAIM BEANLAND[1]

Sir [Fayette County] Novembr[October] the 16 1833[2]

We ar well at preasant. The woman that was sick s[h]e has a child and it is a living. Sir I cant get Mary bed and clothing under $35 and Mr [. . .][3] has takin his thing all ovr. With the bed and other extras expensis will amounting to forty or fifty dollars which I must have. And sir I dont think that it write for me to by them on my own expenses. And sir I want to [k]now whethir you ar willing to pay for them, for if I have to by all these things you may send another man in my plase for I dont think it is write for me to be at all of that expensis. Write to me and let me [k]now what I m[a]y do, for I do ashure you that I will not run you to any expensis with out your consent. And you must let me [k]now what I must do, for I do not think it is write for me to make out this way. These things sir I bought, 3 blankets and had them charged to you. Write to me with out fail and let me [k]now, for I cant stand at what am.

E BEANLAND

Addressed to Columbia. The address on the envelope was written by someone other than the writer of the letter.

1. He had recently succeeded Herbert Biles as the overseer of Polk's Fayette County plantation. He went to Mississippi when Polk bought a plantation there and remained in his employ for several years. Beanland used virtually no punctuation marks, observed few rules of capitalization, and was capricious in his spelling. His letters have required more than the usual amount of editing for the sake of clarity. See John Spencer Bassett, *The Southern Plantation Overseer as Revealed in His Letters* (Northampton, Mass.: Smith College, 1925), *passim*.

2. Although Beanland wrote the date as November, the letter was postmarked October 16; moreover, Polk made a notation on the back to the effect that he answered the letter on October 31, 1833.

3. What appears to be a proper name has not been deciphered. The last name could be "Isaril," but no person with a similar name has been identified.

FROM BENJAMIN CLEARWATERS

Winchester [Tennessee]. October 19, 1833

A Revolutionary War veteran and pensioner, Clearwaters informs Polk that he is moving from Dickson County to Hall County, Georgia. He wishes to have his pension payments transferred from Nashville to Hall County. Clearwaters indicates that he left some pertinent papers with Mr. Robinson, Polk's nephew.[1]

Addressed to Washington. This letter, not in Clearwaters's handwriting, is in an unidentified hand.

1. Polk had no nephew named Robinson.

FROM JOHN W. CHILDRESS

Dear Sir Murfreesboro, Oct 20th 1833

I returned from Alabama on yesterday and succeeded partially in my business there. I found upon an examination of the land office that we had 4 quarter sections of land and one half quarter. I have sold one quarter for $1633, one half down, the balance in twelve months, another quarter for $5 pr acre payable in one & two years, and another for $300 payable in twelve months.[1] I called by your house to get a power of Attorney and you had just gone to the District. I of course had to give bond for title and in one case was required to give security. I done so and told my security that I would send a deed as soon as I got home. If you come bye here on your way to Washington, we can all make the Deed together. If not, you must make a Deed before you leave home, and send to me. I have so far gone without any written authority from you. You will please make a Power of Attorney for yourself and Sarah, such as you would have made before I started, have it proven and certified in your county & bring it with you. I will give you further particulars when I see you. We are all well and expect you up soon.

J W Childress

Addressed to Columbia.

1. See Childress to Polk, February 2, 1833.

FROM JAMES WALKER

Dear Sir, Washington City Octr. 20 1833

I have been here a few days, and find that we shall have competition in our stage lines to our hearts content. [John] Donley is mysterious, and from circumstances I am satisfied that he intends to bid against me, but he has no idea that I so understand him. He seems very much dissatisfied with Mr. Grundy's election—thinks Mr. G. a nullif[i]er, and an ungrateful man. His idea of gratitude seems to me to be very singular for I imagine Donley is one of the last men that ought to speak lightly of Mr. Grundy. Be all these things as they may, *I am under no obligations to* Mr. Donley and he has disregarded the propositions I have made to avoid competition with him, I shall at this time pay off the old debt I owe him. So you may set it down that Donley at this time looses his Tuscumbia & Huntsville lines, *or gets them by a compromise* that will ruin him, and from the consequences of which Harry Hill & Bob Armstrong[1] *cannot save him.*

How these things may operate upon *my interests* time will develope. I may have risqued working for nothing but have made no arrangement by which I can sustain actual loss. Kinkle & Caruthers[2] of Alabama (Clays friend) and Brown[3] & myself fully understand each other. They *operate on Donley,* but we are interested one half. We shall make a strong pull for the line from Memphis to Nashville, and from Bolivar to Florence & Jackson to Randolph, and if we loose we shall have the consolation of knowing we done our best.

I saw the President & Maj [William T.] Barry on Friday and was kindly received by both. I am satisfied that I shall get all that I am *fairly entitled to,* and with this I am content.

As to *your views,* I have as yet had no opportunity of acting. Several persons were present when I saw the President, and I had no opportunity of speaking of you, as I wished. I am to see him again to-morrow and may then have the opportunity. If no opportun[i]ty offers to-morrow, I must postpone it until Maria[4] & Myself are here again about the last of the month. This will be too late for me to communicate with you at home, but if I obtain any information that I think will be of service to you I will leave a letter for you in the Post Office here before I leave.

I have not seen Wm. B L[ewis]. When at Nashville I saw some thing which led me to believe there was a perfect understanding between Bell, Eaton, Armstrong, Foster[5] &c. which makes me feel very cautious in saying any thing to L[ewis] upon subjects in which your & Bell's views may clash. If I can do you no good, I must be careful to do you no harm. I think two parties are organising in the Jackson ranks—one for Van Buren and the other for Dick Joh[nson].[6] What say you to Dick Johnson & his *dark* lady for the [pre]sidency? You will understand more of this when you reach here. I am for the Dutchman of these two.

I left Maria & Mary[7] well at Philadelphia on the 16th. Mary is under the direction of Dr. Physic,[8] who takes much interest in her case. He has not yet said whether he thinks he can do her good.

I am in rather better health than usual—in good spirits, let my luck be as it may.

JAMES WALKER

Addressed to Columbia.

1. Harry R. W. Hill was a wealthy Nashville commission merchant and steamboat owner who moved temporarily to New Orleans during 1833. Robert Armstrong, a Jackson supporter, served as Nashville's postmaster for sixteen years, 1829–45.

2. A stagecoach company of Huntsville, Alabama.

3. James Brown, of Jackson, had received small mail contracts prior to this time. He had been associated with Samuel Polk in surveying in the Western District. Brown was on the board of the Jackson branch of the new Union Bank.

4. Walker's wife, Jane Maria, and Polk's oldest sister.

5. Ephraim H. Foster was a prominent Nashville lawyer. He became a leader of the Whig Party in the state and subsequently served in the United States Senate.

6. Richard M. Johnson of Kentucky. While some Tennesseans did show a preference for Johnson over Van Buren, Johnson's presidential aspirations were not greatly encouraged elsewhere.

7. Walker's ten-year-old daughter.

8. Philip S. Physick was a famous surgeon on the faculty of the medical department of the University of Pennsylvania. The nature of Mary's ailment has not been determined.

FROM FELIX GRUNDY

Dear Sir, Nashville, Octr 21st 1833

I am at present confined to my house by a rheumatic affection in my back. I have written a letter to Silas Wright[1] on the subject referred to.

My intention at present is to leave home on this day two weeks and travel thro East Ten. a little circuitously—send my boy back from Wythe Courthous [Virginia] and take the stage &c. I may be in Columbia to defend Coffee[2] before I go—that will depend on circumstances. I shall be here I presume when you arrive at this place.

Write to me, which road you go. Will Mrs Polk go with you?

FELIX GRUNDY

Addressed to Columbia.

1. A New York political leader who had recently served one term as Polk's colleague in the House of Representatives. The subject to which Grundy refers may have been the speakership, although both Grundy and Wright were then in the Senate. Wright became an increasingly important figure in the Democratic party, so much so that he was proposed as Polk's running mate in 1844, but he refused and instead ran successfully for governor of New York.

2. This seems to be a reference to one John Coffee who was tried by the circuit court in Maury County and sentenced to be hanged for the murder of his wife.

FROM WILLIAM POLK

Dear Sir: Raleigh Oct 22d 1833

On my getting to Chapel Hill I sent for William, and upon interogating him with regard to his wants and debts, I found both to be considerable. Since which I learn that he is quite destitute of shirts and some other cloathing which I deemed necessary he should be furnished with immediately. I wrote him last week to come down and to bring his unpaid accounts. He has done so and I find his debt to one house for goods &c. upwards of $80—that his board is for the present Session unpaid; and I presume upon some other small debts. He has an account here with a Merchant Taylor of $40 and for purchases made of a Merchant about $19. —making an agregate of debt *due* of about $180. His want of cloathing I considered as indispensable and have therefore advanced him the whole of the money sent by me viz. $80 which as you will observe not half meet his present wants.

WILL POLK

Addressed to Columbia. It was opened by Adlai O. Harris and forwarded to Polk in Washington by Samuel P. Walker on November 13, 1833. This letter has been published in McPherson, editor, "Unpublished Letters," *North Carolina Historical Review,* XVI, 77, and in Paul H. Bergeron, editor, "My Brother's Keeper: William H. Polk Goes to School," *North Carolina Historical Review,* XLIV (1967), 198.

FROM JAMES WALKER

Dear Sir, Washington City Octr. 22 1833

I yesterday had the opportunity I desired of conversing with the President in relation to your views. *He gives in to them I think decidedly and frankly.* He says that an objection is made that *he* is from Tennessee the President of the Senate[1] is also from Tennessee, and that it will not look very modest to ask the speakership for the same state. He rather ridiculed this objection, and said it was made for the benefit of the *Georgian.*[2] He thinks no very correct opinion can be formed until the members assemble here, and is of the opinion you ought to be here as early as practicable—is looking for you early in November. I asked him the question distinctly whether urging your views would interfere with the views or arrangements of *the party*. He answered unequivocably that it would not (and I thought he personally prefered that you should suceed in preference to any other person) but said we would talk the matter over further to-day when Mr. [James] Brown & myself dines with him. I have not yet seen W. B. L.,[3] but expect to see him to-day at the Presidents. If the opportunity offers I will ascertain his feeling upon the subject, and probably can guess at his course of action. My judgement is that he will be found under the Bell, Foster & Eaton influence, and that you are to expect nothing from him. Nor should I care any thing about him. I am satisfied the old chiefs feelings are for you & I do not think L. will dare to cross him, & perhaps he may not wish to do so in this instance.

I direct this letter to you at Knoxville, expecting it would not reach you at home. I think I shall not be able to reach you with another letter at Knoxville, and before I leave here will deposite a letter in the City post-office addressed to you when here in which I will particularly give you all the information I think may be of service to you.

I shall leave here to-night or to-morrow morning for Pha. and return here again with Maria about the middle of next week and shall remain so long as my interest and views requires it. As to our prospects here I can form no accurate opinion. I think our prospects fair & feel confident of getting a fair chance, and know the *old man* will see us righted, if we get into any difficulty. I received your letter from Somerville, was glad to hear of the health of all at home; but regret very much the sicknss and danger of George Moore's child. I must not *nor will not* loose his services, so long as providence permits him to live, but if necessary I will move him up to my other plantation, and let him superintend both. But I have no fears but my plantation where he is will be healthy, so soon as the effect of such an immense clearing is over.

I regret that your farming operations goes on badly. I hope you will be able to make some arrangements to change your luck. If you do not rather than you should break up, I think

I would make an arrangement to secure you $1000. for the use of the property as it now is pr annum[?].

James Walker

Addressed to Knoxville.

1. Hugh Lawson White.

2. This is perhaps a reference to James M. Wayne who was considered a likely candidate for Speaker of the House.

3. William B. Lewis. Walker's estimate of what course of action Lewis might take was correct. After most of Polk's friends had come to distrust Lewis, Polk seemed to have hoped for Lewis's support.

FROM ANDREW A. KINCANNON

Dr. Sir Fayetteville 27th Octr. 1833

My particular friend Doctor Hickman[1] of this place is very desireous of obtaining a warrant for his son to West Point. Inge has commited himself to Esqr. Haynes[2] of Corner[s]ville in favour of his son and can do nothing for young Mr Hickman from this district farther than to recommend him.[3]

Will you be so good as to inform me whether your District is represented at West Point, and if it is not, what would be the chance for my young friend?

He is now about seventeen years old and has a fine constitution—Is very stout and active. His education is quite a good one for our place, and in all particulars can & will be well recommended.

Please write on the recpt. of this.

A. A. Kincannon

Addressed to Maury County and forwarded to Washington.

1. Elliott Hickman was a Jackson presidential elector in 1832.

2. James S. Haynes, a merchant, was among the first settlers in the Cornersville area.

3. Both of the young men, William Hickman and Milton A. Haynes, received appointments and entered West Point in 1834.

FROM WILLIAM L. S. DEARING

Columbus, Mississippi. October 28, 1833

A resident of Wilson County, Tennessee, encloses a deposition concerning field notes that he lost while surveying in Louisiana and for which he is seeking remuneration.

Addressed to Washington.

FROM NATHAN GREEN[1]

Dear Sir, Nashville 28th Octr. 1833

The Rev Joseph A Copp,[2] the Cumberland Presbyterian minister at Winchester will be run for Chaplain to your House, at the approaching Session of Congress. Mr. Copp is a man of Talents and education, and is a very interesting Preacher. I have no doubt but that when you know him, you will be exceedingly pleased with him. He unites the urbanity of the gentleman with the gravity and dignity becoming a Christian minister more happily than any man I have seen.

His friends wish to commit him to your charge, & to engage you to bring him forward. Aware that a nominee is looked upon in some degree with the same sort of favor with which the person who makes the nomination is regarded, I cannot but hope you will not only be disposed to support Mr. Copp, but that you will bring him forward, and use your great influence for his election.

Please drop me a line in reply, directed to Winchester, for which place I set out tomorrow.

NATHAN GREEN

Addressed to Columbia and forwarded to Washington.

1. An eminent Tennessee jurist who was a member of the state supreme court at this time.

2. An able minister who was later invited to serve a church in Nashville but moved to Ohio instead. He was not chosen chaplain, although there were several letters written in his support.

FROM EPHRAIM BEANLAND

[Fayette County]

Dear Sir November[October] the 30th 1833[1]

I received yours on the 28th. We ar all well at preasant. Sir you want to [k]now what I have ben doing. I cum on verry slow in geting out my coton crop. Since you left I have maid seven bails which nomber 5 weighs 550 and nomber 6, 504, nomber 7, 484, nomber 8, 486, nomber 9, 550, 10 nomber 488, nomber 11, 500. This is all that I have wei[gh]ed. I have anough for another lode pict out. I have sent 5 bails to Memphis and I do ashure you that as soon as I get your crop to market I will. It will take me 8 more days to get over the first time a picking but I get it all wher[e] I go[2] now.

Sir did you see John Beck[3] as you went home? He cum to me and he had 20 sheepe, 12 ewes, 6 weathers, 2 rams which he sayed that you bought and he further sayed that he was a owing of you and so I kep the sheepe. If you did not by them I shal be verry sorry that I took them and Sir if you by any thing else send a fiew lines if you please.

I am sorry to tel you that the sorrel mooel[mule] is ded. He yaed down in the Stable and died and Sir if you ar a going to sind Garison down I would like to se him. If you could se the coten i [k]now you would send him if you co[u]ld. I cum on verry slowly. I must let you [k]now of won day work. Jack picked out 169, Jim 189, Ben 184, Rubin 175, Aderson 170, Hardy 170, Wally 160, Seaser 159, Barley 109, with all hands amounting to 1874 pounds. Sir when you write please to write a plain hand if you please Sir.

EPHRAIM BEANLAND

Addressed to Columbia and forwarded to Washington.

1. Beanland wrote the wrong month on the letter. It was postmarked at Somerville on November 1 and again at Columbia on November 7. Polk noted that he received the letter on November 26, 1833.

2. The last three words were written "wherigo."

3. Beck was a resident of the section of Maury County that was soon to become a part of Marshall County.

FROM JAMES CAMPBELL[1]

Dear Sir Winchester Tennessee 30th Oct 1833

Your friends here, myself among the number, are anxious to have The Reverend Joseph A. Copp of this place appointed one of the Chaplains to Congress, & hope you will lend us your influence to have it done. Copp is a classical scholar, of extensive acquirements, exemplary piety, agreeable manners, & I know will be acceptable to the H of R as a chaplain. Will you speak to your brother members in his behalf?

JAMES CAMPBELL

Addressed to Columbia and forwarded to Washington.

1. Campbell, of Franklin County, served several terms in the General Assembly.

FROM ADLAI O. HARRIS

Dear Sir Columbia 31st Oct 1833

Knowing the Enclosed Letter to be from Mr Walker I took the Liberty of opening and Dr [John B.] Hays & myself read it.[1] Thinking it might yet find you at Murfreesboro I send it there.

Dillahunty[2] is doubting whether he can make the exchange you agreed with him about. He says that he gives up all of these matters to his overseer & that his Overseer is unwilling to give Garrisson for Herbert. I will make this arrangement for you in some way.

Nothing new. Saml. P Caldwell[3] is getting better.

A O HARRIS

Addressed to Washington.

1. This is probably the letter from Walker to Polk, October 20, 1833.

2. Edmund Dillahunty was a prominent Maury County lawyer and judge.

3. Fifteen-year-old son of Dr. Silas M. and Lydia Polk Caldwell.

FROM ROBERT L. CARUTHERS[1]

Dear Sir Lebanon Nov. 3rd 1833

I take the liberty of recommending to you as a suitable person for chaplain to the H. of R. in the next congress the Revd. Mr. [Joseph A.] Copp of this state. He is a minister of the Cumberland Presbyterian denomination. He is in my estimation, & I have heard him preach frequently, & been often with him as a companion in the social circle, a first rate man & preacher. His prayers & sermons are characterized by pith, eloquence, learning, perspecuity, & *brevity.* He is too modest to thrust himself forward as most men do for office, & if he be elected it must be on the strength of his claims & the exertions of the friends which his claims may secure him. He will always[?] be restrained by his sense of propriety, from any the least mingling of politics with the sacred things with which he is called to deal. I know you would be well pleased with him on acquaintance. I will be pleased to hear that you shall have given him your support. I will set it down as a favour partly done to me. The Church to which he belongs has never had the honor of furnishing Congress with a Chaplain. Why should it not?

ROBT. L. CARUTHERS

Addressed to Washington.
1. A prominent lawyer and judge in Wilson County.

FROM ADLAI O. HARRIS

Dear Sir Columbia 4th Nov 1833

Jno Moore[1] started yesterday with Garrison to your place and agreed to go on with him to the plantation. Dillahunty would not agree to take Herbert in his place. (I cannot see what his objection really was for there is very little difference in their sizes and Herbert is certainly the most active boy.) Dr [Daniel] Stephens exchanged Osburn with me for Herbert and I have sent O. to Dillahunty.

No news from the District since you left here.

I have rented your office to Hilliard[2] for a confectionary (not a Liquor store) and he agrees to make some very good improvements at his own expense and pay $75 Rent. I spoke to Cooper[3] whose store is near to it and seems to be desirous to have such an establishment there.

A O HARRIS

Addressed to Washington.
1. This is probably John T. Moore, a Columbia businessman.

2. Unidentified.
3. Matthew D. Cooper, a well-to-do Columbia merchant.

FROM THOMAS P. MOORE

Dr Polk Harrodsburg [Kentucky] Nov. 5 [18]33

I send you the *latest* correspondence between Letcher[1] & myself. Come by & we will go on together. My regards to Mrs. P.

T P Moore

Addressed to Columbia and forwarded to Washington.

1. Robert P. Letcher was a member of the House of Representatives, 1823–33. He contested Moore's election in 1833, and the House eventually decided to seat neither of them. Letcher won in a special election in 1834. The enclosure mentioned was a large printed sheet of correspondence between Letcher and Moore entitled "To the people of the 5th Congressional district."

FROM WILLIAM L. NEAL[1]

Dear Sir Elkton [Giles County] 7th Novr. 1833

You will pleas pardon me for my intrusion if it is an intrusion. You will leave this state shortly for the City of Washington at which place I wish you to make enquiry if there is any person in this Cuntry that is a regular maker of Hygrometers, if not if I can get an exclusive right to make them as I am perfectly acquainted with making them together with the meterials. You will do me a favour by giving me your Idea on the subject before you leave home.

Wm L Neal

Addressed to Columbia and forwarded to Washington.
1. Unidentified.

FROM JAMES WALKER

Dear Sir, Washington City, Nov. 7th 1833

I have been unable to ascertain any thing since I wrote you at Knoxville in relation to your prospects for the Speakership. I have seen the President frequently, and W. B. L[ewis] but once, and that at Dinner at the Presidents—had no opportunity to sound him. My opinion is that it would meet the Presidents individual wishes for you to be selected, but how it is with others of the party here I cannot say. Mr. Van Buren has been here and very much at the Presidents for the last 3 weeks. I have seen him often and I like him, and believe he is to be our candidate for the Presidency, and if it meets your views I think it would be [to] your interest to let him understand that your friends go for him. I regard Grundy's election as fortunate for you in many respects. My judgement is that you ought not to yield your pretentions, and most especially *not at the suggestion* of WBL. The President spoke of the selection of a *new* speaker as a matter of course, and of course Mr. Stephenson[Stevenson] goes to England.

As to my own affairs—you will have learnt that I have lost all my District Routes. I was terribly underbidden. Kinkle, Caruthers, Brown & myself have the lines from Nashville to Tuscumbia and to Huntsville. *We are satisfied,* and regard the course of the Post-Office Department as correct. They seem to be honestly engaged in *retrenching and correcting abuses.*

We have had much to do with Kinkle & Caruthers of Alabama, and have the best feelings towards them. Their friend Mr. [Clement C.] Clay may at some time want your assistance in promoting their views. I shall regard it as a favor done me for you to aid them when in your power, in all things which you consider correct, and for public good.

I think that you, nor especially Mr. Grundy, are under no obligations to Mr. Donley, and when he calls on you to help him, it ought to be clear that he has just claims to what he asks.

We have been treated with much kindness and attention by the President, and feel perfectly satisfied with all our friends here. We have been thrown much in the society of Judge Campbell[1] & family, and are on the best terms with them. I think if you become intimately acquainted with Judge Campbell you would like him very much.

Kindy's[Kennedy's] health is considered too bad for Federal judge. I fear A. Hays[2] has no chance. Lacy[3] has a good deal of strength and *he is your friend.* I have not hesitated to say here at the right time and place that Craighead[4] would not do—that he was at best but a fence man. It had its influence, and I regard him as out of the question but you owe it to yourself and your friends to *speak of him as he deserves*. I will write you from home.

JAMES WALKER

Addressed to Washington. The letter was to be held for Polk's arrival. Meanwhile Walker left Washington.

1. Probably George Washington Campbell of Nashville, who was in Washington in connection with his work on the French Spoliation Claims Commission.

2. This seems to be a reference to Andrew Hays of Nashville, a lawyer and a former district attorney. Hays moved to Mississippi in 1837.

3. Thomas J. Lacy, law partner of Charles W. Webber of Columbia. He did not receive the appointment and soon moved to Arkansas, where he had a distinguished judicial career.

4. Probably David Craighead of Nashville.

FROM JOHN F. GONEKE[1]

Sir

Columbia Novr 8th 1833

Agreeable to promise I herewith enclose the documents respecting my son John and hope they, with your kind assistance will be sufficient to enable him to enter the Academy.

I have written to Honbl. [Clement C.] Clay of Alabama and the Honbl. Baringer from No Carolina[2] on the Subject and also Judge Clayton[3] of Georgia. Your attention to this business will confer a favour on me and my son that will always be cherished with feelings of the deepest gratitude.

JOHN F. GONEKE

Addressed to Washington. In Cadet Application Papers, United States Military Academy (RG 94), National Archives.

1. A music teacher in Columbia who taught piano and harp at Columbia Female Academy. It is unclear whether his son received an appointment to the Military Academy.

2. Daniel L. Barringer, later a resident of Bedford County, Tennessee, was at this time a member of the House of Representatives.

3. Augustin S. Clayton sat in the House, 1832–35.

FROM ADLAI O. HARRIS

Dear Sir Columbia 9th Nov 1833

Mr. Hilliard who rents your Office, has made some calculations as to the probable cost of the improvements that he wishes to make and finds that it will be about $100. He intends to extend the front part of the building out to the street to range with the other Buildings and to put every thing in good repair and wishes to know of you if in consideration of the repairs &c he may calculate on the House for two years instead of one at the rate of $75 pr year.

No news. All well.

A O Harris

Addressed to Washington.

FROM WILLIAM R. RUCKER

Dear Colo. Murfreesboro. Nov. 12th 1833

I take a pleasure in advising you by letter we are all well again. Susan was very little sick after you left us. She as well as the children recovered very fast & I believe that her health is perhaps better than it has been for several months. The measles has spread more or less through almost every family in town. John Childress has not yet taken them & hopes to escape. I know of nothing further at present that would interest you. There has been *a move* that has come to my knowledge on the *political chess board.* The president some time since gave the appointment of Receiver of Publick money in one of the land offices of Mississippi to Mr Savage[1] of Florence who has since become deranged and of course disqualified for the appointment. Captain Savage said that he would write to Genl Jackson to have it transfered to my brother John W. Rucker.[2] I wrote myself to the General on the subject but I have not learned any thing about it. I would be glad you would interest your self about it. Find out what is going & if need be put in a good word for John. You know him and the General knows him. John is kneedy and such an appointment may be of great service to him. Talk to Judge Grundy about it if the president should think of nominating him.

I should have written to you sooner & directed my letter to Lexington Va. but I was very much engaged & forgot it till it was too late.

W R Rucker

Addressed to Washington.

1. William Forbes Savage was probably a kinsman of Samuel Savage, who was one of the first purchasers of land in Lauderdale County, Alabama.

2. He did not receive the appointment. It is not known whether or not Polk recommended him to Jackson.

FROM SAMUEL P. WALKER[1]

Dear Uncle Columbia Nov 13th 1833

Enclosed you will find a letter from Col. Will Polk of North Carolina which Mr Harris opened, read and requested me to forward to you.[2] Nothing of importance has occurred since your departure from this place.

I received a letter from my father this evening saying that he had lost his mail contracts in the District but had obtained the contracts from Nashville to Huntsville & Florence, all of which you will probably have heard before you receive this letter.

Harvey Walker[3] returned a few days since from Missippi [*sic*], but left Andrew Hays[4] behind to *regulate and manage* R. M. Williamson's election which was to take place in a few days. They were very much pleased with the country and it is highly probable that they will move their goods from this place. Johnson[5] and Walker will go below but Andrew will remain here. The people are beginning to talk about who shall be the members of Convention from this county. Yourself and Cobb[6] are spoken of.

Saml. P. Walker

Addressed to Washington.

1. The oldest son of James and Jane Maria Walker. During the 1840s he moved to Memphis, where he became a prominent lawyer and judge.

2. This refers to the letter from William Polk to James K. Polk, October 22, 1833.

3. A son of James Simpson Walker, who was a cousin and former business partner of James Walker. Harvey M. Walker had been a clerk in the store of which his father was one of the partners.

4. Andrew C. Hays, a brother of John B. Hays, was postmaster at Columbia and had once been an associate of James Walker in publishing a local newspaper. Andrew Hays, a Nashville lawyer, was a cousin of the Hays brothers.

5. John B. Johnson, locally known as "Jack" Johnson, established himself in Madison County, Mississippi. See Johnson to Polk, October 14, 1834.

6. Robert L. Cobbs, a Columbia lawyer.

FROM WILLIAM L. S. DEARING

Choctaw Nation, Mississippi. November 14, 1833

Dearing reveals that he is willing to accept land as remuneration for his lost field notes and suggests that a section of his own choosing would be a proper compensation.

Addressed to Washington.

FROM ADLAI O. HARRIS

Dear Sir Columbia 16th Nov 1833

The Legislature have fixed the time for the Election of members to the Convention 1st Monday in April and to meet 1st Monday in May. This is what we might have expected but not what the country desired. The members of course expect from their fixing the time so early that a member of their own body will be elected, but if we cannot get more talents in the Convention than we have in the Legislature I tremble for our Constitution.

They have Chartered another new Bank to be called the "Planters Bank" & have located a Branch at Pulaski and one at Athens E. Tennessee; Capital two millions, Banks to [be] opened 1st January and Directors to be Elected 1st March. The Conditions of the Charter are very much the same as the Union Bank the Same rate of Interest &c.

Andw. C. Hays has just returned from a trip to Mississippi, is very much pleased with the Country and will I have no doubt remove his Mercantile Establishment there. He speaks very highly of the Country, as a Cotton growing region—says that hands can make $500 each. Dr. William Polk came out a few days ago, is making arrangements to settle himself in the Rattle & Snap tract near to Lucius and Leonidas,[1] and has I believe sent to N.C. for his Negroes. Lucius & the Doctor have gone to Mississippi to look out a place to send their hands & intend planting there the next season. They will make a partnership farm.

No late news from N. Orleans. The market was depressed last advice.

The merchants in the neighborhood of your office are so opposed to Hilliard's occupying it as a confectionary that I have consented to take it back & have not yet rented to any body else.

Smith takes the Field he had last year & D Campbell the other.[2]

All well.

A O Harris

Addressed to Washington.

1. Dr. William J. Polk and Leonidas Polk were brothers of Lucius J. Polk, and all were sons of Colonel William Polk of Raleigh, North Carolina. William J. Polk was graduated from Chapel Hill in 1813. He subsequently studied medicine in Philadelphia, and did, indeed, settle in Maury County. Leonidas Polk was graduated from West Point. He attended an Episcopal seminary and moved to Tennessee. In 1841 he moved to Louisiana, where he became bishop of that diocese.

2. Smith and Campbell are unidentified.

FROM ELLIOTT HICKMAN

Dear Sir Fayetteville Nov. 20th 1833

I must ask the particular favour of you to lend your aid in procuring a warrant for my son William in West Point Academy. I should not have troubled you, living out of the District, but for the circumstance of Majr [William M.] Inge having somewhat committed himself to a young man in Giles, not knowing my son would be an applicant, a circumstance he much regrets.[1] Should difficulty present owing to there being several applicants from this district, Genl. Jackson I am inclined to think would aid in furthering my wishes on the subject. Also Majr [John H.] Eaton to whome I have written likewise.

ELLIOTT HICKMAN

Addressed to Washington.

1. See Andrew A. Kincannon to Polk, October 27, 1833.

FROM JAMES C. O'REILLY[1]

Dear Sir Mauray Cty Nov 20th 1833

Will you pardon the liberty I take in requesting you to forward the enclosed to our mutual Friend Dr Campbell?[2] Your friends here are all well. I should be happy to hear from you. Give my best respects to Mrs. Polk.

J. C. O REILLY

Addressed to Washington.

1. Born and educated in Dublin, Ireland, O'Reilly went first to North Carolina, where he was married. He moved to Maury County in 1809 and at this time lived on a farm in the Zion Church neighborhood. His daughter Caroline married A. O. P. Nicholson.

2. The enclosure has not been found. Dr. George W. Campbell was a brother of McKay W. Campbell and had practiced with O'Reilly in Columbia, but at this time he was in Paris, France, where he died. He is not to be confused with the better-known George Washington Campbell, Nashville lawyer and judge.

FROM JOHN BECK[1]

Dear Sir, Columbia Novr. 21st 1833

The note you had on me I discover has been transfered to Evan Young[2] and forwarded to me for payment. He will not take the account I have on you for some sheep you bought of me. I want you to write to Esqr. James Walker to pay me the money or lift the note. He says he will do it if you will write. Your overseer, Beanland, took twenty sheep at two Dollars a piece, and two goats that were to be valued by yourself were taken by the overseer also. You may recollect what you thought they were worth and include that in the amount. I feel a little pressed for money and they will not take Beanlands statement about it and I want you to be sure and write immediately if you please and as soon as you can. I have no fear about the title to the land, and do not wish to be understood as expressing any. My whole object is to avoid the pressure from the inforcement of the collection of my note.

JNO. BECK by M. G. SIMS[3]

Addressed to Washington.

1. The person who wrote this letter for Beck also signed it for him. The first name of this signature is difficult to decipher, seeming to be either "Jas." or "Jno." Since Ephraim Beanland wrote it quite clearly "John" in his October 30, 1833, letter to Polk, that name has been accepted.

2. A Columbia businessman who was one of the first trustees of the Columbia Female Institute.

3. Unidentified.

FROM ADLAI O. HARRIS

Dear Sir Columbia 21st Nov 1833

I have just taken in and paid your a/c with Leftwich[1] of Mt. Pleasant $10 25/100. This is about the amt you supposed it to be and I am pleased to find that they did not intend to profit by the example of our Columbia folks.

Mr Walker has just returned and is making preparations for carrying his new stage line into effect. The Donly agents &c &c take it very hard.

James Booker[2] is just up from the Western District, was at your farm & Mr Walkers. He says that a great many Horses are dying with something like Blind Staggers. Mr Walker has lost four and you perhaps two. Beanland though I suppose has written to you on the subject.

Nothing new. All well.

A O HARRIS

Addressed to Washington.

1. This is perhaps a reference to Dr. Joel Leftwich, who moved into the western part of Maury County about 1830.

2. Son of Peter R. Booker.

FROM BENJAMIN CLEMENTS

D Sir Tallahasee [Florida] November 22d 1833

I am at this place for a Short Stay only. Expect to Spend four & five months in the Section of Country about St Augustine, East Florida.

Sir when I Saw you in Fayetteville Tennessee last I mentioned to you a little matter I wishd. your attention to while at the City this winter for me.

You will please See Col. John McKinley of Ala on the Subject who was present the most of the time & knows much about the fact.

I wish you & Col John McKinley to See the adjusting officer at the City and refer to my accounts with Genl. John Graham[1] & W. G. Parish[2] of Tuskaloosa. Both of those Gentlemen and the Recever[?] at Cahaba allowd. me ten Dollars per day for my Services as Auctionneer at the Sails of public land. Col McKinley was present at many of the Sails & Knows well that I earnd. the amt. & more per day.

But Sirs after the Death of Obidiah Jones,[3] Mrs Jones brought Suit against me for all over three Dollars per day in the Lincoln Circit Court & obtaind. Judgment against me with Interest on the amt. from the time the money was paid.

Now Sir you will please do me the favour at Some of your Leisure hours to call at the office & refer to the accounts of Graham & Parrish & othrs & you will See at once that ten Dollars per day & in Some Instances more was allowd. me. And I am of the oppinion that if a few Statements of fact was made to the officers that the amt would without any difficulty be allowd. to Mrs Jones & a remittance of the Interest in the Settlement of herr accounts or allowd. to me either way will enable me to pay the Judgment. I feel it a hard case to pay the amt. back after Standing so long. Also when I am So Certain that I earnd. more for the Goverment than even that.

Gentlemen if any vacancy Should appear in any little office that you in your goodness might believe your old friend qualified to fill I hope you will please give my name to the President. I mention none. I know of none at this time.

Please let me hear from both of you after the month of February to St Augustine, East Florida—Say in March.

You will hear from me again about January.

BENJN. CLEMENTS

Addressed to Washington. Although Clements seemed to have intended the letter for both Polk and McKinley, he addressed it to Polk.

1. Probably John G. Graham, a brother of William Graham of Alabama and of Daniel Graham, long-time secretary of state of Tennessee. John G. Graham later moved to Texas.

2. William G. Parrish was a native of North Carolina and a former resident of Tennessee. He was for many years receiver of public money at Tuscaloosa.

3. Obadiah Jones, who died in 1825, had served as receiver of public money in Huntsville, Alabama. Clements had been an auctioneer in some land sales which Jones had conducted. See Clements to Polk, February 6, 1830.

FROM JACOB BLETCHER

Bedford County. November 23, 1833

A Revolutionary War pensioner, personally unknown to Polk, says that he has moved from North Carolina and asks help in getting the point of payment shifted to Nashville.

Addressed to Washington.

FROM McKAY W. CAMPBELL

Dear Sir. Columbia Novr. 23th 1833

Some short time since I wrote to Col. Toland[1] of Philadelphia on the subject of some land warrants—among them, were three 640 acre Warrants in the name of "the *Heirs* of James O'Harra." Col. Toland informed me that Mr. James O'Harra had in his lifetime been a merchant of the City of Pittsburg—probably, but that he had been dead many years, and that Mr. [Harmar] Denny[2] of Pittsburg—who is a member of *your Honorable body*—he *thinks*, married the daughter of Mr. O'Harra and would not only be able to give me information on the subject, but would, in all probability feel himself authorised to dispose of these warrants.

My object is to purchase the warrants if I can get them on proper *Terms.* I say to Mr. Denny that warrants of that size are in my opinion, worth about 20 c. per acre and that I would authorise you to purchase them for me. Mr. Denny will probably apply to W. District members to know the price of warrants. You are well enough acquainted with the situation of the country to know the immense difference between the value of large & small warrants—that the good land you know is in small & broken bodies, and is generally claimed by Occupants, few of whom claim or are able to pay for more than from 20 to 50 acres of warrants & the costs of ripening[?] it into a grant &c. However, I wish you to make the purchase for me and authorise you to go as high as 30 c. (thirty) cents per acre if you can't get them for less. Get them for less if possible and on the longest possible time. I would be glad Mr. Denny (on the supposition you trade) would give me untill you return in the fall of next year. I will give such security as you can assure him is good. If the *thing* will *take* Mr. Denny can authorise me to draw the warrants from the Secretary of State & forward them to you, or himself, & he can transfer them as the agent of the heirs &c or he & they may authorise Genl. Saml. G. Smith to transfer them to me. You know the fees will have to be paid before the warrants can leave the office & the fees are considerable. Should I pay the fees they must be deducted from the purchase money. These warrants are usually transfered by blank indorsements—*name of the owners on the back.* Should we make a trade Mr. Denny, or whoever makes the transfer ought to give bond in double amount of the purchase money to indemnify me against any future claim of the heirs of James O'Harra. Do the very best you can for me in this behalf. . . .

M. W. Campbell

P.S. Nothing of importance has occurred since you left. A. C. Hays, H. M. Walker, Duncan & McGimsey[3] have all returned from a visit to Miss. & *all* have *cotton making* fever the most immaginable. 'Tis rumored that L. H. Duncan & Dr. McGimsey, have made stipulations for *Cotton farms.* Our friend Hays, is in perfect *ecstacy.* I think it's understood that H. M. Walker & *Jack*

Johnson will go to the south and also Nelson Kavanaugh.[4] Dr. Barbour (Son of Honbl. P. P. B. of Virginia)[5] is now here & contemplates settling here—not determined. Mr & Mrs. Walker & daughter returned on Wednesday last in good health & high spirits &c. Your relations &c here are all in good health. It is said Mr. McLemore[6] has made a *grand* speculation at the Choctaw Land sales, & it is *attempted* to implicate Genl. Jackson in the matter. The story is that McL. had some private information from the Executive of the time &c. of sales that gave him the advantage of others. This is the cry of the slugard who wishes to reap without having sown—the excuse of those who folding their arms enjoy the cool shades of *Luxery* and *ease,* while the indefatigable John C. was braving the scorching suns of the south and the dangers of a *sickly,* savage, untamed & uncultivated Country. Let *them* wreath under the only thing that could torture *their* mind, *Pecuniary* loss. J. C. McL. has reaped the fruits of his *industry.* (Our *Jackson* is out of the reach of their *puny aspersions.*)

The legislature have chartered "The Planters Bank" 'tis said on pretty much the same principles with the *Union* Bank—Principal Bank at Nashville, Branches at Pulaski & Athens.

M. W. C.

Please seal the enclosed letter and hand it to Mr. Denny if he is at Washington City. If he is not alter the directions & send it to him in Pittsburg. I am sorry I have had to inflict so long a letter on you.[7]

Addressed to Washington.

1. This is probably Henry Toland, a Philadelphia merchant who did quite a bit of business for Andrew Jackson. He remained a friend of Jackson despite a report he made in 1832 that was favorable to the Bank of the United States as a safe place of deposit for government funds. However, the Colonel Toland referred to by Campbell could possibly be George W. Toland of Philadelphia, who later served in Congress.

2. See Samuel G. Smith to Polk, January 27, 1833.

3. John W. McGimsey was a physician in Columbia and had previously been mayor of the town. He soon moved to Mississippi.

4. Unidentified.

5. It is not known how long Thomas Barbour lived in Columbia, but he did practice medicine there for a while. His father, Philip P. Barbour, was at this time a federal judge in Virginia, and in 1836 Jackson appointed him to the United States Supreme Court.

6. An intimate friend of Jackson, John C. McLemore was surveyor general of the state and had extensive landholdings.

7. These three sentences were written on the margin of the first page of the letter. The letter to Denny has not been found, but it seems that Campbell did enclose another letter to Polk that he dated November 25, 1833.

FROM PETER R. BOOKER

Dear Sir, Near Columbia Tennessee 25th Nov 1833

I have had it in view to make some little investment in the Chickasaw Country when their lands are in market, and am mutch at a loss to know when the probable period of the sale will be. I am aware of the impractability of certain and corrct information on this subject from the very nature of the bussness, but think it more than probable that through the Register of the Land office at Washington some information of the probable period can be obtained which will afford me some satisfaction. Again I should be glad to know what construction is placed or will be if it known on that article in the Treaty, giving sections of land to the Chiefs, whether their reserves will be confined to their place of residence, or whether they will have the privilidge of selecting other Sections. Any satisfaction that can be given me on these subjects will be kindly acknowledged.

My Son James Booker has just returned from the District. He was on your plantation; he think your manager Beanland is going on well with his bussness in a way that will please you. He had the misfortune to loose two of his mules with the blind staggers a disease that has been fatal to stock in that neighbourhood this season of which you have doubtless been informed.

P. R. Booker

Addressed to Washington.

FROM McKAY W. CAMPBELL

Col. Polk [Columbia] November 25th 1833

You will no doubt recollect that I mentioned to you that I would be glad my brother Dr. Campbell[1] could [get] an appointment from the Government that would assist him in getting along where he now is, *in a land of Strangers.* Genl. Jackson has the appointment of Secretaries of Legation. If such an appointment is to be made at London or Paris I wish You would mention his name to the President. He is now well enough acquainted with the French Language to transact common business with considerable facility. Any service you can render my brother will be thankfully recd. by *him* and gratefully acknowledged and remembered by Dr. Campbell and his relations & particularly by Your Friend.

M. W. CAMPBELL

Addressed to Washington, this letter was enclosed with Campbell's letter that was dated November 23, 1833, and was mailed at Columbia on November 26, 1833.

1. See letter from James C. O'Reilly to Polk, November 20, 1833, and that from Dr. Campbell to Polk, December 5, 1833.

FROM WILLIAM H. POLK

Dear Brother Chapel Hill N.C. November 25 1833

I received your letter of 21st Oct in which you said you did not know how it was that I spent more money than Col Polks son. I can account for that very easy: he gets all his cloths from home and I have to buy mine. If you will send me money enough to pay all my debts and 150 dollars at the begining of every session I will not ask you for any more and I think it will be little enough.

I owe about thirty dollars more for my winter cloths. I would not have gone in debt for them if I could have got them any other way. If you intend to let me have money to pay my debts you must send it to me as soon as you can for they are pushing me for it and I canot study when I have such things on my mind.

Genl Polk[1] of Salsbury passed through here on yesterday and said that he saw sister Laura and the children and they was very well. Give my love to sist Sarah and tell her she must excuse me for not answering her letter and I will write to her in a few days.

WILL H POLK

Addressed to Washington. This letter has been published in Bergeron, editor, "My Brother's Keeper," *North Carolina Historical Review,* XLIV, 198–199, and in McPherson, editor, "Unpublished Letters," *North Carolina Historical Review,* XVI, 77n.

1. General Thomas G. Polk was the oldest son of Col. William Polk of Raleigh. Unlike his brothers Lucius, Leonidas, and William, he did not move to Tennessee. He had some political success in North Carolina and served in the state legislature.

FROM HENRY HORN

Philadelphia. November 26, 1833

Horn reminds Polk of a letter in which he (Horn) had asked for help in collecting a note of Dale and Duncan of Columbia and inquires as to progress in the matter.

Addressed to Washington.

FROM SAMUEL G. SMITH

Nashville. November 28, 1833

This introduces Robert Wharton, son of Samuel L. Wharton, as an amiable young man of superior business habits who has received appointment as a clerk in the Post Office Department and asks Polk to help him get established in his new job.

Addressed to Washington.

FROM JONATHAN WEBSTER

Dear Sir Noah's Fork, Bedford Cty, Ten. Novm. 29th 1833

"Delays breed dangers," and perhaps it may be so in my case. You will recollect that about the 3d. of Jany. last, you filed my description of the inclined wheel to be propell by water, or Horse power alone or both combined, on the same wheel &c. You will also no doubt recollect that I wrote you relative to this invention of mine several years ago. It now appears that Mr. James Word[1] has obtaind a patent for a part of my invention (to wit) propelling the inclined wheel by water, but not the combination of the two powers on the same wheel & shaft, nor does it appear that the water is recieved or discharged on any plan, though I cannot understand his mode and maner of recieving and discharging the water. I send you his plan inclosed[2] that you may see when he filed his notice, or dis[c]ription as well as the date of his patent, for should both be subsequent to mine I shall contend for my rights. By comparing his description, and dates with mine you will be able to say whether or no I could be successful against him at law. Again, *would I be allowed* to use my invention of propelling the inclined wheel by water, provided my buckets were made different from his, and the water discharged in a different maner, his patent for the principle notwithstanding. Whilst on this part of the subject I will refer you to the circular from the Department of State, 11th specification which I hope you will explain to me.

I know that I shall be entitled to a patent for my other improvements, namely, the combination of the two powers, and the manor of constructing the buckets, and discharging the water, but if I am to loose the patent for the propelling principle, I care but little for the ballance, which I would be wiling to donate to the world.

I beg that you would be careful in your examinations, for on your Judgement depends my further progress in this matter. Terminate as it may, I shall allways consider my self the inventor, original. I kept no copy of my notice which you had put on file, and would thank you to look at it, & send me a copy of the same, as well as the date of Words notice or grant, for dates in this matter are material things.

If you should think my right good to use the principle (to wit) the water power on the inclined plane, I shall be more particular in describing my machine and send on another notice to be put on file, untill I can attend to the business in person.

Would there be any impropriety in send[ing] you by mail a small part of my invention, say one bucket and valve, and so much of the horse plow, all made fast to but two arms, sd. part about 3 inches long and the same wide, two Inches thick, in all weighing not more that 8 ounces—by which a workman could make a model complet, in the City. It was the dificu[l]ty of conveying a model to the office, that proved this great delay.

I am very sorry, that I am compelled to give you so much

trouble, but I hope you will serve me and when I take my seat in congress, I will do you the like favour if called on.

Alll peace in Bedford now. Turnpike Roads and domestic business keep us imployed. Should I hear any thing worthy of your notice I shall give you the earliest information. Excuse hast.

J. WEBSTER

PS Please inform whether or no, you retained my first letters to you in regard to the propelling principle of the inclined wheel, for those letters I think, would be strong evidence in my favour.

J. W.

Addressed to Washington.

1. A resident of LaGrange, Fayette County, Tennessee. A patent for his inclined water wheel was issued to Word on February 26, 1833.

2. The enclosure was a clipping from the Nashville *Republican* of November 20, 1833. The news story included a diagram of the wheel, with a rather detailed description; a statement by Robert Brown of Fayette County that he had one of the wheels in operation in his mill and could recommend it highly; and a statement signed by twenty-one men of the vicinity who certified that they had seen Word's wheel in operation and considered it completely successful.

FROM JAMES C. WILSON

[Washington]. November 29, 1833

Wilson, a clerk in the Engineer Office of the War Department, seeks a clerkship in the House of Representatives and asks that Polk use influence in his behalf.

Addressed to Washington.

FROM JAMES H. THOMAS

Dr Sir Columbia Nov. 30th 1833

I enclosed to you an application for a pension.[1] It being made before the Circuit Court & that court having no seal, I have had it certafied as you will see & send it to you for your certificate that George M Martin[2] is clerk & that it is *all right*.

We have no news, but such as appears in the Papers. Yes

Dr. McNeil[3] was maried on the 28th inst. to Miss Mary Crocket &c.

JAMES H. THOMAS

N. B. Please direct that a *return* to this may be directed to me.

JAMES H THOMAS

Presumably addressed to Washington.

1. This enclosure has not been found, but Polk noted that the applicant was John Langley of Maury County. Langley had served with the South Carolina line during the Revolution and was placed on the pension roll on June 17, 1834. He died during the next month.

2. He was circuit clerk for more than twenty years and was master of the chancery court, 1834–44. At one time he operated a school for girls in Columbia.

3. William McNeill was a Columbia physician whose marital affairs were the subject of considerable interest among Polk's correspondents. See Charles C. Mayson to Polk, May 19, 1832, and William Minter to Polk, December 9, 1833.

FROM EPHRAIM BEANLAND

D Sir [Somerville] December the 1th 1833

We ar all well and I cum on sloly a geting my crop out, the weather is So bad. I have sent 20 bails to Memphis and have got about 5 more pict out which I shal be til Spring a geting out my crop. It apeares I get along verry slow. I do ashere you sum dayes all hands dont pick out 2 hundrd pounds. It is cold and wet and my corne is verry lite tho I have not geathered nun onldy as I used it. It is in the field and I am verry sorry to tell you that Jack and Ben has wrun away on Friday last. On Thirsday nite I maid 1 baile an loded the wgon wich it was a 11 oclock when I left the screw. And then I maid the hands shell a bag of corne which Jack went 5 miles in the neighborhood and broke open a grocery and he was persuied so closely that he left his stick. The man mist flower and sugar and tobacco and whiskey and when they caime I took the casys[?] all up. Ben had sum flower which he told me 5 or 6 positif lyes about and I corected him. And when I got positif proof that Jack did brake open the grocery I corected him w[e]ll which he owned that he did do it and I then set them to worke. And while I went to diner they both left the field and

I have not heard of them since. And Sir your boys has traded so much with white people and bin let run so loose reined[?] that I am compeled to not let won of them of one[1] the plantation with out he askes my leave and then if I think he ought to go I let him go and if not I ceep him at home. As son as I can get my crop out I will. My bailes avereges 450. The box is give away and rather then to have a new won maid I will make my bailes some liter. And in the next letter you shal have the hoal amount of your bailes, the weight and numbers.

E BEANLAND

Addressed to Washington.

1. These words are written quite distinctly. The writer, however, probably meant "off of" or a localism pronounced "offen."

FROM JAMES M. WAYNE

Dear Sir Washington December 1st 1833

I called to see you last evening but you were out. Will it be convenient to you to give me an interview this morning at an early hour? If so, be good enough to name the time and I will call and you will increase the obligation, if it could[?] be before the ordinary[?] church going hour which I believe to be about ten o'clock.[1]

JAMES M. WAYNE

Delivered by hand to Polk's lodging.

1. This note gives every appearance of having been written in haste. It is obvious that Wayne wished to see Polk about the contest for Speaker. Since none of the several candidates would withdraw, it was decided that Stevenson should remain in that post for some time longer.

FROM ARCHIBALD YELL

My Dear Sir Fayetteville Decr. the 1st 1833

Tomorrow is the meeting of Congress and you may imagine my solicitude for the events of that day. Your prospects may be advanced by it, or retarded according to your success as Speaker of the H.R. I have strong hopes tho not without some fears as that Election will turn upon the preference given by the frinds of one of the aspirants to the Presidency. I mean the frinds of Mr Van Buren can & will perhaps turn the scale & should they be fishing for Pensylvana I fear they will take up that *Milk & Cider* Mug Dr. Sutherland[1] & that will tend to defeat you as the opposition understand *Him* they will vote for him. But it will all be over before you get this & you will be able to inform me how it all turned out. If the little Dutchman Van goes for you I shall be agreeably disappo[in]ted.

This session will be one of deep interest to the people. You will have the U. S. Bank again to battle & the Expedincy of the Removal of the depos[i]ts to contend with, but our party I hope are sufficnt for them all. "Divide et Impera" will be the policy of the *Antis* & the order of the day. The Next Presidential Election will figure in many of the acts of this Congress.

You will see from the Papers here that subject seems to be broached early in Middle Ten & a push will be made by the frinds of Govr Carroll to procure for Him a Nom[i]nation for the Vice Presidency. How it will take elsewhere I can not even conjecture but hear it takes well with the people. The Polititions Generlly are opposed to Him which has been the case you know for years past. But its said he is pleased with the Idea & is quite a warm Van Buren man. Should he not be as much of a favorite with them He will feel disappo[i]nted & may fall into the ranks of Judge M[c]Lean[2] who will have a formadable party in Tennessee if the contest is made betwn *them & Van.*

The paper at this place has hoisted the McLean & Carroll flag and the *Pulaski Beacon* the *M[c]Lean* & H L. White. The Nashville Editors are hands off which perhaps is the most politick course for the present.

I fear the question of McLean & Van Buren at the next Election in this District will give my frind [William M.] Inge some trouble. It will be made & as much made out of it as posibly. I Judge so from the little "Beacon" coming out for M[c]Lean. The subject of the *Military Academy* will give him trouble. You will see the Resolutions of the Legislature on that subject & he is already comm[it]ted in his Circular. But how he will quit the *Ranks* I cant conjecture—time will tell. I write to you frankly as

I am always in the habit of doing & nothing is said or intended to affect your feelings towards Mr. Inge. He is your frind or so professes & I would not disturb that good feeling, but I shall take the liberty to speak about his course as I may view it which will not I hope disturb our frindship. I know it will not.

The Convention Bill has passed and our District is 3 Jo[i]ntly from Lincoln & Giles. Who are to be our membrs is yet uncertain. In Giles A V Brown & Gordon[3] are spoken of & here Col [James] Fulton & Holman[4] & perhaps Col [Andrew A.] Kincannon; its to be hoped here this election will pass off without much excitement, but if all those men mentiond should be out there are some comtentable matters which will show itsself. I have let politicks alone & attend closely to my practice. There is a Branch of the Memphis Bank located at this place so we shall take a rise its hoped. Our membrs [William] Moore & Thompson[5] have I think sustained themselves well.

Old Friend Vicker[6] thinks he has still a balince behind. How is that upon his bounty land? I expect he is mistaken.

Will you be so good as to present my best respects to Col [Ambrose H.] Sevier of Arkinsaw & to your good Lady and accept for yourself the wishes of your old frind?

Yell

Enclosed I send you $3 for the *Congressional Globe*. One I wish forward to Col Jas Fulton, one to myself & the other to Cols. [William] Moore & [Ira] McKinn[e]y. Pardon me for troubling you with such menial service.

PS I have tryed to procure a Bill of the proper size but have failed. I will write to Mr. [Francis P.] Blaire for the Papers.

A. Yell

PS I have just learned that the Legislature or some of them will nominate H L. White for the Presidency!! Its a *Ruse de Guerre* to throw Carroll. There will be a deceiver; its premature.[7]

Addressed to Washington.

1. Joel B. Sutherland of Pennsylvania was a member of Congress, 1827–37.

2. John McLean served as Postmaster General under Monroe and Adams and at this time was a member of the Supreme Court. His court duties occasionally brought him to Nashville, where he had some support as a possible

successor to Jackson. Governor William Carroll and Felix Grundy tended in that direction for a while, but when Grundy was re-elected to the Senate with strong Jackson support, the McLean movement weakened. In September Polk and McLean had conversations in Nashville, which raised some rumors that Polk might become a McLean advocate. Archibald Yell was another Jacksonian who was friendly toward McLean. Yell continued to favor McLean for some months.

3. Thomas K. Gordon was a colonel in the county militia and represented his county in the General Assembly on two occasions.

4. Isaac Holman, an early settler in Lincoln County, had served one term in the state senate, 1829–31.

5. William D. Thompson, a lawyer, was at this time representing Lincoln County in the lower house of the General Assembly.

6. Probably John R. Vickers, a Lincoln County resident and Revolutionary War pensioner. See his letter to Polk, October 18, 1832.

7. These last sentences were written in the margin of the second page of the original manuscript.

FROM HENRY HORN

My Dear Sir Philada. Decem 2d 1833

I am duly favoured with yours of the 28th authorizing me to Draw upon you for the amt of Dale & Duncans note with interest, say $142.24 which I have done this day. For your Kindness and attention on this matter I can only offer you my thanks and assure you of that which you already Know that I am ever and entirely at your service.

Doctr. S[utherland] as I am informed has gone down to Washington but with no expectation or hope of opposing [Andrew] Stevensons Election. It is generally supposed that our speaker will be sent to Europe before the close of the session. I hope so sincerely because I believe in him our country will have an able and efficient Representative. With all those high and noble feelings so peculiar to the People of the Old Dominion he has a clear and just conception of what is necessary to guard the rights of the states on the one hand and preserve the integrity of the Union on the other when he is called by our Venerable friend the President to figure upon another Theatre. Permit me to say that I sincerely hope the House will manifest an enlightened discretion in choosing his successor and that in due time I may have the pleasure of offering you my congratulations as the choice of the House and as the successor of Stevenson. I trust you will continue your patriotic efforts to put down that monster of corruption the Bank. Pennsylvania I am sure will go with you in the holy work.

HENRY HORN

Addressed to Washington.

FROM SAMUEL BURCH[1]

Dear Sir. Capitol [Washington] Dec 3, 1833

After a faithful service of thirty years, I now find myself for the first time in danger of being deprived of my employment, and of being thrown upon the world, with an enfeebled Constitution and Six Small Children and that too, without fault or negligence being charged against me.

You Sir, have known me for some time past, in the line of my official duty. If my conduct has been satisfactory to you, and you believe me as competent as I have the reputation of being, I pray you my dear Sir, to exercise your influence with Mr. Franklin,[2] the newly elected Clerk, in behalf of my continuance in my present office.

S. BURCH

Addressed to Washington.

1. A native of Virginia, Burch was employed in the office of the Clerk of the House of Representatives. His fear of removal seems to have been unfounded, for he retained his position under the new clerk.

2. Walter S. Franklin, a Pennsylvanian, was elected Clerk of the House for three consecutive terms.

FROM BENJAMIN F. McKIE

Columbia. December 3, 1833

The writer says that his father, Daniel McKie, has not heard anything concerning his application for a pension and asks Polk to press the matter.

Addressed to Washington.

FROM JOHN F. McWHIRTER[1]

Head Quarters Jefferson Barracks
Dear Sir [Missouri] December 3d 1833

Accept my apoligy in the outset for what may be said subsequently. Being worried by the unplesantness of my present situation & relying at the same time upon my conciousness of your influence with the head of government, I appeal to you as one who I believe would not hesitate for a moment, when you thought you could in any way alleviate their conditions.

Last spring, I enlisted in the new Regiment of Dragoons, the reason of which I scearcely known, though I suppose it must have been from my depressed situation at that time. I had been reading medicine for a considerable time, which had impaired my health. I had likewise run my purse aground, (having as you know no other resources but my own industry). I was told by a number of persons that my health would be improvd & that in the service I would have ample time to read which I find is not the case—& in fact my constitution is unable to withstand the fatigues, which it is necessary for a soldier to undergoe. I am now sick in hospital & have been for a long time but the surgeon has not a legal excuse to discharge me unless I had a broken bone or something of that kind & even if he could do so consistantly with consience (which I am sure he could) he would not do so in consequence of so many having deserted from the corps.

I now beg it of you as a special favor to use your influence in my favor & this done I believe my discharge can be obtained. Your own influence independent of your extensive acquaitance, with the most influencial men, at Washington, would be fully competent to the task. I will address a short Epistle to the Secretary of War setting forth the reasons why I want to be discharged from the army. I am flatered at present with the prospect of getting some office which might better my condition in a degree but I am fully sattisfied that my constitution will not nor cannot stand the fatigues of a campaign. Especially under the circumstances which will govern that of the Dragoons.

I should not be displeased with the service were I able to undergoe the hardships attendant upon the situation. At the time I enlisted I had not the most distant idea of the service, & in fact I believed that I would be benefitted by the expedition as I yet believe was it not for my health. I am sattisfied that a young man can see & learn a great deal from seeing the far west. But as matters are, & as I have set them forth to you, I shall wait patiently for the moving of the waters. If it is at all practicable I shall be more than happy to get my discharge & if it cannot be obtained through you I know of no other means & will therefore remain in the service & do the best I can.

Be so good as to let me know the result of your efforts which I am persuaded will not prove abortive.

JOHN F. MCWHIRTER

Addressed to Washington.

1. In a letter to Polk, dated June 22, 1845, John F. McWhirter identifies himself as a former resident of Columbia, Tennessee, and as a schoolmate of Polk's younger brothers. Written in Weston, Missouri, where he had settled, the 1845 letter reveals that he traveled widely in the west after leaving Columbia in 1833. It is not known whether he got the discharge he desired, but it seems likely that some of his travels were done while he was in military service. In the later communication, however, he does not mention his military experience.

FROM JAMES N. SMITH

Sir, Covington [Tennessee] December 3d 1833

I write you a few lines to solicit your influence on a subject in which the Inhabitants of this section of the country feel deeply interested. It is with deep regret that we have heard of the Mail Stage being discontinued from Jackson to Randolph on the Mississippi and the Inhabitants of this Town, and its vicinity have memorialized the Post Master General on the subject wishing him to have the stage continued. Randolph is a considerable place for shipment of cotton and other articles and as much travelling from it to the interior of the district and Middle part of the state as any point on the Mississippi in this state—if the same facilities were granted us for the conveyance of passengers.

I know Sir, that your influence is great (in all circles

where you are acquainted) upon any subject that you may feel interested in. And could you feel a willingness to have a personal interview with the Post Master Genl. upon the subject and interfere upon our behalf you could do more for us than we collectively could do by petitioning to him. My reason for addressing you instead of our own Representative[1] is that I know your influence is greater than any new member could have—tho I make no doubt but he has likewise received communications on the subject. By your attention to this business you will confer a singular favor to many, very many of your old acquaintances and particular friends. I should be glad at any time to receive information from you.

JAMES N. SMITH

Addressed to Washington.

1. William C. Dunlap of Bolivar represented Smith's district in the House of Representatives, 1833–37. Smith, however, had lived in Maury County, where he was on good terms with Polk. He had moved to Covington, Tennessee, only recently.

FROM ROGER B. TANEY

My Dear Sir [Washington] Tuesday Decr. 3, 1833

I called this morning to see you but you were unfortunately out. The object of my visit was to say to you, that upon consultation with friends it is supposed that my report of the reasons for removing the deposites, could not with propriety be made until the day after the Presidents message is delivered. It is unusual I understand for a Secretary to present a report on the same day and I wish to conform in this instance to prior usage. My report will therefore be presented tomorrow.

I do not anticipate that any one will expect it sooner. But if any thing should be said on the subject, will you do me the favour to state why it is not in today & to say it will be presented tomorrow.

R. B. TANEY

Marked "Private," this letter was directed to the House of Representatives and apparently was delivered by hand.

FROM JOHN A. ALLEN

Shelby County. December 4, 1833

A former acquaintance, now living south of Winchester's line on public lands recently acquired from the Chickasaws, states that he has sent William C. Dunlap an application for a pension to compensate for wounds received in military service, and he asks that Polk support his petition.

Addressed to Washington.

FROM RICHARD LONG

Farmington. December 4, 1833

A Revolutionary War pensioner, who believes that he is entitled to a larger payment, asks Polk to ascertain the facts of his case.

Addressed to Washington.

FROM WILLIAM P. BRADBURN

Pensacola, Florida. December 5, 1833

A midshipman whose ship has been lost, Bradburn wishes to transfer to a larger type vessel where he would have better opportunity to prepare for his approaching examination. He asks Polk, to whom he is already indebted, to intercede in his behalf.

Addressed to Washington.

FROM GEORGE W. CAMPBELL

Dear Sir, Paris [France] Dec. 5, 1833

The following proposition, which I submit for your opinion, is the result of some months of reflection & examination. Viz. that our government should have some one stationed at Paris, whose business it would be to become acquainted with the scientific institutions here, particularly those in which the sciences are taught, in their applications to medicine & the arts. The profession of medicine in the U. States is without a representative at

Paris. Paris is at present the great reservoir of science of Europe and I might say of the world; furnishing all countries with light, particularly upon the subject alluded to above. But our distance and foreign language, are great barriers in the way of our profiting by what is doing here. But if the government had some person fixed in Paris, to whom our institutions and individuals engaged in the different professions could apply, those barriers would be, in a great degree, superseded. Again, the facilities that such an arrangement would afford our young Americans who visit Paris in search of science, would be very considerable.

There are at this time between two & three hundred Americans in Paris, the majority of whom are students of medicine. They come here without professional experience, generally ignorant of the language; find themselves in the midst of a wilderness of science & scientific institutions, without a pilot to direct the rout they desire to pursue. They blindly wander about until the time expires alloted for their stay, and return home without effecting any thing. It is not expected that Ministers & Consuls would possess the information alluded to; and they are of but little benefit to the student here, or to our institutions at home, on this point. Most of the European states have persons employed to take an account of what is doing here in Medicine and the collateral sciences, to whom those who visit Paris, as well as their citizens at home, can apply with benefit for information.

I have made up my mind to remain in Europe, principally in Paris, for some years, on my own account; and should our government think proper to make an appointment of the kind under consideration, and deem the undersigned worthy of such appointment, he would endeavour to give such a direction to his studies & observations as would enable him to be useful to his countrymen here & at home. Will you be so good as to give me, so soon as convenient, the result of your reflections on this subject, as your opinion, pro or con, will be decisive with me.

After I had left home I wrote back to my brother[1] to send my medical diploma to New York, where I expected to have found it before my departure for Europe. It had not arrived. My brother writes me that he sent it to N. York. I left directions in the post office for it to be forwarded to Paris; it has not arrived. I presume it is in the general post office at Washington. I will take it as a great favor if you will be at the trouble of enquiring & sending it to me, if to be found.

I have been solicited by several of the Americans, to practice among them. Should I conclude to do so, I shall make application to the King to obtain a license, in which event I should be very glad that you would favor me with a letter to Mr. Livingston,[2] stating what you know of my professional standing in Tennessee and the length of time I have been practicing medicine (which is 10 years).

Any communication you may favor me with will be more certain to reach me if directed to the care of Messrs. Wells & co. bankers at Paris.

G. W. CAMPBELL

Addressed to Washington.

1. McKay W. Campbell.

2. Edward Livingston was Secretary of State for two years. He became United States minister to France in May 1833.

FROM NASH LEGRAND[1]

Dear Polk. Norfolk [Virginia] Decr. 5th 1833

We have this morning receid. intelligence of the death of Mr. Burfoot,[2] the late District Attorney for this District. It may seem strange that I should ask you, a representative from a distant state, to instruct yourself about an appointment to be made in Virga. I shall however take the liberty of doing so upon the ground of our old acquaintance and friendship leaving you to act as you please about the matter. The gentleman in whose behalf I would ask your good offices is Mr. McFarland,[3] a native of the District, and recently a resident of this town. I am induced the more strongly to do this for the reason that if he obtains the appointment at all it will be through the voluntary solicitations of his friends. He will not seek it in the ordinary way by getting long lists of recommendations. I have known this gentleman from my boyhood; we were companions at school; we have since been associated in public life and I bear my willing testimony he has talents, has virtues, and has sound democratic principles. I refer you to his friend Jno. Y. Mason[4] as to his qualifications as a lawyer. And as evidence of his standing as a public man, he was with great unanimity elected by the Legislature the Jackson Elector in his District in opposition to a gentleman of great respectability, to whom there was no objection, & who had served as the democratic Elector ever since the days of old John Adams. This was owing to the zeal, ability, and the early stand he took in favor of the election of Genl. Jackson. You will do me a favor, by seeing Genl. Jackson upon this subject yourselff, and making such statements as further enquiries of Mason, Gholson,[5] and others of the Virga. Delegation may authorize you. Do not draw any unfavorable inference of public opinion in our state from the Message of our nullifying Governor.[6] He says that it is his last annual message, and I hope for the honor of Va. it is.

N. LEGRAND

Addressed to Washington.

1. One of Polk's schoolmates at Chapel Hill, Legrand was serving as an agent of the Navy Department and was stationed at Norfolk, Virginia.

2. Thomas E. Burfoot of Richmond.

3. Not otherwise identified.

4. One of Polk's classmates at Chapel Hill, Mason was in Congress for six years, 1831–37. Later he served in the cabinets of Tyler and Polk.

5. Having previously served in the Virginia House of Delegates, James H. Gholson was elected to one term in Congress, 1833–35. Afterwards he was a circuit court judge.

6. John Floyd was governor, 1830–34. He had previously served in Congress for twelve years.

FROM THOMAS P. MOORE

Dr Sir [Washington]. Thursday [December 5, 1833][1]

Mr. Hardin[2] will move to suspend the qualification of either,[3] & to refer the whole subject to the committee on Elections. If this is *done* all my testimonies taken upon the predication of my being the sitting member will be lost, & it cannot be taken again in three months. In the mean time the district is unrepresented. Get a decision upon the question *now* before the House or all is lost. I have placed upon your table a collection of cases which you can examine to report if the subject is not disposed of sooner.

I must not awaken the jealousy of a *certain* person[4] by *too open* a reliance upon you.

T. P. MOORE

Delivered by hand. No address appears on the envelope.

1. On this date, Congressman Benjamin Hardin introduced the motion to which the letter refers. It is believed that this letter was delivered before the House was convened on the same day.

2. Hardin had represented Kentucky in Congress ten years earlier and had only recently been re-elected to that body.

3. Moore's election to the House was being contested by Robert P. Letcher.

4. This reference remains obscure.

FROM A. O. P. NICHOLSON

Dear Sir: Columbia Dec. 5 [1833][1]

Enclosed you will find a letter with a transatlantic destination. I have to ask of you to have it forwarded, if you please, by the nearest and best route, (avoiding always the river route) in the same manner that you have had the goodness to forward other letters for Dr. O'Reilly.[2]

I wish you would examine in the Pension Office for the Declaration &c. of Hugh Allison,[3] of this county. The papers are said not to make out a case which comes within the provisions of the law of 1832. I drew the declaration and had regarded it as a meritorious case, and I would thank you to bestow some attention to the subject. If you are convinced that the law does not cover the case, I would be glad if you would consider whether any relief can be extended to Mr. Allison.

Our Legislature adjourned on Monday last; most of its acts and doings you have doubtless observed in the papers, but you know there are always many things that can never be learned from the papers. For instance, from the papers, you would never have learned that the next presidency had occupied any of our attention—but such was the fact. There was a strong disposition with many members to make a nomination of a candidate. In truth the resolution was actually drawn up to nominate Hugh L. White for President, but upon consultation it was abandoned. The idea was not abandoned from any want of confidence in Judge White, but under a belief that such a measure at this early day might be imprudent. Some were also in favour of nominating

Gov Carrol for the Vice Presidency, but none seemed disposed to venture upon a nomination of either Judge [John] McLean or Mr. Van Buren.

The people are beginning to be interested in the formation of the new Constitution. We have as yet no candidates in Maury. Your name is spoken of by every body, but I have heard no assurances from your friends here that you will suffer your name to be polled. If you permit, you will labor under serious disadvantages and I have no doubt but that strong exertions will be made to defeat your election. It is entirely uncertain who will be candidates. [Robert L.] Cobbs and [Edward B.] Littlefield are a good deal talked of, and several others are thinking seriously about the matter. I feel very well satisfied with my small experiment in politics, and am now prepared to attend to my own business.

If any thing of particular moment should occur, I should be glad to hear from you, and if you should think proper to make any communications to yo[ur] constituents, I should be glad to herald them [to] the four quarters of the country through the Mercury.[4] I believe your friends are all well. Will you do me the favour to give immortality to my name, by presenting my best wishes to Gen. Jackson for his long continued success in filling his high office? And also please present my best respects to Mrs Polk.

A. O. P. Nicholson

Addressed to Washington.

1. No year appears on the letter. The Library of Congress has placed the year as 1833, and internal evidence supports this decision.

2. Dr. James C. O'Reilly was Nicholson's father-in-law. The letter to which Nicholson refers here was probably intended for George W. Campbell in Paris, France. See O'Reilly to Polk, November 20, 1833.

3. No evidence has been found to indicate that he ever received a pension.

4. Nicholson was editor of the *Western Mercury* in Columbia at this time.

FROM JOHN W. CHILDRESS

Dear Sir Murfreesboro. December 8th 1833

I wrote immediately after your departure to George S. Gaines[1] of Mobile, upon the subject of our land certificates and recieved his answer a few days since. He says some certificates were left in his care by my brother, several years since but he does not know the description of them and he thinks they were returned afterwards to him or Major [James] Childress of Tuscaloosa. I have written to him since and possibly may get on the track after awhile. In the mean while you had better examine the land office and see if you can obtain any further information and let me know soon.

We have not heard from you since you left Murfreesboro and are a little uneasy on account of your silence. Dr. Ruckers family have all recovered from the measles and are in excellent health. Mah and myself have purchased the old plantation, and are now moving to it. We give for it $4200 in three annual payments from the 1st Jany. Mah has sold her place for $1800, one third down, and the balance in one and two years. Every thing is so much out of order, it will be some time before we can live in the houses. We are now repairing and moving our plunder and every thing is in confusion. I would be glad to hear from you frequently during the session. Tell Sarah she must write often. I will write to her soon.

We are all well.

John W. Childress

Addressed to Washington.

1. A merchant who had moved from Demopolis to Mobile in 1830 after having served in the Alabama legislature. He had been a representative of the United States at a Choctaw trading station, where he gained the respect of the Indians. At their request, he accompanied them in exploring their new lands west of the Mississippi. He moved in 1856 to Mississippi, where he served in the state legislature.

FROM THOMAS HARTLEY CRAWFORD[1]

Ho. Rep. Harrisburgh [Pennsylvania]
9 Dec. 1833

My Dear Sir,

I have wished for the last year to obtain a situation at the seat of the General Government, equivalent in salary to an auditorship, or Comptroller's office, which would make me entirely easy and comfortable in a pecuniary point of view. The above offices are mentioned as indicating the measure of my wishes, and not as suggesting the removal of any officer. But it had occurred me to as probable, that some changes might be made early in the second Presidential term. I am not certain whether I spoke to you on this subject or not last spring, but during the last session a recommendation signed by all the Penna. delegation but one, was presented to the President by the Senators. Success would be of immense consequence to me. I have written to Mr. [Jesse] Speight, Col Johnston,[2] and one or two others with whom you can, if you think proper, consult. I am disposed to think [James M.] Wayne would serve me, if he could and Mr. [Clement C.] Clay of Alabama. If advisable speak to them. I will thank you to use your influence for me, and let me hear from you soon on the subject.

T. Hartley Crawford

Addressed to Washington and marked "Private."

1. Formerly one of Polk's colleagues in the House of Representatives.

2. Although Josiah S. Johnston of Louisiana was a member of the Senate at this time, this seems to be a reference to Cave Johnson.

FROM THOMAS J. LACY

Dear Sir, Nashville December 9th 1833

Its rumored here that Mr Brown[1] will be made Judge and I may possibly be tendered the office that Gov. Pope[2] now holds, as he is shortly to resign. If its assertained beyond doubt that Mr Brown is to recieve the appointment, then I earnestly solicit your influence in behalf of the situation thats spoken of in Arkansas.[3] I do not wish any thing said or done on this subject, till the other is final acted or determined on, for I assure you, after all, I would *greatly prefer* remaining in Tennessee. Do me the favor to speak of this to Messrs Inge and C. Johnson, for I know they will heartily cooperate with you. I am sincerely gratified for all your past kindness, and I trust it will yet be in my power to make return for your goodness.

Thos J. Lacy

P.S. I will write you again if I am an applicant for the office named. This is only to apprise you of what may happen, & *to ask you to stand in readiness to aid me.*

Addressed to Washington and marked "*Strictly Confidential.*"

1. Morgan W. Brown, a Nashville attorney, was appointed in January 1834 to a federal judgeship in Tennessee.

2. John Pope was a Kentucky lawyer and, at this time, territorial governor of Arkansas, a position he held until 1835. After that he returned to Kentucky and was elected to three terms in the United States House of Representatives, 1837–43.

3. Although Lacy did not get the appointment as territorial governor, he was appointed to a federal judgeship in Arkansas and took his post in April 1834.

FROM WILLIAM MINTER[1]

Sir Columbia Ten Demby 9th 1833

I assume a privilage which I hope will not interfeear with your accostomed good fealing of assisting your neighbour when in your power to do so. I wish you to present those petitions to the patent office & procure the pattents & send them to me in Columbia as early as you can consistant with your other duties. I will pay to your order or direction the amount which I [owe]. You may have to do at any time & will be thankful for the favor. I have made mention of your name to Mr Jesey Bayles[2] Who will probily call on you for some advice & you may look on him as a gentleman. I cannot inform you of any news worth your attention except the Mariage of Dr McNeel[3] to Mrs. [Mary] Crockett & the general good helth of the citizens.

Wm Minter

I shall send a Moddle by the first convnet convayence for the steem engine. If any thing should be lacking pleas to make it known.

Wm Minter

Addressed to Washington.

1. Minter had moved to Columbia with a large family only a short time before. There he operated a small cotton factory.

2. Unidentified.

3. William McNeill.

FROM JOHN T. SULLIVAN

Dear Sir Philada. Decemr 10 1833

The same mail which conveys this letter to you will also carry the Appeal of the "Public Directors" to both Houses of Congress addressed to the Speaker of your House & to the President of the Senate. In this document we have endeavoured to give a history of our stewardship as well as our unceasing efforts to bring the business of the Bank under controul of the Board. You will perceive that we have contended for every inch of ground, and by constant, though unsuccessful efforts, have laboured hard to discharge the duties of our station. The laboured defense of the majority is considered here by all impartial men an entire failure & Mr. Macalester[1] one of the stockholder Directors has this day recorded his vote with ours and against the attack of the majority. He came into the Bank after the greater part of the Report had been read & declined voting "until he had an opportunity of examining the paper." Five thousand copies of the majority report was ordered to be printed at the expense of the Bank, while the minority must print at their own expense.

Mr Van Buren arrived here this evening and will tarry a day or two with us.

John T Sullivan

Addressed to Washington.

1. A native of Philadelphia, Charles Macalester returned there after conducting a mercantile business in Cincinnati for several years. A man of wealth, he became a member of a new banking firm in 1835. He was a noted philanthropist. A college at St. Paul, Minnesota, that subsequently took his name was built on land that he donated for its establishment.

FROM WILLIAM S. FULTON[1]

Dear Sir, Little Rock Decr. 11th 1833

From the regard you manifested for me upon our journey from Washington last spring, I take the liberty to trouble you with my personal affairs. I know how much your time is occupied, and would not make the request, but for the violent course which Govr. Pope is adopting towards me. He is about to resign, and quit the Territory, and, for the purpose of enlisting the opposition to the administration in this Territory against me, he has told them that he intended to have me dismissed from office when he goes out. Now, as he has no family, and is independent, and as I am poor, & have been kept so by his long and repeated absences from the Territory, and have a large and growing family, even if I had injured him, it would be a cruel war upon my wife & children for him to make an effort against my continuance in office. As it is, (for I assure you, I was his friend as long as he would permit me to be so, and never did him harm) as I have faithfully attended to all *his,* as well as my *own* duties, his effort against me is certainly the most unholy act I have ever known him guilty of. His pretended ground for attack, you will understand from the enclosed hand-bills.[2] I believe I have done nothing wrong. I know my intentions were pure. Can you conceive of any thing more cruel than his denunciations, for my differing from him upon a mere question of power? I beg you to see the President. Tell him I defy my enemies. That, at a moments warning, I can prove any charge they can make to be false. I am warred upon, for endeavouring to sustain his friends as well as all his measures. Govr. Pope is secretly opposed to both. Remember me respectfully to Mrs. Polk. I lost almost a father in the death of my venerable friend Genl. Coffee. I rejoice at Marys marriage.[3]

WM. S. FULTON

Addressed to Washington.

1. At this time he was secretary of the Territory of Arkansas. He had lived in Nashville, where he had studied law under Felix Grundy, and had lived for a short time in Alabama. Fulton retained his post in Arkansas until 1835, when he succeeded Pope as governor of the territory. In 1836 he was elected to the United States Senate from the newly admitted state and served until his death in 1844.

2. The point in dispute seems to have been whether or not Pope, as territorial governor, had the power to erect public buildings with funds received from the sale of public lands granted to the territory by the United States in 1831. Since both men retained their places in Arkansas for two more years, it seems likely that they were able to come to some sort of understanding on the subject.

3. John Coffee of Florence, Alabama, and one of Jackson's close friends, had died during the past summer. His daughter, Mary, had recently married Andrew Jackson Hutchings, a kinsman of Rachel Jackson and a ward of Andrew Jackson.

FROM LEVIN H. COE

Fayette County. December 12, 1833

Coe reveals that he is writing at the request of Philip T. Burford, a Revolutionary War pensioner who thinks that he is entitled to more than he is being paid. Burford wants Polk to investigate the case and also to look into the case of a son-in-law who had died in military service while on a campaign under Jackson.

Addressed to Washington.

FROM JOEL R. SMITH[1] TO JAMES K. POLK OR WILLIAM C. DUNLAP

Dear Sirs Huntingdon 12th Decr 1833

Enclosed I send you a recommendation of myself to the favourable consideration of the President of the United States.[2]

The object that I have in view in presenting the enclosed recommendation is that during the spring or summer to migrate to the state of Mississippi or the Arkansas Territory & supposeing that there was or might be a vacancy in that direction & as I intend to remove there that an appointment under the President would very much facilitate my prosperity in a pecuniary way is the cause of my makeing this application.

As to my capacity or fitness to office you are yourselves sufficiently acquainted with me to Judge.

I am not very particular as to the post (if any) that may be assigned me by the president so that it is not a legal one but would like to be receiver of Publick moneys, Register of Lands, or marshall or other appointment that would remunerate me for services rendered.

Both the Hon. Senators are acquainted with me. With Mr. White my acquaintance is limited but to Mr. Grundy I am well known.

I am also known to Col Johnson, Col Bell, Mr. Dicarson[3] & slightly with several other members of congress from this state. Please say to those I have named & the ballance of the Tennessee Delegation that any interest they may take in my welfare will lay me under a very particular obligation to them.

The reason I did not name David (from the river county)[4] was that you are aware that he is not my representative & if he was his recommendation would have but little Influence with *Andrew Jackson.*

On the reception of this please let me hear from you on this subject & any other which you may see fit to write for I have heretofore informed you J. K. Polk that you are my representative in congress in the place of David.

JOEL RIDLEY SMITH

N. B. If the president wishes to know particulars about me You say to him that my mother was a daughter of George Ridley three miles from Nashville & raised by Majr John Buchanan[5] both of whom are well know[n] to the president himself & further that I was out with him in the Creek nation when only 16 years of age. I was one of Genl. Carrolls life guards at [New] Orleans & in the Seminole campaign I was one of Genl Jacksons life guard & further I say not.

J R SMITH

Addressed to Washington. Although the writer included Dunlap's name, it is evident that he was actually directing his letter to Polk.

1. Smith represented Carroll, Gibson, Dyer, and Obion counties in the lower house of the General Assembly, 1831–35.

2. In an endorsement Polk noted that the enclosure was a recommendation from the legislature. The enclosure has not been found.

3. David W. Dickinson.

4. David Crockett was in Congress for his third nonconsecutive term. He had already publicly declared himself anti-Jackson.

5. Ridley and Buchanan are not otherwise identified.

TO ROGER B. TANEY

Sir House of Representatives Decr. 13th 1833

I am directed by the Committee of Ways & Means to submit to your inspection the enclosed memorial of the "Philadelphia Board of Trade" and to say that the committee would be pleased to receive any suggestions or views which you may think proper to make as to the expediency and probable effect on the revenue which would be produced by granting the prayer of the memorial.

JAMES K. POLK

Addressed to Washington. In Letters from Congress, Department of the Treasury (RG 56), National Archives.

FROM JAMES WALKER

Dear Sir, Columbia Dec. 13th 1833

I have been much engaged since my return home, and have not written you, principally for want of something material to say. I am now however at no loss for a subject, and unfortunately very much in the humor of *making complaints.*

When I left home for the East, I had little or no expectation of bidding for Mr. Donly's lines or in any way interfering with him. I had distinctly proposed to him a co-operation instead of competition, and expected him to accede to the proposition. When I reached Washington however, I understood to my satisfaction that Donly & Hough[1] intended to bid for my lines. I therefore felt perfectly willing to enter into the competition, and determined to bid for their lines, and to bid very low. Caruthers & Kinkle, [James] Brown & myself agreed to put in a bid at $4800 for the lines from Nashville to Tuscumbia & from Columbia to Huntsville. The bid was put in in the name of Saml. B. Ewing & Co.[2] and was accepted agreeable to advertisement. It was agreed that Brown & myself were to run the line between Nashville & Mt. Pleasant & Col. [Joseph] Brown's, and have half the pay, S B Ewing, Kinkle & Caruthers to run between Col. Brown's & Huntsville & between Mt. Pleasant & Tuscumbia & have the other half, all the lines to be run in 4 horse post Coaches. About the time our bid was accepted, the officers of the Post Office department manifested some considerable feeling & desire that Donly should be accommodated with his line again, and it was understood that the President desired that the matter could be so satisfactorily and correctly arranged. Caruthers & Kinkle expressed their willingness to surrender to Donly, if some improvements, that they alledged the public interest required, were made in North Alabama. Mr. Brown & myself expressed every wish to gratify the feeling manifested in behalf of Donly and clearly expressed our willingness to assign our half of the contracts provided a contract of equal value was given us in lieu of it. This was said to the President the P M Genl, and the parties concerned. We waited from the 2d of Nov. until the 7th to give an opportunity for an equivalent to be offered to us.

None was offered. Major Donly set up no claim to his contract nor spoke of getting in any other way than by compromise while he remained in Washington. Mr. Brown & myself did not conceive it necessary after an acceptance had been given us to remain in Washington City an indefinite period to protect our rights & prevent advantages being taken of us. The lines from Nashville to Col. Brown's & Mt Pleasant, was fairly ours and we considered it our duty to prepare to put them into operation. We accordingly made arrangements for suitable Coaches, Harness &c. & came home and made all necessary preparations to execute the contract, as our bid had been accepted. Previous to our leaving Washington however, Mr. Donly came to me and requested that we would agree that *Caruthers & Kinkle* should *assign to him their half of the contracts.* I informed him that K. & C. were entitled to the line from Col. Brown's to Huntsville & from Mt Pleasant to Tuscumbia and Brown & myself to the ballance of the road from Nashville to these points, that if it suited all parties we would make no objection to such transfer provided our position remained precisely as it then was, and if any assignment was made it was to be so made that our situation should be the same as it then was, and in no respect altered. This Col. Avery[3] was called on to witness and I again in presence of Mr. Caruthers repeated to Col. Avery what I had agreed to, and requested to know of Col Avery if he clearly understood me, which he said he did, and Mr. Caruthers certainly did clearly understand what I said and meant. This was the state of things when I left Washington. I came home, and made all necessary arrangements to execute the contract. Donly's agent & drivers were fervently, however putting out reports that he had got the lines to which I paid no attention. On my way to Nashville, last week I met Mr. Caruthers in the stage, who informed me that the line from Columbia to Huntsville had been *cut down* to a two horse stage, was retained by them & us & that they had transfered their interest in the Tuscumbia line to Mr. Donly. I enquired how these things had happened, and upon what principle the Huntsville line had been cut down, to which he replied that after we left Washington, Maj Lewis & Eaton had interfered in behalf of Donly, that Maj Barry had become much excited on the subject, and that it was understood the President had requested the contract to be suspended, that they (C & K) were urged to give up their interest, and that the President said that I was satisfied for the *whole* contract to be given to Donly &c. The stage was hurrying Mr. Caruthers, and he had no time to give me further explanations. I was a good deal vexed at what Caruthers said to me, and especially at the line being *cut down* between this place & Huntsville, as this circumstance destroys the daily line between here & Nashville, or so lessens the number of passengers, as to very materially affect my interests, besides the injury to the public. I wrote to Caruthers & Kinkle a hasty and warm letter, in which I complained of bad treatment from some quarter, and desired of them to inform me distinctly what agency Majs Eaton & Lewis had in producing the present state of things, and I observed that if the President had treated me *unkindly* in this matter, I wished to know it. And I also said that after the P M. G. had accepted our bid, & we came home to execute the contract he dared not take the responsibility of taking the contract from us and giving it to Donly and that I would have preferred his taking this responsibility if he had chosen to incur it, to having the contract as it now is. The truth is I never feared that Maj Barry would act incorrectly in this or any other matter, and could not believe that there was any danger of Donly's getting the contracts in any other way than by *compromise* or consent of some of the parties concerned. I am satisfied such was the fact. In reply to my letters Kinkle & Caruthers under date of the 12th say.

About the time you left Washington, we left for Pha. & New York. Our Mr. Caruthers did not however go further than Phila. & returned in 6 or 8 days to the City, found Maj Donly there, and was informed that he was about to get his contracts. Upon enquiry at the Dept and an application for the contracts, according to the acceptances he was informed that doubts had arisen about the correctness of the acceptances, and by order of the P M. G. they stood suspended. Donly claimed them under a general bid, and we understood that Maj Lewis as his friend urged in strong terms the ground taken by Donly and that the President and Mr. Eaton was anxious to have Donly accommodated, not however, upon other than correct principles. In this dilemma, it was intimated by the Department that a compromise between Donly and ourselves would be highly satisfactory, and that they would make some improvements in some of the Alabama Routes, which had been so loudly called for by the people of Alabama, as an equivalent for our interest in the Donly contracts. We said to Col. Gardner,[4] that if he would accept the propositions made in conformity to his proposals, for the transportation of a daily mail between Montgomery & Huntsville, and extend it on to Nashville at a fair compensation, in like manner, that we would give up to Donly his Routes. Owing to the situation of the Department this proposition was rejected. We were then asked what improvements would be satisfactory to us for our interest, and it was stated at the same time that you had agreed to give up to Donly and be satisfied, which we denied, but was told it came from high authority, and could not be denied. We knew however that it was a fabrication imposed on the Department by the party whose interest was to be subserved, and benefitted by it, and so stated our belief to Col. Ga[r]dner & Mr. Brown, without any sort of hesitation or delicacy. You were then considered as out of the question pretty much, but as you had proposed to us previous to your departure from the City that you were willing to accept of Donly in our places, we then stated to the Department what would be satisfactory to us for our interest, and did finally make such an arrangement as was partially satisfactory, but not by any means as we conceive an equivalent for what we gave up, nor should we have done it but to accommodate the feelings and views of the President and others towards Donly. The improvements we obtained were these, the establishment of a line of bi-weekly stages from Elkton to Montgomery Ala. and the route kept up in like manner from Huntsville to Nashville via Shelbyville, Murfreesborough &c. In the mean time the Department had determined to cut down the line to Columbia to a two horse stage which stood jointly between us. These arrangements having been made, we transferred for ourselves & Ewing *our half* of the contract from Nashville to Tuscumbia, that being all we had a right to interfere with, and [. . .] that we concerned we had the right." &c C. & K.

In giving reasons for what they done they remark

If we could have obtained the contracts, we should perhaps have not made any transfers at all. *Suppose though, we had left the City and Donly there, could he not have gotten us out of the way as you were about to be?* How that is though, we cannot pretend to say, and must refer you to the Maj, *who no doubt could explain it to you.*

Caruthers & Kinkle seem to think the whole cause of my dissatisfaction was their having transferred to Donly *their half* of the Tuscumbia line. This is not what I complain of. It is true they had no right to transfer to Donly any part of the line from Nashville to Tuscumbia, except between Mt. Pleasant & Tuscumbia; according to the agreement between them & us, this was all of that line which belonged to them, and we had agreed that they might transfer it to Donly, if they choose. But instead of doing this they transfered him an equal and undivided half and for doing this doub[t]less received from the *Department a very satisfactory equivalent.* This is however a matter between C & K & ourselves; but one in which the Department ought to have something to say & do, if all the facts I state remain undenied, as C & K certainly intimate very strongly that they were forced into the arrangement by the acts of the officers of the Dept.

What I complain of is the *cutting down of the post Coach line between this place & Huntsville.* If this had not been done, I should have troubled you with no communication upon this subject. This act is *very prejudicial* to my & Mr. Brown's pecuniary interests—*is wrong in itself so far as the public are concerned,* and cannot be *quietly* submitted to. It is probably true, that all I can at present do upon this subject is to *make complaint* of the injury sustained, and unavailing efforts to obtain redress, *but at the worst,* it will teach me the folly of remaining in the ranks of a political party that totally disregard my feelings and interests. I have never asked nor expected from those I have contributed to place in power anything but *plain, simple Justice.* I have at all times, and under all circumstances supported the present administration, because I believed that the honesty and purity at its head would secure equal justice to all, without partiality or favor. If favoritism was the order of the day, I had as much right as others to expect it in my behalf, but did not believe it would *intentionally* be extended to any.

The cutting down the Huntsville line may seem to you a smaller matter, (so far as I am concerned,) than it really is. It may be estimated fairly that it will reduce the No. of passengers every other trip between here and Nashville, which amounts to $54 pr. week $2808 pr. annum & $11232 for the contract. One half of this is a clear loss to Brown & myself, without equivalent, and without our consent. Donly sustains no wrong, because the Department paid the equivalent for him, but the contract is worth so much less to him.

I cannot yet believe this injury has been intentionally done us, that it will in some way be corrected or repaired.

JAMES WALKER

Addressed to Washington.

1. John Donly and Joseph H. Hough, both of Nashville, operated stage lines and regularly bid for mail contracts. A rival of Walker, Donly had the

powerful backing of William B. Lewis and John H. Eaton in his quest for lucrative contracts.

2. Samuel B. Ewing was a businessman of some prominence in Huntsville, Alabama. It is believed, however, that the use of his name was a device to prevent rival bidders from knowing the identity of their competitors. Caruthers and Kinkle, stage line operators from Huntsville, and Walker and James Brown, were the controlling interests in S. B. Ewing and Company.

3. John H. Avery was another successful bidder for mail contracts.

4. Charles K. Gardner, a native of New Jersey, was Assistant Postmaster General.

FROM WILLIAM L. WILLIFORD[1]

M[anual] L[abor] Academy [Spring Hill]

Dr Sir Decr. 13th 1833

It is probable that before you receive this letter others will reach you informing you of my wish to obtain the appointment of Surveyor of the lands lately ceeded by the Chickasaw tribe of Indians to the United States. As I am well assured that you can do much in forwarding my wishes, I through the medium of this letter beg leave to ask your assistance again. As I have heretofore been an unsuccessfull applicant, and think it probable that I may not shortly if ever meet with an opportunity of making a similar effort, you will confer a lasting favor on me, one that will not be easily forgotten if you will exercise your influence with the President & Others in my behalf.

New testimonials from the State of Alabama have been obtained and forwarded, to which in addition to those furnished on a former occasion (if I should not have an opportunity of renewing them) reference can be had for the satisfaction of any.

WILLIAM L WILLIFORD

Addressed to Washington.

1. A respected teacher in Middle Tennessee for many years.

FROM OPHELIA C. HAYS

Dear Brother [Columbia] [December 14, 1833][1]

I learned from Mr. Harris with sorrow yesterday that you had given orders for Silvy[2] to be brought back to this place and that she was now on her way here. I had never doubted once that the words spoken by you to me on the subject of her returning would ever be violated. She was sold at a time when I was not properly at myself in point of reason; I mean I was more easly fretted. I own that my temper at any time is not as even as many persons, but still it is as it is, and I do not acquit her. But I expected in the course of time she would see the error of her ways and would be gladly willing to return and live with me which has been the case, as I have learned from severel persons that she with tears in her eyes acknoweledged she had acted not right and would be glad to live with me again.

I gave Dr Hays my concent to sell her it is true, but I told him not to sell her to any of my relations. To tell you candidly I never expected him to sell her, as you may judge from the way I greived about it when I first heard. Dr Hays said when he told me first she is only sold to your brother and he was concious that you never would let her serve any one in the town unless it would be me on a len[g]th of time. I feel as if I had been treated badly by all you, Dr Hays and Ma. I tried to live in peace and did. It is true there has been disturbances, little ones I may say in comparison to former times.[3]

Reckollect that your word to me in the sight of heaven is as firm as if made to men. Dr Hays says he thought it not necessary to bind you up as particularly as if it had been to a person that was not acquainted with his object in sending her away.

When you read this letter you know doubt will think I have said to much but I assure you not more than I feel, for the subject is a sore one to me and always will think and act seriously upon this matter and I will when I see the result know how to feel. As it is I feel injustice has been done bringing her and placing her at Mas. I have said all.

OPHELIA C HAYS

Addressed to Washington.

1. This letter was given no date nor place by its writer. It was postmarked at Columbia on December 14, with no year stated. The Library of Congress supplied 1835 as the appropriate year. Letters from James Walker and Adlai O. Harris in December 1833 as well as internal evidence in the letter itself, make it obvious that it was written in 1833.

2. Sylvia was a slave woman formerly owned by Dr. John B. Hays and his wife Ophelia. Sylvia was sold to Polk after some misunderstanding be-

tween her and her mistress. She had been on the Polk plantation in Fayette County and was now being returned to Columbia.

3. Ophelia Hays's instability was public knowledge in the community. Her four-year marriage had been a stormy one, and in previous letters the possibility of a separation had been mentioned.

FROM JAMES WALKER

Dear Sir Columbia, Dec. 14th 1833

I wrote to you yesterday, a letter long enough in all conscience, but still I have not said all I have to say on that subject.

Mr. Brown & myself were underbid on the lines from Memphis to Jackson and from Bolivar to Florence, on both of which we have about $6 or 7000 worth of perishable property. Whether this property will be taken off our hands or not is yet to be determined. Donly got one of the lines and sold his acceptance for $1000 in hand. We considered that we lost these lines upon correct principles, and were satisfied. John G. Bostick[1] bid for the lines from Mobile to Montgomery & from Montgomery to Fort Mitchell. Before the decisions were made, we were induced to believe that Bostick was the lowest bidder and was in opposition to the Saltmarsh[2] who had in our opinion got our line. He agreed for Brown & myself to have half the lines if they were declared to him, and we sustained his bid. It appeared when the books were opened that the present contractors has underbidden Bostick both lines put together. But Boyd and Horton[3] had a bid in for the line from Montgomery to Fort Mitchell which taken with Bosticks from Mobile to Montgomery was about $600 pr. annum lower than the present contractors (to whom the bid was accepted). Bostick contended that Horton & Boyd's was a good bid, and that them & him ought to have the two contracts—made a good deal complaint & appealed to the President. With this appeal I had nothing to do, and so far as I was concerned, expressed myself satisfied to the President & P.M.G. with the first decision made. I dined with the President on the 2d of Nov. (the day on which the decisions were made). He made some enquiry how the decisions were made. I informed him that I had lost all my present lines, but believed I had lost on fair and correct principles and was satisfied with the correctness of the Department. Some enquiry was made about Donly's luck. I replied that the lines from Nashville to Tuscumbia & to Huntsville were obtained by Caruthers & Kinkle, Brown & myself, and in the course of the conversation observed that we would not have bid for Donly's lines, if we had not found him bidding against us, that we still had no hostile feelings towards him, and as he seemed to want his old contracts so badly, we would *exchange for other contracts of equal value*. This is the full extent and terms on which I ever expressed a willingness for Donly to have his contract. Maj Lewis was present & doubtless noted what I said. You will see the importance of this explanation by referring to the extract I have given you of the letter of Carruthers & Kinkle. My being satisfied with the correctness of the Department up to the time I spoke, could not be construed into a willingness to give up contracts, which I had obtained on the same principles on which I had lost my own.

One decision was made against us which I then thought & still think was erroneous. We had put on stages on the line from Jackson to Randolph on the 1st of July last. Our bid for this line *as advertised* was $2050 and $1175 for a horse mail; Saltmarshs as advertised was $2400 and $1000 for a horse mail. Saltmarshs $1000 was accepted which I did not think was right, on the ground that we were the lower bidders as advertised, and the line ought by no means to have been reduced. We too having only had o[u]r stages for 6 m[onth]s was a reason why we ought to be favored when it could have been done with propriety. It was a hard case but the intentions of the P M. G were doubtless honest & correct.

As I said in my letter of yesterday, the cutting down the line from here to Huntsville, reduces the value of the line between here & Nashville about $1500 pr. annum to Brown & myself. You would of course say it is our interest to continue it in 4 horse Coaches, even at the 2 horse price. Our difficulty is this; Caruthers & Kinkle retain their interest in this line, and when they obtained the line from Huntsville to Nashville by Murfreesborough, it became their interest and policy to keep this line down, and to throw the travel by Murfreesborough. It is unjust that they should do this at our expense or if it is determined to keep this line down & the Murfreesborough line up, the line between here & Nashville ought to be reduced to tri-weekly and we are fairly and honestly entitled to one half the line between Nashville & Huntsville on whatever road it is put. Mr. Caruthers informed me, that as an equivalent for transferring Donly *one half* the line from Nashville to Tuscumbia, the Department made these improvements to the amount of about $7000 pr. annum these improvements were alledged to be necessary, but it is quite clear that they would not have been made at present if Maj Donly had been the lowest bidder on his favorite Routes. It is very certain that the Huntsville line would not have been cut down if such had been the case. I dislike the attitude of a complainer but think much injustice has been done us and that the Department ought either to raise the line from here to Huntsville to a 4 h. coach line, or compel Caruthers & Kinkle to give up to us one half the line from Nashville to Huntsville, as an equivalent for their having this one cut down & destroyed.

James Walker

Addressed to Washington.

1. Probably the same John G. Bostick who was a Jackson presidential elector from Franklin County, Tennessee, in 1832.

2. Orlando and D. A. Saltmarsh operated coach lines in the southeastern states and had been awarded several mail contracts.

3. Unidentified. This probably was a partnership.

FROM JAMES WALKER

Dear Sir, Columbia Dec. 14th 1833

I have written you two letters to-day upon the subject of the contracts. I wish you to show them to Messrs. Grundy & Dunlap (and Johnson if you choose) and upon consulting them make any use of them you think prudent and for my interest. I think it is right for the P M G. and the president to see them or understand their material contents. I think Mr. Brown & myself have been badly treated and we rely on our friends to stand up to us and see that we have justice. I suspect Lewis & Eaton to have meddled in this matter to our prejudice probably owing to some extent to us & our friends being in favor of Grundy in the last election.

Represent my interest in this matter as you think most

prudent upon advisement, and let me know as early as possible what the Post Office Department have to say on the subject.

I do not believe the the President has interfered in the matter at all, but I think it quite probable his name and influence has been used to our prejudice.

I was quite inclined to be a Van Buren man, but if his friends treat my interests so lightly, I had better be off. I must be fairly treated, if not served, what I serve hereafter.

About home matters, I have nothing very pleasant to communicate. Sylvia has reached here, and Ophelia is acting as bad as ever. She commenced it before she knew Sylvia was coming and that circumstance has increased our troubles. We are fearful her and the Dr will part. I hope however this can be prevented and he pursuaded to lock her up and conquer her by force if nothing else will do. I fear that Beenland[1] is too severe with your negroes. Chunky Jack & Little Ben, I heard yesterday, have been runaway for 3[?] weeks, and nothing heard of them. It is said Beenland gave Chunky 200 & Ben 100 lashes, but whether this is true or not I am not sure. I will write to Beenland & Bills[2] by first mail & make all exertions to have them in. George Moore is now here. He will assist in getting hold of them, and will go and see Beenland & try to moderate him. Except severity, I suppose Beenland is doing well enough. My business requires my attention here, or I would go to the District myself.

I will attend to your interest in this county, all in my power for the best, and I expect you and Grundy to attend to my interests in Washington City.

James Walker

Addressed to Washington.

1. Walker regularly misspelled Ephraim Beanland's name.

2. This is probably John H. Bills, merchant and postmaster at Bolivar. He was married to Polk's first cousin, the former Prudence Tate McNeal.

FROM JOEL HENRY DYER[1]

My Dear Sir. Nashville 16th December 1833

It becomes necessary that I should drop you a line. During the last Session of Congress I forwarded the Honl Hugh L. White a memorial asking a pension for the services and sufferings of my father Colo Robert H Dyer[2] dece'd.

At that time I wrote you, and I now beg leave to refer you that memorial. It is needless for me to do more than to point you to the facts contained in that paper.

I well know what can be done for the widow and children of my father will be gone into by yourself. This matter will be before congress this Session. I want you[r] aid and influence in it and remember Dr Sir that I ask nothing for myself, but a mother and sisters require my aid and the assistance of friends. What you may do for them will not be overlooked or forgotten by me. My respects to your lady (my early schoolmate). And accept my good wishes for your health and my aid hereafter in all political *state matters.*

JOEL HENRY DYER

Addressed to Washington.

1. Originally from Rutherford County, Dyer had moved to Gibson County. He served as solicitor general for the Sixteenth District, 1831–36. See Dyer to Polk, December 20, 1832.

2. He had represented Rutherford and Bedford counties in the state legislature, 1815–17, just before moving to West Tennessee.

TO JAMES L. EDWARDS

Sir Washington City Decr 16. 1833

I send you the letter of Jacob Bletcher who desires to receive his pension at the Nashville Tenn. agency, instead of receiving it at Fayetteville N.C. where he has been heretofore paid. Will you examine the letter and inform me whether the transfer can be made.[1]

JAMES K. POLK

Addressed to Washington. This letter is in Pension File S39198 (RG 15), National Archives.

1. See Bletcher to Polk, November 23, 1833.

FROM JAMES WALKER[1]

At home Near Davis Mill Post office,
Dear Sir Bedford County Tennessee December 16th 1833

I write still asking favors. As the tariff is and will Continue to abate It may be that some Eastern Capitalist may wish to take a situation in the west. I have a tract of land in neighbourhood that is as well addapted to the successfull rising of cotton as aney land in the country. It lyes well and is large enough to Suit almost aney gen[t]leman situate in the edge of the uper range. Our country has water power sufficient to opperate machienry advantageously. The land I have offered for sale but as yet have not found a purchasear. My wish is to sell of[f]—if that cannot be done to have it improved and [I] am not able to go into the cotton wool or Flax manufacturing business. If you can find a man that understands either of the above Businesses that wishes to settle in our country please send him on or if it should be thought best to form a company you are invited to take an interrest and have liberty to organize aney companey you plase. It is a healthey pleasent place wher there can be no danger of high water. It will be overshot work supported by small strams of freestone water. It is notorious among us that sheep do better on those lands than our lower lands owing perhaps to the country being a Dryer soil and a greater variety of Sponteneous vegitation. They are tolerable plenty and can be had at one dollar per head. The flease of one year is worth that sum for home consumption. Some time past I opened a correspondance with a gentleman (I have not now his letter before me) I think the president of the Phoenix Manufactureing Company at Patterson New Jersey with a view to introduce if possable the manufactoring of flax and hemp but he put me out of all hopes by, as thought, over rating the cost. It may be that I did not understand him. I believe that business would do better here than either of the other in as much as hemp is one of the shuriest crops that our planters make but I am willing to accept of either and am ready to furnish provisions and Lumber for building.

If congress has not authorised the surveying the land that I applyed for a Surveyors District in I would yet be glad to obtain it. It was for the land ceeded by a treaty held at Perreara Dechine[Prairie du Chien]. I have nothing of a publick nature to inform you of but Look to you for information as I am not takeing any political paper at this time. Please send me som of your Doings at congrees and I pray God to Direct your Course in the councills of this great and riseing republick, believing it is the government of his choice he will aid his servants to perform his will. Therefore you will not turn a Deaf ear to his admonitions. Pleas write me frequently; we are well; fare Well.

JAMES WALKER

Addressed to Washington.

1. A resident of Bedford County who had served as an officer in the county militia. He is not to be confused with the James Walker of Maury County who was Polk's brother-in-law.

FROM ADLAI O. HARRIS

My Dear Sir Columbia 17 Decr. 1833

I have the pleasure to acknowledge the rect. of your favour of the 27 ulto. in which I had hoped to have found that your Speaker was provided for in some Foreign Mission but find from late Washington papers that he is again elected to the Chair of the House.[1]

We have had a remarkably dry fall and have just begun to experience something like Winter. The last few days have been rainy with occasional Snow, and our River is this evening in fine Boating order. So much of our Cotton has however been halled to Nashville in the fine Weather that it will be with much difficulty that we can get my Boats off.

Geo Moore arrived Saturday and on Sunday evening Sylvia and her children. We had been endeavoring to prepare Ophelia's mind for her arrival (for she knew nothing of it until a day or two before she came) but we succeeded very poorly, and in her passion she threatened to write a severe Epistle to you on the subject which I presume she has done. She was so much enraged for a day or two that we feared some bad result but there is a calm now, and we have some hopes that it will continue for a while at least.

I have to day rented your office for the next year to Dr Thomas Barbour son of Judge P. P. Barbour of Va. who has lately settled in our place. He has a small family and has rented Mothers' House on the Hill.

I shall leave for N. Orleans about the 1st January and would be pleased to hear from you if you can find leisure to write.

A O Harris

P.S. Naomi says to Sarah—do write to her for she knows that she is a poor correspondent but that she will endeavour to patch up a Letter during the Session. Mary Eliza is but little improved if any. Ann Maria[2] remains quite lame and but very little better.

A O H

Addressed to Washington.

1. Andrew Stevenson had been re-elected on December 2, 1833.

2. Mary Eliza and Ann Maria, daughters of James and Jane Maria Walker, were ten and six years old, respectively.

FROM RICHARD H. MOSBY

Warren County, North Carolina. December 17, 1833

Mosby, apparently a lawyer, indicates that his letter will be presented to Polk by his friend, Andrew Stevenson. Mosby is serving as an agent for the pension claims of the father of Dr. William F. Smith of Lincoln County, Tennessee. He wishes to know if Polk has received the pertinent papers and what disposition will be made of the pension claims.[1]

Addressed to Washington.

1. The Smith claim seems to have been settled a few weeks before this letter was written, for William Smith was placed on the pension roll in September 1833.

FROM SAMUEL P. WALKER JR.[1]

Sir, Washington City Dec 17 1833

Presuming that from your toilsome avocation, as Chairman of the committee[2] over which you have the honour to preside that you might possibly need the assistance of a Clerk in copying and executing private writing &c. I have taken the liberty of offering you my services, in that line, in which, should you be pleased to accept I will endeaver to give you satisfaction.

For reference as to respectability &c. (it not being my profession) I refer you to Mr Grundy, Mr Silsbee[3] &c of the Senate, or Mr [William W.] Ellsworth, [Daniel L.] Barringer, [John Quincy] Adams of your house.

I reside in C Street, where at all times at a moment's warning, I can be at your command.

SAML P WALKER JR

Presumably delivered by hand to the House of Representatives.

1. A native of Ireland, this Walker was a clerk in the Patent Office of the Department of State. He is not to be confused with the Samuel P. Walker of Columbia who was Polk's nephew.

2. Polk had just recently become chairman of the Ways and Means Committee.

3. Nathaniel Silsbee served as senator from Massachusetts, 1826–35.

FROM GERRARD T. GREENFIELD

Dear Sir [Columbia, Tennessee] 18th December 1833

I receivd a letter from Maryland some time ago. Mr. Grimes and Mr. Baden, informed me, that Mr. Joseph A. Turner would wait upon you with the $5500 for my land and receiv the Deed, which my friend Langtry[1] delivered to you.

I inclose you two memorials which I wished laid before t[h]e Legislature of Maryland. I wish you to write to Mr. Wm L. Weems[2] and direct your letter to Nottingham, Prince George County, Maryland and request him to forward or bring a certified copy of my Aunts Will to you. When you receive the copy of the Will, please put the memorials and the Will, in the hands of the honorable Joseph Kent[3] one of the members of the U. States Senate from Maryland, and who has always professed to be friendly toward me—requesting him to have them placed in the hands of two of t[h]e members of the Legislature of Maryland—a member of each house accompanied with the certified copy of t[h]e Will.

I am sorry to be so troublesome to you, but I trust you will endeavour to further my interests.

I have written to Mr. Grimes that you had t[h]e Deed for Turner and when he paid t[h]e money, he could have possession of t[h]e land, after which, Grimes has his instructions.

After you have attended to the matters mentioned in this letter, I expect to hear from you on the subject.

Please send me any documents you may deem interesting. I hope my business will not interrupt your public time. Our Convention will set t[h]e 3d Monday in May. The elections will take place the 1st Thursday and Friday in March. You have been spoken of, and can be elected, if you will consent. I shall remain at home and attend to my plantation &c. Your friends and relations are well. We are all anxious to hear from you. The Legislature will sit at Annapolis 4 Monday in December.

G Greenfield

Addressed to Washington.

1. Hillary Langtry was closely associated with Greenfield in the affairs of St. Peter's Episcopal Church in Columbia. The Maryland residents mentioned by Greenfield have not been identified.

2. A native of Maryland, Weems moved to Tennessee in 1825 and subsequently settled down in the eastern part of Hickman County. For a bizarre rumor about him see Henry D. Hatton to Polk, October 8, 1834.

3. At this time Kent was a member of the United States Senate. Earlier he had served several terms in the lower house of Congress and had been governor of Maryland, 1826–29. He died in 1837, before his term in the Senate had expired.

FROM ANDREW JACKSON

My dear Sir, [Washington] Decbr 18th 1833 past 5. P.M.

I have this moment been informed that Mr Chilton, & not Mr. McDuffie[1] took the floor on the amendment offered yesterday to your resolution, to instruct the committee on finance or ways & means &c &c. If this be true, it offers a fair opportunity for you, by a short reply and giving your reasons, to call for the previous question. Mr Chilton taking the floor must have been by the permission of the mover of the amendment, as it seems to me, common comity would have yielded place to the mover. It is at once evidence of the intention to smother investigation of the conduct of the Bank, and ought to be met promp[t]ly by the previous question. The time for full discussion is when the committee collect the facts, and report them to the House.

I enclose a private letter from Mr Gilpin,[2] which contains something that may not be unprofitable for you to know.

ANDREW JACKSON

Marked "Private" and delivered by hand. It has been published in Bassett, editor, *Correspondence of Andrew Jackson,* V, 234.

1. Thomas Chilton of Kentucky and George McDuffie of South Carolina were strong supporters of Biddle and the Bank of the United States. Despite the fact that Jackson dated his letter December 18 and spoke of actions that had taken place "yesterday," he seems to be referring to events of December 18, beginning with the presentation by Horace Binney of a memorial from the Bank of the United States with a motion that it be laid on the table and printed. When Binney's motion failed, Polk moved that the memorial be referred to the Ways and Means Committee. Chilton proposed an amendment to Polk's motion, favoring the redeposit of the federal money in the Bank. Using this occasion to speak, Chilton made a pro-Bank speech, at the conclusion of which McDuffie requested Chilton to withdraw his amendment. Chilton agreed, and the House then concurred in Polk's motion.

2. Henry D. Gilpin was one of the government-appointed directors of the Bank of the United States who complained that they were excluded from important decision-making. His letter to Jackson, dated December 16, 1833, expressed hope that the memorial from the minority of the directors to the Ways and Means Committee would provide proof of the misrepresentations of the Bank's official report. He also commented upon the financial distress being brought on by current Bank policies. Gilpin later served as Attorney General in Van Buren's cabinet.

FROM JAMES WALKER

Dear Sir, Columbia Dec 18 1833

I have been very often asked what were your views and inclinations relative to serving in the Convention, and have been written to you on the subject from Mooresville. You know that the election comes on in March & meets I believe in May. That you can be elected without your being here is beyond a doubt.[1] The only question is whether you can leave Congress and come home in time to serve in Convention. I am satisfied now that you & [Robert L.] Cobbs will be nominated and run at all events until we hear from you. And if you think it will not do for you to come home during the session of Congress, Mathew D. Cooper's name will be substituted for yours. This all depends on you. A great number of people will be satisfied in no other way than for you to be in the Convention. Write me fully and particularly on this subject without delay.

James Walker

Addressed to Washington.

1. Walker's confidence of Polk's election, should he announce his candidacy, was widely shared. A. O. P. Nicholson, in his letter to Polk on December 5, 1833, expressed his belief that a strong effort would be made to defeat Polk.

FROM JOHN BARNEY[1]

My dear Sir Baltimore Decmr. 19th 1833

I am requested by my brother[2] who has not the pleasure of a personal acquaintance with you to ask the favor of being informed whether the Bill reported by you as Chairman of the Committee of Ways & Means, making a partial appropriation for the support of Government, includes any appropriation for the first quarter of the ensuing year, for the Navy Department, He being interested in supplies which are suspended untill the Bill shall pass either in anticipation or after the regular session[?].

I am aware how every moment of your time must be absorbed by important business & will not intrude further than to ask a single line stating whether such a Bill as was requested by the Honble Secretary in his Report has been or probably will be introduced.

Jno. Barney

Addressed to Washington.

1. He was the son of Joshua Barney, the famous naval officer of the Revolution and of the War of 1812. John served two terms in the United States House of Representatives from Maryland, 1825–29.

2. William Bedford Barney had served as an officer in the Marine Corps and at one time had acted as his father's aide. Apparently he was employed by the Department of the Navy at this time.

FROM GIDEON J. PILLOW

Dear Col. Columbia December 19th [1833][1]

A period has arrived in the history of Tennessee when every *real* friend to his Country feels an anxious concern for the *future welfare* and *prosperity* of our State. You are already advised that our constitution is about to be changed but whether for the *better* or *worse* time will determine.

In a measure of such deep and lasting moment to the happiness of the country, men of *Talents,* of *experience,* of *correct political principles* and *tried patriotism* should be called into the service of the people. With such apprehensions for the future happiness and prosperity of the state and under such circumstances, you cannot be surprised that your *friends* should be anxious that your name should be placed before the people—not as a candidate—but as the man of their own *choice* to represent this county in the convention.

A communication from a friend of yours placing your name before the people will appear in the Western Mercury before this reaches you, but will be withdrawn if the measure does not meet your approbation. As far as I can ascertain there is a general wish that your name should go before the people. Robert L Cobbs and Col. William Pillow[2] are also spoken of and though some weeks since many others were mentioned as probable candidates for the convention yet public sentiment seems more to have settled down upon *yourself* Cobbs & Pillow.

Be so good Col. as to say to me whether or not you will serve the people in that capacity if they elect you.

As soon as the Winters land Bill may be taken up advise me of this fact and of its *fate* when *that* is *ascertained.*

GIDEON J. PILLOW

Addressed to Washington.

1. The letter bore no year. Internal evidence bears out the Library of Congress decision to place it in 1833.

2. He was an uncle of the writer of this letter and had fought with Jackson during the Creek Campaign.

FROM JOHN WURTS[1]

Dear Sir New York. Decr. 19, 1833

You will I trust excuse an old personal and political friend and associate for troubling you with a few lines in relation to public matters. However much you may doubt the accuracy of my judgment, I think you will give me credit for the sincerity of my motives. Your position in the House of Representatives, must give you a commanding influence upon questions and measures pregnant with much good or evil to the country. I allude to the present state of the currency and money market. I presume not to advise you as to the action of Congress on this subject. But my present position and pursuits, give me a good opportunity to judge of events connected with this matter and I give it to you as my decided and firm conviction, that unless speedy relief can be found, a scene of extensive and distressing ruin must soon occur in the commercial community. It is impossible that this pressure can be long sustained notwithstanding the great prosperity of the country for years past. Indeed that alone has enabled the community to sustain the pressure thus far. Doubts, fear, and dismay now begin to fill every mind, which added to the present scarcity of money, must soon lead to wide spread ruin unless relief is speedily found. I trust therefore my dear Sir, that this subject, will receive your earnest and deliberate consideration, & that your personal and political influence will be used to provide some remedy to check the impending evil.

John Wurts

Addressed to Washington.

1. A lawyer from Philadelphia who had served one term in Congress, 1825–27. At this time he was president of the Delaware and Hudson Canal Company. Blaming economic distress on Jackson's course with regard to the Bank of the United States, this letter appears to have been among the flood of letters that the Bank directors had urged businessmen to write to members of Congress.

FROM JOHN CAMPBELL[1]

My dear Sir [Washington] Treasury Office 20th Dec 1833

See State papers Senate Second Session 17th Congress a letter from Mr. Crawford[2] dated 25th Feb *1823, seven* years after the Bank was chartered in which you will see the doctrine fully asserted of the power of the Sec in transferring public funds from the Bank U.S. to State Banks to sustain the credit of the latter.

J. CAMPBELL

Marked "Private" and directed to the House of Representatives, this letter was delivered by hand.

1. A native of Virginia, he was Treasurer of the United States.

2. William H. Crawford of Georgia had been Secretary of the Treasury on the date mentioned.

FROM JAMES WALKER

Dear Sir Columbia Dec 20th 1833

Your man *Little Ben* made his appearance here last night. He says he knows nothing of Chunky Jack, that he left the plantation before Chunky and does not know what has become of him. His back, I am informed bears evidence of severe whipping. Whether Beenland has acted with too much severity or not I cannot say, but I am fearful he has not judgement enough to keep negroes in proper subjection. I wrote to him yesterday requesting him to moderate, and expressing fears that he had been too cruel.

I am uneasy about Chunky Jack, but hope he will be caught and taken back, or make his way here. The question is what is to be done with them, and particularly with Little Ben, who is now here. It seems useless to send him back unless it is in chains, and then it is uncertain how long Beenland would keep him. I think it strange he suffered him to escape so easily. If he is not sent back it will be a very bad example to your & my plantations. It would be too bad an example for my plantations for me not to send Ben back, if the decision is made by me and whether it is prudent, and agreeable to your wishes & interest for this to be done, I am at a loss to determine.

Mr. Harris must therefore be your representative in this matter, and what he may, or ought to, do is uncertain. You had better write your wishes to him immediately lest the matter should not be determined before you are heard from. I will inform Beenland that Little Ben is here and leave him & Mr. Harris to act upon the subject as they think proper.

George Moore left here yesterday. I had given it in charge to him to get hold of these negroes by all means & return them to your plantation. I will advise him and Maj [John H.] Bills who I had also written on the subject, of Little Ben's being here, and request them to continue their exertions to get hold of Chunky Jack.

I will write you again in a few days respecting my *Stage* business. I expect to hear from Caruthers & Kinkle again tomorrow on that subject. I feel *very sore* on that subject, nor can I resist the conviction that the public & my interests have been sacrificed improperly to promote the selfish views of Caruthers & Kinkle & Donly. If this matter is investigated, as it may be the Post office department cannot avoid much censure. You know that [I] am very tenacious, and restless under a conviction of having been wronged, and that I do not look much to real or supposed future pecuniary interests in my actions on such occasions.

James Walker

Addressed to Washington.

FROM JOHN K. YERGER TO JAMES K. POLK AND WILLIAM M. INGE

Gent. Pulaski December 20. 1833

I have just received a letter from one of the Contractors of the line of stages from Columbia Via Pulaski to Huntsville, who informed me that the line has been *Cut down* from a Post Coach three times a week, to that of a two Horse stage twice a week.

The Citizens of Pulaski, Elkton & Columbia are much interested in this matter, and have received the information with much regret. And when we reflect that a large and important Section of the Country is now to be deprived of mail facilities & accommodations which their enterprise in commerce entitle them to it is received with not only regret but *mortification*. This section of Country has never had its proportion of mail facilities, and to be deprived at this time when it is all important that it should be kept up is greviously hard.

The Town of Pulaski is now rapidly improving. It has a population of about 1200. and from a refference to the nett proceeds of the Post offices in this State it appears that we stand about the 10th. This will also be greatly increased the next year, as a Branch of the Planters Bank of Tennessee will be established here which will be the means of a considerable increase in the revenew from this office.

I am requested by a number of the Citizens of Pulaski, to address, and to solicit you to urge the necessity before the Post Master General of Continuing the present line of 4 Horse Post coaches three times a week.

Hoping to hear soon that you have been successful. . . .

JOHN K. YERGER

Addressed to Washington.

FROM MATTHEW RHEA

Sir Columbia Tenn. Dec. 21st 1833

I take the liberty of calling to your recollection at this time the subject of supplying the different offices of the departments of government at Washington City with copies of the Map of Tennessee. This subject was first proposed to me by Mr Grundy who seemed to think it entirely proper. If not too much trouble, please ascertain what number (if any) of maps *can be disposed of* & may be required for the above purpose, and Seal the within communication for Mr Tanner[1] (number of copies being inserted) and have the same deposited in the mail.

M. RHEA

Addressed to Washington.

1. Henry S. Tanner, a Philadelphia cartographer and statistical geographer, was the engraver and publisher of Rhea's map. Rhea's letter to Tanner

simply requested that the maps be sent to Thompson and Homans, Washington booksellers, for distribution.

FROM EPHRAIM BEANLAND

Dear Sir [Somerville] December the 22th 1833

We'r ar all well and Lisabeth and Mriah has both fine living children and Garisan and the mule has cum long since. And I am sorry to tell you that Jack and Ben both left the plantation on the 28 of November and I have not heard from them since.[1] On the night before I was a bailing until a 11 oclock and Jack went alf and broke into a grocery which he was caught and when I was thoroly convinced that it was him I corected him and I corected him for teling em 5 or 6 positif lyes and whilste I went to diner they boath left the field and I have not heard of them since. And Sir I dont say that I am able to advise you but I do not want any arangements maid for either of them. I want them boath brought back. If they aint they rest will leave me also. I have sent to Maury after them by George More. If they ar theire he will fetch them back. And I also I sent Sillva and her family to Maury. And on Cristmust day I am a going to see George More. He is to be back.

Dear Sir on this day I finished my crop boath corn and [c]oten ageathering and on tomorrow I look for Hardy back from Memphis which he caried the last lode of your coten. I have sum reparing to do which it will take me until neuers [New Years] day and then I shal go begin to clear land. And on this day I sent Jim to Maury and I want Jack and Ben verry much indeade. My corne is verry shorte indeade. I have not got won of my cribs full in the shuck. And you said Sir that you wanted to [k]now how much coten you had in the seede. I cant tell for sum was so wet and sum dayes all hands did not get 200 hundred pounds but they is won thing it is all gind and it is all in Memphis and I have the receits for it ondly the last lode which Hardy will be back on tomorrow. And Sir your negroes has traded with white people and bin let run at so lose rained[rein] that I must be verry close with them. They is a set of white people that lives close hear that would spoil any set of negroes.

Dear Sir I cant give you the amount of your seede coten but

I can give you the weight of the pict coten and the numbers of every baile and the weights of every baile.

No 1	477	No 14	480
No 2	502	No 15	420
No 3	438	No 16	450
No 4	581	No 17	438
No 5	550	No 18	444
No 6	514	No 19	458
No 7	484	No 20	480
No 8	481	No 21	520
No 9	5[52]	No 22	526
No 10	4[98]	No 23	532
No 11	440	No 24	540
No 12	440	No 25	520
No 13	470		

On last Munday I cilled my hogs. My corn was so scearse that I could not feede them any longer which they was 4000 weight of it ondly. It was not verry fat the reason of it I had not corne to ceap it. And sir Dr Edwards caime the other day and wanted me to setle his bill ageanste the plantation which it was $34 and sum sence and I tolde him that I co[u]ld not but I told him that I would let you [know] about the mater. He is agoing to moove away and he wants it setled before he goes.[2]

EPHRAIM BEANLAND

Addressed to Washington. This letter has been published in Bassett, *Plantation Overseer,* 53–55.

1. From this point there is a considerable amount of repetition of what he told Polk in his letter of December 1, 1833.

2. Isaac Edwards, a Somerville doctor, treated slaves on Polk's plantation. Beanland reported later that Edwards had decided not to leave the county.

FROM AARON V. BROWN

Dear Sir [Pulaski] Decr. 22nd 1833

I must beg leave to request your attention to my little business with Thomas Wright the 3rd[1] of Centreville Maryland. I enclosed you my *transfer* from my Father & stepmother, together with a power of atto. to yourself—all of which I presume you have now at the City. I have before me Wrights reply to you stating that about June last the estate would be closed up & that he would advise me accordingly. Write him again & try & close it *finally* this winter for me.[2]

We have recd. the message & "the opening" scenes of Congress—portentous enough—but not appalling. In "the house" the administration will get along well enough but in the Senate there will be frequent & perplexing embarrassments but nothing in my opinion seriously to retard its important measures. A petty warefare, pitiful & malicious, but which will ultimately recoil on those who wage it. The Secretary of the Treasury has done the removal of the deposits all the justice the subject would admit of & has certainly presented it in a very plausible and imposing light.

What of the Speakership? Have no good anecdote on that point for confidential friends? *The four*—whence came they—are they mere forerunners? If so, the quarter whence recd. might illustrate.

Let me know the signs as to the "successorship to the throne." [John] McLean & [William] Carroll you see lead off in my Friend Inge's district. Tell him *all that* will be attributed to him—That he shot the Parthian arrow as he fled to the great Sandhedrim. *Personally* I like McLean myself but *politically* I fear he is *too far off* from us in the South. And how will Van Buren help that matter in the least? One thing I am determined on, that "as to me & my house" we will run mad for neither. Ask Mr Grundy to write me during the Session, what "weight of armor" he intends buckling on in that cause or whether like Achilles he will return to the ships & break a lance on neither side. Now seriously speaking, between Clay & Van Buren, might not one find refuge in the personal worth, & virtue of McLean, although he would greatly prefer some other than either of these, if chance or destiny had not thrown him too far in the rear of probable success. I do not here allude to the leader of nullification, whose ultimate madness & recklessness has excluded him from all the sempathies which his harsh treatment, in the first instance, was well calculated to inspire.

Be good enough to forward me the "Congressional Globe" if

you think it well conducted—*not the Globe simply,* for I have never relished *that* nor *Greens Telegraph,* in the best days of its orthodoxy.

There is considerable excitement about candidates for the Convention.[3] I shall try hard to keep out of it.

I have been absent nearly all the fall through the Choctaw & Chickesaw nations—camping out with "my bed the Earth, my canopy the skies," but after all my excursions I could not get Goldsmith's lines out of my head.

"I still had hopes my long sojourneyings past
Safe to return & die at home at last."

Be good enough to present me respectfully to Mrs. Polk. . . .

A. V. Brown

P. S. Now how comes it that our post rout has been [. . .] in this State? If you and friend Inge cant keep William T. Barry in better order, *we must withdraw our subscription on this* [. . .].

Addressed to Washington.

1. A lawyer in Centreville, Maryland, and Brown's agent in the settlement of the estate of John Beard, in which Brown had a claim. See Brown to Polk, November 23, 1832.

2. The estate was not settled until about two years later.

3. The approaching Tennessee Constitutional Convention.

FROM CHARLES DAYAN[1]

Dr Sir Lowville, Lewis Co. N.Y. Decr. 22 1833

It is with great pleasure I perceive You have taken the mammoth by the horn and have humbled it. The house nobly and honorably sustained You and New York did her duty on that occasion.[2] We have I see one rebel in our ranks, but he is short lived.[3] He has cheated us twice, he never will again. I am much pleased with the prospect in the house formation of committees and the commencement of reform began. Clay cannot sustain himself in the Course he is now pursuing.

His recent attack of the Prest. is execrated by all honest and inteligent men.[4] Webster I should think was taking a more moderate course. He wishes I suppose to be Chief Justice. Will

Maine & N. Hampshire ever consent? If you have time I should be pleased to hear from You.

CHAS. DAYAN

Addressed to Washington.

1. A lawyer in Lowville, New York, Dayan served twice in the state legislature and one term in Congress, 1831–33. Subsequently he was district attorney for Lewis County.

2. This probably refers to Polk's action on December 17 that prevented the Secretary of the Treasury's report on removal of deposits from being referred to the Committee of the Whole House, as proposed by McDuffie. Polk's counterproposal that the report be referred to the Ways and Means Committee was not immediately successful and final action was deferred. It is possible, however, that the reference is to Polk's successful effort on December 18 to have a memorial from the Bank referred to his committee.

3. The identity of the rebel is obscure.

4. This probably refers to Clay's attempt to force Jackson to produce for the Senate a copy of a paper read before the cabinet in September, which outlined his reasons for favoring removal of government deposits from the Bank. Jackson, of course, refused.

FROM WILLIAM T. FITZGERALD

Dr Sir Dresden Tenn. December 22, 1833

I wrote to you at Home last summer asking your aid in procureing for me an Arkansas Judgeship. Judge Clayton[1] has not yet resigned but will do so sometime this winter at what time I cannot tell. Some of his friends & immediate neighbors are I am told applicants and I suppose he will time his resignation to suit them.

It would be by me remembered as a favor if you would talk to the President on the subject & let me know what will be my prospect.[2] I have written to no person from this state but yourself. I should have written to Mr. [Cave] Johnson but he has a friend & Townsman who is an applicant & I expect he will consider it his duty to sustain his application. I think Judge [Hugh Lawson] White will aid me & also Colo R. M. Johnson.

Should you be kind enough to interest yourself for me and should resort to the usual means of getting a recommendation signed by the members I would not wish you (& this inter nos) to ask any of the members from this state to sign it except Judge

White & Mr Johnson if he should not be committed as above supposed. I mean the old members, I know nothing of the new ones except Mr. [William C.] Dunlap & I have no reasons to think he would not be in my favor. I would not now for the office to me & my heirs for the ten generations next following ask any of the them [*sic*] to aid me in this or any thing else, but this in confidence.

The Sovereigns are prepareing to elect their delegates to the Convention. I do not think there will be returned any man of talents from this district. We have some talent among us but as yet none of them are on the field.

I hope our new Constitution will make our executive officer a man of more consequence than he is at present. There will I think be given to the Governor considerable patronage with a negative on the laws &c. If so I should be glad to see you the first Governor under the new Constitution. You can beat any man who has been spoken of in the Western district.

W. Fitzgerald

Addressed to Washington.

1. Alexander M. Clayton had moved from Virginia to Clarksville, Tennessee, as a young man and had been appointed to the judgeship in Arkansas in 1832. After he resigned in February 1834, he returned to Clarksville and shortly thereafter moved to Marshall County, Mississippi, where he had a long and illustrious career.

2. Fitzgerald did not receive this appointment; it went to Thomas J. Lacy.

FROM JOHN CONRAD[1]

Sir   Philada December 23 1833

Being about to publish the debates in both houses of Congress on the removal of the Deposits, and axious to avoid injustice to all the gentlemen engaged in the debate on that question, I beg leave very respectfully to request that you will have the goodness to inform me from which of the papers you prefer having your speeches copied, unless you will grant me the more extended favor of transmitting corrected copies of them, which may perhaps deserve your attention, as in this publication they will assume a permanent form and become a highly interesting portion of the history, and politics of our country.

JOHN CONRAD

Addressed to Washington.

1. At one time, Conrad was clerk of the court of quarter sessions in Philadelphia. Later he was a prosperous publisher, printing among other things, Charles Brockden Brown's *Literary Magazine* and Joel Barlow's *Columbiad*. No record has been found to indicate that he published the debates mentioned here.

TO ANDREW JACKSON

Dear Sir Washington Decr. 23, 1833

Am I authorized in answer to Mr McDuffie to state what I learned from you in private conversation, that in the original draft of your inaugural address written at the Hermitage, your opinions in regard to the U.S. Bank were fully expressed, but on reaching this City, it was deemed adviseable to reserve the expression of them until you should make your first annual communication to Congress? In one aspect of the question as presented by Mr McD. it may be important to make this fact known, but I do not feel at liberty to do so without your permission.

JAMES K. POLK

I would call up & see you but am so much engaged this ev[en]ing that I cannot conveniently.

No address is available. Marked "Private," the letter was probably delivered by hand. It has been published in Bassett, editor, *Correspondence of Andrew Jackson,* V, 234. Jackson's reply was written on the back, and the letter was returned to Polk.

FROM ANDREW JACKSON

[Washington, Dec. 23, 1833]

This for yourself as it is wrote in haste.

The president with his respects replies to Col Polk, that he understood him correctly—that the original draft of his inaugural address, was made at the Hermitage, that his views of the United States Bank then incorporated in it, and also his views of the surpluss funds that might casually arise in the Treasury. These two paragraphs, were by the advice of his friends were, both left out of the inaugural address and were both introduced in his next annual message. It was thought that both these topics were better suited to an annual message, than an ina[u]gural address, and thus you if necessary, may use it. Every one that knows me, does know, that I have been always opposed to the U. States Bank, nay all Banks.

ANDREW JACKSON

No address is available. This letter has been published in Bassett, editor, *Correspondence of Andrew Jackson,* V, 235. It was written on the back of the letter from Polk of the same date and was probably delivered by the same messenger.

FROM LEWIS CASS

Washington. December 24, 1833

Cass encloses a draft of a bill to provide Indian Department expenses for 1834 and also a copy of the estimate upon which the bill is based.

Addressed to Washington. Clerk's copy in Reports to Congress from the Secretary of War (RG 107), National Archives.

FROM WILLIAM MOORE

Dear Sir Mulberry [Lincoln County] 24th Decr. 1833

Mr. William George[1] of this County Recd. a wound at the Battle of Taladega. He says that he once spoke to you on the subject. He says that he is unable to support his Family by labour & that he has not Recd. a pension, but wishes to make application & requests that you assertain the manner he will have to proceed & give him in detail by letter. He was a Corporal in Capt. Porters Compy of Militia under Genl. [Martin] Roberts.

You will write to me. I have but little news. I am anxiously looking to you for something. I am well pleased with the Prest. Message. I think he dealt with Mr. Duane[2] according to his merrits. I am anxious to hear how my Ky namesake has come out with Letcher.[3] I here inclose you a copy of the Report on our Southern Boundry, I wish you to let Mr. [William M.] Inge have the parusal. Consult with him & Colo [William C.] Dunlap as to the course to pursue to prevent the Sale of the land (lying between the two lines) for the benefit of the Indian.

Write me a long letter.

WILLIAM MOORE

P.S. [James] Fulton, [Isaac] Holman, & [Andrew A.] Kincannan are candadates for convention. A. V. Brown & one or two others will be out in Giles. The 2 counties Elect 3.

W. M.

Addressed to Washington.

1. A person by this name, also from Lincoln County, was placed on the pension list in August 1833 for service during the Revolution. It is just possible that William George served in both wars and that the notification that the pension had been granted had been delayed.

2. William J. Duane, a lawyer and active politician from Philadelphia, had served briefly in 1833 as Secretary of the Treasury; he was removed by Jackson when he refused to sign the order taking government deposits from the Bank of the United States.

3. This is a reference to the disputed election in Kentucky between Robert P. Letcher and Thomas P. Moore.

FROM WILLIAM H. POLK

Dear Brother Raleigh N.C Dec 26th 1833

It is now vacation and I came here with the expectation of finding some money but Col [William] Polk says he never received your letter which you said in the letter you wrote me you intended to write to him the next day and I would like for you to write to him as soon as you can. I wrote to you in my last letter that if you would give me 150 dollars at the commencement of every session it would answer and pay all that I now owe. I will tell you how much my board, washing, wood, et cettera comes to in one session.

Board—	$40.00
Washing and bed	$ 8.00
Firewood & candles	$ 8.00
Tuition—	$21.00
	81.00[1]

I do not know whether I can get in on Greek or not. I do not expect that I can and I do not wish to go on irregular. I want to have a good education which I canot get if I go on iregular and I want you to let me go to Nashville where I can join the sophmore class I expect. And after I graduate there if you think I had better go to school longer I will go to any college you think best. And when I am at Nashville I will be near home where you can attend to all things and I have no doubt but what I would do as well if not better there than I can here. I do not ask this of you because I am a little home sick but because I know that I can do better there than I can do here because I am not on a regular standing in college and am not willing and canot go back to another class. I am in hopes you will grant my request.

I saw Mr Alexander[2] and he said he had just received a letter from home and sister Laura and the children were well. You must write to me as soon as you receive this.

WILL. H. POLK

Mrs Polk sends her respects to you and sister Sarah.

Addressed to Washington.

1. Unless an error was made in the listing above, this total should be $77.

2. Probably William J. Alexander, an 1816 graduate of the University of North Carolina and a prominent lawyer in Charlotte.

FROM ANONYMOUS[1]

Dear Sir Philada. Decr. 27th 1833

I have taken the liberty of asking you to read an article Inserted in the "Pennsylvanian" and Copyed into the *'Globe'* 23d May last. I would have sent you the paper in which the article is copied but the Globe is in your house on *file*. It is said MDuffy

[McDuffie] has a large Number of *shares* in (U.S) Bank. Has he sold his 600 *shares?* I sent you [Horace] Binneys[2] speech. Nicholas [Biddle] & his satellites are doing all the[y] can to produce Distress here.

Addressed to Washington. The letter is unsigned.

1. Polk marked this letter "Anonymous." Comparison of the handwriting with that of several of his friends in Philadelphia has given no clue to the identity of the writer.

2. A lawyer in Philadelphia who had served as a director of the Bank of the United States. Binney was a member of the United States House of Representatives, 1833–35.

FROM JOHN WELSH JR.[1]

Dear Sir Philada. Decemr. 27 1833

Having had the pleasure of an introduction to you by my much esteemed friend James Walker Esq whilst in Columbia T. last Summer & still remembering your kindness in directing my way to Chapel Hill which circumstance may recall me to your recollection, permit me to take the liberty of addressing you on the subject of a memorial from the Board of trade of this City praying for the amendment of the 18th Section of the Tariff Act of '32 so that it may Extend its operation to the various changes in duties as provided for by the Act of 2 March 1833. As the Chairman of the Com. of Ways & Means to which it was referred I have thought it possible if apprised of the Advantages of an early determination of it you might have it [in] your power to bring it forward & have the immediate action of Congress upon it.

As you are aware Merchants from the distant parts of the Country may in the course of a few days be expected here for their Spring supplies. We of course are desirous of having the ability to expose our goods for sale. This with regard to such articles as are now in original packages & on which there will be a material variation on duty cannot be done until the decision of Congress on the application & then in Event of the application not being complied with, exportation to a convenient foreign port must be resorted to for the advantage of the drawback. This will cause the Merchant to incur a considerable expense & the Government will Save but little for in Every instance when the reduction is Considerable this Course will be pursued.

You will from the slight sketch of the Subject understand the importance of immediate action to the Merchants of all the eastern cities & the great desire which we all feel that the matter should be disposed of. Permit me then to request your Exertions in their behalf on this point. There is another on which I should be most happy if I could address you with the same prospect of success. I allude to the *cause* of the present distress which our Commercial Community is suffering & which is most rapidly Extending itself to every class of our Citizens & its course will not be stayed until its effects are felt from the Palace even to every Hamlet in our Country, unless the cause be removed.

This is a subject which I am aware has received your attention and it is a matter of great regret to all our admirers in this part of our Common Country, who free from political thraldom can regard this present situation without respect to other influences, that your mind has been led to the conclusions which induce your present course. It would be useless for me by any course of reasoning to attempt to dispel the opinions which you have adopted, but hoping that a few facts which you may not be aware of, may induce you to listen to & believe the bitter cries of distress which must have reached your Ear & then work upon your feelings till exciting your sympathy you will be anxious to avail yourself of the important advantages which your talents & peculiar Situation place in your Control for the purpose of arresting an evil more disastrous in its effects than any thing which has yet assailed our happy Republic, I will endeavour to State them to you.

It was supposed by those in favour of the removal of the deposits from the U S Bk that the State Banks selected in its stead would be able to supply the wants of the Community. Now the fact in this city is that the Girard Bank does not at this moment discount with the same freedom as she did previous to the 1st Oct. when she did not enjoy the Govt. patronage. Merchants who have bonds to pay do not receive the same advantages from her which the U S Bk invariably extended to them & which the Treasury department by publication gave them reason to expect. The other State Banks find their means diminished & each day tending to decrease them still more whilst the excitement in the Community causes them to anticipate a result as fatal to their operations as any thing this Country has yet known. The fears of the people as to the Situation of the State Banks whilst their confidence in the Solidity of the U S Bk not only remains firm but is increased is working sadly to the disadvantage of the former by curtailing their circulation whilst its effect is the reverse with the latter. Stocks of all Kinds are diminished in price & for want of Confidence in the ability of the Institutions to sustain themselves at this Extraordinary crisis together with a disposition on the part of all to refrain from operations of all kinds it is impossible to dispose of the best stocks under an average decline of 20 pct from their prices but 6 weeks since. This circumstance has this day occasioned a Suspension of one of our most extensive Brokers, Men of undoubted capital & unbounded credit, Messrs Benson & Co, who finding that to force their immense investments at the present moment wd. be attended with the most serious sacrifice preferred a suspension which you know to yield to is only justified by most Extraordinary Circumstances.

At this time even Our State could not it is believed effect a Loan at par & the Loan she did effect last year it is now currently rumered that the Contractors men undoubtedly of large wealth will have to postpone its payment. The Union Bk of Tenn. Stock which Commanded freely 6 weeks since ten dollars prem. pr share Cannot now be sold at par & of the Planters Bk their will not one Share be taken East of the Mountains. These are facts which you may weigh & then Contrast it with the other which even the enemies of the Bank here freely admit that all this distress may be correct by a return of the deposits to the U S Bank. If you could but feel it to be your duty to advocate such a measure, how great the debt of gratitude would the people acknowledge to you. But as it is we have nothing to anticipate but a general overthrow of all the best interests of our Country. I should be happy to be of Service to you here.

John Welsh Jr.

Good Cotton 12cts Exchange on [. . .] 4¼.

Addressed to Washington.

1. Not positively identified but probably a merchant of Philadelphia.

FROM LEMUEL PREWITT[1]

Sir [Athens, Mississippi] December 28th 1833

I take the liberty to write you and ask you as faviour to examine Some claims that my frind Samuel Ragsdale[2] has in the Third auditors office. Mr Ragsdale informs me he has previously requested your interference in his behalf. There is three claims and a variety of testimony in support of them and I have faith in justice of the claims and I believe fully that your influence and aid with Mr Plum & Cage[3] ower[our] representors will Be servisable. I would be glad you would write me, and give a shewing of the most interesting policy, that is legisla[t]ing for. I am in fine health and enjoy life with as full a share of happiness as any oald man you know.

LEML. PREWITT

Addressed to Washington.

1. Prewitt moved to the Cave Springs community of Maury County about 1807. After serving in the state legislature for two terms, 1815–17 and 1819–21, he moved with his large family to Monroe County, Mississippi. Two of his sons, Abner and Dyer, served in the Creek War.

2. Formerly a resident of Fayetteville, Tennessee, Ragsdale moved first to Florence, Alabama, and then to Monroe County, Mississippi. He represented that county in the state senate, 1838–41. For information about Ragsdale's claim, see Ragsdale to Polk, December 25, 1828, and Peter Hagner to Polk, March 31, 1829.

3. Franklin E. Plummer and Henry Cage were members of Congress from Mississippi. A native of Tennessee, Cage was a lawyer in Woodville, Mississippi. He served on the Mississippi supreme court, 1829–32, before being elected to Congress.

TO JAMES WALKER

Dear Sir Columbia [Washington] [Dec.] 28th 1833[1]

I have a deed with Harris Executed on my part of William Woodward[2] for the Nelson 100 acres of land in Lincoln sold to him. He has paid up his last note. You will execute it on your part, have it proved or acknowledged before the clk, certified by him for registration, and then enclose it by mail or through

Wm. Martin[3] of Columbia directed to Joel Pinson[4] Esqr. Fayetteville Tennessee, who is to hand it to Woodward.

JAMES K. POLK

Mr. Harris will tell you what I wish about exchanging *Ben* & *Jim*. If *Ben* suits you to keep [. . .] you can have him for *Gabriel*. Skipwith[5] will exchange for *Jim*.

J. K. P.

Addressed to Columbia.

1. Polk headed the letter "Columbia 28th 1833." References in the postscript and in the late December letters from James Walker, Ephraim Beanland, and Adlai O. Harris, suggest December as the proper month, and at that time Polk was certainly in Washington.

2. On July 20, 1830, William Woodward bought from the executors of the Samuel Polk estate a tract of 100 acres of land in Lincoln County. He was to pay two notes of $125 each, the last being due at the end of two years. There was obviously some delay in the payments.

3. Formerly of Fayetteville, William P. Martin was a practicing lawyer in Columbia.

4. Explorer and surveyor of much of West Tennessee, Pinson was a resident of the Swan Creek area of Lincoln County. Later he moved to Pontotoc County, Mississippi.

5. Probably George G. Skipwith, Columbia businessman.

FROM ADLAI O. HARRIS

My Dear Sir Columbia 30th Dec. 1833

You have no doubt been advised by Mr Beanland that Jack and Ben had run away from your Plantation in the District—the cause &c.

I can give you no information on the subject further than I have collected from the negroes Ben & Jim, who a few days ago arrived here. They say that Jack was very badly whip'd indeed, that Beanland salted him four or five times during the whipping, that Ben was also whipd but not so badly. How much of this is true I cannot undertake to say but as highly as I approved of your choice in the selection of an overseer I am very much afraid that he will not treat your negroes as you would wish. As to his other qualifications, there will probably be no objection.

Ben and Jim are both here and both wish to stay here. Ben will not go back. He says he relys on your promise of keeping him here, of selling him or hireing him in this county. He is afraid if he goes back of being whipd. for running away and says that he cannot live with Mr Beanland. Jim says that Beanland is very severe, that he gives them no encouragement—that if they exert themselves to please him they get nothing but curses for it, and on the whole they give a gloomy account of things.

I do not know what to do with them. Mr Walker could not make the exchange you wished. I cannot exchange Ben for a hand to go to the District in his place. Skipwith will hire Jim and will probably give me a hand in his place.

What I shall do with them finally I do not exactly know but will do the best I can and will let you know in a few days.

All Well.

A. O. Harris

Addressed to Washington. This letter has been published in Bassett, *Plantation Overseer,* 55–56.

FROM LOUIS McLANE

Washington. December 31, 1833

This submits to the Committee of Ways and Means a copy of a contract with Matthew St. Clair Clarke and Peter Force[1] for publication of the documentary history of the American Revolution and suggests an appropriation of $35,000 to pay for the work as it progresses.

Addressed to Washington. This letter is in the Papers of Andrew Jackson Donelson, Division of Manuscripts, Library of Congress.

1. Publisher and historian whose most important work was nine volumes of *American Archives,* published 1837–53.

FROM ROGER B. TANEY

My Dear Sir [Washington. December 1833][1]

Will you Do me the favour to call at my house this evening—between 7 & 8 oclock? I wish to show you my annual report on the finances before I send it in.

R. B. Taney

Addressed to Polk at "Clements's" and delivered by hand. The letter is marked "Confidential."

1. The letter bears no date. The Library of Congress places it in 1834, but internal evidence suggests December 1833 as a more likely date.

FROM ROGER B. TANEY

My Dear Sir [Washington]. [December 1833][1]

I am obliged to employ this evening in seeing that my report is ready as I must send it in on Monday. I will be very glad to see you at my house tomorrow evening at 7 oclock. I hope it will suit your convenience to postpone our interview until that time.

R. B. TANEY

The envelope bears no address. The letter was obviously delivered by hand.

1. No date appears on this brief note, but it seems to have been written on the same day as the preceding one. The Library of Congress places it in 1834.

1834

FROM BENJAMIN F. CURREY[1]

Sir [Washington?] [1834?][2]

Having been informed that an act has just passed a third & last reading in your house directing that the Cherokee annuities shall hereafter be paid out to the head men of the Nation I should feel that I was wanting in humanity to the common Indians were I to with hold from your honorable body the following copy of a communication from Colo H. Montgomery[3] Ind Agent to Wm. Hicks[4] President of the Treaty party on the subject of annuities.

"Being called on by you to state when the Cherokee annuities first began to be paid to the chiefs & how much has been paid to them, I believe it was in 1819 that the late Agent Colo. [Return J.] Meigs[5] was directed to pay it in any way most agreeable to the chiefs and in that year & up to the year 1830[?] inclusive it was paid to them.

The amt of annuity up to 1827 $10666.66¢ per annum making	$85333.00
Amt recd by them for the 4 mile purchase	20000.00
Amt for 1828–29 & 30 = $6666.66⅔ per an	20000.00
Amt paid the chiefs per annum for distributing the above to the people $1280.00 = per an for Eight years	10240.00
	$135573.00

Signed H. Montgomery Ind Agt"

Although it will be seen from the foregoing the chiefs received an annual sallary for distributing annuities yet *at no time did the people get any of the money which the chiefs received* & got pay for distributing. *They kept all among themselves* & the people got none. However if even this was right at present there are according to the fundamental laws of the Cherokee Nation East no head men—the term of service for which Cherokee officers were constitutionally elected having long since expired. Consequently the annuity could under this act be paid neither to the rich or the poor. It is apprehended the poor people of the Nation will stand in great need of this stipend & therefore humanity would seem to direct a continuance of the course heretofore ordered by the Hon Secy of War—that of distributing to the heads of families in the proportion their number bears to the whole.

BEN F. CURREY Supt Cherokee Emigration

Addressed to House of Representatives and delivered by hand. The writer seems to have been in Washington at this time.

1. A Nashville resident, Currey was at this time a special agent to supervise the westward move of the Cherokees.

2. The letter bore no date. Internal evidence suggests this date.

3. Hugh Montgomery, born in South Carolina, served as United States Agent to the Eastern Cherokees. He was in that position at least as early as 1828.

4. Little is known of him except that he was an associate chief of the Cherokees for a short time.

5. Meigs was born in Connecticut, served in the Revolution, and pioneered in Ohio. He was for many years the United States Agent to the Cherokees; he died at the Cherokee agency in Tennessee in 1823. He was a brother of Josiah Meigs, at one time the Commissioner of the General Land Office. He is not to be confused with his son or a nephew who bore the same name.

FROM ERWIN J. FRIERSON[1]

Dear Sir Shelbyville Tenn. Jany 1st 1834

I wish to take the Globe in which the Congressional debates are published. The price is one dollar which if you will advance for me and subscribe for it for me, I will refund the amount upon your return home. H. M. Watterson[2] requests me to ask you to perform the same service for him and have the paper also sent to him. Nothing new. [Joseph A.] Kincaid, [Jonathan] Webster, John L. Neill, Sam. Mitchell, Israel Fonveal[3] &c &c candidates for convention.

E. J. FRIERSON

N. B. I want the paper from the commencement of the session.

E. J. F.

Addressed to Washington.

1. A Shelbyville lawyer and, at this time, attorney general of the eighth circuit.

2. Harvey M. Watterson was a lawyer who had been editor and publisher of the Shelbyville *Western Freeman*.

3. All of these men had been mentioned frequently as candidates for various local offices. Neill was a former circuit court clerk in Bedford County. While his middle initial is clearly written in this letter, it was actually *T* instead of *L*. See William J. Whitthorne to Polk, February 7, 1834. The last name, Fonveal, is sometimes spelled Fonville. Kincaid and Webster were the successful candidates.

FROM TERRY H. CAHAL

Dear Sir: Columbia Jany 2. 1834

Brown[1] & Cahal want the Intelligencer. Will you be so good as to send your servant now at once before you forget it & have it forwarded to them for *six months only*. I have heretofore taken it and paid to Norvell[2] at Nashville. We will do that again or you can pay it & we will pay you on your return. I hope you will not neglect this. We send for the Intelligencer because the proceedings of Congress & the Speeches are most correctly published in it. I have not written sooner because there was nothing worth communicating. It might be supposed at a distance, that there must be excitement in Tennessee, and deep interest on the subject of a new Constitution. The fact is not so. I have never seen such indifference manifested about any election in my life as that which is to take place next month. It is hardly talked of. If any man writes to you that there is much feeling about it do not credit it. I assure you the fact is not so. There are to be sure, a few men, such as [Peter R.] Booker, who are in a panic and think the very foundations of Society are about to be subverted and an orderly community converted in a revolution mob by it. They expect to see the rich plundered by the *rabble,* as they are pleased to call the people. I see no reason to apprehend any such danger. I do not think they are sufficiently excited. I dislike to see so much apathy manifested about a matter of such paramount importance. My opinions have been disclosed to you in letters. If you recollect them you know I am no demagogue at heart. You know I have always been in favour of order and a stable—yes & I may say a strong government & its laws enforced at all hazzards. But why am I talking of myself. Pardon it. I want to see some changes in the C[onstitution] of Ten. I want almost all the officers except our Judges elected by the people. I do not embrace that doctrine because it is popular, but because it is right & because I want to give them *the little groat* employmt of their own to attend—So that *damn 'em* they can't interfere with other elections & bring the weight of official influence to bear on the *ballot box.* This may be selfish. I know on that score I have personal grievances enough to warp my judgment aside. But if it be an error, it is one which can never be corrected. The people of *all Tennessee* think with me here. If they did not, I feel strong enough, with the aid of the press to make them do it. The Maury vote *must* go that way. That is bold language & perhaps stronger than you are willing to hear, but I am speaking to a man, to whom it is my duty to tell the truth plainly and whose opinions on these matters I desire to know. Will you tell me what it is, the first leisure hour? If you do not desire that your views should be made public, still I should like to know them for *myself.* If they are *confidential,* they shall forever be treated & respected as such. But still they would influence my vote for a member of the Convention. You know by this time, for you have seen it in the Banner, announced that you are a candidate for a seat there. Your name has been frequently mentioned previous to that where I have heard this subject discussed. It is & has every where been conceded by your enemies that you "could be elected for anything in Maury." If you say you will be at home in time, you are sure to be elected. I need not tell you so & don't do it to gain any credit by it. I've never done enough of that for my own interest. I hope, though, your opinions coincide with mine on the subject of these officers. Were we enemies that would gain my support—were we brothers a difference on this point would lose it. I tell you again I am convinced you could be elected in Maury for anything were a hundred men of fifty times my influence opposed to you and that you are sure to be a member of the Convention if you intimate that you can leave Washington, and I am so far from being opposed to it, that I am in hopes we agree on this point, which is the only thing which could prevent me from supporting you. You know better than I do whether a seat there would be likely to conduce to your elevation in future. It would be nonsense to suppose you have not thought of what so many of your friends have looked to, that is, to be the first Governor under the New Constitution. No man would be prouder to see this & none would support you for it more sincerely and more ardently than the man who now speaks his sentiments to you with so little reserve, provided some of your friends, who are & *will* be my enemies without any cause, did not propogate an opinion, that I did it through motives of interest, *hope or fear*. A proud & a spirited man can not like, *even to seem* to be *made* to do what is right. He would rather of his own will do what he knows is wrong. But if the world thinks he acts without motive, then it is pleasant to perform his duty; his head, his heart & his hand all act harmoniously & cheerfully together. In these last few sentences is condensed the charracter of the writer. But I have said enough—may be too much. One request & I am done. Present my kindest respects to Mrs Polk & be so good as to assure her, if I did not visit her last fall, it was not enmity but pride that kept me away. There were reasons which self respect restrains me from explaining and which she would agree with me were sufficiently strong to keep me at home. I am happy that they will not exist on her return. I wish her to understand that they were not *reasons* produced by her husband and much less by herself, for if I have not always been mistaken in her character *she* is incapable of treating anybody amiss. But she can easily conceive that others over whom she has no control can say *things* of a *gentleman,* which compel him so demean himself as not to let his conduct be subject to be misunderstood. Now I am a better friend than many who would profess everything.

TERRY H. CAHAL

P. S. I cant fold this at last. Say to Mrs P. or hand her the letter & let her read for herself, that the dancing mania has returned to Columbia. I have lately been at several parties where they danced, long as the nights are, till near 1 o'clock. I suppose they think the Cholera is gone forever. Or perhaps it is universal rejoicing at the marriage of Dr. [William] McNeill. If she wants to know who is courting—I am out as a beau about the 27th time & am actually courting two girls at this very time. I do not know which I shall marry because I do not know which I can get—whether either. If I ascertain that I can get either (not a very probable thing) I'll take choice, or perhaps upon due reflection wed neither of them. Marriage should be effected in a business like style upon reflection and not perpetrated in a *passion.*

T. H. C.

Addressed to Washington.

1. Probably Allen Brown. It would appear that Brown and Cahal were in partnership at this time.

2. Probably Caleb C. Norvell, a prominent book dealer, newspaper editor, and publisher in Nashville.

FROM CARUTHERS, HARRIS & COMPANY[1]

Dear Sir, N. Orleans Jany 2d 1834

We have just received your favour of 15th ult. and hasten to advise you in reply of the receipt of fifteen bales cotton for your account, received at different times and sold as soon after as the fair market value could be realized; and we wish all your crop was in, and disposed of at the same rates, for we fear the market will not soon offer as good prices. For the last two months it has been steadily going down and within three days past prices have declined from ¾ @ 1.¢. On the 31st ult. 4000 bales Mi & La.[2] changed hands at 10¼ @ 10½¢ & 10¢. could not be had to day for Tennessee cotton. Recent advices, from the European markets are very discouraging and there are symptoms apparent to warrant the expectation of a reaction soon. Annexed please find sales of your cotton proceeds to credit to your account.

If it is not a matter of too much inconvenience, will you do us this favour to send us occasionally such documents or papers as may be calculated to enlighten us respecting the doings at Washington!

CARUTHERS HARRIS & CO.

Addressed to Washington.

1. Madison Caruthers and Adlai O. Harris had formed a New Orleans mercantile and factorage partnership. They did a thriving business in the Columbia area.

2. Mississippi and Louisiana.

FROM WILLIAM H. POLK

Dear Brother Raleigh N. C. Jan 2nd 1833[1834][1]

I received your letter by the last mail and will certainly pay you the money that you advance when I come to be of age but the way you said you would get it here to me it will be three months before I can get it and you know the session commences the 15th of this month and I have got no money to go back to college until I get that. And if you could write to Col [William] Polk and get the money from him and let him have the money when it comes from Tennessee and if he will do it I can get back to college without loosing any time. And if I have to wait until the money comes, from Mr [James] Walker it would be imposable for me to join my class.

You wrote to me to give you the amount of what I owe; 200 dollars will cover my debts. And as next session is the longest I will need 150 dollars but as the fall session is shorter I will try and do that session with a smaller amount. Col Polk let me have the money that you sent by him when he came from Tennessee and I paid off some of my debts but I still owe 200 dollars. You may be asured that I will pay you the money that you let me have to pay debts. Give my love to sister Sarrah and receive the same your self.

WILL. H. POLK

P. S. As to my geting in college on Greek tis a bad chance but I have tryed as hard as could and find that it is not as easy to do as I thought it was. And as I cant enter college on full standing you had better let me go to Nashville or some other college that

I can enter on full standing. I wish when you write me you would send me a little pocket money as I have not had any money in three months.

WILL. H. POLK

Addressed to Washington.

1. Polk's notation that he answered this letter on January 9, 1834, makes it clear that William had made an error in writing the date.

FROM McKAY W. CAMPBELL

Dear Sir Nashville Jany 3d 1834

You will recollect you had the goodness to pay my years Subscription to the National Intelligencer for one year in advance & started me the paper abt this time last year. I took the Intelligencer principally on my fathers account. As it is now unnecessary to take it longer on that account & I prefer the Globe myself being a *"whole hog"* Jackson man, will you be so kind as to have me *discontinued* as a subscriber to the Inteligencer and send the *Globe* to myself & brother addressed thus. *"A. A. & M. W. Campbell*[1] *Springhill Maury* County Ten." Please pay the years advance for the year we will hand you the money on your return.

I have been confined here to my bed room since the middle of Novr. On the 24th Decr. ult. my Father died at his residence in Maury at the very time when my life was dispaired of by my Physicians and my brother who was there then. Misfortunes seem to visit us in rapid succession. My health is now some better & I am able to sit up in my room & I have some hope of being restored eventually to good health again.

I have no news to communicate except such as you will probably have learned ere this. I hope you will have a less boisterous & more pleasant session than you had last year. I am rejoiced to see my much beloved & much revered Political Father in the *ascendant*. I am much pleased with [Thomas Hart] Bentons[2] *blast* at the whitewash committee's Report—or rather defence of their dear *Idol;* my best respects to Maddam Polk & for yourself accept renewed assurance of my continued regard & esteem.

M. W. CAMPBELL

Excuse this incoherent kind of scrawl I hardly understand it myself.

Addressed to Washington.

1. Archibald A. Campbell was a brother of McKay W. Campbell and of Dr. George W. Campbell, who was in France at this time. Their father was Collin Campbell, who died at Spring Hill on December 24, 1833.

2. It is not clear which of Benton's statements is meant here. He was a constant critic of the Bank and its supporters.

FROM ADLAI O. HARRIS

My dear Sir Columbia 3 January 1834

I have made such a disposition of your boys Ben and Jim as will I hope be Satisfactory; at all events it was the best I could do under the circumstances. Ben had declared that he would not go back to Mr. Beanland again, and no inducements that we could offer him appeared to have any effect in changing his determination and sooner than send him back confined (where he would not have staid perhaps if we had got him there) I have hired him at the Iron Works at $100. per year and have written to Mr. Beanland to hire a hand in his place even if he has to give $100. and have but little doubt he will be able to get a good hand at 80 to 90$. I have agreed that he shall come up when you return and you are at liberty to take him at that time or let him Continue at the Works the year out. Jim has consented to return to the Plantation until your return and has gone back. Beanland has very probably been entirely too severe, but Mr. Walker when he visits the District will I promise go to your place and set all things right. [John H.] Bills in a Letter to Mr. Walker of the 30th ulto. says that Chunky Jack has not yet been heard from. I hope all things may get right after a little and that you may receive no more such croaking epistles as the last two or three that I have written to you.

Maury County appears to be determined to Elect you to the Convention, and if you cannot return we should know it as early as possible.

Col. G J Pillow has a wonderful itching I think to be brought out.

Should it be impossible for you to return [Matthew D.] Cooper can probably be elected in your stead.

A O Harris

Addressed to Washington. Letter has been published in Bassett, *Plantation Overseer,* 56–57.

FROM ROBERT P. HARRISON[1]

Dr. Colonel. Shelbyville Ten Jany 3d 1834

I have just noticed in the newspapers your name announced as a Candidate for a seat in the Convention of this State to revise and amend the Constitution, and I earnestly hope it may be in your power to be one of that body.

Though you know my feelings to well on that Subject for me to say much at this time, we have a shower of Candidates in Bedford (to Wit) Coln *Jonathan* [Webster], Col. [Samuel] Mitchell, Docr [Joseph] Kincaid, Col. John L. Neil, Israel Fonville old Majr. Holt & Aron Gamble[2]—and perhaps there may be some others. There is a considerable excitement in the different counties in regard to who shall be the members, and I sincerely hope such selections may be made as may prove to the interest and Honor of the State of Tennessee.

My Dr. Sir before I close this hasty address I must remind you the conversation that took place between you and myself when I saw you last in regard to my wish to obtain an appointment, under the government in case there should any vacanceys occur that in your Judgement would suit me.

Owing to my misfortunes by *Cholera* and otherwise makes me doubly anxious and knowing that you would have no hesitancy in aiding me in anything of the kind is the cause of my making known to you my wishes &c.

I know not what vacanceys has or will occur during the present congress, but have concluded an appeal of this kind if it availed nothing it would be no injury to any one.

I therefore Submit my wishes & intentions (in confidence) to you for your consideration, with a firm belief that you would at all times take such steps in my behalf, as would be calculated to terminate to my interest and prosperity.

Ro P Harrison

PS. Should you have leasure enough to answer the above, I should be glad to hear from you &c.

Addressed to Washington.

1. For many years Harrison kept a hotel in Shelbyville. In 1836 he became clerk and master of the Bedford County chancery court.

2. The Major Holt mentioned here is not otherwise identified. Aaron Gambill was a Revolutionary War veteran and a Bedford County farmer.

FROM WILLIAM JENKINS[1]

Dear Sir, Thompsons Creek Bedfd. Cty Ten, Jany 3. 1834

I will take the liberty of addressing a few lines to you, for the first time, believing that they will be received by you, as from one whose welfare you are daily studying *to promote* in the halls of Congress.

A sense of duty urges me to address a line to you inasmuch as there has been a *reaction* in my mind in your favour. As *you know,* I did not vote for you at the last election in this district. My reasons were, (and I was honest in my objections) that you were opposed to the *rechartering* of the U S Bank. I then thought your policy unsafe, and dangerous, and as an honest man, I could not give my suffrage to one who held opinions as I believed wrong. But, since, the appearances of the Report of my old friend Mr [Roger B.] Taney (who lived with me, in Fredk. Md.) all my objections to you, and your policy, have entirely subsided. And if the Report alluded to contains fair statements—*Crush it forever!!* It is a *Monopoly* which ought not to exist among us, and I hope you will use your untiring vigilance to *stop an evil,* which is ominious, of such dangerous result. Now Sir, think not strange of this conduct of mine. It is a universal *rule of my life* if I find that I am wrong—*I repent.* And those interested always know it from my own mouth, or pen. Therefore in future, so long as you remain before your constituents for an office, holding the same views as you now do, my feeble support among *my people* will be for you.

In your sending the message to the citizens of this district, you have omitted to send it to three of your friends, than whom stronger friends, no man ever had, to wit, Adam Eules, Nimrod Burrow, & D. P. T House.[2] They feel a little hurt, to be missed. Now I know you cannot think of every one, neither do I suppose copies are printed, to furnish every one. Upon the receipt of this, if you have any more copies please send them, as it will be of service to you.

Since your last election, I have been appointed P M. at Thompsons Creek. My bond has been received at the Dept. I have taken charge of the office & have been looking every mail for my sealed commission. As yet it has not arrived. I would be glad if you would speak to the P. M. General (as tis too delicate for me) and ascertain the cause of the delay, and report it to me forthwith.

I would like to hear from you as often as your other engagements will allow. And should you ever in *"passing up and down"* visit Thompsons Creek, I would esteem it a favour if you could come one night with me at my house.

My family are well.

W Jenkins

Addressed to Washington.

1. Other than that he had lived in Frederick, Maryland, and was postmaster at Thompson Creek, facts revealed in this letter, little has been learned about Jenkins.

2. Adam Eules was an early settler in the area, coming from North Carolina in 1810. Nimrod Burrow was a son of Philip Burrow, one of Bedford County's earliest inhabitants. House has not been identified. The reference to the message is obscure. It is possible that it was Jackson's annual message to Congress.

FROM SILAS M. CALDWELL

Dr. Sir Fayette County[1] Jany 4th 1834

I am now sitting by the fire at your plantation. I reached this place on yesterday Evening and regret very much that I am not able to give you as much information about your business here as should wish. You I suppose have heard before this that Jack

& Ben had ran away from your farm. Two or three days since a man by the name of Hughs who was in persuit of some men who had stolen a Negro on the Mississippi River stoped at a hut on the bank of the River to make some enquiries. Whilst there two white Men & Jack come up to the house to make some enquiries about the same men that Hughs was. That circumstance gave rise to suspicion and they having Jack chained Hughs judged they had stolen Jack and that the other men were partners of theirs took the whitemen & Jack and put them all in Jail in St Helena in Arkansas Territory about 80 miles below Memphis. Jack confessed they had stolen him at Memphis and that he belonged to William Polk[2] and was hired at your farm. They all were going down the River in a scift. He caught them 150 miles below Memphis; they were going to the province of Texas. Hughs got on a steam boat come to Memphis from there here and up to George Moores. I got George to come down and him and Beenland started the evening I got here after Jack. Hughs says it requires two to proove property in Arkansas; in consequence of that I had no time to chat with Beenland.

Mr Hughs charge for apprehending Jack and expenses is about $140. I refused to pay that amount but authorized George if he got Jack to pay him $100 which I thot a fair compensation. I also directed George to sell Jack there if he could get a fair price for him; if he brot him back to take him up to his house and let you have a hand in his place which he will do. I expect he will not stay here. Ben is in Maury & refuses to come back. If Jim is not exchanged he will return. I wrote to day to [Adlai O.] Harris to iron Ben and send him back (Ben is a bad boy). Your negroes here are very much dissatisfied. I believe I have got them quieted. Some others spoke of running away. Harris wrote to Beenland to hire a hand down here in the place of Ben. I judg from that he is not to be sent back. I told Mr. Parker[3] to day to hire one if he could. Harris authorized Beenland to give $100. I directed Parker to give that if not for less. I have not been able to collect any money for you, Beenland being absent and the weather & roads so extremely bad I cant get to Tipton. I saw Carter[4] to day; he has no money but has agreed to pay you Smith accounts & Smith for you[. . .]. I saw Mr. Smith[5] to day; he is willing to take Carter for the

Or[?] debt. The whole face of the country is frozen over. I saw you Merchant to day he is willing to wait until I come down in April. Your account in the store up to the first of this month is $165. In that there is about 13 gallons of whiskey & some coffee I told the merchant I would only pay for 4 gallons, the Balance Fitzgerald[6] must pay also the Coffee.

You[r] account since Beenland came here including the patent Balences, is $35. I will attend to collecting your money & paying you accounts in April when I come down. Beenland has got your crop gathered, made 25 Bales of cotton, has about one of the cribs full of corn in the shucks, about 4 stacks of fodder, Killed 4000 pounds of Pork. He will need at least 50 Barrels corn; it is worth $2.50 Cents pr. Barrel. I know of none for sale in the neighborhood nor has he money to buy with. I expect I shall have some to spare. I will know by April. Beenland has just commenced his new ground. I cant tell how he will do but I am fearfull not quite as well as you expected. I think he lacks stability. I think he has got along badly with the negroes. The negroes say he likes his Liquor, but let that rest as Negro news; if it is the fact it will appear. Elizabeths child died last night; she smothered it somehow. No person knew it was dead until this morning. It was a very fine child, Born the day you & me left this. I had it Buried to day. Maria has a fine boy about one Month old. I Bot you a very fine mule and Brot down with me. I gave $100 for it out of a drove. Your stock looks very well here, your negroes have plenty of Milk. I think if Beenland would be more mild with the negroes he would get along with them better tho I dont know this from observation. I shall leave this in the morning for my farm. Any information I can from you[r] farm at any time I give it to you. Write me as soon as you recive this.

S. M. Caldwell

Addressed to Washington. This letter has been published in Bassett, *Plantation Overseer,* 57–59. Bassett's version omitted some portions of the text, and some of his editing is at variance with the above.

1. This letter was actually posted in Bolivar, Hardeman County.

2. William H. Polk, still a minor, had inherited the slave from his father, Sam Polk.

3. Unidentified.

4. Probably Archibald B. Carter, a resident of Fayette County. Later in the year Polk bought a slave from him. The nature of Carter's indebtedness to Polk has not been learned.

5. Unidentified. It seems likely that he was the same Smith who was a partner in the mercantile establishment Armour, Lake, and Smith.

6. Unidentified.

TO WILLIAM POLK

Dear Sir Washington City Jany 5th 1834

I have received several letters from brother William since I have been here, the last of which was written at Raleigh on the 26th ult. Supposing it possible that he might still be at Raleigh I enclose to you a letter for him. If he has returned to the University, will you forward it to him.

In regard to his debts contracted without my authority and against my express order, I have written to him, that I have no authority as executor to pay them, but that if he will write to me that he will contract no more debts, and that the excess over $300 pr. annum shall be paid out of his own estate, that I would make arrangements to have the money forwarded to you for him. I have written to him, that for the future he must limit his expenses within $300 pr. year, and that if he exceeds that sum the excess must be paid out of his own estate.

I have to request you however to furnish him, with the amount which may be necessary for his next Session's tuition, board and the necessary expenses. His debts already contracted must remain over until I hear from him. If it is convenient for you to make the advance to him of the amt. which may be necessary for the next Session, I will thank you do so, and write to me the amt. that I may cause it to be remitted to you.

William writes to me that he wishes to leave the University and go to Nashville. I have answered him that he cannot be permitted do so, but must remain. I have written him further, as indeed I had before done, that he must employ his vacations in bringing up his Greek studies, so as to enable him to be in regular standing in his class. I hope he will do so, though I confess I have my fears he will not. I hope you will give him such advise and directions as you may think right.

Your son *Rufus*[1] spent a few days here during the holidays. I took him to the President's who treated him with great kindness, invited to dine &c. and I dined with him at the President's. He was very well and is I think a very promising boy. I am sorry to learn that you have been in feeble health since you left Tennessee, but hope when I next hear from you to learn, that your health is restored.

Mrs. P. desires to be kindly remembered to Mrs. P. and yourself.

JAMES K. POLK

Addressed to Raleigh, North Carolina. Letter is in the Polk Family of North Carolina Papers, Division of Manuscripts, Library of Congress. It has been published in Bergeron, editor, "My Brother's Keeper," *North Carolina Historical Review,* XLIV, 199–201.

1. Rufus King Polk, not quite twenty years old, was a student at the University of Virginia at this time. After his father's death, he left school, and in 1835 he moved to Maury County, Tennessee, to take up his inheritance. He died in 1843.

FROM McKAY W. CAMPBELL

Dear Sir, Columbia January 7th 1834

I wrote to you some time since on the subject of some documents belonging to the heir of Mr Francis O'Harra. Col. Toland of Phil. informed me that Mr. Denny a member of Congress from Pittsburg Penn was probably the son-in-law of Mr. O'Harra & would in all probability arrange the business.[1] I should be gratified to hear from you on the business. I notice that the *Immortal "Zip Coon"*[2] has called up his old land relinquishing bill. I hope Congress will not relinquish untill the warrants are satisfied. *Col Polk—I wish* you would be *so kind* as to let me know what division the U. States government will probably do with regard to the Winchester & Thompson lines on the south boundary. Thompsons line you know, is said to be the true 35° of N. Latitude & our State has recognized *it* as her Southern Boundary & has extended her jurisdiction & County lines *to it*. I am *particularly interested* in the decision on the question. I believe myself *& hope* the U. S. will allow it to belong to the State of Tennessee to be appropriated to the satisfaction of Warrants. I would be very *thankfull indeed* for the *best information* you can give me on the subject. If it is relinquished to the state of Ten. our legislature will win the warrant holding by giving it to occupants.

There is another subject Col. Polk in which myself & several of your friends here feel a *good-deal* interested & on which we need your *notions.* It is the construction of that part of the Treaty with the Chickesaw Indians which provides for the sale of their lands. Are we to understand that lands are to be *Sold* without *reserve* to the highest bidder? Or will they be considered as purchased by the United States at Governments price ($1.25) if no individual should bid more? We should be glad to know before hand the notion of the general Government on this subject. I would like to have your notion of the time when the sale will probably take place.

You will no doubt have noticed in the Nashville paper *yourself* announced as a candidate for the convention. You will likewise notice in *our* paper of the 6th Inst. *a call,* or *rather* a nomination which *ought* to have appeared in the W.M.[3] of the 30th ult. We felt authorised to say (not that you were a candidate, but) that you would serve as a *Delegate,* if elected. It seems to be the almost unanamous wish of the people that there should be no candidates, in the usual sense of the word. I have never seen the parties here disposed to unite before this occasion. *All say,* by word & deed, they want *"no Sapling chance." All* seem spontaniously to fix on yourself & Cobbs[4] as the *men.* I look on the other nominations as *rather* complimentary than otherwise.

I had expected the paper I requisted you to send me long since. I am rather surprised, that Mr. Denny has not answered my letter on the subject of the O'Harra Land Warrants before this time. I am anxious to know what to depend on about them. Will you do what you *can* for me toward getting them? Dr. [John B.] Hays started to Nashville early Sunday morning to see Mrs Levin.[5] He could not have got there to see her *alive.* Yes—She's gone! She's gone! "She's from us torn." The aye best woman that e'er was born—but we need not *mourn her* fate. Heaven sure has some favorite Niche for so splendid a Gem of Creation.

M. W. Campbell

Mrs Polk—I have had the pleasure of seeing the *Ladies* of your family connection to day in Company with Dr. Thos Barbour (Son of the Honble. P. P. Barbour of Virginia) and his *lady.* Mrs Barbour was returning the first *visits* of your sisters Mrs. J. Walker, Mrs Harris & Mrs Hays. Dr. Barbour *is* what you would expect the son of our distinguished countryman *P. P. Barbour* to be—a Scholar, learned in his profession & in every respect *a gentleman.* Mrs Barbour is a *plain, modest inteligent* and *amiable* woman. They are both, as I understand, members of the church (Presbyterian) & as I think a valuable acquisition to our society. We have been quite gay here this last month [. . .][6] Cotilion & several private parties. I believe Dr. McNeils getting [. . .] "put life & [. . .] in their heels"—even Mr. *J* Walker said [. . .] more like having a *"frolic"* at the Dr. Wedding than he had done in a great while. Mr. [Hillary] *Langtry* & Miss *Ellen Maguire*[7] attendants had really a pleasant & merry evening. The Old Drs. supper was excellent, his wines &c etc *better* & neither of them dealt with *sparingly.* We *all* partook of them as we ought to do of good things, when they come without money & without price *Freely.* What's past is done gone—let it go—tis well but whats to come grieves *me* & concerns *us old Bachelors* more. 'Tis said the Georgia *Nulifier* has become a *Union* man, expectation is *tiptoe*—& almost every one has a day of their own set for Miss Bradshaw & Mr. Gordon[8] to be married. The weather being extremely severe & unpleasant since Thursday last the *Ladies* have been very much confined, until *today,* they have ventured out a little—*therefore* nothing *new.* There are some, *O,* that would be *men,* have an "itching palm" to be called out as candidates for the convention but the *stupid common such folks,* cant see the *beam of glory,* in *their* (O) *eye,* which they (the people) perceive the motes of *excellency* in *those* they have *called.*

M. W. Campbell

Your relations here with the exception mentioned are all in life & health. Hope you will enjoy yourself this session. I was in great hopes that *Tennessee* would have been in the Chair.[9] Mrs. P, I wish you would [. . .] the Col. for me occasionally about these *little matters.* He has his *head* so full of governmental *"ways & means"*—that he'll never think of my poor little ways & means. My respects to my *Relations* at Washington.

Addressed to Washington.

1. See Campbell to Polk, November 23, 1833.

2. David Crockett.

3. Columbia *Western Mercury*.

4 Robert L. Cobbs.

5. Ann Hays, daughter of Andrew Hays of Nashville, married Lewis C. Levin in 1833. She had visited in the home of Dr. John B. Hays, her uncle, and this seems to be a reference to her death.

6. At this point a part of the manuscript is torn away. Each of the ellipses represents no more than two missing words.

7. A sister of Patrick Maguire.

8. George W. Gordon and Elizabeth Bradshaw were married on January 14, 1834. Gordon was the Georgia nullifier mentioned.

9. Andrew Stevenson had been re-elected Speaker of the House in December 1833, contrary to rumors that he would receive a foreign appointment.

FROM GEORGE W. HAYWOOD

Moulonvert, Bedford County. January 7, 1834

Haywood informs Polk that Samuel Bigham, postmaster at Livingston (formerly Rock Creek), has sold his land and will live on the plantation of Levi Cochran, a young farmer in the section of Bedford that was incorporated into Marshall County in 1836.[1] Bigham wants to continue serving as postmaster if that is legal and Haywood asks Polk to investigate the possibility.

Addressed to Washington.

1. Cochran was a major in the militia and later became a brigadier general. He became one of the leading citizens of Marshall.

FROM JOHN A. MOORE[1]

State of Tennessee Bedford County

Dear Col. Jany 7th 1834

After my respect to you as a worthy and confidential friend I would say to you that my family and friends are Generaly well.

I have not received a letter from you since you have ben in Congress. I would like to hear from you and the news Generaly. Write to me soon as I would be glad to hear from you &c. We have a grate many Candidates out as Deligates for the Convention and Militeary officears. In the 28th Regt I was Elected Col. Commandant without opposition and Captn. [Willie B.] Watkins 1st Mjr over Capt [Henry C.] Hastings a majority of 82 Votes &c.[2]

Bedford County is made a Brigade and Col [Robert] Cannon and Col [Ephraim] Hunter[3] is the Candidates for Brigade General. The Election Comes on the 7th Day of February next. I think Col. Cannons chance Verry good to Be Elected Gen. We have three Canedates out for Lt. Col. in the room of Cannon Majrs. [William] Murphree, [John W.] Hamlin & [William C.] Read,[4] and I think It very Douptful at this time which will be Elected Col. The Election is the 23rd Day of this month. Capt. Arnold and Hamilton[5] for 2nd Majr. Thear is a greate deal said about the Candidates for the Convention. I think Col. [Samuel] Mitchells Chance Verry god for one member as I think he will run well in the County Generaly.

The Candidates for the Convention are Col. Mitchell, Col John Neal[Neill] and Col Jonathan Webster, Dr. Kingcade [Kincaid] Majr Holt[6] and Esqr [Israel] Fonveal &c. I have nothing more I believe that is new worth your attention. Thear is a grate many people maryings. E. J. Frierson is mared to Miss Harison[7] of Shelbyville. I saw your friend Col. Yell a few Days a go and he is will and famley. Nothing more But Remain Your friend and well wisher till Death.

John A. Moore

Addressed to Washington.

1. A native of North Carolina, he was a prosperous farmer in Bedford County.

2. Little is known about these men. Their first names have been supplied from records of the militia.

3. A farmer and merchant who lived at Farmington. He was active in the affairs of Marshall County after its organization in 1836.

4. Names supplied from militia records. The men are otherwise unidentified.

5. Neither Arnold nor Hamilton has been identified.

6. Several Holts held offices in the county militia, and it is not clear which one was intended here.
7. Ann Harrison, daughter of Robert P. Harrison of Shelbyville.

FROM JAMES C. WILSON

Washington. January 7, 1834

A War Department clerk, Wilson pleads for an increase in pay for all government clerks. He points out inequities in the existing pay scale and maintains that with his large family he cannot live in Washington on his current salary.

Addressed to Washington.

FROM JOEL YANCEY[1]

Dear friend Glasgow [Kentucky] Jan 7 1834

How sincerely I do rejoice that you are in Congress at this very critical and important conjunction of our affairs, when I am sincerely sorry to be impelled to say if I tell the truth that there are many intelligent eloquent men in both chambers of the national legislature who under the influence of the most demoniac, exorbitant and inordinate ambitions are indefatigably exerting themselves, to embarrass and thwart the wise patriotic and intense views of our present illustrious friend at the helm, the great Jackson [. . .]. I trust that he by the aid of yourself and other fervent republicans of the Jeffersonian school will triumph over them as he did over the British on 8 January 1815, and that we have faithful [. . .] vigilant and incorruptible sentinels enough in the HR to sustain effectually the principles our good president was elected and reelected on, and that the insatiable thirst of our opponents after undelegated and despotic power, will be Signally rebuked & defeated this very Session, and that the Hydra headed monster the Bank of the US will be effectually decapitated, and exterminated by the generous and inflexible democratic Hercules's in the H R. How glad I am that your motion prevailed to reconsider the vote referring Secy Taneys report on the removal of the deposites to the committee of the whole; and that it is referred to that of Ways & Means over which you preside. Well may Messrs. McDuffie & Binney (par nobile fratrum)[2] dread the developments that will no doubt be elicited by the thorough Jeffersonian scrutiny which I am sure you will make. That very Bank my dear friend is the [. . .] which with its pestiferous influence, has so much defeated the republicans of Ky & elsewhere. I have not the least doubt but it sent money to this district to defeat my election at [. . .]. I watch every Globe with the most intense anxiety to see some glorious victory won by the Whig party. May the God of liberty, virtue & genuine[?] patriotism dwell with you all, and enable you to prostrate the combined efforts of the nullifiers & Clay men, & that you may completely discomfit the Machiavelian intrigues & machinations of the Federal Bank, nullifying & doublefaced party you have to compete with & that your fortitude & resolution may be equal to that of Shadrack, Meshack & Abednego when they resisted the impious proclamation of Nebuchadnezzar King of Babylon and that very Deity who went through the flames with them and rendererd them intangible[?], incombustible & invulnerable to the Tartarean flames will stand by you in your holy struggles for virtue, liberty, & Union, & then Sir you and me and the blessed sons of this dear republic, will stand redeemed & shine conspicuous & brilliant as a pillar of fire amidst a world of benighted despotism, lighting the path of unborn millions to the Temple of liberty; & lend defiance to all the treacherous ebullitions of traitors, & with virtue, union & pure patriotism, will sweep them with the Broom of destruction as rivers of melted Lava from the frater[crater] of Mount Vesuvius do the herbage on that Mountain. My heart is full I write too long. Will you shew this to our friend brother [Andrew] Stevenson Speaker & the rest of our faithful Coadjutors in libertys holy cause, and may God of his infinite mercy preserve the Union of our dear Country entire, as long as the mountains stand & the rivers run.

Joel Yancey

Addressed to Washington.

1. Formerly Polk's colleague in the House of Representatives, 1827–31.

2. George McDuffie and Horace Binney were "a noble pair of brothers" in their support of the Bank of the United States.

FROM WILLIAM G. ANGEL[1]

My Dear Sir Urbanna Steuben Co N Y Jany 8th 1834

I perceive by the Globe that you have been answering McDuffies Bank Speech and that your reply is to be published in pamphlet form for distribution.[2] Dont fail to send me a copy as soon as published. At present I am in the way of assisting my son (a mere boy) to edit a small weekly paper printed in this county.

We have undertaken to expose the wickedness as well as unconstitutionality of the Bank. Any document you may furnish me in regard to the subject will be most gratefully received.

I am gratified to see that you have such a decided majority in the house opposed to that infernal institution. If its corrupting charms can be kept out of the house you will seal the death doom of the monster. I am sorry to see that some of my most esteemed friends take the side of the Bank against the Executive. I dont now suspect them of being in love with the Bank but I fear they are yielding too much to the influence of their dislike of the president on account of the proclamation.[3] I disliked the proclamation but it seems to me that, that dislike could furnish no excuse for me to go with the Bank party if I were now in congress. Every measure should be supported or opposed on the ground of its intrinsic character. I am afraid that some of the votes in congress have been given on other grounds.

A year ago I would have enlisted for life to serve the principles avowed by [Augustin S.] Clayton, [Thomas F.] Foster, [William S.] Archer[4] and the other honest state rights men. How can I account for their votes for the Bank. They declare the charter unconstitutional. How can the president be blameable for with holding the public monies from the custody of an institution which has no constitutional or legal existence? Any other body of individuals in the nation have the same right to demand the use of the deposits as the stock holders of the Bank. What rights have vested in them under a void charter? The law creating the Bank is no more than a blank leaf in the statute book. What *law* then is violated or what *rights* are infringed? I have to express my regret that the Bank charter derives a seeming constitutional existence from the support of the constitutional restrictionists. I esteem the gentlemen I have named. I feel bound to them by the strong affinity of views and feelings mutually entertained by us when I had the honor of a seat with them in the house of Representatives. I still regard them as high minded honorable men having the love of country deep at heart. But I lament that their strong desire to steer clear of Scylla has cast them upon Charybdis. Please write me and send me useful documents &c.

W. G. ANGEL

PS. Direct to the place where this is dated

Addressed to Washington.

1. A member of the House of Representatives from New York, 1829–33.

2. McDuffie's speech on removal of deposits ended on December 23, 1833, and Polk's famous speech began December 30, 1833, and lasted until January 2, 1834. Polk's speech was, indeed, published in pamphlet form and was widely circulated.

3. Perhaps Jackson's proclamation in reply to South Carolina's nullification proclamation.

4. All three were members of the House of Representatives and had been Angel's colleagues in that body. Clayton and Foster were from Georgia, and Archer was from Virginia.

FROM JESSE D. ELLIOTT

Boston. January 8, 1834

Through an unidentified friend, Colonel Earle, Elliott, controversial naval officer at the Battle of Lake Erie and subsequently holder of several different commands, reports that he is sending to Polk a piece of the ship *Constitution.*

Addressed to Washington.

FROM GALES AND SEATON

Office of the National Intelligencer,
January 8, 1834

Sir:

We have read, in a report of the conclusion of your late speech in the House of Representatives, purporting to have been corrected by yourself, as published in the Globe of yesterday, and transferred to-day to the columns of the National Intelligencer, the following passage:

"Was not the bank, to all intents and purposes, the bona fide owner of the National Intelligencer, and, in point of fact, was it not the real, if not ostensible and nominal printer to that House?"

So long as the allegation implied in the question thus put by you, in addressing the Chair of the House of Representatives, was confined to the columns of the party press, which every one knows is not very nice in its discrimination between truth and error, we did not conceive that we were called upon to make any specific reply to it. As, however, these allegations have made such an impression on your mind as to induce you to urge them in argument before the elevated and honorable body of which you are a member, we owe it to you to undeceive you, and, through you, the public, in the matter in question. The charge having been publicly made, from a source so respectable, shall be publicly met and answered.

We therefore do here explicitly state, in answer to the question you have publicly put, that the bank is not, either bona fide or mala fide, to any intent or purpose whatsoever, "owner of the National Intelligencer." We do therefore, also, further state, that the bank is neither the real, ostensible, nor nominal printer to the House of Representatives, and that no one is legally entitled to that honor but the undersigned. We do, moreover, further state, that for the latter suggestion, whatever you have been told (as we have no doubt you have) to the contrary, there is not the slightest foundation, nor even the shadow of a pretence.

Gales & Seaton

Addressed to Washington. The original has not been located; a printed version appears in the *Register of Debates in Congress,* 23d Cong., 1st Sess., 2289–2290.

FROM ADLAI O. HARRIS

Dear Sir Columbia 8 Jany 1834

I have the pleasure to inform you that Chunky Jack has been heard from. He was taken up at Helena A[rkansas] Territory and Geo Moore who it seems got the information has gone after him. I hope after all the difficulties that things may yet go on well at the Plantation and that Beanland may make you a good crop.

The weather has been so excessively cold for the last week that I have heard but little Politics. The general voice says that you must return and I hope that you may be able to lay the Monarch Bank on the shelf and so dispose of other important matters as to be able to leave the Palace and come back to attend to Home affairs.

Naomi[1] says that she is very anxious to receive a Letter from Sarah. All well.

A. O. Harris

Addressed to Washington.

1. Wife of Adlai Harris and sister of Polk.

FROM ISAAC J. THOMAS

Dear Sir Columbia Jany. 8th 1834

We have nothing of a local nature that is interesting. We have had a very cold spell of weather but is now moderating. The health of our county is generally good. Some cases of Typhoid Fever. I again take the liberty to say to you that if you can say any thing to the Honrable Lew Cass that would cause him to give me the appointment of visitor to West Point accademy I would be very much gratified as I have a great desire to visit the North.

Isaac J. Thomas

Addressed to Washington.

FROM JOHN W. YEATS

Fayette County. January 8, 1834

A former resident of Pulaski, Yeats acknowledges letters from Polk and from the Treasury Department and indicates that he has again petitioned Congress for compensation for losses of property during the Seminole campaign.[1]

Presumably addressed to Washington, but the envelope is missing.
1. See Yeats to Polk, December 31, 1832.

FROM GERRARD T. GREENFIELD

Columbia. January 9, 1834

After thanking Polk for assistance in sale of some land in Maryland,[1] Greenfield encloses a deed for the buyer and requests Polk to get the funds due on the transaction transferred to a Nashville bank.

Addressed to Washington.
1. See Greenfield to Polk, December 18, 1833.

FROM JAMES WALKER

Dear Sir, Columbia Jan 9th 1834

Finding that Donly is making every exertion to take advantage of me, and if possible to throw me off the line between Nashville & Tuscumbia, I send you enclosed copies of papers which will show you the true situation of the controversy he has thought proper to bring about. I addressed the P M G. yesterday giving him a very full account of Donly's conduct in this business, which letter I gave him the option to receive as a confidential one or *official* at his pleasure. I think Majr Barry an honest correct man, but I cannot resist the conviction that Majr. Lewis has influenced him to act in this matter unbecomeing the dignified station which he occupies—and my confidence in the Department being somewhat impaired, I do not know what advantages Donly (with the aid of Lewis & Eaton's influence) may take of me. I have always heretofore looked upon Eaton as so far my friend that he would do me justice. I am not now sure of that, unless misrepresentations are made. I therefor send you enclosed copies of a document which Donly required of the agent at Nashville on the 1st. of January—also a copy of the agreement which was made respecting the running of the line which is to "exist until the P M G makes a different decision or order on the subject"—this was inserted at Donly's request, and I have every reason to believe he intends some further advantage of me if he can by any means get it. I am acting correctly in this matter, and do not mean to yield any just right to any influence whatever. I think Donly's next move will be to insist that I have forfeited because I did not take his property on the 1st. of Jany. & make a joint partnership with him. This will be fully explained by the copy of the document I send you signed by M. T. Simpson[1] (the agent of the P. O D) and the copy that I send you of the endorsement on the back of the acceptance to S. B. Ewing & Co. & Lewis that I never agreed to make a *part*nership with either Caruthers & Kinkle *or their assigns.* If the plea *as to property* fails, I think he will next attempt to destroy the character of Caruthers & Kinkle, on account of the manner the mail has been conveyed between Doaks & Natchez, the last contract, and insist, that Walker & Brown's connexion with S. B. Ewing & Co. ought to forfeit their interest in these Contracts between Nashville & Tuscumbia & Huntsville. These are all very foolish efforts as I should judge of intelligent and just men are to be the judges—but I think my interest at Washington requires some attention and *watching,* and I depend on you, Grundy, Dunlap, Johnson & Inge to see that justice is done & no *advantages taken.* From the manner Donly once acted towards your father & me, we know that Donly is capable of any unprincipled act that he thinks will answer his purposes.

I have had an interview with Caruthers in relation to our mail concerns. He has given me such information and explanations, that I am satisfied with Caruthers & Kinkle *for the present.* We agreed on a truce of our quarrel for the present, and if the line between here & Huntsville is restored to its original standing, *all things are to be square between us.* I wish to be friendly with Caruthers & Kinkle on several accounts one of which is that I like them, and Caruthers stood up to me in my trouble with Donly at Nashville on the 1st. of Jan. Another is that Mr. [Clement C.] Clay is their particular friend & you & him I believe are on the best of terms. It is decidedly my interest and feeling for Caruthers & Kinkle to be sustained in all assaults that John Donly, or his friends (or John Bell through this influence) may make on them. Still I do not think the main mail to New Orleans from Nashville ought to be permitted to go by Murfreesboro & Mobile, or that the Coach line from here to Huntsville ought to be permitted to be *cut down* under any circumstances. I feel every confidence that any difficulties will be satisfactorily adjusted between Caruthers & Kinkle and us, and that the Huntsville line is to be restored, which will heal all wounds.

James Walker

PS. I send you the original acceptance to S. B. Ewing & Co. Enclose it to me again, so soon as you find no further use for it at Washington.

Addressed to Washington.

1. A native of Pennsylvania, Michael T. Simpson was in 1835 the Superintendent of the Dead Letter Office.

FROM JAMES WALKER

Dear Sir, Columbia, Jany 9th 1834

I yesterday received a letter from Geo. Moore enclosing one from the sheriff at Helena, Arkansas (80 miles below Memphis) informing that Chunky Jack had been taken up & put in Jail there. He was found in Company with two white men under suspicious circumstances, and all were taken up & confined in Jail, the white men committed for negro stealing, of which from the circumstances related they are doubtless guilty. Moore writes me he was about starting to Helena after Jack, and spoke of selling him, fearful of the bad example of bringing him back among the other negroes, and as Jack had made such a break, he thought there was no security in trying to keep him. I shall be sorry if he does sell him, altho, it may be best so for William,[1] but I do not like under any circumstances to sell property in his situation. But as Moore has gone after him, with the best intentions, if he should sell, we must make the best of it. When Moore was here, I charged him to get hold of Chunky & Little Ben if possible, but did not think of selling, and if he does sell I shall regret it—tho it may be best so for his owner. So soon as I hear more on this subject I will write you. Mr. Harris has written you all about Little Ben, and given you the reasons why he sent him to the Iron-works. If you do not like this arrangement Ben can be taken from the works, and disposed of as you direct. I enclose you a small scrip from the post-office advertisement, which will throw some light on the controversy Donly seems disposed to make about his property. I had an abundance of property taken from our lost Routes, for our part of this line, & was under no obligations agreeable to the post-office advertisement to take any of his property at any time. My letter to Majr Barry will fully explain this matter and perhaps he may shew it to you. I am determined not to yield an inch in this matter, and in no respect to submit to wrong from Donly, but if I am to have much further controversy about it, I would prefer higher game than John Donly.

JAMES WALKER

Addressed to Washington.

1. The slave in question was the property of William H. Polk, brother of James K. Polk.

FROM JOHN EWING[1]

Sir, Washington Jan 10 1834

Having submitted a resolution touching the creation of a National currency,[2] or a National Bank to be solely owned and directed by the several states, it is but natural that I should feel some anxiety in relation to the result. The currency contemplated by the resolution is not prohibited by the unexpired term of the present corporate U. S. Bank charter; nor would the establishment of such a Bank by a law subject to amendment and annual revision, be any infringement of that contract. I am one of those who concientiously believe, that the best interests of the union require a general, uniform currency; and that before the present defective currency, or the present objectionable U. S. Bank charter be allowed to abate, a proper and safe substitute should be provided. The local credit of *state Banks,* will afford no proper substitute to the west for a general currency. Leaving out of view the important consideration of their evident infringment upon constitutional prohibitions, and powers, they cannot give equal currency to their issues, nor extend their credit with equal safety and effect. But, I claim your attention at this time, to the charter of a recent Bank contemplated in Indiana, and with every feeling and disposition to end the present corporate Banking powers of the existing Bank of U States, I beg your attention to the 20th section.

JNO. EWING

Addressed to Washington.

1. A representative from Indiana, Ewing was serving his first term. He became a Whig and subsequently served a second term in the House of Representatives, 1837–39.

2. On December 18, 1833, Ewing offered his resolution in behalf of a national currency of thirty-five million dollars and of requiring the Ways and Means Committee to investigate the expediency of such a program. The House approved his resolution.

FROM ANDREW C. HAYS

Dear Sir, Columbia Ten Jan. 10. 1834

My absence to Mississippi for some time, together with the multiplicity of business attendant on a change of our establishment from this to that state, is my apology for not having written you before this.

I presume that you have been apprised, that your name is in nomination, for one of our delegates to the Convention and will in a short time inform as whether or not you can accept of the nomination. Efforts have been, and are still making to get others out, but as yet without success, the belief that you will *accept,* is the reason why we have not a host of Candidates. Your friends seem to be resolved to run you, and unless your *public duties* be an *insurmountable objection,* I hope you will gratify them. They are impatient to hear from you on the subject.

Your situation as chairman of the Committee of W & M. I hear often spoken of as highly *honorable* and *responsible.* Your appointment to chairman of it was gratifying to your friends, and equally mortifying to your enemies. I have however heard it suggested by some of your *good friends,* that you may not leave the present congress with the same reputation with which you entered—"*they fear* that there is too great might of talent against you on the Bank Question" &c. I am aware that in your present situation you have highly *responsible* and *arduous* duties to perform, as well as talented men to oppose, which will require an active exercise of all your powers. Yet I believe that you have sufficient energy and qualifications to disappoint these *friendly* predictions. Upon this subject, yr true friends here have formed high expectations of your usefulness, and I doubt not but that you will endevor to merit their confidence.

Several articles have lately appeared in the Mercury upon the subject of Convention, some Editorial, others under the head of Communications. Most of these communications are, I believe, from the pen of Mr. [A. O. P.] Nicholson. If you have read them, you will readily perceive their object. It may be that you have not seen them, if so, I take upon myself to say, that the object, is to make the impression that Candidates should announce themselves, make speeches &c. and that it would be out of the question to vote for any man unless he does this. In short Nicholson does not want you to *run,* but wishes himself to be the man. This I know, more from his conversation than from his Editorial articles, but enough is shown in them to satisfy my mind. And here permit me to remark, that he is not to be trusted, he is your deadliest foe, and that too under the guise of friendship—and much more dangerous than an avowed enemy. Never trust him—the old breach, however desirable it once was to some of your friends, cannot be healed. 'Tis true that I once endeavored to effect a reconcilation, but I would not again attempt it, having no confidence in the man—a sly undermining hypocrite I despise.

We have some considerable excitement here, about our Stage Route. Donly's Drivers, and *Creditors* are making much noise on account of Walker & Brown getting the Contract. The people generally, who speak or think about it, are with W & B. They cannot understand how Mr. Donly has exclusive rights, W & B being the lowest bidder & having the acceptance, they are indignant at the unnecessary parade that Donly friends are making about it. Donly's friends say, that in a few weeks W & B. will be removed & the line given entirely to Donly. This no one here believes, yet it shews that some underhanded means are taking by D.'s friends here and at Nashville to drive Mr Walker from the line. Can it be possible, that a Contract between the Government and one of its Citizens can be set aside at pleasure, barely to serve a man, because he has been several years in public employment, and beca[u]se he has the reputation, however undeserving, of doing his duty? Are promises and rewards other than their lawful compensation to be held out to public agents to do their duty? and is all this to be at the expense, & to the injury of the reputation of an equally faithful servant, and one too much longer in public employment?

It is true that Donly has been a faithful Contractor, so has Walker. Walker lost his contract upon fair principals, and like an honorable man gave it up without a murmer. Why should not Donly do the same? Notwithstanding Donlys good qualities as a contractor, there are serious objections to his manner of imposing upon the people of this community, which shews what regard he has to correct principles. Hill,[1] has a deed of Trust upon all his property—his Creditors cannot touch it. Upon the faith of this property he buys, *horses, coaches,* makes stage stands, has work done, and does not pay for it. Complaints of this are almost universal. Under these circumstances, it is not him but the *people* on the road who are *carrying* the mail. He has now gone to Washington, and I am informed has certificates Certifying the mismanagement of the mail in Miss. under the Contract of Kinkle & Caruthers, who are Walkers *partners,* expecting thereby to effect Walker & Brown, *even to removal.* On the first of January his Agent and Drivers at the end of the line seemed resolved to convey the mail, contract or no contract. The truth is they consider themselves as having exclusive priviledges on the road, and I suppose expect the Department to recognize them as its owner or Contractor.

I cannot in this communication say all that I could wish or that I know upon this subject, and have said thus much, knowing to a certainty that attempts are making to trifle with the right & interests of Walker, hoping that you will see that *justice* be done him. *It is all* he *asks—all he wants*—and less than this *he ought not to take.* Nor can I doubt for a moment, but he will receive it, if proper representations of *facts* are laid before the P. M. G.

What I have here said has not been prompted by feelings of interest to myself or prejudice against D. for were I consult my own interest I should wish him *success.* It would enable him the better to pay his debts, & I am a Creditor, but the interests of individuals should always succumb to public good.

My best respects to Mrs. P.

A C Hays

Addressed to Washington.

1. Harry R. W. Hill.

FROM CHARLES D. McLEAN[1]

Dear Sir, Near Memphis, Jany 10, 1834

I have written to Col [William C.] Dunlap, *now* my representative, about a negro woman willed to my wife who absconded from Washington city in 1824; and in my letter requested him to confer with you on the subject. I now ask you to give him your friendly aid and advice to enable me to recover the woman, and children, (if any) or her value.

I hope *"our folks,"* will sustain the President about the *"veto"* and the *deposites*. The old chief's response to Clay's resolution is just as it ought to be—and confers on him additional honor.[2]

Please address me at Memphis. Mrs McLean desires me to say to you that she relies on you to give us your aid in trying to recover Clarissa—or at least to apprize us as to your opinion in relation to the case.

Col. Ed. Ward[3] will no doubt be our member from Shelby county to the Convention.

If occasion ever offers, I will endeavour to reciprocate your many evidences of kindness towards me.

Charles D. McLean

Addressed to Washington.

1. A former newspaper publisher in Clarksville, Nashville, and Jackson, McLean had recently moved to a farm in Shelby County.

2. A Senate resolution presented by Clay had demanded that Jackson inform the Senate whether or not a document concerning the removal of deposits from the Bank was genuine. If the document proved genuine, the resolution required that Jackson provide the Senate with a copy. Jackson declined to comply.

3. Jackson's personal friend and one of the earliest supporters of his presidential candidacy. Ward was a former resident of Davidson County.

FROM A. M. M. UPSHAW

Dear Sir Pulaski Jany 10th 1834

I received some papers a few days since from Mr Clark,[1] I thought we had sent on a duplicate; but find from Mr Clark letter that we had not. You will please say to Mr Clark that I will attend to the papers he sent me as soon as posible. I have commenced taken the nessary steps to get them arranged. I am in hopes you and our Inge will not let McDuffie *Kill* the old Hero this winter.

Pulaski I think has now got to be the third town of importance in the State and we feel that we have been very much injured by the Stages being taken from us. A town that is to have a Bank in it by the first of March and a rail road to Florance, with sixteen large stores in it not to have a stage is out of the question. Tell Mr Barry to send it back, and we Tennesseans will back him.

I would be glad to here from you, perhaps I shall see you before you leave the city. My respects to Mrs Polk.

A. M. M. UPSHAW

Addressed to Washington.

1. Matthew St. Clair Clarke.

FROM DAVID R. MITCHELL[1]

Dr Sir Maury County Jany 11th 1834

These leaves me well hoping they find you enjoying the same. I have drawn up a petition which I inclose to you but I am fearful it is not in proper form as I neaver wrote one before. I write to Dixon H Lewis Esqr, S. M. Mardis Esqr, C. C. Clay Esqr & judge John Murphey.[2] I have wrote on to Alabama to my attorney Francis Bugby Esqr[3] to send on a transcript of the case and his certificate with the judges and opposits attorneys and the shereffs. This case was a grate loss to me besides what time and money I spent while I was in Alabama attending to it. They sold every particle of propertity I had in the World which has keep me in an embarised situation and apears like it will keep me so. I have stated facts as well as I could recolect without a transcript of the case. If you should see I have made a mistake when you get a transcript make any alteration nessessary. Dixon H. Lewis was one of my attorneys who can certify that it was the first case that was tryed establishing the princepal and the [. . .] Line and I as firmly believe that it was the first moving cause to Opothaloholas[4] selling his country as I do [. . .] existance because it striped him of every particle of property he had as the Nation took it and paid the debt and he new he could not hold his station without property and the Nation blamed him for medling with the matter in the way he did and he is naturally ambitious and was forced to sell to rase himself. If I was the cause of the United States gaining the land two or three or perhaps ten year sooner than they would have done why then I should say it would be nothing but justice to give me a small pittince.[5]

If you should not receive any papers from Alabama, if you think there would be any chance with the petition I wish you to make the trial as I am verry much imbarrysed at this time as that oald Cantrell debt has come against me and will put me entirely under the weather if I should not get redress in some way so a little would do me a great deal of good at this time. I got the letter that Opothalohola had wrote to me from the Hon. S. M. Mardis, a friend of mine having put it in his hands for safe keeping, which circumstance I have no doubt but he will recolect and will do all he can for me. If I was in Alabama I could get a grate many certificats stating they thought it was the cause of him selling his land. Dixon H Lewis will do what he can for me. Any communication from you will be thankfully received. Your attention will confer a favour on your friend and well wisher.

D. R. Mitchell

NB. We will ellect you and R. L. Cobb Esqr representetives in our convention. I wish you to speake to the Hon. D. H. Lewis,

S. M. Mardis, John Murphey and C. C. Clay as I have written to all of them.

D. R. Mitchell

P.S. Direct to Snow Creek post Office

Addressed to Washington.

1. A resident of Maury County who remains in relative obscurity. He was a resident of the Snow Creek vicinity and had been a justice of the peace. It is possible that he spent considerable time out of the state. Certainly, this letter indicates a strong tie with Alabama.

2. These were members of the Alabama delegation in Congress. The writer, however, has the middle initial of Samuel Wright Mardis incorrect.

3. A prominent young lawyer in Montgomery, Alabama. The name is often spelled Bugbee.

4. Opothleyoholo, son of a half-breed and an Indian woman, was related by marriage to William Weatherford. He was an important figure among the Upper Creeks during the period of removal to the West. While he was generally friendly toward the whites, he tried to prevent them from defrauding his people.

5. In May 1834 Polk presented to the House of Representatives a petition by Mitchell asking the right of pre-emption in the purchase of a tract of public land in Alabama. This was to be indemnification for expense incurred in prosecuting a suit against a chief of the Creek Indians, obviously Opothleyoholo.

FROM JAMES WALKER

Dear Sir Columbia Jany 11th 1834

Since I last addressed you, I have ascertained to my satisfaction, that Donly has *secretly* and *mysteriously* left for Washington City. What his intentions are, or what advantage he seeks of me I know not, as his movements have latterly if not always been of too dark an order for me to fathom or follow. I have too much other important business to attend to, to follow on after him to preserve and protect my just and *vested rights.* If the Post office department suffers Donly to do me wrong it must be so, and if this should be the case, my controversy will be with the Department, and not with John Donly. It is possible Donly intends to insist that Walker & Brown have *forfeited* because I refused to take an undivided half of his property, on the 1st of January & make a joint partnership with him. I trust

I have sufficiently explained this *property* matter to you, and that you are satisfied that I was under no obligations on any principles to take any property of him on the 1st of January, under the circumstances which occurred, and having property of *our own,* taken from other lines, which we had lost the new Contracts on, we really never were bound to take any of his property, agreeable to the Post office advertisement or to Justice. We were disposed & would have taken his property if he had given us any fair chance to do so previous to the 1st of this month. All this is I think sufficiently understood by you & must be by the Dept.

It seems however that no effort is to be left untried to get me off the road. It certainly is not a matter of great pecuniary importance for us to retain our Contract as it now is, but I consider it a point of honor not to be *jockeyed* off.

It is likely Donly has some new propositions to make in accordance with the alledged public meeting at Nashville[1] and will propose a fast mail from Nashville by Madisonville to New Orleans in 7 days. He has now an acceptance for the Routes from Tuscumbia to Natchez at $15,000. This Contract would completely ruin him. He is determined to *abandon them,* and endeavor to get another contract or come in under the *improvement system* at a high price. When the Postoffice agent was at Nashville, Donly and his friends, said he could not, nor would not execute these contracts at the price he took them at. Mr. Simpson (the agent) advised, and requested him if he *intended to abandon,* to do so then. The question was then asked of the agent, what were his instructions and what would he do in case Donly abandoned. His reply was that in that event he was instructed to give the Contracts to Saml B. Ewing & Co. at their bid (they being the next lowest bidders at $23,500) that if it was Donly intention to abandon, he (the agent) thought he could prevail on (Mr. Caruthers & Walker two of the S. B. E & Co) to take the whole of the property from Nashville to Natchez at a fair valuation, to give him $1000 for his part of the line between Nashville & Tuscumbia, and thus let him out of a ruinous contract and settle all difficulties. After a good deal of chaffering Donly finally declined & went home. After he left town, Mr. Hill, (who had interfered in the matter & who is owner of all the property on the line, by conv[e]yance from Donly and thus prevents its seizure by his crediters) in a conversation with me said that if Donly did not get a higher price for the lines from Tuscumbia soon[?] that he must and should abandon them, and expressed a wish that a fair arrangement could be made for the property, and Donly quit the business. He expressed surprise that the agent would give S. B. Ewing & Co $23,500 and not give Donly the same. I explained to him that Donly had bid them off at $15,000, and if he choose to stand to his bid, nobody had any thing to say. It was his right but if his bid was $15,000, he could on no correct principle be allowed more for the proposed service and if he did abandon that then S. B. E. & Co. became entitled by all correct principles, and the usages of the Department to the Contracts *at their bid,* that although this seemed to him extraordinary it was a correct principle & that it could not be conceded that a man had a right to bid off contracts at less than the service can be performed for and then throw up and bargain for a higher price. Such a principle would destroy the post office department, destroy all competition, and produce corruption to an unlimited extent.

Mr. Hill then asked me if we (S B. E. & Co) in case Donly abandoned, would when we obtained the contracts, sell out to him (Donly) again for $4000 pr. annum. I replied that if Donly abandoned & we got the contracts we could not, nor would not sell out to him again at any price whatever, but if it was desireable to Mr. Hill himself to have the contracts upon the terms he mentioned, I would agree, that if S. B. Ewing & Co. got the contracts, they would put them into complete & proper operation themselves *& then if the P O Dept. sanctioned the transfer proposed,* we would sell out to Mr. Hill or to any other approved responsible man on the terms he suggested, or we would take all of the property at fair and liberal price without any further understanding about it. We did not ask Donly to abandon at all, but if such was his intention, if he would *do so now,* we would make a better property arrangement than at any time hereafter. He (Mr. Hill) said Donly should make some of the arrangements I had spoken of and sent for him. My teams were not placed as they ought to be on the road, and I told Mr. Hill I had remained in Nashville as long as I could or would, and if him or

Donly wanted to see me further, I would be found at Cherry's[2] until after Breakfast next morning. Donly came to see me at Cherry's, we had but little to say on the subject. He went into Nashville & the *public meeting* you saw noticed, was brought about no doubt by Mr. Hill & Co & the editorial article about "for instance John Donly," was clearly in my opinion written by Hill, for the purpose of aiding Donly to make a rise, and to extricate him from his difficulties. This editorial article is calculated to make a false impression abroad as to Donly's real standing here, and as to public opinion respecting the most competent contractors. That editorial article says that the P O. D. ought not to arrange the mails or make the contracts to suit the views of "any particular set of contractors." I agree with this doctrine, and if it had not been departed from solely for the purpose of accommodating the views of John Donly (and not the public interest) the Huntsville Coach line would have retained its original standing, been run by S. B. Ewing & Co according to original contract, and no cause of complaint given to any body, nor would the line by Murfreesborough & Huntsville to Mobile & New Orleans ever have been established. It was to my knowledge a most extraordinary desire on the part of WBL.[3] and the officers of the Dept. to favour John Donly, that produced these results, and seriously affected my interests & public convenience. But enough of this.

I am pretty well satisfied Donly has principally gone to Washington to make a powerful effort to get a higher price between Tuscumbia & Natchez, and to propose a fast mail to New Orleans by way of Madisonville, that he shall have the whole contract to himself, and under some pretext or new arrangement of the mails that Walker & Brown shall be thrown off the road and out of the contract. If any improvement is made we are entitled to that improvement on our part of the road, and I cannot think the Department will under any circumstances deprive us of this right. But we were so worsted by *the compromise* which gave Donly *one half* the Tuscumbia line, that my faith in the Department is very much shaken. I must therefore request you and all our other friends at Washington to keep a good look out for us in this matter. Altho Col. [Charles K.] Gardner permitted our interests to be sacrificed in the compromise I complain of, I think him honest, and that he will not permit farther wrong to be done if he understands the whole case. I would like for you to talk with him freely on this subject.

I understand that Donly sent down his man Dortch[4] to Mississippi to procure testimony that the line between Doaks and Natchez was very badly carried the last contract, with a view of destroying the character of S. B. Ewing & Co., and getting the whole of them out of his way. The line was run by a man by the name of Norman[5] under a contract originally made by Kinkle & Co. The mail has no doubt been badly conveyed on this line, but how this can affect even Caruthers & Kinkle (a part only of the S. B. Ewing Co.) I cannot divine. It is equally true and certain that Donly's own late contract from Tuscumbia to Doak's was just as badly executed as Norman's. Andrew Hays[6] has lately been on those lines and is my authority.

I have no doubt but Caruthers will be in Washington in a short time to represent the interest of S. B. E. & Co. Altho I was dissatisfied with him about *the compromise,* my interest has become identified with his & especially in the S. B. [E.] & Co.'s bids. Donly's object is to destroy Caruthers & Kinkle & W. & B. at one blow. I hope you will have time to protect our just rights. All we desire is *plain open sailing,* and will be satisfied with *stern justice.*

JAMES WALKER

Addressed to Washington.

1. A notice of this meeting was published in the Nashville *National Banner* on January 9, 1834. The editorial article which Walker attributed to Harry R. W. Hill had appeared in the same paper on January 7, 1834. Samuel H. Laughlin, editor of the paper at this time, later claimed that he was not acquainted with the facts when the article was printed.

2. A tavern kept by Jeremiah Cherry at White House, a short distance south of Nashville. Formerly of Columbia, where his father of the same name had once been postmaster, Cherry had become postmaster at White House in 1833.

3. William B. Lewis.

4. Unidentified.

5. Unidentified.

6. This is Andrew C. Hays, of Columbia, instead of Andrew Hays, a resident of Nashville.

FROM WALTER F. LEAK[1]

Sir, Richmond Ct House No C Jany 12 1834

I have recd with pleasure, your reply to Geo McDuffie, on the subject of the deposits; and allow me, as one of the Early Friends of The President, to return you my Humble Thanks for your able Cooperation & support of a Measure, which was called for by The abuses which was created by the Institution Itself; a measure which you have shown, has been sanctioned by precedent, and which never was questioned untill quite recently, and that too by a class of Politicians, who have "Boxed evry point of the Political Compass." I was formerly, the Friend of the Bank And remained such, up to the report of the Government Directors After which, I saw, or thought I saw, something in its Management, at War with the Republican Institutions of My Country. (I allude in part to the appropriation of money To cary on a Crusade with the Government and to the danger respecting such political Interference.) I know the Friends of the Bank tell us, that It acts on the defensive but such Jargon as that will not do for a person of the least political discernment. It is loosing sight of the *True* question, and submerging It into one of minor consequence that of the pecuniary Interest of the Stockholders; for certainly it will not be contended by any Class of Politicans, Nullifiers or Nationals, that the Interest of the Stockholder, was the *moving* principle In the Incorporation of the Bank, but rather was it not created to subserve and only to *subserve,* the Govt. in its fiscal operations. *This* being The main object in its formation, it necessarily follows, that whenever The Govt, thro a coordinate branch or otherwise, believes the Institution no longer desirable as a *mean* to attain the End, That the Bank as such, has no right to complain; much less can she be Justified, in using her Purse to bring into disrepute, the Administration (who as she says) assails her. It is true that the *Interests* of the Stockholders, is intimately connected with the Continuance of the Bank, but their Interests can be viewed in no other light, nor consulted in any other way, than that which Incidentally flows from the Establisment of their Principal. The *Principal* being an excrescence, or likely to become such, on the Body Politic, that which is only *Incidental* ought not to cary on a warfare with its creator. You will of course understand me as speaking of the Executive, as a Coordinate branch of the Law making Power. When he acts as such, It is under the High obligation of official duty. With the same propriety might the old Bank, (upon which by the by, Mr Clay made one of the Best Constitutional Arguments I have noticed, which has had less *lasting* impression upon himself than upon the Community) Complain of the congress of 1811 (I think) who Refused a re-charter. The thing sir, is Indefensible, and I am utterly surprized, how any Man, whether Friend or Foe can approve the conduct of the Bank, in this particular Instance, not to speak of its other Abuses.

I have not written However, to offer any thing like an Argument, to one so Completely Master of his subject, but merely to revive "Old Acquaintance" which was somewhat renewed, on one of my visits to the North, at which time I had the pleasure of your company.

You will probably then, by my signature, have revived "Old Acquaintance" and youthfull associations; you will have recalled To your mind Collegiate Reminiscences, which I Know to you are always dwelt on with pleasure.

Should any thing of particular Interest present itself, during the progress of the session, I should be glad at all times, to have the pleasure of Acknowleging the reception of a letter.

W F Leak

Addressed to Washington. This letter has been published in McPherson, editor, "Unpublished Letters," *North Carolina Historical Review*, XVI, 174–175.

1. Leak was a student at Chapel Hill during the first year that Polk was enrolled there. He served twice in the North Carolina state legislature and was for many years a trustee of the university.

FROM WILLIAM L. STORRS[1]

Dear Sir, Middletown Connt. Jany 13th 1834

If your late Speech on the removal of the Public Deposits should be printed in pamphlet form I would respectfully request of you the favor to send me a Copy.

Wm. L. Storrs

Addressed to Washington.

1. A lawyer and Yale graduate, Storrs was Polk's colleague in the House of Representatives, 1829–33. Later he was elected to the House of Representatives as a Whig. He was a distinguished lawyer, serving as chief justice of the Connecticut supreme court and as a professor of law at Wesleyan University and at Yale.

FROM ROGER B. TANEY

My Dear Sir [Washington] Jany 13 1834

I find myself so pressed with the business of the Department that it will be *impossible* for me to write the report of which you spoke.[1] You must not therefore rely on me for I have much business now pressing which will not bear delay. Yet I will keep my mind on the subject & be very glad to confer with you on the views proper to be taken whenever you will give me the pleasure of seeing you.

R. B. Taney

Addressed to the House of Representatives and delivered by hand. The letter is marked "Private."

1. This was a report upholding the removal of deposits from the Bank of the United States that Polk wanted for use in the Ways and Means Committee. While Taney could not actually write the report, he conferred with Polk regularly as the report was being prepared.

FROM ROGER B. TANEY

My Dear Sir [Washington] Jany 13 1834

Since writing you a note in relation to the report it has occurred to me that the amendment suggested to Mr. McDuffies instruction[1] might embarrass you—if any pledge is given to support it in that form. For you will be driven I think to use the previous question & that would set aside the amendment. Would it not be better that the proposition should come as a substantive seperate instruction after the reference to the committee, and in that form I should give it my hearty support & rejoice to see it adopted.

R. B. Taney

Delivered by hand, this letter is marked "Private."

1. On December 17, 1833, Polk presented a motion that Taney's report on removal of deposits be referred to the Ways and Means Committee. McDuffie offered an amendment that would instruct the Ways and Means Committee to direct that government deposits remaining in the Bank of the United States not be removed from it. Probably as a result of prior planning by Taney and Polk, Seaborn Jones of Georgia presented an amendment to McDuffie's instructions. Its effect would be to instruct the Ways and Means Committee to inquire into the expediency of depositing in state banks federal revenue thereafter collected. Jones presented his amendment the day after this letter was written.

FROM ROGER B. TANEY

My Dear Sir [Washington] Jany 13 1834

Without waiting for the examination which you suggested this morning in relation to contracts heretofore made with the Banks in which public money was deposited, I will make a few remarks on the objection to my power to make contracts with the Banks.

The objection is that although I have the right to deposite the money in the state Banks, yet I have no right to make a contract with them.[1] The argument is beyond measure absurd. Money of the U. States cannot be placed in their keeping without a contract with them. If there was no written agreement the law would imply one. It would imply a contract on the part of the Bank to pay. Could not the U. States sue the Bank if they refused to pay & recover the money? And upon what could they sue but the implied contract to pay? If the Secretary by depositing the money may make an implied contract surely he may make an express one.

The objection therefore that he may not enter into a contract, although he has the right to deposit the money cannot be listened to for a moment.

Is the objection to the form of this contract—to the words in which it is couched? This would be still more untenable. It cannot be pretended that there is any law prescribing the *form* of the contract. If there is a form to make a contract & no prescribed form then the form is necessarily left to the discretion of the party who is authorized to make the agreement.

Is the objection to the substance of the agreement? If the State Banks are selected lawfully as agents, & their duties not defined by law they must necessarily be defined by contract. And the U. States have the same right to take care of their interests in this respect as an individual. This principle is expressly decided by the Supreme Court in the case of the U. States vs. Tingey—which is reported I think in 6 Peters reports.[2] But I have not the book before me and am not therefore sure of the volume.

This seems to answer all the objections to the contract and there is another answer that if Congress disapprove of the terms on the form they can easily prescribe by law upon what terms and in what form it shall be made.

These hasty suggestions will no doubt have occurred to you. But I make them in order to present my own notions on the subject & you will use them if you think proper with the information I promised to give.

R. B. Taney

No address is available, but this letter was probably delivered by hand to Polk in Washington.

1. A few days before this letter was written, Horace Binney of Pennsylvania made a long speech in the House of Representatives in which he condemned the contracts which Taney had made with the state banks and questioned his right to make such contracts.

2. It was actually reported in 5 Peters. In this decision in *United States* v. *Thomas Tingey,* rendered in 1831, Justice Joseph Story wrote the opinion of the court. He clearly stated that the United States may enter into contracts, this right being incident to the general right of sovereignty.

FROM W. F. BOYAKIN[1]

Dear Sir. Berry's Lick, Kty January the 14th 1834

You will excuse me when I inform you that I have been one of your constituents and warm suporters Heretofore in Giles County Ten. During the canvass between you and L M Bramblet I suported you although Residing with Bramblett.[2] You Received the Heartfelt Suport of my Father in Giles Formerly of Maury—Willie Boyakin.

And now Sir all that I want of you therefore is to condesend to write to me and if you can find Leisure without robbing your constituents—to acquaint me of Such Procedings of Congress as you think fit. Also to Send me Such Documents Papers reports &c as are at your desposal, recollecting at the Same time that I am A thoroughgoing Jacksonian. The whole Bent of my influence is given undividedly to the Present Administration.

You must Recollect that Human nature is to grasp at any thing that will associate old Scenes which were Pleasant. Therefore, By a compliance with the above Request you will confer a very Lasting Favour on your unworthy Servant former Suporter and Present Friend.

W. F. Boyakin

P. S. If you oblige me do so to Berrys Lick P. O. Butler County Kty.

Addressed to Washington.

1. Other than the information given in this letter, nothing has been learned about the writer.

2. Neither spelling of this name is correct. It should be Bramlett.

FROM GIDEON RIGGS

Williamson County. January 14, 1834

Revealing that a petition with almost fifty signatures has been forwarded to the Postmaster General asking that a new post office be established at his house, Riggs points out the desirability of that location.[1]

Addressed to Washington.

1. The new post office was established with Riggs as postmaster. The site was very near the Bedford County line

FROM WILLIAM H. POLK

Dear Brother Chapel Hill N. C. January 16th 1834

I received your letter before I left Raleigh, and the ten dollars which you inclosed and if I had not have got that I would have been in a bad way for Col Polk was very sick when he received your letter to furnish me with money for the presant session and was not able to transact any buisness whatever and I remained several days thinking that he would get better and be able to furnish me with the money but he died on the 13th. He had a continual vometing so that nothing would lay on his stomach. He died very easy and retained his senses till the last moment and I thought that it would be better for me to return to Chapel Hill and study by myself so as I would not be to far behind my class and I will not be able to join college until I receive money from you to pay my expenses. I owe the Dialectic Society $15 for my entrence in the society which canot be postponed and I would be very much obliged to you if you will send it on to me when you send me the money to pay my tuition board et cetera which will amount to $100.00 including the fifteen dollars for the Society which you must send as soon as you can conveintly. I received a letter from Samuel and he said all was well and the Jackson College had 166 scollars. Give my love to sister Sarah and tell her she must excuse me for not writing to her and I will give her my reasons for not doing so in a letter before long.

WILL. H. POLK

P. S. I would not request you to send me the $15 for the society if I could dispence with it on any terms.

W H POLK

Addressed to Washington. This letter has been published in Bergeron, editor, "My Brother's Keeper," *North Carolina Historical Review,* XLIV, 201–202.

FROM BENJAMIN E. CARPENTER[1]

Dr. Sir, Phila. Jany 17. 1834

Your favour of the 14th Inst. has been duly received, I embrace the opportunity of tendering you my sincere acknowledgements for this marked compliment.

Let me assure you Sir that I do not flatter when I inform you that the Democrats of the 3d. Congressional District hail you as their Champion in the House, sustaining and defending so eloquently and we hope successfully the constitutional principles and opinions of Jefferson & Madison against a monied Aristocracy.

I further with pleasure inform you, that the Democracy of this District are firm and united in one solid phalanx, and henceforth there will be an end to *Watmoughism.*[2] The Government Directors are our particular friends and great excitement prevails under the impression that the Senate will not confirm their nomination. If not too much trouble have the goodness to inform me on this subject, as well as the probable fate of the Deposits. We hope the Bank will not triumph over the Government.

B. E. CARPENTER

Addressed to Washington.

1. Prominent Philadelphia businessman.

2. From John G. Watmough, a strong supporter of Biddle and the Bank. At this time he was a member of the United States House of Representatives.

FROM JAMES WALKER

Dear Sir Columbia Jany 17th 1834

I have not yet heard from you or the PMG on the subject of my mail concerns. In this matter I feel much solicitude, not that the contracts I am concerned in were so valuable, but because I consider points of honor & character involved in the matter, and because many other persons besides myself have to them important interests at stake. I know not what advantages Donly may be permitted to take of me at Washington in my absence and still have confidence that the PO. Department will do right, notwithstanding J. H E. & Wm B L's influence.[1] But experience has taught me that there is no certainty of this. My mind is made up and I have decided on the different contingencies which may chance to happen. I may see you in Washington this spring. I think Majr Barry an amiable & Col. Gardner an honest man but if they permit Donly to injure me further, I must from self respect go to war with them, and make an exposure of the whole matter in all their bearing on the public interests and individual *vested rights*. I shall regret this alternative, but am determined on it, if it destroys me. I hope that the necessity may be avoided, but if it comes to the worst, I can make a sett *of facts* satisfactorily appear that must sustain me in public estimation. This whole story is not yet known in this country.

We have had no mail from New Orleans for the last 8 or 10 days. Donly & Co. are new Contractors from Tuscumbia to Natchez. I believe the mails are not conveyed at all on this road. Donly has notwithstanding his unpardonable neglect of the routes entrusted to him, gone off to Washington City and will doubtless there pass for one of the most efficient contractors in the West, when in fact he has more outrageously betrayed the confidence reposed in him by the Department than any other man in the West ever did, except his old friend James Edington.[2] I am sure he has not been even so far South, as this place, and from the best information has paid no attention to any of the Southern lines entrusted to him. His drivers are all agents and every thing in which he is concerned is in confusion. He owes an immense amount of money to the people on the road & his property all made over to Harry Hill to prevent its seizure & Harry using his influence at Nashville to push[?] him as the only efficient Contractors in the newspapers & I presume the late public meeting had for its object, the promotion of Mr. Hills interest &c.

Donly instead of going on to Washington to seek advantages of better men, ought to have been attending to the contracts that were given to him, and it will be a shame if he is not yet made to stand up to his bids or abandon the business.

James Walker

Addressed to Washington.

1. John H. Eaton and William B. Lewis were believed by Walker to be firm backers of John Donly.

2. Unidentified.

FROM GRANVILLE H. FRAZER[1]

Sir Nashville 18 January 1834

After my compliments I will advise you that I have just read your Speech of January 2nd on the question of the deposits of the government being removed in defence of President

Jackson for the oald General you know is true to his Country—and to his trust. There is some Collecters passing through this place from Philadelphia & New York and else where from the mercantile houses and banking houses abuseing General Jackson for ordering the deposites to be removed from the United Sts Bank. I only give you this hint so you and your Colegs may be enabled to expose the unmanly course the[y] are taking to obtain a recharter—and endevering to make the ignorant believe that the President is the real cause of the presure. I come through Kentucky last weake and I found that the enemys of the oald General was takeing this step for the purpos of a Lexinaring[electioneering] plan and what was said was not intended for the good of the American people—that Clay, Mcdufee and others was laying great plans at the session to make a Hell of a fus if the[y] could against the President. My last words is to you to stand by the oald General as long as you have a butten on youre Coat.

GRANVILLE H FRAZER

Addressed to Washington.

1. Although he seems to have lived for a while in Nashville, he was for a long time a farmer in Bedford County. Although the spelling here appears to be Frazer, it appears elsewhere as Frazier, and the latter may well be the correct spelling.

FROM JOHN MEDEARIS

Bedford County. January 18, 1834

A Revolutionary War pensioner, Medearis is trying to collect a backpayment that he did not receive.[1] He asks Polk's continued assistance in the matter.

Addressed to Washington. The letter was written by David Yancey.

1. See Medearis to Polk, January 14, 1832.

FROM WILLIAM H. STEPHENS

Sir: Hardeman County Jan. 18th 1834

Once more I take the liberty of addressing you upon a subject, which, although of little interest to you is full of importance to me, namely my application for an appointment to the Military Academy. I have written to the Sect. of War upon the subject, and told him that he could get from you any information respecting me, which information I beg you to give whether he asks it or not.

You know yourself, that by promoting my views, you will not be assisting the son of a rich man, but of one who, being unable to support his large family in Columbia, was compelled to leave some of his children, and for almost the twentieth time, to hunt a new place there to toil and labor, at an age and in a state of health, when men ought to be at rest. But I am not idle myself, anticipating an appointment, I have commenced teaching school, 10 miles West of Bolivar, on Clear Creek for the purpose of obtaining means of getting to West Point, as my father[1] is not able to send me.

I have taken the liberty of writing this believing that you would exert yourself for me; and when you reflect that it will be in accordance with the wishes of some of the most respectable gentlemen of Maury County, I know that you will try to oblidge. . . .

William H. Stephens

P. S. Do you remember my trip for you to Bedford? Exercise half the zeal for me that I did distributing Circulars for you, and I can go to West Point. Wm. H. S.

Addressed to Washington.

1. The Reverend Daniel Stephens.

FROM SAMUEL C. ALLEN[1]

Dear Sir, Northfield, Ms., Jany 20 1834

You have rendered your country a great service by your able & eloquent speech on the Bank. The question now at issue is whether we are to have a moneyed Dynasty? no a Bank Bill Dynasty, in this country instead of a government by the people. Do not despair though the press and the aristocracy which exists by speculation on the honest industry of the people are against you, the people are roused at the core.

There has been a meeting got up at Boston & resolutions

have been passed. Be assured the people are not with them & the party of this interest of which this is a sort of manifestation, is on its last legs. I hope the President will be encouraged to persevere to the end in this thing. It is a question of *power* yes of *soverignty* & there can be no compromise. It must be put down by a strong effort of the public will or it will convert the government which sh'd be the organ of that will into an instrument in the hands of an aristocracy, of the worst kind.

My chief hope is in the personal firmness of the President. I consider this as altogether the most important question which has ever come before the government. I am glad the President seems to be apprised of its importance & to feel the crisis. And he is not a man for *compromises*.

I wish your speech could be read more extensively as it can be in N. E for our presses are most onesided. But still the public opinion will get to be correct in spite of all that is done to mislead it. I beg you will excuse my troubling you. . . .

SAM C ALLEN

P S. May I ask the favor of one your speeches in pamphlet form?

Addressed to Washington.

1. Allen represented Massachusetts in the House of Representatives for six consecutive terms, 1817–29.

FROM ADLAI O. HARRIS

Dear Sir Nashville 20th Jany 1834

I have been requested by some of the friends of Col. W. Barrow[1] since my arrival here to write to you on the subject of his application for soliciter for this district.

It is understood here that Mr Collingsworth[2] will not be nominated again and Col. Barrow is very anxious to get the appointment.

I have but little to do with Politics in any way and in this case have no particular interest for I do not know who the other Candidates are or may be and to make the matter short you know Col Barrow as well as I do, and will know much better what to do than I could advise. It was at the request of Dr Martin[3] that I agreed to write to you about the matter.

Col. B. is a very Gentlemanly Clever man and I have no doubt a man of excellent Sense & as far as I have any thing to say in the matter would be pleased to have him get the appointment.

The steam Boat Memphis arrived here a day or two ago. She brought up from Helena to Memphis your overseer Beanland, Geo Moore, & Jack. I am in hopes that your matters will all go on right now. Dr Caldwell said that he heard of two negroes to hire in the neighborhood and that he has directed Beanland to get them, or one of them to supply Bens place, which I hope he has done.

I am on my way to N. Orleans. Shall start on the Memphis in the morning and was very anxious to have got your speech with McDuffies &c &c on the Deposites but a part only of your speech as reported by the "Inteligencer" has come to hand. Hays is publishing of it and said that he should publish the ballance so soon as he recd it, in the "Inteligencer." He will not publish it as reported in the "Globe."

The Planters Bank stock is nearly all taken. The Bank will go into operation very shortly. Littlefield will be the President, and T J Read[4] I expect Cashier.

Remember me to Mrs. P.

A O Harris

Addressed to Washington.

1. A native of Davidson County, Washington Barrow was practicing law in Nashville at this time. Later in the year he succeeded Allen A. Hall as editor of the Nashville *Republican*.

2. James Collinsworth, a Nashville lawyer, had been appointed by Jackson in 1829 as United States District Attorney for West Tennessee.

3. This is probably Dr. Robert Martin of Nashville, who had been practicing medicine there for several years.

4. Unidentified.

FROM ISAAC J. THOMAS

Dear Sir Maury County Ten. Jary 20th 1834

Permit me to express to you my cordial approbation of the course you have taken & to congratulate you on the eminent

Display that you have made on the very important question now before you in congress (The Deposit question). It is with great satisfaction that I have read till you gave way to the motion to ajourn. Thus far you have sustained every position with clearness & beyond gainsaying. Our District can truly boast of their representative. (I write to you as tho I was in conversation with you.)

We have nothing local that is Interesting. The convention subject appears to produce almost no excitement. You are confidently spoken of as one of our Representative in that Body & you will certainly be Elected unless you let us know that you cannot serve. My sincere Desire is that you will serve if you can consistant with the duties of your present station & we intend to Elect you If we are not otherwise Directed by yourself. R. L. Cobbs is the other that is spoken of. If you have leasure from your Labourious Duties let me hear from you. I know that your present station is laborious. But the promise of our Heavenly Father is That as our day so shall our strength be. With the sincere Desire that the Wisdom of Heaven may guide you I subscribe myself. . . .

Isaac J. Thomas

P.S. We have an unusual wet winter. Tennessee River is higher than it has been for a number of years.

Addressed to Washington.

FROM WILLIAM M. TOWNSEND

Lancaster, Ohio. January 20, 1834

Townsend says that he had an uncle in Delaware whose name was William Polk. After the uncle's death, the widow moved to North Carolina. He asks Polk to help restore communication between him and his relatives.

Addressed to Washington.

FROM JAMES WALKER

Dear Sir Columbia, Jany 20th 1834

The people in the neighborhood of Mt. Pleasant have understood that Donly intended to make efforts to change the main mail from Nashville to Tuscumbia by way of Pulaski, and intersect the present road at Lawrenceburg again. This report has produced much excitement there and a petition or remonstrance has been got up and will be forwarded to you in a few days. I have been requested to apprise you of this and to request you not to permit any change of this kind to be made until you receive the petition, and indeed not at all. Such men as Sansom,[1] and the Polks, are excited and are getting signers to the petition. I told them that I thought the project too ridiculous (if it was intended) to merit serious attention. They say however, that the cutting down the Huntsville line has so much impaired their confidence, that they do not know what to calculate on being done to oblige Mr. Donly.

I hope you will bear in mind, and apprise my and your friends of the fact, that Donly's principal business at Washington is to destroy the reputation of Caruthers & Kinkle, and through them the standing of Walker & Brown and to make some underhanded arrangement by which he will get the whole line between Nashville & Natchez at a high price. We are so identified in bids (S. B Ewing & Co) with Caruthers & Kinkle, that any injury to their standing must now effect us and although I think they done wrong in making the agreement to cut down the Huntsville line to our serious injury I should very much regret Donly's triumph over them. I should be much pleased for you & others, that feel friendly to Brown & me to act in concert with the Alabama delegation, and jointly[?] to sustain the whole S B. Ewing Co. as far as justice will permit. It will be nothing but fair for C. & K. to be heard from before any charges against them are believed or acted on to their injury. The whole controversy about the lower lines will be in a short time fully understood by the Department.

I do not mean by any thing I say that the main *fast* mail from Nashville to N. O. ought to go by Murfreesborough, Huntsville & Mobile or that I abandon our claim to the restoration of the Coach line between here & Huntsville. I think this line ought to be restored, and let the line through Murfreesborough remain as it is, or let all these matters be placed on the footing they were when our *bids were accepted.*

We have had no mail from Orleans for the last 10 or 12 days.

There is said to be a large accumulation of Mails at Doaks Stand. Donly's bid was accepted from Tuscumbia down. It is said, and I believe truly that he has not attempted to perform under the new contracts, and every thing is in confusion on those lines. Notwithstanding this dereliction of duty Majr Donly has Darted off to Washington I suppose to make more new contracts, which he will comply with when he returns home, if it suits his whim or interest. Harry Hill and Col [Robert] Armstrong notwithstanding represent him, as perhaps the only man to whom important mails ought to be entrusted. Is it not extraordinary that such a man as John Donly has always proved himself to be should have high standing and consideration by the head of a Department *under this administration.* One or two fine Teams & Coaches sent to Nashville has effected wonders for him.

JAMES WALKER

P.S. Beanland & Geo. Moore have returned from Arkansas with *Chunky Jack.*

Addressed to Washington.

1. Probably Darrel N. Sansom, a physician and businessman at Mt. Pleasant, Tennessee.

FROM WILLIAM L. WILLIAMS[1]

Sir, Pension Office January 20th 1834

I have the honor to address to you as Chairman of the Committee of Ways and Means, the following communication.

For the execution of the Pension Law of 7 June 1832, it was necessary to employ several temporary clerks in the Pension Office. Among others I was thus employed. The business which has been assigned me, has been of the most laborious nature, such as to require constant attention and hourly application at my desk, and I can truly say, that I have never lost a day or an hour without a good and sufficient reason rendered to the head of the *Bureau.* While such has been my situation, I have been receiving a salary of *800 dollars* per annum; the same with those who are by no means my equals in point of character, or efficiency in business. For my standing in society I respectfully refer you to the Senators & Representatives of No. Ca. my native state, and can produce my private correspondence & college certificates & degree; for my competency, and application as a clerk, I have been requested by Gen. Ward[2] of New York, to refer you immediately to him. I have had to execute the business of the New York division in the office which numbers a fourth part of the pension claims, and often have I assisted in keeping up the other divisions.

My motive in addressing you this letter is to request, that you remunerate me for my services. My redress can be alone obtained through the committee; for, should the Commissioner of Pensions & Secretary of War be disposed to increase my salary (which they well know I richly deserve) all those who have been receiving the same would attribute it to partiality, or expect theirs increased likewise—although not one of them is half so efficient. *Some of them too, are protegees.*

At the close of the present Session, I shall have laboring for 18 months, and I earnestly & respectfully ask five hundred dollars. If you think that too much, any thing you may advise.

I have now stated my request, which is urged from no consideration of a private nature, but upon the broad grounds of superior ability, expedition & attention to business, as can be testified to by any one connected with the same office. *The hire should be worthy of the laborer.*

Permit me, Sir, in conclusion to say that I shall at the commencement of the summer become a resident of Tennessee, whither my Father removed from No. Ca. eighteen months since; and inasmuch as our family will, in all probability, be an influential one, whenever I shall in any way have an opportunity to increase your usefulness and popularity, I shall take great pleasure in doing so. In the event of your presenting my request, and urging it by your influence, you shall receive the homage of a most grateful heart.

W. L. Williams

P. S. I have mentioned this subject to several members of Congress, who all agree in thinking that my request will be granted & all of whom referred me to you. I hope you will see Genl. Ward, and use me in all respects as one who may become one of your constituents & warmest friend. I do not wish a clerkship but merely what my services are worth. A Temporary clerk, it seems to me should be paid more than one who is permanent. Mr. Cambreling[3] told me that whatever you recommended would doubtless be acceptable to the Committee. Do something for me if you please Sir.

Addressed to the House of Representatives and delivered by hand.

1. Nothing has been learned about Williams except what is revealed in this letter.

2. Aaron Ward served six nonconsecutive terms in the United States House of Representatives, 1825–43, and was a member of that body at the time this letter was written.

3. Churchill C. Cambreleng was a member of the Ways and Means Committee at this time.

FROM WILLIAM DAVIDSON

Dr Sir Charlotte N. C. January 21t 1834

Your letter from Tennessee inclosing your account Current and also your letter from Washington has been Receivd.

At the time your letter from Tennessee came to hand I was on the Eve of setting out for the north. I Took the papers with me intending to see you in Washington. I arrived there on Sunday 8t of Decemb. My business Being urgent, I made no stop but pushed on to New York. I was detained longer there than I Expected, and on my return being pressd for time having to be at home on or before the 11t of Januy and having to come by Raleigh, I again passd. through Washington without stoping, On new years morning. So you see I have passed you Twice without seeing.

The object of my Journey to the north was to make some disposition of my Gold mining property. And having Effected an arrangement, I had To return immediately with one of the Gentlemen to Confirm the arrangement, and am now engaged In attending to that business. This arrangement will Relieve me in a Great Measure from pecuniary embarasment to which I have been subject for some Time past. I have been so much perplexed in my affairs for some time, that I have [not] been able to Give that attention To all my Concern that I Could wish.

As soon however as I Get my present arrangement Completed, I will have More Leisure, and will have Every thing settled to your satisfaction. I have not yet sent a power of att. To Mr. Frierson,[1] but will do so as soon I Can attend to it. He has sent me a verbal message by Wm. McCormack,[2] that several of the debtors are desirous of paying up, as soon as they Can Get Titles To their Land.

I will attend to all matters as soon possible, and for reasons above mention and my absence from home, you will Excuse my not writing you sooner.

WM DAVIDSON

Addressed to Washington.

1. Probably Samuel D. Frierson, a Columbia lawyer who took care of Polk's affairs from time to time.

2. Unidentified.

FROM JOHN H. DEW[1]

Dear Sir. Lebanon Tennessee January 21 1834

I have just finished reading the stenographic *report* of your *Speech,* delivered in the House of Representatives and concluded on the 2nd Ins. in reply to Genl. McDuffie of South Carolina; Upon the resolutions in relation to the removal of the public Deposits from the Bank of the U.S. by the Secretary of the Treasury; and the Communication from the President of the U.S. to his Cabinet upon the same subject. Your argument in defence of the Executive for the exercise of an ordinary power, expressly conferred on him by the Constitution of the U.S. and fully sanctioned by precedent & custom evinces a most intimate acquaintance with the multifarious movements that have been made upon the great American political *Chess board* from the organization of the Government to the present *Crisis*. You have shown most incontestably, from laborious research into the public records and documents that the President and his Cabinet have in all things acted strictly within the sphere of their Constitutional duty and rule of action. As I was the author of the preamble and resolutions which were acted upon by the late General Assembly of Tennessee upon the subject of rechartering and of removing from the Bank of the U.S. the public Deposits, you will be apprised of the reasons I have for rejoicing to see the policy I earnestly advocated so ably defended as it has been by you. That the President in this official act has acted the part of a faithful sentinal & public servant & the Secretary has in all things acted in good faith & that the measure is expedient and warrented by the peculiar circumstances of the case I am fully satisfied in my mind. So fair as I have heared an expression of opinion from the citizens of this county your Speech is greeted with enthusiastic applause.

Today with astonishment, great surprise and deep mortification and regret, I see that Morgan W. Brown Esq. has been appointed by the President with the advice and consent of the Senate Judge of the Federal Court vice McNairy resigned. As the Episcopal Minister always prays, Good Lord deliver us from this besetting sin, and national curse. Tell me Sir, where was the Senators from Tennessee, Messrs. White & Grundy? I hope you will not doubt my sincere devotion & attachment to the Prest. and his great political favoritisms, but for this nomination I do most severely oppose. This Sir, is one of Maj E.'s Kitchen movements. Tell Grundy I am done with him. His friends in the Legislature had to fight through fire & persecutions on every side and who was the vilest of his vile persecutors M. W. B. and him to sit & fold his arms and not to oppose the confirmation of the appointment of a man, that was never so much as a respectable county court Lawyer to be our Federal Judge dont work well with me I do assure you.

The subject of electing Delegates to the new Convention has absorbed all things here. I am sorry to inform you that the watch word here, is *reform, democracy without reserve, and an entirely new system of Government.* I hope the wisdom of the patriots of Tennessee will see that you may easily destroy a good thing by giving too much physic and in solid doses, you will say they ought to be broken dooses.

Present my best respects to Col B. Peyton, tell him the puff that reached us upon his maiden effort was thankfully received,[2] we flatter our selves *"the half has not been said"* and that I command him to put his talents to the money exchangers, and to return them (for he has no less than ten) to his constituents with *usury*. Acknowledge from me to Col. D. Crockett from the River

Country the receipt of the "Report of a Committee of Directors of the Bank of the U.S." under the franking privilege. Tell him I decidedly give his favour the preferance of all others of the like kind I have heretofore received, not for any intrinsic merit in the report but the donor gives its relish. Tell him however he is "*barking* up *the wrong* tree." I am Anti Bank to all intents & purposes, "but *for him to go a head.*"

Present me respectfully to the Honb. Senator White & Grundy & representatives Cols, Bell, Forester, Dickinson, Dunlap, & Johnson,[3] and receive for your self my highest esteem & regard.

JOHN H. DEW

P.S. I should like to receive the Speeches in *phlet* form.

Addressed to Washington.

1. Dew was a lawyer in Wilson County who had twice served his county in the lower house of the General Assembly. Later he married a daughter of Joseph Herndon and moved to Maury County. He was elected to a single term in the General Assembly from Maury County, 1841–42.

2. Perhaps Peyton's brief speech of January 16, 1834, which concerned pension laws.

3. These were all members of the Tennessee delegation in the House of Representatives.

FROM HENRY HILL

George Town, D.C. January 21, 1834

Identifying himself merely as a former consul, Hill encloses a newspaper article that he had written on the question of removal of government deposits. He expresses hatred for despotism, especially that of a monied power.

Addressed to Washington.

FROM JOEL R. SMITH

Dear Col Huntingdon 21st January 1834

Sir some month since I addressed to you a letter in which was enclosed a recommendation of myself to the President which I hope came safe to hand but not hearing from you on the subject I am fearfull that it has miscarried.[1]

If you have ere this rcd. it please let me know as soon as practicable, particulars as fair as you know them yourself.

I have this day read very carefully Mr. Clays speech on the Deposit question[2] and if I am politician sufficient to judge I would say that the mountain was in labour & produced not a rat but quite a puny mouse. For rest well assured that I have never read a speech which was so full of vile slander & a speech which was so little called for from the senator who made it.

I will give you much merit for the course which you have thus fair persued on the deposit question & will give you one of Davys expressions, that to go a head & fear not.

JOEL R SMITH

Addressed to Washington.

1. See Smith to Polk, December 12, 1833.

2. Clay's long speech was concluded on December 31, 1833.

FROM SAMUEL P. WALKER

Dear Uncle Columbia Jan 21st 1834

I have intended to write to you for some time but have defered it from day to day until I fear you have heard from other sources, all the news which our town and county afford. Stages, the Convention and the removal of the deposites are, at present, the only subjects of public interest. Major Donly and my Father are at war about the mail contracts from Nashville to Tuscumbia and Huntsville and public sentiment is so much divided that the excitement was never before equaled, unless by a Congressional election. A public meeting has been held at Nashville for Donly's benefit, composed of nearly the same individuals who once before attempted to rule the whole country. There is no telling what may be the result; it has now become a matter of character more than of interest and I am firmly convinced that my Father would spend an immense sum of money and time rather than fail to accomplish his object.

Next is the convention. Who are to be our representatives? is a question dayly asked and as currently answered Polk & Cobbs. The people about Moorsville and in the upper end of this County *swear* that they will elect *you* anyhow; as to the other they are not so particular. Messrs Nicholson and Cahal are waiting impatiently to hear from you and in case you should not suffer your name to be run, one, or perhaps, both of them will be candidats. If you cannot leave Washington it is thought by your friends here that Mr. Cooper can be elected. The Editors of the Mercury seem sedulously to avoid saying any thing more about you than they can possibly help, either as a candidate for convention or as to your course in Congress. Mr Nicholson seems to be too much taken up in praising himself to think of any thing else. "Althoug the yougest member in the House I have discharged my duty with credit to myself and honour to my country" and such stuff as this has filled his columns ever since his return from Nashville and has completely disgusted all who read his paper.

The politicians of our town anxiously wait for the mail every day to hear from Washington. Your speech in answer to Mr McDuffie on the removal of the deposites has been received and is highly applauded by your friends whilst your enemies are silent. It is now late at night and I have no time to say more. Give my love to Aunt Sarah and tell her that I will write to her in a short time and give the marriages, deaths &c.

SAML. P. WALKER

P.S. I was in the Printing office to day and saw a circular from David C. Mitchell[1] announcing himself a candidate for convention. Webster, Kincade and Israel Fonville are the candidates in Bedford.

S P W

Addressed to Washington.

1. A prominent citizen of Mt. Pleasant.

FROM SILAS M. CALDWELL

Dr. Sir Mount View [Maury County] Jany 22nd 1834

I understand you have instructed Mr Walker to sell Ben & buy you another boy. He is also authorized to sell Wally and that he intends to Keep Ben himself and let you have Wally in His stead. Take Wally & if you should afterwards feel disposed to sell him I will buy him as he has a wife at my plantation. But my advise to you is to keep your negroes. Dont be discouraged if they dont like the Mississippi. On examination I will have enough of open land on my farm for both of our hands to cultivate in cotton next year, and can next Winter clear enough for corn. I can arrange things in such a way as to make your negroes profitable to you. You can either rent out your plantation or sell it. Mr. Walker has directed Beanland to hire a hand in the place of Ben. I will be down at your plantation in March and if your business is not going on right I will attend to it. It is probable Beanland may get along better when he gets the negroes all straight. Any information I receive from your Farm between this and the time I go down I will give you. Write to me as soon as you Receive this.

S. M Caldwell

Addressed to Washington.

FROM WILLIAM J. CRANS[1]

Dear Sir, Philada. Jany. 22nd 1834

I have the honor of transmitting to you a copy of the proceedings of the meeting of your fellow Citizens of the First Congressional District of Pennsylvania, and of presenting their sincere thanks to you for your able defence of the Administration.[2]

Your late course has been such as to enhance the feeling of admiration the Democratic party have always had towards you, and a feeling of Pride never fails to shew itself when they refer to the Champions the people have in the House, among whom none stand more conspicous than yourself.

Wm. J. Crans

Addressed to Washington.

1. A merchant of Philadelphia. For some years Crans had a shoe store in the Southwark area of that city.

2. The enclosure was a printed account of the proceedings of a meeting held in the District of Southwark on January 20, 1834. Since the document gave approval to many supporters of Jackson, it is likely that it was rather widely circulated among members of the Jackson party.

FROM GASPARD RICHARD[1]

Dear Sir: New York January the 22nd 1833[1834][2]

I have the honor to send you the printed Extract of the first part of my Memorial to Congress.[3] If you will have the goodness to read it with due attention, I have the confident hopes that you will find that new plan to be the best which could be found to correspond to the great question of this Session of Congress, concerning the settlement of the United States Bank. According to your station as Chairman of the select Committee of Ways & Means I have the honor to solicit your favour to be interested to bring my new plan forward to the knowledge of the Members of Congress, and to the people generally to know if the Constitutional Bank, and the second Company will not be the best to be Incorporated at the Session of Congress, to be a new Act of the Bank Law; and for the Constitutional Bank to be the mother Bank of this Nation, and for a substitute of the United States Bank existing.

The 18th inst. I had the honor to send a letter to Mr. [Churchill C.] Cambreleng my Representative to Congress with my solicitations to communicate the letter to you. As I have not received any answer to my letter, I think it to be my duty to give you all the information of my new plan for your own satisfaction by sending you my printed Extract.

Mr. Cambreleng had presented the second part of my Memorial to General Jackson the President of the United States since the Session of 1831. By those means I have the confident hopes that the President of the United States to be in favour to have the Constitutional Bank to be Incorporated at this Session of Congress, to make a complete reform of the United States Bank, and all those Banks of speculation of this Country who have the power to bring the distress on every class of people of the Nation by curtailing their accommodation of Discount to excite the people to advocate in their favour to have their Charter renewed or prolonged, as the Banks of this City have done in the Session of 1829. Now the United States Banks and their Representatives have had the advantage during this Session of Congress to deliver their long speeches.

Pray Sir: dont you think it is the best time to bring my Memorial forward to the knowledge of the Members of Congress to the standing Committee of the whole States of the Union to make a comparison between the United States Bank, and the Constitutional Bank, which of those two will be the best for the future prosperity of this Nation?

When the Constitutional Bank will be Incorporated to begin their operation by manufacturing the current paper money of this Nation to create their own Capital Stock of 200 million of Dollars, and that great Capital Stock to be destined to support the three fourths of the most industrious class of people to procure them constant employment; dont you think it will be the best way[?] to releive them of their distressing condition?

When the Constitutional Bank will be Incorporated at this Session of Congress, and when the United States Bank will have no hope to have their Charter renewed, they will soon conceive it to be their interest to renew their accomodation of discount during the term of their Charter. And it is to be expected that the local Banks will do the same. On that account the sooner you will be interested to bring my Memorial to the reading of the Standing Committee, they will deliberate on the subject. According to your Office, you have the power to present the report of your respective Committee, and I hope it will be in favour of the Constitutional Bank and the second Company, to be Incorporated at this Session.

Dear Sir: I will esteem it as a great favour if you will do me the honor to send me an answer to this letter.

GASPARD RICHARD

Addressed to Washington.

1. Unidentified.

2. This is an obvious case of giving the wrong date early in a new year. See Richard to Polk, February 3 and June 4, 1834.

3. This document has not been found.

FROM JAMES WALKER

Dear Sir, Columbia Jany 22d 1834

I received last night a letter from Franklin L Smith,[1] in which he encloses a power of atto. to Mr. [Adlai O.] Harris & requests that Wally may be sold for cash, as soon as it can be done, and the money remitted to him to pay off the debts. He thinks him worth now $600 cash, which is what he will command here. Smith says:

"I take this course with exceeding regret, as it seems to be your opinion that it would be better to sell the house & lot, but really I have put off the auditors of the estate so long that I feel ashamed to do so longer while there is available assetts."

If you choose to take Wally at the price say $600, you can remit the money to Mr. Smith, and Mr. Harris will execute a bill of sale to you on his return from New Orleans, say about 1st of April. If it does not suit your Cash arrangements to purchase Wally, and return Little Ben, perhaps it would be better for you to sell Ben, as it is likely he will do no further good on your plantation. I am satisfied that Evan Young will give $600 for either Wally or Little Ben, and put them at the Iron works, which is a good place for negroes. Let me hear from you on this subject, as you see Wally *must be sold.*

I saw a letter from Beanland to Mr Harris, which is about one half oaths &c. He swears he will have Ben or leave the plantation, and have his wages. It is strange that Beanland would tie up your negroes, whip them most unmercifully, then let them run away. He make no exertions to recover them, and when I advised him that Ben was here, he made no efforts to get him, but insults & abuses here because we I suppose did not take Ben to him *in chains,* as there was no other way to get him there, and if we had sent him, there is no security that he would have kept him a week, or made any exertions to get him if he runaway again.

I did not know until a day or two ago, that Dr. Caldwell was your agent, as to your plantation business. He knew Ben was here before he went to the District, and ought to have done what he thought proper with him. I shall advise Caldwell to get another overseer for you, and will try and be satisfied that he gets one that will do. Beanland has not got sense enough, and it is likely he too drinks too much.

So soon as I get my mail business settled & difficulties with Donly so arranged that, I can leave home I will go to the District, spend some time there, and before I leave, see that your business and my own there is in such condition, that we can make reasonable calculations on fair crops &c.

Donly is the Contractor from Tuscumbia to Natchez. This mail or part of the line has entirely stopped. We have no mail from N. O since the 1st Jany. The fault is clearly John Donly's, and still be has gone on to Washington, and himself and other gentlemen of high standing and influence will then contend that he is the proper man to entrust with important contracts. His bids were not at prices *high enough,* and the commercial world must be thrown into confusion, whilst he is obtaining improvements. Is it possible Majr Barry will sustain Donly in such conduct?

James Walker

Addressed to Washington.

1. A lawyer who handled the Marshall T. Polk estate in Charlotte.

FROM WILLIAM CARROLL

Dear Sir: Nashville January 23, 1834

I have this moment finished reading your speach on the removal of the public deposites, and altho I am not in the habit of complimenting public men for the discharge of their duty, yet I have pleasure in saying to you that I consider it a temperate, able and successful vindication of the President. Allow me to add that this is almost the universal sentiment here. As the mail is about closing, I have only time to say, that I hope to have the pleasure of seeing you in March at Washington. Be good enough to write me on receipt of this all the news. Present me respectfully to Mrs. Polk. . . .

Wm. Carroll

Addressed to Washington.

FROM EDWARD W. DALE

Dr Sir Columbia 23 Jany 1834

At the request of Doct. Sansom I have procured some names to the enclosed remonstrance which he requested I should and also herewith enclose it to you requesting your kind attention in presenting to the Postmaster Genl.[1] I am myself inclined to the hope that the fears of our friends at Mount Pleasant are groundless. We are at present verry much in the spirit of making a rail road from this to the Tennessee River. Indeed our citizens genuinely seem to be more alive to this project than at any former period. We have determined to open Books for subscription for the capital stock and to procure the services of a first rate practical engineer to survey the route & make an estimate of the expenses of construction. Do you know an Engineer that you think would suit us and that could be obtained, if so at what cost would his services be? We shall wish the survey and estimates to be made on the most approved plan of constructing such works. Any information that it may be in your power to communicate to us on this subject is respectfully solicited. We are all to pieces as to money matters in this country. The Bank will do nothing and so we go.

E. W. DALE

Addressed to Washington.

1. See James Walker to Polk, January 20, 1834.

FROM GEORGE M. DALLAS[1]

My Dear Sir, [Philadelphia] 23 Jan. 1834

The bearer, Mr. S. Morris Waln,[2] is a particular friend of mine, who has recently suffered a great deal by fire, and whose memorial, praying to be relieved from the payment of duties on certain wines he imported and which were destroyed, has been referred to your Committee. May I beg you to give the subject as early attention as your other engagements will justify, and to facilitate Mr. Waln's progress as much as your views of the merits of his application will permit?

It will give me great pleasure to hear of your health, and of your remembering. . . .

G. M. DALLAS

Addressed to Washington and delivered by hand.

1. Trained in law, Dallas had practiced in New York and in Philadelphia. He had been mayor of Philadelphia and had served two years in the United States Senate. At this time he was attorney general for his state. Later he

occupied several important diplomatic posts and was elected vice-president on the ticket with Polk.

2. Importer and commission merchant in Philadelphia. See Waln to Polk, March 4, 1834.

FROM ARCHIBALD YELL

Fayetteville A[rkansas] T[erritory]
My Dear Sir Jany the 23d 1834

I have not herd a word as yet, from Washington. The cause I am unable to conjecture; I will confess to you frankly I am placed in a Situation by my coming on here, with the expectation of office that has rendered me unhappy; that I am almost a fit subject for a *Mad House*. Here the news preceded me, that I was to be the successor of *Eskridge*[1] which has prevented me from entering into the practice, and at home Ten[nessee] I have quit a good practice, which will leave me without means of support for a Wife & four children, save the exertions which I shall be compelled to make either here or in Tennessee. I have come to the conclusion that the President *has changed his determination* & that I am to rely on my own exertions. To remain here after so *sore* and *mortifying a defeat,* will be more than I can bear; & to go back to Tennessee among my old friends under the disappointment will be a trial that nothing but the care of my family will induce me to forgo. I have been deceived in myself all my life. I thought I had some fortitude but I was mistaken. I shall leave here for Tennessee in about 10 days: what is to be my fate God only knows. From a friend at the Rock[2] I have just learned that a Lawyer Mr Ball[3] from this place has left here for Washington City for the purpose of procuring the office himself and preventing my geting it. He must rely on the influence of Col Sevier or he may attempt to misrepresent me. If he dos let me know all. Keep a look out for this man. You have no doubt done your duty. I can not ask you to do more.

A. YELL

Addressed to Washington.

1. Thomas P. Eskridge, a native of Virginia, had been judge of the superior court in Arkansas but declined renomination. Yell replaced Eskridge on the bench in January 1835. Eskridge died the following November.

2. Little Rock.

3. This is probably a reference to William M. Ball, register of the land office at Fayetteville, a post he had held since 1832. Serious charges were brought against Ball in February 1836, but he was renominated and confirmed shortly thereafter.

FROM WILLIAM P. MARTIN

D Sir. Columbia 25 January 1834

I am informed that at an early period of the present session of Congress an Atto. Genl. for this District will be appointed. Col Washington Barrow of Nashville I am informed is an applicant. I know nothing of Col Barrows qualifications as a lawyer. I know he has native talent little inferior to any young Gentleman within my acquaintance. If you can be of any Service to Col. Barrow by bestowing it you will confer a favour on me. No news. Col. Polk runs well for the Convention. Be so good as to let me hear from you occasionally.

WM P MARTIN

The citizens of this County both captalists & others are half deranged upon the subject of a *rail road* from this place to the Tennessee river. They are adopting energetic measures & *now* seem greatly disposed to commence forthwith.

MARTIN

Addressed to Washington.

FROM WILLIAM J. ALEXANDER

Charlotte, North Carolina. January 26, 1834

Alexander notes that his letter will be presented to Polk by George W. Featherstonhaugh, currently engaged in some geological and mineralogical investigations.[1] Alexander wishes an assay office to be established by the government in his part of the state because individuals involved in gold mining are suffering from the cupidity of the merchants or speculators. He indicates that he has already talked with Henry W. Conner, North Carolina Congressman, about the establishment of such an office.

Addressed to Washington and delivered by hand. The letter has been published in McPherson, editor, "Unpublished Letters," *North Carolina Historical Review,* XVI, 175–176.

1. Featherstonhaugh, an Englishman, spent many years traveling in the United States and, 1834–35, made a geological inspection for the War Department. He is well known for his writings, particularly his *Excursion Through the Slave States* (London, 1844).

FROM JOHN H. KAIN[1]

Knox County. January 26, 1834

A Knoxville physician, born in Connecticut and a Yale graduate, Kain reveals his plans to move to New York or New Haven and asks to be considered a candidate for appointment as postmaster or collector of customs.

Addressed to Washington.

1. Two of his sisters had married Peter and Enoch Parsons.

FROM BURD S. HURT[1]

Dear Sir, Hurt's Cross Roads Ten. Jany. 27th 1834

I see your name announced as a Candidate for the Convention which I have understood, has, been by your consent. I beg leave to assure you, it meets with the approbation of the citizens of Maury generally, so far as my knowledge extends provided it will not interfere with your present office or station.

Notwithstanding the people express great confidence in you, as an officer that has been long tried. Yet a great desire is manifested to ascertain from you if possible, your views on the alterations, or amendments, which you deem wd. be necessary to be made to our Constitution. If it wd. suit your convenience to serve us in the Convention Would it be inconsistent to give us some of your views on the subject in the Western Mercury, or the Nashville Republican?

Perhaps it wd. not be expedient for you to make any publication on this subject occupying the station you do. It is with you to decide.

I discover you have very strong opposition to the Administration, to combat with. But I trust your Cause will end in victory.

B. S. Hurt

Addressed to Washington.

1. He was postmaster at Hurt's Cross Roads in the northeastern part of Maury County.

FROM ROBERT MACK[1]

Dear Sir Columbia Jany 27th 1834

From your declining to come into the Convention, it appears you will have your hands full till late next spring, but I hope not so full that you can attend to the inclosed propectus,[2] as you kindly promised you would at parting.

You know Col., that a man may have a prospectus turning up in his office, or folded in his pocket Book, and never get a Subscriber: *Activity, Yankee* activity, is all such matters. Your situation among the members of Congress, and men of fortune, and literary taste, from all parts of the Union attending in Washington, gives you an opportunity to do much for me in this matter, without encroaching on your business hours. Moments of recreation, or intervals of business in Congress Hall, is best adapted to applications of this kind, as a thing suited to be done *by the bye*. The Members, and Heads of departments, & all that mass of superior, and gifted men, who will spend this Winter in your City, are the very men whose names, whose patronage I wish. Because, if condemned by them, I may rest contented, and not be at the trouble to appeal, unless it be to posterity, the last hope of unfortunate poets. I need not say that the *Presidents* name, at the head of those mentioned, would be both an honor, and pleasure.

The work is now in the press, and I hope to be able to send to your care, a Box containing what may be needed in Washington, some time in April, perhaps sooner. You will therefore see the necessity of *"doing what you do quickly"* and send by the last of March, at farthest, the number of Copies wanted—That is information of the number.

Uncle Sams back is broad. I therefore send on two extra prospectuses, one for George Town, and one more particularly for Baltimore, if your kindness would extend to having them attended to there, by Bookseller or otherwise, as opportunity may serve.

You are at the head spring of news so I will not send Coals

James Knox Polk and Sarah Childress Polk. These paintings were done by Ralph E. W. Earl during the 1830s. They are in possession of the Polk Memorial Association and hang in the Polk home in Columbia, Tennessee.

to New-Market. Only I will say—Cobbs, D. C. Mitchell, & Cahall, are *Out* for the Convention, and as you will see by the last Mercury, Littlefield & T. J. Porter have a call. Will they come out? If they come out will they be *called effectually?* Cant say as to either point. How many more candidates there will be, I have no idea or who they will be but I think a good many more is likely.

It is not *precisely* the business of the Dellegation from Tennessee, to attend to the success of my Poems I acknowledge, but tell *Bell,* and *Grundy,* and *White,* and *Johnston,*[3] that I think it somewhat their business, and shall hold them in some degree responsible, that is as far as relates to the Subscription. As to the work, or what the world says of it, I shall not ask them to say a word for I know a Book that needs defence, cannot be defended.

An outline on the work might be serviceable, but I have not time to give a satisfactory sketch, and less is worse than none. However, the names of the principal pieces may be of use. They are as follows

(1) An irregular Ode on the Death of Washington
(2) Danville Ball—in imitation of Burns' holy fire
(3) An elegy on the Death of J H Davies—irregular ode
(4) Discription of the Battle of *Marengo* by Boneparte—irregular Ode
(5) Kyle Stewart—in Spensarian Stanza Cantos 1 & 2 And perhaps truth Tribunal. Dont know. It might toutch the Congress Hall too hard for my good. Shall take an advisore. In all these pieces (strange to say) there is no humor. Danville Ball is all that can raise a smile. All the rest is mournful—Bloody—moral—grave—censorius and reforming.

Mrs Mack is not present but requested me when I wrote to give her compliments to Mrs. Polk. Pray make them acceptable together with my own. . . .

Robt. Mack

Presumably addressed to Washington although no envelope has been found.

1. A lawyer and judge in Columbia, Mack was a member of one of the

pioneer families in Maury County. He sometimes took care of Polk's legal cases when Polk was absent.

2. The prospectus stated that the book of poetry would contain about 250 pages and would sell for $1.50. Space was left at the bottom of the page for the signature of subscribers.

3. Despite the spelling, this seems to be a reference to Cave Johnson.

FROM GIDEON J. PILLOW

Honble James K. Polk Columbia Jany 27th 1834

Understanding that James Collinsworth, the present United States District Attorney for West Tennessee, will not be renominated to that office, I take the liberty of presenting through you to the consideration of the President, Col Washington Barrow of the Nashville Bar as a Gentleman of high Character and Standing in his profession, and Eminently qualified to discharge the duties of this Responsible office.

Col Barrow is of the Allumnis of the Nashville University, and is known to the President as being of high promise.

I earnestly commend his claims to your attention, and bid you to be assured that your friendly aid in placing them before the president will be kindly remembered by Col Barrow, and will confer a lasting personal obligation on your Friend. . . .

Gideon J. Pillow

Addressed to Washington.

FROM JOSEPH BROWN

Dear Sir Cave Spring Maurey Cty Te Jany 29th 1834

I have taken my pen only to Say that I feel glad that you have been enabled to Defend the Cause of the Presidents Removing the Deposits, but there is One trait of Great men that is Condesention which I alwaise beleaved you possesed and I feel like I do want you still to keep in mind that my Claim May be got thrue in the midst of Bussell, if you Can take time to attend to it altho you no Doubt have much to attend to. But my Claim is the prise of much Blood and the sheding of that procured much

Western Cuntry from which the goverment has Received much Revenue. But my peopel is gone. They Cannot be Brought Back, but the value of the property ought to be paid. But I will clos. Please to write me on the Reseption of this. My family is well.

JOS. BROWN

Addressed to Washington.

FROM WASHINGTON BARROW

Dear Sir Nashville Jany 30th 1834

It is thought here, upon what ground I do not know, that Jas Collinsworth will not be reappointed as United States' District Attorney for West Tennessee. In this event I am an applicant. Although personally unacquainted with you might I not ask your influence & good offices with the President, in my behalf? I have an acquaintance with many of the Bar in Columbia, some of whom have proffered to write to you on this subject. My claims character & qualifications are not unknown to the President & are well known to Mr Bell & others of our delegation. I hope I shall be excused in saying that my appointment would be highly gratifying to a large connection in this & other counties. Hoping that you will excuse the liberty I have taken. . . .

W. BARROW

Addressed to Washington.

FROM J. A. W. ANDREWS[1]

Dear Sir State of Tenn Maury County January 31st 1834

Having heard of the Congressional Globe and wishing to get all the knowledge respecting the acts of Congress that I can I take this method of getting it forwarded to me. If it will suit you to send it on I will settle with you for it on your return to Maury.

I have nothing to write that is new. We are still expecting you to be one of our delegates in Convention. The candidates in Giles & Lincoln are Messrs A. V. Brown & T. C. Porter of Giles[2] & Fulton, Edmiston, Kinkannon and a talk of Col Holman in

Lincoln.[3] There may be others but I have not heard of them. You & Cobbs I expect will have no opposition.

I have not had much news from the city this session of Congress but from the little I have had I presume you have a stormy time of it in Washington which is as I anticipated when the old Hero put Clay's Land bill into his pocket & removed the deposites to the state Banks. But sir all will go right and if men will sneer a little let them do it. It is all that they can do. With the Hero & Statesman at the helm of affairs we can bid their defiance. But I have already written more than I intended and will close by requesting you not to forget the Congressional Globe as I am very anxious to get it. Send back numbers & oblige your friend & constituent.

J. A. W. Andrews

N.B. Please direct it to Cornersville P. O.

Addressed to Washington.

1. Unidentified.

2. Thomas C. Porter, a farmer, had moved to Giles County from Davidson County many years before. He was elected.

3. James Fulton, William Edmiston, Andrew A. Kincannon, and Isaac Holman. It has not been ascertained whether or not this William Edmiston was a near relative of the resident of Davidson County who bore the same name. The last name is spelled Edmunson by other correspondents.

FROM ELIJAH H. BURRITT

New Britain, Connecticut. January 31, 1834

This elder brother of Elihu Burritt requests a copy of Polk's speech on removal of deposits from the Bank of the United States.

Addressed to Washington.

FROM HENRY HORN

My Dear Sir Philad. 31t Jany 1834

The friends of the administration here are becoming heartily tired of the protracted debate in your house upon the Deposite question, and are exceedingly apprehensive that further delay may prove injurious perhaps ruinous to our cause. The change of but few votes will be necessary to turn the majority against us, and we know not what means may be resorted to in order to effect the change. A memorial in favour of Restoring the deposites to the Bank of the U States is now in a course of preparation here that it is said will reach from the Capitol nearly to Georgetown. I am sure at least it would serve to festoon the Entire Hall of the House of Representatives. It is signed by people of all ages and conditions and it is said of all colours. I know that petitions emanating from the quarter which these do if piled upon your table to reach the loftiest dome of your house would not shake the determined resolution of some of our friends. But there are others who I fear would quail under this supposed expression of the popular will upon the question and is it not a dangerous experiment to put their firmness to the test? I am aware that even if our opponents should get the upper hand of us in both houses, the Roman firmness of the Old Hero would not be shaken in the least. He would send back the edict to the house in which it originated. But for Gods sake do not compel him again to throw himself into the Breach to save his Country. Let the popular Branch of the Legislature at least sustain him in his patriotic course.

If we still have the majority do my dear friend rally our forces, sustain the previous question, and relieve us of this awful state of suspense.

Henry Horn

Addressed to Washington.

FROM EPHRAIM BEANLAND

Dear Sir [Somerville] February the 1 1834

Wear all well and I am sorry to in forme you that Elisabeths childe is dead and I have got Jacke at home. I got him out of Heleny[Helena] jaile in the Arcansis which he cost verry near $200 and as for Ben he went back to Maury and Mr Haris has sent him to the iron works and I think that Haris dun rong for I ought to of had him hear at the plantation. This night I will finish fensing my newground, and loosing the work of them to fellows, I have not clearde a fot of land as yet and they has so much timber fallin in the plantation that I must go to cleaning up my old land for loosing Ben it is felt verry sensiable and when it is so wet that I cant work in the old land I will clear. I [k]now that it will take me 1 month to get the timber of one the old land and in that time I must begin to plow which I do not think that I can clear much. I have fensed about 65 acers tho you can tell it is 650 wan way and 525 the other. And Garison is a verry weakly boy and I will take good cear of him. The winter is verry harde and colde and my negro shoes is worn out but I am a mending them to make them last as long as poseable and my dear Sir my corn is but little. I am oblige to fed it on consequence of the winter binge so harde and as for byinge corn they is none hear in the neighberhood to sell under $3 per bariel tho it is cheaper on big Hatchy but by sowing oats and be saving with my corn I want to do with out bying as little as posiable. My stock loocks very bad. I shood like for you to rite to me and let me [k]now what to do in the respect of corn for it is rising daily. Mr Haris rote to me and dyrected me to hire a fellow in Bens place and I did not do it because at the hyringe they was fellows hyred at $130 and another thing Ben ought to be brought back to the plantation for he is a grand scoundrell and I do not think that he ought to be befriended in any such an maner. Now if I corect any of the others any they ar shore to leave me thinking if they can get back to that will do for they must be youmered[humored] to as well as Ben and Sir I do not think any such foolishness as this is write for I caime hear to make a crop and I am determined on doing of it. And Sir on yesterday I seen DR [Isaac] Edwards and he told me that he was not a going away this year but wold still remaine in the neighberhood this year. If you please rite to me and let me [k]now about these fiew things. Nothing more. . . .

E Beanland

Addressed to Washington. This letter has been published in Bassett, *Plantation Overseer,* 61–63.

FROM WILLIAM L. S. DEARING

Natchez, Mississippi. February 1, 1834

Conceding that his chance of obtaining relief for the loss of his surveying notes is small, Dearing requests Polk to introduce a bill that would grant him pre-emption rights to a section of land in Mississippi or Louisiana.

Addressed to Washington.

FROM HILLARY LANGTRY

Dear Sir Columbia 1st February 1834

The enclosed pension certificate of Capt. David Dobbins was sent me today with a request to forward it to you with his best respects and thanks for your attention and he wishes further to trouble you to ascertain the difference in service between himself and Benjamin Carter of this county and for what reason the amount of their Pensions vary![1] Having thus executed my commission I will take a short view of matters & things in general. We have recd your communication declining a seat in the convention with great regret for several reasons. First we cannot easily supply your place, & second your acceptance would have prevented a number of candidates who however unfit are now and will be out. But Sir your reasons and motives have been duly appreciated and the importance of your situation to the country at this time fully considered not only as regards the Bank U S but also in preventing the passage of money bills creating an unnecessary expenditure of public money which may be better employed in relieving the community from the pressure likely to be applied by the Bank. On receiving your letter a few of us heretofore opposed to Mr Littlefield met and believing him the man best qualified who had a fair chance of being elected called on him to serve. He is now lying sick in Nashville and we have not yet recd his answer. In the mean time we have this day had two speeches on the subject, one from T. H. Cahal offering himself on the altar of patriotism for his country's good and one from G. T Greenfield ready to oppose him if no one better qualified offers. Should Mr Littlefield decline as there is every reason to suppose he will, there will be an effort made to unite upon Mr M D Cooper and should that not succeed Coln. Wm Pillow will be called as a firm independant man who can stay at home and beat any opponent who presses himself into the service, but I forgot to say that David C Mitchell has issued a circular announcing himself and his opinions which are really not very objectionable. Of Mr Cobbs we feel pretty certain, but there others yet to enter the lists who you will hear of in due time.

We are considerably excited on the subject of a rail road to Ten. River and from the number and wealth of those who appear seriously interested and convinced of its utility and practicability it would seem there will be little apprehension of its not being completed. Books will be opened here the 17th Ulto. when the true test will be applied. No local news of importance.

With best respects to Mrs Polk. . . .

H. LANGTRY

Addressed to Washington.

1. The writer perhaps made an error in the name of one of these persons. No Benjamin Carter is found on the pension list for Maury County, but his father, Daniel Carter, along with David Dobbins, had been placed on the pension list during the previous year. The pension allotted to Carter was slightly larger than that to Dobbins.

FROM WILLIAM B. TURLEY[1]

My Dear Sir Bolivar February 1st 1834

Permit me to thank you for the valuable present you have made me in your admirable & as I think unanswerable defence of our venerable & patriotic President & the secretary of the treasury against the impotent and malignant attack of a set of reckless and disappointed politicians. You have nobly done your duty and we all here with but few exceptions exclaim strike on and spare not till that vile excresence of our government, the U S bank, be eradicated. The course pursued by Mr Calhoun & Mr McDuffy if truely astonishing, only to think that men who have heretofore had the confidence of the people, men of acknowledged ability, should be willing to destroy our government rather than pay duties raised by a law unquestionably within the words if not within the spirit of our constitution, and yet support with clamour that vilest of all vile violations of the principles of our Federal union, the U S Bank. It is enough to make one lose confidence in public men. At least it must destroy Mr Calhoun & his followers in the estimation of all true men, for political consistency is a jewel for the loss of which nothing can compensate. I feel that the days of the U S Bank are numbered & I rejoice at it; if it could have succeded in the present contest, it would have been our master & not our servant. When it does fall may it fall like Lucifer to rise no more. You must forgive me for thus trespassing upon your valuable time, for after reading your speach I could not consistently with my feelings do otherwise.

WM. B. TURLEY

Addressed to Washington.

1. Turley was born in Virginia but moved to Nashville as a boy. He attended the University of Nashville, read law with William L. Brown, and began practice in Clarksville. In 1829 he became judge of the eleventh circuit, a post that he held when this letter was written. He served with distinction on the state supreme court, 1835–50.

FROM JOHN WALLACE

Philadelphia. February 1, 1834

Wallace, who is not identified, informs Polk that supporters of the Bank, including many city employees, are using bribery and personal threats to get signatures to a petition that will be forwarded to Congress.

Addressed to Washington.

FROM ARTHUR T. ISOM

Maury County. February 2, 1834

A veteran of the War of 1812 has heard of a petition asking that the post office be removed from his store. He is confident that it contains few names of respectable people and asks Polk to forward him a copy.

Addressed to Washington.

FROM ISHAM G. SEARCY

Tallahassee Florida. February 2, 1834

A friend of Polk who had once lived in Rutherford County requests copies of speeches by Thomas Hart Benton[1] and Polk on the question of removal of government deposits from the Bank.

Addressed to Washington.

1. Benton's long address was concluded January 7, 1834.

FROM JOSEPH URY

Tallahassee, Florida. February 2, 1834

A resident of Jackson County, Florida, identifies himself as a former acquaintance of Polk's and reveals that his wife has died, leaving five children. He asks Polk to help him obtain appointment as an Indian agent.

Addressed to Washington.

FROM LOUIS McLANE

Washington. February 3, 1834

Citing the confusion of records in the State Department McLane again requests additional clerical help.

Addressed to Washington. This is a clerk's copy in Report Books, Department of State (RG 59), National Archives.

FROM WILLIAM H. POLK

Dear Brother Chapel Hill N C February 3rd 1834

I received your letter of the 27th enclosing me the other half of the hundred dollar bill and have paid all of it away for Board & Tuition et cetera and am now without a farthing in my pockit. You requested me to state the amount of my debts at presnt. When I wrote to you from Raleigh I stated to you that two hundred dollars would clear me of debt but I was mistaken, it will take $250.00 at least. I am in hopes you will not think that I by differing in my statements wish to receive more than is actualy necessary. You will be so kind as to hurry it on as soon as you receive it from Tennessee for I think that I have suffered enough for my folly. How is it posable for me to study when I am in debt and have not the money to pay them off? Whenever I step out of my room I meet some one I owe. It is imposable for me to look him in the face for I know that he thinks it is time I was paying him. If you will look at my situation you canot help but know that I am at presant one of the most miserable creatures on earth. I do agree to pay all that I expend over three hundred dollars out of my own estate.

WILL. H. POLK

Addressed to Washington.

FROM GASPARD RICHARD

New York. February 3, 1834

Richard refers to his letter of January 22 and asks if Polk has formulated an opinion on his proposal to establish a Constitutional Bank Company as a substitute for the Bank of the United States. He urges Polk to arrange a meeting with Churchill C. Cambreleng and Martin Van Buren to discuss the proposal. It is his hope that they will in turn visit President Jackson to lay the matter before him.

Addressed to Washington.

FROM RICHARD H. MOSBY

Warren County, North Carolina. February 4, 1834

Mosby asks what papers Polk has received on the claim of Dr. William F. Smith and whether or not Smith has recognized Mosby as his agent in settling that claim.

Addressed to Washington. This letter has been published in McPherson, editor, "Unpublished Letters," *North Carolina Historical Review,* XVI, 176–177.

FROM NATHANIEL SMITH[1]

D. Col. Athens Tennessee 4th Feby 1834

I have lately been informed that it will be necessary to have a medical man attached to the party of Emigrating Cherokees that will Shortly leave the agency for West of the Mississipi. If that is the fact I take the liberty of recommending through you to the proper Department for that appointment Doct. Edmund Pendleton Lipscombe[2] (a Grandson of the Celebrated Judge

Pendleton of Virginia).[3] He is a young man of Talents that has been Somewhat wild & unsteady in his habits untill lately. He has become quite Steady & married and bids fair to become a useful member of Society. Any Service that you can render him in procureing Him the appointment will be Greatfully remembered. My Respects to Col. Thos. H. Benton. *You & Him* Well done thou Good and faithful Servants.

NAT SMITH

Addressed to Washington.

1. Smith had represented Grainger County in the lower house of the state legislature for one session. Polk was a member of the lower house at the same time. Smith later was superintendent of emigration of the Cherokees at Calhoun, Tennessee, and seems to have been serving in some capacity in Indian affairs at this time.

2. Other than the information given in the letter nothing has been learned of him. He did not get the appointment sought.

3. Edmund Pendleton presided over the Virginia supreme court of appeals from 1779 until his death in 1803.

FROM WILLIAM F. SMITH

Sir, [Lincoln County?] Febry. 4th 1834

I forwarded by Col [James] Standifer, whom I met in With-Town West Va.[1] the balance of the papers I was able to procure during my visit to the East in October last & should be extremely obliged to you to hear the probable result of your exertions in my behalf &c.

I expect the public Deposit Hurricane must by this time be subsideing. Your Masterly Speech on that subject pleases me better than any act of your whole political career. You preached the funeral of the Bank but it seems that the vault has not yet recd. its *rites,* the last laying on of hands seems hard to succumb to.

Col. Isaac Holman, Wm Edmunson, Col. James Fulton, & A. A. Kincannon from Lincoln & A. V. Brown, Mr. [Thomas C.] Porter & E. Jones[2] from Giles are Candidates for the convention from this District.

WILLIAM F. SMITH

My best respects to Maj W. M. Inge.

W. F. SMITH

Presumably addressed to Washington although no envelope has been found.

1. Wytheville, Virginia, lay on one of the most widely used routes from East Tennessee to Washington, D.C.

2. See J. A. W. Andrews to Polk, January 31, 1834. The Jones mentioned here was possibly Edward D. Jones, but, if a candidate, he withdrew before the election.

FROM ROGER B. TANEY

Washington. February 4, 1834

Explaining that Congress has appropriated money for extra compensation to two judges in Florida without specifying which of the four federal judges should receive the pay, Taney asks for clarification and suggests appropriate action.

Addressed to Washington. This is a clerk's copy in Letters and Reports to Congress by Secretaries McLane, Taney, and Woodbury (RG 56), National Archives.

FROM ALFRED BALCH[1]

Dear Sir, Nashville 5th Feby. 1834

Genl Jackson was kind enough to send me a copy of your speech delivered on the removal of the Deposites from the Bank of the United States. I cannot forbear the expression of my gratification that you have met this question with firmness and discussed it with ability. For after a laborious & painful examination of it, I have long since come to the conclusion that if the govt does not put down that establishment—that establishment will be in effect the govt.

There is in the speech of Calhoun on this subject infinite ingenuity & subtlety.[2] But it might be answered. Now he & Clay are endeavoring to put Van Buren out of their road and if this cannot be effected Calhoun would then go for a southern League were he not afraid that his own blood would first atone for his treason as it surely would. Calhoun is immeasurebly a worse man than Clay. His ambition is like a devouring flame.

The Methodist Bishops, Itinerant and Local preachers &

class leaders throughout the north west are taking the field in favor of McClean.[3] We will soon set the Blue stockings—the old & new side Baptists & Cumberlands upon them and cut them up. Their pans are already primed & their triggers cocked.

For myself I entertain for McClean a warm personal regard. But, if his friends will have war we shall return it with the knife & the knife to the hilt. For I make no terms with mortel man when the interests of Van Buren are brought in question. For ten years—even whilst the old Crawfordites lay in the ditch totally overthrown, I have laboured for him incessantly night & day "in season and out of season" as the apostle saith, & I hope to see my wishes consummated on the 4th of March 1837.

No alternative is now left, unless we wilfully pass from our hands the power which we now hold into those of Clay & Calhoun or McClean, but to rally around Van Buren, and advocate a national convention.

It is impossible for me to believe but that Jackson will escape from the storm which is now raging around him triumphantly. If the politicians are against him the *people* are with him.

ALFRED BALCH

Addressed to Washington.

1. Prominent lawyer of Middle Tennessee who had at one time lived in Columbia.

2. Calhoun addressed the Senate on January 13 on the question of removal of deposits.

3. John McLean.

FROM THOMAS J. LACY

Dear Sir, Pulaski February 5th 1834

I thank you for your admirable speech which I received a few days before I left home. It has added greatly to your reputation, both among your friends, & those who have heretofore been opposed to you. There is but one opinion in relation to its merits, and that is, its one of the very best of our congressional efforts, replete with arguments, illustration, and facts, abounding in just & noble sentiments, clothed in appropriate & felicitious diction. I am happy to see it so generally & highly praised & recomened by all our prints. I intend in a short time to review it myself, & *speak of it & its author as I think & feel* and in a manner I trust that will be of some little service to both. I send[?] you the Republican of 1st inst. in which you will see an article signed Pinkney—read if you have time, & after you have done so, *show it if you please to the President.* It contains nothing but what is gleaned or suggested by your speech, but I hope it will not on that account be the less valuaded. I intend visiting Washington this winter if I find it practicable. My best regards to Mrs Polk, & so wishing you health, happiness, & success in all your undertakings. . . .

Thos. J. Lacy

P.S. I am here attending to the cases of Lester[1] on the part of the state. The trial will not possibly come on. Your speech is all the rage here as well as at Columbia, &c &c.

Addressed to Washington. The letter is marked "Confidential."

1. This is perhaps a reference to German Lester, a Pulaski lawyer.

TO LEWIS CASS

Sir Ho. Repts. Feby. 6. 1834

I desire to be informed whether in your opinion the effect of the refusal of the Bank to surrender the possession of the Books, papers & funds, to meet payments under the act of June 7th 1832, will be to postpone the payments to those entitled, until the Books &c. shall be recovered from the Bank; Or can the Department in your opinion furnish copies of such Books &c. and other funds to the deposite Banks authorized under the mint order to make the payments. The act of June 7th 1832 makes a standing appropriation whereby it is to be carried into effect. Will you inform me also whether the funds now in the hands of the Bank have been drawn from the Treasury, by warrants under this standing appropriation; and also the amt. of the funds set apart for the purpose of carrying into effect now in possession of the Bank. If the whole of the information asked cannot be immediately given, will you be good enough to furnish me with that part of it which can be given without delay. I wish it, if it suit your convenience to day.

James K. Polk

Addressed to Washington. Letter is in the Letters Received by the Secretary of War (RG 107), National Archives.

FROM ANNE NEWPORT ROYALL

Washington. February 6, 1834

Anne Royall, controversial publisher of the newspaper *Paul Pry* (1831–36), acknowledges receipt of money from Polk.[1] She cautions that she is under no obligation to him and also complains of Polk's reluctance to pay. She concludes with disparaging remarks about Clement C. Clay and Samuel W. Mardis, Polk's friends in Congress from Alabama, saying that they had been converted to money religion.

Delivered by hand to the House of Representatives.

1. Appended to the letter is Royall's statement that she has received $2.50 from Polk in payment for a subscription to *Paul Pry*.

FROM JAMES H. THOMAS

Columbia. February 6, 1834

This Columbia lawyer asks whether or not Polk has received the pension declaration of John Langley, who had served in the Revolution.

Addressed to Washington.

FROM WILLIAM T. BARRY

Washington. February 7, 1834

Barry informs Polk that information sent to him earlier about hiring extra clerks in 1833 was incorrect. He complains that the appropriation for the salaries of clerks is presently the same as it was when the Post Office Department had half the work it now has. Barry concedes the relative unimportance of a request for a new engine house.

Addressed to Washington. This is a clerk's copy in Postmaster General Letter Books (RG 28), National Archives.

FROM WILLIAM J. WHITTHORNE[1]

My Dr. Friend Shelbyville Tenn Feby 7th 1834

I write to you to give you a short history of some of our local affairs in Bedford, as relates to candidates Elections &c. We had an Election For colonel commandant in our Regiment the 5th on the 5th Instant. Candidates John T. Neill and James C. Record,[2] formerly of your county, Record Elected by Eight votes. To day, we had an Election for Brigadier General, Candidates Robert Cannon of Shelbyville, and Ephraim Hunter, of Farmington. Cannon, Elected by 5 votes. We have a Host of Candidates for the Convention. Coln. Saml. Mitchell, Coln. Webster, Coln. [Aaron] Boyd,[3] Doctor Kincaid, Sqr. Fonville, Major Holt, Sqr. John Thompson, and it is highly probable, there may be some others in a few days more.[4] I think Coln. John T. Neill is, also a candidate. Realy this State of Bedford of ours is a prodigious place for candidates; of all these it is my impression that Mitchell and Kincaid will be Elected as the representatives from this County.

Our County Court is in session. Every thing going on smooth, and Extremely fine Weather for the season. My Dr. friend I have also to inform you that the Cloud which hung over myself for some time past is about to pass over and Brighter prospects before me. By the death of an uncle of mine I am Enabled to pay all my debts, and have Something left. My neighbours about Farmington begin to say again that this Whitthorne is a first rate fellow. I realy feel Renewed, Regenerated, and almost feel a new Impulse to push ahead again and regain all my former Energies (but Enough of this). I give you this Early information of the Elections in order that you may Know how to address These Right Honbl. Gentlemen. I expect to Keep a close look out for any thing of this Kind and let you Know any thing that I think would Be to your interest. I am yet in the notion of going some further to the South or West. If you can procure me any appointment in the Creek, Chicasaw or Chocktaw nations or any of the Territorys, you will please to do so. I believe you can do almost anything you want to do and I believe you never forsook a friend or forgot a favour and under this belief I have strong hopes that you will procure me some appointment. Give my best respects to Mrs. Polk. Tell her little Jim is going to make a fine fellow. You will please to tender my best respects to my friend Mr. Inge. . . .

W. J. WHITTHORNE

Please to let me hear from you as soon as convenient.

W. J. W

Addressed to Washington.

1. A merchant at Farmington who was one of Polk's most loyal supporters. The "little Jim" mentioned at the end of the letter was Whitthorne's son, who had been named for Polk.

2. A resident of Farmington, Record became prominent in Marshall County when it was organized in 1836. He was designated a commissioner to lay off and sell lots in Lewisburg.

3. A resident of Chapel Hill; not otherwise identified.

4. For other speculations on the probable candidates see Erwin J. Frierson to Polk, January 1, 1834, Robert P. Harrison to Polk, January 3, 1834, and John A. Moore to Polk, January 7, 1834. For a later list and a report on the results, see James McKisick to Polk, March 7, 1834.

FROM CARUTHERS, HARRIS & COMPANY

New Orleans. February 8, 1834

This letter, in the handwriting of Adlai O. Harris, reveals the sale of ten bales of Polk's cotton and the crediting of $429.67 to his account. It comments on the inferiority of West Tennessee cotton and predicts a drop in cotton prices.

Addressed to Washington.

FROM ADLAI O. HARRIS

My Dear Sir New Orleans 8 Feby 1834

I arrived here on the 2d Inst. and am getting pretty well initiated into the minutia of the commission business and am very well pleased with it. This city has improved so much since my last visit here that it has become quite a pleasant residence. I shall however not remain here very long perhaps not later the 15 March, as our business will require my attention in the upper country where I must confess I would much rather be. The cotton market is very gloomy indeed and unless there is some way found out to dispose of English Bills I do not know what we are to do—for the purchasers are compeled to suspend operations unless they can sell Bills.

My very best respects to Mrs Polk.

A O Harris

Addressed to Washington. This letter was enclosed with the Caruthers, Harris & Company letter of the same date.

FROM SAMUEL G. SMITH

Dr Sir Nashville Feby 8 1834

Your favour of the 23rd Jny. came this morning. I send you the reports made to the Legislature from our two Banks. They have not materially varied since that time I expect.

The call on the stock in the Union Bank made fifty dollars on the share paid in. Thus you see one half the capital has been paid.

It is all the information we have in this office touching your inquiries. Previous to the establishing the Union Bank we had no other than the State Bank and for the last four years the amounts of notes in circulation by it does not exceed fifty thousand dollars.

Messrs Yeatman & Woods Bank[1] being private we have no means of information but I am informed that their bills on New Orleans amounts to near nine hundred thousand. They deal in bills exclusively, much of it in Alabama & the W. District. From the United States Branch Bank we have no information but that you will get from the Statements already before you.

I am informed that the circulation of notes on the Branch Bank has increased notwithstanding the curtailment of discounts.

Our Banks hold few of the notes of other Banks as they are not receivable.

The abundant crop of grain with a large quantity of live stock exported for the last four years and the advanced price in the market has afforded a plentiful circulating medium principally in the Sections of the State not engaged in raising cotton or within the immediate influence of the Bank. Much of this particularly west of the Mountains is in specie.

It is alleged that the policy of the Banks making their notes payable at other places will drive the specie from circulation but as yet it has had no such tendency. I presume the past notes sustain no greater loss than was paid for drafts on the eastern cities.

It is understood here that the Branch Bank is directed to cut down her discounts two hundred thousand Dolls. This I immagine is not considered here as an act of necessity but because she has the right to do so. They have been taking bills for the runing notes and this call will not be so serious with those who have been prudent.

In taking a view of the pecuniary situation of the country I can recur to no period when it was more favorable.

SAM G SMITH

The speeches are published in part in the newspapers so that they are not read with the same interest or advantage. If you have some of yours in pamphlet please send them as I may hand them out to your friends.

The business of your Comee. must throw many documents in your way any of which I shall read with interest.

Presumably addressed to Washington, but no envelope has been found.

1. Joseph and Robert Woods continued operations of this bank after the death of their partner, Thomas Yeatman, in the summer of 1833.

FROM JOSEPHUS C. GUILD[1]

Honl. J K Polk Gallatin 9th Feby 1834

I have twice read your speech on the Deposits. You have with Mr. Benton not only triumphly sustained this important measure of the President but have done honor to the state you represent and placed your self upon an eminence that few have the good fortune to reach.

Such speeches as yours and Bentons among the people will soon convince the opposition that they have lost instead of gained by the argument.

Accept of my best wishes for your happiness. . . .

J C GUILD

Addressed to Washington.

1. At this time Guild was a young lawyer in Gallatin; later he enjoyed a distinguished career as a judge. He also wrote a book of reminiscences, *Old Times in Tennessee.* He was a close friend of Balie Peyton.

FROM ANDREW C. HAYS

Dear Sir, Columbia Ten. Feb. 9th 1834

Some weeks since I wrote you upon the subject of Mr. Walker's difficulties with his mail routes &c but am pleased to learn from your communications to him, that the Department are acting in good faith toward him. His *routes* at this time are in successful operation, and what has not been done in this country before, his stages has not ceased to run during the *winter,* and worse roads I have never witnessed.

I said something with regard to the Convention, and the *wishes* of yr. friends as to yr. being a candidate &c. You addressed a letter to Mr. Walker upon the subject, which you will see published in the Mercury. Mr. W. was from home when yr. letter arrived. I opened it, and believing that the state of things here and your own interests required its immediate publication, I took upon myself the responsibility and had it done. Previous to the receipt of this letter, we had an almost perfect calm upon the subject, it being conceded on all hands, that yourself and Cobbs would be the Delegates, but the moment your determination was made known, an extraordinary excitement was the consequence. Mr. Cahal *instantly* announced himself. Several others were called upon through the paper, all of whom *declined—modestly* alledging as a reason want of *capacity* instead of the *true* one, want of *popularity.* Dr. Thomas, has since had himself announced. D. C. Mitchell, Dr. T., T. H. Cahal & R L. Cobbs[1] are the only candidates at this time clearly in the field.

Efforts are making to unite the two opposite parties here upon M. D. Cooper or Col. Wm. Pillow. Cooper appears to be the choice of *our* folks. In a few days it will be determined which shall run—if, *either,* and I think, Cobbs and one of these two gentlemen will be the Delegates. Cahal, however, will be hard to beat, principally because neither of his compettitors will have an oportunity of mixing with the people, the election being so close at hand, and he is but lately from among them. He came to my office late last night, and introduced the subject of the election, observed that *"Col Polk's friends* ought not to against him *so hard* as he feared they were doing—that he was the fast friend of Col. P. and always had been, &c.—that he was as able to serve him in any of his views, as either of his *compettitors"* &c.—that "he doubted not but you would be a candidate for *Governor* and if he had no other *influence* he could *write* and what he wrote, could be published" &c. I replied "that this was an election of so much importance, *party feelings & prejudices,* should not be suffered to operate, and that so far as I was informed, your immediate friends so regarded it and upon this principle they would act. If it so turned out that they voted *against him,* it would not be from any hostility or personal opposition, but because they believed it to be their duty." Many of them I had no doubt would support him. "And many oppose him—this was to be expected"—and that "Your relations & particular friends, should certainly be allowed to exercise their priviledges, without endeavoring to make a party question of it." He seemed not disposed to press the subject & it was here dropped.

The annunciation of your name for Convention in the Whig & Banner (of which you justly complain) was done as I afterwards learned upon the authority of Mr. Booker. When it first appeared I observed the *improper* manner in which it was done, and wrote immediately to the Editor, requesting him to give such explanation as would shew to the public, that it was not authorised by you. Feeling pretty certain, that it had proceeded from some one in this quarter, I requested him to say from what point he received[?] his authority. He done so, but in so awkward a manner that I almost regretted having said any thing upon the subject. It is now however, all past, and understood.

By reference to the "Mercury" you will see that I have attended strictly to your several requests.

Your speech, and the numerous commendations of it, is furnishing a happy influence in your favor here. It is a source of much satisfaction and rejoicing on the part of your friends, and equally mortifying to your enemies, particularly, to *those gentlemen,* whom I *mentioned* as having been making *predictions* with regard to your success during the present Congress, nor do I let a single occasion pass to give them a *hit* upon this subject. In short, this speech, has done more for you than any other act of your public life, and I feel gratified that it is so, because the prophecies of some folks are not fulfiled.

Your favor enclosing the *caricature* was received yesterday. I have it posted up in my office and it affords considerable amusement to all who have seen it. Do not fail to send a copy of any similar publications that may be brought forth. Also be so good as to send me a copy of the Plan of the Hall of Rep. such as you sent to Knox[2]—with names of members.

On yesterday we had a very large and respectable meeting at the Court House, to take into consideration, the propriety of Constructing a *Rail Road* from this place to Tennessee river at some point near Carrollville Ten. Several speeches were delivered and resolutions passed, among the resolutions it was determined that Books should be opened on Monday the 17th for the taking of Stock, at which time the Citizens of this & the adjoining counties were invited to assemble at the Court House for further deliberations. Resolutions were also passed inviting the Commissioners of the Florence & Pulaski rail Road companies. A delegation from Florence attended our meeting on Saturday, among whom were Mr. Tarply, Judge Weakly and Mr. Dillahunty.[3] Mr. Tarply made a most ingenious argument, the object of which was to induce us to join the Florence company & terminate our road at Florence—they propose to meet us half way. He failed however to convince the meeting of the propriety or advantages of the connexion owing principally to the fact of Colberts Shoals being in the way. You cannot immagine the degree of excitement that exists upon this subject. It has already had its influence upon the price of property here, not a doubt being entertained but that all the Stock will be taken. The Nashville people are greatly alarmed at its probable success and well they may be, for if it does succeed Columbia will in a short time not only be what Nashville now is, but greatly ahead of her in commercial importance. We will then have superior commercial advantages, and this in connexion with our rich fertile & healthy country cannot fail to make Columbia equal our fondest anticipations.

Your relations and friends are all well. Present my best respects to Mrs. Polk and for yourself receive renewed assurances of my high regard.

A. C. Hays

Did you receive my letter?

Addressed to Washington.

1. Cobbs and Cahal were elected.

2. Joseph Knox Walker, Polk's nephew.

3. Collin S. Tarpley, James H. Weakley, and Harvey Dillahunty. Weakley had moved to Florence in 1817 from Tennessee and worked with John Coffee as a surveyor of public lands. After Coffee's death, Jackson appointed Weakley to succeed to the position of surveyor general of Alabama, a post that he held until 1851. Dillahunty was a lawyer in Florence.

FROM JAMES H. PIPER[1]

Dear Sir, Knoxville Feby 10th 1834

I wish to obtain the appointment of a visitor to the Military Academy. I have long wished for an opportunity of inspecting that institution, and of becoming acquainted with the course of study and system of instruction furnished there.

Should it be agreeable to you to aid me in the prosecution of my wishes, I will be deeply and sincerely thankful for your kindness.

Please to present me to Mrs. Polk in the most acceptable manner; and accept for yourself assurances of the very high respect and great personal regard. . . .

James H. Piper

Addressed to Washington.

1. Formerly a resident of Columbia and president of Columbia College, Piper was at this time president of East Tennessee University.

FROM ROGER B. TANEY

Washington. February 10, 1834

Having heard of a proposal to increase the salary of the chief clerk in the State Department, Taney asks for a similar increase for the chief clerk in the Treasury Department.

Addressed to Washington. This is a clerk's copy in Letters and Reports to Congress by Secretaries McLane, Taney, and Woodbury (RG 56), National Archives.

FROM ARCHIBALD YELL

My Dear Sir Shelbyville Fby th 10th 1834

I must congratulate you on you very able an temperate speech on the Deposits & the High standing you have acquired by it not only in the Nation but at Home in Tennessee.

I am requeted by Col Sam'l Clay[1] to ask you to make some examination in the proper departmt to assertain if the name of his Farther John Clay a capt in the *Revly* War can not be found. The name of Capt Thos Clay is published & he thinks the name is wrong & that it is his Farther *John Clay.*[2] Your attntion to this matter & leting him know will verry much oblige your frnd &c.

(*Confidntial.*)

I have had an offer for my prpty in Fayettville which I think I shall accept. If so I shall (strange to tell) return to Arkinsaw & settle in Washington Conty where I can make as much mony as I can here & have good health & where I can be, if anywhere, some service to the Admtration & his *Successors.* It will in a few years be admtd into the Union as a State, when a struggle will be made for the ascendency & I intend to be there & take a hand. I have there mny warm friends & old acquantences who are very desirous that I shall return. I haid not less than 6 personal Tennessee frnds in the last Legislater that would go the Hogg for me for any thing.

I have but little acquantence with Col [Ambrose H.] Sevier tho I once lived in his Town but he was most of the time in Washington. I wish you to see him & converse with him on the subject & see what his feelings are, & let me know confidentially. If I could form a partnership with Sevier in the practice for 12 months it would be of service to me & not injure him. If he talks in such a way as to autherse you to say so, you may propose it for me. All this I wish done without leting my *frind Inge* know any thing about it for if it should turn out that I should not go, he migh[t] use it in a *future Contest.*[3]

During this session I shall enclose to the Presidnt some lettrs from my Arkinsaw frinds directed to you & I wish you to presnt them.

I am not asking for office at present but I wish the Presdnt to be informd of my standng in this Territoy & that I go there to suppot his Admtratn & the Successon of *Van* for Presidnt & *Dick Johnon*[4] for Vice Presde, that Bank must go or we must & our *Party.*

I am making mony wher I am but sir I am sorry to say I am not contended. I must engauge in the coming struggle & here I can do no good—but there I can if I am not verry much mistaken.

If you see proper you may say to the Presidnt what is my intntion & that I will shortly forward him some letters for the Territory. There is no office at this time in the Territory that I want. If the office of U.S. atto should be vacant I would accept it if no perticuler frind was an applicant, but I am perticuler or choissy about it.

I go to make sumpthing out of the admsion of the Territory into the Union.

Sevier can be of infinite service to me if he is disiposed. A partneship with him is all I would wish—not the prophits but the character[?] & acquantence that I should form by it. You can say to him what you think prudnt on that subject & let me know &c.

Please let me here from you shortly & write me in that frank & firm manner you have heretofore done.

Bob Cannon was elected Brgr. Genl over Col [Ephraim] Hunter by 5 votes.

A. Yell

Addressed to Washington. This letter was so hastily and carelessly written that it was virtually impossible at some points to decipher it. It is believed, however, that the basic meaning has been faithfully represented.

1. A resident of Shelbyville who was a colonel in the Bedford County militia.

2. There seems to have been such an error as suspected. John Clay was placed on the pension roll in 1833 and drew his pension in Rutherford

County. No person named Thomas Clay appears to have drawn a pension in Tennessee.

3. Yell makes it clear that if things did not work out satisfactorily in Arkansas he would return to Lincoln County and run against Inge.

4. Martin Van Buren and Richard M. Johnson.

FROM ZACH B. ZIEGLER[1]

Dear Sir Philadelphia, Feb 10th 1834

I have been instructed by the Committee of Correspondence, to present to you the inclosed copy of the proceedings of a meeting held by the Citizens of the "Third Congressional District," for the purpose of expressing their sentiments in relation to the all important question of a restoration of the Public Deposits, and the consequent recharter of the U.S. Bank.[2] You will perceive by the tenor of their Resolutions that the People in this section of the country have arisen in their strength, and with a determination which cannot be subdued have expressed their firm intent to shake off the golden fetters by which they were bound, and regain those rights which had been wrested from them. To you who has been the Pioneer of their cause in the House and to those who have acted in conjunction with you, they look with confidence, for a speedy termination of the question, by a steady adherance to the measures of our patriotic Chief Magistrate, and the Secretary of the Treasury, relative to that institution. The noble stand which you have taken, merits and will receive our abiding gratitude and we want but an opportunity to give you such an earnest as will prove the truth of our present professions. On the speedy and final settlement of this great question most undoubtedly depends the future prosperity as well as perpetuity of our Republican institutions; it will unquestionably decide whether the government is to be administered by the sovereign will of the People, and by them alone, or on the contrary, whether an irresponsible monied corporation, usurping that power, shall in future conduct the operations of that government; and control the Nation with its despotic sway, to the total subversion of those great and immutable principles upon which our Republic was founded, and for the maintenance of which our sires had pledged their all.

Our country will be preserved; the invincible spirit of Democracy headed by the Hero who has preserved it from a foreign foe, aided and assisted by a Benton in the Senate and a Polk in the House will again prove unconquerable by a signal triumph over a domestic enemy. In my humble opinion the far famed evils of the Pandora box are slight in comparison to those which have been poured upon the community by the proscriptive course of the Bank not only in the present [un]merciful application of its screws but by its former specimens of fair business transactions. Many who would have considered it as the highest insult under heaven to have been called *slaves* have become its *serfs,* men who have been decidedly opposed to a recharter of the Bank were compelled to sign memorials in favor of a restoration of the Public Deposits by their *honorable* creditors the Bank men. Many instances might be cited w[h]ere coersion was used to procure the signature of individuals; but the case has already been so ably discussed by both Houses as to warrant the belief that they are in possession of all these facts. I therefore beg your indulgence for having thus long trespassed on your valuable time. Permit me to express my thanks for the copy of your very able speech which you did me the honor to send. The committee add their assurances of high regards.

ZACH B. ZIEGLER

Addressed to Washington.

1. Except that he was a printer in Philadelphia, nothing has been learned of him. It is likely that he was connected with some newspaper in that city.

2. This enclosure has not been found. It was probably similar in nature to that enclosed by William J. Crans in his letter to Polk, January 22, 1834.

FROM SAMUEL BIGHAM

Livingston. February 11, 1834

Bingham reports that he has sold his land to Thomas Ross and will soon be moving to Levi Cochran's place. He has heard that there are objections to his continuing as postmaster and therefore wishes to resign. He indicates that he has appointed Ross as the assistant to handle the duties until some final decision is made.[1]

Addressed to Washington.

1. There were objections to the appointment of Ross as the postmaster on grounds that he was a supporter of Henry Clay; see George W. Haywood to Polk, February 16, 1834. A man named Thomas Ross became one of the first justices of the peace in Marshall County; it is probable that he is the same person who is mentioned here. For other references to this matter see Haywood to Polk, January 7, 1834, and Bigham to Polk, February 22, 1834.

FROM LAURENCE LOLLER

Berlin, Tennessee. February 11, 1834

An Irish immigrant who had moved to Tennessee in 1818, Loller asks for help in establishing correspondence with relatives remaining in Ireland. He expresses hope that some of them might join him in America.

Addressed to Washington.

FROM JOHN G. MOSBY

Richmond, Virginia. February 11, 1834

The writer reveals that he has learned from his brother, Richard H. Mosby of North Carolina, that Polk has talked to Andrew Stevenson about the claims of James Smith of Virginia and asks what information Polk has on Smith.[1]

Addressed to Washington.

1. See John G. Mosby to Polk, March 1 and March 23, 1834.

FROM ARCHIBALD YELL

Sir Fayetteville Febyth 11th 1834

I wrote you on yesterday from Shelbyville informng you of my determination to return to the Territoy. On my return home this evning I found a letter from my friend Judge [William] Fulton Secty of the Territoy informg me that Judge [Alexander M.] Clayton had returnd to Tennessee & would resigne without delay, as he is informed. I furthr learn that Sanl Roan[1] the present District Atto will be an applicant. If so & he is appointed as Claytons successor you are requested to present my name to the President for the appointmnt of U.S. Atto &c.

Should Roan not be appointed Judge, as an applicant then I would accept of the Judgship if you & my othr frnds thought me qualifyed for an Arkinsaw Judge. But I should prefer the office District Atto, as I could settle in a section that I should prefer & as I should not hold eithr long for I go there to take a hand in Politicks.

I wish you to see Col *Sevier* & tell him what I have written you. I should like to have his influence if he is not unfriendly & otherwise enguaged. I have this eving written to Fulton who says he will if I desire it forwrd to the President a recommendatn & take an interest in the matter himself. I shall request Fulton to send them to Sevier or the Presidnt—they will reach you on about the 25th of April.

I deem it unnessay to forwrd from here a recommendation. The Presidnt knows me & you & my othr frnds can guess at my qualifications &c.

If I should get the appontmt I will not hold it 2 years. I shall try my hand at sumpthng else by that time. That Territoy must come into the Union full blooded *Jacksonian.* The Senate must be got back to its original purity or things will work badly.

On the recpt of this you will please inform the Presidnt of my intntions & applicatin.

I know I have exausted your patience by repeated questions & solicitations.

A. Yell

Addressed to Washington.

1. Samuel C. Roane was a native of Tennessee and a nephew of Archibald Roane, an early governor of Tennessee. Thomas J. Lacy succeeded Clayton, and Roane retained his position as United States District Attorney.

FROM NATHAN GAITHER[1]

Dear Sir. Columbia (Ky) Feby 12th 1834

I have watched with deep interest the movements of Congress. I regret the inclination of some men in our Country, to keep up the political storm and I regret more to see our senior branch of the legislative body flying out of their orbit; it presages no good. While they proffess great care in guarding against executive usurpation it has been obvious to all, they wish to absorb all power themselves and become the very Tyrants they proffess to abhor in others. The Bank & deposits seem to be the absorbing subject. The people will sustain the president upon that question and if the distress so falsely set forth by Bank friends was real the people will say like the surgeon to his patient when extracting a carious tooth, bear the pain a moment it will never pain you again. The pettyfogging argument urged by some that the Bank is the Treasury of the U.S. is laughed at by almost every body, and they think it is a bad cause that require such absurd grounds for its basis. The doctrine relative to the executive department is to well settled now to be disturbed as to its unity altho it has a plurality in Council. I have read your view upon that point. It is too clear to be disputed. The president will fill his cup to over flowing with his countries gratitude by strangling the Monster. By it the Country will be rescued from despotism and our free institutions preserved. He never falters in his duty and therefore I put down those declarations in the opposition when the bulk is to found false. You have no aid from my successful competitor. I know him *well*. I believe I displeased Blair[2] & others by my vote on the force bill and thereby was not aided in the struggle. I have nothing to regret upon that subject nor my views upon the proclamation. I have been the advocate of principle and the land marks were plain in the political history of my Country. But my attachment to the president was not diminished and the good he had done the cause was so paramount that nothing but a disavowal of his Message doctrines could have thrown me from him. You see our legislature is about making a Bank. It will be well received by the people opposed to the whole system. I take the state institutions as the lesser evil. You see the nomination of Johnston[3] in this state it is the sentiment of our Country. His is a tryed friend and they know him; Van Buren stands high with most all but the Nationals.

I look forward to the presidential election as the crisis in our government. I hope the friends to the good cause will not divide. I am sorry to see so many of our old friends voting with those men now that two years ago they would have thought their political ruin was inevitable if their names were recorded with theirs.

I have no political aspirations but feel much as a Citizen upon the success of our Country. I expect to remove from this early in the spring but shall be glad to hear from you how things are going if you can spare the time.

Present me to the president if it does not exclude business. Let him know that we go with him upon the deposit question as well as all his Message principles, vetos & all. I am consuming too much of your time.

NATHAN GAITHER

Addressed to Washington.

1. After representing Kentucky in the United States House of Representatives, 1829–33, Gaither lost in his bid for a third term.

2. Francis P. Blair.

3. Richard M. Johnson.

FROM EPHRAIM BEANLAND

Dear Sir [Somerville] Febuary the 13th 1834

Wear all well and I am sorry to informe you that I do get alonge so slowly. I have started my plowse, ondly 4 of them yat and on this day a weak ago Hardy left his teame standing in the field and on last night I got him home. And on this morninge Jim and Wally when I calde them they both answered me and I tolde them to starte there plowse and they boath started to the stable and I have not hearde of them since which I had not struck them a lick nor thretened to do it nor in fact I did not [k]now that they was insulted any way. And Dear Sir I will be canded with you if Ben is not brought back Mister Haris had beter take the rest of them untill I get Ben. I [k]now that they will run a way untill I get Ben and you will do me a never to be forgoten if you will have Ben sent to me and in the saime tim oblige your self. If he is not sent heare and maide stay all the rest of the fellows had beter be sent to Maury for I will be damde if I can do any thinge with them and they all ways in the mads and if you do any thinge in ths matter I want you to do it as soon as posiable and you will oblige your friend.

E BEANLAND

Addressed to Washington. This letter has been published in Bassett, *Plantation Overseer*, 64–65.

FROM PETER HAGNER

Washington. February 13, 1834

Hagner acknowledges Polk's letter of the day before and informs him that James Smith is not entitled to commutation pay. He encloses Smith's papers.

Addressed to Washington. This is a clerk's copy in Congressional Letters Sent, Third Auditor's Office (RG 217), National Archives.

FROM ARCHIBALD YELL

Sir Fayetteville Feby th 13th 1834

Enclosed I send a letter to the Presidnt which I wish you to hand him. Its on the subject of the appoitmnt I wrote you a few days since. You can learn what he will be disposed to do & wrte me.

I have to day written to Col Sevier who will take some steps either for me or be disposed to throw obstacles in the way.

I can do better in that Territory than I can posibly here.

I have not written a word to Inge nor shall I. He is under no obligations to me nor will I place myself under any to him. The balance of the Delegation from Tennessee (Crockett excepted) I think likly would be for me.

In the District for Convention I think Fulton, Porter & Kincannon[1] will be elected.

YELL

Addressed to Washington.

1. Yell's predictions were accurate. James Fulton and Andrew A. Kincannon of Lincoln County and Thomas C. Porter of Giles County were elected to represent the district in the constitutional convention.

FROM JOSEPH BROWN

Maury County. February 14, 1834

An old resident of Cave Spring writes at length about his hopes of compensation for property losses in Indian campaigns, alleging that the correct amount of his claim is $750.

Addressed to Washington.

FROM SAMUEL W. POLK

Jackson College [Spring Hill]
Febuary 14th 1834

Dear Brother

I have returned to Jackson College to persue the studies of another long but not unprofitable session.

I expect you have so much buisness to attend to that you have no time to spend in perusing letters, but as none of the family seems to be writing I thought I would make an attempt although there is not much to write about.

On Saturday last there was a meeting in Columbia for the purpose of making a rail road from there to Tennessee river, on wich there was several speeches made. Mr. Cahall has declared himself a candidate for the convention, as he says by the solicitation of many friends. His circulars are now in circulation. Mr. Cobbs I expect will be one of the conventoners but he has not declared himself a candidate as yet. There is a good many more solisited but I believe none of them are willing to serve. I believe if any of them thought they could be elected would willingly permit there name to be runn.

I expect you have heard of the death of Col William Polk[1] who died a fiew weeks since. It grieved Lucius and Leonidas very much to hear the death of their father and a thing so unexpected. Annis Looney[2] died on Monday of an inflammation of the brain. It is supposed to have been occasioned from a fall from a gig.

Dr. [John B.] Hays has given out the notion of moving up to Mothers and has risolved to try it another year.

On the subject of the College we have now one of the graduates from Nashville who has taken Mr. [Benjamin] Labarees place and Mr. Labaree is now president. I recite all my lessions to him and do not think I could be bettered at any other institution, whilst I recite to him. I am now studying [. . .] majors and Salust. I will enter the sophomore class next session. Remember me to sister Sarah and tell her that she must not forget how to write altogether.

SAMUEL W. POLK

Addressed to Washington.

1. He died on January 14, 1834.

2. Unidentified. She was probably a member of the family of Abraham Looney of Columbia.

FROM JAMES WALKER

Dr Sir Columbia Feb. 14th 1834

I send you a letter just received from George Moore which advises of Hardy's running away &c. I am at a loss to know how to remedy the difficulties at your plantation, and to know whether fault is in the negroes or overseer. I hope in a week or 10 days to get my stage business so arranged that I can go to the District, and when I go there, I will endeavor to find a cure for the present difficulties. Your negroes must be put under discipline, and if Beenland really cannot manage them, I must make an effort to get a man that can. I have no authority from you to act, as I might judge necessary for your interest and to be certain that I am conforming to your wishes, write to me particularly on receipt of this, addressed to Bolivar. When I go out I shall remain some time in the country as long at all events as my affairs or yours requires my presence. Beenland can have Ben on application at the Iron works, but as Wally must be sold, it will perhaps be as well to sell Ben in place of him, as Ben says he will not serve you under Beenland. I am not sure that to sell some of your most refractory negroes to *real negro traders* would not be the best thing you could do to reduce the ballance to subjection, and if *Chunky* Jack, could with propriety be sold it ought to be done. I do not know whether Chunky is at your plantation or not. I heard Moore had swapped another hand for him, but from his letter I infer he is at your plantation.

When I go to the District (which will be early in March) I will consider your affaires, as my own, and risque your being satisfied with what I may think for the best, under such circumstances as may exist.

I have run stages on the Tuscumbia line all winter, and packing[?] the mail to Huntsville three times a week, since I received notice of its restoration. The roads are now getting better, and I hope to have our part of the road run in five Post Coaches in the course of next week. A considerable alteration has been made by Mr. Simpson (the Agent) in the running of the Tuscumbia line. This has rendered it necessary for me to put on an additional Team and change sevral of the stands. Upon the whole the Mail keeps me quite busy, and I cannot leave home until I get it all perfectly regular, and I want Majr Donly to arrive at home, that I may know fully the result of his trip to Washington. I cannot think there is any chance of his injuring me there. Still I do not like to leave him, until all results are known.

There is much confusion here about members of the convention. Cooper is not yet at home, and we are at some loss to manage Williamson Smith's[1] pretensions. We hope however to beat Cahall, and if we do this, we shall probably be satisfied. Your speech on the deposite question has given very general satisfaction to your friends, and although I am a U.S. Bank director, I am perfectly satisfied that Gen'l Jackson is right in *crushing the monster,* tho I still think a national Bank upon correct principles is the true doctrine. The recent instructions however to the Western Branches, satisfies me that the *present* Bank is not entitled to public favor.

I have not time however to write on politics. But we have hitherto agreed on all political questions except the Bank (and partly on that). I think we should not now disagree on that.

JAMES WALKER

Addressed to Washington.

1. Matthew D. Cooper had been mentioned earlier as a possible candidate and as one whom the Polk partisans would support. Williamson Smith, a Polk supporter whose friendship seemed important, apparently had only recently revealed his candidacy. He was later elected to the state senate and represented Maury County, 1839–41.

FROM HORATIO COOP

Bedford County. February 16, 1834

After thanking Polk for assistance in procuring a military pension for him, Coop insists that he is not receiving all compensation due him.

Addressed to Washington.

FROM EPHRAIM D. DICKSON[1]

Sir. Dresden Ten 16th Feby 1834

Our Sham representative[2] in your house has inundated his District with Clays & McDuffies speeches which is having its influence on society here. We are not all newspaper readers or it would have no effect (this you might know by the member we return). I wish you if you have any of yours more than you wish to send your constituents to send me 100 or more to this Office & I will distribute them to advantage as I have the charge of the post office here. Also the same No. of Col. Bentons. Please shew this to the Cols. Benton & Bell as they with yourself are my old acquaintance & friends.

EPHRAIM D. DICKSON

Write me the fate of the Cols. Land bill.

Addressed to Washington.

1. He was a member of the first county court in Weakley County and was at this time postmaster at Dresden, the county seat.

2. David Crockett.

FROM GEORGE W. HAYWOOD

Dear Col Moulonvert [Bedford County] 16th Feb 1834

You will find enclosed a petition to the Post Office department from a great number of your constituents praying removal of the post office from the late residence of Saml. Bigham Esq to that of Maj William Davis.[1] You have been aprised no doubt ere this time what has led to this procedure. It is thus, Esqr Bigham the late post master at Livingston has sold his land to Thos Ross whom the people do not like well enough to have him continued as postmaster. Since his removal to the office nearly all the papers have been discontinued or transfured to Macon & Cornersville. Mr Ross is very unpopular in his neighbourhood & as an evidence of that fact you need only to glance at the manes[*sic*] on the petition for the removal of the office. I Believe that it has been an universal rule with the department never to continue an officur or appoint one who is opposed to the present administration of the governmet. You know that Ross is a Clay man & has allways been violently opposed to Gnl Jackson & to yourself in all of your elections & now is the time to pay him in his own coin when you will be at the same time complying with the wishes of so maney of you constituents in this neighbourhood. The petition is a little awkwarly writen but still it conveys the wishes of the neighbourhood on the subjets which it embraces.

As to my own part it would be more convenent for me that the office should be continued at Livingston but I am allways willing to yield to a majority & so far as it can be ascertained I am confident that it is the universal wish that the office should be removed to Maj Davis's. This will be the nearest rout also for both mails being directly on the rout from Franklin to Cornersville & not more than one hundred yars out of the way of the Shelbyville & Waynesboro rout as meisured by Esq Bigham.

We were much pleased at you masterly speach made on the deposit Question. Well done thou true & faithul servant you will have your reward.

G W Haywood

N.B. It has been just ascertained that Mr Ross has gotten up a little petition or reccommendation to the department reccommending him as a suitable person for Post Master. It must be reccollected however that this recommendation does not come from the neighbourhood which supports the office but from Cornersville which is even out of our congressional district. We are rather too high minded in this neighbourhood & understand our rights too well to permit ourselves to be imposed upon in this kind of stiele. What are we to suiffr our selves to be govened by a [. . .] grovling living in such a place as Cornersville! Has it come to pass that we shall become the vassals of susch a *fellow* as Thos Ross & one or two of compeers. Shall the will of the majority be thus trampled under foot when it is execised in so good and so just a cause? In a word shall Thos Ross have the powr of making the people knuckle to him wether they will or not!

G W H

Addressed to Washington.

1. This petition has not been found. The move was accomplished, and Davis became postmaster.

FROM MOSES DAWSON[1]

Dear Sir Cincinnati 17th Februay 1834

It was with great pleasure I received your esteemed favor of the 4th Inst. both on account of the general information it contained and the highly flattering terms in which you write of my good friend Mr. Lytle.[2]

When such men as yourself and your worthy Coadjutors in Congress support and sustain our venerated President his measures must be approved of by these truly republican patriots who elected him.

Seeing nothing to the contrary in your letter I took the liberty of publishing as well to shew our friends here that all is right in your House notwithstanding the defection in the senate as to let his constituents know that Mr Lytle had acquitted himself so well in defense of their favorite President. I therefore hope for your excuse for taking that liberty with your highly valued communication.

We are at present in no small [. . .] here on account of the illiberal and oppressive conduct of the United States Branch Bank. Some of our superficial frinds affect to fall off from the party on the ground that the Bank should either be rechartered or another one be established and indeed there is no little dissatisfaction with some of our true friends arising from apprehension that if the Bank be put down and no substitute raised in its place there may considerable difficulties occur to our commercial interests.

I have myself been reflecting on the subject and am somewhat anxious that something be done to give a currency to the country that would occupy the place of the present. People have been so accustomed to the convenency of having a currency of equal value at all points of the Union that they are extremely apprehensive of trouble loss and inconconvenience when they will have nothing but the notes of the various Banks to travel with over the Union. As a substitute for the notes of the United States Bank I have been thinking of an issue of treasury notes to the amount of the year's revenue—say from to twenty to twenty five millions. They would of course be paid to the offcers of the Govenmnt, Members of Congress and for all other expencis. They would be taken in paymnt of all revenue and dues to the Govenment. And if the credit of the Bank of the United States was established in its partial connexion with the Government surely the treasury notes must obtain unbounded credit when that govenmnt would be responsible for their redemption entirely and all within one year.

There is another circumstance to which I would beg your attention and that is the relative value of Gold and silver. From the Circumstance of Gold being of more value in Europe than in this Country compared with silver would it not be well to reduce the standard weight of the Gold Coin of America so as to more nearly to assimilate that value to that of Europe? It appears to me that there is a heavy expense incurred in the Coining of Gold here which is entirley lost in the melting pots of the European Gold smiths and it strikes me that if the standard was brought up to that of England alone it would prevent the exportation of Gold specie as well as encourage a gold circulating medium. These I confess are crude ideas on this subject but I have been induced to revert to it in consequence of having perceived some time ago [. . .] kind of inclination on the part of Congress to do something in the business.

I fear my dear Sir that I have been over prolix in this letter and have too far encroached upon your valuable time. Therefor after thanking you for you kind letter I subscribe myself. . . .

Moses Dawson

Addressed to Washington.

1. An Irish-born newspaper editor in Cincinnati, Dawson was an ardent Irish nationalist and had been forced to flee from Dublin, where he had helped devise a school system for that city. After a brief stay in Philadelphia, he moved to Cincinnati, where he became the editor of a paper that he made into a strong antifederalist sheet. As a firm supporter of Jackson, he came into conflict in his columns with Charles Hammond. He and Hammond, however, remained friendly in their personal relations.

2. Robert T. Lytle, born in Ohio, became a lawyer in Cincinnati. After serving in the Ohio legislature, he was elected as a Jackson Democrat to the United States House of Representatives, serving 1833–35, and failing of re-election in 1834. At this time he was Polk's colleague in that body.

FROM KENNETH L. ANDERSON

D Sir. City of Balt[imore] Feby 18th 1834

The matter I mentioned you this morning I should be much obliged by its complesion. I am well satisfied that the president is much engagued at this time and often applied to for office by his friends that his conclutions as regards his friends in Tennessee is more dificult to arive at than in any other state. But as I mentioned to you this morning my friends Colo. McKisick, Gilchrist & Yell[1] had mentiond me to the Genl for the appointment of Marshall of Midle or of West Tennessee, I think in 1830, or at any rate about the time of the appointment of the present incumbent, and before these Letters could have reached him I noticed the appointment of Colo [Samuel B.] Marshall[2] of Nashville. To be canded with you I consider myself qualified for that office and am in such circumstances of life that an office producing a little cash answers me much the best. I would not knowingly do any man in or out of office injustice. But I am not satisfied that the president could not do a worse act than to give us an appointment in Bedford in the neighbourhood of his friend Colo. A.E.[3] However I leave the *whole* matter to you. Should you be of oppinion that my being appointed would be productive of good I shall thank you to give it your attention. Should you be of a contrary oppinion do nothing in it and at the same time be assured I shall certainly remain the same and unchangeable. I am unwilling that any other man should see this letter or know anything in relation to it.

K. L. Anderson

P. S. You must take time within 2 weeks to write me. On this subject Let me hear from you.

K. L. Anderson

Addressed to Washington.

1. James McKisick, William Gilchrist, and Archibald Yell were among Polk's most loyal supporters in Bedford County. McKisick was county clerk, and Gilchrist was a lawyer who at one time had been in partnership with Yell.

2. He had been appointed United States Marshal by Jackson in 1831.

3. A sarcastic reference to Andrew Erwin, who was strongly against Jackson and Polk.

FROM McKAY W. CAMPBELL

Dear Sir Columbia Feby 18th 1834

You must—I know you will, excuse me for troubling you with a letter when you are so very busy—when you see it is mostly on my favorite hobby a *Rail Road* from this place to Ten. River. I tell you *Sir* with pride & pleasure that Yesterday (17th Feby) was to the *County* of *Maury* the *Birth Day* of *her Commercial Freedom.* Yesterday the Books were opened for taking of Stock in the Columbia Rail Road. Four thousand shares of Fifty Dollars each was necessary for the incorporation of the company. The business has gone on *Gloriously* nearly *Five thousand shares were subscribed.* My Revd. & *Esteemed* Yea, I may say *my beloved Friend—Leonidas Polk*—made the very best speech that could be made on the occasion on the opening of the Books. He also addressed the people at Mt. Pleasant on Saturday last on the subject & made the best speech I *ever heard.* My *Dear Sir* I tell you he is the *first* man in the country & the only man in our District who I would heartily support for the exalted station you now occupy shld. *you,* from *any* cause, retire from it. He is like his *noble father* who I Lament to say has passed that *bourne* from whence there is no return—a *man* of *Soul,* of *Patriotic* firmness, that must & will attach the people to him—add to these his unassumed his native dignified plainess & courteousness of *manner.*

Col. Polk we will probably be under the necessity of importing the *Rails* for the Road (notwithstanding a *poor fellow* offered to *Split & furnish 5000* rails for *Rail Road* by way of doing his part) and we I suppose, must have an act of Congress in our favour allowing us to import them free of duty, unless there is some general provision on this subject. Will you be so kind as to *attend particularly* to this *matter for us? If a special act is necessary, have one* passed for our benefit at the present session allowing us to import the Iron necessary for the construction of *"our Road"—free* of *Duty.* The Road will be built. It is the most popular *measure* that ever has been agitated here. *It annihilates Partyism.* Don't forget to remember this *matter.*

The Subject of a convention is almost lost in the Rail Road. The moment your determination on this subject was known here Mr. Cahal became a candidate. So long as it was understood that yourself & Cobbs would serve if Elected there were no other candidates nor would not have been had we been permitted to have kept your name before the people. Since your name has been withdrawn they are out like *Burns'* cattle "in shoals & nations." *You ought* to have *been there* Col. Polk—with the assistance our *Rail Road* would have *given You* we would have had the *seat of Government* fixed at *Columbia.* I recd Your letter & must thank you for your attention. Nothing new. Will you *or not* send me the paper I requested You to send me?

The mail is closing & so must I close this letter.

M. W. CAMPBELL

Say to Judge Campbell[1] we are all well.

Feby 19th. I was too late for Yesterdays mail. Say to you that yesterday swelled our R. R. Stok subscriptions to abt. $300,000. I think we will get nearly ½ million this week. We have a Rail R. Ball on 22nd. Property is already rising in anticipation of the R. & will of course fall in Nashville. Col Pittival[2] C. Engineer of Charleston S. Carolina is now here & has been engaged by the Comy. to make a recognaisance of the rout between this place & Ten. R. will set out on that work today. He surveyed the Jackson (W[estern] D[istrict]) & Mississippi rout. The W.D. people have a right to extend their Road to Ten. R. & they intend meeting our Road *there.* This will connect us directly with the Miss. R. You will see at once that this will make *our county* the very *core of the Heart* of Ten.

Give my kindest Respects to Mrs. Polk and to Judge Campbell—for I rec. a letter from him 17th informing me that Mrs. C. & her Daughter were in Philadelphia.

M. W. CAMPBELL

N.B. Will You send me the speeches of Clay, W.[3] & Calhoun of the Senate & the most considerable ones in your house in Pamphlet form?

Addressed to Washington.

1. George Washington Campbell.

2. Formerly of South Carolina, John B. Pettival had served as resident engineer of the Charleston and Columbia Railroad. In Tennessee he surveyed

the route from Jackson to the Mississippi River and several routes from Columbia to the Tennessee River.

3. There were no less than five men in the Senate whose surname began with this letter. The reference, however, is probably to William Wilkins of Pennsylvania, who made a speech on the deposits question on February 5 and 6, 1834.

FROM EBENEZER J. SHIELDS

Pulaski. February 18, 1834

Assuring Polk that the pension papers of Lawson Hobson, which had been returned to Tennessee for correction, are now in order, Shields asks him to certify the signature of chancery court clerk Charles C. Abernathy.[1]

Addressed to Washington.

1. See Shields to Polk, September 28, 1834.

FROM SAMUEL G. SMITH

Dr Sir Nashville Feby 18 1834

We are looking to Congress with no ordinary interest and in common with the people of the union, Tennessee look to you as occupying a situation of the first importance, so far as regards the support of an administration with which they are inseperably identified. In defiance of the many dificulties you have to encounter we are sanguine in the expectation that you will be able to sustain the course of the President until time to test by experienc the position he has taken. I presume the people are now aware of the object of the opposition and put the present controversy upon the ground of a struggle for the recharter of the Bank. I do not profess to be a polititian nor give out opinions upon questions of great state policy but I am inclined to think public sentiment is by no means settled in Tennessee as to the next presidency. Many of those who have some pretention to understand public feeling here seem to be silent and stand aloof as not being informed of the views of the aspirants in relation to the policy of the present administration. The opinion that those who are much in the confidence of the president or resident with him are not familiar with the people of his own state or inclined to keep him in the dark.

If such is the fact of which I profess to be ignorant it is entirely uncertain what course Tennessee will take. That she will sustain the sound republican doctrine I have no doubt but should there be two professing the same or more she may be very much divided or turn upon some new and unexpected connection in organizing the parties. That the anti V B strength is increasing I have very little doubt but to what extent I am unable to say.

You no doubt have been informed of the interprising spirit prevailing in your district on the proposition to construct a Rail Road from Columbia to Tenn River. Should there be vacant land on the rout is it within the policy of the administration to appropriate it for the road so far as it may be actually covered by the tracks or road, taking into consideration the peculiar situation of the tittle which the general government has to the land claimed from North Carolina with its incumbrances? Should all these concur to justify it no doubt your constituents would be gratified to see you had taken some notice of it. Thus far I am inclined to the opinion that a majority of the candidates for the convention are for electing the judges by the Legislature. Much difficulty may arise from other opinion but with prudence I hope we may have a constitution more favourable for stability and republican principals than was antisipated.

SAM G SMITH

Addressed to Washington.

FROM JAMES WALKER

Dear Sir Columbia Feb. 18th 1834

I have received yours of the 2d. I received your letter of the 16th of January, on the 18th was just starting to the Iron works on business of some importance, and do not recollect acknowledging the receipt of this letter & enclosure. Immediately on the receipt of the order restoring the Huntsville line I commenced sending it three times a week. I hope by Sunday to have my part of the line in stages. I have been unfortunate in my post Coaches. The vessel on which they were shipped from New York in a storm at Sea, threw overbord all except two bodies & 1 set of wheels. Mr. Hough is supplying the defects, but it will be several weeks before they are ready for the road. I have however now two post Coaches on the road, one a very fine one manufactured by Hough in Nashville—the other one of our District Coaches repaired. I have now 10 Teams on the road two coaches & three light stages, and hope by the middle of March to have three additional fine coaches. The schedule has been entirely changed, and the present manner of running requires on our part two more Coaches, and one Team more than the manner of running under the proposals. I have careful steady and experienced drivers (our District boys) and I hope to make no failures unless some extraordinary accident happens to justify it. But from the treatment Mr. Donly has received, I should suppose the best and most advisable way of obtaining high standing, with Maj Barry, would be to make failure upon failure, to totally stop all mail communication between New Orleans & Nashville for a full month, to the ruin of commercial operations, between those places, to employ the most worthless and dissipated men to transport the mail, and then post off to Washington and ask of Maj. Barry, to take away a fair contract from some individuals, who were in good faith performing their duty. If such is to be the rewards of failures, and total unworthiness of public business, Maj Barry can and will soon drive the worthy and efficient from his service. It is degrading too, to men conscious of high standing, to have their *just rights,* and fair contracts, jeopardised to favor so utterly a worthless man as John Donly—and even if the thing is not done, or when done is corrected, still it is a *tantalising* that I do not see how to excuse.

The course you have taken in all this matter, is *very satisfactory to me,* and I am obliged to you for your close attention to my interests. You have represented Mr. Brown & myself in that manly and fair manner which I wished. So many strange things have occurred in this business, that I am at a loss to know when the trouble will be over, nor how much assistance may be necessary from the ballance of the Tennessee delegation friendly to Brown & myself. I have however great confidence in the justice and intelligence of the President. I rely too, much on Col. Gardner, and the representations which I have much reason to believe Mr Simpson (the agent of the Department) will make.

Mr. Simpson has travelled our lines, seen what kind of men, Teams & managment we have and I think made himself well acquainted with all our different characters & pretentions and I think his opinion is a decided one.

The conversation you relate as having passed between Majs Barry, Lewis & yourself is certainly very extraordinary. Maj Barry must certainly have taken too much wine, for he never could cooly advance such doctrines, and be competent for the station he holds. What is it to me whether Donly forfeits his contracts or not? And if he does forfeit contracts & bids which I had no concern in is that any reason why I should take his forfeited contracts *at his foolish and dishonest bids,* or have taken from me other contracts, which he has no just claim on, and which I am faithfully executing on the faith of contracts with the proper officers of the government? Before bids were accepted was the proper time for Maj Barry to think of its being best for the whole contracts from Nashville to be in the hands of persons who are friendly. Maj Donly fixes his affections on a particular line, and because he has not got it becomes unfriendly, to those who have, and Maj Barry must take away the just rights of others, to please this *spoilt pet,* and thus place the contracts between these designated points in his hands, and then it would all be in friendly hands. But I see you understand this matter perfectly and there is no use in my furnishing you with arguments to sustain our position.

You ask me to say whether we (S. B. Ewing & Co.) would be willing to take the contract from Tuscumbia to Natchez at Donly's bids. To this I answer unhesitatingly, No—we cannot begin to think of it. We had nothing to do with making the bids, and will under no state of circumstances, take the contracts at them. We will however take the contracts at our own bid, and put them into operation as soon as practicable after notice is given us to do so. But if our bid is accepted at this late hour, we want to be permitted to go on peaceably and quietly to execute our contracts, without being continually harrassed by Donly's efforts to get the P M.G. to take from us what contracts he has thought once his duty to give us. I do not however wish you to officially apprise the P M.G. of this determination. If he thinks proper to make this proposition let him do it to me in writing officially, and if he chooses annex it as a condition, that if S. B. Ewing & Co. do not take the contracts at Donly's bids—that *Walker & Brown* are to forfeit their interest in the line from Nashville to Tuscumbia. If such is to be the alternative it ought to be fully known and understood, and put down on paper officially signed, that bidders may see & know how far they are to calculate on security in purchasing property &c, after their bids are accepted, and that we may truly understand what kind of a government we live under.

The mail is waiting and I have not time to close this letter. I will write you again to-morrow. I enclose you a letter received from Harry Hill in January. When he says "he certainly bid off the whole line agreeably to your own statement largely under any other bids" he says what is not true for I never made any statement to him or any other person about the bids for the whole line. I do not know them. I told Hill what we got from Nashville to Tuscumbia, and what was the bid of S. B. E. & Co. from Tuscumbia to Natchez and this was all I told him. These were *separate* and *disconnected bids* & so were Mr. Donly's and all were decided on their merits with a strong disposition in the department to decide every thing in Donly's favor that could with propriety be done.

James Walker

Addressed to Washington.

FROM JAMES WALKER

Dear Sir Columbia, Feb. 18th 1834

Whilst I was writing this morning the mail came in earlier than usual & I was compelled to close without saying all I had to say.

You will see by Mr. Hill's letter & the one I enclose you from Col. [Robert] Armstrong[1] that even Donly's best friends acknowledge him to be in the wrong, and admit that he misrepresented the bids (Mr. Hill does this). The truth is at the public meeting at Nashville & in signing the memorial that Donly took on, the people only understood themselves as protesting against sending their mail to New Orleans round by Murfreesborough & Huntsville—they never understood themselves as requesting the P M. G. to take away our portion of these lines and give them to Donly. Present this question plainly and fairly to the decision of the people of Nashville & I would be willing to abide the result. These things are however matters of no consequence. If Maj Barry requires me to take Donly's bids or he take away our portion of the Tuscumbia line, I want you to clearly know that *I shall not under* any circumstances take Donly's bids from Tuscumbia down but will take S. B. E. & Co's.[2] I am however very willing to take the whole line from Nashville to Tuscumbia at the present price & let Mr. Donly have nothing to do with it. He had nothing to do with the original bid, and why does Maj Barry hire K. & C.[3] from the public crib to transfer to Donly (put upon me a scoundrell for a partner) and then speak of giving Donly the ballance because Donly chooses to act an illiberal & unfriendly part towards me. If the contracts from Nashville to Natchez ought to have been all in the hands of one company why was it not *so advertised* and why were not the bids *so accepted.* Donly has the contracts from Tuscumbia down at his own bids, what more does he want? The post-office Department purchased out Kinkle & Caruthers part of the contract between Nashville & Tuscumbia & paid for it without his being any thing. This would seem humoring enough for any spoilt child. I hope he has no [. . .] to my house & home nor any of my plantations, as I think Maj Barry has just as much right to give him any of these as what he asks. I understand Maj Barry to speak of giving Donly *our part of the line* to induce him to stand up to his bids cooly made for the lines between Tuscumbia & Natchez and on which he has made failures that would have ruined any other man. If he were even to do this, what security is there that Donly will even then be satisfied until his pay is raised. But enough of this; I know you understand the case fully and I rely upon you to see that no advantage is taken of us. I shall attend to my duty faithfully, and regularly pass all mails that are delivered to me. If Maj Barry becomes guilty of so great an oppression as to take the mail from us, it must be so. I am too weak to contend with the government. But the power cannot be taken from me of contending with Donly, and I am cooly and deliberately determined to run the road, in five Coaches, and with superior Teams & drivers for the next four years, *mail or no mail,* and if Maj Barry wrongs me, I will expose that wrong to the people, and to their representatives in Congress and ask of Congress to render justice for injures inflicted by an officer of the government. This whole story, including the circumstances under which C & K transferred to Donly their interst in the Tuscumbia line, would not look well in print. I do not wish to be understood as threatening, but you know I never can forgive an intentional injury, nor cease to seek to punish those who improperly inflict them on me. This matter must now take its course and the consequences of my action on it, is to rest upon myself & my children.

This stock for a *Rail Road* to the Tennessee River will be taken—near $300,000 is now subscribed & the road will be made & a new era take place in this county.

James Walker

Addressed to Washington.

1. The Hill letter was not found. The Armstrong letter said that Hill held claims on Donly's property but was not necessarily Donly's agent. Armstrong admitted that there was confusion on the line south of Tuscumbia, but he said he was at a loss to explain it.

2. S. B. Ewing and Company.

3. Kinkle and Caruthers.

FROM JAMES M. LONG[1]

Benton Missi [Yazoo County]

Dear Sir

Feby 19th 1834

In all probability there will be a va[ca]ncy at this place in the P. Office Department. The young man who holds it now is going to Virginia this spring I think will resign as he at present only keeps it by deputation.[2] I will receive it as a particular favor if you can consistently with your knowledge of me, recommend me to the head of the department. I have written to my friend W[illiam] C. Dunlap. As it has been some time since we have been acquainted permit me to bring myself to your recollection. I was raised at the Fishing Ford Duck River. My Father

Richard Long[3] Lives 3 miles north of Farmington and Brother Brumfield & Thos.[4] I expect you have but little time to read apolages.

James M. Long

Addressed to Washington.

1. It has not been learned how long the writer had lived in Mississippi. His family was known to Polk, and at least one of them was on his mailing list for government documents.

2. The vacancy did not materialize. The incumbent, Robert L. Adams, remained postmaster at Benton for several years more.

3. See Richard Long to Polk, December 4, 1833, in which he asks about a pension for himself.

4. The brothers are not further identified.

FROM JAMES WALKER

DR Sir Columbia Feb. 19th 1834

I received the enclosed letter from Beenland[1] a few days since. I replied to him that upon receipt of your letter requesting it, I had instructed Mr. Ferguson[2] to give Ben up to him. He will get him on application. I however informed Beenland that I had advised you of the necessity of selling *Wally* and that you might prefer selling Ben in his place. Therefore it would be as well for him to delay going after Ben, until he heard from me or you again on the subject, as he would have Wally in Ben's place in the mean while, and if it was necessary or for your interest he had better if in his power hire another hand in Wally's place. I informed him that you had full confidence in him and that he had nobody to please but you, that he must get his negroes under subjection, and if any more of them runaway, get them again by all means, and if there was reason to believe they were attempting to get entirely away to confine them in Jail, and in case of emergency I would take the responsibility of selling any of them —but if I sold I would sell to nobody but a regular negro trader who would take them to the lower country. I informed him that I would be in the District early in March, and would spend some time with him, and aid and assist him all in my power to get the plantation in proper discipline and to stop this propensity of running away—and if nothing else will do, some severe examples must be made. As soon as I can know that all matters are arranged & settled down between Donly and me, I shall leave my stage business in charge of Neville & Groves[3] & spend some weeks in the District, attending to our three plantations. I am anxious to be there when my crops are planted, and when there I will take the same interest in your plantation that I do in my own & whatever I am satisfied is for your interest to do, I will without hesitation take the responsibility of doing. I will consider your plantation and affairs as my own, and act for you as I would for myself. This you may rely on. I much regret that Donly's extraordinary conduct and the more extraordinary countenance which the P M G. gives him, should render it necessary for me to be here now instead of being in the District as I very much wish to be.

The more I reflect on what passed between Maj Barry & you, the more extraordinary his conduct appears. In fact, I can hardly restrain my contempt. It was just such a conversation, that before alarmed Caruthers and made him go into the *compromise* transfering Donly one half this line. After this was all done he was informed that the Department had no intention of reversing the decision on the bids—but wanted to bring about a compromise for Donlys accommodation. I have no compromise to make except that I am willing to take the whole line from Nashville to Tuscumbia at *our* original bid and further that we will take the contracts from Tuscumbia to Natchez at *our bids*. I will not take any at Donly's bids, but I do not care for this to be known positively at the Department. Whatever propositions they have to make let them do it to us officially in writing and anser the penalty of refusing to take Donly's bids.

If Mr. Caruthers when he goes on, as I expect he will, makes a contract on a/c of C. & K. & W. & B. to convey the mail between Tuscumbia & Natchez & Madisonville, I will stand up to the agreement he makes. The post office Department can get clear of Donly (and I think all of them except Maj Barry wish to get clear of him) and get much better and more efficient contractors in his place. If we have anything to do below Tuscumbia Mr. Brown will take Neville down, and go down and attend to our portion of the business, and both you & [William C.] Dunlap know that both James Brown and Toliver[?] Neville are very efficient men.

JAMES WALKER

Addressed to Washington.

1. This letter was found. It has been published in Bassett, *Plantation Overseer*, 63–64.

2. This appears to be someone at the iron works where Ben had been hired.

3. Neville and Groves, obviously trusted employees of Walker and Brown, are not otherwise identified.

FROM SPENCER CLARK GIST

Washington. February 20, 1834

A midshipman from Knoxville, Gist explains his petition to Congress for additional compensation and asks Polk's aid. He acknowledges that he probably should have turned for help to Luke Lea instead.[1]

Delivered by hand to the House of Representatives.

1. Lea was a member of the House of Representatives from Gist's district, 1833–37. See Gist to Polk, May 10, 1834.

FROM THOMAS WATSON[1]

Sir, Reading Room, Newbern, N.C. 20th Feby. 1834

You will confer a favor on many of your friends here by addressing a copy to the Newbern Reading Room, in pamphlet form, of your Speech on the Deposite Question. The favor will be increased if you will at the same time, transmit pamphlet copies of the Speeches on the same subject by the Hon. Mr. Benton, the Hon. Mr. Forsyth, and the Hon. Mr. Rives.[2] Excuse this liberty: it is taken under the belief that you will readily pardon it.

THOS. WATSON
Proprietor Newbern R. Room

Addressed to Washington. This letter has been published in McPherson, editor, "Unpublished Letters," *North Carolina Historical Review,* XVI, 177.

1. Editor of the *North Carolina Sentinel,* which was published at New Bern.

2. John Forsyth and William C. Rives were senators from Georgia and Virginia, respectively. Rives resigned two days after this letter was written but returned to the Senate in 1836. Forsyth resigned his seat in June 1834 to become Secretary of State, a post he held until 1841. Forsyth's speech was made on January 27 and 28, 1834. Rives delivered his speech on the deposit question on January 17, 1834.

FROM ELIJAH HAYWARD

Washington. February 21, 1834

This informs Polk that the reason Daniel Graham[1] had never been paid for obtaining information about vacant lands in Tennessee was that Graham had never submitted an account.

Addressed to Washington. This is a copy and is not in Hayward's handwriting. A second clerk's copy is in Miscellaneous Letters Sent, Bureau of Land Management (RG 49), National Archives.

1. Graham was Tennessee's secretary of state, 1818–30.

FROM SAMUEL BIGHAM

Livingston. February 22, 1834

Bigham notes that a number of citizens of the area have forwarded a petition to the Postmaster General asking that the Livingston post office be moved to William Davis's place. George W. Haywood has also written a letter to that effect. He states his opinion that if either the Macon or Livingston post offices should be discontinued, the one at Macon should be closed.[1]

Addressed to Washington.

1. Neither post office was abolished at this time. The records for 1835 show William Davis as postmaster at Livingston (formerly Rock Creek) and Benjamin Williams at Macon (formerly Beech Plains). On February 8, 1834, Thomas Ross had taken the oath as assistant postmaster at Livingston.

FROM WILLIAM CARROLL

Dear Sir: Nashville, Feby 22, 1834

I take the liberty of addressing you on a subject in relation to which it is probable I ought to be silent. It is known to you that nearly three years ago the President promised me the appointment of Minister to Mexico as soon as circumstances would authorise him to make it. A letter which I recd. from Major Eaton this evening informs me that the President believes the relations between us and Mexico now require that the appointment should be made[1] and that he will make it if the Committee of Ways and Means report a bill for an appropriation and succeed in passing it. As Chairman of that committee you have much in your power, but I do not wish you to do any thing to promote my wishes which you may deem inconsistent with the interest of the country. Allow me however to say that the whole western country feels a deep interest in obtaining the fine Province of Texas, and I believe that it is also the desire of the President. A more propicious time for the attainment of this object cannot be expected. A revolution has terminated very recently. The Republic is in debt and must have money. But on this point you know more than I do. Major Eaton has advised me to visit Washington, which I shall do, and expect to leave here if nothing happens to prevent it about eight or ten days hence.

In one or two conversations between you and myself in relation to the Mission to Mexico, you were kind enough to promise me your friendly aid, on that account I feel less delicacy in writing to you than I otherwise would. Will you do me the favor to address me a line at Pittsburgh to the care of Mr. George Grant[2] Merchant?

As I hope soon to see you, I will only add a tender of my respects to Mrs. Polk. . . .

Wm. Carroll

Addressed to Washington.

1. Contrary to information that Eaton seems to have sent to Carroll, the minister to Mexico, Anthony Butler, was not recalled until some months later.

2. Not otherwise identified.

FROM JOHN CHISHOLM

Florence, Alabama. February 22, 1834

Thanking Polk for a copy of his speech on removal of deposits, Chisholm asks him to look into the pension application of William Kenada and says that he has already written to John McKinley about it.

Addressed to Washington.

FROM POWHATAN GORDON

Williamsport. February 22, 1834

A farmer in the western part of Maury County and later a member of the General Assembly, Gordon writes to Polk about the mail route from Williamsport to Franklin, informing him that the citizens have a strong interest in this new route. He asks for Polk's assistance.

Addressed to Washington.

FROM JAMES WALKER

Dear Sir Columbia Feb. 23d 1834

Yours of the 7th was received during my absence a few days since. Its contents are surprising, and the views expressed by Maj Barry are certainly *very novel* in the history of our government. If he does as he says he will, it will be one of the most outrageous acts of oppression ever yet in this country done by the government to any of her citizens. Look at it. The government invites her citizens to come forward, and enter into competition for the performance of public service. They do so, competition is gone into fairly, openly and honorably between experienced men. One sett of men are declared to be the best bidders, and the government accept their bids, order them to commence the service, to procure the property necessary thereto, and pledge themselves in a convenient time to enter into detailed contracts. The individuals thus situated retire to their homes, and diligently commence the execution of the contracts assigned them, incur a heavy expense for property of no other use to them. It however happens that an irresponsible man who has been *petted* and spoilt by the government, has with a hope of future favors, put in bids that he is not willing to stand up to. He requires to induce him to comply with propositions deliberately made, that he shall have the contracts of other individuals faily made, and at their prices. These individuals are required to take off his hands the bids and property of this unworthy individual (whose failures and incompetency are notorious) or surrender up their own contracts to another letting.

Can such doctrines be sustained at this day, and under this administration? Are the rights, interests, and *feelings* of individua[l]s, in the strict performance of their duty to be thus sported with?

Your letter has convinced me that it is not only necessary for Mr. Caruthers, but for me also to visit Washington. If a contract can be satisfactorily arranged and we can have any assurances of being permitted to keep it in peace after we have put our men & property on it, I am willing to undertake upon fair terms and on proper principles to transport the mail jointly with Caruthers & Kinkle, between Tuscumbia & Natchez, and if required between Jackson & Madisonville. I will do any thing that an honorable man ought to do to aid and assist the operations of the Department, but I will be *forced* and threatened into nothing. If Maj Barry chooses to take the responsibility of re-advertising and reletting the contracts he has once accepted to us, he must do so. I cannot contend with the government of my country, but the poor priviledge of telling a plain story cannot be taken from me, nor can the people of this region be prevented from believing the facts of the case. But I *cannot* believe Genl Jackson will permit such an act, or if he by possibly should, it cannot be possible that Congress would permit such an outrage to be inflicted on private rights.

But I hope to see you shortly. As soon as I can leave home with any sort of propriety, I will set out for Washington. I suppose Caruthers will go with me or meet me there, and if we can see any way by which we will be safe in executing the contracts, between Tuscumbia and Natchez, we will do so and the Department shall have no further trouble about that mail. We cannot convey the mail in Coaches, or even 4 h[orse] stages for the sum mentioned, but perhaps some satisfactory arrangement can be made to convey the mail *dry,* and in good time, for the amount of money that is spoken of. We will do any thing that is right about it but cannot be asked to make a ruinous contract. I will write you again in a few days. Expect to start in something like a week. Caruthers in now in N. Alabama, expected home in a few days.

I hope we shall be able to make an arrangement that will be satisfactory to all parties (except Donly & friends) and it is to prevent much *future vexation,* and contention, that I consent to neglect important business at home and visit Washington at this time. I go myself because I think I can have personal access to the president & I know he will have the thing done right when he understands it.

James Walker

Addressed to Washington.

FROM JAMES WALKER

Dr Sir Columbia Feb. 24th 1834

I cannot but feel much irritation at the course Maj Barry has thought proper to pursue in relation to Donly. I am however silent on the subject, and have only said that I leave for *Philadelphia* next week. I see no use in any public excitement about it. I have every confidence that Genl Jackson will make him act correctly in the premises. At all events, let what will come of it I shall feel better satisfied to personally make known to the President the true state of the case. If Maj Barry does as he says he will I should feel it a duty I owe to myself, and to my children to petition Congress for redress, and to reveal all the *facts* that have transpired in relation to this extraordinary matter. I can make out a case and clearly prove that the Department purchased[?] (by making contracts with C & K. and improvements they would not have otherwise made.) C & K's interest in the Tuscumbia line. Donly gave no equivalent for it, the P. O. Dept. did & I know how much. Upon no correct principle can the P. M. G. interfere with *my* contracts, because Donly or any body else fails to comply with propositions deliberately made. I am alone responsible for my own acts, and those I voluntarily give the power to act for me. But enough of this, if my contracts are re-advertised & relet, I should never know when to stop in efforts of vengeance and Maj Barry's character would be destroyed, let my fate be as it might. The *facts* are on my side, and new and important principles would be involved, which it would be unbecoming any freeman tamely to submit to.

Some allowances are however to be made. Real difficulties exist, but these difficulties might be removed by the stroke of a pen. Donly fails to comply with his propositions. What next? Is it not clearly the duty of the PM.G. to employ the next lowest competent bidders if they are *now* willing to be employed at their bid? If the bid, in the manner advertised produces too great an expenditure, then the manner of conveying the mail may be changed, and a contract *agreed on* with all proper stipulations. There are so many various ways in which the mail might be conveyed, and at different prices in different ways, that it is impossible for any amicable and satisfactory adjustment to be made of the whole difficulties, without the personal presence of both Caruthers & myself. I think by both of us going on, some agreement can be made that will ensure the regular transportation of the mail between Nashville & N. Orleans. I am disposed to make such an arrangement on fair terms and if the *manner* can be agreed on, perhaps the $16000 will answer for compensation. But of this I am not sure until I see Caruthers. Corn &c. is very high & difficult to be had in Mississippi. Mr. Brown is recently from that country. I shall see him before I set out, and know better the lowest sum which can be afforded. I want nothing extravagant or unreasonable, but my pride will not allow me knowingly to go into a *loosing contract,* even to save what I have, and am justly entitled to. All circumstances convince me that it is necessary for me to go to Washington immediately, and place these matters beyond uncertainty in some way. I either wish to be permitted to execute my contracts in peace or have them taken from me, if it is to be done. This *dog life* I will not stand. I intend to be prudent and silent and to treat the affairs of the P.O. Dept with becoming respect.

James Walker

Addressed to Washington.

FROM JAMES WALKER

Dr. Sir Columbia Feb 26 1834

I recd yours of the 12th just on the eve of going down the line to make arrangements to supply a stand &c. It will be time enough for an umpire to be agreed on, when a contract is made, *that is to be stuck to.* I have written to you two long letters on this subject which partly communicate my veiws & feelings. I am now arrangeing my business with all possible dispatch and will set out for Washington in a few days. In the mean while I wish to be understood as neither accepting nor declining the PMG's propositions but I tell you I will not take Mr. Donly's bids unless the manner of conveying the mail is changed but will do any thing that an honorable man ought to do in like circumstances.

I am satisfied of the necessity of visiting Washington, and think all things had better remain as they are until Caruthers & myself arrive. The PMG can have the mail conveyed with certainty between Tuscumbia & Natchez but I see no reason why private individuals should actually loose money to save the government or to preserve contracts *already decided on.*

I hope you can keep all things as they are until I reach and then we must settle the ballance of the controvsy as we may. I am confident I can explain the whole matter to Gen. Jackson so that no difficulty will occur.

JAMES WALKER

Addressed to Washington.

FROM DAVID T. CALDWELL

Charlotte, North Carolina. February 27, 1834

A physician in Mecklenburg County and son-in-law of William Davidson, Caldwell reminds Polk that in 1831 he was sent a note to collect from William and Thomas Harding,[1] a copy of John McKnitt Alexander's will, a deed from Joseph McKnitt Alexander[2] to Walter S. Pharr[3] and Caldwell, as well as a deed from Pharr and Caldwell conveying more than 900 acres of land to John W. Jones, resident of Randolph, Tennessee, and trustee of Tipton County. Caldwell has learned that Jones has not received the pertinent papers from Polk and asks Polk to forward them immediately.

Addressed to Columbia. This letter has been published in McPherson, editor, "Unpublished Letters," *North Carolina Historical Review,* XVI, 177–178.

1. Probably brothers of John Harding and uncles of General William Giles Harding of Belle Meade, near Nashville.

2. John McKnitt Alexander, who died in 1817, lived in Charlotte and had participated in the famous Mecklenburg Convention in 1775. His son, Joseph McKnitt Alexander, was educated at Princeton and became a doctor.

3. A Presbyterian minister in Mecklenburg County.

FROM WILLIAM H. POLK

Dear Brother Chapel Hill N.C February 27th 1834

I would have written to you sooner but I have been expecting an answer from the Faculty in relation to my Greek every day but did not receive one until this morning in which they said that they could not let me in for it would be setting a precedent which they could not hearafter avoid for after letting me in they could not refuse any person else that applied hereafter. I have now determined to give it up altogether and make no more trials and submit my case to you. If you think it will be better for me to remain here and go on through College on irregular standing than to go to any other College where I can enter on regular standing and get a complete education, and if it is not to much trouble give me your reasons for thinking it will be better for me to remain. And if you can convince me that it is better to stay here and receive part of an education than to go elsewhere and receive a full one I will not open my mouth about leaving here again.

I will be very much obliged to you if you will send me on Messrs Calhoun's, Benton's, Clay's & McDuffee's speeaches as I am very anxious to read them and not taking any paper I have not been able to see them. I have not received a letter from home this session, and therefore cannot give you any information concerning our relatives at home.

WILL. H. POLK of Tennessee

P.S. You must answer this letter as soon as you can and may send me any other speeaches you think it worth reading.

W. H. POLK of Tenn

Addressed to Washington.

TO LEVI WOODBURY

Dr. Sir Washington Feby 27th '34

I see from the Intelligencer of this morning that the Bill to Regulate the Deposites, has been ordered to a third reading in the Senate. It will probably pass and come to the House to day. I will have it referred to the Com. W & M. May I ask your attention to the Bill? You will find it published in the Intelligencer of to day.[1] I should be glad to see you upon the subject at such hour after the adjournment of the House this evning as may be convenient to you. Will you do me the favour, to designate the hour & place where I can see you this evning?

JAMES K. POLK

Addressed to Washington. This letter is in the Papers of Levi Woodbury, Division of Manuscripts, Library of Congress.

1. Polk seems to have erred in his date. The available issue of the *Intelligencer* for February 27, 1834, did not include a copy of the bill mentioned.

TO LEWIS CASS

Dear Sir, [Washington] Feby 28th 1834

I recommed James Guest of Maury County,[1] Tennessee as worthy of the appointment of Cadet, in the Military Academy at West Point. He is a poor young man, and the orphan son of a soldier of the last war, who was in the battle of Tippacanoe, and in the southern campaigns, under the command of General Jackson. He is upwards of sixteen and under twenty one years of age, good moral character, and highly worthy of the patronage of the government and I hope he will receive the appointment, which I solicit for him.

JAMES K. POLK

Delivered by hand to the Secretary of War. The letter is not in Polk's handwriting, but the signature is his. This letter is in Cadet Application Papers, United States Military Academy (RG 94), National Archives.

1. James L. Guest received the appointment only to learn that he was too young to enter the academy. He became a prominent citizen of Columbia. See Guest to Polk, May 10, 1834.

FROM A. W. BILLS

Millersburgh, Kentucky, March 1, 1834

Bills commends Polk for his position on the Bank and regrets the silence of Senator George M. Bibb of Kentucky. He also says that he has forwarded to Thomas A. Marshall a petition in support of the claim of James Busby for commutation pay.

Addressed to Washington.

FROM JOHN G. MOSBY

Richmond, Virginia. March 1, 1834

This introduces the bearer, John Thompson of Virginia,[1] and asks Polk to discuss with him the problems surrounding the claim of James Smith.

Addressed to Washington.

1. A notation on the envelope by Thompson says that a hasty departure from Washington will prevent his handing the letter to Polk in person.

FROM JAMES WALKER

Dr Sir Columbia March 1st 1834

I have just returned from arranging a stand between here & Lawrenceburgh. It became necessary for me to purchase an occupant claim, to build stables, houses, purchase corn, Hay &c in the neighborhood of Mt. Pleasant & haul out. With the present schedule it is impossible to run this line as it ought to be without incurring this expense, and *uncertain* as all matters are in relation to mail business, I thought it best to make arrangements as they should be at once. I have not yet heard from Caruthers & Kinkle, and presume that Caruthers is yet in So. Alabama. I also wrote Mr. Brown on Sunday last, and requested him to come up immediately as I particularly wish to consult him as to the line between Tuscumbia & Natchez, and I wish him to remain on these lines until I can go to Washington & return, as there is no telling what difficulties might occur if both of us were absent. It would therefore be impossible correctly to give a definite answer to the P M. G. until these gentlemen are seen or heard from and this may be assigned as a reason for not giving a positive reply until I reach Washington. My mind is however fully and deliberately made up on the subject. I will *not accept* the propositions, on the terms proposed nor will I ever agree that my failing to comply with bids & propositions made by John Donly in which I had no concern, can in any degree affect or forfeit contracts rightfully and fairly obtained by me, which we are in good faith executing, and in doing which we have incurred an expense of from 7 to $8000. I am irritated on this subject—my patience is worn out & I feel like there was a *smothered flame* consuming me. The very silence I yet deem it prudent to preserve on this subject makes me feel more intensely the wrongs, which have been inflicted, and I am impatient to be off to Washington to see Maj Barry face to face. He *cannot,* he *dare* not readvertise the line from Nashville to Tuscumbia. Gen'l Jackson is too great a man to permit it. Even the threat I consider an indignity and a positive wrong. If Maj Barry does what he says he will him or me one utterly looses our reputation in public estimation. The issue will have been made by him and we must each abide the result as we may. I am conscious in this whole matter of having neither wronged, nor attempted to wrong any body, nor done any act which I cannot face. I will not *tamely* submit to a palpable wrong from any quarter. I rely on Gen'l Jackson for a just and proper settlement of all these difficulties. If this just expectation fails me, I rely on myself for the ballance.

Upon more reflection, I believe it is impossible for the main N.O. mail to be conveyed on the road between Tuscumbia & Natchez with less than 4 horses. The expense of a 4 h[orse] stage or coach cannot be borne for less than the bid of S B Ewing & Co. $23520. Corn is worth now from 1.25 to $1.50/100 pr. bushel & exceedingly difficult to be had at that price. I do not want the line from Tuscumbia down, at less than our bid, and if even our bid is accepted, we must have some assurance that the controversy is then settled, and that when we have the contract made it is a contract of binding import. What safety or propriety is there in our making contracts with the present head of the Department, when such a fellow as Donly can influence him to take them away from us and re-let them? It requires the investment of too much money, in horses & stage property, for our fair contracts to be thus *sported with.* There is another very important consideration—we have now 10 steady valuable men as stage drivers, whose living is dependant on us, whose interests is idenfied in our fortunes. Are they too to be thrown out of employ to gratify a man utterly unworthy of public confidence?

The P M. G. can settle all difficulties by accepting the bid of S. B. Ewing & Co. and giving us proper time to put men and property on the road and an assurance that *it is a contract.* As to Donly's property although he deserves nothing from us, there would I presume be no difficulty in our taking what is suitable at a fair price. I have no[w] so arranged my affairs, as to be able to start to Washington at a days notice & only wait to see or hear from Caruthers & Brown. I expect to set out next week, and hope to see you shortly after receipt of this.

James Walker

Addressed to Washington.

FROM S. MORRIS WALN

Philadelphia. March 4, 1834

Calling attention to a bill that would exempt him from paying duties on certain wines that had been destroyed by fire, Waln asks that Polk prevent the bill's getting lost in a committee.[1]

Addressed to Washington.

1. See George M. Dallas to Polk, January 23, 1834.

FROM ANDREW HAYS

Dear Sir Nashville March 5th 1834

Mr William T Brown[1] of this place is a candidate for the situation of Judge [Alexander M.] Clayton in Arkansas, he having resigned.

He is a man of great individual worth and highly respectable professional attainments. He is poor and has a wife and three children and no appointment could give more universal satisfaction in Tennessee.

Any services that you may render him will be thankfully acknowledged. . . .

ANDREW HAYS

Addressed to Washington.

1. A Nashville lawyer, Brown did not receive the appointment. In March 1835, however, he became United States district attorney for West Tennessee, and he was judge of the sixth circuit, 1836–38. Later he moved to Memphis, where he was a leading lawyer.

FROM JAMES WALKER

Dear Sir Columbia, March 5th 1834

I received a letter to-day apprising me of the return of Mr. Caruthers from So. Alabama, and that he would meet me at Nashville on Tuesday next (the 12th) to accompany me to Washington. Although it is totally impossible for us to accept the propositions of the P M.G. or quietly to submit to the alternative mentioned, still the trip we contemplate, cannot fail to produce a full and final settlement of the whole matter. We hope that our trip may save us and our friends some unpleasant feeling, and at all events we will feel conscious of doing every thing which we ought to have done.

JAMES WALKER

Addressed to Washington.

FROM SAMUEL H. LAUGHLIN

My dear Sir, Nashville, March 6, 1834

You may rest assured that the drudge who edits a daily newspaper has but little time to devote to letter writing, and still less to devote to amusement and attention to out-of-doors affairs. On the present occasion, however, I must trouble you with a line.

I have it from Judge Clayton, of Clarksville, lately a Judge of Arkansas, that he has resigned his office.

William T. Brown of this city is an applicant I understand for the office. He is one of our *natives,* but has lived in Georgia, and has become poor and lost his patrimonial estate in standing by his friends. He has excellent capacity, first rate ambition & industry, and most unblemished moral character. Mr. Grundy knows him well. If you can aid in procuring him the office, you could not interest yourself for a more deserving man. We have no better lawyer here of his age, & he is not too young.

S. H. LAUGHLIN

Addressed to Washington.

FROM EPHRAIM BEANLAND

Dear Sir [Somerville] March the 7th 1834

I did not rite to you on the firste of the month. My reasons was that Squire Walker detained me on Wally acounte which in his last letter said that he had solde Wally and that he must go to the Iron works which he shall starte amediately. Dear Sir wear all well and have bin since the last letter and I have got all of the negroes at home but Jim. I have got Jack and I have got Hardy and I wente to the iron works and got Ben and on last Monday I got Wally which they have all bin runaway and I have got them all backe on the plantation and since I brought Ben back they all apear satisfide. Ande Squire Walker rote me a letter which I redit to all of them which he sayes that they shall stay heare or he will sell them to negro trader and by otheres in there plases which they do not like to be solde to a negro trader. I thinke that they ar all very well aware that if they go to runninge away that it will not do for I am determined to brake it aup. This set of white people that they had so much corispondance with I have broke it aup intierely and they ar verry well satisfied and crop time is now heare and if Jim goes to Maury he must be sent back to me for I have not time to go after him but I wante his servisis verry much in deade.

Not longe before Jim run away G More wanted him to make sum gates and I sente him theire and he run away from him and cum home and then he left me with out a cause which if he goes backe I wante him sente to me. Dear Sir you wantd to [k]now how I cum on the last month. I have got all of my olde grounde broke aupe and my coten grounde baded aup but about 40 acere. I will have it all in tolerable good auder this weake but the olde newgrounde that lies on the creake that is nothinge done to it yet. On monday next I comence in it which I thinke that it will bringe good coten. I thinke that I muste plante the rise of a hundred aceres in coten and the ballance of my olde grounde in corne and as for my newgrounde is verry backwarde, I do not thinke that I can get in more than 20 aceres at moste if that much but I shall get in as much as posiable. Loosinge Wally I hate it but he is oblige to go so Walker sayes. On to morrow I am a goinge to the alection and if I can hire a boy on reaseble termes I shall do it and if not I make the beter youce of the hands that I have got for I am determened on makinge a crop. To the hands that I worke I thot your lande is verry good for coten. I have sode 10 acares in oats which they loock verry fine and my corne is verry scearse. My stock loocks bad on the scarsity of corne, my sheepe looks well and they is 9 lambs, and as for my horses is ondly tolerably. The gray mare is intieraly unfit for farm service which I put my horse in her place and he workes finley and I have got a firste rate set of runinge plowse and in fact I thinke that every thinge is moovinge on verry well at this time which I am glad to say so. If you wante any thinge done let me no it. Nothing more but youres respectfully.

EPHRAIM BEANLAND

Addressed to Washington. This letter has been published in Bassett, *Plantation Overseer*, 65–67.

FROM ELBERT HERRING

Washington. March 7, 1834

The Commissioner of Indian Affairs sends lists of blacksmiths employed by Indian tribes but states that he does not have the names of three blacksmiths appointed in 1832 in compliance with a treaty with the Choctaws.

Addressed to Washington. This is a clerk's copy in Letters Sent, Bureau of Indian Affairs (RG 75), National Archives.

FROM JAMES McKISICK

Dear Sir Shelbyville 7th March 1834

I wrote to you some time ago on the subject of old Major John Pattons[1] Pension claim. We had a conversation on the subject in this place last summer, the understanding between us was that I was to remind you by letter of the subject after your arival at Washington. I done so, but I presume that owing to the pressure of other business you have not as yet had time to direct your attention to that subject. I informed you that I had wrote to the Secretary at war who had answered my letter & informed in his answer that Jacob Pattons[2] pension claim had been examined & that further allowance could be made. You will observe Sir that John is the name of the man who I represent not Jacob. John Patton claims in his declaration for two years services, whereas the pension certificate he has received allows only about $23 annually. It seems to me there must be some mistake about the matter, if so you will do an old soldier who is in great need a particular favor by having it corrected.

Inclosed you will receive a communication from my Mother to Genl. Jackson. About two years ago she took a notion that as my decd. father had been a Soldier of the revolution & had been wounded & disabled in the defence of his Country, that some provision ought to be made by government for her, and she frequently applyed to me to make her out a communication to the President on the subject. I always put her off in same, saying at some future time it would be more proper. Finally she became impatient & applyed to some person else to make out her communication, & handed it over to me to forward through you to the president. I had a wish not to send it, but she has become so importunate on the subject that no alternative is left me but grossly to equivocate or absolutely refuse, which refusal would have been very mortifying to her. I would greatly prefer that you would not submit it to the president. She will inquire tho every time she sees me if I have heard or received my answer from you on the subject. You might say in a letter to me, among other things, that you had received my Mothers communication to the president which would be attended to so soon as a favourable opportunity presented itself. Something like this would quiet her for a while at least.[3] Our Election for delegates to the convention is now progressing. The die will be cast this evening. We have nine candidates running Mitchell, Webster, Kincaid, Neill, Holt, Boyd, Squire Fonvielle, Squire Thompson & Col. Erwin.[4] Your old *Friends* Erwin and Kincaid have *locked* Horns and are perfectly at issue upon several important points of constitutional policy; I will drop this letter evening & perhaps I can tell you then who is elected.

Saturday morning 8th. The Election is over, Kincaid & Webster are elected; Kincaid got an overwhelming majority over all the other candidates. This is not verry strange in Bedford County, but in any other part of the civilised world it would be passing strange. Write me a long letter as soon as convenient. I would like to know as much about matters and things generally as you can communicate, It was understood Mr. . . . . [*sic*] was to make a speach on the deposit question, it seems tho those who anticipated it were disappointed. He seems to have been verry active for a long time. He may be collecting combustable matter which will explode after while, but it seems me that his speeches sustaining the administration are like Angels visits.

JAS. MCKISICK

Addressed to Washington.

1. John Patton was receiving his pension in Bedford County. It is not clear whether or not he received an increase in the allowance.

2. Jacob Patton was drawing his pension in Monroe County, Tennessee.

3. This letter was found in Polk's papers. Apparently he followed McKisick's instructions and did not deliver it to Jackson. Jane McKisick obviously was personally known to Jackson.

4. See William J. Whitthorne to Polk, February 7, 1834. Andrew Erwin apparently entered the contest quite late.

FROM WILLIAM D. QUIN

Paterson, New Jersey. March 8, 1834

Quin asks for a copy of Polk's speech on removal of bank deposits as well as a copy of his report supporting the Secretary of the Treasury's removal of government deposits from the Bank.[1] Commending Polk warmly, he urges him to continue his fight against the Bank.

Addressed to Washington.
1. Polk had submitted the report to the House on March 4, 1834.

FROM ORANGE H. DIBBLE

[Washington]. March 10, 1834.

Dibble, formerly a canal contractor in western New York, writes concerning his contract to build a bridge across the Potomac. He states that he has Jackson's word on the matter and considers that good enough, despite the attitude of Charles F. Mercer, Virginia congressman, and others. Dibble reports that he has incurred large expenses and liabilities in preparing to begin construction and recommends an appropriation of $300,000 for the forthcoming year. He declares that should Congress not support the contract, he will suffer serious losses.[1]

Addressed to Washington.
1. Congress did not approve Dibble's Potomac bridge contract, and for several years he was involved in recovering money which he had spent on the project. Meanwhile he was appointed postmaster at Buffalo, New York, a post he held for several years.

FROM GEORGE W. TERRELL[1]

Dear Sir: Paris West Tenn March 10th 1834

I received under cover of your frank a short time since, a copy of the able speech made by you in reply to McDuffie on the deposite question. It is but sheer justice to say to you that Tennessee may well be proud of her gifted son, who is able, in the hour of dread trial to meet, ay, and to foil, in debate the mighty champion of the opposition, and I might, perhaps, with propriety say, the Charles Fox[2] of America, and to sustain, and triumphantly vindicate the Administration of her favourite *Chieftian.*

You know well that I cannot do any business thro my immediate representative in Congress,[3] therefore when I want any thing done I must apply to some other member—and as I have ever had reason to regard yourself as a friend, I must request the favour of you (in conjunction with Mr. [Cave] Johnson) to attend to a matter of interest for me there. When the President was in Nashville he said to me that he had intended (in consideration of my father's services &c) to give me some good appointment, under the general government, and would do so as soon as an opportunity offered—he spoke then of the appointment of Charge des Affaires to some of the Courts. But after waiting near two years and hearing nothing more of it I withdrew the application. Judge Grundy wrote me, a good while ago, that the President would still do so; I have learned that Judge Clayton of Arkansas has resigned if so, I would be pleased to fill that vacancy, if my friends think my qualifications such as to Justify them in recomending me. I am getting to be a pretty good lawyer and I would promise one thing—so to qualify and conduct myself that my friends should not have cause to regret their exertions in procuring the appointment for me. Will you be so kind as to have an interview with the President, and learn from him what his disposition is at present on the subject, and communicate the result to me? It may be that my withdrawal of the application (for I did it under excited feelings) may have put him out of the notion of giving it to me at all—if so I would be glad to know it.[4] I am aware of the weight of your influence with the President, and therefore am anxious for you to see him on the subject; and should it ever be in my power, you may be sure of the favour being reciprocated. Should this office be disposed of one in the new Territory about to be laid off in the North West, would be equally acceptable.

I wrote to Mr. Johnson, some time ago, requesting him to pay you some money that I borrowed from you so long since, and about which, you no doubt think strange of me. Permit me therefore (in congressional parlance) to explain; in the first place I left the money with Mr. Holland[5] in 31 at Nashville and did not know but what it was paid until long after you were gone. I then wrote to [William T.] Fitzgerald to pay it, but he could not spare the money. Last fall I expected to see you at Nashville but did not do so but by way of slight compensation, I have paid the taxes on some land you have in our county, and will continue to attend to it for you.

As soon as may comport with your leisure, I will be under obligations to you if you will call upon the President and write me the result of the interview.

G W Terrell

P.S. If Majr. Eaton is in the City, I think it is not improbable he would aid you in the application to the President which you know would give it great additional weight.

G W T

Addressed to Washington. The letter was posted in Huntingdon.

1. He was a leading attorney in Paris, Tennessee, at this time.

2. A political figure (1749–1806) who has been called England's first great statesman of the modern school. Fox was a fine speaker, but his independent attitude prevented his reaching the great eminence in his government that he probably merited.

3. David Crockett.

4. Apparently Terrell's patience gave out. Shortly after this letter he moved to Texas, where he was an important figure in the Republic of Texas.

5. Unidentified.

FROM JOEL WEBSTER[1]

Dear Sir Shelbyville 10th March 1834

Our election for delegates to the Convention is over. Kincaid and Webster is elected, the popularity of the doctor is astonishing as he advocated a reduction of the Counties throughout the State, and each County to have a Representative in the general assembly.

I discover from the papers that the Deposite question Still occupies your time in Congress. The proceedings of the opposition in the Senate appears more like a faction, than a deliberative body acting for so great a people as ours. From observing that the people of several of the States are misrepresented in the Senate, a thought has suggested itself to my mind that it would be right to amend the Federal constitution so as to give the election of the Senators directly to the people. I am willing the Senate should retain all the power they now have; the election by the people would save all the expence attending the process in the Legislatures, and the honest yeomanry of the country would not be as easy acted on by logrolling and chicanery, as the few men composing the Legislative bodies. If your views accord with mine, and amendments are proposed this Session, let mine be among them. Please say what the vote would probably be on the deposite question, in the house of Representatives.

J WEBSTER

Addressed to Washington.

1. He was a son of Col. Jonathan Webster of Noah's Fork, Bedford County.

FROM J. M. NEELY[1]

Sir Dresden Weakley County 11th March 1834

Feeling that our district is unrepresented or what is worse misrepresented in Congress if your convenience would possibly admit of it I would request that you would send to this place some of the most important documents of Congress.

You know Crocketts course, and he has not the magnanimity to send anything on the administration side of the questions agitated there.

A few good documents sent to Majr. Ephraim D Dickson Post Master in this place or to myself or both, a few to Mr. Andrew S Harris Post Master in Troy, Obion County, or to Majr. Lysander Adams[2] (of the same place) or both might be of service, at the least would be thankfully received.

J M Neely

Addressed to Washington.

1. Unidentified.

2. Adams had opened the first store in Troy about 1824. Troy was designated as the county seat of Obion County at about the same time.

FROM NATHANIEL SMITH

Dr. Col. Athens Tennessee 11th March 1834

Our old friend Col. Wm. Hogan[1] wants the appointment of emigrating Agent for the Coosa District of the Creek Indians. Any Service that you can render him in procuring the appointment will be greatfully remembered.

Nat Smith

P.S. We could not Elect Meigs[2] to the Convention. He was beat by a Mr. Neil[3] quite an ordinary man. The prejudice run so high against Lawyers that we could not head it.

Nat Smith

Addressed to Washington.

1. Hogan had served with Smith and Polk in the lower house of the Fifteenth General Assembly, representing Campbell and Claiborne. In the next General Assembly he represented Claiborne County in the lower house. He did not receive the appointment sought. See also Hogan to Polk and Grundy, March 12, 1834.

2. Return J. Meigs moved from Kentucky in 1823 and practiced law in Nashville. In 1834 he became a special agent to the Cherokees and was residing in McMinn County at this time.

3. John Neal, a farmer, represented McMinn County in the constitutional convention.

FROM ROGER B. TANEY

My Dear Sir Washington March 11 1834

Since I saw you last night I have reflected on the conversation which passed between us. Our friends in Congress must decide on the course proper to be taken but as you are kind enough to desire my views it is my duty to state them. My impression is that the resolutions ought on our part to be proposed in the order they stand and if the three first are postponed to take up the fourth, the proposition should come from the adversary & not from us & that we ought not to assent to it. I think a firm and steady course is the true one & that a decision that the Bank is not to be rechartered and the deposits not to be restored would put an end to the contest.

R. B. Taney

Delivered by hand. This letter was marked "Private."

FROM KENNETH L. ANDERSON

D Sir Shelbyville 12th Mar 1834

I had intended to have written you on my arival which was the 4th Inst but then concluded I would wait until I could give you the result of the Election in this county which has termanated quite diferent to what I had Expected in this defeat of our mutual and esteemed friend Colo. [Samuel] Mitchell by over 100 votes which has been assigned to diferent causes by diferent persons. The real cause I myself believe to be his want of energy and his supposed hostility to new counties as is manifest from the facts that he remaind in this place both days of the Election and received but little over 100 votes in the entire Western part of the county. These two considerations proves to my mind that had he have use the means he was bound to his friends to have used he would have been Elected with ease. However our partie is now looked on by the other side as completely used up as the saying is with the Exception of yourself. Though I am inclined to beleave that hereafter our people will not beleave there friend is safe until he can prove it by the Certificate of the Shff., which I think is the only safe evidence to receive. Kincaid & Webster are the delegates. Cobb & Cahal in Maury which you will have seen before this reaches you.

Your friends are in good health. I have presented you to them, as well as Messrs Grundy & Inge. They will write you frequently they say and entirely Excuse you for not adressing them. Mention me to Judges Grundy & White and to my particular friend Inge. Present me to Mrs Polk and accept for yourself my best wishes.

K L. Anderson

P.S. You must let me hear from you Soon.

Addressed to Washington.

FROM WILLIAM HOGAN TO JAMES K. POLK AND FELIX GRUNDY

Gentlemen Athens Ten 12th March 1834

I am in the act of moving to Talladega County in the Creek Nation. I have spent the last winter there. I expect there will shortly be an Emigrating agent appointed for the Indians, they are selling their Reservations. The Indian Country has been divided into two locating Districts the Coosa & Tallapoosa. It may be that two agents may be appointed if so I should like to have the appointment for the Coosa District.[1] I am veary in every Respect except Girls and if you are not under obligations to some other person your interferance in the procurement of that office for me will do me a favour that shall not be forgotton. Write me to Talladega Alabama.

WM HOGAN

Addressed to Washington.

1. See Nathaniel Smith to Polk, March 11, 1834.

FROM JOHN A. THOMAS

Dear Sir Fort Wolcott, Newport R I March 13th 1834

There has been lately received at this Post the copy of a Bill now before Congress, entitled "a Bill to equalize the pay of the officers of the army & navy of the U States."[1] It is of course the wish of the Army, that it will not pass, into a law. You will confer a favour by letting me know the probable fate of the Bill.

Please send me a copy of the document called for by congress stating the names of Cadets &c &c appointed since 1827.

J A THOMAS
Bvt. 2d Lt 3d Regt. Arty

Addressed to Washington.

1. The bill was introduced by John G. Watmough on February 28, 1834. It was sent back to the committee and amended, but no further action was taken on it during that session.

FROM ALLEN BROWN

Dear Sir, Columbia, March 14th 1834

I send you the Declaration of William Gordon, which I hope you will have the goodness to present to the proper Department as soon as your convenience will allow. You will do the old Soldier a favor by having it acted on speedily, send me the certificate if you have a long Session. I hope you will be in at the death of the *Bank,* and in huntsman's style bring home, the tail in your hat. Public interest is much excited here on the subject of a railroad to the Tennessee River. We had subscribed in this county, in Six days upwards of four hundred thousand dollars, a sum it is said, amply sufficient to construct the road. The county is able and we *will* have the road. Our civil engineer returned a few days since from a survey of the route and he says we have money enough subscribed to build it, and its completion will deliver us from the wrongs and oppressions of Nashville and make us a free and prosperous people.

Cobbs and Cahal are our members to the Convention. I fear your inability to be in the Convention may be the cause of much permanent injury to the Country. A. O. P. Nicholson was a candidate, and *beaten* thank God. This country owes you much for the conspicuous part you have taken in the destruction of that monster the Bank.

ALLEN BROWN.

Addressed to Washington.

FROM ELIJAH H. BURRITT

New Britain, Connecticut. March 14, 1834

Burritt asks for a copy of the Ways and Means Committee report on the removal of deposits. He notes that as a former newspaper editor he has supported the administration strongly. He fears that many people in his section favor Webster's proposal.[1]

Addressed to Washington.

1. Burritt had edited a paper while he lived in Georgia. A few days after this letter was written, Webster introduced in the Senate a bill to extend the charter of the Bank and to restore federal deposits after July 1, 1834.

FROM CHARLES CALDWELL[1]

Dear Sir, Lexington Ky. March 15th 1834

Though personally unknown to you, I take the liberty of addressing a note to you at the request of Dr. G. W. Campbell, of Columbia, Tennessee (now in Paris) with whom I believe you are well acquainted. Dr Campbell informs me that he has written to you himself, on the same topic,[2] to which I ask, when convenient to you, a moment of attention.

The Doctor informs me, that there is a large number of young Americans now in Paris (the case is always so) who have repaired to that seat of science and the arts, to prosecute the study of medicine; but who, being strangers in the place, new to the world, especially the *great* world, and having no one to guide their movements in the proper channels, are wandering from place to place, occupied almost exclusively with objects of novelty and curiosity, and wasting their time unprofitably, and many of them ruinously, as relates to *reputation,* no less than to *health* and *funds*. That such was the case, I perceived, much to my regret and mortification, when I was last in Paris, in 1821. For want of some one to steady and direct them, many young Americans, of fine minds, good families, and not badly educated, appeared to me to be on the road to ruin.

Dr. Campbell suggests that it would be a measure of great usefulness, to have some one appointed to take charge of such of these young men, as might choose to put themselves under his care (and many I am confident would rejoice in the opportunity) that he might erect a rallying point for them, give them due counsel as to their studies and modes of improvement, and do for them all that the youthful most require, when they are strangers in a large city, and a foreign land. In all this, I perfectly concur with the Doctor. That great good would result from the establishment of a sort of American Medical Consulate in Paris (call it by any other more appropriate name) I am confident. And I know of no one better qualified for such an appointment than Dr. Campbell. Should you think fit to broach this matter to the President of the United States, to whom I have the honour of being known, do me the favour, I pray you, to say, that such are my views respecting it or perhaps he will take the trouble to throw his eye over this letter.

Respecting the general policy of the measure proposed, I have nothing to say. Of that, yourself and the President will much better judge. Personally I see no objection to it; as I presume no salary would be expected, the incumbent depending for his remuneration on fees received from the gentlemen benefitted. The mere appointment by the government, and the sanction and weight thence derived, would, I presume, be deemed sufficient, as the office would thus be rendered honourable, at least, if not lucrative. But on these points Dr. Campbell has probably expressed his own views to you.

Excuse, I entreat you, the trouble I have give you. . . .

CH. CALDWELL

Addressed to Washington.

1. A native of Tennessee who studied medicine at the University of Pennsylvania and then taught there, 1810–19, Dr. Caldwell in 1819 founded the medical department at Transylvania University. He continued there until 1837, when he founded the Louisville Medical Institute, forerunner of the medical school of the University of Louisville.

2. See Campbell to Polk, December 5, 1833.

FROM ISAAC EDWARDS

Dr Sir Fayett Cty Tennessee Mar 15 1834

I hop the present pressure of money will be a sufficient apology for addresing you on that subject. The amt of your medical Apct[?] is small its true but evry little assists. It is $[. . .].[1] If convenient would be more than obliged to you, to remit it by the first mail, at which time I will receipt the Apct. and hand it to Mr. Beanland. I saw him a few days past, he informed me the Negroes ware all well and they have been so all the winter. He is going on very well and bids fair to make you a good crop.

I EDWARDS

Addressed to Washington.

1. A smear at this point has made the amount illegible. It seems to be of two digits and was probably $25 or $75.

FROM MOSES DAWSON

Dear Sir Cincinnati 16th March 1834

I congratulate you on your able report and your pithy resolutions on the question of the great mammoth of corruption and tyranny the Bank of the United States and most sincerely do I pray that your Collegues in Congress who have so far nobly supported you will not swerve from the course they have so worthily commenced.

You will probably hear of a memorial prepared by a meeting

of the Bankites here on the 24th ult. but which has never been forwarded till this day having had to undergo the operation of signing. You will be told that the meeting was called without regard to party and that many signing the call were of the original friends of Gen. Jackson and impressions will also be attempted to be made that the meeting itself was composed of a great number of Jacksonians. To explain all this is the object of this letter. It is admitted that a few who had voted for General Jackson in 1828 were at the meeting but most of these men seceded from the cause on the publication of the veto on the Bank-bill and any that voted for him in 1832 who attended that meeting were completely under the trammels of the Bank. Yet still there were not 50 of any kind of Jackson men at the meeting and that meeting did not consist of more than 700 by the best information I can obtain. Now Sir it is certain that there was at least 2661 opposition men in the City at the last election. There therefore must be as many or more of them turned against the Bank as there are Jackson men in its favour since only 700 could be had to attend the meeting. So much for the meeting. Now for the manner of carrying its instructions out.

That this meeting was composed of all the oppositionists in favour of the Bank in the City no one entertains the least doubt but that a known Jacksonian should preside and that the other officers should be taken from the Jackson ranks has to be explained. The Bank question has always been a matter of contention between the parties—the Clay men for the Bank the Jackson men against it. To make the meeting the more effective then it became necessary to induce a belief that a change had taken place among the latter. Jackson men then must be made officrs of the meeting in order to operate upon the country people in this district and state as well as upon the party in other states. For this purpose also the Chairman and other officers were empowerd to appoint Committees from the Wards of the City and Townships of the County for the purpose of obtaining signatures to the memorial. And those men acceeded to the scheme and appointed active Jacksonians on their committees but in this they reckoned without their host. Not a man of them would act but on the other hand were so irritated that they set about to have a counter meeting.

Finding their mistake in these appointments they set about to employ hirelings to perambulate the country for signatures to be paid by the hundred names they might procure. Schools were entered and the names of Children taken, travellers in public inns and Bar rooms were taken though neither resident in the district or the state. Steam boats were boarded and all who would sign whether black white or gray, resident or nonresident in the state or district, were taken and by these means about 4000 names have been appended to the memorial. I should have mentioned however that many persons were induced to sign whose bread depended on those who asked them. A certain factory was entered in the absence of the principal and the hands most indignantly refused to sign and hoisted the holders of the paper out of the concern. These men met the principal in the street and complained of their bad success with his men. He turned them back and threatened his people with dismissal if they would not sign. This carried the point and the poor men submitted and with heavy hearts signed the papers. Such Sir have been the means resorted to by these advocates of corruption and such has been their success—and all this to operate upon our worthy representative and to induce him to believe that a majority of his constituents have changed their minds on the subject of the Bank. But attend to the sequel. The patriots who had been insulted by being named as committees to procure signatures to the memorial called meetings of the wards and Townships to appoint delegates to meet in convention and to express their sentiments in opposition to the men of the Town meeting of the 24th ult. This convention was held on Thursday last in which all the Townships, with one exception, and wards were represented by a large number of delegates say 178 and a large number of citizens not delegates. The Convention was unanimous in reprobation of the course pursued by the Bankites and in approbation of the measures of the Administration in the cause. The proceedings will be forwarded by tomorrows mail.

The memorial of the Bank men will be forwarded this day addressed to the Vice President of the United States, for finding that extra postage would be charged if addressed to Mr [Robert T.] Lytle as was at first done they changed the envelope and directed the Package to the Vice President.

The above history of this proceeding of the Bankites may be believed as a true state of the facts as they occurred.

Moses Dawson

On examining the polls for last election I find the number to stand thus—for Mr Lytle 4642 for his opponent Mr. Pendleton[1] 3681. Now allowing all the signatures to the Bank memorial to be genuine which is far from the fact, it would leave a majority against the Bank of 411 so that Mr Lytle still continues to be sustained in the course he has taken against the Bank—as may seen by the following.

The number of the memorialists are said to be 3956 or 275 more than voted for Mr. Pendleton. Take this 275 from the 4642 who voted for Mr Lytle and we have remaining 4367 which is 411 more than has signed this memorial and there is little doubt but if the truth was known more than 1000 of these signatures were spurious, children, negroes and non residents of the district or state.

Previous to mailing this letter I have understood that the packet containing the memorial has been again withdrawn from the Post office.

M. Dawson

Addressed to Washington.

1. Nathanael G. Pendleton, father of the better known George H. Pendleton, had been Lytle's opponent in the election of October 1832, in which Lytle was first elected to the House of Representatives. Subsequently, Pendleton served one term in that body, 1841–43.

FROM WILLIAM H. POLK

Dear Brother Chapel Hill N.C March 17th 1834

I have not received an answer to my last letter and thinking perhaps that you had forgotten it as you will recollect in my last letter that I requested you to give me your reasons for forcing me to remain here, I am in hopes that you did not think it wrong in me to make such a request of you. I would not have done it had I have been able to think of any reason sfficiently strong to have influenced you so strongly against my leaving this institution. The time has now come where something must be done for I cannot and will not remain here any longer than this session for I am determined to have a good education or none. I am willing to go to any institution in the U.S where I can enter regular but would prefer going to Princeton College N.J. where I can enter the Freshman Class next June and promice you that if you will let me go to shut myself up in my room and study hard for four years, and you may rest assured that I will fullfill my promices. If you consent for me go write to me immeately and I will commence studying Greek or rather looking over what I have got. There is a young man in my class that is going to leave here for Princeton who will join the Freshman Class there. You will think perhaps that I am very capricious on account of my asking you to go to so many institutions and that I would not be stisfied any where but I can assure you that if you will let me go to Princeton I will be contented at least if I am not you shall not know it. I am obliged to bring this letter to a close for the bell has just rung for recitation. Give my love to sister Sarah. You must give me an answer this as soon as you can.

WILL H POLK of Tennessee

Addressed to Washington.

FROM PETER WAGER[1]

Sir: Philada. March 17th 1834

Altho a personal stranger to you, I am sure you will pardon the Liberty I take in addressing you. It is for the purpose of asking the faver of you to please to send me a copy of your able report with the documents when printed.[2] Permit me to congratulate you Sir, on the prospect before us of being amply sustained by the people. . . .

PETER WAGER

Addressed to Washington.

1. A resident of Philadelphia, Wager was a government director on the board of the Bank of the United States. President Jackson submitted his name for reappointment, only to have it rejected by the Senate on February 27, 1834, and again on May 1, 1834.

2. Wager is referring to the "Removal Public Deposites" report submitted by Polk in behalf of the House Ways and Means Committee, March 4, 1834.

FROM SILAS M. CALDWELL

Dear Sir Beanlands[1] [Fayette County] March 18th 1834

I arrived here this eveng and found your people all well. Your negroes have been doing very bad. Jim & Wally[2] both have been away two or three Weeks. I have Bot Wally. Jim got to Columbia, was caught. John Shaddon[3] got here with him this Evening. Beanland thinks they will stay now at least he is in hopes they will. He has got on with his Business very well, agreeable to his chance. He will have all his cotton land ready to plant by the first of next month. He is now planting corn and will be able to get his old ground planted in fine time. He wont be able to get in more than thirty acres of new ground. He has about 60 acres fenced. He thinks he will have in cultivation about 100 acres of cotton and that quantity in corn. His horses & mules are in tolerable Order. He will not have corn Enough. There is none in the Neighborhood for sale at any price. I expect to let him have what corn he may want. Your people has plenty of Milk. I think if the negros will stay at home Beanland will make you a good crop. I think he is anxious to do so. I expect to go to Tipton to see Durham[4] about that money. I promised to pay your store a/t in Sumerville when I come down this time. If I dont collect I shall have to beg days[?] for you some longer.

I expect to remain here until I plant my cotton. I will be here before I go home again. As soon as I get home I will write you again and let you know how your farm comes on and how I succeeded in collecting your money. I have not seen Carter[5] since I came down. I dont know what he will do.

S M CALDWELL

Addressed to Washington. This letter has been published in Bassett, *Plantation Overseer,* 69–70.

1. This was the name that Caldwell frequently gave to Polk's plantation while it was under the overseer Ephraim Beanland.

2. The name *Ben* was written and smeared out, and the name *Wally* was substituted.

3. Shaddon lived near Columbia in Maury County. He seems to have been a substantial landowner and probably operated a plantation of his own.

4. Col. Thomas Durham established a town in Tipton County which

was named Durhamville in his honor. Durham had bought some land from Polk and still owed Polk money. See Caldwell to Polk, April 11, 1834.

5. Probably Archibald B. Carter.

FROM SAMUEL A. GILLESPIE[1]

Dear Sir Madisonville Mississippi 19th March 1834

Haveing gone into an arrangement with our Relations John & James Gillespie[2] of the Neighbourhood of Natchez to Enter in to the Land Speculation in the Chickasaw Nation at the Sales of the land, as they are to furnish the funds it involves upon me for my part to Examine the Lands and be in possession of good information by the time the Sale may come on & I write you this letter Requesting the favour if you can possibly obtain it to let me Know at what probable time they Will be Sold. As you are a favourite with Genl. Jackson I am of the Opinion he will answer any Questions you might ask him on the Subject. As it will take three or four months work or Longer to obtain a Genl. Information of the Country which is a Longer time than has been usually Given in the public notices of Sales in this State & Alabama also assertain when the Bal. of Lands that yet Remains unsold in the Chocktaw count[r]y this state will be sold.

Should you be able to obtain this information it is a Great accomodation to me & will be Kept to my self. Write me to Columbia where I Shall be in two or three weeks.

S. A. Gillespie

Addressed to Washington.

1. Formerly a prominent dry goods merchant in Columbia, Tennessee.

2. Not otherwise identified.

FROM DAVID R. MITCHELL

Dr Sir Columbia March 19th 1834

I drew a pertition some time in January and sent on to you[1] and also wrote to several of the members from the state of Alabama but have recd. nothing from you sence. Please write to me and let me know wheather you Recd. it or not. If you have

Recd. it please let me know what is has been done with as I feel Verry anious to hear from it as I am in destress.

D. R Mitchell

Addressed to Washington.
1. See Mitchell to Polk, January 11, 1834.

FROM McKAY W. CAMPBELL

Dear Sir. Columbia March 20th 1834

According to the request of Capt McKie I send his application for a pension to you.[1] He says You promised particularly to attend to it. His application was first made while he lived in Alabama and failed for various reasons. The present may require Your aid to pass tho I think it has enough in it to justify a very liberal allowance &c.[2] The old man Kilpatricks[3] duties as a *preacher* called him out of our reach during this court & he is the only clergyman in all this county that has any considera-able acquaintance with Mr McKie.

This is a *great* day *here*. Directors for the Columbia Rail Road Company have been elected to day. The votes have not been half counted out, will consume most of *tomorrow* to finish counting. Leonidas Polk, H. Langtry, J. Walker, Allen Brown, P. W. Porter, E. W. Dale, will, I think, certainly be elected.[4] Booker, Cooper, Plummer, Sansom, Looney, Skipwith, Kirk, Boddie, Buckner & Nicholson[5]—of these it is uncertain who will make the 7 others required. Scarcely any thing thus far talked about *here* at this time but the Rail Road & matters connected with it &c. No common place matters transpiring worth your notice. Some Town property of value has changed hands since Mr. Walker left. Mr. Plummer & Dr. [William] McNiel have exchanged dwellings. Plummer gets McNiels Residence & the store room he occupies, for his brick dwelling lot &c.

I must write you again shortly and chiefly for Mrs. Polks benefit, as it is natural she would be grateful to know how our *famous city* of Rail Road *renown* is doing. But I fear the Mrs will become so deeply interested in politics & especially the deposit or "vexata question" that she will loose sight of us.

Your attention to Mr. McKies matters will oblige him no doubt. . . .

M. W. CAMPBELL

N.B. I return some papers with Capt. McKie's application bonds because they were before the comr. on with his first application. I dont think them necessary & have taken no trouble to have them renewed &c. Mr. Cook[6] the principal witness is dead.

M. W. C

Addressed to Washington.

1. See Andrew Matthews to Polk, February 3, 1833.

2. McKie was placed on the pension list on May 5, 1834.

3. Joshua Kilpatrick, a Methodist minister who lived at Bear Creek in Maury County.

4. Campbell was correct in this prediction.

5. Peter R. Booker, Matthew D. Cooper, James R. Plummer, Darrel N. Sansom, David Looney, George G. Skipwith, John Kirk, Willis H. Boddie, Anthony H. Buckner, and A. O. P. Nicholson. David Looney, son of Abraham Looney, had worked in Hillary Langtry's store; became a successful businessman in Columbia; later, moved to Memphis. Kirk, a business partner of Edward H. Chaffin in Columbia, became mayor of the town. Boddie and Buckner were residents of Mt. Pleasant. Boddie moved from North Carolina; he became one of the wealthiest men in Maury County. Buckner at one time served as postmaster at Mt. Pleasant. Boddie, Buckner, and Nicholson were the three not elected at this time.

6. Unidentified.

FROM JOHN W. M. BREAZEALE[1]

Dear Sir: Athens Ten. 21st March 1834

Both our acquaintance and correspondence seems to have been for some time suspended. But, suffer me to renew the correspondence, though we may be placed in a situation that cuts off all other intercourse.

The crisis in which the republicans of the present day are strugling, is a trying and fearful one, and I think I may venture the opinion that, every true patriot is looking on with anxious solicitude. Shall a monied aristocracy parelise all the energies of the government, prostrate the *Independence* of the people, and render them the willing instruments, of their own degradation, and perhaps, final overthrow? This question is to be answered by the final result of the present controversy, which has been waged by the U.S. Bank, upon the president; upon his friends and supporters every where; and in short, upon every one who would not succumb to this mamouth institution. I will not flatter; but the course you have pursued on this great question, deserves as I hope it will receive, the approbation of every true republican.

But Sir; after we get through the present struggle, as we must, and I hope successfully, another must occur, involving consequences, if not as dangerous, at least as perplexing. Who is to have the support of the republican party in the next Presidential election? On this subject, I have no information that would autherise me, even to conjecture what your opinion may be. But notwithstanding this, I can perceive no impropriety in communicating mine and leaving it to your discression whether to communicate yours in return, or not, as you may think proper.

I have long been of opinion that the only means to put an end to that distracting and dangerous party warfare, now raging throughout the country, is to be found in the choice the great republican party make in the next Presidential election.

To me it seems obvious, that if a leading partizan is elected, all the antagonist parties will unite in waging war upon him and his administration. And it is my decided opinion, formed upon mature consideration, that there is no man in this nation, after Gen Jackson shall have retired from the executive chair, that can get along with the administration of the goverment under such circumstances. It is my deliberate opinion, that it is the magic of *his* name, combined with his *great moral courage and superior energy that now holds this union together.*

But you may ask can a man be found whose tallents, experience and orthydox principles, would autherise his election to this exalted station, who is not to be found among the leaders of some party? I answer, in my opinion there can. *And Judge White is that man.* He is not a heated partizan, and he has latterly been placed in a situation, by his election to the chair of the senate, that kept him aloof from the excitement. But I will not trouble you with a rehersal of facts with which you are better acquainted that I am.

My object in writing this letter is to consult with you upon the subject, if you think it prudent to give me your opinion. And if you think with me, I would suggest the propriety of your causing (through some friends, who accord with us in sentiment) Judge White name to be brought before the people, by means of communications in news papers, in such a way as to ascertain whether the people will take him up. I do not think Tennessee should manifest too much anxiety on the subject, especially at an early period, but I can perceive no impropriety in using proper means to test public sentiment.

If the Richmond Enquirer would take up Judge White, I entertain no doubt he would be surported by Virginia; and very probably by the whole South. Kentucky would prefer him to Van Buren, and the New England states will support him, in the event they have no candidate resident in some one of those states.

The oposition, or anti Jackson ranks are in confusion just now, fearing they will not be able to bring forward a man who can successfully compete with Van Buren, and it is very manifest, from the various persons named as candidates even by the friends of Jackson, that there are many who are not satisfied with Van Buren. Now then, is the time to rally all ranks and parties, and harmonise the great body of the people, once more if possible. And I am greatly mistaken if Judge White is not the man on whom they will be most likely to unite. He has already been named in Alabama, and spoken highly of in other sections of the Union. Let us follow suit and not cast away the advantages we have it in our power to obtain.

I have no news worth your attention. We have made rather an unfortunate selection of members to the convention, from East Tennessee. In the West I think they will do pretty well as far as I have heard.

I have removed from Kingston and settled in this place, therefore you will direct your letters accordingly.

I have written in hast and no time to copy.

John W. M. Breazeale

Addressed to Washington.

1. A former resident of Roane County, Breazeale represented Roane and Morgan counties in the General Assembly of 1829–31. He had recently moved to Athens, where he was to edit the *Tennessee Journal* for several years.

FROM THOMAS P. MOORE

My Dear Sir Fullers [Washington] March 21 34

I have two constituents here Jno Bruce & ——[1] who have been waiting for three months for the action of Congress upon a bill for their benefit. It is only 7 in the rear, has passed the ordeal of the Committee on Claims, & is every way just. Can you possibley let these worthy fellows have a chance to get their Bill through on tomorrow? *They are now out of money. I receive no pay & may soon be in like condition.*

T P MOORE

Addressed to Washington.

1. Moore left a blank where the second name should have gone. John Bruce is unidentified.

FROM JAMES BROWN

Dear Sir Nashville 22d March 1834

Enclosed is a letter to James Walkr which you will please hand him or forward to Phila as the case may require. Its contents are not of much importance, but he would I expect like to know that Mjr Donley and us are still geting on smoothly. Nothing new or extraordinary has transpired since he left.

JAMES BROWN

Addressed to Washington.

FROM JOHN W. JONES

Randolph, Tipton County. March 23, 1834

Having learned from David T. Caldwell that certain deeds, as well as a copy of John McKnitt Alexander's will, had been sent to Polk, Jones asks that the documents be forwarded to him.[1]

Addressed to Columbia.

1. See Caldwell to Polk, February 27, 1834.

FROM JOHN G. MOSBY

Richmond, Virginia. March 23, 1834

This acknowledges Polk's letter but disagrees with the Third Auditor's opinion that the heirs of James Smith are not entitled to commutation pay. Mosby urges Polk to examine the case further.

Addressed to Washington.

FROM JAMES OSBURN[1]

Dear Sir March 23th 1834 near Cornersville Tenn

As we generally hear from you thro the medium of the newspapers, and as you seldom hear from us thro such means, I think it necessary to advise you of some of our sayings, doings & opinions personally.

We, I speak of all those with whom I have conversed on the subject, are getting mighty tired, as the Kentuckians says, of our Governor William Carroll: his private character and conduct, it is said, have worn him out and distroyed his popular reputation with all Ranks of our people from the lowest to the highest. As governor of Tennessee, a man ougt to do honour to the office, and ample justice to the eleviated character of the state and we certainly have not had more than six or possibly seven, Governors who have been equal to these things. Cassaday[2] says he brought Carroll out in the first instance, and was certainly instrumental in making him Governor, and that he is now convinced of the truth of what he was then told, viz: that he might, and ought to have been, much better employed. In order to prevent any of the "small Fry" of politicians from putting themselves up for the office, and as Carroll will certainly not again be elected, it is desired that you signify distictly your willing to acept and execute the duties of the office of Governor of Tennessee, unless something shall intervene of sufficient importance to preclude the proprity of your so doing.

I wish you to write in such a manner as to enable me, and others of your friends to give gradual publicity to the spirit and tenor of the communication. Such a letter is looked for from you by more persons than myself. Our Convention will meet in May next; and we expect much contention on some important point. The East Tennesseans, at least some of them, the little brotherhood are about trying the experiment of a constitutional claus for the emancipation of the slaves. Is it not astonishing some times to see with what sanctified and pious enthusiasm we can bear other peopels misfortuns and give away other mens property? These people having nothing to lose on this point and can in no way be injured, by the letting lose such population among us. I will send you the proceedings of a meeting, shortly to be held on this subject.

James Osburn

N.B. I saw Mr Winow[3] on yestedy he request you to cal at the Globe office and pay his subscription for the Globe and he will pay you on sight.

J. O

Addressed to Washington.

1. Osburn was known as one of Polk's firm supporters. During the next year, he came into political prominence when he obtained a copy of the famous letter that John Bell wrote to Charles Cassedy in which he revealed Hugh Lawson White's attitude toward a national bank. He sent a copy of the letter to Polk, and it was highly publicized.

2. Charles Cassedy had at one time served as secretary and clerk to the commission which set the boundary lines of the Creek cession.

3. Probably Henry Wineow, Osburn's neighbor. It was from Wineow that Osburn obtained the copy of Bell's letter to Cassedy.

FROM JOHN A. THOMAS

My Dear Sir Fort Wolcott Newport, R Island March 23d 34

I have lately applied to Gen Gratiot[1] for the situation of assistant Instructor of Tactics at the Military Academy and beg your kind intercession in my behalf. It is my desire to acquire a thorough knowledge of my profession; And to become well versed in the fundemental principles upon which such a knowledge greatly depends.

The facilities (you are well aware) for such attainments are more abundant at the Academy than any Post in the Army. It is consiquently a matter of considerable importance to me that I should obtain the situation. I will take it as a particular favour if you will speak to Gen Gratiot on the subject. I have conversed with Col. Thayer[2] & he entirely approves of it, and has kindly offered to give me any recommendation that I may require. He will I expect be in Washington in a few days. If you would trouble yourself to inquire of him about my qualifications, claims, &c you might probably be enabled to make a recommendation more advantageous. . . .

J. A. Thomas
Bvt 2d Lt 3d Arty

Addressed to Washington.

1. Charles Gratiot was graduated from the United States Military Academy in 1806 and became a career officer. At this time he was Inspector of the Military Academy.

2. Sylvanus Thayer was graduated from West Point in 1808, and from 1817 until 1833 he was Superintendent of the Military Academy. He instituted many reforms and has been called the "father of the Military Academy." He finally resigned in protest against actions by President Jackson that he thought were undermining discipline and hurting the institution. At this time he was in charge of fortifications at Boston.

FROM STEPHEN ADAMS[1]

Dear Sir Winchester T. 24th March 1834

I must take the liberty of saying a few words to you on the subject of the deposites, U.S. Bank &c. from the active, and prominent part, you have taken in the great question, which has, and still adjutatates, the country to such an unprecedented degree. I suppose it will not be uninteresting to you to know the sentiments of the pople of your own State, as well out of your district, as in it; you however, tested the question at home last summer. In this section a few merchants, and enemies of General Jackson, are opposed to the removal of the deposites and in favor of the recharter. Hundreds however who were in favor of the Bank, previous to the present Session, are now decidedly opposed to it. The effort they have made to *force* its recharter, has rendered it verry unpopular; we now look upon it as a struggle between the people and the Bank. If the Bank should succeed we may expect it to rule. If the people succeed (as I hope they will) they may still govern themselves.

During the last Session of our State Legislature, you will recollect, the question was presented in the Shape of resolutions. I voted against the Bank, but was told that I differed with the majority of my district; the truth is, a majority at that time thought nothing about it. At this time I think there are about one hundred against the Bank to one in its favor. The people here are willing to sustain the man who has on so many occasions, shewed himself worthy of their confidence, and to whom we all owe so large a debt of gratitude. We will sustain him at every hazard; he has often risked his life for his countrys good, he has *dared* to opposed the *monster* for the liberty of his fellow citizens. Yet the menials of the Bank, talk of *assassination;* what sacrifise would not Tennesseeans make, for the man to whom they are so largely in debt—any, I hope. I have been one of General Jacksons warm but humble friends & admirers from my youth up but my dear sir, I never knew his intrinsic worth, so well, until within a few years past. If that man had not been President, what would have been the Condition of our beloved Country, at this time?

It is not for me to say, my opinion however is that the Union would have been dissolved. If not, it would have been a condition not worth preserving. I will not trespass upon time to follow these suggestions to the causes which produced the opinions. Suffise it to say that it does not go down well with us in the Country to hear our favorite abused and threatened with assassination in his old age. In fact I loose all patience when I think of it. I have been in North Alabama lately and they are as unanimously in favor of the course persued by the President as we are here. I discover all the friends of the administration are much pleased with your course, and you have my sincere thanks, for the ability & zeal with which you have supported the masures of the administration, and I have no doubt I express the feelings & sentiments of four fifths of the people of Tennessee.

STEPHEN ADAMS

Addressed to Washington.

1. Born in South Carolina, Adams moved to Franklin County in 1812. A lawyer, he represented Franklin and Warren counties in the senate of the General Assembly, 1833–34. Soon thereafter he moved to Mississippi, where he had a distinguished career as a jurist. He served one term each in the United States House of Representatives and the Senate.

FROM WILLIAM P. DUVAL[1]

Dear Sir Tallahassee [Florida] March 26th 1834

I have ventured on a liberty in enclosing the within letter which I trust you will forgive. I know how much you are engaged by your public duties and how anxious and trying have been your labours during the present session of congress. I am as anxious as a parent can be to obtain leave of absence for my son in law Mr Price[2] the Inspector of the port of Apalachicola. His health and my daughter's require them for a time to leave their home. I do not believe they can ever recover from the effects of the disease common to that post if they remain another summer there in their present condition. They have lost their only child a most promising boy six years old. I beg of you with the feelings of a father that you will oblige me so far as to present the enclosed letter to Mr. Taney and obtain the temporary leave of absence solicited.

I have been with you in heart and judgement throughout the protracted discussion on the Bank question and the deposits and rejoice sincerely at the very able defence and argument you delivered on this subject. I have never so much desired a seat in Congress as at this time. I feel the danger which so daringly threatens the happiness and liberty of our country and if there was not another man in this nation who would do it humble as I am I would never cease to denounce this monopoly of curses—*the Bank.*

I look on the politicians of the day, who have changed their principles at least as often as their coats as so many devils hirelings, who for pay will fight under any banner. The president will I hope be sustained by the people. As to the merchants—when was it ever known that patriotism with them interfered with *trade.* I look on all large citys as corrupt and the smaller ones as apeing the larger. My only hope is in the purity of the agricultural community and I thank god they constitute 19:20ths of the nation. I well remember the crys, speeches, and public meetings, when the old Bank was put down. The present are factsimilies of the occurences of 1811.

I trust yet, that Virginia will return to her principles. A few desperate and designing men have placed her in a most ridiculous attitude—That of declaring the Bank *unconstitutional* and yet denouncing the president and Secretary of the Treasury for not supporting an Institution established in violation of the solemn charter of the nation.

The very state of things designedly created by the Bank to force a recharter, is, and ought to be sufficient warning to honest men of all parties, to unite in putting it down. This Hidra has I trust met with a Hercules that will yet strangle the Monster.

WM. P. DUVAL

Addressed to Washington.

1. Born in Virginia, Duval had moved to Kentucky, where he practiced law. He served one term in the United States House of Representatives, 1813–15, and in 1822 was appointed governor of the Florida Territory. He was still governor at the time this letter was written; later he moved to Texas.

2. Not otherwise identified.

FROM SEABORN JONES[1]

My dear Sir Steamboat Baltimore 26 Mh 1834

While I was dressing in my room this morning I heard a Gentleman who lives here say to one who came in the Stage with me that a committee was going this day to Washington & that they intended to make Colo McKim[2] resign or vote for the restoration. As I do not know the man & as I cannot tell whether it be true or not let not my name be known or this published. You can tell Colo McKim to put him on his guard for the Gentleman said in addition that one of the Committee offered to lay any wager that Colo McK. woud do one or the other.

SEABORN JONES

Addressed to Washington.

1. Jones, of Columbus, Georgia, was in the House of Representatives.

2. Isaac McKim of Baltimore, Maryland, also was in the House of Representatives at this time.

FROM SEABORN JONES

My Dear Sir Baltimore 28th Mch. 1834

You have no doubt heard that the balance of the loan ($700,000) of the Penna. State Stock has been taken. As you may be in some doubt as to the truth of that Statement which you have seen in the Newspapers I have written to dispel them. I have it from unquestionable authority that it has been taken by the Agent of Rosthchild. This is some disappointment to the Bankites. I shall be in Washington tomorrow night.

SEABORN JONES

Addressed to Washington.

FROM LOUIS McLANE

Washington. March 29, 1834

McLane describes investigations begun earlier by Edward Livingston concerning the relative financial burdens borne by Americans and Europeans for the purpose of government. He highly approves of the project and asks for appropriations that will permit it to continue.

Addressed to Washington. This is a clerk's copy in Report Books, Department of State (RG 59), National Archives.

FROM EPHRAIM BEANLAND

Dear Sir Aprill the 1 1834 Fayette County Ten

We ar all well and have bin so since I rote the last letter and Sir I can say to you that I think that I am getinge on tolerable well at this time. I have all of the negroes at home and I did thinke that they all would of stayed but on Munday last I toock aup Jacke to corect him and he curste me verry much and run alf before my face which in runinge 2 hundred yards I caught him and I did not [k]now that he had a stick in his hande and he broke it over my head the 3 lick which I stabed him 2 with my nife and I brought him backe to the house and chainde him and I have him in chaines yet. In a fieu dayes he can go to worke ande he further more swares that he will at never stay with the Polke family any more. I can worke him and I intende to do it. I sente for Dr Edwards and he examaned the places where I stabed Jack and he sayes that they are not dangeres by any meanes.

Dear Sir you wante to [k]nowe how I am acominge on with my crop. I am dun plantinge all of my oalde grounde corne and it is cum aup very well the firste that I planted and on to day I will get half dun a planting coten which I will get done this weake if the weather holds good and as for my new grounde I have 10 acares of it broke up wan time and the negroes has run away so much that I coulde not do any more and I do ashore you that I Shall get in as much as I can and loosing Wally I did not like it but he was oblige to go. I thinke that I can get my crop in the grounde in good time. In aworde I am doinge tolerable well at this time tho I sayit my self. I wante to see you at your plantation very bad in deade. Nothinge more at this time. . . .

BEANLAND

Addressed to Washington. This letter has been published in part in Bassett, *Plantation Overseer,* 67–68.

TO ROGER B. TANEY

Sir House of Representatives April 1st 1834

The Committee of Ways and Means request that you will communicate to them your views together with any plan which you may think expedient or proper, for the future management of the revenue, and up keeping of the money of the United States, in the event, Congress shall determine that the State Banks are to be employed as the future depositories and fiscal agents of the Government. And more especially, they request that you will state the probable effect of the plan you may recommend, upon the currency, your opinion as to the competency of the State Banks to perform all the duties of fiscal agents of the Government, which the public service may require to be performed; and also the mode of their selection, what legal provisions, if any, may be necessary to protect and secure the public interests therein, and the duties and services which they shall be required to perform.

JAMES K. POLK
Chr. Com. W. & Ms.

Addressed to Washington. This letter is in Letters from Congress, General Records of the Department of Treasury (RG 56), National Archives.

FROM JAMES H. THOMAS

Dear Sir, Columbia Ten April 8 1834

I am aware that you have little time to devote to local matters, but you will excuse me for this time. I sent you a Declaration for a pension for John Langly some time ago.[1] I sent it to you to certafy that G. M. Martin is clerk &c. I have never heard from the application tho. a long time has elapsed. Mr. Langly is anxious to hear—be so good as to write me immediately how it is.

It may be you have never reced it. I have heard that Guess has a warrant for West Point & also it is said, that he is not old enough to go yet & that he will probably not go until next year (now I dont *know* this to be so). I dont know whether Wm. Stephens has a warrant or not but if he has not (& I believe he has not) & any appointments are yet to make, if Guess should not go, I think you would greatly aid a promissing youth by procuring Stephens a warrant.[2] Nothing but my entire confidence in the talents & persevering spirit of the boy & my great anxiety for his welfare could make me thus trouble. Thus any attention you may find it convenient to give to his application will greatly oblige a thankful family & be gratefully remembered. . . .

JAMES H. THOMAS

Addressed to Washington.

1. See Thomas to Polk, November 30, 1833.

2. See James L. Guest to Polk, May 10, 1834, William H. Stephens to Polk, January 18, 1834, and Daniel Stephens to Polk, January 19, 1833.

TO A PHILADELPHIA COMMITTEE

Gentlemen Washington City April 10th 1834

I have had the honour to receive your letter inviting me, in behalf of the democratic citizens of the City and County of Philadelphia, to participate with them in the celebration of the birth day of the author of the declaration of Independence, at a public dinner to be given at the Washington Hall on Monday the 14th Instant.[1] I regret that my public duties here will prevent my attendance, and beg you to carry to those whom you represent, assurances of the pleasure with which (if the obligations of official duty permitted) I should have joined you in the festivities of that interesting occasion. Participating fully with you in those feelings and sentiments which have prompted the proposed celebration, at this most interesting period of our political history, I beg to convey through you, the enclosed sentiment.

May The principles of Thomas Jefferson never be overthrown by the blighting influence of an irresponsible monied corporation which seeks by its power, to controul public affairs, and rule the destinies of the nation.

The political principles of Thomas Jefferson! They can never be overturned or destroyed by the corrupt power of an irresponsible corporation which seeks by its money to controul public affairs, and rule the destinies of the nation.

This is an unsigned draft in Polk's handwriting.

1. This letter has not been found.

FROM SILAS M. CALDWELL

Dr. Sir Somerville April 11th 1834

I stayed at your plantation last night. Beanland has finished planting Cotton on the fifth also has planted all the Old ground corn. He is now Breaking this new ground. He will plant about 35 acres of new ground. He is sufficiently Early with this Crop. Your cotton will be up next week. I think he has upwards of 100 Acres in cotton and about 100 Acres in Corn. I have furnished him with what corn he will need. The negroes are all Well & at home and if they stay there he will attend his crop. I collected your Money of Durham $287.50/100 and have this day Settled your a/ct with Smith &c. in this place. Also with Smith for the [. . .]. Mr. Carter has paid no money except one or two Smith a/cts.[1] You have no a/cts here which are required at this time. I expect to leave this for home in a few days. I will attend strictly to your Business until you return and then for Reasons which I will give you, I will resign my commission. If you would attend to me as I have to your Business I should have receved a letter or two from you ere this time. I have been Badly treated, not By you. You will please Write to me on the receipt of this.

S. M. CALDWELL

In great haste

Addressed to Washington.

1. See Caldwell to Polk, January 4, 1834.

FROM WILLIAM B. LEWIS

D Sir, Washington 11 Apl. 1834

Enclosed herewith is a statement of Mr. Eakin,[1] my chief clerk, which gives the information I promised you last evening relative to the imployment of a supposed *extra* clerk in the office of the 2d. Auditor. By this it will be seen that I have no more clerks employed than are authorized by the act of Congress of Apl. 1818; and I assure you that it is *impossible* to keep up the business of the office and furnish the information called for by Congress with a less number. The business in my office has increased within the last 12 or 18 months, at least 25 per cent, for the reasons stated by Mr. Eakin.

I see it has been said in debate that the clerks do not go to the offices until 10 in the morning & leave at 3 oclock in the evening. This is a great mistake, so far at least as it regards the office of the 2d. Auditor, and I presume it is equally so with regard to the other offices. In the summer season of the year I am at my office every morning about 8 oclock, and in the winter a little after 9—and my clerks get to the office about the same time I do. I name this for the purpose of correcting an erroneous impression as it regards what is considered "office hours."

W. B. Lewis

Addressed to Washington.

1. James Eakin, born in New Jersey, had served for several years in this capacity and continued for several years after this letter was written. The statement mentioned was not found.

FROM ELEAZER EARLY

[Washington]. April 12, 1834

A former clerk of the House, Early offers himself for appointment as secretary of the committee examining the affairs of the Bank and seeks to enlist Polk's support of his candidacy.

Addressed to Polk "at Clements's" and delivered by hand.

FROM ROBERT MACK

Nashville. April 12, 1834

Mack notes that he is having his books bound and will be ready to send a quantity of them to Washington soon. He wishes to know how many subscriptions Polk has secured and to which book dealer he should send copies.[1]

Addressed to Washington.

1. See Mack to Polk, January 27, 1834.

FROM ROGER B. TANEY

My Dear Sir [Washington] April 15. 1834

I understand that Congress will do no business today or tomorrow in consequence of the death of Mr. Dennis.[1] I hastened my letter to you this morning as I know you are anxious to press forward this business but I would be very glad to receive some information from New York before I send it in & as nothing will be done before Thursday—do me the favour to return me the letter & you shall certainly have before 9 oclock on Thursday.

R. B. Taney

Delivered by hand. The letter was marked "Private."

1. Littleton P. Dennis, a member of the House of Representatives from Maryland, had died on April 14, 1834.

FROM ROGER B. TANEY

Washington. April 15, 1834

In a very long document, Taney discusses the problems involved in the shift of government deposits to state banks and suggests methods of meeting these problems. He denies that the Bank of the United States ever provided a satisfactory circulating medium and accuses that institution of deliberately trying to undermine confidence in state banks by circulating false rumors. He argues that the great evil of the currency is the disproportion between paper in circulation and coin to redeem it, and proposes actions that would alleviate the situation and restore stability of paper circulation. After setting forth suggestions as to the method of selecting banks to receive government deposits, he maintains that if a broad and sure foundation of gold and silver is provided for the system of paper credits the alternate seasons of abundance and scarcity of money will disappear.

Addressed to Washington. The original of this letter has not been found. A printed version is in the *Register of Debates in Congress,* 23d Cong., 1st Sess., Appendix, 157–161.

FROM ABRAHAM WHINNERY[1]

Cain Hill Washington County Arkansas
Teritory April the 15th 1834

Sir,

You may think it somewhat strange for me living at so great a distance and in remote part of the world to be troubling you at this time, seeing by the newspapers that you have warm times in congress but I am happy to find your standing by the old Genl. at so important a crisis and truly gratifyed to find you meet with the approbation of your constituents and the American people generally. Seeing that there is likely to be a Vacancy in the Teritory of Judge of the circut court I have just received a letter from my old friend Col. Yell, that if [Alexander M.] Clayton resign his office Sam Rhone,[2] U.S. Attorney will be an applicant to fill the vacancy of Clayton and should this be the case Col Yell would accept the office of U.S. Attorney for this

Teritory.[3] If it is consistent I would like for you to use your influence in behalf of Col. Yell. There is many of your old friends in this County as well as his and I know it would meet there approbation. I speak in behalf of a great many of them living here. The reason I have prefered writing to you instead of Col Sevier is that you are acquainted more intimately with Col. Yell than he is and I preferred writing you on that account. Hosts of certificates might be forwarded in his behalf but I deem it unnecessary. I hope sir you will do me the favor to urge his claim.

A. Whinnery

Addressed to Washington.

1. Whinnery was for several years a member of the Arkansas territorial legislature. In 1836 he was a member of the constitutional convention that gave the state its first constitution. The signature of this letter is badly slurred, and it has been interpreted several ways. On another letter from him, however, Polk wrote the name quite clearly. Moreover, no person by the name of Whinny or Whinry, two of the ways it has been interpreted, was found to have resided in Washington County, Arkansas. One Abraham Whinnery had once lived in Polk's congressional district, being a colonel in the Tennessee militia in the late 1820s. Doubtless this is the same man.

2. Samuel C. Roane.

3. Thomas J. Lacy succeeded Clayton, and Roane continued in his position as United States Attorney.

FROM JEREMIAH CHERRY

White House [Williamson County]

Dear Col. April 16th 1834

James Guest is to Young by 12 mo. Try & get the Secretary to postpone the appointment one year, and in the mean time the boy shall be better quallified. You know all the good reasons why the poor boy should be appointed that I do—let out all your links for him if it will avail. I feel verry anxious for him to get it—both on account of the boy & in spite of P. N.[1] of Columbia. Mr [Andrew C.] Hays of Columbia has wrote to you on the subject & all the news about Bank breaking &c.

J. Cherry

I have wrote to [David W.] Dickinson, [John H.] Eaton, [Thomas H.] Benton on the Subject.

Addressed to Washington.

1. This is possibly a reference to Pleasant Nelson, an innkeeper in Columbia who had served as the town's recorder for two years, 1830–32. He was later clerk of the circuit court.

FROM JESSE D. ELLIOTT

Boston. April 16, 1834

This naval officer raises objections to the navy pay bill recommended by John G. Watmough and points out what he considers inequities contained therein.

Addressed to Washington.

TO WILLIAM H. POLK FROM JAMES K. POLK AND JAMES WALKER

Dear William Washington City, April 16, 1834

We have consulted together much, and anxiously endeavored to come to a conclusion in relation to you that we hope may have a beneficial influence on you now on your destiny through life. In reading over your letters it is painful to perceive that your whole mind seems to be ingrossed to effect the object of getting money. We unfortunately too perceive that you seem to think that the money you ask for is your own and that you have a right to do as you please with it, and pledge yourself to account fully, when you are of age. It is true that if we were to yield to your wishes we would be but permitting you to spend your own money, but we should violate a most sacred duty which we owe you, our own family reputation, and betray the confidence reposed in us by your father. You may think this strange language —it is nevertheless true, and if you come to be the man we yet hope you will, in after life you will be satisfied that the course we find it necessary and our duty now to pursue; although it causes you present mortification, is the only one calculated to promote your real interests and to make you a valuable man. You have strength of mind and talents to make you an ornament to our family, if your energies and faculties are properly applied and directed. It is with pain we perceive that your whole mind seems to be engaged in extravagant desires to spend money and from the amount you request to pay off your debts, we fear that you are getting into habits that must inevitably destroy you.

We have upon deliberation concluded upon a course that imperious duty and necessity renders necessary to pursue towards you. We propose to inform you what that course is and to assure you that we are unalterably determined to adhere to it. We will endeavor to do you all the kindness we can until you come of age and then what you are to be depends on yourself.

In the first place then we yield to your wishes to leave Chappel Hill at the end of the present session and go to Nashville, there enter College regularly with a view to graduate at that or some other good institution. As to *money* we will be rigid, we will under no circumstances permit you to have more than $300 pr year which must pay for your education and all expenses. Our own experience satisfies us that this amount of money is sufficient to render your appearance genteel and you in every way comfortable. This sum will be annually furnished you by Mr. Walker in such manner as you may need and will, you may rely on it, not be exceeded. As we deem this amount sufficient and that more would be injurious to you, we shall take pains to prevent your mother from letting you have even a cent and all others from advancing with a hope of your repaying when of age. We have also consulted upon the propriety of paying your present debts in North Carolina incurred without our sanction, and have concluded not to do so. Your creditors must wait until you are of age and then depend on your honor. We are aware that this decision will be mortifying to you, but it is one produced by painful necessity. If mortification and want of money will alone teach you the proper use and value of money and time we must inflict the pain. When you left Tennessee for North Carolina we informed you that we could not sanction or permit the means of spending more than $250 which we considered sufficient for a decent support with proper care at the school at Hillsborough. If when we lay down rules of expenditure, you totally disregard our wishes and injunctions mortifications [. . .] to us all it must be borne. And your pledge to pay all excess honorably when of age does not relieve us of the duty to withhold the means of your destruction. You may think it strange that we say that furnishing you money agreeably to your wishes would destroy you but the fact is so. If you were furnished money freely or your contracted debts paid the time you ought to employ in hard study would be taken up in extravigance and frolic & the acquisition of destructive habits.

We fondly hope that you will yet live to see the day when by the Salutary influence of the rigid course we have deemed it our duty to pursue, you will have arrived at a station in society to feel the benefit of it and properly appreciate our motives.

No address is available. This is apparently an unsigned draft in Walker's handwriting of a letter actually sent. It has been published in Bergeron, editor, "My Brother's Keeper," *North Carolina Historical Review,* XLIV, 202–204.

FROM LEWIS CASS

Washington. April 17, 1834

Informing the Ways and Means Committee that a large sum has been deposited in the Treasury for Indian contingencies, Cass argues that the money should be applied to the payment of annuities alone.

Addressed to Washington. This is a clerk's copy in the Reports to Congress from the Secretary of War (RG 107), National Archives.

FROM MATTHEW ST. CLAIR CLARKE

Washington. April 17, 1834

Clarke complains of inadequate reimbursement for the publishing project in which he is engaged. He notes that he has supplied information elsewhere about the progress and expenditures on the project.

Delivered by hand. The letter is in the Papers of Andrew Jackson Donelson, Division of Manuscripts, Library of Congress.

FROM ISAAC K. HANSON[1]

Sir, [Washington] April 17th 1834

I take the liberty of calling your attention to the mistakes made by some members in relation to the expenses of living in this City. The fact is, that every article in the grocery binn, and marketting, remains as high now, as during the last 2 years, *Tea and Flour excepted;* Beef, Veal and Lamb have been 25 per cent higher for *some months* than for the last 2 years. *I know,* from my own experience, that $1000 is insufficient to the maintenance of a family in sickness, which will visit all, and in health. If the opponents to General Jackson wish to ride into power over the prostrate fortunes of men, who find it difficult to keep out of debt, upon $1.000 annually, let them be careful, (*for their own sakes,* I mean) to hide the cloven foot of ambition, and to *admit* the truth in relation to the expenses of living. I respectfully, thank you for your efforts to counteract the schemes of these men, and earnestly hope that you will be successful.

I K Hanson

I refer you to Col R M Johnson and to Mr Stoddert of Md.[2]

Delivered by hand.

1. Hanson was a clerk in the Register's Office, Treasury Department. He was a native of the District of Columbia.

2. John T. Stoddert of Maryland was at this time a member of the House of Representatives.

FROM ISAAC K. HANSON

Sir [Washington] [April 18, 1834][1]

Conscious of the faithfulness with which I perform my duties as a Clerk at $1.000 in the Register's office, Treasury Department, I displayed perhaps too much sensitiveness to the attacks of the opposition members upon the character and conduct of the Clerks, without an opportunity being afforded to *them* of a *defence.* Under these feelings, and having no property except my *Salary,* and no legacy except my *reputation,* such as it is, to bequeath to my *unoffending* and *helpless* family, in the event of my death, I took the liberty yesterday, of writing to *you,* and hope that I did not act disrespectfully. To *you* the Clerks are mainly indebted for their preservation from ruin which to *me* as one of them, would be the inevitable effect of a curtailment below the sum of $1.000. I refer you to Mr Stoddert of Maryland who is acquainted with me.

I. K. Hanson

Delivered by hand.

1. No date appears on this letter. The Library of Congress erroneously supplied 1830 as the year in which it was written. Internal evidence, particularly Hanson's letter of April 17, 1834, is the basis of the date here supplied.

FROM JAMES WALKER

Dear Sir Philadelphia, April 20. 1834

Mr. Goneke requests me to drop you a line or two, which will serve as an introduction of his son to you. He has a particular wish you should take his son to the Presidents, and give him the opportunity of paying his respects to him. I have said to him that I knew you would take much pleasure in gratifying his wishes.

The citizens here, and especially the mercantile community are certainly deranged, on the subject of the Bank and in their extravagent hostility to the President, I think the city of "steady habits," has at this moment forgotten *her interest,* and may at no very distant day find that her intollerance in politics, has been the means of taking from her that ascendancy in Western trade she has been so anxious to retain. You know that I am a modest man, and rather averse to obtruding my opinion among strangers, and in a community with whose politics I have no right to interfere. I have however already found myself engaged in several warm controversys from the simple fact of my mildly denying that the President was an ursuper, a Tyrant, a dotard, a military despot and flagrant violator of the Constitution.

I arrived here on the same evening that the news reached that the President had communicated a message to the Senate, *protesting* against a resolution which had passed that body.[1] As I wished to spend but a few days here, I called that evening upon some of my mercantile friends, and was present when the annunciation was made to several, and of course can judge of the manner that the information was generally received and remarked on in this polished city.

One scene will give you the idea. I was in the counting room of a mercantile establishment, a gentleman stepped in full of news, and accosted those present, with "Have you heard the news: Jackson has denounced the Senate, has personally abused certain Senators, and accused them of misrepresenting their states and threatened them oh, a most high handed measure. He certainly is a madman, where will he stop."

"The man certainly is mad, who would have dreamt of such a high handed measure, such presumption and Tyranny and especially now when Jacksonism is completely down. It is down here, down in the North, *completely down in the north,* as the New York election proves, and if not yet down in the west, soon will be. He cannot hold out longer than fall. When the Representatives return to their constituents, they will find them *suffering under such a pressure* that they will be compelled to return their seats, to vote for a re-charter of the Bank."

A part of these gentlemen, knew that I was a Tennessean, and therefore *ought to be* a personal and political friend of Gen'l Jackson, and therefore although I am averse to medling in politics in a Strange country, I considered it but due to self respect, and to the venerable patriot at the head of the government to remark that:

> "A gentleman on board from Baltimore had kindly lent me a paper containing the document alluded to. I had read it with much care, and my deliberate conclusion was that it done honor to the head and heart of its author, that it was a calm, dignified and sensible state paper, worthy of the chief magistrate of the American people, that the President had done nothing more than *place the saddle on the right horse.* And such would be the judgment of the American people and of posterity."

The truth is I think that this is one of the ablest papers ever issued by Gen'l Jackson, and one which the occasion called for most imperiously.

Messrs. Preston, McDuffiee, Webster, Duane &c. have been haranguing the people here, and producing all the excitement in their power. Preston is considered the greatest and most eloquent man, and is most admired, because he denounces the President most boldly, and as they say here happily quotes Davey Crocket, Jack Downing[2] &c. It is beyond all doubt that a most violent struggle is making and will be continued by the opposition, and all exertions (I fear with too much success) will be continued to keep up the monied pressure, and depriciation of the notes of the state Banks. The doctrine is to force the people to compel their representatives "to truly represent them."

JAMES WALKER

Addressed to Washington.

1. On March 28, 1834, the Senate adopted a resolution that Clay had introduced, censuring Jackson for removing the deposits from the Bank. Jackson wrote a vigorous protest which reached the Senate on April 17, 1834.

2. A fictitious character created by Seba Smith, a Maine newspaperman. Downing was a Down East Yankee whose rustic speech and homespun wisdom made him an outstanding figure in the development of American humor. Smith made Major Downing a confidant of Jackson, and, from this point of vantage, Downing satirized Jacksonian democracy.

FROM SAMUEL G. SMITH

Nashville. April 21, 1834

Smith asks for a copy of the Tennessee census of 1790 and 1800. He notes that the information is needed for the forthcoming state constitutional convention.

Addressed to Washington.

FROM ROGER B. TANEY

My Dear Sir [Washington] Monday Morning April 21, 1834

I wish very much that you would show my letter to you on the currency to Mr. Seaborn Jones today.[1] He has given much attention I know to this subject and has much valuable information. I would even delay the report for a day longer than you propose in order to give him an opportunity of examining deliberately my letter before you report.

R. B. TANEY

Delivered by hand. The letter was marked "Private."

1. See Taney's long letter to Polk, April 15, 1834.

FROM LEWIS CASS

Dear Sir, [Washington] April 24. 1834

I forgot last evening to state that I wished to talk with you about the estimate for the appropriation for removing the Creeks before the Committee took up the subject. Be good enough to retain the paper in your hands, as unofficial, till I see you.

LEW CASS

Delivered by hand. The letter was marked "Private."

FROM BENJAMIN PHILLIPS[1]

To The Honble. Polk Washington City Aprile 24th 1834

Having heard your ready answers to the opposition and the able manners you were prepared to answer them on all questions put to you on the appropriations bill your clear head, Sound memory & honest heart will Carry you through. John Q Adam's objections and all sorts of [. . .] objections notwithstanding I never heard a man do or Speak more to the purpose than Judge Joel B Sutherland[2] this afternoon on taking the sense on the bill without putting it off or postponeing [. . .] longer he done honour to The Cause & himself. The Speaker Sustained himself nobley from the repeated attacks of the opposition and Particularly the Virulence of John Q Adams & the Intemperate expression of Horace Binney of Philadela. (Mr Binney dont know there was a man in the Galleries acquainted with his powers of intelect and Judgement and who can put him down in Physics and Politicts.) Nor do Mess Clay, D. Webster & Presston know that Andrew Jackson & Marten Van Beuren Can answer the question how the Public Confidence can be sustained without a United States Bank or a national Bank or without an issue or emitting Treasurery loan bills on Dallas's plan or a paper Currency and leve the national revenue untouched and a metalic Currency in Circulation among people without distress in the Commercial or Manufacturing Interest or agricultural interest and this great Problem that cannot be solved by Webster, Clay & Calhoun & these wise men in the Senate will be laid before the American people for their decision to say is Andrew Jackson & Marten Van Beuren men who understand national interest or not that they Shall Stand before the American people as Statesmen and guards & virtuous guards of the nation's Treasure. I now ask Mr Henry Clay, Danl Webster & John C Calhoun to answer the question and they may call to their aid all their Party and Nicolas Biddle to help them.

When They are palled and Jammed in the difficulty of the Solution the President Andrew Jackson & Marten Van Beuren will lay the answer before the people and appeal to their Judgements, Yes and before this well learned Senate & the national Voice of the people in Congress in the House of Representatives. Look Senators what you are about.

BENJ PHILLIPS of Phil

Delivered by hand to the House of Representatives.

1. Although this letter is listed as anonymous by the Library of Congress, it appears to be from one Benjamin Phillips of Philadelphia. If this is correct, he was probably the shipwright living on Swanson Street.

2. Sutherland participated in a lively debate on the appropriation bill on April 24, but his remarks were not found in the *Registerr of Debates in Congress.*

TO JAMES L. EDWARDS

Sir Washington City Apl. 27. 1834

I have certified as to the official character of the Clerk whose signature appears to the Enclosed declaration of Wm. Gordon. In looking over his declaration and your remarks in relation to it, it appears that he has stated with precision his services for 7½ months, and adds that he served another term of *about* 4 weeks. If the letter be rejected, still I suppose he would be entitled to a pension for 7½ months. If I am right in this, will you cause his pension certificate to be issue for that time.

JAMES K. POLK

Addressed to Washington. Letter is in Pension File S3403 (RG 15), National Archives.

FROM JOHN McKENZIE

Hico, Carroll County. April 27, 1834

A Revolutionary War pensioner, McKenzie asks Polk for help in getting compensation for government use of his slaves in the 1790s. He has already enlisted the aid of Felix Grundy and Cave Johnson.

Addressed to Washington.

FROM MICAJAH BULLOCK

Sir, Lexington Ten. April 28. 1834

By the resignation of Mr Wendel[1] Post master at Lexington, Tennessee, the office at this place is now vacant, and the appointment of another Postmaster will shortly devolve on the head of the Post office Department. Amon[g] the applicants for the office, is Col. John Mclellan,[2] a gentleman of intelligence and strict integrity, possessing very superior business qualifications; in short, every way qualified to make one of the best in the department that could be selected, for the appointment he is desirous of obtaining, in this place or its vicinity. This opinion is founded on an intimate acquaintance with this gentleman of nearly three years since his becoming a citizen of Lexington. Knowing him as do I can most cheerfully recommend him for the appointment of Postmaster at Lexington. Should you, Sir, feel yourself at liberty to aid in procuring his appointment you will by so doing much oblige. . . .

MICAJAH BULLOCK

Addressed to Washington. This letter was actually posted in Huntingdon, Tennessee.

1. This is D. D. Wendel and should not be confused with David Wendel, postmaster at Murfreesboro.

2. A Lexington businessman. Bullock's spelling of this name seems to have been in error. McClellan did not receive the appointment; Wendel was succeeded by James Banks.

FROM BOLING GORDON

Dear Sir Williamsport April 28, 1834

I have had the pleasure to receive through your friendly agency a copy of the report of the Committee of Ways and Means on the Subject of the Deposits for which please receive my thanks.

It affords me great pleasure also to find the measures of the administration on that subject and that of the recharter of the United States Bank have been sustained; and that for the present at least, a death blow has been given to that corrupt institution.

You will receive within a few days, a petition from the citizens of Williamsport and its vicinity asking of the Post Master General an alteration in our mail arrangement so as to make it depart and arrive at *Columbia,* instead of Mount Pleasant as at present; also, that it should depart from Columbia for Clarksville via of Williamsport on every *Saturday* Morning.[1]

The considerations which operate in favor of this change are obvious and conducive to general interest, and when it is recollected that the change in the *points* of departure was heretofore made to accommodate the mail contractor and not at the suggestion or wish of the public, its return to the former points can not be objectionable. At Columbia the mails concentrate from different quarters on different days of the week which by the contemplated change we would generally receive without that detention which is unavoidable at Mount Pleasant owing to their having a tri weekly mail only and that directly on the Northern and Southern route. Heretofore, and until the recent change in the time of *departures,* we have considered our selves as being in *three* days journey of Columbia, and *five* of Nashville; but now, our Columbia papers at Williamsport (a distance of twelve miles) are about five days old while those of Nashville reach us on the ninth day.

The contemplated change will bring the papers &c both from Nashville and Columbia on the third day, they being printed on Thursday evening in Nashville, reaching Columbia on Friday, and Williamsport on Saturday, a day too, which suits the convenience of the people.

As this route extends principally through Mr. [Cave] Johnsons district, it would be well to mention this subject to him and say that I have made it known and no where is there any objection to the change. The Citizens of Centreville and the lower part of Hickman County receive their letters and papers in due time by a mail that departs at Franklin on Saturday, and reaches Centreville the same day, while those of the County of Dickson receive by the way of the Western District, mails three times a week. These, I hope, are sufficient reasons to induce the Post Master General to make the change which is so much desired by a respectable portion of yours and Mr. Johnsons constituents.

I was in Columbia on yesterday and as far as I could learn your friends were generally well. No discovery has yet been made in relation to the robbery of the Bank.[2]

You will please present me very respectfully to Messrs Johnson, Inge, Dickinson, Bell & Peyton; also to Messrs White & Grundy whom I should have mentioned first, and say that I feel my self under great obligations to them for the favor they have frequently done me in the transmission of public documents.

B. GORDON

Addressed to Washington.

1. See Powhatan Gordon to Polk, February 22, 1834, and Marshall P. Pinkard to Polk, May 3, 1834.

2. On the night of April 11, 1834, Parry W. Porter, cashier of the Union Bank in Columbia, had been assaulted and his keys to the bank vault taken. About $19,000 was taken from the vault, and the robber escaped without being seen.

FROM LEWIS CASS

[Washington]. [May 1834][1]

Cass promises Polk certain materials pertinent to appropriation bills and suggests that explanations of appropriations be given only if objections are raised. He also suggests that the committee not engage in extensive discussions of contingency funds.

Addressed to the House of Representatives and delivered by hand.

1. No date appears on this letter. The Library of Congress has suggested May 1834. This date is supported by internal evidence and other correspondence.

FROM EPHRAIM BEANLAND

May the 1st 1834 Pleasant Grove
Little Muddy, Fayette

Dear Sir

We ar all well at this time with the exception of Ben havinge the rumatism but I thinke that he will be about in a fiew dayes to go out and on this day I will finish scrapinge out my cotten the first time however finish scrapinge where it was wanste. I thought that I had the best prospect for a crop that I ever had in my life but the froste cut it very close. I do ashure you I never saw as great a destruction with frost in my life tho yet I think I can get a tolerable good stand provided there is no more froust and there is no other axident to hapin to it. My corne looks tolerable well and as for the new grounde I have got it broke aup wan way and on the 17th they caime a storm which it did throwe me back verry much. I have got the timber all aup of my coten ground and on to morowe I will comence a cleaning aup my corne land being thrown back with the storme so much that it dose apear like I can not be able to get in any new grounde but if I can get in 25 or 30 acares I will be shore to do so if posiable. Takinge every thinge in to consideration I believe that I can get in 35 acares. My negroes all of them stayes with me and they apear like they are very well satisfied. I make the moste buter and have the most buter milke that I ever saw and I have got the finest oats that I ever saw in my life. Nothing more. . . .

E. Beanland

Addressed to Washington. This letter has been published in Bassett, *Plantation Overseer,* 71.

FROM [BARRIE] GILLESPIE[1]

Huntingdon. May 1, 1834

Gillespie writes in behalf of his friend, John McClellan of Lexington, who is an applicant for a position as postmaster. He notes that McClellan had served previously as acting postmaster and thus is acquainted with the duties.[2] Gillespie asks for Polk's aid in this matter.

Addressed to Washington.

1. Presumably this is Barrie Gillespie, a resident of Huntingdon; his given name does not appear on the letter.
2. See Micajah Bullock to Polk, April 28, 1834.

FROM ROGER B. TANEY

Washington. May 1, 1834

Taney suggests that appropriations to cover expenses of the government of Florida be approximately doubled. This would make up the deficit from the previous year and would allow for the increased expenses predicted by the governor of the territory for the current year.

Addressed to Washington. This is a clerk's copy in Letters and Reports to Congress by Secretaries McLane, Taney, and Woodbury (RG 56), National Archives.

FROM JAMES WALKER

Dr Sir Wheeling [Virginia] May 2d 1834

I arrived here this morning and found a steam Boat just ready to start and shall be off in a few minutes. Tell Caruthers if he has not left that this is the best & quickest route. In looking over my papers I find the enclosed which I neglected to hand to you.[1]

JAMES WALKER

Addressed to Washington.

1. The enclosure was a note from John C. Wormeley expressing the desire for appointment as one of the commissioners to select lands for Chickasaw Indians who chose to remain in the Nation.

FROM JAMES L. WALKER[1]

Dear Sir Columbia May 2d 1834

You will find enclosed a note on Mr W T Barry which belongs to Mrs Towler.[2] Mr Barry has promised to pay the Bal. due on this note this Spring and as I understand made the request when the first hundred Doller which is the last credit on the note was paid that he should have an opertunity to do so as I understand at Washington. Please present him with the note and if paid, you will oblige me by placing the amt in the hand of Saml. Jones[3] of Baltimore, he being the surviving partner of Talbot Jones & Co. There is considerable Interest on this note I must ask the favor of you to calculate the Interest. You will oblige Mrs. Towler and your humble servant by attending to this matter. I want this money to my credit in Baltimore.

JAMES L. WALKER

NB. We are now looking for Mr Walkers return your friend our uncle. My respects to Mrs Polk.

J. L. Walker

Addressed to Washington.

1. James Walker's nephew, who was active in Columbia business affairs.

2. Mrs. Julia Towler had moved to Columbia from Kentucky. Later she was married to Moses W. Houston. She died in Maury County in 1853.

3. Not otherwise identified.

FROM MARSHALL P. PINKARD

Williamsport. May 3, 1834

Complaining of the delay in getting mail from Nashville, Pinkard asks for one direct mail per week and suggests that Williamsport mail depart from Columbia rather than from Mt. Pleasant.[1]

Addressed to Washington.

1. See Boling Gordon to Polk, April 28, 1834.

FROM WILLIAM H. POLK

Dear Brother Chapel Hill N.C. May 3rd 1834

I received your letter this morning and was struck with astonishment when I came to the part where you said that you could not pay my debts and the reason you asigned was that you did not want to encourage me in extravagance. I will not pretend to deny but what I was extravagant when I first came from home but I was young and unexperienced and had no person to curb me and being naturaly of an extravagant disposition I rushed headlong in debt unmindful of the future sorrow that awaited me, but when I wrote to you for money and you laid before me the consequences which must naturaly follow from such procedings the truth flashed upon me. I repented, and I deny that I have since been to extravagant and I will prove it to you satisfactoraly, to do this I will be obliged to lay before you my whole conduct since I left home. Now in the first place I came to Chapel Hill and wishing as you may say to apear large I rushed heedslessly into debt to a large amount. And when I wrote to you for money fearing that if I gave you the whole amount of what I owed you would not pay any of them therefore I only sent you a little more than half of what I owed thinking that I could get the ballance at some other time and you refusing to let me have any I spent the money which Coln Polk left when he went to Tennessee to pay my next sessions expences only retaining enough to pay my College fees paying my board money away to satisfy my creditors for a while and thus things went on until I went to Raleigh last winter seeing that something must be done. I came to the determination to give you the whole amount of what I owed and this apearing so much larger than it was when I first wrote to you, you could not but think that I valued your admonitions but little, but I improved by them and altered my course but still foolishly continued to keep you in the dark with regard to the real amount of my debts and thus you was led into the erroneous impression that I was still exstravegant. Hoping that the explanation which I have given will be satisfactoraly I will proceed to make one request of you which after the explanation that has been given I hope will be granted. My request is that you will let me have part of the money if not all as there is some debts whch cannot be suspended. My board money I must pay before I leave here and I owe the society[1] 18 or 20 dollars which will disgrace me if I do not pay before I leave. I think if you can let me have 150 dollars I can satisfy my creditors for the present. If you cannot do it any other way I request of you to lend it to me and I will pay it back when I come of age. I will close my letter by giving you my thanks for permision to leave here.

W H Polk

P. S. The session Closes the 20th of June, but I think that I had as well start as soon as you can make the necessary arrangements for there cannot be any thing learned from now until the end of the session as we are reviewing and it will only be spending money for nothing. You will oblige me in answering my letter as soon as posabil.

William H Polk

Addressed to Washington.

1. The Dialectic Society.

FROM LOUIS McLANE

Washington. May 5, 1834

In reply to inquiries made in relation to the mission of Jeremy Robinson to Havana, the Secretary of State writes at great length about efforts to recover documents relating to Florida that had been taken to Havana despite the agreement with the Spanish to leave them in Florida. He clarifies the roles of Robinson, Richard K. Call, William Shaler, Richard J. Cleveland, and Nicholas P. Trist in retrieving important records.[1] McLane explains also that a suit involving a huge tract of Florida land depends upon access to some of these records.

Addressed to Washington. This is a clerk's letter-book copy in Report Books, Department of State (RG 59), National Archives.

1. Robinson had been appointed to the Havana mission in 1832 and stayed there until he died in November 1834. Call, a Florida lawyer who later became governor of that state, had undertaken a special assignment to Cuba in 1829. Shaler and Cleveland, former partners in overseas trade, served as consul and vice-consul, respectively, at Havana. When Shaler died in 1833, he was succeeded by Nicholas P. Trist, who remained in that position until 1841.

FROM ROBERT MACK

Columbia. May 5, 1834

Mack expresses some impatience at not having heard from Polk about the number of copies of his book that should be sent to Washington. He concedes that Polk is doubtless very busy in Congress but urges him to help with this venture. Mack indicates that he is sending 100 copies to Mr. P. Thompson of Washington.[1]

Addressed to Washington.

1. Probably a partner in the book firm of Thompson and Homan.

FROM JOHN Y. MASON[1]

Dear Sir. Pha.[Philadelphia] May 5th 1834

I thank you for your esteemed favor. Our position has been taken with great care, and maintained with temper & firmness. I gave in a letter to my most valued friend, [Joseph W.] Chinn, a hasty sketch of our proceedings, and he writes me, that with my permission he had shown it to you. He expresses doubt as to our right to inspect the books out of the presence of the Agents of the Bank. On this point I have great confidence, because our character, as a public tribunal forbids the idea that an improper use would be made of the privilege, and a contrary construction of our power, would make the Comee. dependant on the Bank for the discharge of that duty which lies at the basis of all the others. For it is most obvious, that if opposed to the inspection, the Bank could and would render the inspection nugatory and wholly ineffectual. We have not however decided, that we will include them, on the contrary asserting only our right to do so. We have expressed the hope, that nothing will occur to render it necessary for the Comee. to exercise the power in order to fairness fullness and dispatch in the transaction of our business. The Bank insisted on their Comee of acting in *conjunction* with us, in our investigations and inspection. We refused to admit their right to do so, giving the assurance above mentioned. To the offer of their room, they attached that condition; we concluded that as they had refused us a room for their exclusive use and occupation, we would sit at our chamber until further order, and called on them for certain extracts, necessary to conduct our investigation, and *required* them to produce certain of their books for inspection at our committee room. In reply, the Board of Directors has *refused us the extracts.* 2 has *refused* to submit their books to our inspection out of the Bank, and 3 declare, that they are not aware that they had declined giving us a room for our exclusive use and occupation, but insist on being present. We have thus fixed their refusal to suffer their books to be inspected out of the Bank and to furnish us statements and extracts, without which our examination is a mere farce. We have this morning adopted a resolution, declaring that we do not waive our rights as asserted, but fully to exhaust every mode of discharging our duty, that we will proceed to the Bank to-day at 1 o'Clock to make the inspection. [John] Sergeant unofficially replied, that they his Comee. cd. not be got together to-day, but wd. answer us to-morrow morning. We however determined to go to the Bank and demand of the President and Cashier in the Bank, an inspection of certain books, the expense book &c. They replied verbally, that they were not authorized to comply with our request, but desired a half hour to reduce their answer to writing, which was granted and we retired. To-morrow we shall go to the Bank again, and will meet the Comee. again. It is not our purpose to ask them to retire, but call for the books, inspect them, propose to make extracts for ourselves. This I have no doubt will be refused. We will then request them to retire for the Comee. to deliberate. This too will be granted but they will claim to carry out the books. We shall request them to leave a particular book as its presence will be necessary, in the deliberations of the Comee. in determining, whether the extract shall be taken. This I presume, will be also refused. What then is the practical advantage of our attempting to proceed farther, until the House shall have decided that we are wrong in our position for if we be right, then there is a breach of Charter. Will not a report of their difficulties interposed by the bank to an investigation of charges of the most grave and serious import to their character and conduct, of their arrogance in claiming equality with the House of Representatives, and of acting jointly with their Comee. in performing the only duty which gives Congress an efficient control over them, have a greater effect, than any disclosures which we can make? I think, our proceedings will show to the whole country, that Congress cannot exercise an efficient control over such an institution—that its supervision is nugatory, its examinations void & the power of the Directors, or of the president if they choose, unlimited, unchecked, & irresponsible.

Show this to Clay, Mardis, & Chinn in confidence, & burn it. [William M.] Inge is much better, but has been extremely ill.[2]

J. Y. Mason

Addressed to Washington. The letter is marked "Confidential."

1. Mason had been appointed to a committee to investigate the activities of the Bank.

2. These two sentences were written along the margin of the first page of the letter.

FROM RICHARD C. ALLEN[1]

Sir, Tallahassee Florida 7th May 1834

Information was received here a few days since, through the Delegate in Congress from this Territory, that the nomination of

James D Westcott[2] jr Esq. to the office U. States attorney for the Middle District of Florida, would be opposed in the Senate, upon the ground of alledged *incapacity* and a deficiency, generally in those qualifications and legal attainments requisite to a correct and proper discharge of the duties of the situation.

I cannot believe that any gentleman who has had a fair opportunity of judging of the qualifications of the nominee, and who is disposed to do him justice in this respect, would urge or offer such an objection; and I am quite certain that no gentleman of the profession in this District would hesitate to admit that he is well qualified to discharge the duties of the office, however opposed some of them may be to him in politics. For myself I am decidly of opinion there is no gentleman in the District (and there many verry highly respectable) better qualified in the most extended sense of the terms than is Mr Westcott. I can assure you also that the appointment of Westcott will be acceptable to the mass of the people of the District of all parties and especially so to the friends of the Administration.

I hope the motives which prompted this hasty note will serve as an apology for obtruding myself upon you in this matter. My sole object & wish, is to prevent imposition and injustice, so far as the expression of the opinion of one so humble as myself will contribute to that and I have known Mr Westcott and practiced in the same courts with him for more than five years, and I am fully satisfied not only that he is well qualified but in every respect worthy the situation. I have written to Judge White & Judge Grundy today[?] the forgoing facts. Should my wishes in this regard accord with your own view, and you could find it convenient to further them you confer a favor on me.

R. C. Allen

Addressed to Washington.

1. At one time a surveyor and land speculator, Allen became a large stockholder in the Union Bank of Tallahassee and was at this time cashier of the Central Bank of Florida. Later he became a federal judge and was important in the statehood movement in Florida.

2. Westcott, born in Virginia and educated in New Jersey, was at this time secretary of the territory of Florida. He received the confirmation of the Senate and served as attorney for the Middle District of Florida for two years. Later he served in the United States Senate, 1844–49.

FROM ROBERT MILLS[1]

Dear Sir [Washington] May 7 1834

I would take the liberty of calling your attention to an error in the wording of that clause in the appropriation bill which reads "23,000$ &c for the Custom house in Baltimore." It should read 23000$ &c for the Custom house *Stores* in Baltimore. Perceiving by the Baltimore papers that Mr. Heath[2] is under a mistake on the subject also, I have deemed it my duty to call your Attention to it.

I would express a hope that the house will restore the clauses altered in Com. of the Whole, relative to the Custom houses, to their original standing as reported by you. Where Free stone was proper for the [. . .] Custom house in inland towns, granite would be more proper for those built near the sea Coast and under the influence of the Salt.

ROBT. MILLS Architect

Delivered by hand to the House of Representatives.

1. The first native professional architect in the United States, Mills was an exponent of Greek revival. After designing buildings in many leading cities, he crowned his success by winning in the competition to design the Washington Monument. He studied under James Hoban, Thomas Jefferson, and Benjamin Latrobe. In 1836 Jackson appointed him Architect of Public Buildings.

2. James P. Heath, a Baltimore lawyer, was at this time serving his only term in the House of Representatives.

FROM LEWIS CASS

Washington. May 8, 1834

Cass explains that the difficulty in getting information about employment of blacksmiths for the Indians is due partially to two fires that occurred in War Department records.

Addressed to Washington. Clerk's copy in Reports to Congress from the Secretary of War (RG 107), National Archives.

FROM JEREMIAH CHERRY

Dear Col. White House Ten May 8th 1834

This morning James Walker Esqr Breakfasted at my house on his way home, and observed that you could not understand my letter to you, on the subject of James Guest appointment. I know not what I wrote for I had wrote several that night & was tired of writing, but I ment for you to use your influence to get the appointment postponed. I received a letter from our Friend A C Hays the day before I wrote to you on the subject, stating that I had better write to you, Mr. Dickerson [David W. Dickinson], and any other member or acquaintance that would have any influence with the Secretary and to get letters wrote here by some of my friends to theirs in Washington to the same effect. I wrote to Dickerson, Eaton as my acquaintances, and to Col. Benton as a friend of the boys Father and if I had of known any more I would have wrote to them on the subject as I felt verry much interested in the boys appointment and his welfare hereafter. Mr Hays I expect, and know I did, thought it a pretty considerable matter and the more weight thrown in the scale the greater the prospect of success, not in the least doubting your influence with the Secretary or your willingness to do a favour for Mr Hays, James or myself—and if I did wrong in writing to more than yourself, you must attribute it to my ansiety for James's appointment. I knew not how to write on the subject but, L. Polk[1] told me the other day that a transfer of the warrant could be made as there was a number of appointment made that would not take effect perhaps in a year or more.

Your Friends & relations in Columbia are well. Mrs [Silas M.] Caldwell I understood yesterday was unwell. My wife is there now on a visit. Dr Martin formerly of Columbia was married a few days ago to Miss Duglass of Nashville.[2] Myself & Family injoy good health & hope that you & yours enjoy the Same.

J. Cherry

In one part of my note to you I said something about spiteing P.N.;[3] it was only that he has always said the connection was too unpopular for you to interest yourself for them.

C.

I would like to hear from you. I know not how to write a letter.

Addressed to Washington.

1. Probably Leonidas Polk since he was a graduate of the Military Academy and would have been better acquainted with such affairs than his brother Lucius J. Polk.

2. In May, in Davidson County, Robert C. K. Martin and Priscilla Douglas were married.

3. Probably Pleasant Nelson.

FROM SPENCER CLARK GIST

Knoxville. May 10, 1834

Gist inquires as to the status of his petition to Congress for extra compensation and asks about the fate of the navy bill introduced by John G. Watmough.[1]

Addressed to Washington.

1. See Gist to Polk, February 20, 1834, and Jesse D. Elliott to Polk, April 16, 1834.

FROM JAMES L. GUEST

Dear Sir Columbia May 10th 1834

I return you the commission which you were kind enough to procure for, and forward to me, only because I yet want one year of being as old as required. I shall be 16 years old in June 1835, and will take it as a great favor in you, and the Secretary of War to receive the present commission and have it renewed a year hence. In the mean time I will endeavor to improve in my education, so that I can be certain to stand the requisite examination.

James L. Guest

Addressed to Washington. The letter is in the handwriting of James Walker, but it was signed by Guest.

FROM JOHN Y. MASON

Dear Sir Pha.[Philadelphia] May 10th 1834

The Committee having failed in procuring an inspection of the books of the Bank, has determined to return to Washington.

When I last wrote you, we had determined to meet the Comee. of Directors in the Bank, to perform that duty.[1] I anticipated that they would submit the books, but refuse extracts. In this I was disappointed, they took a bolder ground. We submitted calls for specific books, they replied by producing a preamble & two resolutions, *requiring* the Committee to furnish them the charges and specifications, touching which the evidence was wanted & objecting to furnish any book, unless they thought the charge amounted to a violation of charter. We replied, by informing them, that our duty was to *inquire* whether charges should be made and a prosecution had, that we were not authorized to prefer charges, & had none to make, that our duty was one of inquiry merely and requested a specific answer to our calls. The answer was a refusal to submit them, unless in the mode & for the objects which they had stated. We then issued a subpn. duces tecum[2] summoning the President and Directors severally to attend us at our room and bring the certain books; they attended, but did not bring the books & gave in a paper signed by each, refusing to bring the books, and *refusing to testify, because they were parties.* So ends the investigation. Quem deus vult perdere prius dementat.[3] Can their own friends sustain them? Many of them here, not in the Directory, it is believed, will condemn them. I shall probably be in Washington on Tuesday. Inge is much better.

J. Y. MASON

Addressed to Washington. The letter is marked "Private."

1. See Mason to Polk, May 5, 1834.
2. *Subpoena duces tecum* is a writ requiring a witness to bring with him, and to produce to the court, books, papers, or other records.
3. Whom the gods would destroy they first make mad.

TO LEWIS CASS

Dr. Sir Ho. Repts. May 12. 1834

The General Appropriation Bill passed the House this morning and has gone to the Senate. The House has also concurred in the amendments from the Senate, to the *Army Bill,* and the latter only wants the signature of the President to become a law.

On tomorrow I hope to be able to procure the consideration of the *Indian* and *fortification Bills.* If the statements relating to the Indian Annuity Bill which you promised, are prepared, I would be glad to have them this evning. I would be glad also to have an estimate of the appropriations required to carry into effect the Indian Treaties recently ratified by the Senate,[1] to the end that I may move them as amendments. Will you send me a draft of the amendments with the estimates, and also a copy of the Treaties?

If any reductions can be made of the amounts proposed to be appropriated, by the Bill reported for *fortifications,* without injury to the public service, I would thank you to suggest them in the course of the day. If any reductions can be made, I should think it adviseable to make them.

James K. Polk

Addressed to Washington. Letter in the University of Michigan Library.

1. This probably refers to the treaty signed with the Pawnees on October 9, 1833. A delegation of Chickasaws was in Washington when Polk wrote this letter, but the treaty with them was not signed until May 24, 1834.

FROM POWHATAN ELLIS[1]

Dear Sir — Louisville [Kentucky] May 12. 1834

It gives me great pleasure to have an opportunity of making known to you my friend Richard M Gaines Esqr[2] of Natchez. He visits Washington and will most likely remain with you ten or fifteen days. Any civilities you may have it in your power to extend to this gentleman (whose character & worth entitles him to yr confidence) will confer a personal favor. . . .

Powhatan Ellis

Addressed to Washington.

1. Born in Virginia, Ellis began the practice of law in Lynchburg before moving to Natchez in 1816. He was a former member of the United States Senate, but at this time he was federal judge for the state of Mississippi. Later he was minister to Mexico.

2. A Natchez lawyer who was at this time state attorney general.

FROM GEORGE W. HAYWOOD

Dear Col. [Bedford County, May 12, 1834][1]

You behold enclosed one more communication on the subject of the Post office in our neighbourhood.[2] I for one do not want the office abolished altogether but would rather it should be continued where it is now located if it could be done without doing to much violence to the wishes of the people &c. the practice heretofore pursued by the Department.

G. W Haywood

Presumably addressed to Washington, but no envelope has been found.

1. This letter bore no provenance nor date. The date of May 12, 1834, has been supplied by the Library of Congress. This date is accepted here on the basis of internal evidence.

2. The enclosure was a copy of a letter that Samuel Bigham wrote to the Postmaster General under the date of May 12, 1834. The letter contains information on distances and directions of roads serving the various post offices involved. Bigham obviously favored locating the office at the home of William Davis.

FROM LEWIS CASS

Dear Sir, [Washington] May 15 1834

I called to see you last evening on the subject you and Judge Clay spoke of. I would go down again this morning, but I have a particular matter to attend to which will retain me. If you are coming up this way this morning, I will thank you to call for a moment on the same matter.

Lew Cass

Delivered by hand.

FROM DAVID JARRETT[1]

Dear Sir Denmark Tennessee May 15th, 1834

Please to Send me Some of Mr Benton's Speachs on the Subject of Speacia Currancy—Also Some of the Presidants Protests to the Senate. We take but few news papers which is the only chance we have to get any thing from the Republican Side. The male bags has bene loaded for months past with the oposition prints from our representative, but they are Sent to such persons who scarcely read any thing, and many[?] packags are not red by any person, but used in this plas as rapping paper. If Crockett gets his land bill through he is Statesman of while he lives under all circumstances & in behalf of our Country, I think it would be best to Voat against it at the preasant Session or postpone the final decision until another Congress. I do wish that you & Mr C Johnson would furnish this District with the reports of the Committes & Speachs of the administrative party, for I again tell you that Col Crockett has flooded this district with the Speaches of Clay, Calhoune, Webster, Wilde, Chilton[2] &c &c. Who pays for all of the fine paper, and the printing? It must *Cost* a *great deale*.

Our Country is healthy, Money plenty, & a fine prospect for a Crop.

What is the matter with the postmaster, does he lack Capacity? Is he presisely honest? Will he finally injour the Administration materially? Many of Jacksons warmest friends believe that their is Something wrong in this matter. We know that he has failed to let our Contracts agreeable to advertisements, and Change the rout and gave more than twise as much as he ought to give. I believe that the President is Imposed on in Some instances. Mr Grundy ought to examine the Situation of the Post office & report, & if he neglects to do this, it must be through design, & he will be considered designing and unfaithful.

D Jarrett

Addressed to Washington.

1. An early settler in Madison County who had been involved with Sam Polk in locating and surveying lands.

2. Richard H. Wilde and Thomas Chilton were members of the House of Representatives from Georgia and Kentucky, respectively. Both were favorable to the Bank and therefore were considered unfriendly toward Polk. Chilton's speech on the deposits question was given on December 18, 1833, one of the earliest on the subject. Wilde did not deliver his speech in the House until March 18, 1834.

FROM JAMES WALKER

Dear Sir Columbia, May 15. 1834

I reached home on the 8th in 9 days from Washington found all well except Ann Maria, and your Sister Eliza. Ann is I hope better, but her case is a very doubtful one. Eliza is in quite bad health, but is understood to be better within a few days. The Doctor [Caldwell] started out to the District, when we had the frost here on the 27th. My crops in the district were not injured by the frost, but Shelton has nearly been ruined since by a hail storm. I first heard that your crop was ruined by the frost, and afterward (I am inclined to think more correctly) that you were not much injured. I think Beenland will find no difficulty in getting seed to replant as much as necessary, and as Dr. Caldwell has gone out to attend to his & your interest I think you may be satisfied that your chance for a crop is as good as others. He will be at home in a few days, and will advise you what your prospects are. On my arrival I found Donly in Mississippi. Of course I must wait here until he returns, to make property arrangements with him, and to know of Mr. Longhbad[?],[1] when it will be proper for us to take possession of the lower line. It may therefore be some time next month before I can go to the District where I am very anxious to be.

I received on yesterday your letter enclosing Lieut Lea's.[2] Our Rail Road company (or rather Directory) have as I think very precipatately appointed Col. Pettival chief engineer at a high salary. Col. Pettival seems to be a clever and a scientific man, but I cannot ascertain that our people have anything like sufficient information about him, to justify putting all our interests in his charge. The truth is we have in the Railroad made a bad commencement. Allen Brown, David Looney, W. Porter &c have the ascendancy in the board, and are as wild as bucks. Their operations thus far look more like a disposition to divide the spoils among themselves, than setting about to make the improvement like honest sensible men. Dale & Plummer much to my surprise and mortification go with them. On one side I find A Brown, D. Loony, P W Porter, G. Skipwith, Dale, Plummer, & Buckner (in place of Sansom) *they rule.* In opposition to their views is Langtry, Cooper, L. Polk, Booker.[3] I of course think with the minority and if we cannot by some energetic course change the plan of operations, my judgment is that our Rail Road project will be a splendid failure. However I do not despair. Our minds are made up to a course that I think will govern them. If we fail we can but resign, and break up the project for the present, but a Rail road will be made very shortly from here to the Tennessee River whether this Co. make it or not. I should like to have Mr. Lea in our employ. His family is a guarantee that we could rely on him, his being a native Tennessean, would insure a more disinterested devotion to our interests, and especially as our work is but the commencement of the great work in Tennessee. Besides we have had Col. Pettivals opinion and inspection of the road. I would like to have additional light and an additional mind capable of giving us proper [. . .] information. I will submit Mr. Lea's letter to our board on Saturday, and if they take no order[?] on it I will forward it to the Jackson Co. As I have said enough about our Rail Road prospects to throw a doubt over them, I will write you again next week how we stand, whether our prospects are good to accomplish the object or whether all is lost.

JAMES WALKER

Addressed to Washington.

1. Unidentified.

2. Albert M. Lea was graduated from the United States Military Academy in 1831, after which he served on topographical duty. At this time he was en route to Iowa for duty on the frontier. Later he was chief engineer of Tennessee and a member of the faculty of East Tennessee University. He moved to Texas and subsequently served as a general in the Confederate army.

3. See McKay W. Campbell to Polk, March 20, 1834.

FROM THOMAS P. MOORE

D Polk Fullers [Washington] (Friday) [May 16, 1834][1]

I know you have your hands full yet I *must* trouble you. I have been confined for two days & may not be able to go out tomorrow. I hope you have a meeting tomorrow night. If so get the persons whose names are enclosed to make a part of it.[2] And if you can ascertain the day on which Hamer[3] will report, rally our friends & impress them with the importance of avoiding the Committee of the Whole. Once there & it will never be heard of again. Explain to Hamer & Jones[4] the kind of motion necessary to get it on the table printed, & the order of the day for a [. . .] day. Recollect that not *a seat* in Congress only, but my character is at stake! I never when in or out of Congress refuse to work for my friends. If you can send me a list of those who will *probably* be absentees next Tuesday pray do it.

T P Moore

Delivered by hand.

1. This date is suggested on the basis of actions in the House of Representatives. It was on Tuesday, May 20, 1834, that the House voted not to refer the election matter to the Committee of the Whole House.

2. A list with some twenty names was enclosed.

3. Thomas Lyon Hamer, a House member from Ohio, was chairman of the Committee of Elections that was considering the disputed election involving Moore and Robert P. Letcher. This committee brought in a report favoring Moore, but the House called for a new election, which Letcher won.

4. Seaborn Jones of Georgia was on Hamer's committee and favored the majority report of that committee.

FROM ANDREW JACKSON

[Washington] May 18th 1834

The president with his respects to Col J. K. Polk, requests to see him tomorrow morning at ten oclock A. M. to make to him and some other gentlemen, who he has requested to be present, a confidential communication.

Delivered by hand to Polk's boardinghouse. The note is not signed, but it is in Jackson's handwriting.

FROM JAMES BRIGHT

Dear Sir, Mardisville Alabama May 21st 1834

I have often had it in contemplation to write you since I have been here, but my engagments have been such that I have never found it convenient till now.

I have been here ever since November last, with the exception of about three weeks in visiting my familly, first engaged in locating the Indian reservations under the treaty of the 24th March 1832,[1] and now engaged in certifying their contracts for the sale of their reservations. In the execution of this duty, I have had a great deal of trouble and many difficulties to encounter, But under all the circumstances, I have no reason to complain. I have got along fully as well as I expected. I have had the good fortune to enjoy uninterrupted good health, otherwise I never could have accomplished what I have.

In the execution of this duty, I can hardly hope to escape censure, having such a variety of interests to represent, and the organ thro which a vast amount of property and money must pass from hand to hand, and perhaps many disappointed in their most sanguine hopes. There seems to be a greater variety of ways and means invented to commit fraud upon the poor Indians than ever was on any other occasion and with all the plans we have been able to invent, and great care and caution I have no doubt in many instances, we have been imposed upon and they defrauded and deprived of their just rights.[2]

In rendering justice to the Indians, I have in some instances incured the displeasure of some of the citizens, but this is what I always expected, and if I had have undertaken to have pleased them I must have done the Indians injustice.

There have been some complaints made to the Secretary of War, thro some of the members of Congress from this State, but it is nothing more than I expected as the persons who made them felt a deep interest in the matter. But it was on a subject which I had fully explained to the Secretary. I am in hopes it may not become necessary, but if it should, I must call in the aid of my friends at Washington, and by whom I have no fears of being sustained as far as I deserve. As I have no personal acquaintance with Genl. [Lewis] Cass who has from time to time (as far as my engagements would admit) been apprised of my proceedings here, if it should become necessary you would say to him what in justice to your feelings you know of me.

My engagements have been such since I have been in the nation, I have had but little opportunity of knowing any thing about our public affairs, but from observations I occasionally hear fall from others, I am afraid things are not going on so well at Washington.

By the death of my much esteemed friend Genl. [William] Polk, my son[3] who is still in N Carolina is left without a guardian, and from my engagements here and being an entire stranger in that Country I have not been able to select another. He is still at Hillsborough, have you any acquaintance there whom you could recommend & whose friendship might be engaged? If you do please inform me and should you make N. Carolina in your way in returning to Tennessee and could find it convenient to call and see him it would be very gratifying to John, and for which I would feel myself under additional obligations to the many I have already recd. at your hand—and if you should not pass that way, if you should at any time find it convenient to drop him a line by way of advice I know it will be acceptable.

If you have leisure sufficient from your public duties, it would be very gratifying to receive a line from you directed to this place.

J Bright

Addressed to Washington.

1. Under the terms of this treaty, the Creeks ceded to the United States all their lands east of the Mississippi River.

2. Reports made in 1836 and 1838 bore out the worst of Bright's prophecies. The frauds, however, were only a part of the harassment of the Creeks. Ample proof was found that they were even abused physically by unprincipled white men who sought their lands.

3. John M. Bright, later a prominent political figure in Tennessee, was at this time a student in the Bingham School at Hillsborough. This was the same school attended by William H. Polk when he was preparing to enter the University of North Carolina. Bright was graduated from the University of Nashville and studied law at Transylvania in Lexington, Kentucky.

FROM WILLIAM H. POLK

Dear Brother Chapel Hill N C May 21th 1834

I have been expecting a letter from you for some time in answer to the request I made with regard to the loan of some money to pay off some debts the payment of which cannot be delayed longer than the close of this session which will close on the twenty sixth of June and by letting me have the money before that time you will confer a favour on me which will never be forgotten and which I hope some day to be able to return. If you can make it convenient to send me that accompanied with the money to pay my expences home by the 12th of June as I fear there will be so many people here at the examination that it will be very difficult to get a seat in the stage for five or six stages after the 26th and by that means I will be delayed on the hill for at least ten days. You will please give me an answer to this by the next mail after you receive it.

WILL H POLK

Addressed to Washington.

FROM POWHATAN ELLIS

My Dear Sir — Lexington Kentucky May 23 1834

For the benefit of the health of my family I propose spending the summer here or somewhere else in the state. Will you have the kindness to forward such docts as you can spare and if you have leisure moment I should be exceedingly gratified to learn what is the present state of parties in Washington. Who are the prominent men for the next Presidency on both sides of the question and what will be the probable result? I know your time is much engaged in attending to your public duties and therefore will not press this request upon you if it is not entirely convenient. Mrs Ellis unites with me in kind regards to Mrs Polk.

Drop the enclosed letters in the post office. If however it is an abuse of the franking privilege send them to the post office by your servant & have the postage charged.

POWHATAN ELLIS

Addressed to Washington.

FROM McKAY W. CAMPBELL

Dear Sir — Columbia May 26th 1834

I rec'd a few lines from you informing me that Capt Daniel McKies pension had been granted & sent on.

It was taken from the office on Saturday last—taken to him. He has sent in this morning (Monday) by his son[1] with a wish that It should be returned. The old man is very much vexed indeed that the Department should offer him a pension of the trifling sum of $26.66 per annum & this sum is by some mistake made payable at Lexington Kentucky. The old man rebells against such treatment—Says he would not receive such a "picattoon" allowance.

There is certainly some mistake about the matter. It is only for $26.66 & made payable at Lexington. Now the old man proved in the Declaration that I drew for him, & on which you seem to think the claim was granted, at least fifteen months service, (perhaps 18 months) *positively* & *unequivocally*. From the mistake in making it payable at Lexington, I am induced to believe there is some mistake in making it out & filling it up.

It is with much reluctance that I trouble you with this matter again, knowing as I do that you are & have long been under an almost insupportable press of business. But the old man requests that I should present the matter to you again & request you to give it the best attention you can—have the matter re-examined, revised & corrected. I cant understand how the Comissioner happened to allow Capt. McKie only 26.$ pr. An. when he positively states that he served 15 or 18 months & greater part of the time in the capacity of an officer. Will you do the old man the kindness to cause the matter to be reinvestigated and on the declaration which I made out for him at the March Term 1834 of our County Court—not any papers Matthews may have sent[2]—have it made payable at Nashville. Write to me what can be done for Capt. McKie, as soon as you learn & have leisure.

Nothing new in politics here but what you will see in our papers. The indignation we feel here at the course persued by the *Conspirators* in the Senate is inexpressable. You can guess what light we would view such men as Clay, Calhoun & Webster when we see them descending, from their exalted seats as Senators, with D. *Crockett* & Poindexter & *such* hanging on as Yelpers *discending down down* into the *Rable* of large cities to raise a *hue & cry*.

I suppose if *Clay* &c. succeed in putting down the people &

the *Present* President of the United States that the *actual* President of U.S. which they will make (Esqr. Biddle or the Bank) will fix on them Clay &c. handsome pensions or annuities as having been faithfull soldiers during the *"War of the Revotion"* by which the present generation will have *lost* or rather *sold* to *Squire Biddle* or the Banks (J. Q. Adams [. . .][3] perfection) what our ancestors wre[sted] from the hands of Tyrants & paid for [. . .] their lives & blood. I must believe that Clay, Calhoun & Webster (who are the *Soul* of mangy pack that yelp for pay or something worse) are the most corrupt & basely unprincipled men on *Earth.* They are certainly now in a state of feeling that they would rather see their country *Sunk,* into the lowest abyss of anarchy & confusion, internal war & bloodshed, & even fall again under a foreign Yoke than that General Jackson should succeed in his glorious triumphs over their corrupt base machinations. That the God of bravery may (as he has [here]tofore been) be a Stay & Buckler [. . .] our beloved Patriarch & that we will find ourselves safely landed on [. . .] top & our Jackson still alive at our head is the prayer of his *friend.* Excuse me for running into this effusion for when I touch I know not when to stop.

M. W. CAMPBELL

Addressed to Washington.

1. Benjamin F. McKie.
2. See Andrew Matthews to Polk, February 3, 1833.
3. Portions of the last page of the letter have flaked off. The ellipses represent perhaps no more than a word each.

FROM JAMES WALKER

Dear Sir Columbia, May 29th 1834

Mr. Kirk is desirous of building on the ground he purchased from Marshall.[1] He is affraid however to join our buildings, as [Adlai O.] Harris's & yours are considered somewhat dangerous. He therefor proposes that you & Harris take down your buildings & rebuild three stories, and that I take down or repair the corner[?], and also make that 3 stories, the whole building to correspond with the Brown's. The most of the old materials can be used and the expense will not be very great. Houses are so plenty for the business of the place that you & Harris cannot rent much longer unless your buildings are made better and I am inclined to think if any one would agree to Rent your House for 5 years, on condition that you would repair or rather rebuild it, it would be your interest to do so. Harris is disposed to go into the arrangement. I do not think I will take my house down, (as my cellar is a good one, and I can see no necessity for taking down but perhaps may) but I will put on the other story, and make it correspond with the ballance. Let me have your views on this subject. Donly has been absent since my return home. I yesterday received a letter from him dated Clinton Mi. proposing for me to go down to Natchez and commence ascertaining the value of the property there. As we all live in this country I think it would be more proper for him to come home, and for us to choose our men so that no trips might be made without avail. But we will think about it and decide in a day or two.

Nothing new in politics. I have been at Nashville and have spoken of things *as they are* at Washington, as much as prudence would justify. The people here certainly view the controversy between the Bank and the government very correctly. I am sure that the parties may yet be counted in this quarter as 500 for the administration to 1 against it. It is *impossible* for a bank party to start up here; if any are foolish enough to try it their political destruction is inevitable.

I hope Anne Maria is much better. Mary [Eliza Walker] about as usual. Maria's health is delicate, but I hope her prospects are better than they have been for several years. Poor old Bob[2] is a maniac—compelled to be chained down. *Oph*[elia] has much of the D'l about her.

I have seen a late letter from Beenland to Dr. Caldwell. His prospects are represented as pretty good considering the frosts & storms, that have injured us all more or less.

James Walker

Addressed to Washington.

1. Before his death, Marshall T. Polk had sold a lot in Columbia to John Kirk.

2. Unidentified.

FROM EPHRAIM BEANLAND

Dear sir [Fayette County] Juine 1th 1834

We ar all well and have bin since I last rote and I am sorry to informe you that I have got A bad stand of coten. I have got a good stand on 50 acares it is ondly tolerable good and on the rest of the crop is verr indiferent which I planted over the second time and it caime aup verry well and it all dyed which I have put it in corn 15 or 20 acares and my newe grounde corn is come aup verry well I think. I have got in 35 or 40 acares and my oald ground corene is promising and I say it is cleane and the most of it loocks well. Sum of it is as high as my head and I have the finest oats that I ever sawe, 10 or 12 acares which I have bin feedinge my work horsis intirely on them for 3 weaks, I have no corne to feede them on. I have 6 bariles of corne that the Dr Calwell[1] let me have and he cant spare any more and I cant hear of any for saile under $3:75 per bariel. I am tolde that Govan[?] has corn to sell at $2:50 per bariel which I am agoing theire in the morninge to get my bred corne if I can. The docter disapointed me verry much for I ingaged 40 bariles and I ondly get 10. My bakin holdes out verry well I thinke, and I think that my crop is in good order and I shold like to see you verry much and when you come I want you to stay hear as longe as you can. Nothinge more at this time.

E. Beanland

This man Shelby[2] that wants to by your farme the information that I got of about the man is, he is nothinge more than a whim and a drunking man at that.

Addressed to Washington. This letter has been published in Bassett, *Plantation Overseer*, 72–73.

1. Dr. Silas M. Caldwell. See Caldwell to Polk, April 11, 1834, for Caldwell's statement about furnishing Beanland with corn.

2. Unidentified.

FROM WILLIAM E. GILLESPIE[1]

Dear Sir Columby 1st June 1834

Doct McGimsey has removed from our Town, and has settled himself permenantly on a farm in the state of Mississippi and he has authorised me to make sale of his house and lots in Columbia formerly owned by Saml A Gillespie.[2] Mr Cooper[3] wishes to purchase the house and lots, and has frequantly conversed with me upon that subject, and I am inclined to believe he and myself will effect a trade, unless I can make a better sale to some other person. I think the property will suit you, as it is certainly the most desirable place for a family residance in our Town and in fact, the most valuable property of the kind in Town. The landed property in our County has risen considerably in the price since we have under taken the rail road and in fact the Town property has also risen very much in the price. Doct [William] McNeil has purchased Mr Plummers house and lot at the price of $7000. McGimseys house is equally as good as that of Plummers, & in addition to that he has two lots connected together, either of which is more desirable and more valuable than that of Plummers. But as McGimsey is anxious to sell, I will give a bargain on the property. Do you not wish to purchase it or trade your house and lot for it? Mr Cooper offered Mr Plummer his house & lot & $4500. cash in hand for Plummers house & lot, previous to the sale to Doct. McNeil. Please write to me upon the subject, on the recpt of this letter, and I will not make a sale untill I hear from you.

W. E. Gillespie

Addressed to Washington.

1. A Columbia lawyer who was at this time clerk and master of the chancery court. His kinship with Samuel A. Gillespie, if any, has not been ascertained.

2. John W. McGimsey had bought a house from Samuel A. Gillespie about two years before. Local legend has it that Gillespie built the house to the specifications of a prospective bride only to have her jilt him after it was completed. Like McGimsey, Samuel A. Gillespie moved to Mississippi. See Samuel A. Gillespie to Polk, March 19, 1834.

3. Matthew D. Cooper, by coincidence, in 1827, had also bought a house from Dr. McGimsey.

FROM ELLIOT H. FLETCHER[1]

Dear Sir. Fayetteville June 3d 1834

I have been engaged for the last ten or twelve years in prosecuting the mercantile business in this place. My business was at one time a prosperous one but a train of untoward circumstances which it would be here needless to enumerate has reduced me to ruin. Everything on earth has been swept away but my good name and what adds a double sting to poverty is the reflection that by an over estimate of my means I have involved in my own ruin some of my best friends.

I am now driven to the hard necessity of seeking a temporary shelter for my wife and child under the roof of her father and he unfortunately is poor and already burdened with the support of a large family. My friends have advised me to study the law. I have made the attempt but here surrounded by creditors, by the friends I have injured—with broken spirits, and crushed pride, eating the bitter bread of dependance I have found the task so beset with difficulties that I have yielded it up as hopeless. I have since endeavored to procure employment without success. In the midst of my despondency it occurred to me today that you had the means to serve me and I trust you have the will. Without any claim upon your kindness save that which misfortune gives, in this my extremity I ask your assistance in procuring me publick employment. I ask for no particular office. I am willing to accept any thing suited to my capacity, any thing that will support me.

I am told a bill for organizing a territory So West of Michigan is in its passage thro the house.[2] I certainly under happier fortunes would feel no desire to live in so high a northern latitude as Huron, but in my present circumstances, I would gladly accept of an appointment there. I take it for granted that you correctly appreciate the attitude I occupy in reference to national politics, I have no political claims on the administration. Yet permit me to say that all my life I have held strictly to the Virginia doctrines. Of course many of the President's measures have met my most cordial approbation, nor need I say that I am anti Bank and anti American System.

I have thus given you a simple statement of my necessitous condition, and a candid avowal of my political creed.

I know that your publick duties are of an anxious and harrassing kind, and how little leisure you have to devote to applications of this sort. I certainly know too, that I have no claims on your gratitude for the past but I know that you can serve me and I confide in your generosity. By stretching out your hand you can raise up a ruined man. Stand by me Col. in this extremity and tho. it may not be in my power at any time to requite the obligation still to my last day I will acknowledge the debt. I confide everything to you. If you are willing to interest yourself cordially in my behalf I take it for granted that the President would refuse no application (more especially an act of grace) made by you.

I leave it to you to determine on the propriety of making the application at all, but if it be made I trust it will be done at your earliest leisure. I repeat that I have no prediliction for Huron. I have suggested employment there because I thought it likely that its vigourous climate would make offices there less sought after. Certainly I would on many accounts prefer other portions of the Union.

I am told it is the practice to accompany applications for office with recommendations. I will merely say that if be necessary I can procure in this state proper testimonials as to character and I trust as to fitness.

I would likewise suggest that if there should not be time to send back that my very particular friend Mr Inge would gladly take upon himself the trouble of drawing up a reccommendation. Mr Grundy will sign it and I would reckon on Messrs. Bell, Peyton & Dunlap, tho my personal acquaintance with the two last gentleman is but slight.

Let me intreat of you the favour to acknowledge the receipt of this letter immediately; to me it is every way important to know the worst at once.

Excuse this scrawl—for I write in haste and with a bad pen. I will write to Mr Inge by this mail if I can finish my letter before the mail closes.

ELLIOT H. FLETCHER

Addressed to Washington.

1. Fletcher was a merchant in Fayetteville. It is possible that he was a kinsman of Thomas H. Fletcher, who had once practiced law there. See Archibald Yell to Polk, June 4, 1834.

2. Several bills dealing with that area came before the House, and it is not clear which one Fletcher was speaking of, but the name Huron appeared later in his letter, and it seems likely that he referred to the bill reported by the House Committee on Territories on April 12, 1834, which used the name Huron.

FROM WILLIAM H. POLK

Dear Brother Chapel Hill N.C. June 3rd 1834

I received your letter this morning enclosing me one half of a hundred dollar bill for the purpose of bearing my expenses home. I also received ten dollars a few weeks ago which I thought I had acknowledged the receipt of in my first letter until I received your letter. I will start home in a few days after I receive the other half of the bill. Give my love to sister Sarah. You must excuse me for not writing a longer letter as the mail will close in a short time.

William H Polk

Addressed to Washington.

FROM GASPARD RICHARD

New York. June 4, 1834

Richard reminds Polk that in January he sent him a printed extract of his memorial to Congress in behalf of a Constitutional Bank Company. He reiterates his intention to secure a sound, uniform paper currency for the country. He hopes that Polk agrees with his proposal as the best way to relieve economic distresses.

Addressed to Washington.

FROM ARCHIBALD YELL

My Dear Sir Fayettville June the 4th 1834

The Honorable station which has been assigned you this Session of Congress as the champion of the Republican Party has made it nessary that your whole time should be employed to sustain it. I should not now trouble you with minor matters, but for the appeal I have to make in behalf of our mutual friend, Col E H Fletcher.[1]

You are apprised that once he was in easy circumstances but by an unforeseen change in buisness, he has like many others been brought to poverty, with nothing left but a good nam & an unsuled reputation. Thus thrown upon the world without a dollar he has to make his way through this cold and uncharitable world, & more than all an amiable & intelignt wife has to bare with him his misfortunes.

His situation maks it prudnt that he should settle in a country where his prospects would be more flatering than in Tennessee, & where he could cultivate and bring into useful opperations a rich & cultivated mind. He has made rapid progress in reading law in which he has been engaged for the last twelve or eighteen months and would now be qualifyed to take a respectable stand at the Bar in Tennessee or else where.

Nothing is wanting but to place him in a situation where he will not be shackeled by his surrounding difficulties but left free to act and he will some day become a useful man and an ornament to society.

I then ask a "Boon." Procure him a place that will give a home and support to a disconsolate wife & make hapy an Honorable but unfortunate adventurer. To be able to secure a small pitance for his family he is willing to encounter all the dangers and hardships insident to a settlmnt in a new Country. The pleasurs of society he will willigly yeald, to be placed beyond the constant view of a mass of avericious creditors.

My best feelings are enlisted for an amiable but disponding family and could you but be an eye witness to all the misfortunes that surround them, I should have no fears that your bosome would remain unmoved while it would be in your power to relieve them, which I have every reason to believe from the relation you occupy in the ranks of the party & the confidence of the Presidnt. On your exertions and sempithies the result depends, therefore anothr *medium* has not been sought to solicite the President, not that *he* would be less zealous, but the chances of success less shure.

This favor is not asked on political ground as you are assured he has never been the personal friend of the Presidnt, but is most decidedly with the Admnitration upon the grate question that divide the party at this time. I mean he is Anti *Bank,* and Anti Internal Improvmnt and but for his early prejudices he would now have been a thorough going supporter of the Admtration.

We are not aware of any vacancy at present that you could precure. The new Territory of Huron will create many new offics and even there he will willingly go, to enable him to support his family. Should there be a vacancy in Arkinsaw that he could fill, I am certain he would much prefer it, but as it is a matter of favor he will not decline any that may be precured for him. This appeal I make to your liberality & magnimity and pray it may be crowned with success.

Mr Cormack[2] & myself will leave here by the 1th of July for Arkinsaw where I shall make my future home. But be assured. Let my lot be cast wherever it may, you will always have the wishes of you old friend for your success & prosperity.

Be so good as to present me to your good Lady and accept for yourself my kindest wishes.

A. Yell

Addressed to Washington.

1. See Fletcher to Polk, June 3, 1834.

2. Possibly Samuel W. Carmack. Carmack had moved to Florida but had retained a home in Fayetteville.

FROM JOSEPH M. NOURSE

Georgetown, D.C. June 11, 1834

Having served as Register of the Treasury from 1790 until 1829 at very low pay, Nourse has made claim for extra compensation and requests Polk to help get quick action on the matter.

Addressed to Washington.

FROM WILLIAM J. ALEXANDER

Dear Sir Baltimore June 16th 1834

Mr John W Huske[1] who will hand you this note is a gentleman of the bar from the town of Fayetteville N C. He will stay a few days in Washington and as he is a stranger may stand in need of a friend. Any attention you may give to him will by me be deemed a personal favor to myself. Present me most kindly to Mrs Polk.

Wm J Alexander

Addressed to Washington and delivered by hand.

1. In addition to being a lawyer, Huske was for many years president of the North Carolina branch of the Bank of the United States.

FROM GEORGE A. WAGGAMAN

[Washington]. June 20, 1834

The Louisiana senator asks if the Quartermaster General has reported to the Ways and Means Committee concerning funds for building barracks at New Orleans.

Delivered by hand to Polk at the House of Representatives.

FROM WILLIAM G. CHILDRESS[1]

Dr Sir Nashville June 21 1834

Your favr of the 11 Inst is this moment recd. and as I fear the time is short between this and your adjournment I hastene to give you but a short and concise reply. The convention of the State of Tennessee is now in session and has been for five weeks and but little as yet done, tho. I believe I can venture an opinion as to the result generally. I believe the principle of the old Constitution fixing the basis of representation will be continued with an increase of members; I believe the valorem principle of taxation will prevail, and that the Judges of the State will be put in for a term of years & I fear a short period; this I oppose. I am for the old plan with the addition of the privilege of removal by an address &c.

Some Excitement prevails here upon the subject of politicks of the Genl. Government one of which items is the result of the election of Speaker vice Mr. Stevenson resigned.[2] The warm *Jackson* men here are somewhat mortefied and the opposition are verry much elated—the Bank party go with the opposition. I am inclined to the opinion that some exertions are or have been made to Keep down or stifle enquiry; some days ago I recd. a New York paper with some remarks upon the subject of the election which I showed & read to the Editors of the two papers here, which was passed by in silence. Your verry particular friend E. H. F.[3] I am informed is gratified at said result. James Bell of this place has made a large failure and it said here his Brother

John goes with him.[4] The amt is said to be from $50.000 to $75.000. after the [. . .] is exhausted. I think it verry doubtful whether his elevation is to benefit or injure him, time only will tell as I think exertions are making on both sides but the greater for him. The failure will I think prove prejudicial.

The Jackson men from E. T. are quite indignant.

W. G. CHILDRESS

Addressed to Washington.

1. Sarah Polk's cousin and a political leader in Williamson County. At this time he was a member of the state constitutional convention. He served one term, 1835–37, in the state senate.

2. Andrew Stevenson presented his resignation to the House on June 2, 1834, whereupon balloting for a successor began. Polk and John Bell were in strong competition throughout, and on the tenth ballot Bell was elected.

3. Ephraim H. Foster.

4. James Bell and his brother John married sisters of David W. Dickinson of Rutherford County. James Bell established a mercantile business in Nashville, borrowing heavily from the Bank of the United States. When his business failed in 1834, he signed over his interest in his father's estate to John, who had endorsed his notes. James then moved to Carroll County, Mississippi. In 1841 he fell from a steamboat and was drowned in the Mississippi River.

FROM JAMES A. CRAIG

Haw River, North Carolina. June 21, 1834

A college classmate, now a physician, writes in behalf of a patient who is a veteran of the Revolutionary War. He informs Polk that he has forwarded the necessary papers to Washington and asks him to inquire as to their arrival.

Addressed to Washington. This letter has been published in McPherson, editor, "Unpublished Letters," *North Carolina Historical Review,* XVI, 178–180.

FROM RICHARD PETERS[1]

D Sir Philadelphia June 21 1834

I observe that an amendment has been proposed in the Senate to the appropriation bill to allow $400 for recording the proceedings of the Supreme Court.

The object of this proposition is to have the opinion of the court recorded by the clerk, and I do verily believe that it has been introduced on the suggestion of Duff Green who wants to have the opinions copied so that he may print them in an Ephemeral Law Journal, thus giving circulation to that opinion, in an imperfect form, as they will be without the statements of the cases in many instances as also without the points argued by counsel. Such a course might lead to much error, and it will very much affect the sale of the regular reports, which even with the sum attended by benefit to the reporter, do but barely pay for the labor of preparation and the cost of publication.

The measure, if its object is to preserve the opinions of the Court, is unnecessary, as by the [. . .] rule the original opinions are to be deposited with the clerk of the court. Thus the expense of recording is a waste of public treasure.

As the Chairman of the Committee of Ways and Means I have deemed it my duty to make this communication to you, that you may as the [. . .] of the bill to [. . .] act in the matter as you think proper.

RICH. PETERS

Addressed to Washington.

1. Son of a prominent jurist of the same name, Peters succeeded Henry Wheaton as Reporter of the United States Supreme Court. In that capacity he published seventeen volumes of *Reports,* covering the years 1828–43.

FROM BENJAMIN F. BUTLER[1]

My Dear Sir Washington June 24t 1834

There is a bill before your house, from the Senate, for the relief of Wm. A. Duer, John Duer, & B. Robinson,[2] Trustees of the estate of Lord Stirling,[3] making some compensation for his revolutionary services, in which many of the citizens of the State of New York, & among others your humble servt. take an interest. The bill passed the Senate almost or quite *unanimously,* & Judge White who examined the subject with great care, could give you satisfactory information in respect to its justice. I do not venture to ask you to move its consideration, because I am aware how many other bills may have equal or stronger claims upon your attention, and yet I take the liberty to add that such a proposition from you would probably prevent a delay till next session. . . .

B. F. Butler

Addressed to the House of Representatives and delivered by hand.

1. A former law partner of Martin Van Buren, Butler was at this time in Jackson's cabinet as Attorney General. He also served briefly as Secretary of War under Jackson. Long a Democrat, he followed Van Buren into the Free Soil Party in 1848 and later joined the new Republican Party. His latter years were spent in the practice of law in New York.

2. William A. Duer and John Duer were brothers who had distinguished legal careers in New York. Beverly Robinson, another New York lawyer, was William's brother-in-law and law partner.

3. William Alexander, grandfather of the Duer brothers, despite his title, joined the American army during the Revolution and served as a brigadier general. He was prominent in social and financial circles in New York. The bill mentioned in this connection was passed and signed by the President before the end of June 1834.

FROM ROGER B. TANEY

My Dear sir [Washington] June 24 1834

Many thanks for your vote.[1] I congratulate you on the successful manner in which the House of Representatives will terminate the conflict.

R. B. Taney

Addressed to the House of Representatives and delivered by hand.

1. This seems to be a reference to the favorable vote taken in the House on June 24 on the bill regulating the deposit of federal money in local banks. Polk had introduced the bill on April 22 and had spoken at length in its support on June 20, 1834.

FROM ROGER B. TANEY

My Dear sir [Washington] June 24 1834

I am very sorry to hear that you are sick but the labours you have passed through this session are enough to break down a man of iron.

The reason you assign for omitting the provision I suggested had escaped my recollection. I admit its force. At the same time, if any of the opposition should propose such an amendment, would it not be well to offer no opposition to it on our part?[1]

In relation to the harbor bill, my chief fear was that it might be laid on the table altogether or provisions introduced in it *insidiously* to compel the President to veto it.[2] My object was merely to converse with you generally on the principles of the bill without pretending to interfere with any particular item in the Bill.

R. B. TANEY

Delivered by hand to the House of Representatives. The letter is marked "Private."

1. It is unclear which amendment Taney meant.

2. A harbor bill had been under discussion for more than a month. The bill was laid on the table on June 19 and was taken up again the following day. Polk seems to have shared Taney's fear that the bill would not survive if it were burdened with amendments. The House, however, accepted the bill on June 23 by a large margin.

FROM JAMES WALKER

Dear Sir Nashville June 24th 1834

Upon receipt of yours of the 11th I concluded to come here, and endeavor to effect the objects suggested. I have been yesterday and to-day pretty much engaged in making efforts to have articles republished in the Banner in an editorial shape, but without success. There is no alternative but to have them published as *communications*. James Grundy has Hunts[1] promise to do this, and has promised to attend to it particularly. I have requested him to be particular in the communication he makes to deny that you were the candidate of, or choice of the men designated by the opposition as the kitchen concern. This matter will be attended to here and at Columbia not exactly as I wished, but I think in a way that will effect the object desired. The question can at all events be raised, and investigation will satisfy the people that Bell was the candidate of the opposition and committed to the Bank. I have conversed freely with W. G. Childress,

Bass,[2] and others; and I think the correct impression is making. However B. has many warm and powerful friends here and all the Bank influence will be for sustaining him and this Nashville is a most wretchedly Bank ridden population. I think Bell can be beat and I have done all I could prudently do to cause him to be unmasked. It would not do for me to be known in the matter, as it might be attributed to you, and to an interference out of our own District. I have therefore been very cautious. There is no doubt but the result of this election has, and will most seriously affect B. D. & P.[3] There is no possibility of doing any thing with Hall[4]—but if we can get the Ball in motion and the discussion commenced, Mr. B. will be placed in a very awkward predicament. I reserve many things for personal communication.

JAMES WALKER

Addressed to Abingdon, Virginia.

1. James P. Grundy, a son of Felix Grundy, was practicing law in Nashville. W. Hassell Hunt was publisher and part owner of the Nashville *National Banner,* of which Samuel H. Laughlin was editor.

2. John M. Bass, son-in-law of Felix Grundy, was a popular and successful businessman as well as a leader in Nashville civic affairs. He was mayor of Nashville in 1833 and subsequently was president of the Union Bank of Nashville.

3. John Bell, David W. Dickinson, and Balie Peyton were members of the Tennessee congressional delegation who were considered unfriendly toward Polk.

4. Allen A. Hall began publishing a newspaper in Nashville about two years after moving from North Carolina. After serving as editor of the Nashville *Republican* for a number of years, he was associated with the *Republican Banner.* He became a strong supporter of Bell and of the Whig party.

FROM LEWIS CASS

Washington. June 25, 1834

Cass explains that delegations of Indians to Washington were promised funds for expenses and estimates the amount that should be appropriated for that purpose.

Addressed to Washington. This is a clerk's copy in the Reports to Congress from the Secretary of War (RG 107), National Archives.

FROM ROBERT MILLS

[Washington]. June 25, 1834

Mills requests that Polk confer with Webster concerning the appropriations for custom houses and, if possible, recommend that the sums reported by the Ways and Means Committee he restored to the appropriation bill.

Delivered by hand to the House of Representatives.

FROM [ANDREW C. HAYS]

Dear Sir Columbia Ten 28 June 1834

I write merly to say to you that I have enclosed you a paper to Knoxville Ten which you will call to get.

Mr Walker tells me that he has just written; from his letter you will know all the news worthy your attention.

My best respects to Mrs Polk.

In haste.

Addressed to Abingdon, Virginia. This unsigned note is not in the handwriting of Hays, but it was sent under his frank as postmaster at Columbia.

FROM JAMES WALKER

Dr Sir Columbia June 30, 1834

Believing that a letter will still reach you at Abingdon, I again write you, without having any thing particular to say. From the National Banner containing nothing of the kind that James Grundy told me he had the promise of having inserted, I suppose that the Nashville editors cannot be induced to publish any thing that they believe will affect Mr. Bell. I used every exertion to have the articles reprinted there without personally requesting it. If I had personally made a communication and requested its insertion, it is probable it would have been done—but if I had done this the relation I sustain to you, would have given B. or his friends the power to charge that you had caused it to be done. The manner it has been noticed here, and at Florence I think will do. I think there can be no doubt but it will be properly attended to at Bolivar and Jackson.

You may rest assured that you have lost no standing with the people of Tennessee on account of the result of the speakers election. You can in my opinion beat any man in Tennessee for Governor. You can beat Bell, it seems to me, as badly as you beat Bradford & Porter.[1] I believe you can beat him in Davidson county. As you have been and yet are rivals he ought to be content to give the people of Tennessee an opportunity of deciding on your respective merits and claims on their confidence.

From the time I came home I had invariably expressed the opinion that you would be beaten by Bell, and that he would beat you by going over to the opposition in effect. Your friends are therefore not disappointed, and although they regret the result, they rejoice that your course has been such as they can most heartily approve. Although you have been beaten, they consider you as occupying far higher ground than Mr. Bell, and if he or his friends view it differently, they ought to give the people of Tennessee an opportunity of showing who they esteem most.

We are only in tolerable health. [Jane] Maria is complaining and Anne Maria in very bad health.

James Walker

Presumably addressed to Abingdon, Virginia, although the envelope is not available.

1. In the congressional election of 1833, Polk had defeated Theodorick F. Bradford and Thomas J. Porter by a wide margin.

FROM WILLIAM W. TOPP[1]

Dear Sir Columbus Mi. July 1st 1834

The *Postmaster* Mr. *Sims*[2] of this place, about an hour Since made his exit to another world. There will, now, be many applicants for this office, and among others your humble servant is an applicant for that appointment.

I have lately located myself in this place and should be pleased to have the management of the Post Office in this place. It is now becoming lucrative. I shall feel under many obligations to you, for your assistance in this business. I have abandoned the practice of medicine entirely. I hope you will give me your aid.

W W Topp

Addressed to Washington and forwarded to Columbia.

1. Formerly a resident of Pulaski, Tennessee, where he had practiced medicine, Topp was known personally to Polk.

2. John B. Simms served only a short time as postmaster at Columbus. It is probable that Simms was known in Tennessee because his death was reported in the Nashville papers. Topp did not get the appointment.

FROM THOMAS AND GEORGE W. MARTIN[1]

Dear Sir. Pulaski July 8th 1834

We have just recd a letter from Doctor W. W. Topp of Columbus Mississippi, formerly of this place apprising us of the death of the Post Master at that place, with a request to write to a few of our friends asking their assistance in procuring for him the appointment. You are personally acquainted with Doctor Topp and know him to be a man of business and a gentleman of the highest respectability and standing. The exercise of your influence in his behalf will much oblige. . . .

Thomas & G. W. Martin

Delivered by hand. No address appeared on the envelope.

1. Thomas Martin, a successful merchant, moved from Virginia to Sumner County and, in 1818, to Giles County. He was married to Nancy Topp in 1824. George W. Martin was probably a brother of Thomas Martin although this has not been established.

FROM JOHN W. FOWLER[1]

Dr Sir Memphis Ten 11t July 1834

About the 11th of January last I learn that a negroe of yours was taken from Hellena Jail Arkansas Tery which Negroe it appears was stolen from your possession by a man by the name of John Bickerstaff[2] who was also lodged in the same prison to be further delt with as the law required. A short time since (only a fiew days before he was to have had his trial &c) he made his escape from prison and is at this time lurking about this place. This is therefore that you may be apprised of this fact that he is here among us and no one having authority to arrest him and that you may persue such course as you may think best. I would sugguest that you cause the govenors proclimation to issue &c.

J. W. Fowler
D. Shff. Shelby County

Addressed to Columbia.

1. In addition to being a deputy sheriff of Shelby County, Fowler was at this time an alderman in Memphis. He was not personally known to Polk.

2. Not otherwise identified.

FROM CAVE JOHNSON

Dear Sir Clarksville 15th July 1834

I promised to write you a word on my return. The aspect of affairs here are as favorable as we could wish them. The course of our opponents at Washington is perfectly understood and properly appreciated. Should you choose to be before the people of the State, I think you might rely as much upon this section of the country as upon any other, so much divided as we are upon all questions. The Bank, tariff & internal improvement party do not muster verry strong but when added to the Foster[1] party are pretty formidable. Hewlings[2] friends here (the Cheatham[3] influence) have fallen out with him & intend to beat him for the Legislature. The truth I suppose to be, that Hewling intends to be Judge in the place of PWH[4] & Cheatham's friends intend to make Martin[5] & I hope my friends will be able to defeat both by retaining PWH—if he desires it. When thieves fall out honest men will get their rights. If I choose to run again, I shall probably have no opposition.

I met [John H.] Martin[6] of Gallatin at Bowling Green, who informed me that some of Mr. [Balie] Peytons friends were much dissatisfied with his course against you as candidate for Speaker & by way of apology he informed them, that you was too intimate with the Nullifyers or had thrown yourself into the arms of the Nullifyers, something of the kind; the precise phraseology I do not recollect. [William C.] Dunlap & myself corrected the matter to him. He thinks you enjoy the confidence of that part of the State in a verry high degree (& he is a warm friend of B[ell] having practised law in partnership with him). The excuse that Mr P. made sufficiently attests that fact.

We had a pleasant trip—spend two days at the White Sulphur. There was but few ladies & those of the homeliest the world ever saw. We had no mishap except getting my hat run over by the Stage & my pantaloons torn.

Give my respects to Madam & tell her *I am content* with my bachelorship.

C. Johnson

Addressed to Columbia.

1. This refers to the following of Robert C. Foster Sr. and his sons, Ephraim H. Foster and Robert C. Foster Jr. The latter was a lawyer in Franklin who represented Williamson County in the General Assembly several times.

2. Frederick W. Huling.

3. Richard Cheatham of Robertson County.

4. Parry W. Humphreys, for whom Humphreys County was named, was a particular friend of Cave Johnson, who had studied law in his office. Most of Humphreys's long career was spent on the bench, but he served one term in the House of Representatives, 1813–15, and was narrowly defeated for a seat in the Senate by John H. Eaton in 1817. In 1836 he moved to northern Mississippi for reasons of health and died there about two years later.

5. It is uncertain which Martin is meant here, but he is not the one mentioned in the following footnote.

6. John H. Martin was a native of Virginia who had served under Jackson in Indian wars and at the Battle of New Orleans. He practiced law at Glasgow, Kentucky, until 1826, when he moved to Nashville and became associated in practice with Henry A. Crabb and John Bell. After Crabb became a judge and Bell was elected to Congress, Martin became a partner of George S. Yerger and was associated with him in editing his famous *Tennessee Reports*. In 1836 Martin moved to Vicksburg, Mississippi, where he practiced until his death from yellow fever in 1841.

FROM ALBERT M. LEA

Dear Sir, Newport, Ky. July 22, 1834

You were good enough to say that you would write me in relation to the demand for my services as Civil Engineer in Tennessee.[1] Duty now calls me to the Upper Mississippi, but I expect to be in Memphis in a few weeks, where I shd. be very happy to hear from you.

Please give my regards to Mrs. Polk.

A. M. Lea, of Tenn.
2d. Lt. Dragoons

Addressed to Columbia.

1. See James Walker to Polk, May 15, 1834.

FROM WILLIAM C. DUNLAP

Friend Polk Bolivar July 26th 1834

I arrived home on the 18th Inst after a very unpleasant travel in the Stages. [Cave] Johnson & myself were crowded out at the White Sulpher Springs and detained two days and I remained two days at Paris. The subject of your election was the subject of conversation all the way home and it was a sourse of regret to all the friends of the administration that you were not elected. Mr Bell is looked upon by all as the opposition candidate and the antis claim him wherever I was and here I have been asked how it happened he was elected, if it could be that the administration had lost so much that an opposition man could be elected.

We met at Boling Green Ky. John H Martin of Gallitan who informed us the citizens of Sumner were complaining very much at Peyton for voting for Bell and against you untill they received letters from Mr Peyton informing them that *you had thrown your self into the arms of the Nullifiers* and therefore he could not vote for you. This reason appeared to be a sufficient justification for his course. Johnson & myself both authorised him to say that it was false and that there was but one of the Nullifiers Majr Felder[1] who voted for you and his objection to Bell was that he could vote for no man in favour of the Bank and Bell being a Bank Man he could not vote for him. We did not learn to whom the letters were written, both of us intended to ask Martin but neglected to do so. Martin is the particular friend of Bell but no great fondness for Peyton.

My Constitutents appeared much pleased to see me and gratified at my sustaining the Executive, and one of them who lives in the country came to Town to see me and said he had come just to tell me he had no doubt I had returned with a *clear conscience.*

Tell the Madam there is no longer any hopes of my being her *uncle.* Your Aunt was married on the 22nd Inst. to Wm H. Wood of this county.[2] He is a merchant of steady habits, good looking young man, not very remarkable for smartness, is rather what is called a *good chance.* Your relations are all well and expect you to bring the Madam with you when you visit the District.

Write me when you will be here as I should like to be at home when you are here and as there has moved into my District several young Ladies I wish to visit them and may be absent if I did not know when you expected to be here.

W C Dunlap

Addressed to Columbia.

1. John M. Felder represented South Carolina in the United States House of Representatives, 1831–35. He had served many years in the legislature prior to 1831 and returned to that body in 1840 and served until his death in 1851.

2. Benigna Polk, the youngest daughter of Ezekiel Polk, married William Henry Wood in Hardeman County. Wood is not otherwise identified.

FROM JAMES FORGEY

Mt. Pleasant. July 28, 1834

This long-time resident of Maury County, having heard that Polk intends to sell his land and slaves in Fayette County, expresses interest in buying. He expects to visit that area in a few days and will examine the property at that time.

Addressed to Columbia and delivered by hand.

TO JAMES L. EDWARDS

Sir Columbia Ten. July 31st 1834

Will you inform me what decision has been made in the case of *Samuel Hillis* (alias *Hillhouse*)[1] an applicant for a pension under the act of 1832? His amended declaration was forwarded to your office some-time during the last fall or winter.

James K. Polk

Addressed to Washington. This letter is in the Historical Society of Pennsylvania.

1. See Edwards to Polk, October 8, 1833.

FROM EPHRAIM BEANLAND

Dear Sir [Somerville] August the 2 [1834][1]

On yesterday yours caime to hand and you wanted to [k]nowe howe I was ageting on and howe we all ware and what the prospects I have for a crop. My corn is good and my cotten is promisin at this time. I have seean grown boles in it yesterday nearly waste high. I have sum good cotten and sum indifferent and to take the crop all togeather I am afraide it is two fine. It is in the right stage to make a firste rate crop or to make A sorry won. If we have a good dry season crops will be fine and mine is good I think tho my stand is not good tho I think I will make a fare crop if the season is dry and on tomorowe I am agoinge to see Dr Calwell and see what the chance for bagin and rope and make the arangements about it and as for the newe gin I never have seean the man nor heard from him and I am a goinge to see about it when I goe down and as for the runing geares that is hear they ar no Account and I cant make out with them at tawl and I am sorry that you ar not cominge down for it is imposiable to make out with them and as for payinge for them I would not give a dam for them for I tore them all to peases to pick the last yeares crop the cogs was all wayes aworkinge out and the runinge geares that is hear I cant under take to picke a crop with them and if the new gin is as indifferent he shant leave it in the gin house and I rite to you and let you [k]nowe as soon as I get back. We ar all well and I have sode 4 acares of turneps. Nothing more at this time.

EPHRAIM BEANLAND

If you please rite a note to my step fatheres, Peter Williams Esq livinge on Sillver Creake[2] and dyrect him to send my brother Edward[3] to me as soone as posiable for I have got an opinige in Sumersville in A Le and Smithes[4] store for him and I think it is a good place and I donte want him to delay. Send your note to

Jim Bendens[?] the firste opertunity. Please do this faveour and you will oblige your friend.

E Beanland

Addressed to Columbia. This letter has been published in Bassett, *Plantation Overseer,* 73–74.

1. The year has been supplied on the basis of internal evidence.

2. Silver Creek was southeast of Columbia in the part of Maury County that was included in the forming of Marshall County in 1836. Peter Williams had been a tavern keeper in Rutherford County prior to 1820; in 1836 he was a member of the first county court of Marshall County. His wife was Polly Beanland, widow of Edward Beanland who had died in Maury County about 1815.

3. In a letter of September 2, 1834, Beanland calls his brother Gibson or Gipson. Bassett reads the name Gefson and assumes that it was a shortened version of the name Jefferson. See Bassett, *Plantation Overseer,* 74.

4. Armour, Lake, and Smith.

FROM JOHN W. CHILDRESS

Dear Sir Nashville Aug 2nd 1834

I recieved your letter yesterday informing me you will not be at Nashville this week. I brought a Murfreesboro paper in my pocket expecting to see you here, and will enclose it from this place. There is nothing of interest here. Mr Bell has been invited to an explanation dinner and refuses to accept as you will see by yesterday's paper, and takes occasion to deny every thing that has been said of him in the papers. It is thought by some here that he refuses the dinner that he may be invited to the Jackson dinner and make his speech there. How that is I am unable to say. The president has not arrived, but is expected about Sunday. I will go home to day and will probably go to Columbia with my family in 3 weeks.

John W. Childress

Addressed to Columbia.

FROM WILLIAM BARNETT[1]

Dear Sir Waynesboro. Aug 6 1834

I have anxiously waited all the late Session of Congress to hear from you on the subject of my *Pension* application and have not heard One word from you or Mr Inge. Will you be good enough to inform me what has been the result?

Permit me to congratulate you most heartily on your safe arrival home, after the very boisterous Session through which you have passed, and in which you bore so conspicuous a part and upon the great manifestations of approbation which you are receiving from your fellow citizens. . . .

WM BARNETT

Addressed to Columbia.

1. A person by this name was listed among McMinn County pensioners as having been placed on the pension roll on February 5, 1834. It is not clear whether or not this is the same person.

FROM WILLIAM G. CHILDRESS

Dr Sir Nashville August [9] 1834[1]

I recd. your favour of last week covering a letter to Majr. Jno W Childress. I learn from you that you design visiting this place in a few days. The President has arrived as I presume you have learned; last night Majr. Eaton arrived & this morning before he was out the Hon. J. Bell was here looking for him. He found him & has got him to go with him to day to the Hermitage. I am informed [John B.] Forester & [David W.] Dickinson accompanied the right Honobl. I have had a talk with Eaton & to no purpose as I believe. I have seen Grundy & we wish you to be here on Monday next & remain a few days. I wish you to stay with me on Sunday night & ride in on Monday morning &c. More when I see you.

W. G. CHILDRESS

Addressed to Columbia.

1. The day of the month has been supplied on the basis of the August 9 postmark.

FROM JAMES L. EDWARDS

Washington. August 11, 1834

Replying to Polk's note of July 31, Edwards states that the Samuel

Hillis papers were returned to Charles C. Mayson for further documentation and have not been returned to Washington.

Addressed to Columbia.

FROM JOHN McKINLEY

Dear Sir: Florence [Alabama] August 13 1834

Your letter of the 2 reached here during my absence at my plantation which must be my appology for not answering it earlier. You say you fear you will be forced into a controversy with Mr Bell, in relation to the late election of Speaker, & wish a Statement, from me, of certain facts which came within my knowledge, previously to the election. Should it become necessary to the maintainance of truth & justice for me to make a statement, I will do so without hesitation. But I hope that will not be the case. I have seen Mr Bells letter, to which you allude. And although there is a pretty strong imputation against the unsuccessful candidates, it applies as much to the others as to you; & therefore it can not be necessary for you to take it to yourself, whatever may have been his intention.

I do not wish to make any statement which would have the appearance of volunteering my evidence against Mr Bell. (You may state that he did refuse to submit to the friends of the administration his claims to the Speakers chair, That he did state that he did not expect to be elected by the administration party in the House, That he did not expect to get of that party more than 25 or 30 votes, That he was supported by the opposition & elected by them, That you did without the least hesitation consent that the administration party, in the House, should determine who should be run, & that you would support such person, And that you were considered, by all parties, as the administration candidate, & was supported by that party.)

Should these facts be denied then call on me & I will state the facts as they occurred.

J. McKinley

Presumably addressed to Columbia, but the envelope is not available.

FROM SAMUEL BURCH

Washington. August 14, 1834

Acting in the absence of Walter S. Franklin, Burch informs Polk that the records of Congress that he requested have been mailed to him.

Addressed to Columbia.

FROM ABRAHAM H. QUINCY[1]

Hond Sir, Georgetown D C Augt 15th 1834

Having been witness to many of the agonising scenes of the revolution I have observed the spirit with which families of ease and fortune bore their reverses in hopes of acquiring and transmitting liberty to their progeny and independance to their Country, I am greatly agitated with a view of the present state of the political affairs of our Nation. It is however with much gratification that I reflect upon the ceaseless patriotic exertions of the Polks, the Grundys, the Wrights, the Bentons and others of the last Congress, who so nobly stood opposed to the flood of corruption and torrents of abuse created by Bank influence and treasonable design. If the people were not in earnest in their opposition to the Clays & the Calhouns they should not have let down their hopes & thereby have raised their ambitious resentment to raging fever. If they did not mean to support Genl Jackson in the integrity of his intention to veto the existance the Bank they should not have tampered with him. All who knew him, knew him to be a man of *purpose* that his very soul was the model of integrity. Presuming upon the efficacy of the Press, our opponents aimed at, and have acquired, its complete monopoly. I avow that there is but one essential interest in our day and yet this one interest is totally neglected in its legitimate means of support. Our revolution was accomplished, our liberties gained, and our Nations grandur attained by association of exertion and identity of purpose, and no man can presume that these important principles can be maintained at less cost, or with less integrity of purpose. The true and responsible watchmen under God over the liberties and welfare of nations are the men of the middle walks in life. The fashionable are fools, the wealthy are timid, and the ambitious are mad men, while the dependence of the poor leads to political inaction and dangerous servility. Our men of the middling standing have lost the fine spirit of Englishmen by aiming for distinction and bringing their children up with such high notions as makes them hold in too low estimate the democratic qualities of our constitution. Few of these who were born to wealth in and before the period of our revolution, carried their heads so high as our modern fippenys. In those days we esteemed it for our honor to be ruled well, & that rule was esteemed the best by the Hancocks, the Washingtons, the Lees, & the Lafayettes that most widely difused the blessings of civil Government. Men who rise from low life to wealth and notice, should ever be esteemed while patriotic, but when assuming high pretentions, should be held in *abhorent contempt.* Liberty is seldom called to struggle with *gentlemen*—a fact illustrated in the recent senatorial and Bank attack upon her. Nature sometimes manufactures gentlemen without the help of fortune, but fortune oft confers her favours upon fools. If a change is seriously intended in the form it must be revolutionary, for our government is the government of all, or from its principles it must be the government of none at all. To direct this whirl wind will require mightier men than now lead in the opposition, & on such alone as arise from the ashes of social life & civil liberty. A French Revolution must be a play thing compared to a civil war among so many interests as this country would present—two millions of negroes claiming long abused rights of birth and two millions of religionists under a foreign political head, sworn (as they value salvation) to exterminate every & all fellow beings that are not as big fools or as big rouges[rogues] as themselves. All parties seeking their strength in the divisions among their opponents will give us a full sample of War, pestilence & famine in or through as many successive centuries as have been apportioned to poor Africa. If Legislation is to believed in all she uttered[?] the last Session, our picture is not too high coloured and if she is believed but half, reason will supply the balance. I presume no gentleman will deny that the prospect is strong that the Federal perversion of the Press is fully answering all the designs of that faction. They sicken at the prosperity of the nation, and like the progenitor of their infernal spirits can never be happy but in the misery of all others; they have never favoured a salutary national measure, and placing themselves on the fashionable side of society, have produced a species of palsying infatuation in our National concerns. This is not a powder & ball campaign, but to be conducted by moral, not physical means. No reflecting mind but must know that if the Electors of our country could be kept correctly informed of the designs of the parties they would at once spoil the hopes of a Banking Senate and a rougish aristocracy. Now sir, as it is a fact that the money of the people and the Ear of the People is compleatly at the disposal of their most deadly enemy, can we counteract this mighty power but by an exertion commensurate with it? And I do venture to say there is not a family throughout the states that would not indulge themselves with a respectable well edited patriotic newspaper published once each week at one dollar pr ann. Such a paper may be put in circulation by companies very extensively, and should its subscription then amount to thirty thousand, a discount can be made of twenty pr cent yearly or a premium of 25 pr cent given in papers for the encouragement of such [. . .]. I have encouraged a son of mine to procure the printing of five thousand copies of a sample or speciman paper called the Republican Counsellor and Universal Newsman, to be edited by a person who edited a paper on the same principles in opposition to fine Striped Federation in Boston in 1808 & 9, & published weekly from the first day of its publication, five thousand copies—2250 of which were subscribed for, and also forty or more members of Congress became its patrons at the same time, that is, this amount of patronage was received the first month, and all its back numbers were demanded. Of this paper said the Honble James Wilson[2] then a member of the United States Senate and Editor of the Trenton True American, "We receive from Boston a paper entitled the 'Columbian Detector,' which we never open but with pleasure, peruse but with delight, nor close but with satisfaction. It is purely political, and its politics are pure, and it has the happy knack not only of adding much to the stack of interesting [. . .] matter, but of cloathing old subjects in a new & fascinating dress, and we can say with the Patriotic Doct. Bentley[3] of the Essex Register, that we regret the sheet on which it appears is not half as large as its objects require and its friends wish."

Added to which appeared about the same time in the Baltimore Whig, Edited by Baptist Erwin Esqr[4] the following remarks, "We receive from Boston a Gassette entitled the 'Columbian Detector,' characterized by fine satire, laconic brevity & wit from which we give the following extracts as specimens." Now sir, let me state, that if this subject can be carried into extensive operations making the Tammany Society of New York the center of its movements, I will subscribe $200 pr ann toward its support, and if needed will support its Editorials gratis. It is believed, however, that it will give its company patrons Revenue & may be extended to a million copies without owning a single Press or haveing any responsibility attached to the parties. Such sir, is the universal moral delinquency produced by the influence of the Bank and its senatorial cooperators, that unless timely check is given to the lying system of modern Whigism and Bank plunder, our country will soon be converted into a political Mad House.

Abram Howard Quincy, Clerk
in the Navy Department.

PS, If I have become tedious from length, sir, your friend Coln James L. Edwards at the head of the Bereau is somewhat chargable, being as he is a next door neighbour to me in Gay Street Georgetown D. C. Chatting in the evening together, he assured me that the Hon Mr Polk was a gentleman of great *patience* as well as pleasantness.

A H Q

Addressed to Columbia.

1. A native of Massachusetts and a member of the famous Quincy family. While engaged in mercantile pursuits in Boston, he began publishing the *Columbian Detector* in 1808. Later he moved to Maine, where he published the *Northern Light* for several years. Since 1832 he had been a clerk in the Navy Department.

2. James J. Wilson of New Jersey had served in the United States Senate from 1815 until 1821. He edited the Trenton *True American* for many years and served as Trenton's postmaster from 1821 until his death in 1824.

3. William Bentley, a pioneer in Unitarianism, lived in Essex County, Massachusetts. He was noted for frequent contributions to the Salem *Register*.

4. Baptist Irvine was editor of the Baltimore *Whig* from about 1807 until 1813.

FROM ARCHIBALD YELL

My Dear Sir Fayettville August the 18th 1834

When I saw you in Shelbyville I had only time to mention to you that for the present I had declined my trip to Arkinsas but that I might be so situated as to make my move certain. That contingency was same situation that would enable me to expend at least half the prophits in the support of correct principles. Without it I am too poor. I have a competency to support my family but not enough to carry into effect the views contained in the enclosed letter, which I send you for the information of the party.[1] There is no man in the Union more devoted than Judge [William S.] Fulton to the Prisidnt & the measures of his Administration & eviry thing said thear may be relyed upon. I have forward you his letter that you might consider of the propriety of admting the Territory into the Union in time to do this Admitrn Harm. You can present it, if no change can be effected in the complection of things as they now present themselves & have for the last 12 months.

Altho this letter is a private one yet I can not for a moment believe that I am acting in bad faith in using it for the good of the party—and I am assured he would not complain. If you should think it contains any information that may be of use to the President or the Party you are at liberty to use it as you may see proper; I know you can have no other feelings about it than a desire to promote a good cause. If the President but knew the real situation of Parties in the Territory he certainly would not assist in bringing additional forces against his measurs & just so certain as she is admited the next Session of Congress You will have one or more Bank Senators as we live, Ashly[2] or [John] Pope certain, the 1st anti Jackson as well as Bank & if I am not greatly mistaken Crittendon[3] will come in with one of these if the two partis are not sufficiently strong to carry both Senators. I shall not be the least surprised if [Ambrose H.] *Sevirs* party who are the only true Jacksonians would prove the minority under the state government without some help is given by a Press of the true faith & in the proper section of the Territory. I have got a young man of Talents who will go & take charge of the Paper, Andrew Jackson Greer a son of Vance Greer Deced.[4] He is write in name as well as politicks. I shall imediatly write to Fulton, Johnnson & others and assertain the prospect of patronage & whethr they will help with funds in its establishmnt. I will go one half; Greer will one third. I will not be known in the establishmnt myself but will locate if at all in the same county, and will give it a helping hand.

All my letters from the Territory assure me that Judge Eskridge will not apply for a reappointmnt & will most likely resign this fall; his time expires in the spring. If Roan[5] is appointed his successor I want the appointment of Roan U.S. Atto for Arkinsis if tho the Presidnt thought I could discharge the office of either I would gladly accept. And as my name has been before him & still is for an office in the Territory & perhaps as strongly recommended as any that may be presented; If so and you feel a freedom to assertain the views of the President on this subject it will enable me to determin at once what I shall do. If he gives you assurince of the appontmnt I shall make arrangments forthwith to sind on Greer & will myself follow in a few months & will settle in the *Vacant* Circuit, Washington Cty.

I know its unnessary to make application th[r]ough any other source if you fail in yours, and as the President is acquanted with me personally all that will be wanting will be you asking the office if he is disposed to give it. If he is not—frinds could not save me & further he may have promised or intended the *place* for some frind to whom he has given assurances, all of which you can & will please assertain. On this as on all former occations I hope you will write me the ressult of your application with *candor* & without disguise as upon you application my future moves depend. Your early attention to this matter will confer a lasting favor. Write me as an early [. . .] as you may be able to assertain how things stand &c.

A. Yell

Addressed to Columbia.

1. The enclosure has not been found.

2. Chester Ashley, born in New England, had practiced law briefly in New

York, Illinois, and Missouri before moving to Little Rock, where he continued his legal career. Later he served in the United States Senate from Arkansas, 1844–48.

3. Robert Crittenden, political leader in Arkansas and brother of John J. Crittenden of Kentucky, was a supporter of Henry Clay.

4. Vance Greer was a half brother of Joseph Greer, a Revolutionary War veteran. It appears that Yell was in error and that Andrew Jackson Greer was the son of Thomas Greer of Shelbyville.

5. Samuel C. Roane.

FROM JOHN W. CHILDRESS

Dear Sir Murfreesboro. Aug. 19th 1834

Mr Grundy has been in town several days and the citizens of the county offered him a dinner which he refused. They then by subscription requested him to deliver his views upon the Bank & upon a Bank. Accordingly today at 11 oclock he addressed a large crowd in the court house giving his view in a very happy style against The Bank & a Bank which was recieved by the crowd with demonstrations of joy. Mr [David W.] Dickinson without being requested then arose and made the lamest speech I ever heard from any man. The people recieved it with no marks of approbation and seemed to be displeased that he had obtruded himself upon them. In the mean while wine had been prepard in the room above stairs, and the company were invited to partake, 13 regular toasts were prepared and all drank with enthusiasm. The one in honor of yourself it was remarked by every person was recieved with greater glee than any other, the presidents not expected. Mr Grundy, & H L White were toasted and nothing said of the rest of the delegation except a toast to this amount, "The friends of the Administration, we judge them by the company they keep." Evry body seemed to understand the allusion, and assented to the sentiment hartily. Crockett,[1] [William] Brady & others are making great exertions and it is thought there will be a great falling off from Dickinson. Should you be a candidate for any thing in which the people of this county would have a vote, you would get four fifths of the county against any body.

There was a meeting on Monday to invite the president to a

dinner here. It was first agitated by some of Dickinsons operatives with a view of selecting a committee from their own party. We kept silent, when the meeting was called went in appointed the Chairman & Secretary of our own side, and the Chairman made a good selection for a committee. The committee are Gnl. Brady, Col. Ridly, Elisha Williams, Maj. Dance, Maj [Daniel] Graham & P. I Burres,[2] none of them of the Bell party except Dance. They will go down tomorrow for the purpose of waiting on the president. I should like to know from you, what course the President is likely to take with regard to Mr Bell. Brady has given me some flattering accounts but in such matters I cannot fully rely[?] upon him. I would rather hear it from yourself. It is likely all the proceedings here this week will be published in the paper. It would be well for you to have it republished in Columbia.

Susan recieved a letter from Sarah today. We had declined our visit to Columbia untill the Cholera had subsided. After that if nothing interferes we will be over. Tell Sarah some of you must write to us every day or two untill the Cholera disapears. We will be uneasy if we do not hear often. We are all well at present. Give our love to Sarah and Mary.[3]

John W Childress

Addressed to Columbia. In the Library of Congress this letter is erroneously filed under the date of August 19, 1836.

1. Granville S. Crockett represented Rutherford County in the lower house of the General Assembly for one term, 1835–37. From 1834 to 1836 he was sheriff of the county.

2. Bromfield L. Ridley represented Warren County in the lower house of the General Assembly for one term, 1835–37. He later moved to Murfreesboro. Russell Dance, a Murfreesboro merchant, succeeded Polk as clerk of the state senate. Williams and Burres are unidentified.

3. Mary Childress, niece of Sarah Polk and John W. Childress, was the orphaned daughter of Anderson Childress. She was reared by her paternal grandmother.

FROM JOHN F. GONEKE

Dear Sir [Mt. Pleasant] August the 19th 1834

I was in Columbia last Monday with the view of seeing you respecting my son Johns warrant for admition into West Point

Academy. I left him in Virginia instructed to go on as soon as he would hear from me. You would confer a particular favour on me if you would inform me on the Subject by next mail if convenient. He and myself are verry desirious of obtaining the warrant for admition. I am oblige to go to Alabama on some particular business and might be detained longer than I wish before I could return Columbia. I have directed Mr Lewis G Lanier[1] to take your answer out of the Post office at Mt Pleasant. He will inform me or my son immediately on the subject.

John F Goneke

Addressed to Columbia.

1. Unidentified.

FROM WILLIAM P. BRADBURN

Norfolk, Virginia. August 20, 1834

Bradburn says that he is attending a court-martial growing out of the loss of the vessel on which he served and asks that Polk help him get an assignment to a ship bound for the Mediterranean.

Addressed to Columbia.

FROM ELLIOTT HICKMAN

Fayetteville. August 20, 1834

Hickman admits that records of troops disbanded do not carry his father's name but insists that his father did serve under Thomas Polk[1] during the Revolution and that his service can be proved.

Addressed to Columbia.

1. Ezekiel Polk's brother and James K. Polk's great-uncle.

FROM ROBERT J. NELSON

Nashville. August 20, 1834

Having heard that his father served as a captain during the Revolutionary War, Nelson asks Polk to investigate possible benefits accruing from that service. He also seeks information on relief laws relating to lands purchased in Alabama.

Addressed to Columbia.

FROM WILLIE BLOUNT[1]

Dear Sir, Nashville Augt. 22d. 1834

I have just time to say that your speech on the Bank at the close of your late session transmitted under cover by you a few days since is recd.[2] The perusal of which affords me great pleasure. It will be placed on my files of papers of value at home and often read. Any communication from you at any time on any subject will be very acceptable. . . .

WILLIE BLOUNT

Addressed to Columbia.

1. Elderly former governor of the state, Blount represented Montgomery County in the constitutional convention of 1834. He died within a few months after this letter was written.

2. Probably a reference to Polk's speech on June 20, 1834, regarding the regulation of federal deposits in local banks.

TO ANDREW JACKSON

Dear Sir Columbia Augt. 23rd 1834

I have caused *Mr Gilpin's* speech[1] to be republished in the Columbia paper, and now return to you, as you requested, the original in pamphlet form. It is an admirable speech and ought to have extensive circulation. It has not as yet, I believe been republished in either of the Nashville papers.

Public sentiment in this part of the State upon the subject of *a Bank* as well as *the Bank* is sound, and the intelligent men here are delighted with your sentiment at the Nashville Dinner. I see from an Editorial article in the Banner since the dinner that the Editor[2] professes a concurrence in opinion with you and a willingness to sustain you in your opposition to the incorporation of *a Bank* as well as, the recharter of *the Bank*. The Republican so far as I have observed has been silent, except the mere publication of the proceedings on the day of your reception at Nashville. Perhaps he may yet speak.[3]

The people every where are becoming satisfied that an *incorporated National Bank* under any modifications or restrictions which can be imposed, can afford to the public no security against its corruptions and its abuses. Indeed it may well be doubted whether it be in the power of human legislation to impose restrictions or forge chains strong enough, to confine a power such as that which may be wielded by thirty five millions of money, with the ability to extend its discounts and bring the country indebted to it, to double that amount. The restrictions of any charter which can be framed will be disregarded, as they have been by the present Bank. Its money may be used for corrupt and other purposes than the legitimate business of Banking, as has been done by the present Bank, and still it will have, as this Bank has, purchased advocates, and aspirants to high public station to sustain it, however grossly it may abuse its power, and however corruptly it may use its money. Any new concern, if not immediately, would very soon pass into the hands of the owners of the present Bank, for the most obvious of reasons—that they are possessed of the wealth and constitute the aristocracy of the country; and in less than three years Mr Biddle would be at the head of the new as he is of the old concern. Our past observation proves too, that any incorporated Bank will probably become an engine of political party. The old Bank of the U. States was in the hands of *foringners and of the Federal party,* and the whole weight of its power and influence, it is known, was thrown into the scale, against the administrations of Mr Jefferson and Mr Madison, in their measures of restriction, which preceeded the war, adopted for the national defence and to protect the national honour. That Bank was owned in great part by forigners and that portion of our own citizens, who afterwards thought it "unbecoming a moral and religious people to rejoice in our victories over our enemies." The present Bank is owned and controlled by the same persons or by their descendants entertaining the same political tenets. Any new Bank would go ultimately into their hands, and be wielded as a political engine, for corrupt and base purposes.

But rely upon it, the great contest in which your administration has been engaged is not yet over. The indications are I think unerring. The letter of *Webster* to *Biddle*[4] and the responses amounts to an invitation to the latter to make out and prepare the Report for the Senate's committee and send it to the chairman at Boston. Such Whitewashing as this, will not satisfy the public. The annunciation of the Bank since the adjournment, to extend its discounts and bring the country indebted to it from five to ten millions, was necessary to enable it to perform another serving operation whereby it could oppress its debtors, and produce more panic. But the country are already familiar with this operation and it must fail of its effect. The greatest outrage of which it has been guilty is the withholding from the Treasury the dividend upon the Government stock, under the false pretense that it is retained for damages, upon the French Bill when it is demonstrable that the Bank is entitled to no damages either in law or equity. But all these movements go to prove that the managers of the Bank and their political allies are resolved to make another desperate and I trust a last & expiring struggle for the perpetuity of their power.

They may dispair and I think will, of success, in obtaining the recharter of *this Bank,* and I should not be surprized, if the opposition rally next winter upon the more specious proposition to charter *a new Bank,* and that will be the battle we will have to fight. I mistake the signs or the question of *a new Bank,* will be the next test of the opposition to your administration, and if I mistake not that is to a question even in Tennessee, and it is to be regretted that the public press in the state do not take bolder and stronger ground than has yet been taken. For myself I think there is no substantial difference between the two propositions—*a Bank* or *the Bank,* and for one I am ready to meet the question in either form. I have no fears of the result in either form it may present itself. We have but to be vigilent and victory is certain. My reliance is not so much upon the politicians, as upon the great body of the people, who are every where sound to the core.

James K. Polk

Delivered by hand. This letter is in the Papers of Andrew Jackson, Division of Manuscripts, Library of Congress. A copy, not in Polk's handwriting, is in the Polk Papers.

1. This probably refers to the speech made by Henry D. Gilpin at Philadelphia on July 4, 1834, which was subsequently published.

2. Samuel H. Laughlin was editor at this time but was replaced by George C. Childress within less than a month.

3. Allen A. Hall was editor at this time; a few weeks later he was succeeded by Washington Barrow.

4. Polk is probably referring to the Webster-Biddle letter of July 8, 1834, in which Webster informed Biddle of the investigation of the Bank that had recently been authorized by the Senate. The letter indicates the areas of inquiry to be made by the Finance Committee of the Senate, which Webster headed. He also enumerates the various materials and records of the Bank that the committee might need to examine.

FROM EPHRAIM BEANLAND

Near Sumersville Pleasant Grove Plantation
August the 24th 1834

Dear Sir

Wear all well with the exception of Casy. She is agetinge better. Jim and Enykey[?] all have had the congestif fever and I think shortly they will be able to go to work. On tomorowe I shall go to picken out cotten and as fr my crop I cant say any thinge about it. Dr Calwell is hear and he has seean it all and he can tell you whether it is a good wan or not. Sir I understand that J Walker Es shold of sayed that you ware agoing to sell out your farme and if you are I would like to [k]now it. My reasones is this, that I do expect to followe the busness for a liven that I nowe followe and I have got a good opertunity of makinge A ingagements for next year and do not think that it is rite for you to make other ingagements untill I consulted you on the subject. If you please rite me A fiew lines on this subject if you plase. I do not want you to think urge an ingagement for next year with you ondly that I am had three applicationes for next year and if you cant cum I want to [k]nowe wheather you want to imploy any person for the next year.

EPHRAIM BEANLAND

Addressed to Columbia and delivered by hand. The envelope bore the inscription "favored by Dr. S. Calwell," and it is presumed that Caldwell delivered it to Polk. This letter has been published in Bassett, *Plantation Overseer*, 76–77. In Bassett's version of the letter, by some curious error, one line of the text appears after the polite ending.

FROM JOHN W. CHILDRESS

Dear Sir Murfreesboro. Aug. 24th [1834][1]

I recieved a letter not long since from my uncle James Childress of Tuscaloosa, informing me that he had found the Certificates of our Lands in Alabama, in the hands of George S Gaines, of Mobile, and further that he had recieved several applications to purchase what remains and that it can be sold for 5 or 6 dollars pr acre. As the time is near when our notes in Alabama will fall due I should like to know what arrangements are to be made for their collection, and what is to be done with the remainder of the land.

As it is probable we will not visit you before you go to the Western District, I shall not have an opportunity to see you. I will now say to you that you will greatly oblige me if you will call, as you go down at Col. Willis's,[2] nine miles this side of Jackson, on the Cotton Grove road, and ask him to make a settlement with you for me, of the last years rent of the farm for which he is acting as agent. If he can not pay the mony request him to make out and send a statement of the whole affair—(viz) the price rented for, what the cotton sold for and all expenses attending it, the cost of improvements specifying the articles &c. It is about three days ride from Columbia to Willis's & if you will call and stay all night you will find him a clever man. Be so good as to say to him that Mr Williams[3] also requests that he will send by you the arrearages, for the year 1832 and that he has seen advertised for the taxes a tract of land belonging to him in Weakly County, for which Col. Willis is agent, and requests him to attend to it. If you have time go over and see the land I designed living on, (it is but a few hundred yards off) and give me your advice as to the propriety of settling on it next year, as it is my intention to leave here if I can.

I received your letters to Dr. Rucker and myself yesterday and was truly glad to hear that the Cholera had not been so bad as we had anticipated. I hope you will continue to write us every mail whilst it lasts.

I enclosed by todays mail to you a paper from this place, containing an account of the proceedings of the Grundy meeting.

The Bell folks take it in high[?] dudgeon. The paper also contains an Editorial and a piece communicated, upon the subject of the intended suppression of the presidents toast at the Nashville dinner. The piece signed O.P. was written by Brady, tho he does not wish it known to any person but in strict confidence. It is denied here by the Bell folks that there was any intention on the part of the Editors to suppress it.

Give my love to Sarah & Mary.

JOHN W CHILDRESS

Please enquire of Willis if he has rented the farm this year and for what price.

J W C

Addressed to Columbia.

1. Childress failed to put the year in the date on this letter. The Library of Congress has filed it under 1835, but internal evidence proves that 1834 is the correct date. See especially Childress to Polk, August 19, 1834.

2. This is perhaps Flemming Willis, who served as postmaster at Cotton Grove in the 1830s.

3. Perhaps Elisha Williams.

FROM JAMES STANDIFER

Dear Col Mount Airy [Tennessee] August the 25th 1834

If I have neglected writing you I have not forgot you. I found my family and friends all well, my folks had a fine crop groing. Crops are fine in this section of country. (I have attended two courts and talked with some of the [k]nowing ones. I have not seen the first man but what says they would rather have James K Polks standing than John Bells, Speakers place and all. The people are for the man that stands up Boldly for the President and his measures. They are for no other sort of a man these times.) T. J. Campbell[1] complains very much at the way the speaker was made. I have taken some pains to assertain the feeling of the people of E Tennessee, and I believe the strong brese will bloe rite. Give my best respects to Mrs Polk and except to your self the esteam of your friend.

JAMES STANDIFER

Addressed to Columbia.

1. Born in Rhea County, Thomas J. Campbell had served as clerk to the

state house of representatives before becoming a member of that body, in which he was serving at the time this letter was written. He was a Whig elector in 1840 and served one term in the United States House of Representatives. Failing of re-election, he again became clerk of the house in 1847 and served until his death in 1850.

FROM ROBERT M. BURTON[1]

Dr Sir. Nashville August 27th AD 1834

I have been informed through Mr Harris that you were at the Springs recruiting your health in order to brace up against that worst of diseases the cholera—which I regreet to learne is afflicting various parts of Maury. Mr H informs me that you are desirious to know the state of politicks in this market. *"The Bank as well as a Bank"* are both in a collapse state. No medicine can revive such a project. The Presidents toast was the last finishing stroke. The little dogs have since that memorable day ceased to yelp. I was in company with Epham F.[2] he remarked, We are [. . .] down—Grndy & Polk are to rule this State. The Bank will have to go down but that he would prefer [. . .] might it leave [. . .] to the last. It was fortunate for the State that it so you politicians of the true faith happened to meet here at the time you did. The seed has been sowed ad a good crop I have no doubt will be yielded. Mr Grndy was at Murfresbro last week and corpsed the Bank, had the funeral dirge of *A Bank* sung and left the place. Litle Davy[3] had to say not my will but thine be done. Laughlin has now passed the Rubicon, he says he will push the war into Africa if so the litle gentleman of the other press will have to fall in or be fairly drummed out of service. The President handed him Mr Gilpin's speech which he said he must publish. It has been done most reluctantly. The old Chief has been in Nashville for the last two days, his health has much impoved and he emphasizes with still more force that a Bank is as objectionable as the Bank and that Polk for the hard service done in the cause deseres a Medal from the American people. There is no man in this nation more deeply seated in the affections of that old soldier than you are—and I was not mistaken when I infored you of the vry favorable point of vew that you stood in before the whole people of Tenessee. It is said here that Bell is to publish some account of his actings and doings. How he is to set about the matter or in what way the attack is to be brought on is as yet in the dark. Should an assault be made in which you are directly or indirectly implicated—Charge bayonet instantly and victory will be yours. The gentleman seems uneasy—he has no quiet days and many slepless nights. There is an awful day of reckoning a head!!

I stumbled on a caucus last night of Bank men, the object was to lay a plan to bring out Hugh L White for President. They proposed to me to have him nominated by the convntion. I understood them at once as being the opposers of Van Buren. They proposed to open a correspondence on the matter. The whole arrangement was broken up. Nothng will be done.

Mclaine[4] will be here next week. The subscription to the Marksman stands as it did when you were here At[August]4. ending with Mr [. . .] name. I have impressed it on old Edmondson[5] to have it put in the desk of the Bar room before Mclaine arrives to see his feelings. I believe he will turn out to be a cider mug. We have hammered away al day at the seat of governmt nothing done. It will not be located. Friday we expect to get off. I long for the day of deliverance, it is time we were at home. We have only had three fights amongst us and two of our members are taking their liquor freely. Poor Cobbs, I fear he is undone forever. Maury [County] is rather in a cripled condition at this time, one member with a broken arm and the other not as sober as I have seen men.[6] Our Constitution I expect will go down pretty generally with the people.

It is said that in the letters addressed to the President inviting him to a dinner at Murfreesboro that somthing is said about silent centinals in the hour of danger. I have not yet seen the correspondence. Little David it is thought will bid adieu to politicks by not presenting his claims to the people again. If H L White could be run successfully for the Vice President without interfering with the prospects of Van might it not be done [. . .]?

I have written you this scrawl very hastily ad without any correction but when you reflect that I have been penned up all day until I am perfectly exhausted in mind and body you will have abundant charity for all defects. The Governor is yet indisposed. I am afraid he will not be in order for the heat. Believing that he has more [. . .] ad [. . .] than I have I should like to see him contended[?] for the money. I believe he can take the money with a lame arm. The magazine must be kept well supplied with powder so that when the match is applied the Bank ad its man must go together. A committee from Huntsville waited on the President to invite him to a dinner which he declined. He will be off for the City by the 10th—so will Mr Grndy. I should be pleased to hear from you at a leasure momet.

Robert M Burton

Addressed to Columbia.

1. A Wilson County lawyer who was representing his county in the constitutional convention at this time. He was one of Polk's acquaintances at Chapel Hill. Burton moved to Tennessee in 1823 and began practicing law at Lebanon.

2. Ephraim H. Foster of Davidson County.

3. David W. Dickinson of Murfreesboro.

4. Justice John McLean of the United States Supreme Court was to preside over the United States circuit court for West Tennessee. He was being mentioned frequently as a possible successor to Jackson.

5. This is probably a reference to William Edmiston whose name was often spelled incorrectly. Edmiston had served in the Indian Wars and at New Orleans under Jackson and then had settled as a farmer in Davidson County. After Jackson retired from public life, Edmiston became a Whig.

6. Robert L. Cobbs and Terry H. Cahal were Maury County representatives to the constitutional convention.

FROM ANDREW BEAUMONT[1]

My Dear Sir WilkesBarre [Pennsylvania] Augt 31 1834

I experienced much pleasure at the receipt some days since of a copy of your speech on the Bill to regulate the deposits as a token of your friendly remembrance which I reciprocate by sending a paper containing the proceedings of our Genl County meeting. The preperation for the great Battle to be fought in Penna is making with great activity & bustle on both sides. But the tone of either side is vastly different. One the one hand the sturdy honest Republican yeomanry of the country come up to the lines full of that courage and confidence which a just cause always inspires; but on the other hand all that clamour & confusion reigns by which a wicked and unholy purpose is always characterized. I feel confident Penna will do her duty. Genl Anthony[2] is thought to have endangered his success by the unfortunate heresy of 'A Bank' which you recollect he advocated in his speech. He so writes to me and I see such remarks made in the papers printed in his district. I hope he will not be defeated thro' this indiscretion. I remonstrated with him, Miller & Laporte[3] upon this fatal error but they all knew too much, having been members of successive Legislatures who resolved and reresolved that the U S Bank was a blessed institution. They may all hereafter be reelected and I defeated but it will not convince me that they were right and I wrong. Our friends in this district are confident but I await the great Teacher Time. I should be pleased to hear from you and your opinion of the general result of the western elections.

A. BEAUMONT

Addressed to Columbia.

1. After holding several political posts, including that of postmaster at Wilkes-Barre, Beaumont was elected to the United States House of Representatives, serving two terms, 1833–37. Later he became commissioner of public buildings in Washington.

2. Joseph B. Anthony, a lawyer of Williamsport, served two terms in the House, 1833–37, and then served as a state judge for many years. His pro-Bank speech was delivered on May 19, 1834.

3. Jesse Miller and John Laporte, from Landisburg and Asylum, respectively, had both been elected to Congress in 1833, and both were reelected. Miller, however, resigned in 1836 to become First Auditor in the Treasury Department, a post he held until 1842. After leaving Congress in 1837, Laporte became a county judge and later was surveyor general for Pennsylvania.

TO ANDREW JACKSON

Dear Sir Columbia Sept. 1st 1834

I have had the perusal of a letter from Judge [William S.] Fulton, the Secretary of the Arkansas Territory to Col. *A. Yell* now of Fayetteville Tenn. urging him to remove to that Territory. *Fulton* regards it as important in reference to the political character of Arkansas when she shall be admitted into the Union (which will probably be in a year or two) to have the aid and assistance of men of influence and character, and decided in their politics as Col. Yell is known to be. He thinks there is danger, without proper attention, that one or both the Senators of the new State, may be Bank-men and opposed to the measures of your administration. *Col. Yell* writes me that he is very desirous to emigrate to the Territory and would at once do so, but he is poor & has a family to support, and fears he would find himself embarrassed in his circumstances, unless he could receive from Government some office—the emoluments of which would aid in supporting him.[1] He says that the only reason which induced him to resign the office (Receiver of public monies) which you gave him a few years ago, was his extreme ill-health at that time, and the apprehension that he could not survive if he remained there; but that his health is now entirely restored, and he is resolved if he possibly can to settle himself permanently in the Territory.

It is suggested to me that Judge [Thomas P.] Eskridge (one of the Territorial Judges) will not probably desire a re-appointment and may possibly resign this fall; his term expires in the spring. In that event, I think *Col. Yell* qualified for the office & should be much pleased to see him appointed. Or if the present atto. of the U. S. for the Territory (Mr Roan)[2] should be appointed Judge he would be pleased with his office, that of atto. of the U. S. Col. Y. has ever been a consistent and zealous supporter of your administration; is now right in his politics in all respects; is a highly honorable & worthy man. To receive either of the offices indicated would be of service to him.

There are I believe numerous testimonials now on file in his behalf, which were forwarded to you, when he was recommended for another office some years ago.[3] You moreover know him personally. I know how unpleasant it must be to you, to be annoyed by numerous applications for office, and I would not trouble you with this, were it not a case in which I feel a peculiar interest. If it should be consistent with your sense of propriety I shall be much gratified if he could receive one or other [. . .][4] appointments indicated when a vacancy [. . .] occur.

JAMES K. POLK

Addressed to Washington. Letter is in the Papers of Andrew Jackson, Division of Manuscripts, Library of Congress.

1. See Yell to Polk, August 18, 1834.

2. Samuel C. Roane.

3. See Polk to Jackson, April 22, 1829.

4. At this point a part of the manuscript is torn away. The two ellipses represent about three or four words.

FROM CAVE JOHNSON

Dear Sir, Clarksville 1st Sept 1834

I recd yours of the 25th on yesterday. I will reply to it as soon as I am able to sit up long enough to do so properly to be used if necessary. I have no objection to your using my other letter except it was written hastily, as to the facts I have no doubt they are correctly stated. Enclose me a coppy of the portion that you think may be useful to you. I hope to be well enough in a few days to attend to it. I shall regret to get into any controversy with our colleagues but shall be at all times ready *to give the truth* when necessary whatever may be the consequences.

I have ordered our paper a week or two since. You have seen the New Chickasaw treaty.[1] Eaton has purchased the Salt Lick reservation at 1.25 & of course Lewis gets the money & has made Winchesters line[2] the true line between us & the Chickasaw—thereby giving them 215,000 acres worth a million to which our warrant holders were entitled—ratified too without opposition. I have asked Grundy what I shall say in defence of him to those people, who supported him & me *to a man.* I have been greatly troubled since I saw you with rheumatism & it is now difficult to turn myslf in the bed or get up without assistance. I am anxious to get to Hickman the 2nd Monday in Sept. but fear I shall not be able to do so. I do not expect to vote for the new constitution. Public opinion I think much agst it here.

CAVE JOHNSON

Addressed to Columbia.

1. This treaty with the Chickasaws was signed in Washington on May 14, 1834. It modified the Treaty of Pontotoc, 1832.

2. This line was surveyed in 1819 by James Winchester, who was commissioned to run the correct line between Tennessee and Mississippi. His

line was too far north and was not accepted as the state boundary although it was accepted as a boundary of Chickasaw lands. The final line agreed upon as the boundary between Tennessee and Mississippi did, indeed, add some 215,000 acres to Tennessee, but it was encumbered by Chickasaw claims. The Lewis mentioned was possibly William B. Lewis.

FROM JAMES PARKER[1]

Dr Sir Perth-Amboy [New Jersey] 1 Sept. 1834

The receipt of your remarks on the Deposite bill reminded me of what I had often intended but hitherto had omitted; to write and give you as far as I could a general Idea of our Political matters in this quarter. New Jersey is beginning operations for the Election which takes place on the 14 October and there seems to be no likelihood of a want of exertion on either side. I have been since my return in various parts of the State (the Northern half) and find our friends united and firm, and from what I see and hear, I feel confident of our success in the Election for members of the House of Representatives which is by General Ticket. Each party holds a Convention next week to select the Tickets and discordant opinions and Interests will exist among our opponents; with us I have no reason to anticipate any differences of opinion. The Bank is as you will see given up and well it may be, for its cause is hopeless in an open Contest. As to our Senator we may gain our General Ticket and yet lose a majority in the Legislature owing to the Circumstance that we have several counties in which the parties are very closely balanced, while our strong Counties have large & certain majorities. I think we can count with Certainty on Seven Counties (one half) sending one half our whole Number of members. Of the doubtful Counties our friends assure us one and perhaps two more. I therefore count with much Confidence on our Senator. Mr. Frelinghuysen[2] has a strong Interest in our part of the State but it will be counterbalanced in the southern part, and upon the whole I was told by a man who knows that section well and *not one of us*, that the Circumstance that Mr Fs time was out would operate against the Anti-Jackson Interest.

In Pensylvania I have no doubt of an accession of members on our side. Colo. Watmough[3] is shaking in his seat with many others. The Jackson money, as it was called in Derision, operates well & it ought to do so. Our opponents make a great Noise in New York but they are, as they naturally must be, disunited in Fact. Pull off their wigs and such a motley set never was congregated before. The more Noise and swaggering you see in New York on the part of the Wigs the more signal you may expect their defeat to be. The City is perhaps doubtful and may verify Mr. Jeffersons saying that Great Cities are great Sores upon the body politic (tho I do not believe this), but the Country is sound and you will see it.

In Rhode Island it seems to be settled that Mr Burges[4] has lost his chance for the Senate. The majority of 6 in assembly is more than counterbalanced by a majority of 8 or 9 in senate. The object now is to keep Mr Potter[5] out by running an Anti Mason. The End I do not venture to predict but no Bankman will come from Rhode Island to the senate I believe.

Maine comes up next. I know nothing, but I think I may venture to predict that her Election will be the Commencement of a series of victories to our Cause progressing South West to the Potomack.

You see at any rate that one man in this quarter is not discouraged and I cannot tell how many more feel & think with him. I have been pleased to see the true account of your southern Elections which have been so misrepresented at first by the [. . .] Editors that some of our friends almost believed the South & West was against us. As matters progress, I may write you again.

James Parker

Addressed to Columbia.

1. Having served numerous nonconsecutive terms in the New Jersey legislature, 1810–27, Parker became mayor of Perth Amboy in 1829. At the time of this letter he was serving his first term in the United States House of Representatives. He was re-elected once and thus served in that body 1833–37.

2. Theodore Frelinghuysen of Newark was a Princeton graduate. He served in the War of 1812 and was for a dozen years New Jersey's attorney general. He had been elected to the Senate as an Adams man and, as herein predicted, was not re-elected.

3. John G. Watmough was defeated in his try for another term in the House of Representatives.

4. Tristam Burges had served for ten years in the House of Representatives but, as Parker predicted, he did not win a Senate seat.

5. Elisha R. Potter had been prominent in Rhode Island politics for almost forty years. He had been twice elected to fill vacancies in the House of Representatives before serving three consecutive terms in that body, 1809–15. After many years in the state legislature, he ran unsuccessfully for a Senate seat in 1832 and again two years later.

FROM EPHRAIM BEANLAND

Pleasant Grove Plantation [Fayette County]

Dear Sir August [September] the 2, 1834[1]

We ar all well with out it Casy she is verry lowe at this time and I have pict out 6000 weight of cotten and on yesterday I started my gin with the old running gear tho I can make out with them untill the newwuns is maid which I will have them as soon as posiable. I got a letter from Silleman[2] and he says that he cant repaire the running gear tho the is no repairinge to do for I will have newwuns maid and them that is first rate. Sir I shold like to see you hear before you sell out for I think that you have bin mistaken in your place. I want you to hire a [. . .] boy and rite a note to my step father and dyrect him to send Gibson[3] hear forthwith as sone as posiable for I cant get A L and Smith[4] to weight any longer than next Friday weake. Please do this and I will pay you when you come downe. I am agoinge to baile cotten to night.

Beanland

Faile not if you please to let Gibson [k]nowe of it.

Addressed to Columbia. This letter has been published in Bassett, *Plantation Overseer*, 74–75.

1. This letter is so badly blotted and smeared that it is virtually impossible to decipher. The date, however, is written August 2, 1834. Bassett assigns the letter to August 3, 1834. The content of the letter clearly shows that it was written after his letter to Polk, dated August 24, 1834. Since Beanland sometimes continued dating his letters in a given month long after it had ended, it seems almost certain that it was written in September rather than in August. The envelope is clearly postmarked September 3.

2. In September 1832 Polk had agreed to sell a tract of land in Madison County to Thomas N. Silliman. A part of the bargain was that Silliman was

to deliver to Polk's Fayette County plantation a saw gin, a cotton screw and press, and running gear for the cotton gin. Silliman seems to have lived at some distance from Polk's plantation.

3. See Beanland to Polk, August 2, 1834.

4. Armour, Lake, and Smith.

TO HUGH LAWSON WHITE

My Dear Sir: Columbia, *Sept. 2d,* 1834

I received your letter of the 26th ult. on yesterday.[1] I am surprised and astonished at the information which has been communicated to you—*that one of your oldest and most valued friends, now high in office,* has said that *"he will denounce you as soon as it is ascertained that you are willing to be a candidate," &c.* There must be some mistake about it. It certainly cannot be so; and unless your information comes in a most unquestionable shape I should be slow to believe it, but should much sooner suspect that the communication came from an interested source, or from one having some object to effect, by separating in feeling at least, old and long tried personal and political friends. It has not been a great while since the person to whom I presume you must allude, gave public evidence of the estimate in which he held your private and public character; as well as of your capacity for high office, by his willingness to have you associated with him in highly confidential and responsible public relations. This opinion of you was, *I know,* long since that time unchanged, and I have never had any reason to believe, for one moment, that his former confidence in you was in the slightest degree impaired. I would much sooner suspect the accuracy of my information therefore, than yield for an instant to the impression which the information itself is calculated to make upon your mind. Nothing could pain mutual firiends[*sic*] more, than the idea, that anything could occur, to break up, or in the least disturb the intimate relation of private friendships which have existed for more than forty years, or to separate those now in the evening of life, who for so many years have acted together upon public affairs, and who have always agreed—with perhaps unimportant exceptions—upon all measures of public policy, and especially those which have engaged the public attention, during the present and pending Administration.

James K. Polk

Presumably addressed to Knoxville, but that information is not available. The original of this letter has not been located. The letter has been published in Nancy N. Scott, editor, *A Memoir of Hugh Lawson White* (Philadelphia: J. B. Lippincott & Co., 1856), p. 254.

1. This letter has not been found.

FROM JOHN D. GONEKE

Sir. Horse Pasture Henry County [Virginia] Sep 3 1834

I should have written to you before this time but as I did not expect a commission before next June[1] I posponed it untill the present moment and I only wish to let you know that Father has changed his minde and has left me in Danville and if you will be so kinde as to use your exertions in obtaining it and send it to me at Danville, Pittsylvania County Virginia and in doing so you will oblige your Obediant Servent.

John D. Goneke

P S Write to me by the next mail and let me know if James Gest[2] accepted of his commission and wether thear will be any vacansyes for this year. Direct your letter to Horse Pasture, Henry County Va as I am going to school hear at present.

J D G

Addressed to Washington.

1. This refers to his application for admission to the United States Military Academy.

2. James L. Guest of Columbia. See Guest to Polk, May 10, 1834.

TO JAMES L. EDWARDS

Sir Columbia Ten. Sept 4th 1834

On the 28th of April last I enclosed to your office the amended declaration of Daniel McKie for a pension. A pension certificate was returned to me for between $20 and $30 per annum, which I enclosed to the claimant, who immediately returned it to me stating that there must be some mistake as to the amount; that if he was entitled to any thing, he must be entitled to a much larger amount. The statement in his Declaration he said was for a much longer service, & a part of the time as an officer, than to entitle him to the pittance which had been granted to him. His pension certificate too was made payable at Lexington Ky. instead of Nashville Ten. from which circumstance he supposed there must be some mistake as to the person, or that there may have been some other applicant of the same name with himself, residing in Ky. Upon receiving his certificate I handed it to Mr. *Sylvester*[1] one of the Clerks in your office—informing him of these circumstances, and requesting that there might be a reexamination of the case. Mr Sylvester returned the papers to me with the certificate, stating as well as I remember that no correction could be made. At all events, whether he returned the certificate to me or not I had some conversation with him upon the subject. My impression is he returned the certificate to me, and that I enclosed it again to the claimant. In this I may be mistaken as the old man states he has never received it.

Will you have the office examined and write to me fully in regard to it? In reexamining the claim, you may find two declarations in the office. The first was prepared a year or two ago and was defective. The second was an amended or perhaps an entire new declaration. The last is the one on which the claimant relies & that one was sent to your office by me on the 28. April last. The applicant is a highly respectable man & is desirous to know in what condition his claim stands. Will you inform me on receipt of this?

James K. Polk

Addressed to Washington. This letter is in the Maine Historical Society.

1. Henry H. Sylvester of New Hampshire was a clerk in the Pension Office for several years during the 1830s.

FROM SAMUEL H. LAUGHLIN

My dear Sir, Nashville, Sept. 4, 1834

My information from the Hermitage is, that the President leaves early next week for Washington. Will you be up to see him before his departure?

You will see that [Allen A.] Hall is out upon Maj. Lewis[1] (of your town) to-day in a column or two, and defending (and as he thinks sustaining) Bell against the whole world. If Lewis will press him for his authority—whether it is from Bell himself—he will have to answer; but I think *now* before the end of next session of Congress is, perhaps, not the right time to let matters be pressed home.

Mr. Grundy has left for Washington. My man Hunt is timid and scared; but I have got Carroll, Bass, Gwin[2] (the parson) and others on him, demonstating to him that war to the knife is the duty of the Banner.

Hall has been forced out on the publication of Gilpin's letter (not a very appropriate pretext) to declare war against the Bank and *banks*—if he speaks truth.

Tomorrow I lead the way to the course I shall take about the Presidency. Hammond[3] has misconceived me, and given good occasion for *taking the shoote*[?] in explanation to our Ohio friends. I shall go ahead.

I should like to see you, and if you come this way before the President leaves, I should like to visit the Hermitage with you. I have not been there yet. I intended to have gone up this week, but I learned that Mrs. Jackson (Andrew's wife) was very ill, (Report says she is better to-day) and I was unwilling to intrude. I have feared too, that going there at this juncture, might look like seeking favor of some kind, of which God knows I am innocent.

I say again I should like to see you. A few city subscribers have bolted and withdrawn since I commenced operations the other day. A few more will follow. To keep my publishers up and in spirits (I have no interest or very little in it and that is on their account) I should be very glad if you could send in the names of a few, or get others to do it soon. Let others do it. Write a line to Johnson to do the same.

I take my Presidential course now, because McLean is here. You will see that I am cautious and neither commit myself or any body else, though the end I aim at, is plain to those who understand any thing of matters ahead.

Please present mine and Mrs. L's compliments to Mrs. P. and accept for yourself my best wishes.

S. H. Laughlin

Addressed to Columbia.

1. Micajah G. Lewis and Felix K. Zollicoffer had recently began to publish in Columbia a paper called the *Observer*. Lewis withdrew before the paper was a year old.

2. Governor William Carroll, John M. Bass, and James Gwin. Gwin had served as Jackson's chief chaplain at New Orleans. He was the father of Senator William M. Gwin of California and of Samuel Gwin.

3. Charles Hammond, Cincinnati newspaper editor.

FROM SAMUEL H. LAUGHLIN

My dear Sir. Nashville, Sept 6, 1834

I wrote you the other day when I was only informed privately of the contents of Mr. Hall's article, in reply to the Observer, and before I had an opportunity of examining it in detail. I find that it contains an unwarrantable attack on you, and made not in pursuance of the original grounds of the controversy. I have been requested to republish the article. I have done so with a disclaimer of meddling in the dispute between the editors, and reserving the right to copy Maj. Lewis' reply to present article.[1] I think that matters ought not to draw you or Mr. Bell into the controversy. It ought, if possible, to be avoided at this time I think. It is exceedingly imprudent in Hall to take a course rendering apparently necessary for you to authorize any statement to be made. I hope you will look to such reply as the Observer ought to make, without coming yourself into the controversy *now*. I have no knowledge how far Hall may act upon *advice*. Six or seven of Bells friends however made me a particular request to republish, which I have agreed to do to-day.

In the present state of affairs, Tennessee, in her delegation in Congress, should present the *appearance* of harmony at least. If the worst comes to the worst you know my feelings on the subject, in which there is no mistake; but I must consult Hunts' interest with the *mercantiles* of this blessed town, among whom Bell has his partizans. I am glad I was requested to publish Hall's article; it opens the way for all Lewis'. Let me know your view, and, if you can, come up as before requested.

SAML. H. LAUGHLIN

P.S. Why does Mr. Lewis, although for Judge White, which is

all well, take occasion to speak rather ill of Van? I don't understand it. I should like for him to copy my article of yesterday headed—*indications.*

Addressed to Columbia.

1. See Laughlin to Polk, September 4 and September 9, 1834.

FROM SAMUEL G. SMITH

Dr Sir Nashville Sept 6 1834

As far as has come under my observations our political aspects is very much as you left us.

We have no difinate expression or move from any quarter. What will be the tone of those who may be before the people is yet to be disclosed. The President I am inclined to think will leave Tennessee without any correct knowledge of things in his own State. The people are with him and he is so far as relates to men and measures uncompromizing and occupying the position where you saw him. I visited the Hermitage but owing to his sick family had but little conversation with him. Majr [Andrew Jackson] Donelson was absent but I will yet see him as he remains for a few weeks and I left a message that if he was disposed to hear the politics of Tenn he must call and see me.

You will have seen the course of our press's. One professes an open opposition to the Bank but as yet he has not taken the strong grounds to show the corrupt influence exercised nor has he adverted to the danger of such an institution operating upon the public mind and the purity of that state of public sentiment which must result from a metalic curency.

I look for more from him before we can depend upon an able support from that quarter. The other you will see is out for our representative. This artickle is intended to be the foundation of a contest I have no doubt but I am not in the confidence. The Governor is spoken of for Congress & this press intertains a bitter hostility towards him. What will be the course towards the Bank & the administration I am unable to say. Is it probable that there will be any turning[?] along in Tennessee when the whole character of the administration is staked upon this question?

Do they expect to assure the President on it & claim to be

his friends? Such a course cannot be put down on the people if the issue is fairly made.

The cry that the Bank is down is only to lul to sleep those who are opposed to it. The Indian department & every other branch of the Government is to be attacked in order to weaken it & then press the Bank through. We have suppressed resistance here that will act when occasion offers. Such a course if persisted in must ultimately draw out all the facts & the administration will I presume stand by its friends.

When it is known that there is no reconciliation[?] then other matters such as persecution & hobbies will be resorted to. The whole support of the Administration wants concert.

The feelings & patriotisms can be found with the democracy & we will get it out before Spring.

A full crop plentiful money Market & success of the State Banks will prepare the way for a cordial support on the part of the people. If war is to be made either directly or indirectly upon the President or those who stood firm by him under the most trying circumstance I prefer it to be open. Let every man speak out. I hope to hear from you.

SAM G SMITH

Addressed to Columbia. A note on the margin of the last page of this letter has not been deciphered.

FROM CHARLES K. GARDNER

Washington. September 8, 1834

Gardner reveals that Henry D. Hatton, a planter of Prince Georges County, Maryland, wishes to get information about his sister who lives in Middle Tennessee and will write directly to Polk.

Addressed to Columbia. The letter was enclosed in that of Henry D. Hatton to Polk, October 8, 1834.

FROM ALVIS Q. NICKS[1]

Dear James Talladega [Alabama] Sept 8th 1834

Providence has placed us many miles distanced from each other but old acquaintance should never be forgotten.

My friend Wm. Y. Lundie[2] is an applicant for assistant emmigrating agent in the place of Mr Hogan[3] who declines accepting the appointment to remove the Creek Indians.

I want you to see the President & tell him he must appoint him. This favor will be the same as if your old friend had received it.

A Q Nicks

Addressed to Columbia.

1. Nicks had moved to Talladega from Lincoln County, Tennessee, only a few months before this letter was written. He became attorney for the Creek Nation and later was elected to the Alabama legislature. He probably knew Polk while he was still a resident of Lincoln County. He is one of the few correspondents who addressed Polk by his first name.

2. Unidentified. There is no record of his having obtained the appointment.

3. It is unclear which of two men named Hogan is intended here. William Hogan of Athens, Tennessee, had asked Polk to help him get such an appointment. See Hogan to Polk, March 12, 1834. On the other hand, John B. Hogan of Mobile, Alabama, occupied that position in 1835. Perhaps William Hogan declined the appointment, and it was then given to John B. Hogan. No connection between the two Hogans has been established.

FROM WILLIAMSON HAGGARD[1]

Bedford County Tennessee

Dear sir Sept the 9th 1834

After my compliments to you and family there is one request I make of you, that is I wish you to compose a speech for me and the Topic of which I wish to be on Republicanism and against the Nulification. My reason for wishing you to make the Speech is that you are well acquainted with the procedings of the Nulifiers, And it has been my pleasure always to be for the Republic and against those that did not belong to that order.

There is to be an Exhibition at or near fathers some time in Oct or Nov next and I wish you to compose a tolerable lengthy one and send it to Shelbyville by male as soon as you can have an opportunity of doing so and you will oblige your most sincere friend.

It is verry sickly in this neighborhood at this time, crops is indifferent in places. I will add no more. I shall look for that speech as soon as you can make it.

WILLIAMSON HAGGARD

Addressed to Columbia.

1. Unidentified. This letter has the earmarks of a request from a schoolboy. It is probable that the writer was the son of the Samuel Haggard who had lived at Davis Mills for some years.

FROM SAMUEL H. LAUGHLIN

My dear Sir, Nashville, Sept 9, 1834

Your friendly letter of the 7th. instant is before me. I thank you for the information it affords me, and for the views which you have been pleased to communicate in relation to the controversy between the Columbia Observer, and Nashville Republican. I act upon the *cautions* and keep my eyes open. Every movement I see in the camp of your apparent enemies, I will note. Confidentially, you shall from time to time hear from me.

It has been suggested to me to-day that Hall did not write his article—that Eaton was about &c. I do hope for the honor of the Gov. of Florida,[1] that he has something else to do than to employ himself in writing puffs and squibs for a newspaper. Time will show.

The President left the Hermitage this morning for Washington, via Knoxville. This foolish, indiscreet pushing of Judge Whites name for the Presidency may have something to do with his movement in that direction. I have not been at the Hermitage for the reasons I stated to you. Hall has been there. The President gave him the correspondence between Biddle & Woodbury which I publish to-day, with directions to furnish me a copy forthwith. He did not do it til he had it put in type himself. As he got it on Saturday, I could have published it yesterday; but that did not suit him as he could not publish before to-day. I have gotten it out as soon as the Republican any how. The people will now say, it is well the Deposites were removed *in time* or perhaps the Bank would have laid hands on them also under some pretext.

As the President is gone, you need not come up. However

much I might desire to see you, I would not, under any circumstances, impose the trouble on my own account.

But, I wish to see you; and for that purpose will avail myself of a kind of quasi invitation. I have to attend your great Railroad Meeting, unless something occurs in the mean time to prevent more than I am now aware of.

I esteem your correspondence entirely confidential.

No news here—none—none.

S. H. LAUGHLIN

Addressed to Columbia.

1. Eaton had recently been appointed to that post.

FROM SEABORN JONES

My dear Sir Geo Columbus 10th Sept. 1834

I have recd a copy of your last speech upon the deposite question for which you will accept my thanks. I had hoped before this to have sent you a copy of mine upon the gold Bill[1] which was printed about the time I left Washington, but by some strange accident [Francis P.] Blair has sent them on to me.

Having heard of the death of Judge Johnson[2] of the Supreme Court I have presented to the President the name of Judge Wm H. Crawford as his successor. If not inconsistent with your feelings & opinions I would be glad if you would join me in recommending him to the attention of the President to whom I have this day written. I admit Mr Crawford's mind was injured by his severe illness in 1824, but I know it is yet strong. I think he is competent to discharge those duties for I have practised under him several years since he came from Washington. Mrs Jones joins me in best respects to Mrs Polk. . . .

SEABORN JONES

P. S. I know he drew up the opinion of the Judges in the case of State of Georgia vs Tassell for murder[3] (for I was in his room while he was writing it) and I have no hesitation in saying it was better than Marshalls or McLean's upon the same question in the Cherokee Case in the Supreme Court. If you can get the opinion (it was published in many papers) do read it & Judge for yourself.

S. Jones

Addressed to Columbia.

1. Jones gave his speech on June 1, 1834, and on the same day the gold coin bill passed the House. The bill established various standards, weights, and values of gold coins. It became a law shortly thereafter.

2. William Johnson of South Carolina was appointed to the Supreme Court by Jefferson in 1804. He had recently died in New York.

3. In 1830 a Cherokee Indian named Corn Tassell was convicted of murder in Hall County, Georgia. At this time the United States and Georgia were at odds over the question of jurisdiction in Cherokee lands. Since this murder had been committed in Cherokee lands recently annexed to Hall County, friends of the Cherokees attempted to take the case to the United States Supreme Court. Georgia, however, was determined to uphold her jurisdiction and submitted the case to a convention of Georgia judges, of which William H. Crawford was a member. The judges upheld the conviction, and Tassell was hanged. Crawford was asked by his colleagues to write the opinion of the group, and it is to this opinion that this letter refers.

FROM EDWARD KAVANAGH[1]

Dear Sir Damariscotta Mills, Maine 10th Sept. 1834

Our State elections took place on the 8th Inst. and I have already received sufficient returns from my District to satisfy me that my opponent[2] has been elected by a majority of about 300 votes. There were more than 8000 votes thrown and the result can not astonish any one who has been acquainted with the previous political character of the District. So great an excitement was never before known in this region, and I had to encounter the opposition of nearly all the shipping interest in this section. Moreover two presses which had heretofore supported me were bought up by Partisans of the Bank, (one of them 3 weeks before the election,) and they will remain under their control. I have no doubt of the reelection of Hall, & Mason & Smith,[3] and of the success of the Republican Candidate for governor.[4] We shall soon have returns from the other Districts. There will certainly be 5 if not 6 Repub. Members of Congress.

Edward Kavanagh

Addressed to Columbia.

1. A lawyer who had served in the legislature of his state before his election to the House of Representatives, Kavanagh later became governor of Maine.

2. Jeremiah Bailey of Wiscasset, who served only one term, 1835–37.

3. Joseph Hall, Moses Mason Jr., and Francis O. J. Smith were all serving their first terms in the House of Representatives, and, as indicated here, all were re-elected.

4. Robert P. Dunlap, the Republican candidate, was victorious. After serving as governor, Dunlap won a seat in Congress. See Kavanagh to Polk, September 15, 1834.

FROM LEONARD JARVIS

My dear Sir Ellsworth [Maine] 11 September 1834

Our elections for state and federal officers was holden on the 8th and we have already received sufficient returns to give us the assurance that all is safe. We shall elect our governour & shall have a majority in both branches of our legislature. I fear that we shall lose the congressional district which is represented by [Edward] Kavanagh. This however is no source of Triumph to the Wiggs or of surprise to us. The wonder was that he ever was elected. His personal popularity has hitherto sustained him in a district which was known to be against us. Many who could not vote for him would not vote against him. But in the late election when every man was brought to the polls, where no one was permitted on the side of the opposition to stay at home the defeat of Kavanagh was made certain. Mrs Jarvis unites with me in offering her regards to Mrs Polk. . . .

LEOD. JARVIS

Addressed to Columbia.

FROM CAVE JOHNSON

Dear Sir, Clarksville Sept 12th [1834][1]

Enclosed I send you the statement which you desire. I said nothing of Ben Hardins[2] statement, because I have written him on the subject believing that he will give me a more full statement & also thinking it prudent to ask his permission to give it tho there was nothing private in the conversation.

I think it would be well if you can do so to let pass every thing for the present, at least leave the matter *to the Editors.* Next winter you can get all & more than you wish. If a controversy is gone into now, will it not seal up the mouths of all in Washington next winter & besides *you ought* not to come out until your defence is palpably necessary.

The controversy is obliged to come on in the next congress & it would be better for you if it be possible to let it be between other parties.

You will of course [see] the defence of him in our Clarksville paper. They will be driven to the defence & to stand unaided by the administration. The opinion of our Editor represents the sentiments of 50 or 100 opponents of the administration.

My health is verry bad yet. I am just able to crawl out of my bed & to town & back.

My widdow would have thought she had been born to bad luck if she had concluded to come.

C. Johnson

Addressed to Columbia.

1. The date here was supplied by the Library of Congress. Its correctness is substantiated by internal evidence in this and other letters. See especially Johnson to Polk, September 1 and October 2, 1834.

2. A Kentucky member of the House of Representatives. In a short time he became a Whig.

FROM CLEMENT C. CLAY

[Huntsville, Alabama?] Sept 13th 1834

As regards the course of Col. Bell I hope he will not render it necessary for you to defend yourself in relation to the late election of speaker. If he has the stock of prudence which I have alway thought belonged to him, he will not impose that duty upon you. I did intend to have had a conversation with him to urge upon him (as I had uniformly done with other aspirants) the *propriety* and as I thought *the duty,* of submitting to the friends of the administration the question—who should be *our* candidate for the speakers chair? But having been informed by Mr [Henry] Hubbard of N. H and by my colliegue Col. McKinley that each of them had proposed the same thing and that he had declined entering into any such arrangement I deemed it useless and did not make the proposition directly. I certainly considered him the candidate of the opposition mainly; and believed he was considered by many, if not all of our political friends. Some of the Presidents friends I have reason to believe voted for Col. B. and desired his election. But I think and believe it was understood by others, the proportion was verry small. Indeed, his refusal to abide by the determination of the majority of the friends of the administration whether he should run for speaker, was conclusive to my mind that he did not rely on *them* for his election.

This is a copy of an extract from a letter that apparently was received by Polk. The copy is in an unknown handwriting and contains neither provenance nor address. The original letter has not been found.

FROM CAVE JOHNSON

Dear Sir, Clarksville 13th Sept. 1834

I recd yours of the 9th inst to day. I have noticed the articles in the Republican to which you allude purporting to be editorial and presume that allusion was made to you in one or two places in the article. I can feel no hesitation in giving you the truth so far as I know it of any transaction falling under my own observation whenever the same shall be necessary.

I have heard much said here as well as at Washington of the contest between you & Col. Bell for the Speaker of the House of Representatives, particularly as to the support which each of you received. It was supposed many months before the vacancy actually happened, that it would take place & several individuals friends of the administration were spoken of as suitable to fill the vacancy—among the number you & Col Bell were esteemed the most prominent. None seemed to doubt that if so many friends of the Administration were run, that the election would be finally settled by the votes of the opponents of the Administration, who would of course cast their votes upon the man least acceptable to the President & his friends. This was a result which the friends of the Administration wished to evade and therefore it was proposed that the friends of the Administration should have a meeting that the strength of the several candidates should be ascertained & that the strongest should be run as the candidate of the Administration party and the others should yield their pretensions and support him. You unhesitatingly determined that you was willing to have the election submitted to the friends of the Administration & let them decide who should be the candidate & that you would support the man thus selected. You was considered I believe finally by all parties as the Administration candidate & so far as I knew, heard, or believe every vote which you received except one was given by the friends of the Administration. Majr. Felder of South Carolina told me he had voted for you because of your course agt. the Bank of the United States, which he believed unconstitutional.

I understood from members who conversed with Col Bell upon the subject & whose names I can give if necessary, that he refused to submit his claims to the Speakers chair to the friends of the President & in consequence of his refusal no such meeting was holden. He received the votes of the opponents of the administration & was elected by them in conjunction with a few votes received by him among the friends of the administration.

C. Johnson

No address is available. It is believed that this letter was enclosed in the same envelope with the one dated one day earlier.

FROM BENEDICT J. SEMMES[1]

Dear Sir, Prince Georges County Md 14th Sept: 1834

Mr. Henry D. Hatton a highly respectable citizen of this county, desires to correspond with you, on a subject of great importance to him. You may repose full confidence in his integrity and veracity, and any service you can render him, will be gratefully acknowledged by me.

B. J. Semmes

Addressed to Columbia. This letter was enclosed in that of Hatton to Polk, October 8, 1834.

1. Semmes was a native of Maryland. He had practiced medicine and had engaged in agriculture. After serving in the Maryland legislature, he was elected to the United States House of Representatives, where he served two terms, 1829–33.

FROM EDWARD KAVANAGH

Dear Sir Damariscotta Mills, Maine, 15th Sept. 1834

In my last I gave you information of my defeat in this Congressional District; it is now *feared* that [Leonard] Jarvis[1] has also lost his election. The result is quite uncertain. Jarvis and I represent a vast extent of Seaboard in which is owned the principal part of the tonnage of the State. The pressure has fallen very heavily on that interest and many Ships are lying at the wharves unemployed: yet I verily believe that a majority of our constituents, whenever a *fair* expression of their opinion can be obtained will approve the course which we have taken in supporting the measures of the administration. It is impossible in the short limits of a letter to detail the schemes resorted to all for the purpose of affecting our elections. We have however the consolation to say that the Republican Candidate for governor has beaten the Federal Candidate (Sprague)[2] by more than 2000 votes, and a Republican majority has been secured in both Houses of the State Legislature. For Congress we shall have elected *four* members; in one District there was no choice on account of a division among our Friends: that District may be set down for the administration, so that if Jarvis has been defeated our representation will stand 5 for the administration and 3 opposed.

I have thought that this intelligence might not be uninteresting.

EDWARD KAVANAGH

Addressed to Columbia.

1. Jarvis won, despite Kavanagh's fears.

2. Peleg Sprague, having served three terms in the United States House of Representatives, was serving a term in the United States Senate while a candidate for governor. He was defeated by Robert P. Dunlap.

TO JAMES L. EDWARDS

Sir Columbia Tenn. Sept. 16th 1834

I herewith enclose the Declaration of Charles Alexander[1] for a pension, and as he is very poor, I must ask the favour of you to examine it, as soon as received and forward his certificate, if a pension be granted him to me, for him.

JAMES K. POLK

Addressed to Washington. The letter is in Pension File S21599 (RG 15), National Archives.

1. See Alexander to Polk, June 16, 1832. Alexander was a veteran of the Revolutionary War who had moved from his native North Carolina to Tennessee in 1814.

FROM SAMUEL JACKSON HAYS[1]

Dr. Sir, Jackson [Tennessee] 16th Sept. 1834

This is to ascertain the time when you contemplate visiting your plantation, and whether you will pass thro' Jackson on your way. I have business in the neighborhood of Memphis & have concluded to defer my trip until I can hear from you. If you should still feel disposed to sell, it is quite probable we may trade, should your land prove to be on examination of such character as is represented. The open land presents a considerable inducement to me, as I must have cotton land for the ensuing year.

Please write me by the return mail whether I may expect you here, or at what time I may certainly meet with you at Somerville. Make my respectful salutations to Mrs. Polk. . . .

S. J. HAYS

Addressed to Columbia.

1. A nephew of Rachel Jackson and a younger brother of Stockly D. Hays, Samuel Jackson Hays became a wealthy planter who was reputed at one time to have owned a thousand slaves. He became a general in the Mexican War.

FROM JOHN T. STODDERT

Wicomico House [Charles County, Maryland]

Dear Sir Sept. 16th 1834

It gives me pleasure to extend the circle of your acquaintances by making known to you H. D. Hatton Esqr of Prince Geor. County Md. He is a gentleman of fortune, family & high respectability. In politicks, he is sound & firm, according to your view of men & things.

Mr Hatton has some relatives in your County & may need your friendly aid in opening intercourse of [. . .] or business with them. Any services you may be able to render him will be duly appreciated. . . .

J. T. Stoddert

Addressed to Columbia. This letter was enclosed in that of Hatton to Polk, October 8, 1834.

FROM ARCHIBALD YELL

My Dear Sir Fayetteville Sept the 16th 1834

I received your letter this evening with a mixture of disappointed pleasure. I had not calculated on the promise of the office with much certainty, but from your letter I feel very assured that the office will be offered & therefore I will in the course of a few weeks so soon as I can arrange my affairs leave here for the Territory & locate in the *Circuit.*

I have written to my frinds in Arkinsas for letters & I have no fears of being there well sustained & have requested them to forward their letters to Washington City direct.

Can you procure me the frindship of Judge [Thomas] Lacy? It will perhaps be of Service to me. I have not acquaintance sufficient with him to call on him; do in that matter as you think proper but if it can be procured here it may & will prevent his recommending any other from the Territory.

I regret that it has become nessary for me too leave here so soon as I have at this time a good practice and buisness that I should like to wind up before I leave here but under all the circumstances I shall leave it in the hands of some of my friends and locate my self imediately in Washington County, and then there can be no room of grumbling on the score of Non Residents!!

I wish frind *Sevier* had droped me a line, or would he have been more deffinate. You say he will write; the first time you see him jog his memory on the subject. Should any thing occurr worth notice please write me. You must take with you to the City my obligations to the old *Chief* for his *promise* & you must take charge of the matter while there. I shall trouble you with my correspondence or letters to the President from the Territory if they do not forward them before I get on to Little Rock.

I see with regret that my old frnd & College mate *Hall* Republican has come out with a long defence of Col Bell in the nature of an individual attack on you for which last Week myself & three others *discontinued* our *paper* & I told him my reason for it. 1st, that he that was not for us on the Bank question was against us; 2d that I viewed that defence as intended to injure you & support Mr Bell. We [. . .] therefore now to seperate on those conjecturs. Here you have lost nothing by the publication, nor will you any where but I was vexed & discontinued the paper. Perhaps without [. . .] cause but I can but suspect his *Bank motives* & yet believe they will keep up a fire on you as long as they think they can do you any harm &c.

A. Yell

Addressed to Columbia.

FROM JOHN W. CHILDRESS

Dear Sir Nashville Sept 18th 1834

On my arrival here today I learned that Col. Laughlin was drunk and had been so more than a week and therefore was not responsible for the omission to publish the answer of the Observer as he had promised. And further that his editorial term has expired and he has been dismissed from the department. Through one of the hands in the Banner office (John Philips)[1] I also learn that Mr Bell & Mr Hunt have of late become intimate, that it is probable Washington Barrow[2] will be employed as Editor, and the whole concern will be in the field for Bell so soon as an opportunity offers. However of this you can better judge from the next numbers of the paper. It is however certain that Laughlin has nothing more to do with the paper, for his name is stricken from it. I delivered your letter to Genl Smith, and he promised to make the necessary inquiry and call on me tonight. He was not apprised of the fact that Laughlin was dismised when I saw him. He told me he would write to you at Bolivar, and can give you his views. If you think it important to retain his friendship you must not evince too much solicitude about Gov. Carroll, for there is great hostility between them. He seemed to think Bell had been tampering with the Banner and had no doubt he would move the world to triumph. Situated as things are at present I am unable to do any thing by staying here. There is nobody to whom I could apply as Laughlin is out of the question. I do not know what plan to advise, for the purpose of giving circulation to your defence. Perhaps, if you can arouse your friends to the task, they can by writing letters to their acquaintances in different portions of the State procure a general circulation for the O[b]server. And until that can be effected, you could have extra copies printed and sent out. Every thing shall be republished in the Murfreesboro paper and it would be well, through your friends at Bolivar to have the same done there. I have seen since I came here, the Prospectus for a newspaper to be published in this place, called the Reporter by Long[3] and John Philips the nephew of Judge Philips.[4] Philips tells me if he can procure enough subscribers to commence with, he will take sides warmly and publish every thing necessary. If you think it important to have a press here it would be well to make some exertion to give him a start—if not the whole exertion should be used for the Observer. I have no doubt Bell is making great efforts to increase the list of the Republican. He had a conversation this evening with John D Martin[5] and soon afterwards I heard Martin say he intended to change the Banner for the Republican. I would be glad if you would apprise me from time to time of all the movements &c.

I will go home tomorrow.

John W. Childress

Addressed to Bolivar, Tennessee.

1. Other than information given below, nothing has been learned of Philips.

2. In November, Barrow became editor of the Nashville *Republican,* not the *Banner*. George C. Childress had recently become editor of the *Banner*.

3. Medicus A. Long had practiced law in Shelbyville in the 1820s. He became editor of the Sparta *Recorder and Law Journal,* and in 1835 he became the publisher of the Nashville *Union and American.* He returned to Shelbyville, where he was elected to one term in the lower house of the General Assembly. After an unsuccessful candidacy for the United States House of Representatives, he moved to Florida.

4. Formerly a resident of Rutherford County, Joseph Philips served in the War of 1812 and then moved to Illinois. He was a member of the supreme court in Illinois, after which he moved back to Rutherford County.

5. Although Childress wrote the middle initial as it appears here, it is thought that he meant John H. Martin.

FROM JOSEPH THOMPSON[1]

Sir, Shelbyville Sept 18th 1834

I take the liberty of informing you that I have removed from Shelbyville to Livingston Ala. and I calculated to have seen you before I left Tennessee but as it has been out of my power to see you I have taken the liberty of writing. There will be a vacancy in Livingston in three or four months for Post Master and I have taken the liberty to solicit your influence with the post master genl.[2] I do not think there will be any other except myself with the exception of *one* man who is an anty Jackson man and a Nulerfier and as I have a tolerable hard time with the nulifers you will pleas do the best you can for me. Let me hear from you on the subject in Livingston Alabama.

Jo Thompson

I would refer you to Col Michell, Mr Gilchrist Esq & E. J. Frison[3] as to my integrity, &c. I will leave Shelbyville before this reaches you. You will please let me hear from you on the subject as early as posible. You must excuse me for troubling you as I should not have done so had my [. . .] not have been cast among strangers.

J T

Addressed to Columbia.

1. Little is known about Thompson other than that he had lived in Bedford County for some time and was acquainted with Polk. Within a few years, he moved back to Shelbyville.

2. See Thompson to Polk, December 30, 1834.

3. Samuel Mitchell, William Gilchrist, and Erwin J. Frierson, all of Shelbyville.

FROM WILLIAM GARRETT

Giles County. September 19, 1834.

Garrett, a Giles County postmaster who had moved from East Tennessee, asks Polk to resubmit a claim for property lost in the War of 1812, saying that Hugh Lawson White and Joseph Anderson could supply information as to the circumstances.[1]

Addressed to Columbia.

1. Anderson was United States senator from Tennessee, 1797–1815, and served as First Comptroller of the Treasury, 1815–36. See Garrett to Polk, December 12, 1834.

FROM JOHN THOMSON[1]

My Dear Sir New Lisbon [Ohio] Sept. 19th 1834

Your good and friendly letter of the 23d. ult. was recd. in due time, and I should have given an earlier reply had I not waited to obtain more correct information to communicate to you, in relation to the political conditions of our state at the present moment, than I was in possession of at the time your communication was recd. I am truly rejoiced to hear that your state is still unmarred in her political principles, and that she is still uncompromising in her hostility to the Bank, and I trust to a Bank of any kind, to be created by congress.

As far as I am informed, (and I have been much engaged since I came home in learning the public sentiment on that subject) I am perfectly satisfied this state is sound to the core in opposition to that corrupt, and corrupting institution, the U. S. B.

We will elect our Governour Lucas[2] with ease, and we will increase our majority of members in congress from this state.

The old Jackson set 11, in number will be elected except Genl. McLean, whose case is rather doubtful. Majr Allens is also some what doubtful,[3] but the other 9 including my humble self will I trust be reelected, though you know of the 9, we have lost our friend [Humphrey H.] Leavitt he being now on the Bench in this state, but there is little doubt a Mr Kilgore of our side will be chosen in his room, and as to [Robert T.] Lytles prospects I have a letter from a friend in that district who is well qualified to Judge, which states they will be able to reelect Lytle though the Bank party are doing all in their power to prevent it.[4]

But as to the opposition members I will state that from the best information I can obtain, Mr. Bell will be beaten by Mr Kennon who was in the 21 & 22 congress from this state and who you know was one of the three that voted against the Bank in the 22d congress.[5] Mr. Spangler will without doubt be run out by a Mr Collerick[Colerick], and Mr Crain it is confidently asserted will be run out by a Mr Helfinstine[Helfenstein] of that district, and Mr Sloane it is believed will be run out by a Mr Rice. There is also strong hopes that Mr Vintons district will be represented in the next congress by Mr House[?], whom you might have seen in the city last spring, and who was at that time a mail contractor. He made some publications against [Thomas] Ewing of our state, on his P. O. report.[6]

From the above you will perceive there is no doubt of Ohio electing her democratic Governour and at least a majority of members to the next congress.

The fact is we can hardly hear of a change against us, when we hear, and know of many in our favour, perticularly on the Bank question. The toast given by the old Hero at Nashville must have been a thunder-Bolt to your neighbour Beall[Bell], but of this it is perhaps best to say little at this time as we need all our strength in the field at the next conflict, for you may rest assured the great battle is yet to be fought on the floor of our Hall in the City of Washington, and the only way that leads to victory is through the Ballot Box in the states.

There is one thing I wish you to accomplish in your state, and that is to run out that disgraceful creature in human shape, Davy Crockett, for he is unworthy of the station he now occupies, even if he came on the Democratic side in politicks.

At a late meeting of the stockholders of the Bank of the U.S. a resolution was passed authorizing the President & Directors to apply for a renewal of its charter, and there is no doubt they will make the atempt, and there is as little doubt they will adopt measures, and use means (no matter how corrupt) to have a congress elected favourable to a recharter. It therefore behooves us to be on the alert, and to use all honourable, and just means to defeate them in these macinations.

Our election will be on the 2d Tuesday of next month which is the 14th, and as soon as the result is known here I shall give you the information.

Give my kind respects to Mrs Polk, and rest assured I am still your most sincere friend. . . .

John Thomson

Addressed to Columbia.

1. Born in Ireland, Thomson came to the United States while quite young. He studied law and moved to Ohio, where he began practice. He served as a Democrat in the House of Representatives, 1825–27, failed of re-election, but was returned in 1829 and served four consecutive terms.

2. After serving as governor of Ohio, 1832–36, Robert Lucas was appointed territorial governor of Iowa, where he remained the rest of his life.

3. Jeremiah McLene of Columbus was re-elected, and William Allen of Chillicothe lost. Allen subsequently was elected to the United States Senate.

4. Daniel Kilgore of Cadiz was indeed elected and was re-elected two years later. Lytle was also re-elected.

5. William Kennon of St. Clairsville defeated James M. Bell of Cambridge.

6. Thomson's predictions here were inaccurate. David Spangler of Coshocton, Joseph H. Crane of Dayton, Jonathan Sloane of Ravenna, and Samuel F. Vinton of Gallipolis were elected. Colerick, Helfenstein, Rice, and House are not otherwise identified. Thomas Ewing was in the United States Senate, where he served until 1837.

FROM SAMUEL G. SMITH

Sir Nashville 20 Sept 1834

Your favour by Majr [John W.] Childress came to hand in due time and I delayd writing until the Republican of today came out. You will no longer be at a loss to know what course is to be pursued towards you. I was formerly as I considered upon intimate terms with the Editor[1] but recently have had no intercourse in a friendly or confidential character. Upon all occasions I protested against you being brought in & he so expressed himself, but could there have been a doubt previously the paper of today determines for itself. Since it was published without his knowledge I called upon Mr McLemore[2] & stated to him it was a matter deserving the interference of the friends of the administration in which he agreed & said he had spoken freely to some of those concerned & requested them to refrain from any attack upon you, but it seems there is a settled determination to continue it. I then called upon Mr Hall & stated to him that you nor your friends could submit to such a course, that they would defend this attack and that I could not agree to see a warfare against you when you are in no way connected with this district or our representative, that I had concluded if the district was content with him I should be, but there was no justification on his part to assail you. He stated that a man was to some extent responsible for the acts of his friends & he with Col Bell had been attacked in the first instance.

I assured him that the Columbia paper was under the control of the Editor & you had nothing to do with it—this I had always stated to him. He said that the Govr. & Grundy intended to rule the state & he protested against it. I stated to him a war upon you could not reach them, but he seemed disposed to indentify all in the [. . .] when in fact they are not mentioned. I stated to him that falshoods were stated in relation to your visit here to caucus against B. This he was ready to contradict me.

The conclusion of our interview was his opinion that a controversy was inevitable. I assured him that so far as you were concerned an overwhelming majority of the people of Tennessee would speak out and that Mr B would be found guilty of a failure to support the measures of the administration and that I was at no loss to determine as to the feelings of the President in a controversy. This seemed to iritate him but he said a few days before the President left he had become satisfied that Mr B would give him an efficient support. I have no doubt the President was informed that Mr B would go for all the measures so warmly discussed last winter & that the comtes. would be arranged to his satisfaction but I do not think he is to be thus managed. I have no doubt also that he was assured Mr B would support Mr. V.

for the Succession. Thus you see the exertions to reconcile him. The Editor of the Banner has been drunk for weeks & I am told is dismissed.[3] I called & could get no satisfaction but the result is that they will not republish the articles from the Columbia paper.

This is as I expected. The truth is I can view it in no other light but a determination to keep up the hostility commenced against you eighteen months since. You will see from the Republican that he does not intend to give it an insertion as the Columbia paper did. I am inclined to think George Childress will take charge of the Banner[4] although not known here, but unless I am deceived this is a plan to control both presses for I am confident he is under the same influence. However time will prove & I hope I am mistaken. I shall know as soon as he commences if he does intend to pursue the same course.

I shall write you occasionally as they progress. Let me hear from you.

SAM G SMITH

Addressed to Bolivar, Tennessee. The letter is marked "Private."

1. Allen A. Hall.

2. Probably John C. McLemore of Nashville.

3. Samuel H. Laughlin had been drinking heavily and was, indeed, dismissed as editor.

4. On September 22, 1834, just two days after this letter was written, George C. Childress was announced as the new editor of the *Banner*. Childress had lived in Rutherford County but had moved to Nashville, where he continued the practice of law. He remained as editor of the newspaper for a relatively short time and then moved to Texas, where he helped draft the Texas declaration of independence.

FROM JOSEPH HALL

Dear Sir Camden [Maine] Sept 22 1834

Presuming that a word of information upon the result of our recent election will be interesting I give you the following.

[Robert P.] Dunlap the Democratic candidate for Gov is reelected by a plurality of 3379 votes. Senate 15 Dem 8 Federal. Sommerset County no choice, entitled to two. In the House 94 Democrats members 66 federal. Twenty six Representatives districts remain to be heard from, a majority of which will return Democratic members.

Members of Congress elect[1]

Cumberland District	F[rancis] O. J. Smith	Dem
Oxford District	M[oses] Mason jr	"
Kennebeck "	G[eorge] Evans	Fed
Lincoln "	J[eremiah] Bailey	"
Penobscot & Sommerset "	G[orham] Parks	Dem
Waldo "	J[oseph] Hall	"
Hancock & Washington "	L[eonard] Jarvis	"
York District No choice	a Democrat will be returned.[2]	

JOSEPH HALL

Addressed to Columbia.

1. All of these were incumbents except Bailey.

2. John Fairfield of Saco, a Democrat, was elected. He later served as governor of his state and as United States senator.

FROM JAMES WALKER

D Sir Columbia Sept. 22d 1834

You have no doubt already seen the Republican of Saturday, and formed your opinion of its contents.[1]

Although the Editor makes sundry insidious insinuations intended to prejudice you in public estimation I see nothing that requires you to come out over your own signature. Lewis is at the Camp meeting. I have not yet seen him, but will do so, and consult as to the best manner of noticing this last production, which I think must be from the pen of Bell or John H Eaton or both.

I am much frustrated in my business and agitated in my feelings by the sudden death of Mr. Satterly.[2] He left here on Tuesday apparantly well—staid that night at Mount Pleasant. On Thursday morning he was taken at Turner's (8 miles beyond Lawrenceburg) with *Cholera* and died in 11 or 12 hours. His loss is considerable in my business, and I lament it much on every account. We are all about as well as when you left.

JAMES WALKER

Addressed to Bolivar.

1. This refers to an editorial by Allen A. Hall of more than six columns in length in which he replies to an editorial of comparable length by Micajah G. Lewis that had recently appeared in the Columbia *Observer*. Hall said that Lewis had written statements that he knew were untrue and had thus goaded Hall into making a reply that he would have preferred not to make. He insisted that he had no ill feelings toward Polk and was writing only to defend Bell. It is clear throughout, however, that as a loyal supporter of Bell he would defend him even to the point of attacking Polk.

2. An employee of Walker, Caruthers, and Company, probably a stage driver. It is believed that he was not a resident of Maury County.

FROM CLEMENT C. CLAY

Dear Sir, Huntsville [Alabama] 23d. Sept. 1834

Agreeably to your request I enclose a *mere* statement of *facts,* in regard to your conduct in the election for Speaker—leaving the *inferences* to others, if you should have occasion to use it. Indeed, the *inferences* are so obvious that no one can mistake them—and I think it always better for *a witness to avoid an argumentative statement* even regarding the effect desired. If I have omitted any *fact* you deem material, write immediately, and, if in my power, it shall be furnished. I have retained a copy & can make out a new statement with the necessary additions. In the meantime suffer me to suggest—*take good care to put your adversary in the wrong.*

C. C. Clay

P.S. Mrs. C. joins me in best regards to Mrs. P. & yr self. She will not accompany me this fall but I should be glad to join you in a mess.

C. C. C.

Addressed to Columbia. The letter is marked "Private." The letter following was enclosed with this one.

FROM CLEMENT C. CLAY

Dear Sir, Huntsville, [Alabama] Sept. 23d. 1834

Yours of the 15th instant. was recd. on my return home a day or two ago, after a weeks absence. I regret, extremely, that you have reason to expect to be assailed, in reference to the late election of Speaker of the House of Representatives; and still entertain some hope that the result may be otherwise. As an act of justice to you, I am willing to furnish a statement of such facts, as came within my knowledge, in regard to your conduct before, and pending, the election.

In common with many other supporters of the administration, I deprecated any contest between our political friends, for the office of Speaker fearing that any division among ourselves might result in a triumph of the opposition. To that effect, I frequently expressed myself to you, and others; and suggested such modes of obviating a collision of that nature, as occured to me. It was proposed that it should be ascertained, which of the aspirants to the Speakers chair met the approbation of a majority of the friends of the administration, and that, whoever he might be, *he* should be supported by our political friends generally, and that all the other candidates of our party, should withdraw. I mentioned this proposition frequently, to you and others; and was anxious that it should be acquiesced in by all our political friends. To me, you invariably, throughout the session, expressed, and in all other respects indicated, your ready assent to that proposition; and your perfect willingness to retire from the contest, if your pretensions were not approved, and preferred, by a majority of the friends of the administration. I suggested this mode of preventing division among ourselves to two other gentlemen, who were considered candidates, each of whom expressed his willingness to acquiesce in the result. I had also determined to name the subject to Colo. Bell, and so expressed my purpose; but, before I did so, was informed by several members of the House, that Colo. B. had declined submitting the question—whether he should be a candidate to a majority of the friends of the administration, and, therefore, I did not make the proposition.

I am, of course, unable to speak, positively, of the political character of *all* who voted for you. Those who voted for, or supported you, within my personal knowledge, were *all* decided friends of the administration; and I do not recollect to have *heard* that you received more than *one vote from the opposition.*

C. C. Clay

Addressed to Columbia. This letter was enclosed with Clay's other letter of the same date.

FROM ARCHIBALD YELL

Frind Polk Fayetteville Sept the 23d 1834

I shall leave here in a few weeks for the Territory to remain until next Spring, when I expect to return for my Family. I have no fears of being well sustained from my new home. Already they are commited & will not recommend another, but to make things doubly shure I have written to sevirl of them to again write to the *President*. That will be done forthwith. Judge [Thomas J.] Lacy is a favorite with the President and could be of grate service to me if he could be prevailed on to give me a letter, perhaps you can arrange that. At all events I shall make no attempts through any other quarters; my acquaintance with Lacy will not authorise me to write him on the subject, or I would do so. In that matter do as you think prudent & I am contented.

I shall be recommended from Arkansis by Judge [Benjamin] Johnson[1] the Fatherinlaw of Sevier, Judge [William S.] Fulton, Genl Montgomery,[2] [. . .] Smith,[3] Majr Rector[4] & Frank Armstrong[5] and many others not known to you or about over the Teritory but who have standng at home and from the County. I shall settle in Washington. I shall precure the Letters of Whinery, John B. Dickson, Dr Bradford[6] all family of Bradford with others with whom you are unacquinted. The most of the Letters I shall precure after my arrivl in the Territory will be sent to the care of *Polk & Sevir* the policy of which you will understand. I shall not ask of Sevir to intermeddle in my behalf as I am not disposed to place him in a situation that will make him desert some old and tried frind in the Territory who may possibly be applicants. And further tho we are frindly I am not willing under the present state of things to be thought under obligations perticularly to *Sevir*—for as yet there is no determining who is the *Simon pures*. Should he bolt on the Bank question and go with *Uncle Dick Johnson* we shall be in opposition. That I do not anticipate at this time but as I am untrameled and aloof from their local parties, I am not disposed to form any *entangling alliances* except with those on whom I can rely. I expect to take with me from Here young *Andrew Jackson Greer* a young man of fine talents & pure politics who will take charge of a Press if one can be got up in the West. Of Course I shall not be known in it but it must be established when it gets under way. I should like to have the Press to do the Printing of the Laws of Congress "By authorty" and such other little jobs as Maj Barry might throw in the way. I will write you imediatly on my arrivl at Little Rock, and will then be able to give you more specifically my strength and who will be applicants from the Territory. I will also write you what will be the feelings or course of the Delegate Sevir that you may act accordingly.

I received the Columbian that contained the Editors "Comments" on *little* [Allen A.] *Hall.* He has used up little *Allen* and if I am not very much mistaken his frind with Him. I can speak for this quarter of the State, and so far as his letter has been read it is conclusive aganst *Bell.* He has even made me, more *steadfast* in my suspicions; and before its ended Monsier Bell will turn Anti-Jackson or I am verry much mistaken. I have never been until of late the warm supporter of Billy Carroll but He now has my harty & warm good wishes for his success if he encounters Bell for Congress as its said he probably will.

I wrote a tart letter to Hall & discontinued his Paper [. . .] the appearence of his first Number, and so did severil others from this place, & subscribed for the *Banner* but I believe we have not made much of a swap except on the Bank question.

I should like to hear from you often. If you have seen *Lucius Polk* tell him to write me if he has any further perticulars to say in relation to that matter.

I have written letters to Will Dunlap & Forrester & Grundy.[7] They are the only Members of Congress that I could have write to. You must do the rest.

Present me to your good Lady. . . .

A. Yell

Addressed to Columbia.

1. A brother of Richard M. Johnson of Kentucky.

2. William Montgomery, a prominent resident of Arkansas who was made a brigadier general of the territorial militia in 1830.

3. Unidentified.

4. Elias Rector, a member of a politically prominent family in Arkansas. At this time he was United States Marshal for Arkansas Territory.

5. Francis W. Armstrong, formerly of Tennessee, was a brother of Robert Armstrong of Nashville. He served as agent to the Choctaws in the west until his death in 1835, when he was succeeded by still another brother, Capt. William Armstrong.

6. Abraham Whinnery and John B. Dickson were members of the territorial legislature. Bradford is unidentified.

7. William C. Dunlap, John B. Forester, and Felix Grundy, all members of the Tennessee delegation in Congress.

FROM SAMUEL KING[1]

Dr. Sir No. C. Oakville Sepr. 24th 1834

Having no other means of information than that which is derived thro our Public Papers, I was truly surprized in the Summer of 1833, when I saw it announced that the President was taking preparitory steps for a removal of the public deposites. Those feelings were the more induced from the reflection that the House of Representatives had so recently passed a *vote* on that question, & the short interval that would occur until the annual meeting of Congress. At first I believed it to be a mere slang gotten up by his opponents nor did I believe it possible until the measure was consumated. I then predicted, that whatever might be the political effects of that measure, the value of his Administration was at an end. In this I still fear I was not mistaken. Of his right to do so, I never entertained a doubt, and visioned it as a question of policy. Whatever may be our political feelings, we subvert the object for which our Government was formed when we lose sight of the public good. Whether from our disposition as a people, or the nature of our compact, our history proves that our most violent agitations have arisen from personal annimosities. This has always impressed on my mind the great importance of a rigid adherence to the several Departments of our Government, and if I mistake not, it was the great stumbling block to national liberty in the British Government, until due regard was paid to the judicial arm of that Government. It seemed to me from the outset of this interminable controversy, that the Bank question ought to have been referred to the Judicial department, and for the additional reason, that no Legislative act could take place until the termination of the Charter. And what does all this crimination & recrimination amount to—it is yet a mere matter of opinion, as inflexibly adhered to by one side & the other, as the day it commenced. Supposing the House of Repr. had have concurred with the Senate & adopted the Resolution eventually approved of by that body, what would it have effected? It would still have left him the President with all his functions unimpaired. I really have thought my dear Sir, it forms one of the most unfortunate epochs in our history; and has given an importance to a mere creature of the Government, that they otherwise would not have had.

My reflections on the durability of our Government induces me to believe that our existence depends on giving a more inflexible character to our Institutions, particularly those that relate to money matters.

I cannot but feel sanguine in the system I took the liberty of suggesting to you in our short ride from Farmington to Shelbyville,[2] nor can I see how the public interest can be [. . .] & promoted, by the Revenue of the Country, but by the adoption of such a plan. It is with much deference that I dissent from the Executive in placing the deposites in the local Banks. In addition to the fact staring us in the face of the loss we have sustained, surely we are not free from the most serious apprehensions—this is apart from that deception that will be practised on the Government, by failing to comply promptly with the orders of the Government. I have it from your own language, that N. Biddle entered into a negotiation through an Agent sent to Europe when our debts should be paid, with the Revenue of the Country at his command, notwithstanding, the order of the Government. If the President of one institution, resorts to such a subterfuge, how much more is it to be expected of fifty? I leave it with you, and you can better imagine than I can, how many ten thousand artifices will be practised. The coyness of those institutions to receive those deposites, arises from the fear of too much of their Paper getting afloat; but let that mammoth die, and you will soon see a scramble for the deposites, and should your reliance succeed to admiration viz. a specie circulation, it will be found to fall far short, for observe in such a state of things, we shall see the States extending their charters so immoderately, that if the amount of specie was as plenty as Brick bats it will not be commensurate to such exigencies. Permit me now, to put the question to your candor, is it to be doubted, but all those States that are favored with the deposites will patronize the Executive that patronizes them; nor can I perceive, how such a system, avoids Constitutional scruples to a greater extent. If the following surmises are within the limits of a feasible plan, why not establish a national Bank, with a branch in each State of the Union. Make the Genl. Government the principal & include the States in proportion to their population, with power to appoint Directors corresponding to their amt. of Stock. Let all the Stock be owned by the Genl. & State Governments, & exclude individual interest & of course transfers.

You will observe that I entertain no doubt of the Constitutional power of Congress to Charter a Bank, and should you ask why I prefer the plan above suggested, I would say that I entertain the hope that we would then have a circulating medium of such a character as it ought to be—not liable to such fluctuations—rescued from that selfish spirit, which one day makes emissions excessive, and the next day curtails, thereby effecting their purposes in society at pleasure—throwing into, and calling out of circulation what sums they please. If there were no restrictions imposed on the States to emit *money* (for I must call it money) the circumstances that Congress is only competent to regulate commerce would imply they had the right to regulate the article by which it was carried on. This would appear to my mind to be as clear as the right they have and exercise, to build Ships "to establish a Navy." How the idea was ever conceived that the States had a Constitutional right to Charter Banks, has always been a matter of surprize to me. I have always viewed the prohibitions of the first Art. 10th Sect. as definitive, and I suppose were a State to claim the right of granting letters of *marques* that there is not Court in the nation, but would condemn it as unconstitutional. Sir, I do not believe there is a Christian people on Earth so much imposed on as the people of the U. States. Twenty five authorities claiming the power of emitting money thereby compelling society to pay at least 6 pr.Ct. & swindling for as much more as possible on the circulating medium of the Country. And so far as the deposites are serviceable to those miserable institutions, they are paying on their own capital.

There are no periods of our history more dissimilar, than those when Charter was granted by Congress & the period when a renewal was applied for last. At each of those periods the Treasury was overwhelmed with debts and it was then necessary to sustain the Department. Those institutions were then relied on as means for that purpose and answered admirably well. The Treasury is now free of embarrassment, the national debt paid in point of contemplation, and all the Government wants from the assistance of the Bank is to act as an auxiliary.

You will of course perceive that I have indulged in that freedom of opinion, which I know you approve, on points of honest difference.

SAMUEL KING

P.S. You will notice that No. Carolina is claimed by both political parties. The other day I saw a nullifier that is elected a Member to the next Sess. of Assembly, who boasted they would number *fifty* strong, who with the Unionists would form a majority, and that they could vote the Jacksonians down. I asked him what they would do next, who would they then go with, he observed any party that would oppose Jackson and Van Buren. From all I hear, I think it not improbable but they will elect Swaine present Govr. Senator. I have no idea that he is more than one degree from a nullifier. I shall be disappointed if Brown or Mangum are elected again as Senators.[3] But under those calculations I think there is a clear majority against the Bank. There are so many political maneuvers, that I cannot conjecture who No. C will go for as President, but I can see no prospect of success for Martin V. Buren. Please favor me with a letter & tell me who yr. State will go for. If you think fit, show this scrawl to the Mr. Polks.

SAMUEL KING

Addressed to Columbia. This letter has been published in McPherson, editor, "Unpublished Letters," *North Carolina Historical Review,* XVI,

180–185. McPherson's version includes several paragraphs that are believed to have been a part of some other letter or document.

1. King had represented Iredell County in the North Carolina legislature for several years.

2. King had been in Tennessee during the summer of 1834.

3. David L. Swain continued as North Carolina's governor until 1835, after which he became president of the University of North Carolina. Bedford Brown and Willie P. Mangum were returned to the Senate.

FROM GEORGE W. TERRELL

Dear Sir Paris West Dist Septr 24th 1834

I recd a short time since some documents from you for which, please accept my thanks. It has been rumored here that you will probably be a candidate for Governor at our next election—if this be true I wish to know it. There can be a great deal done in this quarter for you, if you wish to run, and your friends would like to know the certainty of the matter that they may be preparing the way—the people here think you were some how or other badly treated in the late election for Speaker of the H. Rep. This is a deep and pervading sentiment in the minds of the community here. Please drop me a line on this subject.

I have directed Mr. Zollicofer[1] who has some money of mine in his hands, to take up the due bill you have so long held so patiently on me. I am really ashamed that it has lain so long, and have twice attempted to get it taken up by gentlemen from this section in Congress, but failed in both.

G. W. Terrell

Addressed to Columbia.

1. Felix K. Zollicoffer of Maury County was at this time editor of the Columbia *Observer*. He later edited other newspapers, including the Nashville *Banner*, 1850–52. He became a Whig and served in the United States House of Representatives, 1853–59. He was killed in the Battle of Mill Springs in 1862.

FROM ARCHIBALD YELL

My Dear Sir Fayetteville Sept the 25th 1834

This mornings mail brought about a *bushel* of Republicans enough to supply all Lincoln. It can not be possible that halfe that number is sent to any other county in the state, if so the Tax is not an inconsiderable item for they all had the stamp *Free!* Along with those *Bell* dockuments I received two sheets in reply to my letter that I mentioned to you that I wrote to *Hall,* asking a discontinuence of his Paper and give him my reasons for it. The whole letter to me is a very extraordinary one; and if I am not grately mistaken it develops some of the deep and settled designs against you; if his statements are to indicate the course that ther party designs. He may tho. speak without authority, but I fear not. If he is to be believed, you ought to be put on your guard against a design to ruin your political prospects and if posible to bring you in Collision with the President, which I hope to God you may avert. But perhaps I may be two suspicios and not comprehend propely the misterious sentence to which I allude. That you may better understand the subject which preceeds it, I will remark he states, that it is impracticle in your & Bells frinds to fall out; that Mr. Grundy & Gov Carroll will only be the persons benefited by it; & they will drop you so soon as they find you can be of no further service to them. Then comes the following.

"And now mark me Yell for a Prophit. In less than six months there will be a split between Carroll & Polk.[1] Nay there will be a split between Polk and the *President!!* Coming events casts their shaddow before. But Polk by no earthly posibility can continue to maintain his present position in the event of certain future contingences which are *obliged* to take place; wher this, I repeat, the policy of driving myself and others who were sensearly desirous of serving him in anything, that did not go to the injury of Bell, into opposition to him? Yet such is the inevitable result of the course pursued by his frinds *myself* among the numbers &c."

If I understand this misterious sentence, it is an indication that you are to be Removed from the Head of the Committee of *Ways & Means,* if any thing else I can not discern it, Tho. you will really see and understand it and I hope be able to meet all and every "Contngency" *that are "obliged* to take place." How they are to bring you and the President in collision I am at a loss to conjecture. And yet they say that your frinds & I among the rest have brought this about. I brought it about, because I discontinued his paper is strange sort of logice to me. I hope you have not taken the same view of the course of your frinds; I know you will not. There is some *Hellish* scheme concocting to bring you in collision with the President and then they are safe. Do you conjecture what it is? If not you should be on your guard and it seems to me you ought to apprise the Presidnt that a design is formed to bring about a division, tho. about the course you ought to pursue I have intruded my own views without perhaps knowing even the allusion. Your better Judgment will enable you I hope to stear clear of *braking* with the *President*. I dont look upon *Halls* letter as a confidential one and you may therefore use the Extract in such way as you may think your safety may require.

I think from the verry higher dudgeon in which they took my discontinuence of the Paper they may *opperate* upon me also with the President. If they can destroy your standing with *Him* then nothing will save me but my being too small game for them. I am not in their way. You are.

A. Yell

Addressed to Columbia.

1. See William Carroll to Polk, December 19, 1834.

FROM CHARLES CASSEDY

Livingston, P. O. Bedford Co. Tenn.

Dear Sir Sept. 26 1834

A temporary inflamation of the eyes, which has incapacitated Doct. [George W.] Haywood from writing you himself, induces him to request the favor of my pen, on the subject of his claim against Th. G. Bradford.[1] I have requested Maj. [William B.] Lewis, of the Treasury Dept., if possible, to bring about a consent, on the part of Bradford, that a portion of the pay he derives from the Treasury, may be secured to go by installments to the payment of this demand, by bringing the President's *rule of political equity,* which says "no man shall remain in the official employment of the government, if he can oust him, unless he pay his just debts when practicable," to bear on him. In the event of this arrangement being made, Mr. Lewis will advise you of it—in order that you may, which you are earnestly requested to do, attend to the security for the payment of the debt, which you can do with little trouble; and, as to the amt. of the Judgments & Interest, it will be easy for you to procure the transcripts from the gentleman to whom you confided them. If Bradford refuses the accommodation just named, you are requested by Doctor Haywood to prosecute his claim against him; &, in fact, to do all you would do in a case of your own, of a similar character, and he will sanction the proceeding. If you can, on fair terms, comprimise, you are authorised to do so; if not act in a professional capacity, by bringing a suit.

I inclose you *one* pamphlet, no doubt *of hundreds* which have lately arrived in your district, to produce unfavorable impressions of your conduct while on the Bank Committee. The work is not calculated for this meridian; it will operate opositely to the way intended by the *donor*—so much for the folly of faction, like rascallity, it is always *short sighted.*

CHARLES CASSEDY

Addressed to Washington and forwarded to Columbia.

1. Thomas G. Bradford was a clerk in the office of the Secretary of the Treasury, a position that he continued to hold for several more years. Earlier he had edited the Nashville *Clarion*. The nature of the claim against him has not been ascertained.

TO SARAH POLK

At the plantation [Fayette County]

Dear Sarah Sept 26th 1834

Within an hour after I wrote to you on yesterday, I sold my land to Mr Booker for $6,000—one half down at Christmas, and the other half upon a year's credit. To day I have bought *Mariah's* husband and have some expectation that I may be able to get *Caesar's* wife. My crop is better than I expected. There is a fair prospect that it will yield me including corn & cotton both, about $2,500. *Beanland* has done well considering the trouble he has had with the negroes. *Old Jack* is now gone, without any known reason and has been away for near three weeks. No account can be had of him. I fear he has taken another trip to the Mississippi River.

I will send up *Jim* & *Ben* with old Mr *Moore* (George's father) who will start on Monday. I will give them a letter to *Mr. Harris* requesting him to deliver them to their owners. I find negro clothing very high here, and will write by them to Mr Harris—requesting him to buy for me, their clothing and send it down with Old Mr Moore who will be returning with a waggon. I am resolved to send my hands to the South, have given money to *James Brown* to buy a place & have employed *Beanland* as an overseer. I am determined to make more money or loose more one. I have been kept exceedingly busy since I got here, have not been off the plantation except to a neighbour's house on business. I have received no letter from home, and have seen no newspaper, and of course know nothing of the character of the publication, which the Editor of the Republican had promised to make before I left home. I determined not to perplex myself about it, until I had done my business. I hope to be able to get off on tomorrow evning or the next day; and I think I may have an opportunity to sell my land near Boliver, and will probably be detained there for a day or two, and will then come directly home. I bought Mariah's husband a very likely boy—about 22 years old for $600. and paid for him with the notes I held on his master for land which I sold him several years ago.

James K. Polk

P.S. I will write to Mr Harris giving him a statement of the articles I wish sent down for the plantation when Old Mr Moore returns. If he is not at home will you see to it, and get *Saml. Walker* to buy them for me upon the lowest terms he can. I have written for enough to make two suits round. The negroes have no idea that they are going to be sent to the South and I do not wish them to know it, and therefore it would be best to say nothing about it at home, for it might be conveyed back to them.

J. K. P.

N.B. Since writing it occurs to me, that I will have to go a day or two out of my way, with the hope of getting a negro in payment of a debt due me by Silliman to whom I sold land.

J. K. P. Sept. 27. 1834

Addressed to Columbia. This letter has been published in Bassett, *Plantation Overseer,* 77–78.

FROM D. C. TOPP[1]

Dear Sir, Bollivar Sept 26th 1834

I have been informed that you are at your plantation in Fayette County at present and desirous to sell it. I shall leave here this evening for La Grange and will if possible to-morrow or next day ride up to see you. Should you leave however, this part of the State before I have an opportunity of seeing you inform me in a note which you will please leave at the Post Office in Sommerville who will be authorised to sell your plantation for you and your price &c.

D. C. Topp

Addressed to Somerville, Tennessee.

1. A former resident of Giles County and probably a relative of William W. Topp, who had moved from Giles County to Columbus, Mississippi. See William W. Topp to Polk, July 1, 1834, and Thomas and George W. Martin to Polk, July 8, 1834.

FROM WILLIAM C. DUNLAP

Sir Bolivar Septr 28th 1834

Yours of the 12th Inst. I recd. on my return home from a visit to one of the counties in my District.

You request me to state to you what was your course and Mr Bell in relation to the election of Speaker to the House of Representatives last Session of congress.

So far as came within my knowledge or as I heard from others your conduct was highly approved by all your political friends You unhesitatingly agreed to leave it to the friends of the administration who should be the candidate for Speaker. The only objection I heard to Mr Bell's course was that he refused to leave it to the friends of the administration who should be their candidate.

You were considered as the favourite candidate of the President and in the election you only received one opposition vote, Majr [John M.] Felder, and Mr Bell received a large majority of the opposition votes. They opposition claimed to have beaten the Presidents candidate. It was generally understood that Mr Bell was in favour of a National Bank; I never heard him express any opinion on the subject.

You are at liberty to use my extracts from my former letter to you.

W. C. DUNLAP

Addressed to Columbia.

FROM EBENEZER J. SHIELDS

Pulaski. September 28, 1834

Shields reminds Polk that pension papers of Lawson Hobson have been sent to Polk and urges that he write directly to Hobson, who is uneasy lest the papers be lost.[1]

Addressed to Columbia.

1. See Shields to Polk, February 18, 1834.

FROM JAMES STANDIFER

Dear Col Mount Airy [Tennessee] September the 29th 1834

Your faver of the 12th Instant has been reseved; it will at all times give me pleasure to give a statement in support of an honest Injured mans charractor such as I think you to be, should you be attacketed by anyone worthy of notice, but until then it perhaps will be best to say but little. Mr Bell never spoke to me about the election of Speker that I recollect, I supposed he [k]new my course. I very distinctly recollect at different times to heare you say you was opposed to have a division in the Jackson ranks for Speker, and perticular a division amongst the Tennessee deligation and that you was willing to leave it to a majority of the deligation from your one State, which I understood some of Mr Bells friends refused to do. The conversation about Mr Bell being elected by oppisition votes that they counted as well as any other votes I understood was to Majr

Walker.[1] I never heard of but one vote being given to you that was opposed to the Presidents administration and he was opposed to a recharter of the bank. I did not understand ther was any doubt at Washington who the oppisition voted for. It was said they shook hands and exulted at ther success, tho it is true some good Jackson men voted for Mr. Bell. I shall feel my self Justifiable to give you a more formal statement should Mr Bell attack you, but unless he dose I would not wish my name to go to the public. I shall be pleased to hear from you when it soots your conveniance.

JAMES STANDIFER

Addressed to Columbia.

1. Unidentified.

FROM ALFRED FLOURNOY[1]

My Dear Sir Pulaski Septr 30th 1834

Your favour of the 11th Inst. was recvd some days since, and would have been answered forthwith except for a heavy calamity which has befallen my family, one that has interrupted all my family arrangements—a misfortune that to me is irreparable. You may perhaps have heard before this of the death of my wife.[2] My dear friend you cannot well imagine how desolate I am. I have six little children, and there is not a man perhaps in existance, who is less qualified than myself to take charge of such a family. My wife was an excellent manager and had the exclusive charge of my household. I had been a great deal about from home and ever on my return I found all to my satisfaction. I am at a loss to know what is best for me to do—the more I reflect, the more gloomy and discontented I feel.

The suggestions in your letter has been attended to. You need have no apprehensions of opposition or concern[?] from this quarter. If you should desire any thing from our little paper if you or any of your friends will forward any article to me it shall be attended to. Our Editor[3] entertains for you the kindest feelings & will be disposed to aid you in all he can. I trust if you are forced into a controversy you may be able to anihilate your enemies. I calculate on being in Maury in 8 or 10 days, if so, I will do myself the pleasure of visiting you.

A. FLOURNOY

Addressed to Columbia.

1. A Pulaski physician with whom Polk had been on friendly terms for many years.

2. She was a daughter of John Hamlin Camp, a Giles County physician who had served several years in the state legislature. Two other daughters of Camp had married two brothers of Alfred Flournoy.

3. This is apparently a reference to Alston B. Estes, at that time editor of the Pulaski *Tennessee Beacon*. Estes had recently been connected with the Columbia *Western Mercury* and was certainly known to Polk.

FROM CAVE JOHNSON

Dear Sir, Clarksville Oct. 2nd [1834][1]

I enclose you Ben Hardins letter from which you will see he remembers nothing and evidently does not wish to remember any thing.[2] He said precisely what I told you but I was fearful that he might not choose to remember.

We shall have to get some how a new paper in Nashville. Do you know any thing of the Reporter?[3] Majr. Hise[4] would like to have a hand in it. He is with us in our State affairs but agt. us in general politics & promises to conform. He would like to go to Washington & write letters as a Co-editor. He writes a good paragraph & might do us much good, if connected with a prudent discreet Editor.

I have been very sick, confined to my room & bed with rheumatism the last 8 or 10 days. I think it more than probable that I shall be unable to go to Washington this winter and am thinking seriously of resigning my seat.

C. JOHNSON

Addressed to Columbia.

1. The Library of Congress has supplied the year, which is supported by other letters. See Johnson to Polk, September 1 and September 12, 1834.

2. This letter is available. Hardin said that he had no recollection of the conversation at White Sulphur Springs to which Johnson had referred. From the tenor of the letter, it is clear that Hardin was not committed to Polk although he still claimed to be a Jackson man. See Johnson to Polk, July 15, 1834.

3. The *Reporter,* to have been put out by Philips and Long, seems never to have been published. See John W. Childress to Polk, September 18, 1834.

4. Although John P. Heiss was later connected with the Nashville *Union,* he was still a resident of Philadelphia at this time.

FROM EPHRAIM BEANLAND

Dear Sir [Somerville] October the 4th 1834

On last nite I got home from the Arkensis and I hearde of Jack but never co[u]ld get Site of him and it Is suposed that he is in Shauney villige[1] which I was advised to not go theire for they is A den of thieves and to tell you the fact I donte thin[k]e that you will ever git him. I sene John Bigerstaf[2] in Memphis which I rote a letter to Jisco[3] the Sherif of Philips County Arkensis Teritory that he was heare and as for Jack he has got alonge with them theves and I thinke that the chance is bad of getinge of him.

It has bin a raininge for 5 dayes studdy. I am afrad that the cotten will turn alp but sorry. I thinke if you and Booker[4] can trade It would be best for you for I am afraide that it will be sorry. I shal make 6 bailes to day. Silaman[5] caim hear and I sent the gin back and I also bought a negro boy from for $600. The boy is 22 years olde and I told his that I wold give $5 hundred dollars for the boyes wife and 2 chilldren. Please to rite to me and let me [k]nowe sumpthing on the Subject. We ar all well at this time.

E Beanland

Addressed to Columbia. This letter has been published in Bassett, *Plantation Overseer,* 79.

1. Shawnee Town, on the west bank of the Mississippi River near Memphis, was a favorite haunt of fugitives, black and white.

2. Unidentified. There were families by this name living in Fayette County at this time, and it seems likely that he, too, had lived there. See John W. Fowler to Polk, July 11, 1834.

3. Although Beanland wrote this clearly, the correct name is Henry L. Bisco, Phillips County sheriff, 1832–36. Bisco moved from Virginia in 1825 and quickly became involved in political affairs in Arkansas. He served in the territorial legislature, where he was a strong supporter of statehood for Arkansas, and established a newspaper at Helena largely for the purpose of

promoting statehood. He was a member of the convention that gave Arkansas its first state constitution.

4. Peter R. Booker of Maury County. Booker's son, James, had shown interest in lands in the Western District, and this land might have been purchased for his benefit.

5. Thomas N. Silliman.

FROM SAMUEL KING

Oakville, North Carolina. October 4, 1834

King expects his son to cultivate land on the Hatchee that he owns in common with John C. McLemore and wishes Polk to notify McLemore. After asking about crops in the Hatchee region, he inquires about the question of the bank deposits. He closes with a prediction that Virginia will not re-elect Benjamin W. Leigh and that North Carolina will elect David L. Swain.[1]

Addressed to Columbia.

1. Leigh, senator from Virginia, was re-elected in 1835 but resigned his seat in July 1836. Presumably King alludes to efforts to elect Governor Swain to the United States Senate; these were unsuccessful as Bedford Brown was re-elected.

FROM SAMUEL W. MARDIS

My dear Sir Montevallo [Alabama] October 4th 1834

Your welcomed letter of the 22nd Augt (Strange to tell) never came to hand until last evening. I was much pleased to find amidst *friends, public dinners* &c that I had not been forgotten & only regret that the tardiness of the mail should so long have post-poned those sensations of pleasure which as usual were well calculated to excite in the [. . .] of *disinterested friendship.* The delay in the reception of your letter is regretted on another account. I fear that my failure to reply may have been attributed to indisposition to do so, or negligence on my part. I beg that you will feel assured that I have not a friend within the circle of my acquaintance by whoes attention, I would feel more favoured, or whoes good opinions would be more highly prized than those of yourself. I am happy to say to you that notwithstanding the gloomy prospect, Mary Eliza stood the journey quite well; reached home in safety; found our dear *children* in good *health,* as likewise our *friends.* And if you will now shut your *eyes* and stop your *ears;* I will tell Mrs Polk *privately* what has happened since our arrival. Oh! that she could see the *beautiful plump little creature, my feelings overcome me;* I cannot *prosecute the matter further, its name is Ann Yates Mardis.* I thank you for the Presidents sentiment. It is in character with the distinguishing public acts of his whole life *frank bold and independent.* I have been noticing with solicitude the course that the friends of Mr ——[1] were about to take & have been fearful that they would attempt to divert public attention from his recent acts and the attitude that he does now occupy in Congress by endeavouring to make up a false issue between you & himself; and thus, in the heat of a personal contest to cover up and conceal from public view his real & true principles, if in truth he has any. I am pleased to find that you so well understand his plan & highly approve of your determination to act on the defensive. You say that it has been insinuated that you were supported by the *Nullifiers* for *Speaker* to *the House of Rep.* Nothing could be more false than this charge. I took a deep interest in your election, and know of my own knowledge that not exceeding three of them, voted for you, at any time & that they were violent *anti-Bank* men, and assigned (at least two of them) as a reason why they voted for you, that *you were honestly opposed to the Bank.* It is with pleasure furthermore that I bear testimony to the fact that through out the canvass for the *Speakers chair* (so far as I was enabled to judge) that you neither deviated to the right or to the left or endeavoured to conciliate either the *Nationals* or *Nullifiers;* but your conduct was during the whole period marked by that industry & zeal for the success of the leading measures of the Administration which won for you the confidence & esteem of a large proportion of its friends. I know furthermore from frequent conversations with you on the subject that it was a prominent object with you (if successful) to take the chair untramelled by and uncommitted to the opposition, free to pursue in the chair the same course of conduct in referrence to the measures of the Administration, that you had pursued on the floor of the House.

This leaves my constituents in a good humour as it does Mary Eliza, children, & myself in good health. What rout will you go; & when will you start? Mary Eliza sends her love to Mrs. Polk, & talks of meeting her at Washington at times; not positive. Let me hear from you soon. Shelby County is the County of my residence. Mention me kindly to Mrs Polk. . . .

SAM W. MARDIS

Addressed to Columbia.

1. A rather obvious reference to John Bell.

FROM JOHN W. CHILDRESS

Dear Sir Murfreesboro October 7th 1834

On yesterday it being the first day of the Circuit Court Mr Bell addressed the people of Rutherford. A few of his friends had collected the people in the Court house by making proclamation that there was to be a speech delivered and then introduced approbatory resolutions and offered him a dinner which he declined. Notwithstanding there was a large crowd in the room, who had gone there to hear a speech, there were but six or seven that voted for the resolutions and two against them. He delivered his speech after court adjourned in the evening to a respectable auditory. He was greatly excited and become very furious applying harsh and unbecoming epithets to those who had questioned the correctness of his course in Congress. I do not recollect that he made any remarks pointing particularly to you, except that the other candidates for Speaker had treated him gentlemanly, leaving it to be inferred that you had not. That he heard no complaints of him from either of the other gentlemen. He vaunted greatly his adherence to principles, his unwavering support of the president, and said distinctly, and in these words, that had he not been true and firm to the administration, he could have changed the small majority in the house upon the Bank question by going over and taking his friends with him and thereby have defeated all the measures of the President. He boldly charged that influences had been exerted upon the President, to get him to withold the nomination of Stevenson at the beginning of the session because it was discovered that he would be elected at that time and that it was attempted to postpone it again after the Bank question had been settled. But he took care to qualify his remarks by saying that the President did not suspect the trick, & that any man may have been duped in the same way. He stated that various plans had been tried to estrange him from the President and to draw from him a disapproval of his (Bells) course. That he was supported by a large portion of the Jackson party, with the exception of six or seven individuals had the confidence of the whole party & would have recieved their votes had the balloting gone on longer. He intimated that unfair tricks[?] had been resorted to, to defeat him but did not say by whom. He evaded his Bank Speech in 1832. Said that he was willing to give Jacksons experiment a fair trial, and if it did not answer the wants of the people, that then he *might* be in favor of a national Bank. That he had no idea that a metallic currency would answer the purposes of a circulating medium and almost said it was Demagoguon in any one that would say so. I have attempted to give you the outline of his speech as well as I could in a letter. His friends here & elsewhere are making great exertions to create the impression that it is a personal dispute between himself and you & that you are urging the attack.[1]

The 'Observer' is too prolix & uses too much repetition—he should be more careful in writing his pieces. The article in the Pulaski paper is the best I have seen. I have heard nothing from you since I left Columbia. Write me and let me know the state of affairs. Give our love to Sarah & Mary.

JOHN W CHILDRESS

Addressed to Columbia.

1. Bell's speech has been variously reported, but it was generally agreed that it was not one of his better efforts. It attacked Polk only by innuendo, and it could also be said to have had a strong anti-Jackson tone. Bell wrote Jackson about the speech, indicating that in his excitement at Murfreesboro he might have gone further than he had intended. It is clear, however, that Bell was not yet ready for an open break with Jackson. The account given here by Childress was probably as fair an interpretation of the speech as is available. By contrast, see William Brady's account in his letter to Polk, October 13, 1834, and William R. Rucker's in his letter to Polk, October 12, 1834.

FROM HENRY D. HATTON

Hatton's Hills, Maryland. October 8, 1834.

Hatton, a Maryland resident who is personally unknown to Polk, writes a long, rambling letter, asking for information about his sister, who is a resident of Hickman County. He charges that she is incompetent and that William L. Weems had married her and taken her away secretly in order to acquire property left in trust for her by her father.[1]

Addressed to Columbia. This letter enclosed three letters: Charles K. Gardner to Polk, September 8, 1834; Benedict J. Semmes to Polk, September 14, 1834; and John T. Stoddert to Polk, September 16, 1834.

1. The marriage had taken place about two years before this letter was written. Weems, formerly of Maryland, was a friend of Gerrard T. Greenfield. He later developed Bon Aqua into a popular watering place and health resort.

FROM THOMAS J. LACY

Dear Sir, Nashville Oct 9th 1834

Heretofor, I have been unable to furnish you with the information you desired, owing entirely to my indisposition. I am now only able to go about a little, but as my courts are siting am compelled to leave here in a day or so, and shall go directly to Helena. As soon as I get there you shall hear from me fully; for I then can give all the perticulars in relations to the land of that country.[1] I shall get there in six day and you can get a letter in ten afterwards so you can tell what best for you to do before you proceed to Washington. I shall return to stay a week in December in this state. My best regards to Mrs Polk. . . .

Thos J. Lacy

Addressed to Columbia.

1. Polk had asked Lacy for information on entering and purchasing land in Arkansas. See Lacy to Polk, December 4, 1834.

FROM EPHRAIM BEANLAND

Dear Sir Near Summersville Fayet Oct 10, 1834

We ar all well but Loosy and Any they aint able to go to picken out cotten yet and it has rained all moste everry day since you left hear. The weather is nowe fine for cotton for the last 3 days. I am glad to hear of Jack. I say sell the oalde scounderel tho if you wante him worked send him on and I will take good care of him and secure him. I am glad to hear of you a byinge 5 negroes. My cotten is a goinge to turn out well I thinke if I can get it out but I do ashore you that I cant get it out in time if I donte get more hands than I nowe have got. I have sent 10 bales to Memphis and on this morninge I have started my gin. I cant get out my crop in time if I donte get more help for when I run my gin I have not got but 7 hands. Please to send Jack to me and I will ceap him if it is posiable and as for Reaveses boy he will take $600 for him.

I nowe see parson Reaves[1] and he is hear and he says if you send Jacke heare he will cill him for he says that if his boy Fill wold not run away he wold not take $1000 for him for he is a rite smarte blacksmith and A good shumaker and a good huar. The boy Fill will live with you. I would advise you to by him, he can be broke from runninge a way. This is the 2 time that he ever run a way in his life and Jack went theire and got him alf. He will take $600 for him and I wante you to sell Jack and never let him come heare no more for they is a greate many of the neighbers is afraide for him to come hear. Reaves will be theire in a fieu days and he wants to sell his boy which I have barginde for him at $600 and I thinke he is verry cheape boy. I bought him for you and if you ar afraide to I am not. By him be shore he is such a handy boy.

Sir, Silliman came heare and I sente the gin back and I bought a negroman from him and the boy is 22 years olde weighinge 180 to 185 pounds. He is warented to be sounde healthy and a rite handy boy which I was to give him $600 for him and he was to send him on with out faile and the boy has a wife and she can be got for $500 her and 2 children which I tolde him if I liked hear I would give it. Rite to me and let me [k]now what to do. I have paide the Blacks Smiths acounte with oute payinge oute won dollare in cash. I got the receite in full ande I give the pony for the oxen which I have got a good teame now and I have loste won milke cowe since you left. Nothing more. . . .

E Beanland

Addressed to Columbia. This letter has been published in Bassett, *Plantation Overseer,* 80–81.

1. Unidentified. From information in this and other letters, it would seem that he was at this time a resident of Fayette County but that he had probably moved there fairly recently from Maury County.

FROM JOHN H. BILLS

Hon James K Polk Bolivar Oct 12. 1834

Mr. Samuel Rogers, assignee of H W Keeble, Requests that you send him through me a title to the 100 acres of Land I sold Keeble for you.[1] He holds your bond. It is understood that Keeble has paid George Moore, he showed me a Recpt of Moore's to that Effect.

If however that is not *valid* Rogers requests the title sent and with it Keebles note which he pledges himself to pay. *I will guaranty that he does so,* he manifests some impatience about it.

Jno. H. Bills

PS. I have not succeeded in getting our Printer to *Speak* yet, but think I will do so on Wednesday next.

Young Alexander & my son have both Recovered.

B

Addressed to Columbia.

1. The land had been sold to Humphrey W. Keeble in September 1832. See Bills to Polk, September 5, 1832. Rogers is unidentified.

FROM WILLIAM R. RUCKER

Dear Coln. Murfreesborough 12th October 1834

I have for some time been so professionally busy that I could not get even a few moments to write to you. John Childress however has had leisure & I suppose you have by him been apprised of the passing events of this Neighbourhood. You have seen one Murfreesborough paper & have noted its contents. The Labors of A Citizen to prove that there has been a conspiracy to injure Coln Bell with the Citizens of Rutherford and the Nashville district and to impress upon the people the idea that

Mr Grundy's visit & Speech was intended to injure Coln Bell & not to advance the interest of Jackson's administration.[1] You have no doubt perused with some interest the pieces under the Signature of D. J. O. challenging Coln Bell & his friends to show good reasons for the Honble Speakers silence at the last trying Session of Congress. These things have made the Speaker very wrathy & on the first Monday of the Circuit Ct having been summoned by some of his adherents he made a most vehement & flaming tirade against his enemies at the head of whom he makes no scruple in placing his Honorable collegue who contested with him for the honor of the Speakers chair. This speech was the most intemperate and ill advised defence that I ever heard. I have not learned that even his best friends have approved of it and I am confident that he will lose a good many friends in consequence of his abuse of you & especially of Genl Jackson. I would be very glad if I could furnish you with a complete copy of the speech, but If I could even give you every word you would lose more than half because I could not impress upon you his temper shown by the most bitter & revengeful countenance, stamping, raving, and the most pugnacious thrashing & sawing with his hands & arms. Mr Keeble[2] has given a short though very imperfect synopsis of the Speech and I would greatly have prefered that he had said nothing about it than to have done it so badly. I heard only a small part of the Speech but as Genl Brady heard it all & has a good memory I had spoken to him to write out for me as complete a synopsis as he could with a view of sending it to you. I will get in the morning & get John to copy it and forward it to you with this letter. From what I have heard Brady read I have no doubt that he has done Bell ample justice & in some places covered his folly & softened his asperity. This Speech if published will plainly designate the atitude in which the Honble Speaker stood & still stands towards Genl Jackson & his administration. Coln Bell was just invited to a dinner by a Committee which he declined but determined to make a Speech. A copy of the proceedings was made out for publication—but it was not furnished to our Monitor & we suspect it will most likely be published in Nashville. James Brown[3] their Secretary went to Nashville last week but it did not appear in the last paper. Perhaps he is waiting for Bell to write and his speech to appear along with the other proceedings. If the whole matter is not stated it will be advisable to have Brady's version published.

I was talking with Brady this evening about the propriety of your coming up here (now that Sarah is here) & by invitation of some of your country friends to make a speech on the subject of the abuses of the Bank & in defence of the administration. I know a great many who would be very much gratified to hear you and it would be desirable that you would not say one word about Mr Bell or the Speakers election. It would mortify him & his friends exceedingly and really I do not see that you ought to pay any attention to his [. . .] speeches. They will all recoil most certainly & effectually upon yr. enemy by your passing them by without noticing them. However further aggression may make it necessary to come out but that time has not yet arrived.

If you should think of coming up you ought to come early next week when our court will most probably be still in session. My family are well. But Mrs. Childress is right sick. I was to see her last night though she is not at all dangerous. Old Daniel Bowman[4] the last Elector visited the President a day or two before his departure for Washington and not knowing the way he got Brady to go with him. To old Bowman whilst there the President was more [. . .] in his condemnation of Bell's course the last Session. The old Elector spoke of what he heard when he came back and Coln. Bell in his Speech spoke of the Old Farmer being draged to the Hermitage to pick up a crumb against him. You will find the allusion to Mr Bowman in the synopsis. Brady does not wish it to be known that he wrote out the Speech. Perhaps it may be necessary to have it understood if published that it was done by one of Coln. Bells friends—for as I said before it does him as far as I heard ample justice. I did intend to copy this, but it is late & I am in hopes you will be able to understand me.

W R Rucker

Addressed to Columbia.

1. For an account of Grundy's speech, see Brady to Polk, October 13, 1834.

2. Edwin A. Keeble was editor of the Murfreesboro *Monitor*. He was in the process of closing out his business, and the paper ceased publication at

the height of the controversy over Bell's speech. The imperfect synopsis of which Rucker speaks appeared in the *Monitor* on October 11, 1834.

3. Unidentified.

4. An old and respected citizen of the county, Bowman had been a justice of the peace as early as 1813. He was a presidential elector in 1832.

FROM EPHRAIM BEANLAND

Dr Sir. Sommerville Fayette County Octobr. 13th 1834

Agreeable to my communications to you a few days past, I have Mr. Reeves[1] boy for you. You will therefore pay over to him Six hundred dollars in United States paper, clearing Mr Reeves of all expenses, and he will execute a letter.

EPHRAIM BEANLAND

N.B. Sir you will.[2]

Addressed to Columbia. Although Beanland signed the letter, it was written by somebody else.

1. This is the same person referred to as Parson Reaves in earlier letters. Note the different spellings.

2. This incomplete sentence has not been explained.

FROM EPHRAIM BEANLAND

Dear Sir Near Sumerville October the 13 1834[1]

On this day I sawe parson Reaves and I did make the bargin for his negroman Fill which I thinke him well worth the $600 and parson Reaves will be theire in A fieu dayes and he will call on you for the money. You can see the boy and if you thinke that the boy will soote you be shore and by him for he is a good hande with the brand and a verry good shumaker and A rite smarte blacksmith and I thinke that if he is taken to the Misippi he can be broke from runninge away. I was aufered $700 for him to day by a trader but I tolde him now. If you ar not pleased I am sorry of the trade. He is to warent that the boy is sounde and to make the bil of saile. They is severel that wants the boy and I tolde him that you wolde give him you nited States money. Rite and let me [k]nowe how you ar pleased with the trade and also the trade of Silamans boy. I was to give $600 for him and I thinke that he is as big as Jim, 22 yeares olde, boathe warented to be sounde and stoute boyes. We ar all well and my cotten is a opninge finely and I cante get my crop oute in time if I donte get more hands. I thought that was the best thinge that colde with Silaman was to by his boy he was home and I have note hearde from him. Ples let me [k]nowe howe your pleased with the 2 trades. I am shore that the cotten will make as good a crop as you thought it would.

Ephraim Beanland

Addressed to Columbia.

1. This letter and the previous one bear the same date. It also repeats some information. No satisfactory explanation has been found for this apparent duplication. Since only one envelope has been found, however, it seems likely that the two letters were sent under the same cover.

FROM WILLIAM BRADY

[Murfreesboro]

My dear Sir Monday Evening Ocr. [13] 1834[1]

Since you passed through our Village on your way home, we have had a variety of political movements. Mr Grundy came amongst us and was heard by the people with delight; for he talked to them in a plain and common sence strain; and upon subjects in which they felt an absorbing interest. The currency—the Bank and a Bank was ably reviewed by Mr G and the measures of the administration lost nothing of their lustor in the hands of the orator. He spoke of no one harshly, and left the Speaker of the House of Representativs unmolested in the possession of his civic Laurels.[2]

After Grundy left here the whole hive was in an uproar and battle[?] lines were written, and messengers dispatched to head Quarters at Nashville giving information of Mr G. movments. The Speaker and his frinds could see nothing in the circumstance of Mr G visit here, than an attempt at his distruction. And therfore a clumsy writer in this place had orders to assail Mr. Grundy. If you have seen the Monitor printed at this place you will have seen how the task has been performed.[3] The writer who subscribes himself a Citizen of Rutherford County is said to be Hoover—the son of Old John,[4] the vindictive contemner of the President and all the measures of his administration.

I omitted to state to you, that after the conclusion of Mr Grundy's speech the Representative from our district[5] essayed to make a speech. It was said by his friends to be a total failure. The only thing which I recollect of his saying was that he cheerfully subscribed to the views and doctrines advanced by Mr G. and intimated that while Mr G was enforcing his principles in the Senate of the U S. that he, Dickinson was not less zealous in the other branch of Congress.

We had been threatened with a castigation from the Master Spirit himself *and* [. . .] Mr Speaker Bell reached our Town on Sunday evening (*Week*) previous to the sitting of our circuit court. His fiew friends were active to attract public attention towards him, and hundreds of invitations were given to our citizens to call upon the Speaker which went unheeded. At Elevn OClock it was announced that a public meeting would be held in the court house, tho the object was not stated and after incessant bawling for one hour, the meeting was organized by Mr Fletcher[6] taking the chair. Henderson Yokum[7] the same individual, which you may recollect of seeing at the Railroad meeting in Columbia, offered some resolutions (without comment) and the question was taken—four voting affirmatively and three in the negative. So it may be said that the question carried; which it would not have done had the voice of the crowd spoken. The object of the Resolutions as expressed was to [. . .] the Honbl Speaker—but the whole affair resulted in a Speech, delivered in the same day. All his kinfolks and his fiew friends assembled to grace his triumph. But how sad the disappointment. The orator sank below expectation, and his warmest admirers were constrained to speak in disapprobation of his effort. He satisfied none not even himself, for it was evident after the close of his *Philipic* that he was disturbed and unquiet. His speech was marked by bad temper and a weak manner. He evidenced the most consummate arrogance at one moment and cringing servility at another. When alluding to those who may have doubted his political integrity, he used no milder terms than hypocrites, base and unprincipled *cabal* &c—

and had you have heard him, you would have been somewhat at a loss to seperate the Presidnt of the US. from the rest of his traducers—for the *Speaker* made an indiscriminate slaughter of all his enemies. Parts of his speech were so palpable, and variant from the truth, in relation to the *President,* that I felt it my duty to address him a letter upon the subject; in which I detailed the subject matter of Mr Bell speech. If he would so speak of the Chief Magistrate, you may well suppose that all others less conspicuous who should dare stand in his way receivd a thurst[*sic*]. However there was nothing open, nothing tangible —*inuendo* was the weapon he fought with.

The impression the Speaker has left behind him is other than favorable; and his visit here has not advanced his own or his brotherinlaws cause.

It has been suggested that a speech from you at this place would advance the cause of our friends; and I am of this opinion for the State of the public mind is such, that you would meet with a warm reception. The people would like to hear you upon the subject of Banks and currency and such other matters as might suggest themselves to your mind touching the policy of the Genl Government in relation to retrenchment &c. If you have the time we should be glad to see you amongst us.

I had something to say to you about another matter relating more immediately to myself, but I will defer it for a personal interview.

Permit me to say to you that my prospects in the County of Rutherford were never so bright as at this time. I do not over calculate when I put down my majority ovr Davy here at 800. Now if Williamson will only give me a few crumbs his defeat is certain.

S[h]ould it be in your power to visit us we should be glad to see you before the end of this week.

Wm Brady

Addressed to Columbia.

1. Brady put no day on the letter, but it was postmarked on October 14, which was on Tuesday.

2. Grundy spoke at Murfreesboro late in August 1834.

3. This letter appeared in the Murfreesboro *Monitor* on September 6, 1834.

4. John Hoover was an early resident of Rutherford County. In 1822, while Murfreesboro was the state capital, he was appointed by the legislature to a commission to supervise the building of a courthouse to replace the one recently burned. The name of Hoover's son has not been learned.

5. David W. Dickinson, referred to later in the letter as Davy. That Dickinson was Bell's brother-in-law and that Brady hoped to replace Dickinson in Congress perhaps account for Brady's apparent desire to connect his political fortunes with Polk's. Polk was warned later by John W. Childress that Brady could not be trusted. See Childress to Polk, December 20, 1834.

6. Probably John D. Fletcher who later represented Rutherford County in the state legislature for two terms. Afterward he moved to Franklin County, where he was again elected to the legislature.

7. A West Point graduate of 1832, Henderson Yoakum resigned his commission in 1833 and returned to Rutherford County. He was mayor of Murfreesboro, 1837–43, during which time he also served one term in the upper house of the state legislature, 1839–40. He moved to Texas in 1845, practiced law at Huntsville, served in the Mexican War, and in 1855 published a two-volume history of Texas. An ardent expansionist, he strongly supported Polk during his presidential administration.

FROM EPHRAIM BEANLAND

Dear Sir Near Summersville Oct the 14 1834

When we parted you sed that I had better sende olde man Charly and Loosy back to Maury which I have got a good chance to sende them by Rily Johnson.[1] I was to find him corne and foder which he got it heare and I thoughte it was beste to sende them on before the colde weather. Ande if he is pute to any trouble you will pay him for it. Loosy and the olde man Charly will note be of any servis heare and I sente them backe. I gave him as much corne and foder as he woulde cary and he comes 12 miles oute of his waye with them. You can settel it he cante aske much for his trouble. Please see Peter R Booker ande get him to bringe my bed from Goodrumes[?] for I am oblige to give the won aupe that I Have got. Please faill note to get my bed on Bookers wagon and sende it to me and I will be under lastinge obligations to you.

I am pickinge oute cotten slolly at this time. I thinke that I have got 18 or 20 Bailes but I have got 11 bailes made and my runingear has broke and I cante stop from pickeinge oute cotton ande my cotten is a opninge verry well indedde and I cante get it oute in time to go away for I muste go to Maury won time more. Any how if posiable when Bookers hands come downe I wante to go backe if posiable tho I will note leave heare undly when it is conveinante. I am willing to let it alf A goinge to the laste but I do ashore you that I mus come backe and see mother.

We ar all well at this time ande I donte thinke that I am half done pickinge oute cotten. I wolde like for you to by a place that has good warter if posiable. I thinke that Seasers wife will go yet with him if he woulde preswade hear a littel more.

E Beanland

Addressed to Columbia. This letter has been published in Bassett, *Plantation Overseer,* 82–83.

1. Unidentified.

FROM JOHN B. JOHNSON[1]

Dear Sir, Madisonville[2] [Mississippi] 14th Oct 1834

On Monday I arrived home safe but have been a little indisposed, too much so to ride out in pursuit of the information you desire but have made every enquiry that I could since I reach home. Lands are selling at from 10 to 15 Dollars, payments one third down (on paper that ought to command cash) and the other payable in one and two years. I cannot describe any farms in this neighborhood minutely but there are a great many for sale of various sises. The land in this neighbourhood is not considered first quality. Of the Madison Cty land as you have already learnd, the lands near Vernon & Livingston & Vernon are better but sell from 15 to 20 Dollars and they are considered much more sickly & scarce of water, but nearer to navigation. The nature of our business is such I find since I have returned that It would not be prudent or convenient for us to become partners of yrs in a farm for reason, Harvy[3] has purchased the sight for the mill and in fact I am moore pleased my self with the prospects of a steam saw mill since I examined one at Columbia than after I looked at Shelbys. There is considerable improvements since his was constructed.

I think your best plan would be to come to Miss. and if you are pleased you can purchase a farm on time if desired and have your business attended to. If you should settle near us we would take pleasure in rendering you any assistance in our power. Lands will continue to rise in my opinion and I believe all concur in the same opinion. Doct. Gillespie[4] purchased recently the sixteenth section near Cantion[Canton] at about Sixteen Dollars on long time, I think one 2 & three years perhaps longer. There is none of It cleared. It is said to be very good. What I have said cannot avail you much but I could doe no more if I wer to ride throe the county having conversed with men whose Judgement is better and who have had experience. Your had better come down.

JOHN B. JOHNSON

Addressed to Columbia.

1. This is the same person mentioned in Samuel P. Walker to Polk, November 13, 1833.

2. Madisonville was located in Madison County, Mississippi, as were the other places mentioned in the body of the letter: Vernon, Livingston, and Canton.

3. Harvey M. Walker, formerly of Columbia. See Samuel P. Walker to Polk, November 13, 1833.

4. Samuel A. Gillespie. See Gillespie to Polk, March 19, 1834, and William E. Gillespie to Polk, June 1, 1834. Gillespie had moved from Columbia to Mississippi about two years before.

FROM JOSEPH B. BOYD[1]

Jackson College Maury Cty Tenn

Hon Sir October 16th 1834

The object of this letter is to enquire of you whether or not there is a vacancy in this congressional district to send a student to West Point Academy and you being the representative of it, I thought you would be the proper person to enquire of; and being perfectly disposed to conform myself according to your instruction you cannot oblige me more than by communicating me whether or not there is a vacancy and what are the qualifications required of a youth before permitted in the insitution. In the mean time I am solaced with the hope of possesing your friendship.

Although very ignorant of the politicks of our country I am

sensible how beneficial you have been to it since my recolection.

I rely on your friendship to excuse the trouble of answering to this letter as I am under the necessity of calling for your information. I pray you to except assurances of my high veneration and esteem for your person and carecter.

JOSEPH B BOYD

Addressed to Columbia.

1. A son of Aaron Boyd of Chapel Hill, Tennessee. In 1835 Polk vigorously supported Joseph Boyd's appointment to the Military Academy. Boyd was graduated from West Point in 1839. He served in the Seminole War and later became a lawyer in Nashville.

TO WILLIAM R. RUCKER

My Dear Sir Columbia Oct. 16. 1834

Your esteemed favour of the 12th was received on yesterday, accompanied by a brief sketch of what Mr B.[1] is reported to have said in his late speech at Murfreesboro'. From your account of it, and that which I have received from other sources, the speech was a most extraordinary one, such indeed if the sketch contains an accurate synopsis, it places him clearly and unequivocally at issue with the policy of this administration, and as he has chosen from what you say, and from what I see contained in the sketch sent me, to make a thrust and indiscriminate attack on others, it is but justice that the true account of his speech should be published to the world. This I would think important. If it be published however, it can only be done with propriety in the first instance, at the place it was delivered. If it should be published at Murfreesboro, it would of course through that channel make its way to the public. The allusions to myself are indirect and by innuendo, and not such as probably I would be justified in noticing. When in my own judgment or in the opinion of my friends it is proper for me to come forth *I am prepared, fully prepared.* As to coming to Murfreesboro after Sarah I do not think it will be in my power. I doubt too the propriety of my going up voluntarily at this time and under the circumstances. Might it not look like volunteering were I to make a speech? Might it not be regarded as following him up, to answer him?

My opinions upon the great question of the Bank in any form in which it has or may present itself, are publickly known and I could have no objection to repeat them any where & every where, but my doubt is, as to the propriety of my visiting Murfreesboro' at this juncture. I do not doubt from any apprehensions I have, as to the consequences or effect on the public mind, which might be produced as to myself personally. I am armed with truth and a conscious rectitude of my own conduct, and am at the defiance[?] of those who have or may assail me, and this they will see if they ever do render it necessary for me to come forth in my own vindication. If they intend by what they say or do, to attack me I wish them to do it openly and not by insinuation and innuendo.

I am very sorry to hear that Mrs. Childress[2] is sick but hope she is not seriously so.

James K. Polk

Addressed to Murfreesboro. The letter is marked "Private."

1. John Bell.
2. Mother-in-law of Polk and Rucker.

FROM ANDREW BEAUMONT

My Dr Sir Wilkes Barre [Pennsylvania] Oct 17 1834

We have beat the Whigs otherwise Tories in our district by about 700 or 800 majority. It seems the Bank selected my district as the point of their most furious attack. They mustered all their powers of men & monies to crush me & bragged of a majority in my own county of 800 against me, but my friends gave me a majority over the Bank candidate (their most popular man Judge Shoemaker)[1] of upwards I believe of 300. I thought you would take a little interest in my fate & thus trouble you. We shall carry 18 out of the 28 of the Penna delegation. The question has been fairly put, Banks or no Bank. There has been no compromise as some of our men of easy virtue would have it last winter between *the* Bank & *a* Bank.

A Beaumont

Addressed to Columbia.

1. Charles Shoemaker. Not otherwise identified.

FROM ARCHIBALD YELL

My Dear Col Fayetteville Oct the 18th 1834

I wrote you a few weeks since, a letter informing you of a conspiracy which has been formed against you at Nashville, which letter I hope you have recived. I presume you are absent from home or I should have heard from you. My dear Sir those Nashville people are determined to sustain their party & put you down if money will do it. I have no doubt *Laughlin* has been managed out of the Banner and a more pliant *Bank man* selected & in less than 2 years Mr Bell and his whole pack will be out for *A Bank* of some description and as *Hall* intimates in his letters you will be displaced from the Head of the *Comt. of Ways & Means* if Bells reelected but how it is they are to bring you and the President to issue I cant concive. If they can do that then I shall not be longer amazed how it was that *Bell beat you.* They can do any thing!!

I shall leave here for the Territory on Tuesdy next & shall remain there until spring. I shall then Return & take my Family.

Judge Fulton writes me *Eskridge* will probably Resign in a few weeks so soon as he gets through his Circuit which will be about the 2d week in Nov. If I could be Nominated early this faul or winter to take effect the 4th March at which time Eskridges Term expires it would greatly accomodate me as I could then Return this winter & take my Family before the Courts in the spring. Otherwise I shall have to Remain until sometime in May before I could get off if I am appointed.

Judge Lacy wrote me he thought the Term expired the 4th March next. I shall leave this matter to your management at Washington tho. you will be much troubled this Winter.

I wish you to keep me informed of how things are progressing after your arrival at the City. You will be apprised[?] of my great anxiety to know the *Result* as early as possible. Write me to Fayettville Washington County A.T. I will write you again from Little Rock.

A. YELL

Addressed to Columbia.

FROM SAMUEL H. LAUGHLIN

My dear Sir, Nashville, Oct. 20, 1834

I wrote to you some weeks ago, in reply to your favor of the 11th ult. and informing you that imperious circumstances had made it my duty to put an end to my connexion with the Banner. Those circumstances were such (in part) as I did not conceive it to be my duty to lay them before the public. They were private. 1st. My contract expired about the middle of last month by its own (written) terms, and was only renewable in case of mutual agreement. 2d. The proprietors of the paper and myself had disagreed *toto calo*[1] on every important point of national policy which had become the subject of public discussion in the last twelve months—the deposites—Bank—Presidency &c. &c. as we disagreed about the previous questions of the several vetos &c. The truth is, Mr. Hunt cannot and does not approve of any of the prominent acts of the present Executive: he hates the President. Under these circumstances, we could not agree and my course was daily wormwood to his taste. He finally determined that he would rather run the risk of letting his paper go to the Devil, than see it stand up for the man he hated in his heart. He is also for McLean, and he is for *any man* before Van Buren, whom he hates more cordially than even the President. About the end of the year the Bell Controversy arose, and he and the other Bell (Bank) men here soon saw they had nothing to hope from me, although they were aware that I had excluded some severe peices written against that gentleman, and which were offered by responsible authors. Still they saw that a contest might arise in the District in the course of the next electioneering Campaign, and that I would adhere to my principles and political friends. Negociations were entered into. After consultation upon consultation, and casting about for an editor—a hand plant—in which Mr. Bell took a full share, Mr. Childress, a clever young enough in his way, was pitched upon, and Hunt, whom I had saved from ruin in a pecuniary point of view by procuring him about $5000 for public printing, but who was still upon the point of open insolvency, standing under protest &c. was *somehow* put in funds to settle with me and promptly pay up my salary at the end of my year. I was glad of this. For under the circumstances I was determined to be off several days before a final explanation took place. I saw what was at work. Childress was pitched upon because he has called himself and is called a Jackson man, and because by selecting him the Chief Justice,[2] whose brother-in-law he is, would be propitiated, and consent for me to withdraw. I withdrew at the end of the year, and only allowed it to be announced that my engagement had expired. I could not have renewed it if I had wished it, for I expressed such a wish to Hunt a month before, and I discovered as I believed, shortly afterwards—after he had *consulted*—that he had rather not. I did not intend it upon *any terms* unless I had the *sole* control of the paper under the advice of my own friends. Hunt and others wrote foolish articles in favor of the Bank. These I declined to publish, and that was another source of discontent. The Banner is now a prostitute, open to the embraces of all politicians of all parties, but is the peculiar mistress of the Bank and Bank men; and so I have quit her bed and board. Thus matters stand here with the Banner.

I am urged from various quarters to establish a paper. I have not the means even if I had the will to enter the arena. Two Journeymen printers here have issued a prospectus written by one of them and have obtained three hundred voluntary subscribers in a few weeks.[3] With this I have had nothing to do. There is here, however, an experienced printer, who is a tolerably efficient editor, who has had propositions made to him to buy the Republican. He is wholly unable to make the purchase, but some of our first men want him to make it, but they are men, who, though high in office (some of them) never advance any money to any body for any purpose, unless in the course of profitable trade. I have kept myself aloof—out of sight. The man I speak of is Long (formerly editor of the Sparta Law Journal) who is of excellent habits, and has energy and industry enough for any undertaking. I have put him upon finding out and feeling pulses in this business while I stay at home or out of town at my mother-in-laws. Some persons however sent for him and advised him to buy Hall out with whom I have had no connexion—Sam Smith[4] for instance. Hall will sell—must sell I take it, being very much embarrassed. But I have no money, and Long has no money, and, I think it likely we can get none. If I could raise the money, I would advance it to Long to purchase, and I would take the paper and devote my whole time, and all the little talents which God has bestowed upon me to its management as an editor, pay or no pay. Bell and the Bank men have placed me in a situation of collision with the publishers of the Whig compelling me to withdraw. Both papers now virtually belong to him and them. We—the people—the honest politicians of the Country have no metropolitan paper—of circulation all over the State—into which they can look for a fair expression of the sentiments of the great Jackson republican party; and this state of things has been brought about by the agency of a little money. Fletcher[5] has been a manager in it and I could name others of like stamp.

If I had some money, I could cause either the Republican to be purchased, or could cause the mortgages with which the Banner is shingled over, to be taken up, and force a control however reluctant (or sale) of that establishment.

Without the possession of one of these presses, or the control of one of them, the Presidential question, and the question of a *future* Bank will create great trouble here. Without one of them, or another paper here, Van cannot, I fear, carry this state. Besides they, as at present arranged, hold the lash over all our local politicians, and controul our local politics to an extent truly alarming.

For myself I do not seek any office. I write in haste as the mail is closing, and because I have been busy in court to-day.

Do you know why Childress who is ambitious and implacable, does not love Jackson, or his measures, say what he may? He was a pressing applicant for the office of District Attorney, when Collinsworth's term last expired, and is not of a nature to love the man who did not give it to him.

Now, Sir, if I could see you and Grundy and Johnson together as I did last summer, I would propose a plan—a feasible plan—to get one of these presses, that could not fail. I would have it before spring, and in operation—in full operation against all plotters, U. S. Bankites—State juntas—and corruption in all high places. But I cannot see you all.

As I have no secrets however with you, I will just say, that if our friends in Congress, New Yorkers &c. and other friends at Washington, would make contributions as loans so as to enable me to raise a sum that would buy Hall out at a low cash price—for so he will sell—I would come to Washington after the meeting of Congress & try the experiment. The Office shall be worth more than the sum paid for it and shall be bound for the repayment in time to a common trustee, or in any other manner deemed proper. In time and labor for the common cause, I will risk and pledge my time—my whole time if necessary—for the next three years. I wish to show the puny Banking drivellers here, that they can be beaten at their own game, and that the public will mingle contempt with the detestation in which good men already hold their miserable contrivances.

Altho I scribble in haste, what I write is upon the most mature reflection. I have expected a letter or I would have written you sooner. I have been in the country where I am trying to settle a little establishment so as hereafter to make my own pigs, turkeys, corn and potatos.

Let me hear from you. I will write to Johnson and to Fulton of Lincoln. Will you write to Inge. Whatever I do is confidential. Every thing here must be done by Long, if *I am the least suspected, no contract can be made. Hall will be paid not to sell, and will be indulged for his debts.*

The refusal to republish Lewis'[6] articles after I went out, was a dirty trick.

S. H. LAUGHLIN

P.S. I have written to Grundy.

Addressed to Columbia.

1. Diametrically, or by the whole extent of the heavens.

2. John Catron became chief justice of the state supreme court in 1831 and served until the position was changed under the constitution of 1834. Jackson appointed him to the United States Supreme Court in 1837.

3. This is perhaps the same prospectus that was mentioned in John W. Childress to Polk, September 18, 1834.

4. Samuel G. Smith and Laughlin did not see eye to eye on the proper procedure in trying to establish another paper to combat the Nashville press, which was believed to be completely under Bell's influence. Smith had little confidence in Laughlin because of his drinking habits. See Smith to Polk, September 20, November 20, December 18, and December 28, 1834.

5. Perhaps Thomas H. Fletcher.

6. Micajah G. Lewis of the Columbia *Observer*.

FROM JOHN H. DUNLAP

Paris, Tennessee. October 21, 1834

A Henry County lawyer reports that his brother, William C. Dunlap, has forwarded to him a small note on John W. Cooke,[1] payable to Polk. Cooke has disclaimed knowledge of any indebtedness to Polk, and the writer wishes to know what to do next.

Addressed to Columbia.

1. At this time Cooke was judge of the ninth circuit. It is possible that this small debt is related to the business affair of some years before between Cooke and Joel Childress. See William R. Rucker to Polk, August 26, 1828.

FROM ARCHIBALD YELL

Friend Polk. Memphis Oct the 21th 1834

I arived here to day in good health & shall on tomorrow cross ovr into Arkinses. I will write you again on my arrivel at the Rock & give you the prospect of help from the Territory.

Before I left home Frierson & Gilchrist Fulton & Cormack[1] promisd to write you letters to the President which you will forwrd or take them on yourself. I must again urge you to have the Nomination made as early in the Session as possible. If I am Nominated I shall expect to return to Tennessee for my Family so as to get back by the first Court the 1th Mondy in April. Should I be disappointed, the sooner I know it the better for me. You are apprised of the sacrifice I am now making by my absince—in a pecuniary [. . .] as well as absince from my Family.

I learn here that a *Union* has probibly taken place between the Govr Pope & Mr Crittenden—if so & the Territory is admited you may put down Arkinses as *Anti,* & 2 Bank Senators—in the persons of Pope & Crittenden; of the state of parties I will write you more fully from Little Rock.

I hope to hear from you often.

A. Yell

Addressed to Columbia.

1. Probably Erwin J. Frierson and William Gilchrist of Shelbyville, and James Fulton and Samuel W. Carmack of Fayetteville.

FROM EPHRAIM BEANLAND

Fayet county near Summersville Pleasante Grove
Dear Sir Plantation Oct the 23th 1834

On yesterday I received boath of yours and you wished me to pay parson Reaves for his boy Fill. He lefte hear sum time since to go to Columbia which I dyrected him to go to you ande you wolde pay him for his boy. And as for Seasers wife she sayes that she wonte leave hear master. So you neade note to weighte on hear. She has bin verry sick.

And as for Sillaman was to of sent his boy on sum time since and he has not done it and he was to of rote to me and he has not done it. And as for olde Mister More has not got downe yet. As soone as I get the notes that you have againste Silaman I will go and see him. I thinke that me and him can settle the matter with oute you to sue him. I [k]nowe that I can get a good trade in the boy and as for the woman I will attende to hear when I go over and also try and settle with him for the scrue and for the runin-gear for I do thinke that I can come as near the worth of it as any other man and I tolde him when he was hear that I wanted to settle with him and when I go I shall attende to the matter.

And as for my cotten has rotted rite smartely in the fielde but it will turne oute well I thinke. I have sente 15 bailes to Memphis and I will have oute 20 by Saterday nexte and if I was you I would take $2600 for your crop or not lower than $2500. If I was you I would note let A fieu dollars splite the trade. Is nowe wet and the cotten dose not open well since the froste and I cante get my crop oute in time if I donte let more healpe. I wante to geather my new grounde as soone as my waggon gets back from Memphis and as soone as I see Silaman I will let you nowe howe we trade. We ar all well.

Ephraim Beanland

Sell Dick to a negro trader if you please.

Addressed to Columbia.

FROM EPHRAIM BEANLAND

Near Sumersville Fayet County
Dear Sir October the 26th 1834

On yesterday I received yours and you wanted to [k]nowe wheather Fill and Dicy had caime on. They both got to the plantation on last Friday and they ar verry well satisfied and you wish to nowe wheather I was to pay the rewarde or not.[1] I was not. I was to give $600 and pay the Jaill feas. But as for the rewarde I had nothinge to do with it for I do ashore you that I would not pay it for Reaves may be ashor that if I had the payinge of it I would not do it for my bargin was to pay the Jaile feas and he was to make the bil of saile and as for the rewarde Reaves may pay it himself for it is a matter of impartance when I make a trade to make wan at a time. I am Astonished to thinke that would think that I would make such a bargin and donte you pay it a tawl for when I bought the boy Fill I was ofered $750 for him in wan hour after I hand bought him. So I thinke that Reaves juste co[u]ld as reasniable expect the $150 that I was ofered mor then I gave as for me to pay the reward. It is true that I have bin ofered $750 by 2 men for Fill but I tolde them that I bought the boy for you and I was preswaided to take $750 but I would not do no such a thinge because I wanted you to owne the boy and if you did not wante the boy I wold ceape him my seff for he co[u]ld be solde readily for $800 hear and as for Seasers wife she cante be got. I went yesterday and ofered Carter[2] $475 for Seasers wife and see[*sic*] is not willinge to go with you, so I tell Seaser that she dose not care any thinge for him and he sayes that is a fact. Govan[3] sayes that he would of give $800 dollars for Henry if he would of thought that Carter would of solde him so I thinke that we had beter go to negro tradinge. I have bin tryinge to trade the notes that I holde on Durem and on Biles[4] for a boy 15 yeares olde which it will be a good trade if I can and all of the notes is hear and I am agoinge to Sillimans to day and I am ancious to come to Maury I do ashore you. I shold like to nowe wheather you have a wagin acominge down a cristmust or not for I have 1000 pounds to corn[?] if I can make the arangements with you. We ar all well and I am sorry that I sente Casey and Charly aup. You said to send them the firste.

Dear Sir, I will see Silaman on this nite and amedetely I will let you nowe what we do and on laste Friday I was at the Doctors plantation and C C Jones will be in Maury on the 4 of nexte month and he has a negro girl for saile and I ast him if he would take his owne notes for the girle and he did not say and if you will minde you can get a good bargin and gave him his owne paper for the land that Gorge More solde him. If Booker will give you $1.25 per bariel for your [c]orn and gether it take it up in cash and on a credit of 12 monts. $1.75 if you geather it or if he will geather it you take $1.5[0] per bariel. I have made 18 bailes of coten. They has bin a goodeale of wet and if Booker I will give you $2500 for your crop take it. When you see the doctor give him my beste respects and tell him that I had as live go with him to the Missippi as any other man and I am ancious to nowe where I am a going. I wante my bed sente dwne by Bookers wagen. Olde mister More has brought all of your articles.

EPHRAIM BEANLAND

Addressed to Columbia. This letter has been published in Bassett, *Plantation Overseer*, 83–85.

1. This was probably a reward that had been offered for the return of Phil (Fill).

2. Archibald B. Carter, sometimes referred to as Burrus Carter.

3. Unidentified.

4. Polk held notes on Herbert Biles for $175 and on Col. Thomas Durham for $287.50. He had turned the notes over to Beanland for collection. Herbert Biles was Beanland's predecessor as Polk's overseer.

FROM STOCKLY DONELSON[1]

Dear Sir [Nashville] Oct. 28th 1834

Mr Lucius J. Polk is now with us & has conveyed to my sister Mrs. A J Donelson[2] the Information that you would leave Nashville in company with your Lady and family on Wednesday the 5 Nov & that you were kind enough to say you would be happy to take charge of Mrs Donelson, to go in company with your family to Washington &c. I have made arrangements to go with my sister to Washington & we have appointed the 4th Novr to leave Nashville &c. I should be very happy indeed if we could make arrangements to go on together, or if my services can be dispensed with, it will suit me much better. It will be necessary for my sister to take an accommodation stage at Nashville for Louisville if one can be had. If you would consent to this mode of travelling I have thought we could all go on together from Nashville. If however an accommodation stage can not be had, we will as matter of necessity take the stage at Nashville. In that event there would be no difficulty in making our arrangements to go together. In any event I would prefer going as far as Louisville with Mrs Donelson & family & as both parties would there take steam boats; if no other arrangement can be made perhaps from this point, if we can there agree to meet, Mrs Donelson would be less incumbrance to you as Maj Donelson expects to meet her on the road after she leaves the Ohio river. I name it in this way as I know Mrs Donelson would be unwilling to impose herself and family on your kindness to an unreasonable degree. As I am not much acquainted with the best mode of travelling I will submit to you to know whether any arrangement agreable to you can be made by which we can go in company or whether if you were relieved of the trouble until we reached Louisville it would suit for me then to Return. I should be happy to hear from you as soon as your convenience will allow.

STOCKLY DONELSON

Addressed to Columbia.

1. A son of John Donelson Jr. and a nephew of Rachel Jackson. He is not to be confused with the elder Stockly Donelson, who was Rachel Jackson's brother.

2. Emily Donelson had married her first cousin Andrew Jackson Donelson, the Major Donelson mentioned later in the letter.

FROM ARCHIBALD YELL

Friend Polk. Little Rock [Arkansas] October the 30th 1834

I am this far on my way to my New Home, Fayetteville Washington County, and it gives me pleasure to say that I am better sustained here even than I antisipated. I have forward to the President a Joint letter from Judge Johnson one of the Judges of the Superior Court, Fulton Secretary of the Territory, A.H. Sevier the Delegate which is more than I could expect.[1] Col James Conway,[2] Survey. Genl., Col Smith & Judge Crutchfield[3] both the Land offices at this place; Capt Jacob Brown[4] principle Superintendnt of Indian affirs, Liut Collins,[5] Col Wht. Rector[6] who you know; with lettrs from Judge Lacy, Gen'l Montgomery and many others as you will see, enough I should suppose to serve me, if the President has not changed his views. Judge Esk[r]idgs Term expires this Winter sometime not known when precisely; that will be known at the departmnt. I wish to bring my Family here this Winter if posible & I can not leave here until I here from the Nomination. If the President would make the Nomination early in the Session, I could have them on before the spring Courts (1th Mondy in Ap[r]il). Col Sevier is my perticular friend & I wish you to evince my frndshp for Him by your confernce with Him on my matters. I will again write you from Fayettevill A T. Col Sevier can give you all the news.

YELL

Addressed to Washington.

1. A letter dated October 29, 1834, in support of Yell's appointment and signed by several prominent Arkansas citizens is in Letters of Application and Recommendation, 1829–37 (RG 59), National Archives.

2. A member of a numerous and politically powerful Arkansas family, James S. Conway was surveyor general of the territory, 1832–36.

3. Peter T. Crutchfield was serving in the same land office with Bernard Smith. He had become the receiver of public money about a year earlier.

4. An officer in the United States Army who was later involved in some land sales of questionable legality.

5. Richard D. C. Collins went to Arkansas in 1831 as an agent of the Quartermaster General's Department to survey and supervise the opening of a road. He remained there for many years, working on various other roads and on several navigation projects.

6. Wharton Rector, a brother of Elias Rector, was at this time agent to the Creek Indians in the west.

FROM EPHRAIM BEANLAND

Dear Sir Near Summersville Novenber the 1 1834

On this instante I got your notes from C C Jones which I sende to you in this letter the 3 notes is $630[1] and I have geathered my newgrounde corn. They is 120 barels and if Booker is to geather your corn and gives you $1.25 per barel I think that is aboute fair for corne is a seller at $1.50 cents per bariel hear nowe and if Booker is to geather the corne you have don well. We have valied all of your property today and the D[r] Calwells yesterday and on tomorowe we will mach the negroes. And if you please have Wally and his wife sent with me and have Henry and Mariah and little Henry bef left at the Docters. I have made 20 bailes of cotten and I [t]hinke that my crop will turn oute well and I want the Docter to make the necesserry preperations and let us starte on in go[o]d time. If you can I wante you to hire Bookers hands to helpe pick out the cotten and let me get belowe in good time and I should like to [k]nowe where I am a getng to and Dear Sir I am ancious to get a good starte for I wante to make a good crop and on tomorowe I will go to Summersville[?]. I think that my chance is bad at this time to by a negro and I got $300 from Silaman to by a negro and I gave him the ballance of the notes and he was a goinge to see you and settle with you and I have got his receite for the notes. We ar all well.

EPHRAIM BEANLA[N]D

Addressed to Columbia.

1. See Adlai O. Harris to Polk, November 7, 1834. Beanland's letter apparently reached Columbia after Polk had left and was forwarded to Washington by Harris.

FROM WILLIAM K. HILL[1]

Dr Col. [Columbia] 2d Novr. 1834

I did not reach home until ten oclock last night. I have not seen Mr Slaughter[2] since our last interview but will do so in the course of one or two days, and if I do not procure a letter from him instructing you otherwise, I wish the appointment talked of secured for him.

I send you the note (herewith) for the hire of the negro woman.

The old note please leave with some friend and I will pay it off as soon as I return from Alabama to which place I shall go on Wednesday next and shall be absent Eight or ten days.

I will see you if I can as you cross the square this morning.

Wm K Hill

Dr Col.

Have you a negro woman to hire? If so I will give you a fair price for her in advance or Security that it shall be paid at the end of the term (as you may prefer).

Wm K Hill

Delivered by hand. There was no address on the envelope.

1. A Columbia merchant and farmer, Hill was secretary of the state senate almost continuously from 1829 to 1841. He also had been secretary of the constitutional convention of 1834.

2. Francis Slaughter, one of Hill's old friends and a resident of Maury County for many years, was under consideration for a consulship at some point on Galveston Bay. He received the appointment to San Jacinto just before the Texas Revolution. After the revolution he remained at the same post, accredited, of course, to Texas instead of to Mexico.

FROM SHERMAN PAGE[1]

My Dear Sir Unadilla [New York] 2 Nov. 1834

We are Buckling on our armour and like the spartans of old combing out hair & washing our hands & faces preparatory to the battle which commences tomorrow. If God is on our side & he ever has been we will give the Wigglery such a whipping that they will stay Whipped. A better spirit never pervaded the State of N. York than at this time. We feel certain of from 8 to 10 thousand for Marcy.[2]

Sherman Page

Addressed to Columbia and forwarded to Washington.

1. A lawyer in Otsego County, New York, Page had served in the state legislature before being elected to the United States House of Representatives, where he served 1833–37.

2. William L. Marcy was successful in his bid for re-election as governor of New York. He had served briefly in the United States Senate, 1831–32.

FROM WILLIAM GILCHRIST

Dr Sir Shelbyville Novr 3rd 1834

Enclosed I send you the letter of Recommendation for Col Yell to A. Jackson.[1] Please read it, & then seal it.

I would be glad to spend the evening with you, if convenient; other circumstances render it otherwise.

Please let me hear from your freequently from Washington & whatever occurs worth notice I will communicate.

WM. GILCHRIST

Delivered by hand.

1. See Yell to Polk, October 21, 1834. Gilchrist possibly refers to a letter to Jackson dated November 4, 1834, in support of Yell's appointment. It was signed by James McKisick, Erwin J. Frierson, Samuel Mitchell, and Gilchrist. That letter is in Letters of Application and Recommendation, 1829–37 (RG 59), National Archives.

FROM JAMES BROWN

Dear Sir November 4th 1834 Chickasaw Nation

I wrote you a short time since that I expected to buy a tract of land on Tillatoby[1] for you. I have since then examined the land and find it not to come up to the description given of it. I can enter land at goverment price that I would as leave have. I find it all most impossible to find a tract of land that would suite you, that can be bought, in fact such places are very scears & whin I find the body of land, I cant find the owner, and most generaly the good lands are owned in small parcels & by speculators that are non residents & have no agents in the country. I shall be at the land sales 1st Monday in December where it is likely I shall see the most of them & will I think be able to get a tract to my notion. I have bought a section & a half of land of a Chickasaw lying on the Yocknepetauphy[2] but the title to that is as yet uncertain but if I can get the title complete in time & I can do no better for you, I will let you have it so that you will be certain of a place. It is a most beautifull lying tract, has good water a handsome situation to build, a fine running, small creek on one line 500 acres of the 640 tilable that lies well, but it is not quite as rich as I should like to get for you tho it is good 2d rate. The groth is a variety of oak, hickory, dogwood, &c it is very handsome land, and very easey cleared. Hands to be on the place by 1st December could clear as much land by planting time as they could cultivate. It has two or three small cabins, & 20 acres of cleared land. When I have a place certain I will wright Beanland at Sommerville where it is, how to get to it &c. Corn will cost about 75 cents per bushel, there is plenty in the countery for sale. Hoping I shall get a place to suite my own views before I wright you again.

JAMES BROWN

NB. Sales of Chickasaw lands are not yet to be relyed on, as they have not yet got the certificates authorising them to trade nor have they yet got ther entrys made. I think about the 1st of December will bring about some certainty as to the lands. Speculation runns high. I have not been able to stand the prices offered for some of their lands. If I trade with them I must make a profit on the land. The 640 I bought cost $2000 the section. The ½ section not being located cost me $500. I think the trade I have made will be confirmed.

J. BROWN

Addressed to Columbia and forwarded to Washington.

1. Tillatoba is a small creek flowing into the Tallahatchie River.

2. A stream flowing a few miles south of Oxford, Mississippi, and emptying into the Tallahatchie River. This spelling varies only slightly from that of William Faulkner's fictitious county, Yoknapatawpha.

FROM ADLAI O. HARRIS

Dear Sir Columbia 7 Nov 1834

I recd. the Enclosed Letter from Beanland yesterday with the three notes of $210 each enclosed in it which I have taken out and put with my papers until you return.

Not finding any thing in it that I could attend to and expecting the Letter daily with the list of the Valuation, &c I concluded to enclose it to you.

I handed Gregory[1] yr note for the mule. The mule he says is at Dr Caldwells. Your Letter to Caldwell by yesterdays mail I had an opportunity of forwarding to him immediately after the mail came in.

I should like very much to hear frequently from you. Address me at this place until 5th Jany. after that until 20 Feby. at N Orleans.

A O HARRIS

Addressed to Washington.

1. Probably Thomas Gregory of Maury County from whom Polk had recently bought the slave woman, Dicey.

FROM MICAJAH BULLOCK

Lexington, Tennessee. November 8, 1834

Writing in behalf of William Gann of Perry County, an invalid pensioner who wishes to exchange the pension for a grant of land in Choctaw country, Bullock reminds Polk that Gann has previously spoken to him on the matter.

Addressed to Washington.

FROM ARCHIBALD YELL

My Dear Sir Fayetteville A T. Nov th 10th 1834

I wrote you a few lines by Col Sevier and now write you for fear he may not reach Washington before you may want by posibility some information in relation to my office as late Receiver of Public Moneys &c.

When I left the Territoy 2 years since I apponted a Deputy who paid ovr of Pub. Money to my successor Col Chambers[1] the sum of $350. which it seams Chambers nevr deposited to my Cridit & my deputy used $125 so that I am due the Govmt the sum of $475. I fortuntely met Capt Bradford of Lexington Ky the Brother of Mrs Chambers & the Executor of the estate who promptely adjusted the account & I paid him the balence $125 cash, all of which he is to deposite at Louisville to my Cridit & has given me a Recept for that amount which will more than square me with the Govmt. From his Character I have no fear of his doing so if no accident befall him on the way. He was also apprised of the impotence to me of the Deposite, and is my frind & will no doubt attend to it promptly. But my Dear Sir if that matter eithr though nigligence or misfortune should not be adjusted do not let that be an obstacle. Advance the mony & you shall be repaid on *Notice.* Col Sever can inform you all about it. Please give this information to Mers. *Grundy & White* so that the matter may be adjusted before the senaters makes a *final blow*. I give you this information for fear of some *mishap*. Attend to it for me thoughout this matter; you are constituted my true and lawful attorney to do all things according to your own judgmt as if I was personally present, requesting a friendly confidence & cooperation with my frind *Col Sevier*. You will see from the recommendation forwarded to you or the Presidnt by my frind Judge Fulton, that all things here are *easy* & to my astonishmt found Col Sevier one of my warm frind & signed the recommendations.

Judge Eskridge I fear will not apprise the Presidnt that he will remove this winter, in time to let me hear the result & go to Tennessee & return before the courts commence the (1th Monday in Apil). Its now said he will not resign as was expected but will hold on until the end of his Term the 4th of March I believe, but without any wish or expectation of a reappointent. Indeed being He could not get 5 membrs of the Bar in the Territy & perhaps not one in His Circuit to recommend Him for a reappointent; this He knows and will not apply. Col Sever tells me there will be no applicant from the Territory. I did expect *Roan*[2] would have been thro Col Sever, but he is no otherwise enguaged & *Roan* can not get a Nomination so that all things here are as safe & easy as I wish them; you & the President & the *Senater* for the balince.

I found hear on my arrival grately to my astonishmt all partis willing to receive me; even Governer [John] Popee seamed disposed to be frindly. I did not ask the Govenor to interest himself for me because I believe his *name* would have but little influence at this time with the President, and as I thought it quitee likly He would find difficulty enough withe His own case this Winter as it is generally beleived Here as well as *desired* that He should not be Reappointed, the reasons varies according to the Local Parties here—the Sevĕr or Jackson men because he is a whole Hogg Bank man in every shape & no very grate Jackson man, according to my standard. The Crittenden Party because they hate him personally & he has heretofore made war on them. There is a 3d Party here if it ought to be dignified with the name of Party, headed by Govenr Pope in person. Around Him he has a few relations & a few of the disapponted of both the other partis. He is too weak & unpopular to form a strong party but he may pull down & weaken the Jackson party. That He may do to a grater extent than I now imagine, as he has a Press at Command and is himself a man of Talents & will put his shouldr to the wheel. He has now nothing to make by looking back. He will not be received in the ranks of his formr frinds.

If we go into a state govert this Winter, it would be a matter of some doubt whether he ought to be discontinued but if we do not form a state govrmt for a few years to come then I should have no hesitation in determing what would be the policy for the Party.

If Fulton could succeed Him the people would be sattisfyed. He has been long in the Territory & is popular, but if some Man was sent Here from abroad who would not go into politicks with a view to a state govemt & to support the anti Bank Measures of the Admtration he would do us but little good & might weaken our party. Under present existing circumstances Govr Pope might be less dangerous, as there are many of the Bank Crittenden men who never will recognize Pope as their Head. *A Modest Stranger* they might, to effect thir designs. I am giving you a long letter about things that do not interest you. How do you and *Bell* get along? Write me often. . . .

A. YELL

Addressed to Washington.

1. Benjamin S. Chambers had died on October 13, 1833.

2. Samuel C. Roane.

FROM STEPHEN ADAMS

Dear Sir, Athens Mississippi 11th Nov. 1834

I have become a citzen of this place and must ask a favor of you. You will recollect that under the late amended Treaty with the Chickesaw Indians, the President was to appoint an additional clerk; situated as I am, I would be glad to receive the appointment and as I have not the pleasure of a personal acquaintance with the President I would take it as a favor, if you would write to Genrl. Jackson upon the subject.

This end of Mississippi is opposed to nullification, & in favor of Jackson. I have no doubt Mr. Poindexter will be beaten and Mr Black invited to resign.[1] The convention in this State, have nominated Mr. Van Buren for President, & Benton Vice President. If the Democratic party run them, they will receive the vote of this State. Although the role of this State is small at present it will not be so long. I believe this state is growing faster in wealth & population than any other in the union.

I would be much pleased to hear from you.

STEPHEN ADAMS

Addressed to Columbia and forwarded to Washington.

1. George Poindexter and John Black were Mississippi's senators at this time.

FROM JOHN H. DUNLAP

Dear Sir Paris Ten Nov 11th 34

I take it from your letter that unless you have some certainty of getting your money this winter that you wish a note enclosed on John W. Cooke collected. Understanding you thus I have deemed it advisable to bring suit which will be the only means of enabling you in my opinion to get hold of the money. I fear your land will be dull sale however I will endeavour to sell it for the best possible price. I should be pleased at any convenient time to hear from you during the winter.

JOHN H DUNLAP

Addressed to Washington.

FROM JOSEPH THOMPSON

Livingston, Alabama. November 11, 1834

Thompson again seeks Polk's help in obtaining appointment as postmaster.[1]

Addressed to Columbia and forwarded to Washington.

1. See Thompson to Polk, September 18, 1834.

FROM ADLAI O. HARRIS

Dear Sir Columbia 15 Nov 1834

I recd this[1] to day and being very anxious to see the price that your cotton sold for have taken the liberty of opening it. The market will should no doubt continue at about present rates for some time. Dr Caldwell left here on Tuesday morning with *all hands* not forgetting Abe & old Will. All our folks here are in good health.

A O Harris

Addressed to Washington.

1. The enclosure was information about Polk's cotton that had been sold by Caruthers, Harris & Company of New Orleans. While Harris was a member of that firm, he was at this time in Columbia.

FROM ALBERT M. LEA

Dear Sir, St. Louis Nov. 15, 1834

There is a captaincy vacant in the Topographical Engineers. It is the custom to fill those vacancies from the subalterns of the Line. I take the liberty to ask you to do any thing you may think proper to procure the promotion for me. Could I get this situation it might assist me much in those views of Internal Improvement in Tennessee, which have so long been the subject of my thoughts & studies. There can be no objection to my promotion, except on the ground of fitness; in relation to that others can give you better information than myself. My recent promotion in the Dragoons[1] shd. be no bar to my promotion in the Top. Engineers, for the former was thrust upon me, and though an honorable & a responsible service, is not that for which I am best suited. I do honestly think that I could do the country much more service as an Engineer.[2]

I would not have troubled you with this had it not been for the fact, that Officers on the outposts are generally overlooked, when promotions of this kind are to be made.

My respd. complt to Mrs. Polk.

A. M. Lea of Tenn.
2d. Lt. Dragoons.

Addressed to Washington.

1. The promotion consisted of being raised from a brevet to a permanent rank as a lieutenant in the Dragoons.

2. This appointment did not come through, and Lea soon resigned his commission and returned to Tennessee, where he pursued a career in engineering.

FROM HENDERSON WHITE[1]

Jackson Arkansas Territory

Dear Sir November 15th 1834

Waving the necessity of any formal apology permit me to trouble your kindness with a few lines. The nature of this communication requres candour and frankness and I am sorry your knowledge of me is limited. I am informed that the office of Receiver of Public monies at Batesville is or will soon be vacant. If it is congenial with your feelings I wish your influence in my favour for that *office.* If so I request you to see Col A. H. Sevier who I think is partial tward me and who will develop the matter to you and who will give you a history of my reputation in Ark. which I hope together with your knowledge of my parents in Giles Co. & me will justify you in using your influence with the Executive in my favour. A few evenings before I left Columbia I had an interview with you—in which you kindly offered to aid me in Arkansas by giving me letters of Introduction to Judge Fulton &c. I have always been a devoted friend to your and the present Executive and I rely much on your influence with the Executive and if you will exercise your influence in my favour it will be duly appreciated by your friend and humble servant. You must not think me an Egotist or vain when I tell you my partiality for you is instinct and intuitive in me representing the district and state of my nativity and my influence which is not very feeble in Ark. has been exercised to sustain you among the dissenting part not from feeling alone but from principal & a due regard for your merit.

If it is not requiring to much of your kindness write to me after examining this matter. I shall be well recommend by some prominent men in Arkansas, to Bell & Dickinson from Ten.

HENDERSON WHITE

Addressed to Washington.

1. Except for the information contained in his letter, White is unknown.

FROM JOSEPH THOMPSON

Livingston, Alabama. November 18, [1834][1]

The writer has received Polk's letter advising him how to proceed in seeking appointment as postmaster but still fears that the incumbent will be able to pass the office to another.

Addressed to Washington.

1. The Library of Congress lists this as an undated letter. The date was supplied on evidence contained in other correspondence. See Thompson to Polk, September 18 and November 11, 1834.

FROM WILLIAM BRADY

My dear Sir Murfreesboro 20th Nov 1834

Our mutual friends Daniel Bowman Esqr and Benjamin Bowman[1] his son wish to subscribe for the Weekley Globe or the Congressional Globe—I mean the Globe which Blair published at $1 pr week. Will you please have it forwarded to Messrs Daniel and Benjamin Bowman, directed to this place? They have paid me $1 for a Twelve months subscription, which I will hand you on sight. Therefore I would ask you to pay Mr Blair and Reeves[2] for the paper and I will refund. They wish your early attention to this business as they wish to see the Presidents Message and other public documents and they are concerned to see how Mr Speaker Bell diportments himself.

I regret that I did not see you before your departure for the City. I did not get your letter, until I returned from Franklin or I should have availed myself the pleasure of a ride with you, as proposed. I was satisfied with my prospect in Williamson, in my sojourn there and I am induced to believe that D______[3] will not run and that Foster[4] will enter the list. I saw and talked with William G. Childress and I think he will not disturb me. It is not the wish of his friends that he should do so, either in Williamson, or here. If there shall be no conflict amongst us, who hold the same views and look to the same results, there will be no question of the result.

I saw the second Auditor in Franklin. He was in attendance upon the *Governor* of *Florida.*[5]

Speaker Bell was not cordially recd. in the Town of Franklin —as I was told by Olmsted,[6] Childress and others—and was permitted to pass without ceremony, while he trained[?] with his old friends and acquaintances in Williamson.

We hail the coming shadows, or rather light, from New York &c and we think we see in the signs of the times that the Administration will be triumphantly sustained.

I write you while business is transacting in Court and therefore badly.

WM BRADY

Esqr Bowman sends his respects to you.

Addressed to Washington.

1. The Bowman family had lived in Rutherford County for many years, and its members were known personally by Polk. Little has been learned about Benjamin Bowman.

2. John C. Rives was Blair's partner in the management of the Washington *Globe* from 1833 to 1849. Rives reported debates in the *Congressional Globe* from 1833 until his death in 1864.

3. David W. Dickinson.

4. Robert C. Foster Jr.

5. William B. Lewis, Second Auditor, and John H. Eaton, Governor of Florida.

6. This possibly is the Charles G. Olmsted who moved about four years later to Columbus, Mississippi, where he practiced law. In 1833 Olmsted made an unsuccessful bid for the congressional seat of the district of Rutherford and Williamson counties.

FROM SAMUEL G. SMITH

Dear Sir Nashville Novr 20 1834

Your favour of the 12th came this evening. I assure you the delay in writing until this late period has been with a view to ascertain if any thing definite should be done upon the subject of our late conversation. As I anticipated the whole negotiation then on foot for one of the existing establishments failed. I was called upon by the gentlemen proposing to purchase to know if I would act as trustee in the terms to which I assented provided the application was joint from debtor and creditor. At the same time I informed him nothing would be done.

It ultimately turned out that my opinions were well founded. I need only say to you that I am informed he made an offer of $1000 more than was first asked with more prompt payments. The next information I had the establishment was transfered and before the receipt of this you will have seen the debut of the present proprietor. In some few days afterward the gentlemen who had been proposing to purchase called upon me and stated the determination to put an establishment in operation. It seem to be the understanding that L. . g as publisher and L . n as editor[1] were to constitute the association and they were resolved upon making an effort. They stated to me their poverty and a want of aid to put it in operation and asked for assistance.

Taking every thing into consideration; the conversation one of them had with you, the other having married into family connection for whom I had at all times entertained feelings of strong partiality I agreed to render them some assistance and will advise your friend at the proper time what is necessary.

I have been particular to have it understood that this is to be upon the footing of assistance as any other enterprise. This I considered necessary that the establishment might as it should be independent. I am informed their arrangements are for Ln to go on to Washington in a few days, while there prepare his prospectus and that L. . g would meet him at Cincinatti by the first of January to purchase materials. I must confess to you I am not free from apprehension of difficulty. You are aware of the want of steady habits and the charge of subserviency has been urged against him in his former career. That he was subjected to inconsistency upon the Bank question cannot be denied; his own admissions prove it. We must however take into consideration his peculiar situation and allow for the frailties of human nature. I was flattered with a hope that a man of his former character for discriminating intelect and correct intentions will appear[?].

I have repeated to him frequently that the friendship contemplated is amply sufficient to put in operation and with proper attention continue the establishment. He informs me that Mr Bass[2] is in his confidence and proposes if necessary he will come forward and aid in February. This still weakened my confidence. You will perceive he is making friends & confidents without any obligation to aid him and free from any identity in case of difficulty. If he is to sustain the Bank of which *Mr.* B. is president and then as a matter of course to sustain Mr Grundy or thrown into his hands, what will we have done? Will we have aided to sustain the true republican doctrines or placed a press at the disposal of a Monied corporation very odius to the community, charged with extravagant extorsions upon the business & prosperity of the country, and wielded by a single politician who can if so inclined when he pleases stand off and say his hands do not appear in the matter. I estimate these gentlemen for their full merit and with the best feelings for them, but I cannot sanction any step to put this press in a situation to be tramaled and liable to be used for men & not principal. It is within the range of possibility, for the most patriotic & virtuous man to go astray but well settled principals of justice and equal rights are as immutable as the decrees of Heaven. If under the influence of a monied power and subject to be reached by a skilful and well trained politit, high in power it may be the means of such mischief in promulgating false doctrines. I have a great contempt for the dwarfish editorial paragraphs spouting the praise of many favorites or show of liberality in a corporation clothed with exclusive privilege.

The power of the government designed to place the power in the hands of the people upon the principle of equal rights have every species of favorritizm is a departure from & violation of its purity & good faith. Professions of partiality for men of a party amount to nothing; it is the principal to be advocated and every thing like sham and evasions to be exposed. Truth, honesty & correct views and nothing short can stand the scrutiny of time.

If Mr Grundy &c are to understand matters let their hands be tied by identity and aid in undoing in the commencement. Let them hail their profession of friendship to the liberties of the people and sound doctrine, not to be severed at will or changed by vearing from the correct principals. Nor should any one be screened behind a curtain which cannot be hoisted should a bold effort be necessary to put in [. . .] all the aid for the country.

You cannot impress upon him too strongly the great importance of steady habits, firmness of purpose, an independent, fearless & honest adhearence to truth & consistency, an unqualified support of all such measures as tend to sustain the true republican principals upon which the national government should be administered; the right of the individual states not parted with by the [. . .] of the Constitution; and the best interests of the people of Tennessee. A departure from or evasion of these important duties must inevitably and justly weaken confidence and inspire the public mind with more indignant feeling for the servelance[?] of the press than the prevalent corrupt measures of a maladministration. We have an example of firmness integrity and patriotic devotion in our venerable chief magistrate worthy of imatation in all avocations.

A consciousness of his rectitude contributes to the energy & strength of his effort which seldom fails to crown them with success.

You will see him as soon as possible upon his arrival and have the first interview.

Take nothing upon trust or fair promise until your mind is satisfied of the correct motive, and guard against too few communications. I presume Messrs Johnson, Inge and Standifer are your friends but disclosures need not be made to scarcly any one. In the extreme East I know not how the delegation stands to our matters. In the extreme *west,* things may exist in future which would make it *impolitic* to communicate to this *delegation* there particularly as no immediate aid can be expected. The crude suggestions I have thrown out are not intended to dictate or instruct. I hope not to be guilty of such arogance but they may lead you to reflection upon the subject and guard against difficulties in future. I have no object in view but the support of sound political doctrines and the prosperity of our country and in these devotions I acknowledge no superior. I expect to hear from you frequently & in the mean time you shall be advised of what is the current of times in the State.

SAM. G SMITH

Addressed to Washington. The letter is marked "Confidential."

1. This is an obvious reference to Medicus A. Long and Samuel H. Laughlin and to their plans to start a newspaper in Nashville.

2. It should be remembered that John M. Bass was a son-in-law of Felix Grundy.

FROM CARUTHERS, HARRIS & COMPANY

Dear Sir N Orleans Nov 21st 1834

We hand you annexed, sales of Ten Bales Cotton received for your account the proceeds of which we hold subject to your order at any time you choose to command them.[1] The cotton market continues to experience a very animated demand and the sales of the week have been nearly equal in amount to the stock on sale, at an improvement generally of fully a half cent over the price of the previous week, and perhaps more on very fine and choice cotton.

The receipts of cotton up to this time are 91.869 bales against 90.770 bales at the same period last year, and from all we can learn of the crop coming forward we do not think that the total receipts of the season at this port will greatly exceed those of last year, and look with some confidence to a steady support of present prices.

CARUTHERS HARRIS & Co

Addressed to Washington.

1. The enclosure has been found. The net proceeds from the ten bales amounted to slightly more than $600.

FROM SILAS M. CALDWELL

Dr. Sir Bolivar Nov. 25h. 1834

I was at your plantation a few days since. Beanland has made 28 Bales, 25 of them are at Memphis. He thinks he has 10 or 12 more to pick out. Bookers hands has not yet got down. Beanland has been to see [Thomas] Durham But got no money and says he cant pay the money before next March. He is going to move this winter to Mississipi. [Herbert] Biles paid me fifty dollars and says he will pay me by Christmas fifty more. The Balance he will pay in the spring when you return and make him the *Deed*. I have paid Beanland his wages 350 Dollars. He starts to Maury next Sunday. I have given him Sillamans notes and directed him what to do with them. I saw Bills as I passed through Bolivar going down. He had seen James Brown a few days before. Brown had Bot. a tract of Land in the Chicasaw nation of 900 Acres fine lying land but thin Land. Bills could not learn from Brown whether it was for us or not. From what I could understand from Bills if we got it it would be at a considerable advance. I have not received a word from Brown on the subject. I am on my way to Chocchuma to see Brown. I have no idea that Brown will Buy land for us. I expect to buy myself. The fact is I have no confidence in Brown. I expect if he should Buy for us we would have to pay him well for it. If he has not Bot when I see him I will get the money and depend on Buying myself. Beanland has not Bot. any negroes for you. I am not able to tell you when we will start with the hands to Mississippi. It is uncertain how long it will take me to procure the land But as soon as we can get ready I will go. I got down very well with the negroes & stock. Charles, Lucy & Abram I sent to Beanland immediately. As soon as I make a purchase of a farm I will write you fully on the subject and at what time we will start.

Write to me as soon as you receive this to *Somerville*.

S M Caldwell

Addressed to Washington.

FROM BENJAMIN F. CURREY

Sir Head of Coosa Ga Nov 25 1834

Mr. [John] Ridge who bears this communication is one of the Cherokee chiefs. He goes to the city with five other Delegats to open the road & make the way plain for the salvation of his people. By a resort to the original source of all political power he goes clothed with plenary authority.

Another Delegation also goes on headed by Jno Ross.[1] Theirs is an usurped authority holding themselves up as chiefs by resolutions &c after the Constitutional period for which they were elected has expired. Mr Ridge will satisfy you of every important particular connected with their unhappy condition here. Do afford him every facility in your power & confer an eternal obligation on them as well as on your friend. . . .

BEN F. CURREY

Delivered by hand.

1. Ridge and Ross represented two points of view among the Cherokees. Ridge was prepared to negotiate for removal, but Ross was demanding a large payment for Cherokee lands before consenting to final removal. In 1835 Ridge signed a treaty under which Cherokee lands were ceded. Eventually Ross relented and led his people into Oklahoma, where he was instrumental in reuniting the two branches of the tribe. He served as chief of the Cherokee Nation from 1839 until his death in 1866.

FROM WILLIAM BRADY

Dr Sir Murfreesboro 29th Nov. 1834

One of Mr Bell's Editors in Nashville, having published a denial (no doubt by authority) of the correctness of the report of his speech at this place; it was thought best to republish the speech, as given by the Editor of the Monitor, *and the By-stander;*[1] with suitable remarks upon the denial. This was done at some inconvenience, as the Monitor had ceased to exist. I send you a copy and the correctness of the report can be proven by a hundred living witnesses. It is in vain for Mr Bell or his friends to deny the *scope* of his speech; and we should not have heard of such denial, if it had been received favorably at the City of Washington. But, the notes of disapprobation, which saluted him from that quarter, awoke the Speaker from his slumbers and then nothing would do but denial. And he would [. . .] out the *damd. spot*—if sensoring would obliterate it from the memory of the world. The speech as reported by the *By-Stander,* was so favorably received on its first appearance, that it was said to be reported by the Speaker himself, or some devoted friend—and His *Honor* Judge Mitchell[2] was pointed to as that friend. None doubted its accuracy but those who disapproved of all that Mr Bell said and they asserted that it was a milder form than delivered by the Speaker.

My prospects at home for a seat in the next Congress of the U S is daily brightening—and whether it be D______ or Robert C______[3] the people of Rutherford will give a good account of them. If W. G. Childress will hands off—then I know what's *what*.

Doct Rucker is now absent in the State of Mississippi and Maj John W C______[4] in the State Alabama—tho' all well at home.

I have written to the chairman of the Senates Post Offices committee,[5] *Twice, Thrice* in relation to William G. Parrish's claims, against the Gnl Post office department. Will he neglect it and suffer Dickinson to take from me an important friend by claiming superior dilligence? I hope not. Will you speak to Senator Grundy about the matter for me—he will understand it.

Carroll is not yet out and is still wrestling with the rheumatism. Graham[6] has gone down, and will have an interview with his excellency and urge him to action.

WM BRADY

Addressed to Washington and marked "Private."

1. This appears to be the account written by Brady himself. It appeared in the *Monitor* on October 18, 1834.
2. Probably James C. Mitchell, a former congressman, who was judge of the eleventh circuit, 1830–36. In 1837 he moved to Hinds County, Mississippi.
3. David W. Dickinson and Robert C. Foster Jr.
4. John W. Childress. See Childress to Polk, December 20, 1834.
5. Felix Grundy.
6. Probably Daniel Graham of Murfreesboro, a former secretary of state for Tennessee. Later he was state comptroller.

FROM HARVEY M. WATTERSON

Dear Sir. Beech Grove [Bedford County] Nov. 29 1834

Enclosed you will find ten dollars, which you will be so good, as to pay over to Duff Green for my subscription to U S Telegraph, and say to him, that I wish it discontinued at the close of the present year.

Since I saw you in Columbia, I have taken a tour through the State of Mississippi. I was in the town of Jackson during the sitting of the late Democratic Convention, and also made many enquires in various parts of the country, in regard to the feelings of the people towards the Administration, and from what I learned, I am well satisfied that an overwhelming majority are its friends. Poindexter is certain of defeat. This seems to be admitted there by his own party. I was a good deal amused at the closing remarks of a Speech of a member of the Convention. Said he Black ought to be censured—Cage ought to be censured—and Poindexter ought to d——m'd.[1]

Politics apart. I bought a farm in Yazoo county, and calculate upon removing about the 25th Dec. I shall, however, spend 3 or 4 months of the year in this county—from the 1st June to the 15th Sept. I presume you have a good many acquaintances in Mississippi. If so, it would afford me much pleasure to bear letters of introduction to them from you. Should you find it convenient and agreeable to comply with this wish on my part, you can direct the letters to Clinton or Vernon, Miss, where I will be certain to receive them. I would like to become acquainted not only with the politicians of the state but with men of business. Perhaps you know personally some of the following named gentlemen, To wit, Gov Reynolds[Runnels], Gen Hinds, H. S Foote Esq, George R Fall Esq, Robert J. Walker, Esq., Hon Daniel W Wright, Col. J F H Claiborne, R M Williamson Esq Dr Wm L Balfour &c. &c.[2]

No news of consequence in this county at present. The political waters are unagitated. Every thing is perfectly still. Please accept an apoligy for the length of this letter, and also assurances of my friendship.

H M Watterson

N.B. Since writing this letter I discover that I have written the 2d page upon the wrong side.

H M W

Addressed to Washington.

1. John Black, Harry Cage, and George Poindexter, all anti-Jackson, were three members of Mississippi's four-man delegation in Congress.

2. Men of prominence in political affairs of Mississippi. Hiram Runnels, Thomas Hinds, Henry S. Foote, Robert J. Walker, and John F. H. Claiborne

had at one time or another held state or federal posts. Fall was editor of a Jackson newspaper, the *Mississippian.* Wright was a distinguished lawyer and judge. Little is known of Balfour except that he was an early settler in Madison County.

FROM JAMES WALKER

Dear Sir, Columbia Dec 1st 1834

I returned home a few days ago, found all well, except Maria,[1] who had been indisposed one or two days from cold. She may be said now to be well.

I was much surprised at Jackson [Tennessee], on receiving from Samuel[2] a copy of the letter of the Post office Dept. advising us of complaints and censuring us. The truth is, that our line is and has always been in first rate condition, and all our mails have been delivered with the most perfect regularity. What more do they want? We have run it in first rate New York post Coaches, and given a comfort & facility to the travel hitherto unknown. Still we have "disappointed the hopes of the Department." We never promised that the friends of John Donly and John Bell, would do us justice, and if the Department is to frown on us until this description of persons become our admirers, we have but little hope of becoming favorites, or even giving the ordinary satisfaction.

I have forwarded to Col. Gardner certificates from the acting Post Masters at Natchez, Jackson, Columbus & Florence, showing the regular delivery of the mails at those offices since we took charge of it and also a letter from Gov. Reynolds, Genl Hinds, Judge Wright, Col Williams[3] and other distinguished Jackson men of Mississippi, certifying that our performance was highly satisfactory to them & to the people of Miss.

If we had made failures, I should have suffered it the duty of the PM. at the office where the mail was due to have reported it and we should have been advised of the time and place where we had failed. Instead of this we are informed, that complaint has been made from Nashville censured, lectured and asked if we can comply with our contract &c.

I have replied to Col. Gardner as I think I ought to have done. You can see my letters on application to him.

This is a troublesome arduous & vexatious business, and attended with much risque. I think it probable I can employ my time, and money to as much profit otherwise, and enjoy more personal ease and happiness. I would prefer a separation from the P.O Dept. to a continued quarrel & distrust. My pride is gratified, and I am now confident that the public will do us full justice, in any question that may arise on this matter. I should be much pleased to understand what is the feeling in the P O Dept. in relation to us, and if there is a probability of a continued controversy, and want of confidence, it would be agreeable to me *individually* to make terms of separation.

I am willing however to comply with our contract & have always expected to be held to a strict performance of duty. *We have strictly performed our duty,* without [. . .] to ourselves & to the Post office Dept, and greatly to the public interest.

We have received *no pay* for services performed since the 1st of January. I will write you tomorrow on this subject.

JAMES WALKER

This letter was enclosed with Walker's letter to Polk, December 2, 1834. A note on the envelope said that this was a part of the mail which was taken in a robbery on December 9 and that it was not received in Washington until February 27, 1835.

1. Jane Maria, Walker's wife.

2. Samuel Polk Walker, James Walker's oldest son.

3. Thomas Hinds and Daniel W. Wright are doubtless two of the men to whom Walker referred. The third, Reynolds, was probably Hiram G. Runnels; there was no governor named Reynolds. The fourth name, Williams, could have been any one of several persons by that name who were politically prominent in Mississippi at this time.

FROM JAMES HAYS WALKER[1]

Dear Uncle New Haven Connecticut Dec 2d 1834

I did not write to you on Saturday as I had anticipated for the reason that we had not then every thing fixed; but I can say now that we are as well fixed as we could wish to be. We are still boarding at commons, and do not find it so uncomfortable as we had reason to expect. We have received all the furniture which you purchased for us and now room very comfortably.

Saml and William[2] are still reciting to Mr. Davenport and still think that they will be able to enter the class in a week or two without difficulty. Knox[3] and myself are still reciting with the Freshman class, and find that we have men of talent to contend with and that we will have to study hard to hold any sorte of pole with them. Farewell.

J H WALKER

Addressed to Washington.

1. The second son of James Walker.

2. This is a reference to Samuel W. Polk, youngest brother of James K. Polk, and William F. Cooper, a son of Matthew D. Cooper of Columbia. William F. Cooper became one of the most distinguished jurists of the state, serving on the state supreme court and also helping to digest and revise the general statutes of Tennessee.

3. Joseph Knox Walker, younger brother of the writer of this letter.

FROM JAMES WALKER

Dr Sir Columbia Dec. 2d 1834

We have received no pay from the post office Department for services rendered since the 1st of January last, nor has the Department thought proper to forward our contract for execution. What is the cause of this delay I know not.[1] It is unreasonable to suppose that we can get on under the heavy expenditures which our extensive & expensive lines renders necessary unless some mail pay is sent us. I suppose that Walker & Brown is entitled for transporting on one half the road from Nashville to Tuscumbia from 1st Jan. to 9th June at the rates of $4200 pr. annum, one half pay $933.33/100

Whole pay for 21 days or ⅔d month 233.33

Donly had 3 Teams on the road from 9th to 17th June for which he is entitled to about $22 which we can pay to him or let the Dept retain it for him.

One half pay from Columbia to Huntsville

at $2300 pr. annum from 1st Jan. to 1st July	$575.00
	1744.66
Draft returned by James Walker & Co. (same as Walker & Brown) or J R Smith & D Fentress[2] in June last	24.15
	1768.81

This is what I suppose we are entitled to but I am not certain.[3] The contracts were originally taken at lower rates, but in the compromise of the controversies, that arose, the rates were finally fixed at the rates I have estimated at, and I suppose that Donly and us are entitled to pay at the rates finally agreed on. If Caruthers is still at Washington, please to show him this letter, and get him to urge the settlement and payment of Walker & Brown's a/c. If this account was adjusted and I could receive an authority to draw for it in favor of Samuel[4] in February next, it would answer my purposes as I have advanced the money for W & B and the use I have for it is in Philadelphia, when Sam'l goes on[?].

We have drawn some drafts for Coaches & in payment for Donly's property, which were due 15th ulto. which I hope the Department have paid, and forwarded to Walker, Caruthers & Co the ballance of our quarterly pay due 1st of October. If they have not done so I will thank you to request them to do it and if Caruthers has left Washington I wish you would call at the P. Office Dept, and have W & B's a/c adjusted, and either have our pay forwarded, or something on which I can rely on Samuel's getting the money in February.

It may be thought that I have evinced too much sensitiveness under the letter of censure which was addressed us by the Post office Department. When the *facts* are considered, it will not appear extraordinary that I should have felt sore under it. Leaveing out all the circumstances that transpired before we took charge of the whole line, this letter is calculated to make the impression that no matter how good our performance is, or how splendidly our lines are run it will be difficult for us to give satisfaction to the head of the Dept. When I received that letter, I felt conscious that we had been completely successful in restoreing order & regularity out of confusion, and had regularly delivered our mails at all points, was taking passengers thro' in a manner highly satisfactory, and was receiving the thanks of the peopl for the fine line we had put into operation. The line all the way through to Natchez is fully as good as between Nashville & Columbia, and will be found, as to Teams Coaches, steady and skilful drivers, and general good management equal to any in the Union. *No disgrace to the Jackson administration.*

If the P M. G. could be satisfied that our performance would be satisfactory I should like much to put on 4 h. post Coaches between Jackson & Madisonville. If this cannot be done we must accept the offer made & put on 2 h stages at $6000 pr. annum.

JAMES WALKER

Addressed to Washington.

1. At this time committees from both houses of Congress were investigating the Post Office Department and had already found evidence of laxness in the matter of handling postal contracts. It seems likely that these investigations were related to the delay in making payment to Walker and his associates. The reports of the committees, however, did not mention the operations of Walker, Caruthers and Company, or those of Walker and Brown.

2. Probably Joel Ridley Smith and David Fentress.

3. Walker erred either in addition or in listing the amounts.

4. Since Samuel W. Polk was already in Connecticut, this seems to be a reference to Samuel Polk Walker, who had recently married Eleanor Wormeley of Maury County.

FROM THOMAS J. LACY

Dear Sir Helena [Arkansas] December 4th 1834

I wrote you about four weeks since, which I fear you did not receive before you left Tennessee for Washington. In that communication I informed you perticularly in relation to the entry and purchase of land in this Territory. I am fully pursuaded that had you have sent an agent as you contemplated last fall that he could with a small amount of capital have made an investment which in a few years would have been unusualy valuable. There are swarms of speculators in every part of this country spying out the most choise spots, and taking up and purchasing large quanties of land. Time is now of the greatest importance, and whatever you conclude to do should be attended to as early as practicable. Most of the places on the river are already appropriated, or likely to be very soon; but there are still some few that can be had by entry and a few choise spots that can be procured on reasonable terms, by buying out the settlers claims, which gives the right of entry. If you can send down an agent this winter they can be had, or if you can appropriate a sum (say two or three thousand dollars or even a less amount) and intrust it to Mr Biscoe[1] who knows well all the county—a man of buisness & of responsibility, he can lay it out for you to the greatest advantage. I will see its attended to and I am sure you will be highly gratified at the result. Land is rising daily. It now sells at many places on the Mississippi at a high price varying from ten to fifty dollars. Still there are many points not known to the speculators, some on the river, and much that is short distance back, of a fine quality, and that never overflows. Above and oposite Memphis are good tracts (that is howevr considered out of the cotton region), that can be got at a very low price & between this & Memphis, are some, at the Mouth of the St. Francis river, that are excelent, and can be readily obtained. About forty or fity miles below this, at the Horse shoe bend, is a place that is said can yet be had & is very valuable. So also, at or near Boltons; & one place in the Cypruss bend, about one hundred & twenty miles below here. Back of this place & also of Memphis & above & below here on the river between this & Chicot, on lakes & lagoon, are large quanties of land of superior quality & finely adapted to the culture of cotton, which can be entered or purchased at a low price. I shall remain here (with the exception of a few weeks) or on the river all the winter & spring. Let me know you determination, & what arrangements you wish to make, (if any) as soon as you get this. There is I am sure, a rich harvest open & you can without the posiblebility of failure, reap bountifully. If a receiver office of this Territory should become vacant, I shall speak your influence in behalf a worthy man of the Territory. Make my best regards together with my wife's to Mrs Polk. . . .

Thomas J. Lacy

Addressed to Washington.

1. Henry L. Bisco of Helena, Arkansas.

FROM JOSEPH W. McKEAN[1]

Ultima Thule Sevier County A.T.
Dr Colo [December 4, 1834][2]

The enclosed letter to the Presidt you will please hand him. It is concerning the appmt of your mutul friend Col. A Yell as one of our circuit Judgs. Yells appt would be very popular with the People in the Territory. Sevrl of the Bar have Requested me to write to the President as I was personally acquaintd with him. I expect the old man has forgotten me. I would be glad to hear from you & if you have any public documts that you think I would like to see please send them. I like to read anything aganst the Damd *Bank*. You will please say whether Yell will get the appt.[3]

Jos W McKEAN

Addressed to Washington.

1. A merchant in Sevier County, Arkansas Territory. In 1833 he became postmaster of a post office that was transferred to his store. This post office was then named Ultima Thule. He was a member of the upper house of the territorial legislature at that time.

2. The writer placed no date on the letter. The Library of Congress has placed it in an undated group. The month and day appeared on the envelope, and the year has been supplied on the basis of internal evidence.

3. Yell was nominated for the post on January 7, 1835, and was approved by the Senate on January 20, 1835.

FROM CARUTHERS, HARRIS & COMPANY

Dear Sir N Orleans Decemr. 6, 1834

Annexed please find sales of ten bales cotton for your account the proceeds of which we hold subject to your order at any time. We were delayed in delivering the cotton by bad weather & other circumstances or the account should have been handed you earlier.

During the last three or four days the cotton market has been greatly excited with an intensive speculative demand caused by the last N York accounts, and advices of 24 Octo from

Liverpool stating an advance of ½c. in that market. The natural consequence of this increased demand, a corresponding advance in price has taken place, and choice Missi. has brought as high as 18¢ while some is held at 19 @ 20¢ tho nothing over 18¢ for the finest small [. . .][1] been obtained.

We can scarcely hazzard a conjecture respecting the probable result of the present state of the market; we observe however that transactions are chiefly of a speculative character and those who hold foreign orders, the English particularly, decline executing them except in a few instances when orders are peremptory; and under these the operations are limited & reluctant.

CARUTHERS HARRIS & Co

Addressed to Washington.

1. A tear in the manuscript has removed perhaps two words at this point.

FROM ARCHIBALD YELL

Sir Fayetteville A.T. Decer. the 6th 1834

Enclosed I send you the volunteer recommendaton of a large portion of the Bar of this Circuit. There are but four othrs I believe in the Circuit, three of them are my frinds but I have not called upon them for a letter. The other Gentleman Mr. Dickinson[1] I am told is an applicant for the vacant office. He will certainly be without any recommendation from the Circut & I presume from the Territoy except Judge Eskridge should. They are friendly and reside in the same Town.

This recommendation is unexpected to me and I presume has mostly grown out of their opposition to Mr. Dickinson as they all differ with Him in the local politicks of the Territoy. Perhaps I am indebted for this kind favor from the old addage "*not because they love me most,*" &c be that as it may, I feel under obligations for their frindly interference.

I think it altogether likely that the matter will all be over before this reaches you either for "weel or for wo."

I have nothing to write you of interest since my last. I can not leave here until I here from *Washington.* So soon as I do I shall be off for Tennessee; I shall wait with *impatience* and *trembling anxiety.* Present me to my frind Col Sevier and I congratulate old Jackson and our party on the recent elections. We are on *tip toe* to hear from N. York. If she takes the write *shute* all well and the President nom[?] *Van.*

Let me heir from you often perticularly at prsnt.

A. YELL

Addressed to Washington.

1. Probably Townsend Dickinson, who was register of the land office at Batesville, Arkansas.

FROM PRESTON FRAZER[1]

Sir Shelbyville Dec 8th 1834

I regreat that your stay in Shelbyville was so short, and that my situation from hury of buisiness was such that we bearly had a passing meeting. I had a wish to have had a conversation with you on the following. In a few days now I leave for the State of Mississipi to buy a farm, but as that bids fair to become a wealthy and important state I have other views and the place best calculated to give me a general acquaintance would be most desirable and best facilitate my views. As you see I will in a few days be a citizen of Mississipi, and if you thought my claims would justify, in making the effort for me and you knew of no other who stood in the way, the appointment of receiver of public moneys in the Chickasaw nation would give me a general acquaintance with the people in the middle and upper part of the state. The President knows nothing of me. This I leave for your representation. He had some knowledge of my Brother Doct James Frazer[2] who was surgeon in his army at New Orleans and since died in Lebanon. Any communication will find me at Clinton or I would rather it were directed to me to the care of Col Samuel Gwin[3] of that place. Nothing new here more than I believe the President and Col Polk has more friends in Bedford than they have ever had. The new constitution is not very popular.

PRESTON FRAZER

Addressed to Washington.

1. A Shelbyville physician who frequently asked Polk to help him obtain government appointments. He did not receive the appointment sought in this letter. Although he seems to have lived in both Florida and Mississippi for short periods, he continued to keep a residence in Shelbyville. It is not known whether or not he was a kinsman of Granville H. Frazer.

2. Not otherwise identified.

3. A son of James Gwin, the Methodist minister, and a brother of William M. Gwin. Samuel Gwin was appointed register at the Chocchuma land office in Mississippi, where he betrayed his trust and defrauded the government of a considerable sum of money.

FROM ALEXANDER MARTIN

Lincoln County, Missouri. December 10, 1834

Identifying himself as a friend of Polk and a former resident of Maury County, Martin seeks assistance in getting Congress to grant the right of pre-emption to persons who have settled on unconfirmed Spanish grants.

Addressed to Washington.

TO LEVI WOODBURY

Sir House of Representatives Decr 10th 1834

I am directed by the Committee of Ways and Means to communicate to you the enclosed Resolution of the House of Representatives,[1] and to request that you will submit to the committee your views or any suggestions you may think proper to make, upon the subject to which it relates.

James K. Polk

Addressed to Washington. This letter is in Communications from Committees, Senate and House of Representatives, 1833–37 (RG 56), National Archives.

1. The resolution was concerned with possible establishment of branch mints in certain gold regions.

FROM DAVID T. CALDWELL

Charlotte, North Carolina. December 11, 1834

Caldwell has sent to Polk an execution on Thomas Harris, to be levied on land in Bedford County. He is concerned about the transaction and expresses an interest in buying the land for himself.

Addressed to Washington. This letter has been published in McPherson, editor, "Unpublished Letters," *North Carolina Historical Review,* XVI, 185.

TO LEVI WOODBURY

Dear Sir Ho. Repts. Decr. 11th 1834

I send you the draft of a Bill which I have prepared for the sale of the U. S. Bank Stock.[1] If alterations suggest themselves to you, you will oblige me by making them, and returning the Bill to me this afternoon or tomorrow morning, as I wish to bring the subject before the Committee at its meeting tomorrow. If the Supplemental Report[2] is ready, I should think the sooner it was sent in, the better, as I wish to Report the deposites Bill soon,[3] so as to have our business in a state of forwardness, and thereby prevent the press of other business from rendering it difficult to have our bills acted on in proper season to have them sent to the Senate.

James K. Polk

Addressed to Washington. The letter is in the Papers of Levi Woodbury, Division of Manuscripts, Library of Congress. It is marked "Private."

1. On December 16, 1834, Polk presented to the House a bill authorizing the United States to sell its stock in the Bank of the United States.

2. Probably a reference to Woodbury's "Report of the Secretary of the Treasury, on the present system of keeping and disbursing the Public Money." This report was dated December 12 and was referred to the Ways and Means Committee on December 15, 1834.

3. Polk presented a bill to the House on December 16, 1834, that provided for regulation of the deposit of money of the United States in certain banks.

FROM WILLIAM GARRETT

Giles County. December 12, 1834

Garrett reveals that he is forwarding a petition to Congress, for compensation for property loss sustained in time of war. He expresses confidence that Polk will be able to get such a reasonable claim approved.[1]

Addressed to Washington.
1. See Garrett to Polk, September 19, 1834.

FROM ROBERT MACK

Dr Sir Columbia Dec 12th 1834

By this time no doubt you are deeply engaged in business and have little time to spare on private matters. Yet according to your promise I hope you will make some endeavour to circulate my Book among the Members of Congress and the numerous *Noblesse* that will visit Washington this winter: As those are that class of men I wish to pass upon the work. Tho the Ordeal may consume my hopes yet I wish it to take place for I know that if men of taste and understanding do not like it none else will.

To effect this purpose I would suggest the expediency of keeping some of the Copies lying on your Table in your Reading room if not disagreeable. Or any other way or method your feelings and ideas of propriety may dictate.

I have written to Mr Bell and Mr Grundy on the same subject meaning no infringment on any thing but a little of your time and attention which I think on some grounds I might claim from all three. But should the favor asked be an infringment of any thing else, then on intimation the request will be withdrawn.

There is nothing new transpireing here. Indeed if there was the public print would inform you of it better than I can. The old and new Constitutions are begining to excite some interest among the people as the day of final decission of their respective merits draws nigher—both have their faults and both many opposers. But I think the new Constitution will be successful. Its worst features will cause it to prevail. I mean the Advalorem clause by which a host of officers *may be* created and improvements Taxed; and the provision for middle sized Counties by the Operation of which the Minority may give law to the Majority which if not aristocracy is at least destructive of all Republican principles the very basis of which is that the majority shall rule and decide on what shall be law. Again if we take the old Constitution we cannot get it amended. The new we can piecemeal. This weighs much with many and with me.

Do my dear Sir drop me a few lines in your holydays if possible. In the mean time accept of my good wishes. . . .

ROBT. MACK

P S You have heard no Doubt that Dr McNeil is up to the 9 month law if not *over* that is *under*. This shames us sadly poor man!!! But you may not have heard that Miss Crocket is married to a Rich Orleans[?] C. Merchant.[1] Yet such is the fact.

R M

Addressed to Washington.

1. This is probably a reference to the marriage of Edward Chapman and Esther T. Crockett in Columbia on December 4, 1834.

TO LEVI WOODBURY

Sir, Ho. Repts. Decr 12th 1834

I am instructed by the Committee of Ways & Means to submit to you, for your consideration, the enclosed Resolution of the House of Representatives,[1] and to request that you will communicate to the committee your opinion and views upon the subject to which it relates.

JAMES K. POLK

Addressed to Washington. This letter is in Communications from Committees, Senate and House of Representatives, 1833–37 (RG 56), National Archives.

1. The resolution concerned the establishment of a branch mint in New York.

FROM JAMES WALKER

Dr Sir Bolivar, Dec 13th 1834

I have just been advised that one of our Drafts for $1500 (for Donly's property,) has been returned protested for non-payment our credit thus injured in Miss. and we threatened to have our property attached to pay the draft &c. I suppose however they will wait until we can have the time to forward the money & damages to Mi. Whose fault would it be if the mail were to stop from this cause, ours or the Departments.

We have not received a cent of pay since the 1st of January and I stand ready to prove satisfactorylily that our line is as well run & the mails as regularly delivered as any other contract in the union.

Will you call at the Department, & see what they mean. I hope I shall not again have to call on the President on this subject, but I cannot bear to be dishonored & disgraced in this manner, if I can help it. As to performance the facts are with us, and we dread no scrutiny or examination, if fairly & impartially done.

JAMES WALKER

Addressed to Washington.

FROM JAMES WALKER

Dear Sir Bolivar, Dec. 14th 1834

I am so much chagrined & disappointed by the extraordinary treatment that we have received from the Post office Department, that it is hardly prudent for me to write on this subject. You know the circumstances under which we took this contract—something of the difficulties we contended with & surmounted, and you know something of the punctuality & regularity with which we have run our lines. Few contractors have contended with, so successfully against so many difficulties, & no 500 mile of stage line in America was in better condition, and trips more regularly made, when I received a lecture from the Dept informing us that their hopes were disappointed, and that our performance thus far boded, failure &c. in the winter. Never men more unjustly reproached and at the very time it was done, the people on our roads were universally admiring our energy, system & success. This blow was discouraging enough but the failure to pay our draft for $1500, and thus strike a blow at our credit in Miss. (where we are to a great extent strangers) is cruel in the extreme, especially when it is considered that at the time our Bill was dishonored, they actually owed us nearly ten times the amount of it. I may be too sensitive, but this looks so very much like a deliberate disposition to crush us that I cannot but feel most intensely. I have never asked the Department any other favor than to do me justice. I had hoped that *correct* information existed as to our performance, and expected that our operations were to be made in mutual confidence, and a disposition on the part of the Dept. to render us every aid and assistance which was proper. Our part of duty has been *faithfully* done, as I can satisfactorily establish to all impartial men.

I am discouraged. If the Department is determined to break us down, they can do it. I could sustain my ¼th of the contracts without pay & without aid, but I am not sure I can sustain, the whole as I now have to do by my own resources & management unless the Department give us that aid and justice we *had* a right to expect.

I take Col. [Charles K.] Gardner to be an honorable high minded man, (and know nothing to the contrary of any of the officers) perhaps he will inform you what we are to expect from the Department. I wish you would call on him and endeavor to learn why we are treated so differently from all other contractors—what offense we have committed, why it is that our contract has not been forwarded for execution &c. and why we get no pay and why it is that we are lectured and reprimanded, when we are in the most energic & successful discharge of faithful services. If I am to be involved in difficulty by this business I would prefer a retreat before my fortune is seriously affected by it. We have invested about $40,000 in stock &c and our quarterly expenses are from 15 to $18,000. The winter quarter will be a heavy loss. I want to understand the ground we stand on—am willing to go on if we can do so in mutual confidence & harmony. If the Dept esteems us in the way of better men and are determined to get rid of us, the sooner they do it the better *for us*. They have the power. *Final justice I hope to obtain if I live.*

If you think I am too much excited, remember that I never before had my Bills dishonored, nor have been threatened with attachments—nor have I, or any of my concerns ever yet drawn

Bills, but under circumstances authorising a full belief that they would be honored & paid.

I will thank you to write me immediately on this subject. I do not know where Brown is. Dr. Caldwell left here a few days ago for Chocchuma. I hope my crops from present prospect will bring me $10,000, if the season continues good for picking.

JAMES WALKER

Addressed to Washington.

FROM JONATHAN BOSTICK

Chapel Hill, Tennessee. December 15, 1834

Bostick again seeks appointment as surgeon or assistant surgeon in the army or navy. He reminds Polk that when he first applied there were no vacancies[1] and asks for information in that regard.

Addressed to Washington.

1. Polk had written in his behalf on June 13, 1833. See also John Robb to Polk, June 29, 1833.

FROM WILLIAM H. ELLIS[1]

Dear Sir New Haven December 16th 1834

I have taken the liberty to send you with this a Newspaper containing a couple of articles, one on the election of President the other on French affairs which I have marked with a pen. These articles, though they appear as editorials were written by our friend R. I. Ingersoll.[2] I know that he would be unwilling to have it generaly known that he is a newspaper writer but without asking his leave I have ventured to mention it to you, trusting that you will not mention the subject except to particular friends. I should be pleased to see the article upon the subject of the election of President transfered to the Globe, with such remarks as Mr Blair might think proper to make.

If it would not be asking too much of you, I should be pleased to be furnished with the document accompanying the Presidents message, and also the report of the Secretary of the Treasury in relation to the reorganization of the Treasury Department;[3] with such other documents as may be printed relating to revenue, and all matters generaly in relation to the collection thereof.

WM. H. ELLIS

Addressed to Washington.

1. A man of some prominence in New Haven, Ellis was a loyal Jacksonian in a city that had favored Clay overwhelmingly in 1832. He served on a three-man welcoming committee when Jackson visited New Haven in 1833.

2. Ralph I. Ingersoll, a Yale graduate, practiced law in New Haven. He had served in the United States House of Representatives, 1825–33. He was a strong Jacksonian and later served as minister to Russia while Polk was president.

3. The House of Representatives received Woodbury's report on December 8, 1834. The report was referred to a select committee of nine members, and 5,000 copies were ordered to be printed.

FROM ALEXANDER DELAUNAY

New York. December 18, 1834

Delaunay asks Polk to urge prompt action on a petition before the Ways and Means Committee that would relieve him from payment of duties on medical books imported from France.

Addressed to Washington.

FROM SAMUEL G. SMITH

Dr Sir Nashville Decr. 18. 1834

I received in due time the Presidents Message which you were so kind as to send to me. It cannot be otherwise than gratifying to those who have enlisted under his banner in support of sound political doctrines and who have adhered with so much firmness as yourself and some others to the measures of his administration to find that the opposition both in feeling and action are put to silence. I have not heard a single word of exception to the document. Many very inteligent men who have not meddled with politics have said to me it was without exception. It is said here that there has been some movement at Washington between the friends of Judge White and Mr Van Buren.

It is also stated that the strength of the former is very imposing. It is a matter about which I must confess my profound ignorance.

Some are ready to take sides and many are seemingly at a loss to know where to place themselves waiting for further developments. For my own part having no information upon the subject and not knowing the feelings of those of the true stamp with whom I have determined to act, I mean to hear more authentic information on the subject. A few days after my last letter to you I learned that Ln.[1] was indulging in his intemperance and last evening I was informed he had become sober[?] & expected to leave for Washington in a day or two. Such conduct is well calculated to prostrate all confidence in him. Should he go to Washington as I presume he will you can advise me as early as possible as to future arrangements. I think our presses are very much inclined to advocate the claims of Judge White, indeed I am confident their present determination is to do so. I am not now asking you for any opinion or expression of feeling but whenever you may come to any settled determination upon the subject anything you may say will be in the strictest confidence. I have received some communication from different parts of the state to know if my name could be run for the Executive but as yet I have given no direct answer. It is a subject about which I have no feeling myself and only wish that we may have some man who we can rely upon, but those who have a wish upon the subject or are looking to it do not meet my views for the present state of things.

The democracy of Tennessee who have never been wrong in politics were never more steadfast to their principles.

I hope to hear from you frequently.

Sam G Smith

Addressed to Washington. The letter is marked "Confidential."

1. Samuel H. Laughlin.

FROM WILLIAM CARROLL

My dear Sir, Nashville, December 19. 1834

I received a letter last evening from Mr. Grundy of the 7th instant, informing me that he had seen a letter predicting differences between you and myself. I cannot imagine who the writer is, or the motive which influenced him in writing. One thing however you may rest assured of, that he had no authority from me either verbally or in writing for his predictions. I defy the most malicious enemy I have to say that he has heard a single unfriendly expression uttered by me against you. After the conversations between you and myself at the *City Hotel* previous to your departure for Washington, I should certainly be a very base man to entertain unkind feelings towards you. You profered your friendly offices in my behalf, for which I then felt, and still feel the deepest sense of gratitude. Of the sincerity of your friendship I did not then doubt, nor do I now. If at any time I should receive information from a source entitled to credit, of a want of friendship towards me on your part, you may be assured that you shall be the first person to whom I shall communicate the fact. The author or authors of those reports doubtless have their objects in view, but they must look sharp or they will be disappointed, and if discovered their perfidy shall be exposed. You were kind enough to say, when I saw you at Nashville, that you would take the first favorable opportunity of ascertaining the intention of the government in relation to myself. When you do so, please to inform me of the result. A single difficulty is not now in the way of making the appointment, and if it is the intention of the Administration to fulfil a positive promise made four years since,[1] I see no reason for further delay.

The newspapers seem to say but little about the next presidency. I should suppose however from what I do see, that it is the intention of the Democratic party to take up a candidate by a national nomination. In that event no one seems to have as good a chance as Van Buren.

With a tender my kind respects to Mrs. Polk and the expression of wish to hear from you occasionally, I am dear sir. . . .

WM. CARROLL

Addressed to Washington.

1. Carroll had been promised a diplomatic post to one of the countries to the south and had been mentioned as a possible choice to negotiate with Mexico.

FROM WILLIAM J. ALEXANDER

Raleigh, North Carolina. December 20, 1834

The writer supports the appointment of a friend to a government post at the port of Wilmington and seeks Polk's assistance in his behalf.

Addressed to Washington. This letter has been published in McPherson, editor, "Unpublished Letters," *North Carolina Historical Review,* XVI, 185–186.

FROM JOHN W. CHILDRESS

Dear Sir, Murfreesboro Dec 20th 1834

I returned about a week since from Alabma, and succeeded in collecting only $794. of the money due us there. I have the promise of getting the balance soon by means of a check on Nashville, to be sent as soon as it can be procured. The patents for the Land I sold last fall have been found and also for a quarter & half quarter yet unsold. I was offered $8. pr acre for the quarter but was advised to hold it up longer and therefore did not sell. Genl Brady showed me a few days since, a letter from you, in relation to Mr Bells speech at Murfreesboro. You are a great deal better versed in these matters than I am but I will presume to advise you that it would be best not to place yourself too much in the power of Brady. Present circumstances will prevent him from abusing confidence, it is his interest to act honestly, but may not things change after a while that would make it his interest to act differently? If such should be the fact, no motive of integrity will prevent it. He is destitute of principle. He is now procuring certificates of the correctness of the speech as reported in the Monitor! and will be able to get them from men of standing and perhaps from some of Mr Bells friends. [Edwin A.] Keeble in an Extra number of the Monitor vouched for the correctness of the speech, in answer to the Republican, who denied. The certificates therefore will as soon as they can be procured, come out as from Keeble in justification of his report of the speech, and to repel the charge made by the Nashville paper, that the speech was incorrectly reported. The Monitor has been discontinued. The certificates will be presented to the Nashville papers for publication, if they refuse, of which I have no doubt, they will be sent to Washington, and you must have them published. The affair has come to a point, at which energy must be used or more will be lost than gained. I have been enquired of by several of your friends why it is that the Globe the organ of the President espouses the cause of Mr Bell so warmly and why it is that no paper will publish anything against him. It is even suggested that from the presidents silence from the fact of the Globe and all the presidents relations in this State being for Bell that he is really the choice of the President himself. If the people do not get some evidence to the contrary from headquarters soon, they certainly will pretty generally take up that notion. Keeble was hard to persuade to lend his name to publish the certificates. He says he engaged in the matter expecting support from other quarters, but he finds that nothing has been published against Bell except in his & one or two papers of similar circulation and every thing in his favor has been generally and widely circulated. If something energetic is not done, and shortly, these things will create a distrust prejudicial to yourself and will fix down the belief as Bells friends affirm already that the clamor all originated from your being defeated, and there was no cause of complaint against Bell. If the certificates are procured they will be from men of high respectability and will stand any sort of scrutiny. Write me soon upon this subject. Give my love to Sarah & tell her I will write to her soon.

John Childress

Addressed to Washington.

TO MAHLON DICKERSON

Sir Washington City December 20th 1834

The estimate of the appropriations required for the support of the Navy for the year 1835 exceeds the appropriation of the current and former years, for the following objects—viz—"Pay and subsistence of the officers of the Navy & pay of seamen," and "For pay of superindentendants, naval constructors and all the civil establishments at the several yards." A part of this increase—as appears from the letter of the commissioners of the Navy Board accompanying your letter to the Committee of Ways & Means of the 18th Inst. is owing to *allowances* proposed to the 2nd Lieutenants at Boston, New York, Norfolk and Pensacola, and to the Purser at Charleston S. Carolina; and to a proposed increase in the pay of the Clerks of Commandants at Portsmouth N.H. Boston, N.York, Washington, Norfolk and Pensacola, & for pay for an additional Clerk to the Storekeeper at Boston, New York and Norfolk, and for increase of allowances to the officers of the Depot of Chronometers & Instruments at Washington. I desire to be referred to the laws under which such *increased allowances, increased pay,* to Clerks, employment of additional Clerks, is proposed to be made; and also to be informed of the particular reasons which may exist for the proposed increase of *allowances* & *pay,* over the sum granted to the same persons for the same service for the present & preceeding years.

It appears from the letter of the Commissioner of the Navy Board, that a part of the increased appropriation asked for 1835 is owing to an increase of the number of officers & seamen proposed to be employed over the number now in service. I desire to be furnished with a statement of the additional number of each grade proposed to be employed & a detailed estimate of the pay & allowances proposed to be made for such increased numbers; and also to be informed of the reasons for such increased numbers. I observe from the Documents accompanying your annual Report that it is proposed to employ the same number of Receiving Vessels for 1835 that were employed for 1834; the estimate for this branch of the service is however increased to a considerable amount over the appropriation of last year. An explanation of the necessity for such increase is desired.

I desire to be furnished with an estimate more in detail of the several appropriations asked for the improvements & repair of Navy Yards, than that which is furnished by the Documents accompanying your annual Report. Accompanying such detailed estimate it would be desireable to have a statement of the amounts heretofore expended on unfinished objects at the several yards, and the amount which it is estimated it will cost to complete it. For example at the Navy Yard at Charlestown Mass the largest item of the appropriation asked for 1835, the following—viz—"Towards completing Rope Walk $50.000." I wish to know how much has been heretofore expended for this object and how much it is estimated it will require to complete it; and a similar statement for every other unfinished object in the several yards. I observe in the estimates for "improvements & Repairs at the Navy Yards at Portsmouth, Brooklyn N.Y. Philadelphia, Washington, & Gosport" are items of appropriation under the head of "all other purposes." An explanation of what is meant by the general terms *"All other purposes"* is desired.

It is submitted for the consideration of the Department whether the amount asked for the Improvement & Repair of Navy Yards for 1835 may not be diminished without injury to the service.

A statement is also desired shewing the amounts heretofore expended for the several Magazines & Hospitals, for the completion of which, further appropriations are asked in the *"submitted"* estimates, and also a more detailed estimate of the several amounts required for their completion than is furnished by the documents accompanying your annual Report.

A statement shewing the amount heretofore expended under the act of July 10th 1832 for the purchase of tanks, & how the deficiency of former appropriations for this object has been produced.

I desire also to be furnished with an estimate in detail of the appropriations required for pay, subsistence, and all other items of appropriation for the *Marine Corps* under the re-organization of that Corps by the act of the last Session. Accompanying this estimate I wish to have a statement of the numbers of the Corps of all grades before re-organization and subsequent thereto, together with a comparative statement of the pay &c. allowed under the former law and under the re-organization, shewing distinctly in what the increase of the appropriation asked consists. The information which I have requested in relation to these several items of appropriation connected with the naval service for 1835 is intended when received to be submitted to the Committee of Ways and Means to aid them in preparing the annual appropriation bill for the naval service in 1835.

JAMES K. POLK

Addressed to Washington. This letter is in Miscellaneous Letters Received by the Secretary of the Navy (RG 45), National Archives.

FROM JAMES BROWN

Dear Sir Coffeeville Miss December 21st 1834

I have no doubt you have been long since expecting to hear from me as to the success in geting you a plantation. Dr [Silas M.] Caldwell left this to day for the district having purchased a tract of land on Yellabusha[Yalobusha] & in Yellabush County some 5 miles South west of Hendersonville containing 880 acres & has entered 80 acres adjoining, the 880 cost $10. per acres, ⅓ cash & ⅓ in one & two years. It is the best tract of land I have seen in this countery that could be bought. I was very anxious to get a tract in October or November but found it entirely impracticable to get such a tract as I would have, owing to the bodyes or good tracts of countery being so divided by different owners & they non residents. I then concluded to defer the purchase untill the land sales 1st of December at which time I expected to see the land holders generaly & could more readily get a tract to suite. I was mutch releived in finding Dr Caldwell there at that time. We began to inquire into prices, quality, locality &c of different tracts & found as we thought, a tract 40 miles south of Chocchuma that was a great bargin, 1st rate land 150 acres cleared land, only 680 in the tract, price $6. per acres half cash & the ballance in 12 months. The tract was spoken of in such terms that we had no doubt but it would do. The Dr went to see it, buy corn &c and I felt satisfyed that the matter was setled, but in five or 6 days the Dr returned & reported the tract was more overrated & missrepresented than any land he ever saw. I then hunted him up & examined the tract bought. We understood the price to be $5000. cash but no person authorised to sell & the owner lived 100 miles down the valey &

no certainty as to the price but we thought it best to go and see him but when the Dr got there the price was as first stated $10. per acres. We had agreed before he started that if we were missinformed as to price, that the tract was better worth $10 per acres & would suite you better than any other tract could be had for the same money. I had purchased several tracts in the Chickasaw nation that would suite but I ascertained that I could not get the title to them confirmed in time for you. The Chickasaw land committee have done nothing as yet towards confirming trads that have been made, the countery is in great confusion. I have as yet avoided difficutyes & kept myself quite cool as to Chickasaw transactions.

I have been ingaged for a few weeks in undertaking to secure some lands for the Choctaws who were entitled to land under the Choctaw treaty but failed to get it owing to some bade management of the agent in not having there names registered and forwareded to Washington in due time. I shall wright you again on this subject and may want some assistance. I have no doubt that they have been ronged out of there just rights.

I should be pleased to hear from you when convenient or anything occurs that might be interesting to me.

JAMES BROWN

Addressed to Washington.

FROM THOMAS BARBOUR

Columbia. December 22, 1834

After thanking Polk for sending him a copy of a recent presidential message, Barbour urges his support for further appropriation of public lands to meet certain warrants that have been issued.

Addressed to Washington.

FROM JAMES A. CRAIG

Dear Friend: Haw River N. C. 22nd. Decr. 1834

It has been a long time since I have had the pleasure of a letter from you. Why do you not write me? Be assured it would afford much gratification.

What disposition will be made of the French debt? The United States has been a long and lenient Creditor. Indeed recent occurrences in France do not manifest scarcely any dispotition on the part of that Government to pay off the debt in question. But the firm and independent tone used by our venerable president will convince France that she must act and that promptly.

The message as a state paper is generally considered by our party here as the ablest that has appeared in many years. The sentiments it breathes are purely republican. The opposition to the administration in N. Ca. is not as formidable as one at a distance would suppose. General Jackson in North Carolina to day is stronger (I verily believe) than he ever was. The Vote on the Senate Election was a pretty good Criterion. It was said during the fall that Brown could not Run but he nearly doubled his opponent. A very intelligent member of the Senate says from what he can glean this session there will not be any opposition at the next Congressional Election to Mr. V. Buren.

I am well pleased the "old Hero" has made us such a good chief magistrate; you remember no doubt I was one of his early and steadfast friends. I had the honour of drawing up the first Resolution in N. Ca. recommending Genl. Jackson for the Presidency.

I will be glad to hear early from you, and fully on the most interesting subjects of the day.

If different pension agents are to be appointed thro' the several states, will they be chosen from the several states & when? Will they be chosen by the President or Secretary of war?

James A. Craig

P. S. I must ask the favour of you, Dear Colonel, to call upon the Secretary of the Treasury and ask what is to be done in the case of the old pensioner *John Boudy.*[1] The circumstances of the case are these. Boudy has always had the reputation of being a Revolutionary soldier of the *Maryland Line.* La[s]t Winter made a Declaration under the act of 1832, a Certificate was allowed him for full pay, under said act. (B. not then have any Certificate of his service as a Cont. Sol.). In April he drew his pension—on the day he got his pension money an answer to an enquiry arrived from the Register of the Land office for the state of Md. enclosing a Certificate that Boudy had enlisted and served in the Maryland Line till the close of the War. Boudy receives his pay under the act of 1832. In a few weeks afterwards, I wrote to Genl. Barringer, stating the evidence B. had just recd. and requesting to know if it would not entitle him to pension under the act 15 May 1828. The answer was that it would entitle him. Boudy makes affidavit in due form of what he had drawn and makes a relinquishment upon the Certificate & returns it to the Hon: J. L. Edwards—all to the Care of the Hon: D L Barringer (our representative) in July last. Mr. B. wrote me had effected the exchange of Certificates, and had procured one for Boudy under act 1828, that he had thro' mistake placed it in a trunk with his books & papers, that the trunk had miscarried and had not been heard of when he set out for Washington this session, but as soon as he could get his trunk the Certificate should be forwarded to the old man. The Session has again met and 3 weeks transpired and yet the old man can get no word of his Certificate. The old man is poor and infirm and needs his money. If the trunk is not found—will not Mr. Woodberry grant a new one upon Mr. Barringer's affidavit? Please give this matter your early attention and write me the result.

J. A. C.

Addressed to Washington. This letter has been published in McPherson, editor, "Unpublished Letters," *North Carolina Historical Review*, XVI, 186–187.

1. See Craig to Polk, June 21, 1834.

FROM THOMAS W. DYOTT

Philadelphia. December 22, 1834

A native of England and a wealthy dealer in patent medicines, Dyott solicits patronage for a new Democratic newspaper in Philadelphia. Dyott had financed the paper and is eager for its approval by Democrats in Washington.

Addressed to Washington.

FROM WILLIAM L. WILLIFORD

Jackson College [Spring Hill] Ten.
Decr. 23d 1834

Dr Sir

I have just received a letter from Col. Jeremiah Smith[1] of Winchester State of Indiana, informing me, that the office of surveyor general for the states of Ohio, Indiana and Michigan Territory, will become vacant at the close of this month, and that he is an applicant for that appointment. He also requests me to state to you what I know in relation to his qualifications &c.

I have long been acquainted with Col. Smith and know him to be a considerable proficient in Mathematics—his genius is peculiarly adapted to that Science. I consider him not only qualified, but eminently qualified for a Surveyor, both in theory and practice. It may perhap be thought strange why I speak thus positive respecting his qualifications, but the reason will be found in the fact, that he was once a student of mine for a considerable time.

From his mathematical knowledge and skill in surveying it is confidently believed that he would discharge the duties of the Office to which he aspires, with honor to himself and fidelity to the government.

Should you think proper to use your influence with the President to obtain his nomination, or exercise it in any other way to promote his wishes, I am well persuaded, that it will be confering a great favor on one that is worthy, and at the same time be highly gratifying to. . . .

William L Williford

P. S I have written to the President in his behalf from his request. Col Smith is a warm administration man. This however I did not communicate to him. Smith is about 30 years old.

W L. W.

Addressed to Washington.

1. Unidentified. Since the writer of this letter says that he had taught Smith, it seems likely that the latter had been a resident of Tennessee. He did not receive the appointment.

TO LEVI WOODBURY

Sir House of Representatives Decr 23rd 1834

I am instructed by the Committee of Ways & Means to communicate to you for your consideration the enclosed Resolutions of the Ho. Repts.[1] and to ask your opinion & views upon the subject to which they relate. The Committee having referred two former resolutions of the House upon the same subject to your Department, it was deemed proper to give those now enclosed the same direction.

JAMES K. POLK

Addressed to Washington. This letter is in Communications from Committees, Senate and House of Representatives, 1833–37 (RG 56), National Archives.

1. The resolution concerned the possible establishment of branch mints in North Carolina and New Orleans.

FROM LEVI WOODBURY

Washington. December 23, 1834

Woodbury explains the increased estimate of contingent expenses of the Office of the Secretary of the Treasury, stressing particularly the expenses attendant upon the recent destruction by fire of the building that housed the department.

Addressed to Washington. This is a clerk's copy in Letters and Reports to Congress by Secretaries McLane, Taney, and Woodbury (RG 56), National Archives.

FROM ANDREW C. HAYS

Dear Sir, Columbia Ten Dec. 24. 1834

Yours of Nov 10th was received a few days after my return home about the 1st inst. and would have been promptly replied to, but for my indisposition at the time—from which I have not yet entirely recovered. I was attacked with scarlet fever the day after my return, and have been closely confined ever since, until a few days ago, am therefore unable to communicate, hardly the common occurences of the day.

The contents of your letter shall be promptly attended to—of this you rest assured. While I was confined Genl. [Samuel G.] Smith was in town, I did not see him, but presume that if he had desired to confer with me on the subject of which you speak he would have called upon me. He will be here again in a few days. I shall however say nothing to him about the matter unless he broaches the subject first.[1]

I think it more desireable that a Newspaper should be established in Nashville, that will fearlessly speak the sentiments of the people of the State, at this time than it has ever been because I believe that the Press is at this time more under the influence of the *Bank & Bell & Foster* faction than it has *ever been.* There is no improvement of talent in the Editorial Department, and surely some man can be found sufficiently qualified to compete successfully with them—particularly in so good a cause.

You have no doubt seen that Smith, [Daniel] Graham & Dunlap,[2] are all in nomination for Governor. I should greatly regret to see Graham & Smith run in opposition to each other—having always understood that they stand on the same side in our State divisions. I still hope such an event will not occur.

I heard it mentioned a day or two since that Genl. Smith should have said while here "that it would be folly in either of the three to run while Carrol was in the field—that it was usless to try to disguise the *fact* he would beat either or all of them" &c. I am told that he spoke confidently of Carrol's being a candidate, provided the new Constitution was adopted, of which I believe but few entertain a doubt. *Your* friends I do not believe would consent to *your* leaving the District to offer for Governor. I have heard expression to this effect within the last few days.

[Terry H.] Cahal & [A. O. P.] Nicholson I understand, both visited the last Bedford Court. There is considerable talk about it—many surmises &c.—all however agree that both are looking forward to Congress.

I am of opinion that Cahal will be a candidate for the Legislature, and I think too with strong probabilities of success.

[Gideon J.] Pillow I also believe will be a candidate—but have no idea he can be elected. Jefferson Porter, I think is entirely out of the notion of being a public man and should the new Constitution be adopted I think it more than probable he will move to Mississippi. Young Porter[3] has already removed to Natchez.

We traveled from Miss. in the stage in company with Judge [Daniel W.] Wright (he who was nominated by the Democratic Convention for Congress). The Judge mentioned that he had spent an evening in company with Mr. Bell among some Jackson friends, at Natches, perhaps, and that he was convinced from Mr. B's warm declarations made on that occasion, that he was opposed to the Bank and a warm advocate of the principles of Genl. Jacksons Administration. He seemed to much pleased with him. I think however that I convinced him that Bell had acted with great duplicity on that occasion, and that his real sentiments & feelings were the very reverse of what he had represented them to be—that Bell had gotten among a number of warm Jackson men & hence his great profession of devotion to the Administration. I referred to his Murfreesboro speech—to his silence during last session—to the support he received at the hand of the opposition at Nashville—(*which opposition Wright had been just abusing and affirming that there were more of them there than in any two Counties in Miss.*). I also refered him to information obtained of *Green Lewis,*[4] who I met with in Miss. and who had spent some time in the Yazoo valey where Bell had been, and where he had been vociforous and loud in his denunciation of those he called his enemies, on the subject of the Speakers election. So much so that several there understood him as being in the opposition. Judge Wright is a warm [. . .] honest man—devoted to the Administration and personally attached to Genl. Jackson, under whom he served during the war—just such a man as would despise a hypocrite in politics or any thing else. I also mentioned the controversy between our Editors. He requested that I would send him the papers. I have done so, and when he reads them he will give Mr. B. the *go by*—if he has not already done so. He has not yet accepted the nomination and says it is doubtful whether he will. Should he do so I doubt not but he will be elected for I believe him to be the most popular man in the state. Tho' not a man of the first order of talents, they are very respectable.

There is no possible chance for the re-election of Poindexter —any respectable Jackson man can beat him.

You have no doubt seen that the Nashville papers deny the correctness of the report of Mr. Bell's speech at Murfreesboro. Some pains should be taken to set this matter before the people. The Murfreesboro paper may have done so, but not having seen it I am unable to say. If it is not done, it is not yet to late.

Mr. Walker is absent in the District, and has been for two weeks. His family is well, as are also your relations generally. Yet there is considerable sickness still in the country.

Bradly Mays is married to night to Miss Maguire[5]—all the Town invited, and nearly all gone, though the rain is falling in torrents. It has been raining for ten days—*fond of going to Wedings I think!!!*

Thos. Norton[6] a day or two since shot a man, who attempted to pass the bridge without paying toll. It is thought he will recover. If he should Norton will only be sent to the Penitentiary. Should he die he will certainly be hung for there was no sort of excuse for the act.

I have but little more room nor have I any thing more to wright if I had.

My best respects to Mrs. Polk and for yourself assurances of my high regard, and best wishes for the health, prosperity & happiness of yourself & family.

A. C. HAYS

Addressed to Washington.

1. This probably refers to the efforts to establish a newspaper to counteract the Nashville press, which Bell controlled. Smith was apparently still in Maury County at the time this was written. See Smith to Polk, December 28, 1834.

2. Richard G. Dunlap, a brother of William C. Dunlap, John H. Dunlap, and Hugh W. Dunlap of Paris, Tennessee. Unlike his brothers, Richard did not move from the vicinity of Knoxville. He represented Knox and Anderson counties in the state legislature. He withdrew from the gubernatorial race in 1835 before the election. Although John was also called General Dunlap, Richard had a longer and more distinguished military record; he was with Jackson at New Orleans, in the Seminole campaign of 1818, and served in

the Cherokee country in the 1830s when trouble seemed unavoidable there. He planned to take a group with him to help the Texans in their fight for independence, but the fight ended before he was ready to depart.

3. Young J. Porter was practicing law in Natchez, Mississippi. He was a brother of Parry W. and Thomas Jefferson Porter.

4. Unidentified.

5. Roger B. Mayes and Ellen Maguire were married on December 24, 1834.

6. Norton was a deputy sheriff of Maury County at one time and was probably serving in that capacity when this letter was written.

FROM SAMUEL KING

My dear Col. Tenn. Shelbyville Decb. 24th 1834

I am now on my return from the Western District, and seated by a comfortable fire, under the hospitable roof of the Landlord, where we parted last August, just after you gave an acct. of your stewardship to your Constituents: and although I have been very uncomfortable thro. the day, yet regaled with the comforts of an *Inn* & a recollection of our partial acquaintance, I have concluded to drop you a line, as I sought that repose necessary to traveller, after a ride through a very intemperate day.

A few days ago the Presidents Message was handed to me by a friend, which I read hastily by a nocturnal lamp amidst a family crowding around an indifferent *Fire.* I have wondered if the least exception could be taken to it as respects our external relations, or rather if every American would not respond to the sentiments it contains.

Touching the Bank, there will of course be a variety of opinions. I do not claim a more honest difference with the views of the President on this point than many of his friends; but I claim as much. Permit me to make a few suggestions with much defense, on those points so exceptionable to the B. of the U. States. But first, let me premise, that each of the Charters was granted by the different ruling *parties* for the purpose of sustaining the Treasury, as also a Fiscal agent, when the whole energy & strength of the Nation was necessary. Now that the burthen is removed from that Department the national debt paid why not establish a currency free from those exemptions which every unprejudiced citizen must admit. Is the ground more free from Constitutional objections to make a Fiscal agent of the local Banks, than the U. States Bank?

Do you by patronizing those Institutions give a sound & uniform currency?

Do you destroy the influence of Banks, or of money in patronizing, or supporting the Executive; or rather do you not put in the power of the Executive by selecting the places of deposite to control the elective franchise?

Do you exclude Foreign capitalists from making investments in those Institutions?

Do you raise any security against the extent that the states will go to granting charters, and the small bills they will emit?

Do you prevent the hourly imposition that is practiced on the Agricuturalist, by the Merchant getting money by handfulls, to speculate on his labor, which is now the case in buying Cotton from here to the Miss. at about ¾ of its value?

Have you any control over those miserable State Institutions that you select as places of deposite, as to their duration or accountability?

Can you support a specie currency when the States are unrestricted in the number of Charters or their capacity to get the specie [. . .] in their vaults, & give the farmer their rags?

My dear Sir, I fear you will raise a strife between States, that will produce the most dreadful effects. Would to God, I could be in any way serviceable to an Executive that I have honestly supported in all his elections; but I tremble at the prospect. I dread the consequences that await this Republic. You will recollect that no man condemns more unhesitatetingly than I do, the high handed measures of the U. S. Bank; but the inexpediency of the alternatives is to my mind distressing. Why not give a Bank of the U. States, with a branch in each State on the Funds of the government, & exclude individual capital? Please let me hear from you in Iredell N. Carolina. My respects to Judge [Hugh Lawson] White, Messrs. [Luke] Lea, and [William C.] Dunlap. The mail waits.

Sam'l King
of Iredell Cty N Carolina

Addressed to Washington.

TO JAMES WALKER

Dear Sir Washington City Decb. 24th. 1834

I have been so busily engaged in preparing the appropriation bills and those connected with the Bank that I have not heretofore taken leisure to write to you. I have had nothing to do with the management and undercurrents which I understand have been going on here in regard to the next Presidency. I have considered that it was my first duty to attend the important measures committed to the committee of which I am a member. This I have done and shall continue to do, and I am sure my constituents will appreciate my services more than if I were engaged in the intrigues of politicians with a view to my own personal advancement. I have no doubt that my constituents feel and think as I do, upon the subject of the succession, but still they have not commissioned me here to either to engage their voters, to commit them upon the subject or to express their opinions. As a citizen I shall have a right to my own opinion, and whenever[?] there shall be occasion shall certainly exercise it. In regard to our countryman Judge White I have said this, that there was no man to whom personally I have ever had kinder feelings, and that if he was brought forward, or taken up and run by our own political friends, it would give me pleasure to support him, but at the same time I think that the great party now dominant in the country, who have recently achieved so signal a victory, have fought the battle to little purpose, if in the moment of their triumph, they permit themselves to be divided & distracted about men, and thereby perhaps enable our political adversaries to take advantage of our divisions, throw the election into the House,[1] where there is danger that the money of the Bank and the patronage of the Government, would corrupt & purchase votes enough to carry the election against us. It must certainly be the desire of our party, who are emphatically from the policy we advocate the Republican party of the country, if possible to continue united and not divide about men. I think the party should unite if it be possible and run but one man and it would assuredly give me pleasure should Judge White be that man.

Suppose we divide and start more than one candidate, and suffer the friends of our respective candidates to become irritated & exci[ted] against each other; may not the opposition, and will they not take advantage of such a state of things, and at a moment when it shall be too late for us to retrace our steps, and re-unite our friends in favor of any one, suddenly push out a candidate of their own, defeat our election before the people, throw the election into the House and thus stand a fair chance to come into power against the popular will. To avert such a state of things I repeat we should continue united and if possible run but one man. Should Judge White be the man upon whom the party unite, none would support him with more pleasure than myself. Upon this subject, the present moment may be an important crisis. As soon as Congress assembled, many of the opposition members expressed wishes that Judge White should be brought out and announced their intention to support him if he was. Their motive for this, the game they will play hereafter or the object they hope to affect, I know not except— that they would doubtless do any thing in their power to divide & scatter us. That portion of our delegation in Wt. Tennessee, who manifested such unprovoked hostility to me during the past summer; I mean the Speaker, Dickerson &c.[2] probably think they can make something out of this state of things to my prejudice, and for their own purposes, have been zealous or pretend to be so, to bring Judge White out at once and at all events without waiting to consult any portion of the democratic party residing in other states with whom we have so long acted, and who have so long acted with us in sustaining the administration of the present Chief Magistrate. Ought they not to be at least consulted upon such a step as this? But that portion of our delegation probably think that by taking this course they will gain an advantage of me in Tennessee and that by uniting with the opposition Mr B. may be enabled to retain his place here at the next Congress, in the same way he originally obtained it. The East Tennessee part of our delegation very honestly and sincerely desire to see Judge White elected. On the day before yesterday I was informed by Col. [James] Standifer that there was to be a meeting of the delegation, on the night following (last night) upon the subject and was requested to attend. On Yesterday Mr [Luke] *Lea* spoke to me on the subject & told me the meeting was to be at [Balie] *Peyton's* room and urged me to attend. I told him that my attending or not attending was a matter of no consequence; that neither my own opinions or that of my constitutents of Judge White would be changed, whether I attended or not; that I had no commission from my constituents to speak for them; that, that was a matter they would attend to for themselves, when the time came for them to act; that I was very laboriously engaged in the discharge of my public duty as a member of the House; and that I did not regard the proposed meeting as any part of that duty. I told him furthermore that I could not but suspect that, that portion of our delegation who are, without cause given by me so exceedingly hostile to me, were prompted in this movement more in the hope of injuring me, than for any love they had for Judge White. And furthermore I told him, that what was conclusive against my attendance was this—that I could not without loosing all self-respect go into a consultation upon any subject, (unless public duty required it,) with that portion of our delegation who had during the past summer through their organs and tools, so unjustly and wantonly assailed me; and especially when I was informed that the meeting was to take place at the room of a colleague who was crtainly exceedingly unfriendly in his feelings towards me, and who had never invited me to come to it. For these reasons I declined and did not attend. The meeting was held, [Felix] Grundy, [John] Blair & myself absent. [Cave] Johnson attended but will probably communicate to the delegation his views in writing. They entirely accord with mine. I understand that [William C.] *Dunlap* (though I have not talked to him) agrees in his views with Johnson & myself. I write you very *confidentially*—that you may be apprised of what is going on here. From the unfairness with which I have been treated in other things I have reason to suspect that letters may be written home misrepresenting me upon this—probably representing from my absence from the meeting, that I am unfriendly to Judge White—and I look for nothing else than to see some misrepresentation in regard to it, through the Nashville papers. I write you to put you in possession of the facts, that you may in the proper way, and without using my letter publicly, be enabled to put the matter right. I wish you to take so much time from your business—which I know to be pressing upon your time, as to write me your opinion fully & freely upon the subject; and whether you think I have acted prudently or not. I have acted upon my convictions of what was proper, and with feelings of most perfect friendship for Judge White. Can I be affected by it?.

JAMES K. POLK

P.S. I have written in haste—and I fear almost illegibly, but have no time to copy.

J. K. P.

Addressed to Columbia. The letter is marked "Confidential."

1. Polk quite clearly understood that even though Hugh L. White was a Democrat his participation as a candidate in opposition to the Democratic nominee would play into the hands of the Whigs, whose only hope of winning the presidency seemed to be through throwing the election into the House of Representatives.

2. John Bell and David W. Dickinson. Polk frequently misspelled the latter's name.

FROM JOSEPH BROWN

Cave Spring, Tennessee. December 25, 1834

Brown asks news of his son, James Brown, who had been asked by Polk to buy land for him in Mississippi.

Addressed to Washington.

FROM JAMES Y. GREEN

Bedford County. December 25, 1834

After thanking Polk for sending him a copy of a presidential message, the writer reports success with the turning lathe on which his father had obtained a patent.[1] He also inquires about the proper procedure for obtaining a pension for a Revolutionary War veteran.

Addressed to Washington.

1. See William Green and others to Polk, December 16, 1831.

FROM HENRY HORN

My Dear friend Philada. 25 Decem 1834

As I regard you as one of the most vigilante sentinels upon the watch tower of liberty in the House of Representatives and as one of the most intrepid soldiers in the cause of the People I deem it my duty to call your attention to a matter which from the multitude of objects that are continually pressing upon you and the apparent inconsiderable importance of this may possibly have escaped your notice. I allude to the movement made in your House a few days since by Mr [Horace] Binney with view of altering the mode of selecting Juries in our United States district Court.[1] The subject it appears has been refered to the committee on the Judiciary in your House.

In a conversation I had today with the marshall of our district I learned that Mr B was much displeased with a verdict recently rendered against his client and some person was heard to say that it was a Jackson verdict because it so happened that it was given in favour of one of our friends Mr. Henry Toland when in the opinion of every disinterested man that I have heard speak upon the subject the case was clearly and justly with him and the Jury was of a character entirely above suspicion.

The motive of Mr B however for making this effort to strip the Marshall of the power of selecting Juries which has been exercised by that officer without the least ground of complaint I believe ever since the existence of the court itself may perhaps be found to spring from a deeper source than his mere disappointment in the result of the above mentioned trial and it is on this account that I desire to call your attention to it.

Our city and the adjoining districts are still subject to a powerful and corrupting monied influence with which the democracy is obliged to maintain in continual arduous and sometimes bitter conflict. Should Mr B succeede in getting the mode of selecting juries so changed as to oblige the Marshall to make his choice from among the names returned by the assessors of our city and the immediate neighbourhood, when the assessors themselves are chosen throug the influence of the Bank and it founders, what chance of a just and equitable trial can any man suppose the government would have against the Bank before Judges bound to the care of that institution by the strongest arguments of interest and Jurors placed in the box through its immediate influence.

Suppose in defense of our national rights and honor we should be obliged to wage war against a foreign nation and the aristocracy of our commercial cities should as in the War of 1812 array itself on the side of our enemies, what could we hope from Juries drawn from such a source? Defection and treason itself might under such a state of things stalk abroad in our cities and defy the law the government and the people. Nullification might and doubtless would approve of the plan of Mr B. but I believe it is fraught with dangers of an alarming character that strike deep at one of the most inestimable safeguards of the citizen, the trial by an impartial Jury of the vicinage. You will look to it.

When our Bill on the subject of the provisors in the 10 and 12th clauses of the 2d. Section of the Tariff Law of 1832 is reported by your Committee I shall feel much obliged to you for a copy.

HENRY HORN

Addressed to Washington.

1. No mention of Binney's action has been found in the *Register of Debates in Congress* for that session.

TO JAMES WALKER

Dear Sir Washington City Decr. 25th. 1834

I wrote you a long confidential letter on yesterday. I stated to you that I declined attending the meeting and my reasons for it. Since then the fact that a meeting took place and the objects of it has been communicated to ——— and my course is highly approved.[1] The meeting has attracted attention and things as they *really are in Tennessee,* are beginning to be well understood here. He says that if Judge White should be united upon and be the candidate of the party, that then he should be supported by the party, but that any portion of those professing to be the friends of the administration who would bring him or any one else out, & without consulting the wishes of the friends of the administration in other states, will virtually not only destroy him but themselves. The storm I apprehend is to bust upon us, and we in Tennessee must be prepared to meet it. Whatever our personal preferences for men may be, as patriots we should go for the good of the country, and to that end should avoid divisions, and preserve if possible the integrity of the party. If a man from Tennessee should be agreed upon, we should support him; but can we consent to be a small fraction of a party, to be used as a rallying point for the opposition? Can we agree to be the Jackson stalks upon which the opposition are to graft? The person to whom I have alluded and whose hints I have ventured very confidentially to sugest, says he has already heard that it has been dropped out by some one of the opposition, that the plan of their operations, is upon the *Bell* system, alluding to the Speaker's election. I will not be hasty or imprudent in this matter, but may venture to communicate what is passing *to you.*

Since the meeting the other evening Johnson has written a letter to the delegation stating in substance that if Judge White is taken up by the friends of the administration he will support him, but if he is to be run by the opposition nationals and nullifiers, aided by a small fraction of the Jackson party, that his co-operation as one of that fraction is not to be expected; that he intends not to separate from the party but to act with it. Dunlap I understand expresses himself in the same way, but I believe has written nothing upon the subject. Blair is of the same opinion; and Grundy is more excited than I have almost ever seen him, and seems almost ready to come out and denounce the whole movement, as one calculated to divide and destroy the party.

You must write me what is said or thought of this matter in Tennessee, or has it seriously attracted public attention? Is it possible through Andrew[2] to let [Micajah G.] Lewis understand what is going on here, without giving my opinions as coming from me? Let his paper if he chooses advocate the claims of his favorite man, but at the same time abuse no-body else of our party. He could too without any inconsistency advocate the union of the Republican party, and express a readiness, if it becomes necessary in order to avoid a division among ourselves, and the consequent hazard of defeat, to yield his first choice & take his second. The time is not far distant when the friends of the administration in Tennessee must take their ground, & I take it they would be unwilling to be found acting with Massachusetts and against Pennsylvania, and the other states that have uniformly acted with us. I have given you the facts. Do what you can & think prudent in regard to the course of the Observer. The National Convention it is confidentially communicated to me will probably meet in the spring or summer. Will Tennessee send delegates to bring forward the claims of the man she may prefer; but if she fails in having him nominated, will she act with the party and support the candidate of the majority?

J. K. P.

Addressed to Columbia. The letter is marked "Confidential."

1. This appears to be a reference to President Jackson.

2. Probably Andrew C. Hays of Columbia.

FROM WILLIAM BRADY

Dr Sir Murfreesboro' 26th December 1834

I was sick a bed when your Two letters reached me, and now sit up in pain in answering them. I feel solicitious, deeply solicitous about the matters suggested in your communications; and as far as my agency can contribute to strip the veil which now covers the political hypocrite, it shall be effeciently and promptly given. When you pend. your first letter you had not then received the Extra Monitor. That publication was forced upon us, by the appearance of an Editorial in the Republican just before the demise of Allen A Hall. That it was an authorised denial by the Speaker himself I have no doubt; for it made its appearance immediately on his return from the South. The article in question was met as you will see by the Extra Monitor; copies of which I caused to be forwarded to the President and several Members of Congress, and to all the prominent political Journals in the U.S. and many individuals in Tennessee and the other States, who would be supposed to take an interest in the course taken by the Speaker. The article in the Whig and Banner,[1] to which you refer made its appearance some two or three weeks after the publication of the Extra Monitor; and you will perceive how studiously the Banner Editor[2] avoids the remotest allusion to the Editorial of the Monitor. The fact is, a direct and positive denial of the correctness of the report of Mr Bells speech as published, has not yet been made, either publickly or privately, by Mr Bell or his friends, and I assure you that he has no friend in this place, not even Dance;[3] or his, the Speakers, *Chaplain Martin Clark,* who would have the hardyhood to call to question the truth of the reported Speech. I apprehend that we should not have seen these evasive notices of the Speech in the Nashville prints had not rumors from Washington whispered that Mr Speaker had made false and unfounded insinuations against the President of the U S and that the President so regarded them; and hence the necessity of their breaking silence. The Nashville papers presume upon their silence, to escaping from the detection of falshood; for had they come out and specified when any error consisted in the sentiments attributed to Mr Bell in his Murfreesboro Speech, it would have met a full refutation by proof. But the only thing they say, is that the Speaker is too sensible and dignified to have uttered such sentiments—and too faithful to his party to have spoken as he is reported to have done on that occasion. You have put it upon the proper ground; their denials are for a foreign markett; and their silence, or the avoiding a controversy at home is to smother the truth; and to put an extinguisher upon the rising flame that might consume them. The speech as reported can and will be supported by all or nearly all who read it, including many of the old friends and present supporters of his brother [in] law *Dickinson.* James Buruss—the Secretary of the invitation party to Bell, that he should dine with them, says the Speech is correctly reported; as does Currin, Molloy[4] &c and Judge [James C.] Mitchell pronounced it accurate to a fault to me in person and called it an able exposition of the Speakers views as delivered by him on that occasion. You will recollect that the speech contained a flattering notice of the Judge; and I do not know that His honor intended by what he said to include the whole speech, or only that portion of it, in which he was made to figure so conspicuously. The Judge is now absent to the State of Mississippi, and therefore, I cannot know of him what he now thinks of the accuracy of the Speech but on his return, the question will be passd to him, for his answer in a more tangible shape than a mere verble communication. [Daniel] Graham nor [Granville S.] Crockett neither heard the speech; but Col [Bromfield L.] Ridley—Sol Beasly—Bob. Miller,[5] the Bowmans—and a hundred others of equal respectability, with those named in your letter heard the speech, and they will answer. I shall collect the proof, and hold it in readiness, for further action; but why not give the whole of the Extra Monitor to the Globe—or if the Globe refuses, to the North American? How is it with the Globe? If that print is with the President and his friends, to me it has an awkard way of showing of it. It is true that Blair sustains the President personally, and in the main measures of his administration but how is it, that every apologetic article which has appeared in the Nashville papers or elsewhere, in relation to Bells election to the Speakers chair, or his Murfreesboro Speech have found their way into the columns of the Globe? I am not censorious, yet I should think Blair should give both sides or neither. Or is he playing the same game that Bell played so successfully? Is he to reach the Printers chair of the house by the union of the true friends of the President in conjunction with Mr Speaker Bell and his followers? Let the Extra Monitor find its way into the columns of the Globe, and the Speaker must then come out, and disrobe himself of his dignity, and plead to the record, and shall he deny one statement, which is to be found in the report of his speech, which was given by myself, I will fasten the falshood upon him, and there to *stick—stick, stick.* I will be prepared and you shall hear from me. We can expect nothing from the prints at Nashville, for allready, the succession according to their reading, to our present chief magistrate is filled for the next sixteen years. Hugh L. White, comes in next, and then the Speaker will generously condesend to take upon himself the burthens of State—(See the Whig & Banner). Now when you read the fulsome article in that Print, and know at the same time, that Barrow is of the same school, political, moral and Collegiate, what are we to expect from that quarter? I will answer for you, the contempt of silence. Refusal to publish one word, that shall not go to the exhaltation of Bell, and the promotion of their own views and schemes. All the officers, Nation and State, disposable in Tennessee are to be monopolised by their friends & party. And for this purpose *Catron*—(I forget the name of the Stud—Isaacks could aid me) is now on a Tour of observation down East and will hang around the President with all apparent devotion, while his brother [in] law G. Childress[6] Editor of the Whig & Banner at Nashville, will ask the sentiments of Speaker Bell; that he is willing to see the experiment tried &c—and will blow hot and cold with the Bank junto at Nashville. Do I not judge of them rightly and is it not obvious that this is the game the Nashville Press is now playing?

I concur fully and heartily in your views of a press at Nashville about the control of the Bank and mercantile influence of this place. A press devoted to the measures of the National executive and the cause of his successor. A press in a word that shall give the views of the people, untramelled by Bank influence. The times call loudly for such an one, and without it the sentiments of the people of Tennessee, will not, cannot be known, either as to men or measures. And I can see no obstacle in bringing about this matter. The money can be had, and I should think no difficulty would present itself in finding an Editor capable and faithful. If a paper should be established; the Editor should be wholly *de Nashvillized;* free from all partialities, or under the least obligation to her monied Lords, or aspirants for office. What will Mr Grundy do in this business? He tried poor *Sam*[7] and it was a total failure. The truth is Sam lacks moral courage; and when the sound of the Bugle is heard and the enemy shall appear in force—Sam's in the *straw*. Our friends here will engage like true soldiers in the cause. We have but little money—but if that be furnished, we will give the Editor—one that will never flinch, and who will be found ever at his post and with *Ritchie*[8] will be found crying head up under all circumstances.

And I will hazard the suggestion to you, that if a paper should be established at Nashville, that it should come out for Van Buren as the successor of Genl Jackson—boldly and fearlessly. This would put a stop to the petty game now carrying on, headed by Bell as I believe and some of the enemies of the administration, in holding up White for the succession. I am induced to this belief, from many circumstances, which were brought to light during the sitting of the convention at Nashville; and the part bore in them, by E H Foster, and what is now going on in Alabama strengthens my first impressions. A young man in the Legislature of that State—a class mate with Dickinson; (I do not now recollect his name)* and the devoted friend of Bells is the introducer, or mover of resolutions nominating *White* for the Presidency. The credit of this whole movement Mr Bell will take to himself at a proper time, or not, as circumstances shall warrant—not that he really desires the election of White; but White is to be enlisted under the Banner which the party and press at Nashville shall fly—and hence, Mr Childress's proclamation—Jackson, White and Bell—(see the Banner). Now I would strike from the Banner flag—Bell and its precursor White, and insert, Jackson, Van Buren and the people vs the Bank and the Aristocracy. Rely upon my full cooperation in the project of a proper organ at Nashville, that shall disabuse the publick mind; and shadow[?] forth, what is really public sentiment in Tennessee. And I would say to Mr Grundy, that no man in our State has a deeper stake in this matter than himself. His enemies now man the guns at Nashville; and the dissplaced corps wear the same livery; and will he cry peace when the war whoop sounds at the gates of his household? I trust not. Nor do I doubt his course. I have written you under embarrassing circumstances of fever and pain, but I hope intelligibly enough, that I shall be understood. To my friends I have no secrets, and in this particular may want discretion, tho' I shall ever exercise, so much of that principle as not to injure a good cause by improper disclosures. This letter you will regard as written in this spirit—and for your own eye and reflection.

Wm Brady

**Aggricola*

**Phelan,* a graduate at the Nash. University.[9] He is not the introducer of the resolutions, but the supporter &c.

P. S. Before closing this letter, your letter reached me in blank, enclosing the schedule of the members of Congress. I am better today, and will write you again shortly. Carroll is still sick, and undetermined what course he will take. A man diseased in body & mind, will ever hesitate in important matters; to give impetus and force to the inclinations of our minds, it requires the union of health and vigor of intellect.

BRADY

If these views are worth any thing, you are at liberty to suggest it to the President.

B

P. S. Doct Rucker has just stopd in, and informs me that Peyton has written to G. A Sublett[10] of this place, stating that Whites prospects to the succession is brightening &c. Now Sir is this not another proof confirming what I have previously suggested in this letter, that it is a movement on the part of Bell and his friends, to distract & divide—and thereby secure for Bell and the Bank party at Nashville, some influence in Tennessee, with Whites friends. This is all that they can or do expect, and to effect this they would jeopardize the Principles, now in successful opperation sustained and recommended by Genl Jackson and which would also be supported by *Van Buren.* I am told the letter states that the opposition will run no candidate, and that White is more acceptable with all parties than Van Buren—tho' this last idea I do not get from Doct. Rucker. Now Sir, who, with one idea, can doubt that if two friends of the Present administration should come forward, as the successor to the present Chief Magistrate, that the Whigs would not start their man? Nomi—Nomi—and then the evils which the friends of the administration, and those who sustain and advocate the measures, of the executive, would wish to avoid, would be inevitable—an Election in all probability by the House of Representatives. Tho I should not anticipate this under any circumstances—for White, would not get more than two or at most three States.

B

Addressed to Washington.

1. For several months this newspaper carried on the front page the name *National Banner and Nashville Daily Advertiser,* and on the inside sheet it substituted *Whig* for *Advertiser.*

2. George C. Childress.

3. Russell Dance, a Murfreesboro merchant.

4. Jonathan Currin was a Murfreesboro businessman. Burrus and Molloy are unidentified.

5. Beasley and Miller are unidentified.

6. John Catron was married to a sister of George C. Childress.

7. Samuel H. Laughlin.

8. Thomas Ritchie, editor of the Richmond *Enquirer*.

9. Since only one star was found in the text of the letter, it seems probable that Phelan had used a pen name. John D. Phelan was formerly a newspaper editor in Huntsville and was at this time a member of the Alabama legislature.

10. George A. Sublett for some years had published a newspaper in Murfreesboro. He was a member of Murfreesboro's first board of aldermen and was a charter member of the first Methodist church to be organized there.

FROM SAMUEL W. POLK

Dear Brother New Haven Connect Dec th26. 1834

I have been delaying for sometime, to write to you, untill I should enter the Class. It appears to me very long since you left us, and I know you must be very near out of patience waiting to hear from me. And therefore I consider it my duty, to let you know the reasons why I have not written.

We have entered the class, and expect to commence College duties on tomorrow. The reason we have not entered sooner, is that the Algebra studied here is very different from the one I had studied. Surds in Bonnosostte[?][1] is near the beginning, but in Days they are about the middle, but this is not the only reason, why we have not been able to over take them. The other is, that when we were endeavoring to come up with them, they were advancing very rapidly, and we could not have been able to enter at this time, if we had not said two recitations a day, and I hope with this explanation you will not suppose that I have been Idle and not applying myself.

The rest of the boys are well, and if I were to speak the truth, I could not say in good spirits, by no means excusing myself. The rooms are very warm, ours especially. James's[2] stove smokes some but very little. We find Mr Olmsted[3] very clever and attentive to us. We still continue to eat in Commons, and like it tolerable well. We have good but coarse fare, such as students should receive. The weather is very cold and disagreeable we want nothing that would add to our comfort. Write frequently for we dont receive letters often from home. I have not received any yet, and am getting low spirited about it.

SAML. W. POLK

Addressed to Washington.

1. This is obviously the name of the author of an algebra textbook of the time, but the spelling intended is difficult to determine.

2. James Hays Walker, son of James Walker.

3. Denison Olmsted was a professor of mathematics and natural philosophy at Yale. At one time he had been on the faculty at the University of North Carolina.

FROM SPIVEY McKISSICK

Dear Sir [Spring Hill, Tennessee] 28 Debr 1834

I had the pleasure the other day to receive from you the presidents message and was truly gratified to see in my judgment, one of the most dignified communications ever made to congress. We trust that Henry Clay & Co will not be able during the present session of Congress to rise[?] a Bugaboo of sufficient importance to affright those who were so severely worked on during your last session. We have for the last two or three weeks been talking much about our new constitution and am inclined to think from the best information that I can gether it will find but few supporters in the neighbourhood in Spring Hill. So you see we are not very fond of new things particularly when we have to surrender that, that is well tryed civil good.

Our postmaster at Spring Hill[1] is at this time I suspect in Texas. It is said by some that he will not return I think differently however. Should he not come back or should there be applicants for the appointment of Postmaster at Spring Hill I will say to you that should you think me competent to discharge the duties of that office I will attend to it having better health and more leasure than formerly. Your friends and relations so fare as I am acquainted are well. It has for the last ten or twelve days been raining. I think the sun has not been seen but once in twelve days. You never saw as bad roads in Tennessee. Present my respects to Mrs. Polk and receive the same from yours &c.

S. McKissick

Addressed to Washington.

1. Henry Wade was postmaster at this time and was not immediately superseded; apparently he did return and resume his duties. When Wade left that position, he was succeeded by J. O. Potter.

FROM SAMUEL G. SMITH

Dr Sir Mount Pleasant T Decr. 28. 1834

I acknowledge the honour of your favour inclosing me the report of the Secretary of the Treasury. We have nothing of any interest in the way of political news, Washington being the source from which we expect to hear whatever is interesting to the country. I have heard nothing from Ln.[Laughlin] since my last nor am I able to inform you if he is gone or still dissipating at home. Upon reflection I am rather inclined to think that the first of March would be soon enough to commence operations. It cannot now be done in time to give whatever news Congress may afford.

This however is a matter about which I have no settled opinion nor wishes in any way. It is due to you that I express my great apprehensions as to the stability of the man. For my own part so far as relates to any controle he has over his own conduct I have no confidence whatever. If means were placed in his hands to procure the materials for such an establishment I should not be surprised at his failing to do so and wasting the funds. Soon after you left here he called for the contemplated favour to make arrangements and even more than was promised.

I knew he was not ready to go into the arrangements and put him off.

Soon afterward I ascertained that if he had obtained it that another disposition would have been made of it. If he should get the means or material in his hand I have no expectation he can retain them under his own management. What the other man can do time must prove as he wants experience and I fear capacity to manage the finances of such an establishment.[1]

I hope you will endeavour to make some impression upon him as to stability & consistincy. He will assure you of expected aid from men here but it is all idle, he will not get any. They wish to controle him by such profession and the truth is he has had such associations with some persons here that he will & intend to sustain them at the expense of consistincy & every other consideration.

The present arrangement is to meet his friend at Cincinatti in January and this he will do to get the means in his hand. I hope to hear from you soon. Some business having brought me to your district I find the politics of the true stamp.

Many of those in Tennessee who the President looked upon as his warm personal friends in my opinion are in effect against his administration. I regret to think that such a venerable patriot should labour under such mistaken impressions as to men.

SAM G SMITH

Addressed to Washington. This letter is marked "Confidential."

1. It is not entirely clear who the second person was. It is possible that it was Medicus A. Long, formerly of a Sparta newspaper, but a subsequent statement about meeting in Cincinnati possibly means that it was some other person.

FROM JAMES P. GRUNDY

Dr Sir Nashville Dec 29th 1834

My partner Mr [William T.] Brown is an applicant for the Office of Judge in Arkansas.[1] I address you as a friend desiring your influence in his behalf. I have been associated with Mr Brown for about four years in the practice of the Law and I can confidently assure you that no Lawyer in Nashville possesses superior qualifications—both as a sound lawyer and a gentleman.

I hope that you will aid my father in procuring the appointment. He feels the same solicitude that I do—having been acquainted with Mr B. for many years and having always found him on the side of principle.

Any exertions made by you in this matter will confer a lasting favor. . . .

JAMES P GRUNDY

Addressed to Washington.

1. Brown had been recommended for a similar post earlier in the year. See Andrew Hays to Polk, March 5, 1834.

FROM ADLAI O. HARRIS

Dear Sir Columbia 29 Dec 1834

Yours of the 8 Inst came to hand in due time, and should have been replied to some time since, but on application to Mrs [Silas M.] Caldwell who had the valuation of the property refered to in your letter, she promised to furnish you with a copy of it immediately and having sent back some paper for the purpose I presumed she had done so. She did not let me see the valuation.

Mr Herndon[1] promises me to take your stone House though he has not yet determined whether he will take it for a term of years or not. He is to determine & clear the matter, before I leave for N Orleans (15 Jany).

We have nothing new here in the Political World. Commercial matters are at a stand. The feverish state of the cotton market some few weeks ago has subsided and prices have receded about 1½ to 2 p—though I have no fear of much further reduction during the season. The two last mails from N. Orleans have failed in consequence of high water—so that we have nothing late from that quarter. All well.

A O HARRIS

Addressed to Washington.

1. Joseph Herndon, a Columbia lawyer.

FROM HILLARY LANGTRY

Dear Sir Columbia 29th December 1834

Enclosed please receive the petition of a committee appointed by the Rail Road convention asking an appropriation of

$20,000 to lay out and survey the route through this state. I need not bespeak your favourable consideration of or early attention to this document, satisfied that you are ever alive to the interest of your constitutents when they do not conflict with higher and more important duties. Accept my thanks for your polite attention in forwarding me a copy of the Presidents message. It is worthy of the head & heart from which it emmanated and proves that both are ever active for the interests and honour of his country. May he long live to partake of its growing prosperity and reap the fruit of his arduous labours. There is little new here except the marriage of Miss Ellen Maguire to R B Mayes on Wednesday last & several others on the lasso[?]. Give my best respects to Mrs Polk. . . .

H. LANGTRY

Addressed to Washington.

FROM JOSEPH ROYALL[1]

Chocchuma, Mississippi. December 29, 1834

Royall, a former resident of Maury County, reports that another claim has been filed for land to which he has a proven pre-emption. Fearing that float claims allowed to orphaned Choctaw children will be given preference over prior claims of occupants, he asks Polk's help.

Addressed to Washington.

1. This name is sometimes spelled Royal but in this letter it was clearly written as above. See Samuel H. Williams to Polk, December 13, 1832.

FROM THOMAS SMITH

Nashville. December 29, 1834

The writer, a state senator from Jackson County and brother of Samuel G. Smith, seeks Polk's help in behalf of an invalid pensioner who has moved from North Carolina. The agent at Nashville has paid him for time since the transfer was accomplished, but the pensioner claims he has not been paid for the period 1827–31.

Addressed to Washington.

FROM WILLIAM P. BRADBURN

Pensacola, Florida. December 30, 1834

The writer expresses great appreciation for the many favors Polk has done for him and after reviewing his career from the time he was a printer's apprentice, he expresses the hope that he will return to Tennessee in a few months with a star on his collar.

Addressed to Washington.

TO MAHLON DICKERSON

Sir Ho. Repts. Decr. 30th 1834

I have not received an answer to my letter addressed to your Department, eight or ten days ago, requesting to be furnished with certain information and explanations relating to the appropriations proposed for the Naval Service of 1835.[1] The Committee of Ways and Means have delayed acting upon the subject until the information requested was received. They are aware that much longer delay in bringing forward the appropriation bill, may operate injuriously to the service, and with a view as far as practicable to prevent further delay, I am instructed to request that the information asked in my former letter may be communicated to the Committee as soon as the convenience of the Department will permit.

James K. Polk
Ch. Com. W & Ms.

Addressed to Washington. Letter is in Miscellaneous Letters, Naval Records Collection (RG 45), National Archives.

1. See Polk to Dickerson, December 20, 1834.

FROM S. JONES

Hollidaysburg, Pennsylvania. December 30, 1834

Jones, superintendent of the Pennsylvania Portage Railway, writes in opposition to a House resolution by Augustin S. Clayton suggesting possible remission of import duties on locomotives and locomotive parts.[1] He argues that such action would encourage large purchases of English locomotives and thereby do serious harm to American manufacturers.

Addressed to Washington.

1. Clayton had offered the resolution on December 16, 1834, and, after some debate as to which committee should receive it, the House tabled the resolution on December 19, 1834. Jones probably had not yet learned of the House action.

FROM CHARLES W. MORGAN

Washington. December 30, 1834

A navy captain asks Polk's support of a bill that would equalize the pay of navy officers.[1]

Delivered by hand at House of Representatives.

1. Debate on a bill to regulate and equalize the pay of navy officers had received some prominence in the preceding session of Congress and was resumed on December 16, 1834, with John G. Watmough of Pennsylvania as its chief supporter. After much debate, the House approved the bill on February 18, 1835.

FROM JOSEPH THOMPSON

Dear Sir Livingston Ala Deb 30 1834

Enclosed you will find the resignation and recommendation of the postmaster at this place.[1] Fully relying on your influence in this case I hope you will give it your prompt attention believing with your influence and the within that it would not be nesasary to send a petition from this place, but should it be nesasary for me to take any other steps in the matter you will please inform me at as early a period as posable.

My friend Saml B Boyd[2] of this place formerly of Tennessee has wrote by the same mail to the Honl. Luke Lea [. . .] and Standifer[3] if they can be of any service. I have no doubt you may command their influence.

Jos Thompson

Addressed to Washington.

1. Polk noted on the envelope that he had written to the Postmaster General and had handed the recommendation to Samuel W. Mardis of Ala-

bama. See Thompson to Polk, September 18, November 11, and November 18, 1834.

2. Probably related to the well-known Boyd family of Knoxville. In 1839 he was elected to the state senate from Sumter County, Alabama. His election was contested, however, and the legislature ruled the election invalid.

3. Luke Lea and James Standifer were members of the House of Representatives from Tennessee. The illegible word appears to be a proper name and logically could be assumed to be that of another Tennessee congressman.

FROM WILLIAM J. ALEXANDER

Raleigh, North Carolina. December 31, 1834

The writer introduces a mail contractor from North Carolina and asks Polk to use his influence toward a renewal of his contract. Alexander also reports the resignation of Romulus Saunders, the state's attorney general, and expresses the hope that a successor will soon be selected.[1]

Addressed to Washington and delivered by hand. This letter has been published in McPherson, editor, "Unpublished Letters," *North Carolina Historical Review,* XVI, 187–188.

1. John R. J. Daniel, a Halifax County lawyer, was chosen to replace Saunders.

INDEX

SUMNER
WILSON
RUTHERFORD
WARREN
BEDFORD
LINCOLN
FRANKLIN
MARION
HAMILTON